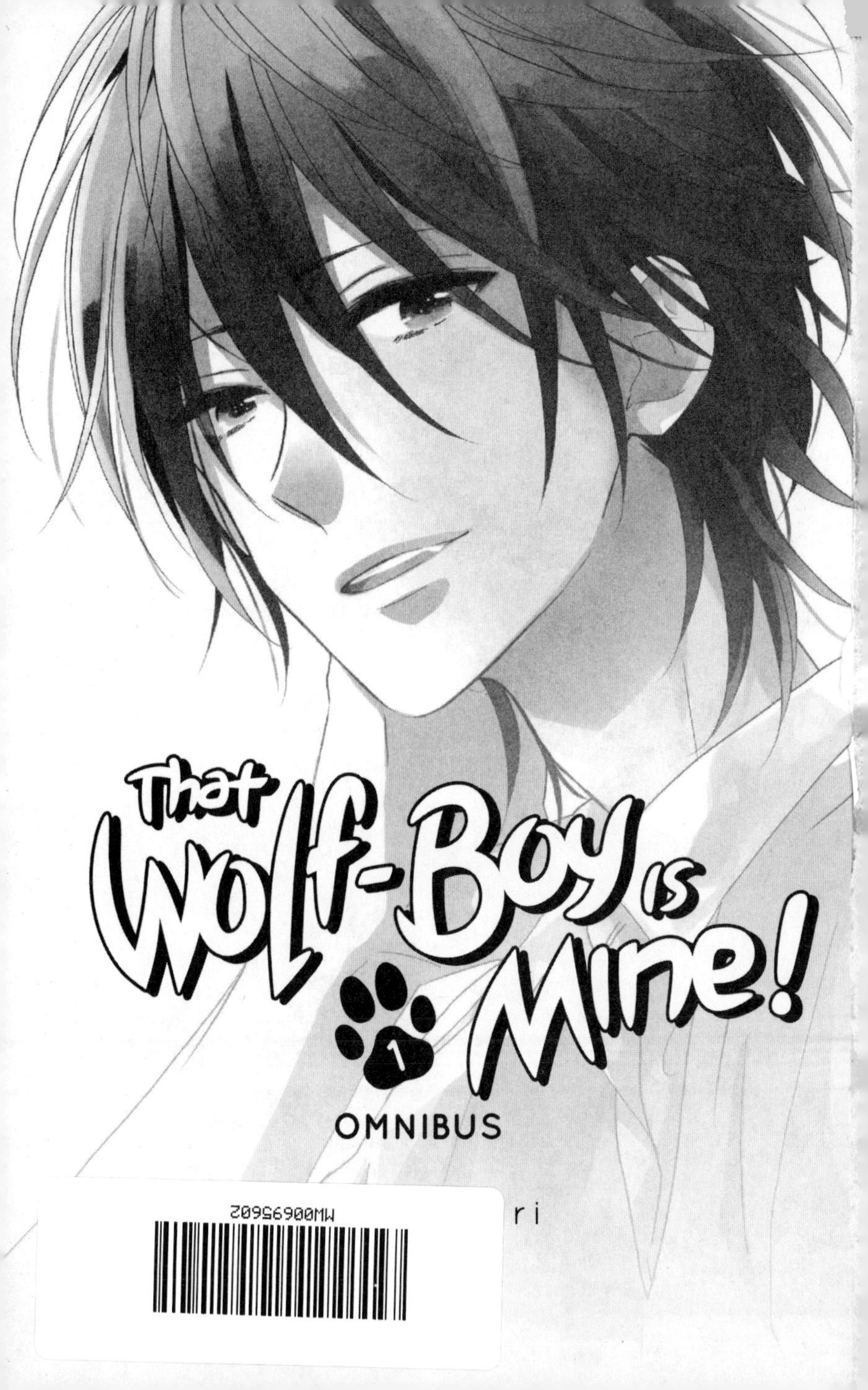
That Wolf-Boy is Mine!
1
OMNIBUS
r i

That Wolf-Boy is Mine!

Contents

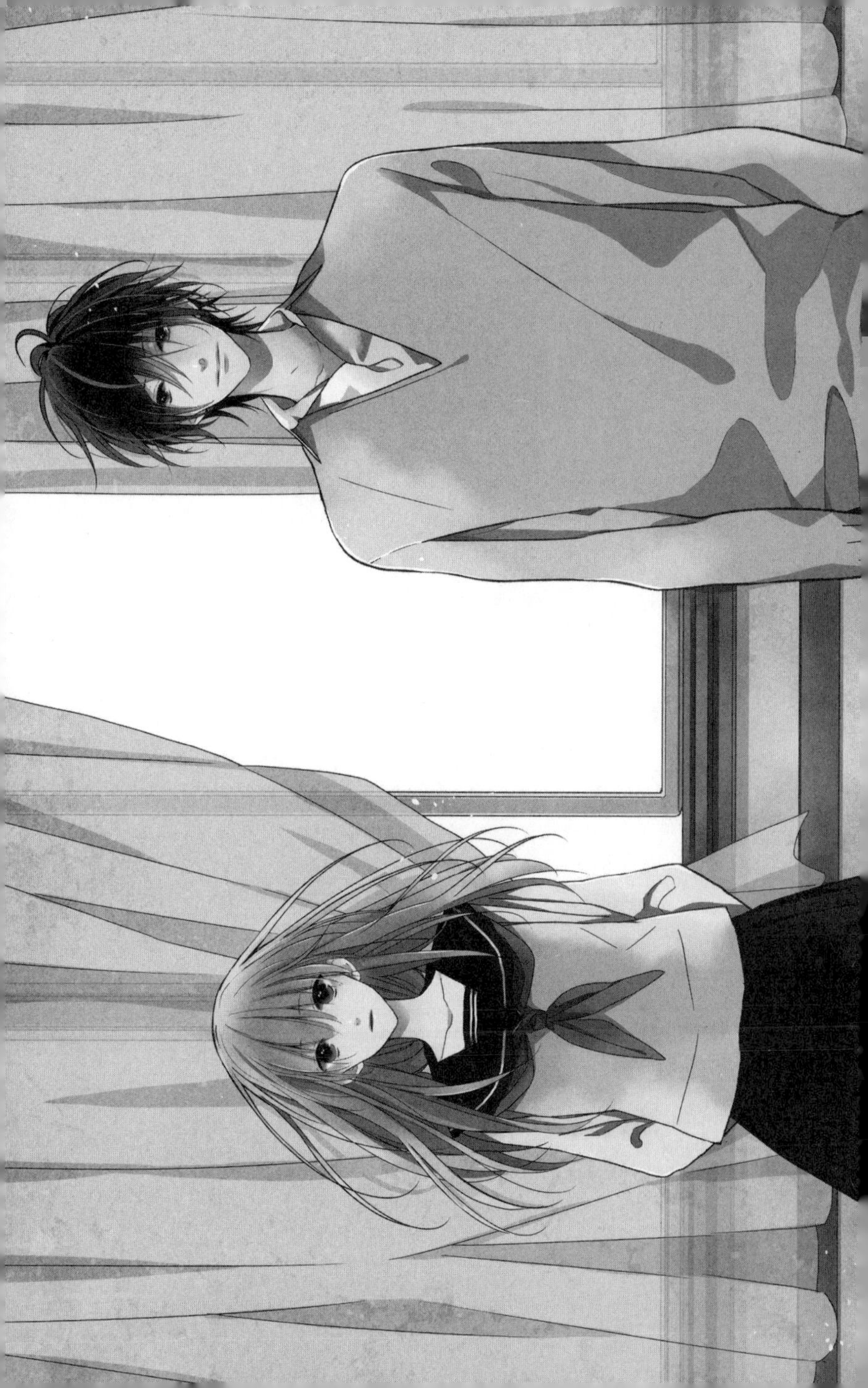

That WOLF-BOY is Mine!

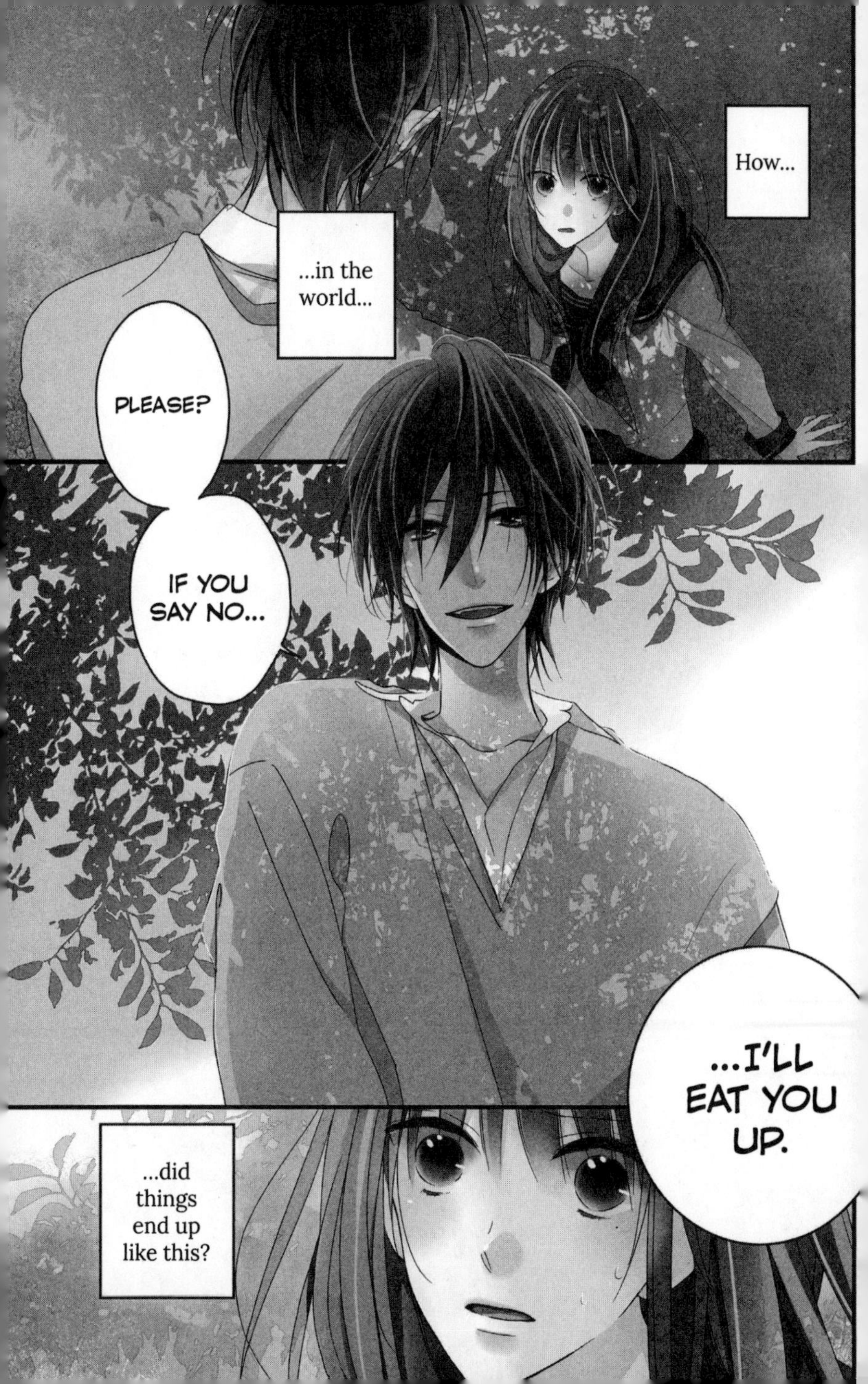
How...
...in the world...
PLEASE?
IF YOU SAY NO...
...I'LL EAT YOU UP.
...did things end up like this?

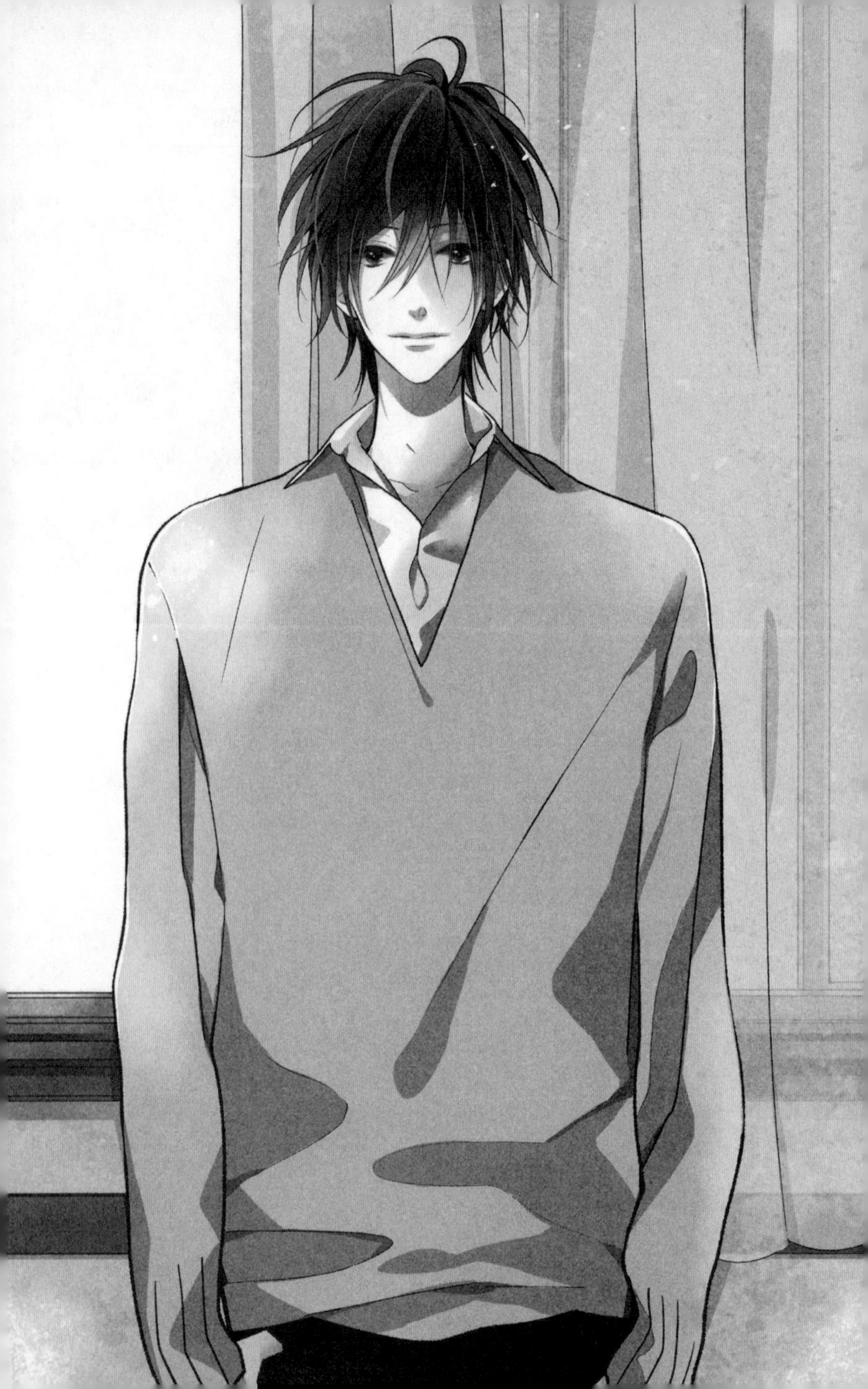

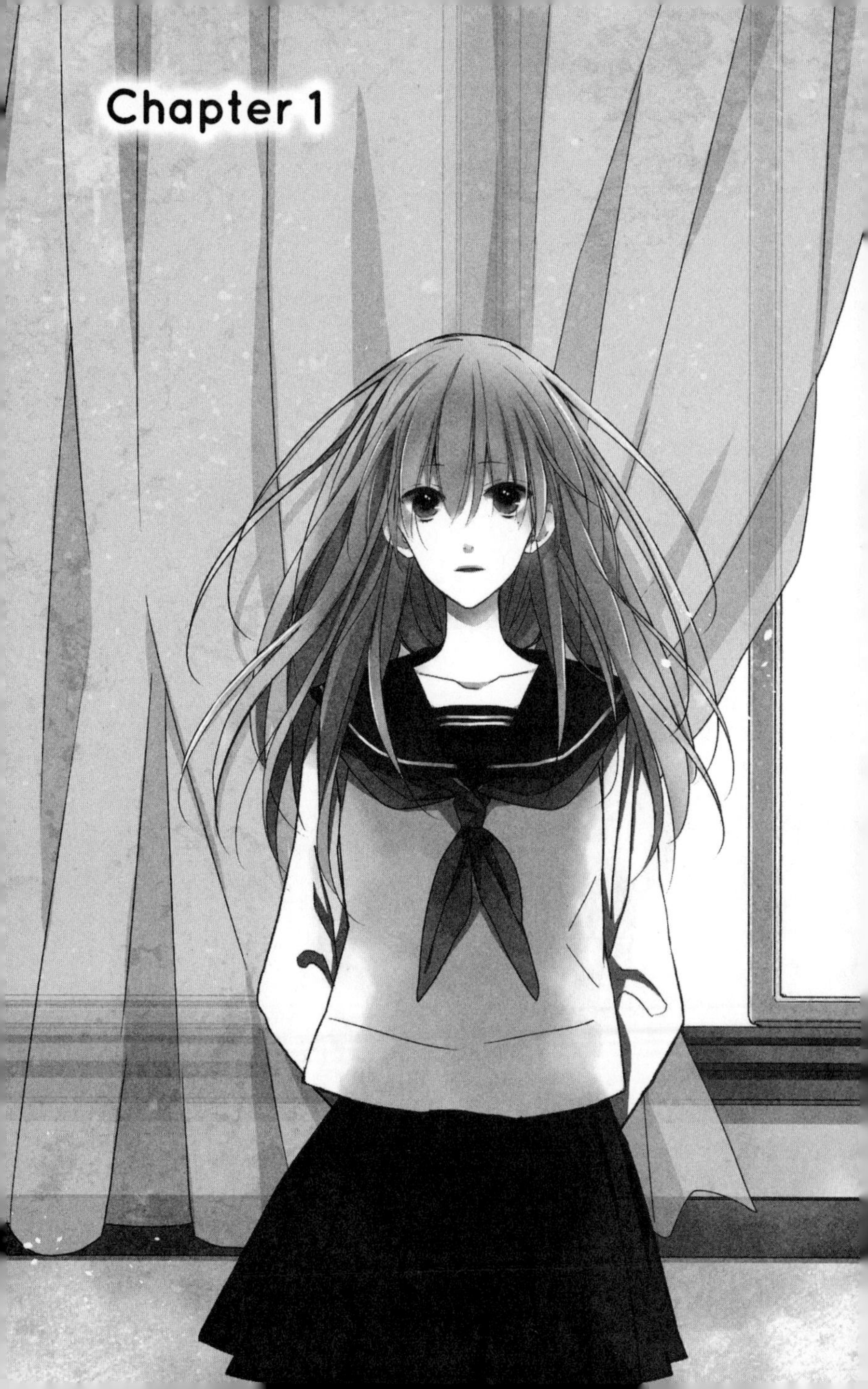
Chapter 1

That Wolf-Boy is Mine!

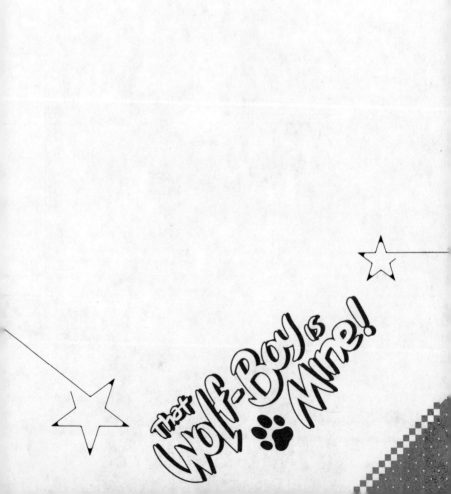

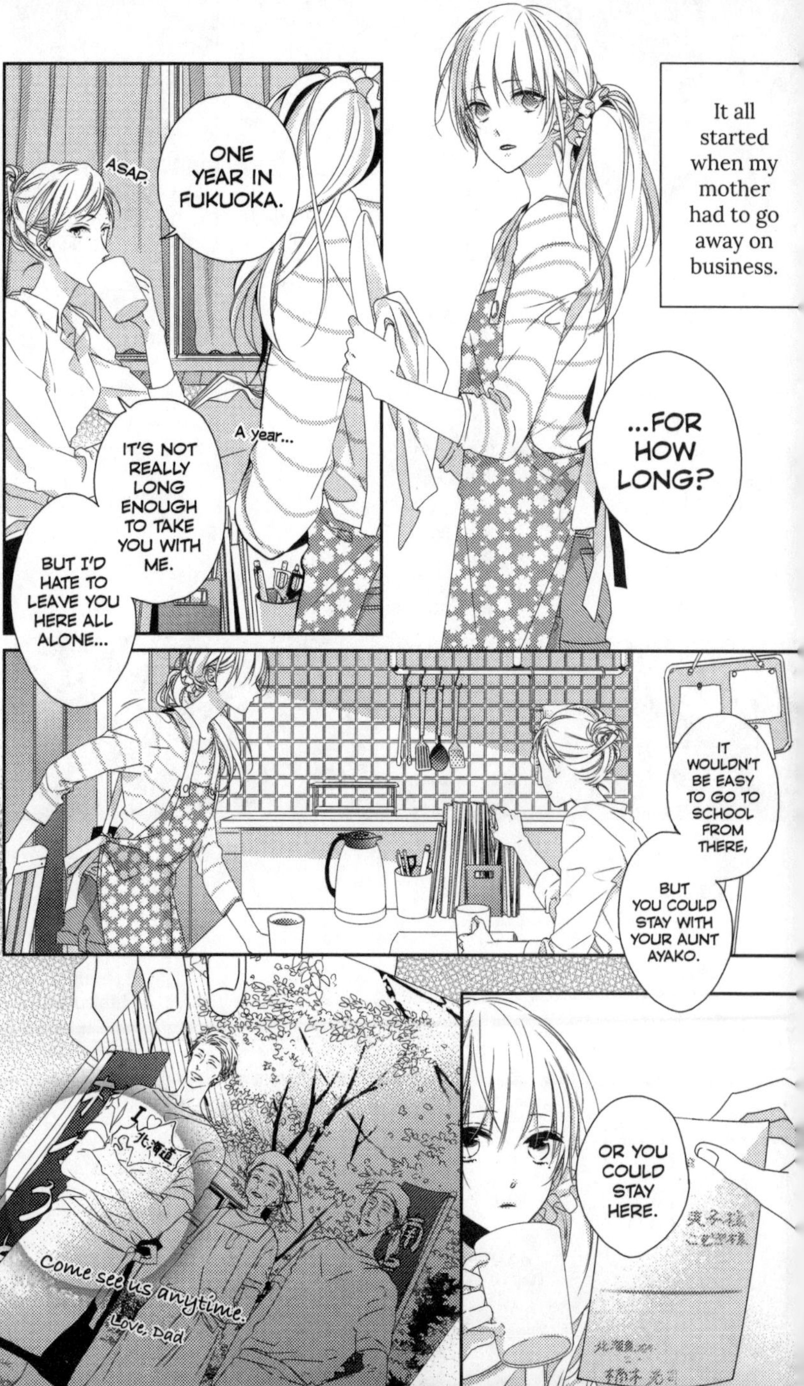
It all started when my mother had to go away on business.
...FOR HOW LONG?
ONE YEAR IN FUKUOKA.
ASAP.
A year...
IT'S NOT REALLY LONG ENOUGH TO TAKE YOU WITH ME.
BUT I'D HATE TO LEAVE YOU HERE ALL ALONE...
IT WOULDN'T BE EASY TO GO TO SCHOOL FROM THERE,
BUT YOU COULD STAY WITH YOUR AUNT AYAKO.
OR YOU COULD STAY HERE.
Come see us anytime.
Love, Dad

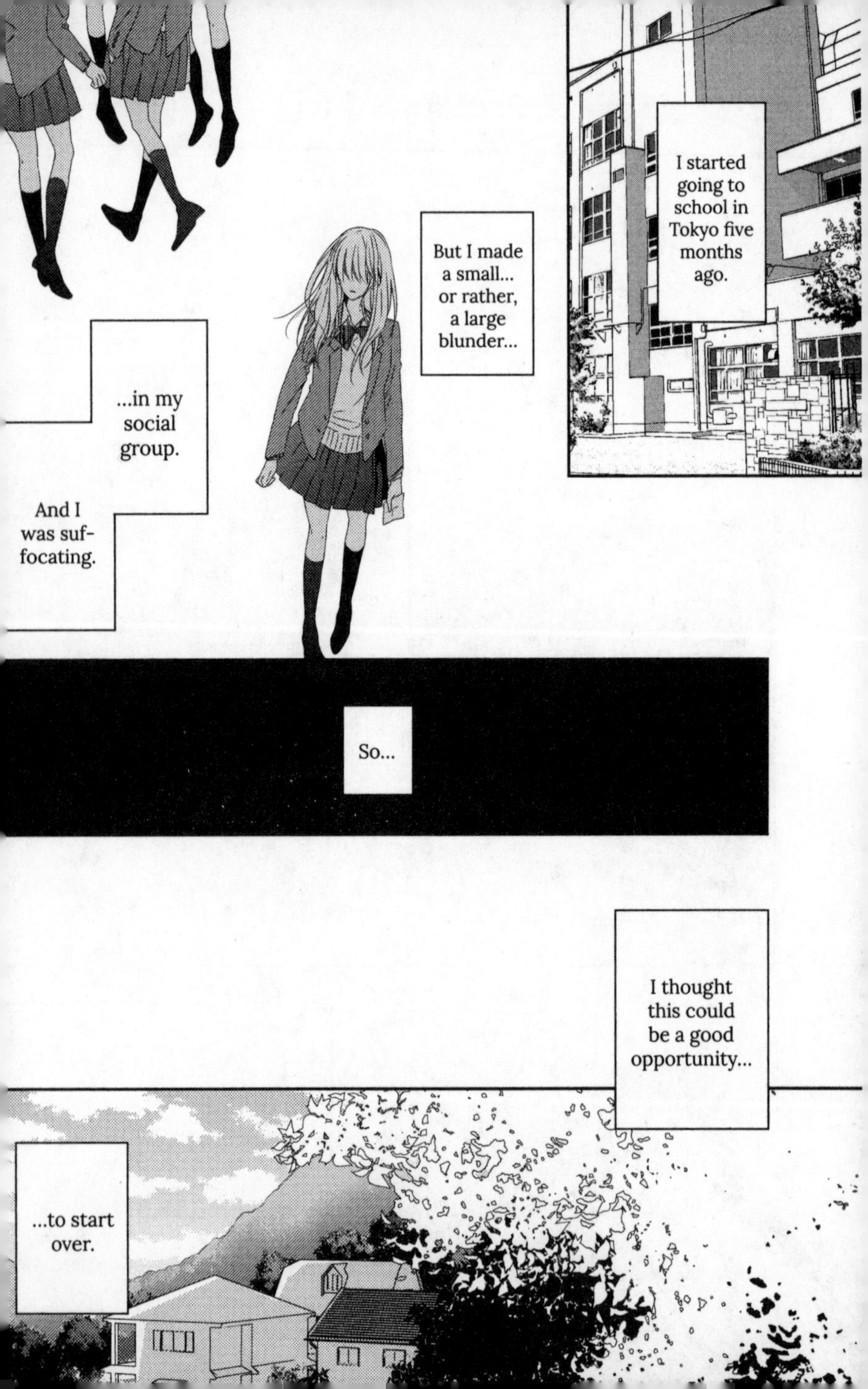
I started going to school in Tokyo five months ago.
But I made a small... or rather, a large blunder...
...in my social group.
And I was suffocating.
So...
I thought this could be a good opportunity...
...to start over.

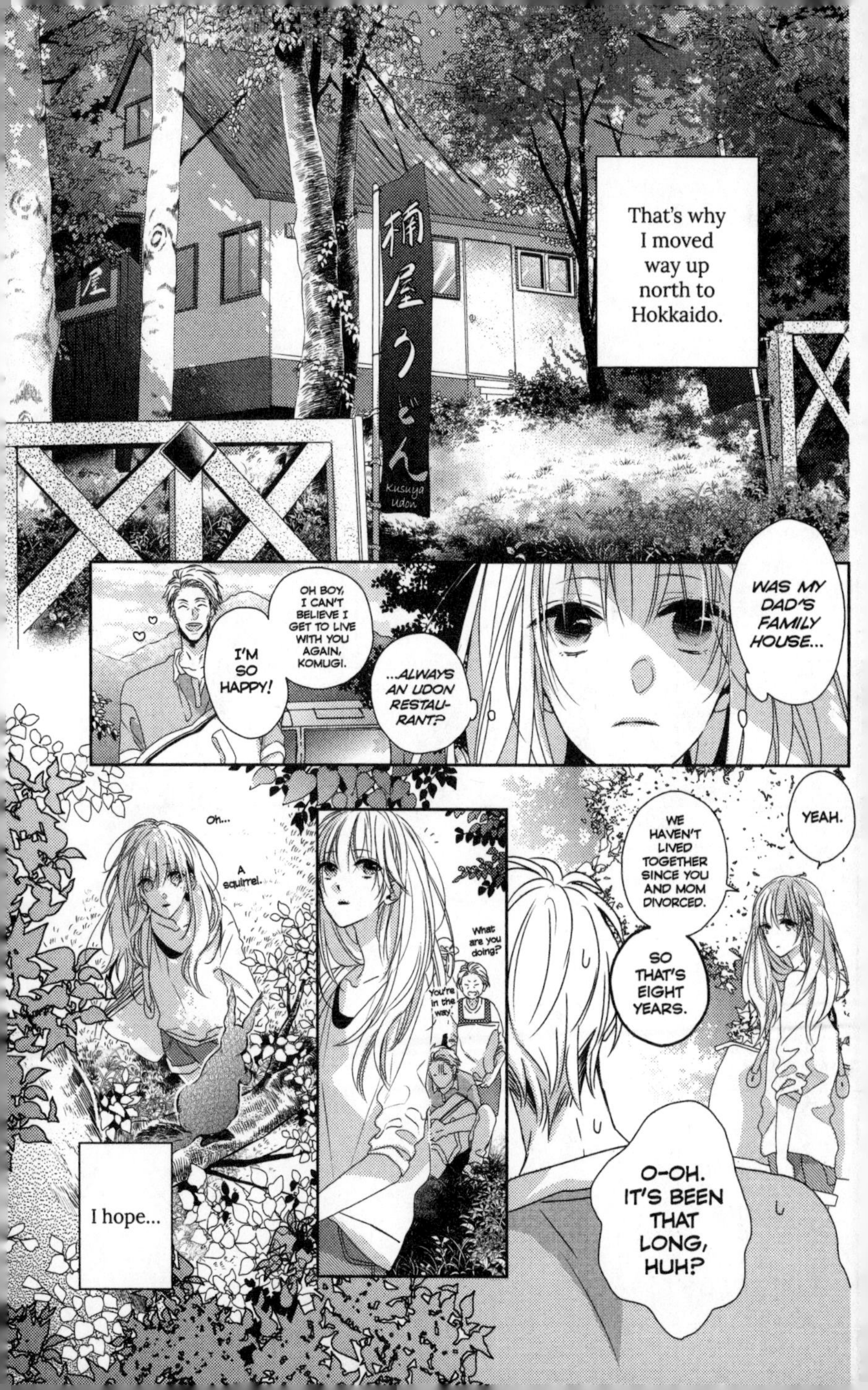

That's why I moved way up north to Hokkaido.
楠屋うどん
Kusuya udon
屋
WAS MY DAD'S FAMILY HOUSE...
...ALWAYS AN UDON RESTAURANT?
OH BOY, I CAN'T BELIEVE I GET TO LIVE WITH YOU AGAIN, KOMUGI.
I'M SO HAPPY!
YEAH.
WE HAVEN'T LIVED TOGETHER SINCE YOU AND MOM DIVORCED.
SO THAT'S EIGHT YEARS.
O-OH. IT'S BEEN THAT LONG, HUH?
What are you doing?
You're in the way.
Oh...
A squirrel.
I hope...

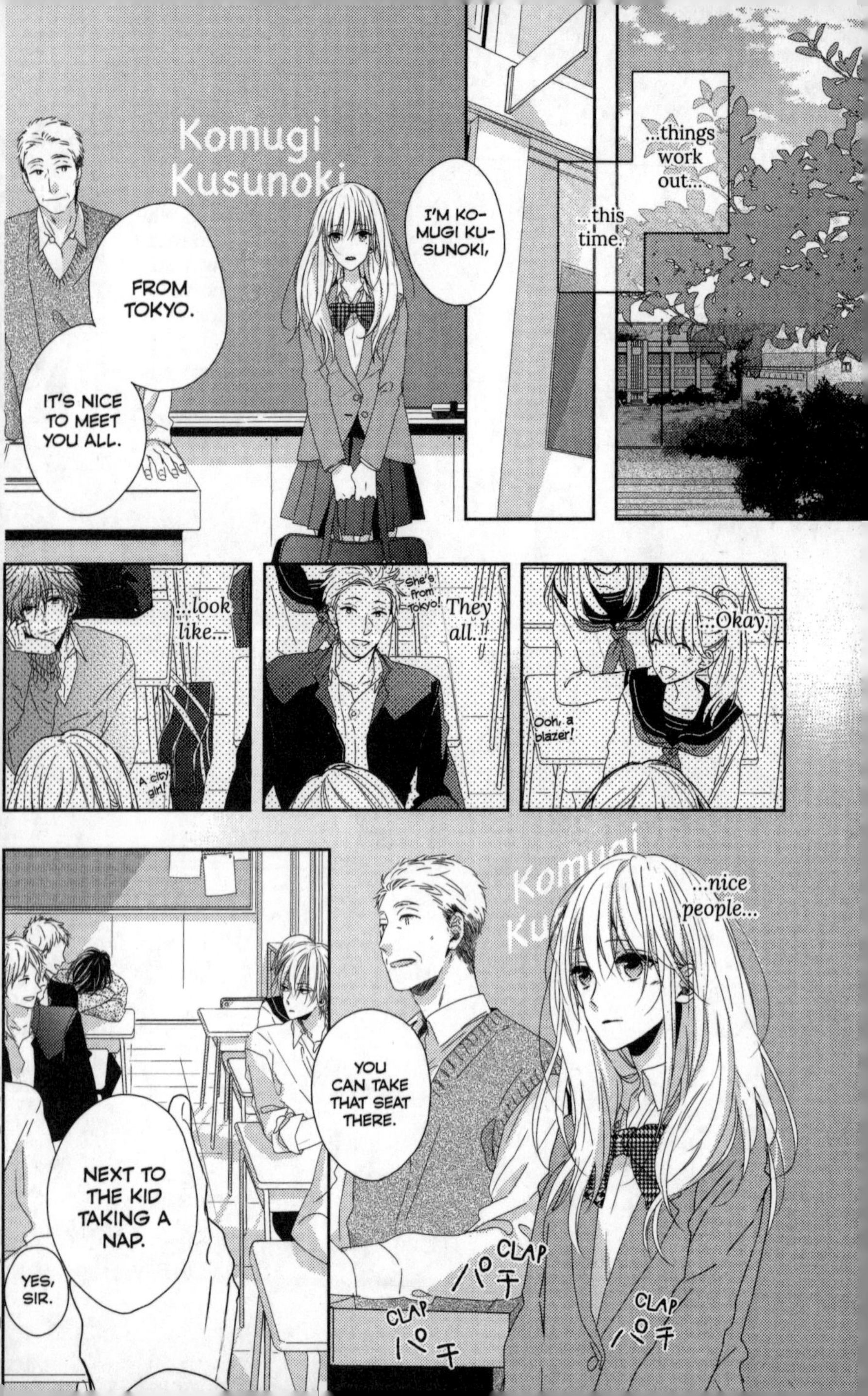
...things work out...
...this time.
Komugi Kusunoki
I'M KO-MUGI KU-SUNOKI,
FROM TOKYO.
IT'S NICE TO MEET YOU ALL.
...Okay.
Ooh, a blazer!
She's from Tokyo!
They all...
...look like...
A city girl!
...nice people...
YOU CAN TAKE THAT SEAT THERE.
CLAP パチ
CLAP パチ
CLAP パチ
NEXT TO THE KID TAKING A NAP.
YES, SIR.

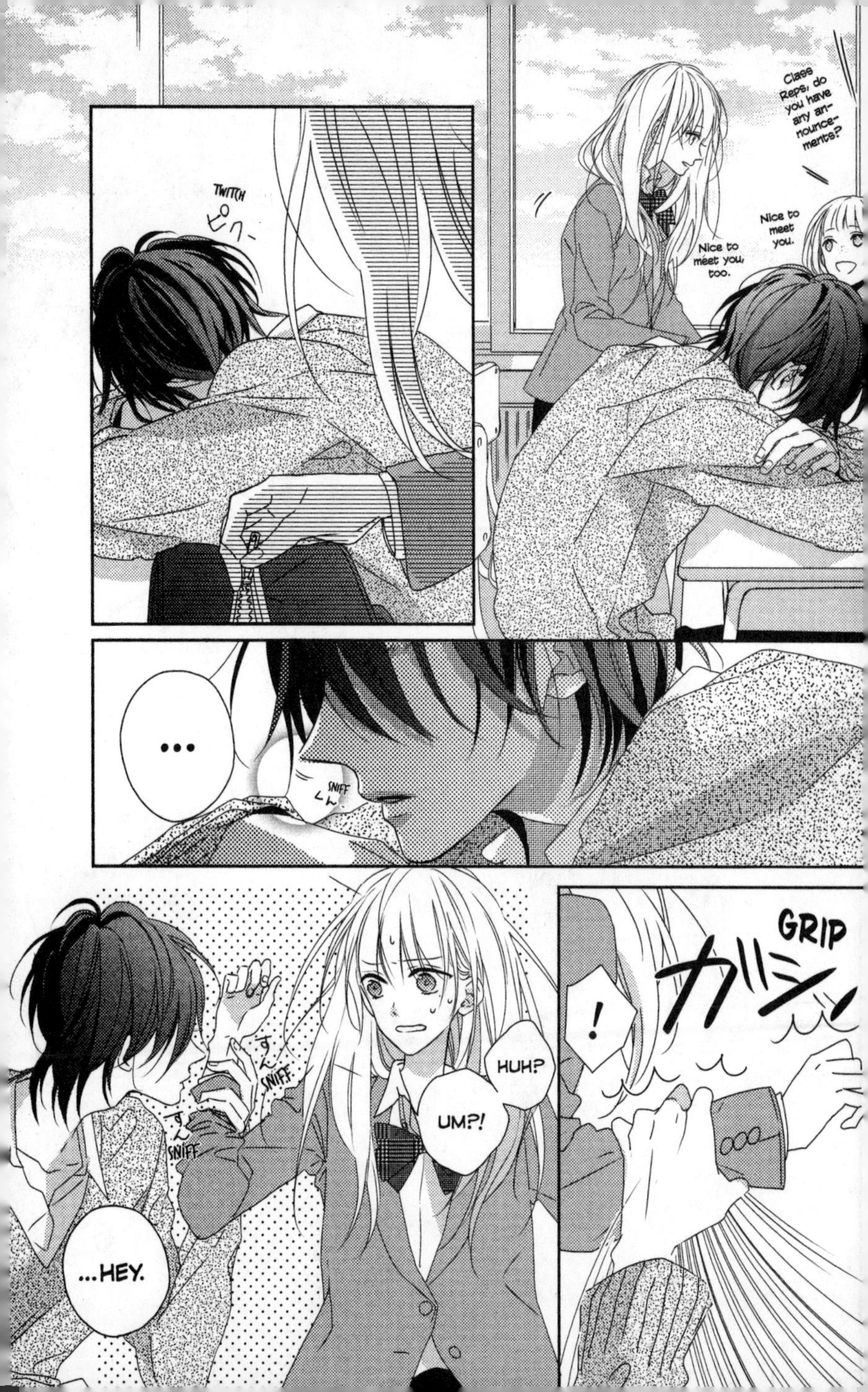
Class Reps, do you have any announcements?
Nice to meet you.
Nice to meet you, too.
TWITCH
...
SNIFF
GRIP
!
HUH?
UM?!
SNIFF
SNIFF
...HEY.

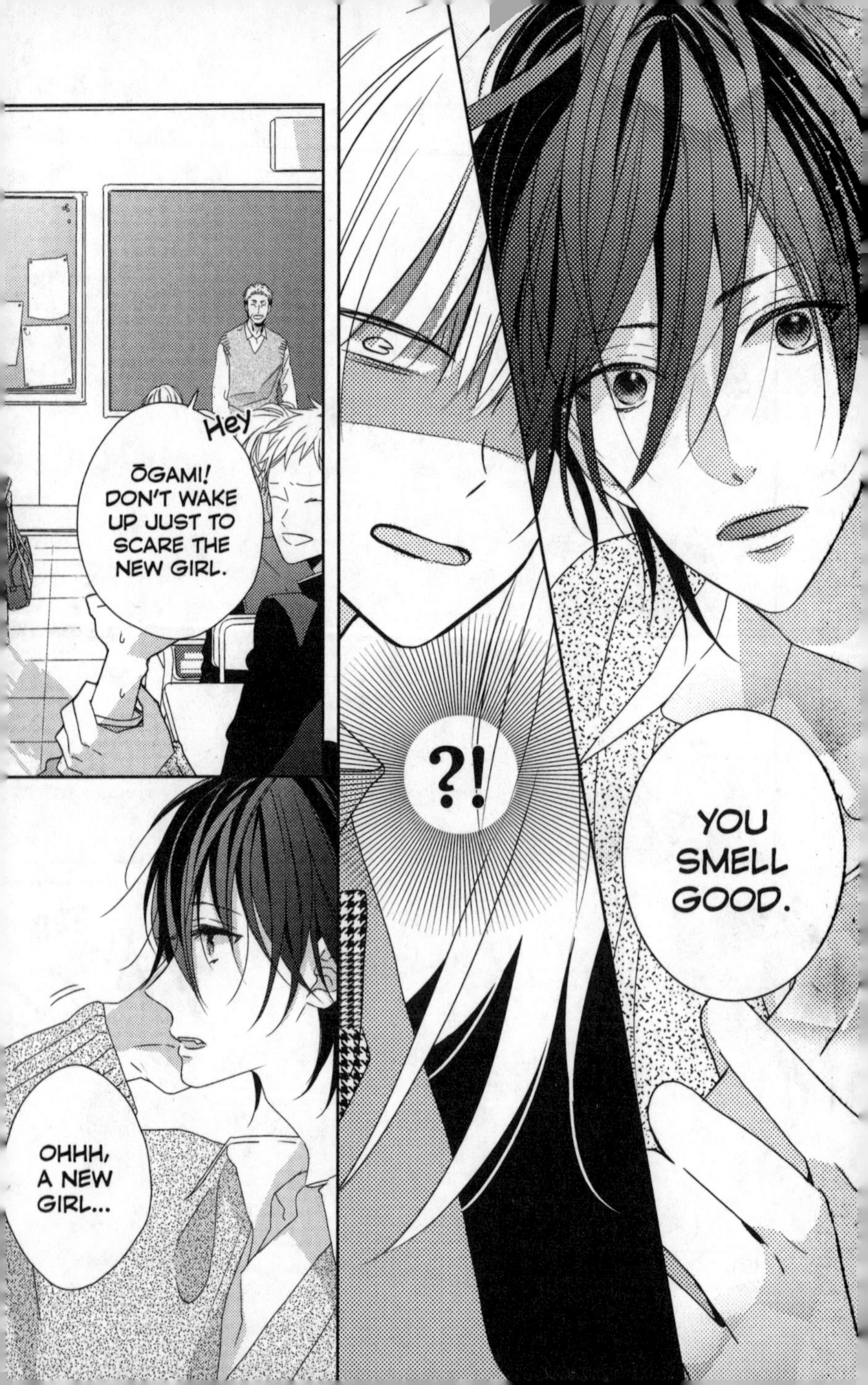
YOU SMELL GOOD.
?!
Hey
ŌGAMI! DON'T WAKE UP JUST TO SCARE THE NEW GIRL.
OHHH, A NEW GIRL...

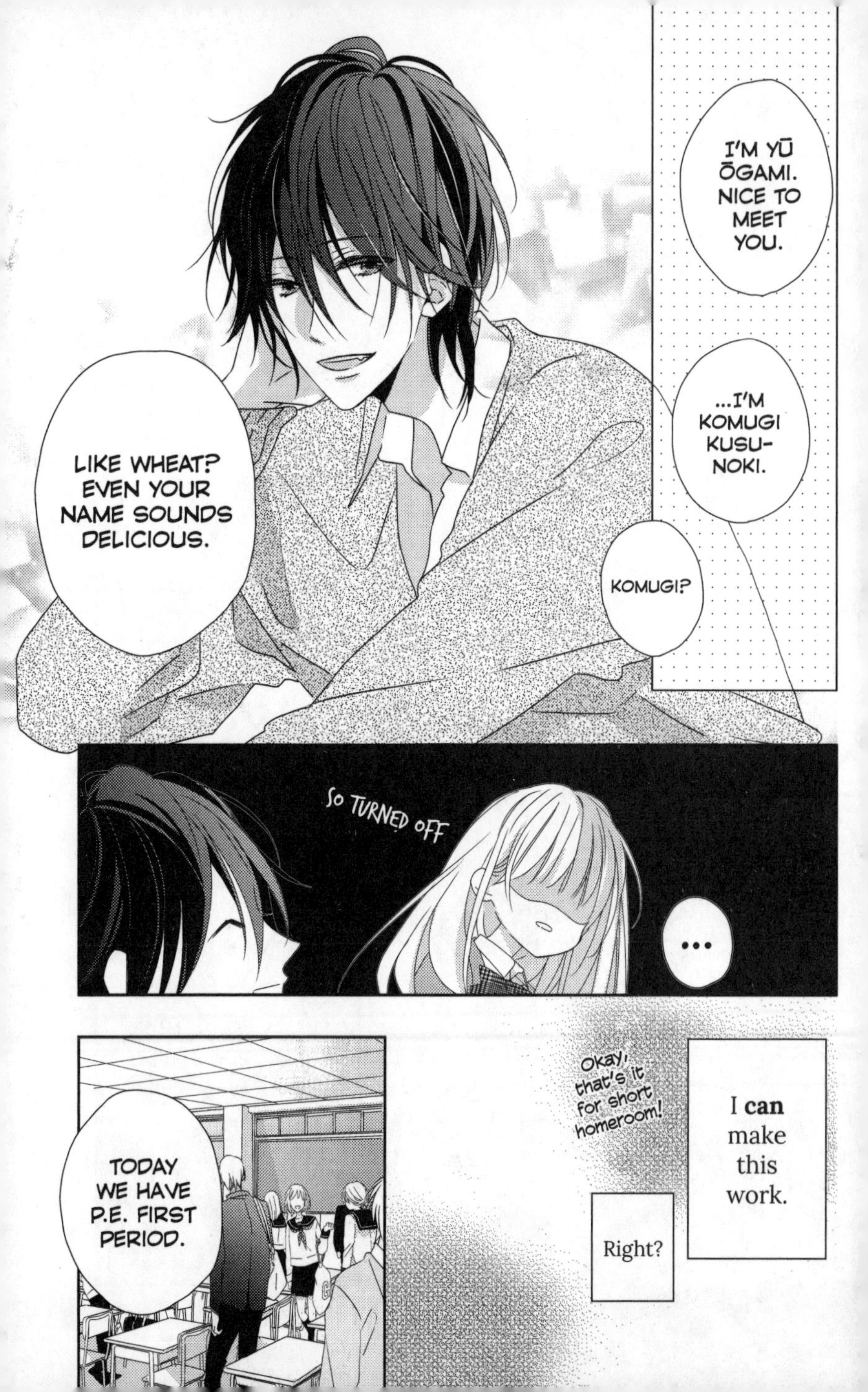
I'M YŪ ŌGAMI. NICE TO MEET YOU.
...I'M KOMUGI KUSUNOKI.
KOMUGI?
LIKE WHEAT? EVEN YOUR NAME SOUNDS DELICIOUS.
...
SO TURNED OFF
I **can** make this work.
Right?
Okay, that's it for short homeroom!
TODAY WE HAVE P.E. FIRST PERIOD.

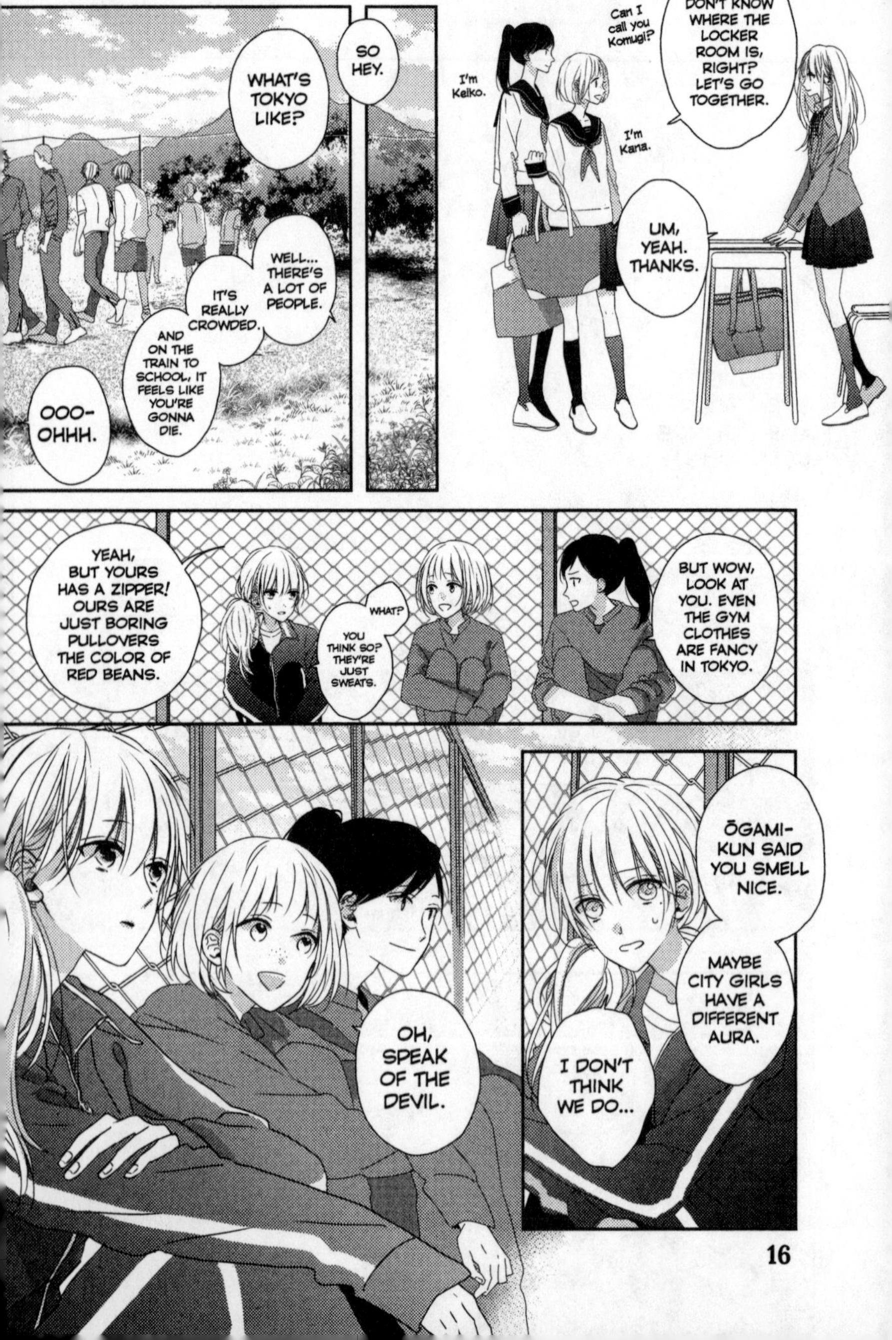
YOU DON'T KNOW WHERE THE LOCKER ROOM IS, RIGHT? LET'S GO TOGETHER.
Can I call you Komugi?
I'm Keiko.
I'm Kana.
UM, YEAH. THANKS.
SO HEY.
WHAT'S TOKYO LIKE?
WELL... THERE'S A LOT OF PEOPLE.
IT'S REALLY CROWDED.
AND ON THE TRAIN TO SCHOOL, IT FEELS LIKE YOU'RE GONNA DIE.
OOO-OHHH.
BUT WOW, LOOK AT YOU. EVEN THE GYM CLOTHES ARE FANCY IN TOKYO.
WHAT?
YOU THINK SO? THEY'RE JUST SWEATS.
YEAH, BUT YOURS HAS A ZIPPER! OURS ARE JUST BORING PULLOVERS THE COLOR OF RED BEANS.
ŌGAMI-KUN SAID YOU SMELL NICE.
MAYBE CITY GIRLS HAVE A DIFFERENT AURA.
I DON'T THINK WE DO...
OH, SPEAK OF THE DEVIL.

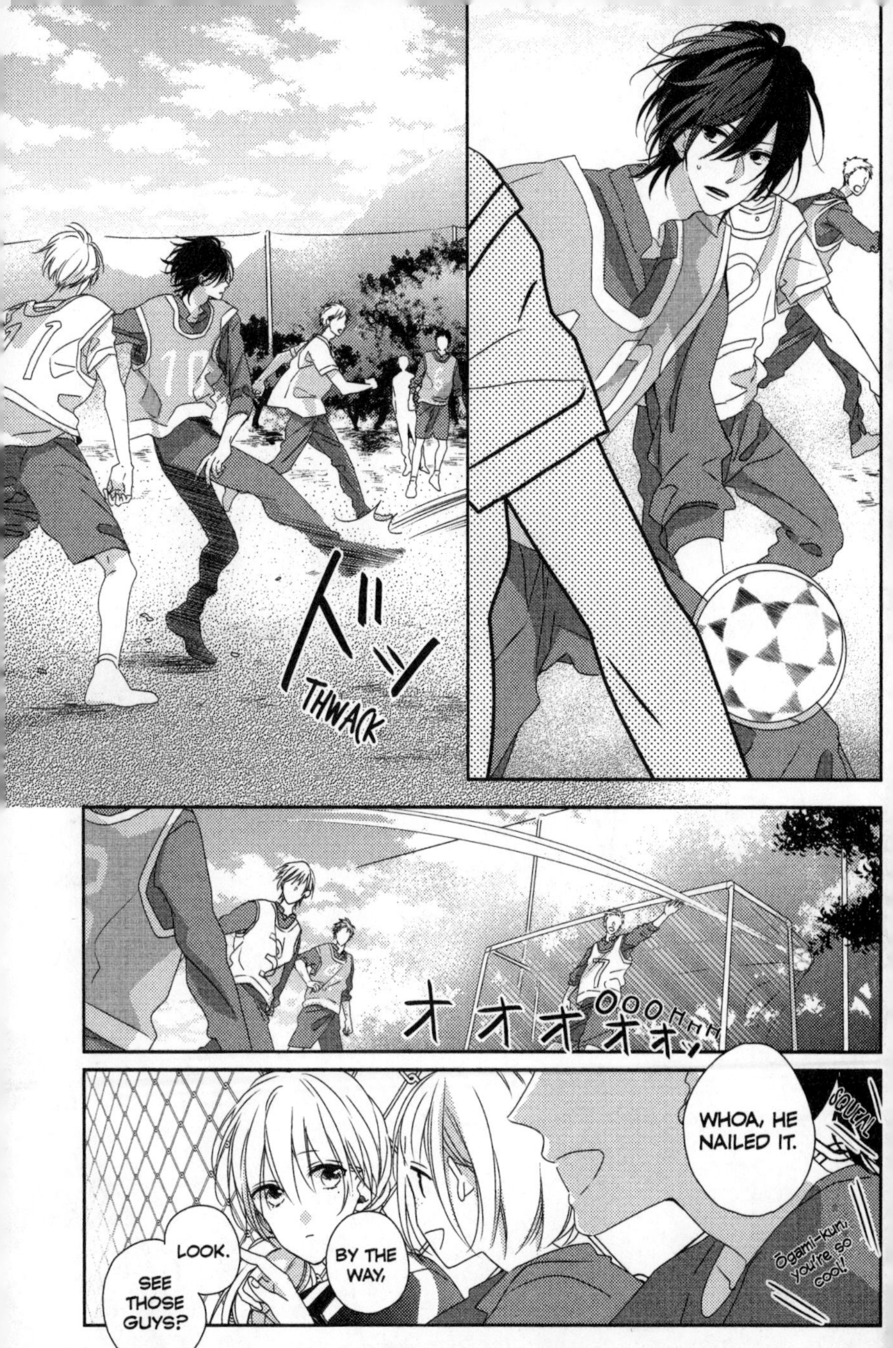
ドッ
THWACK
オオオオオッ
OOOOHHHH
WHOA, HE NAILED IT.
SQUEAL
Ōgami-kun, you're so cool!
BY THE WAY,
LOOK.
SEE THOSE GUYS?

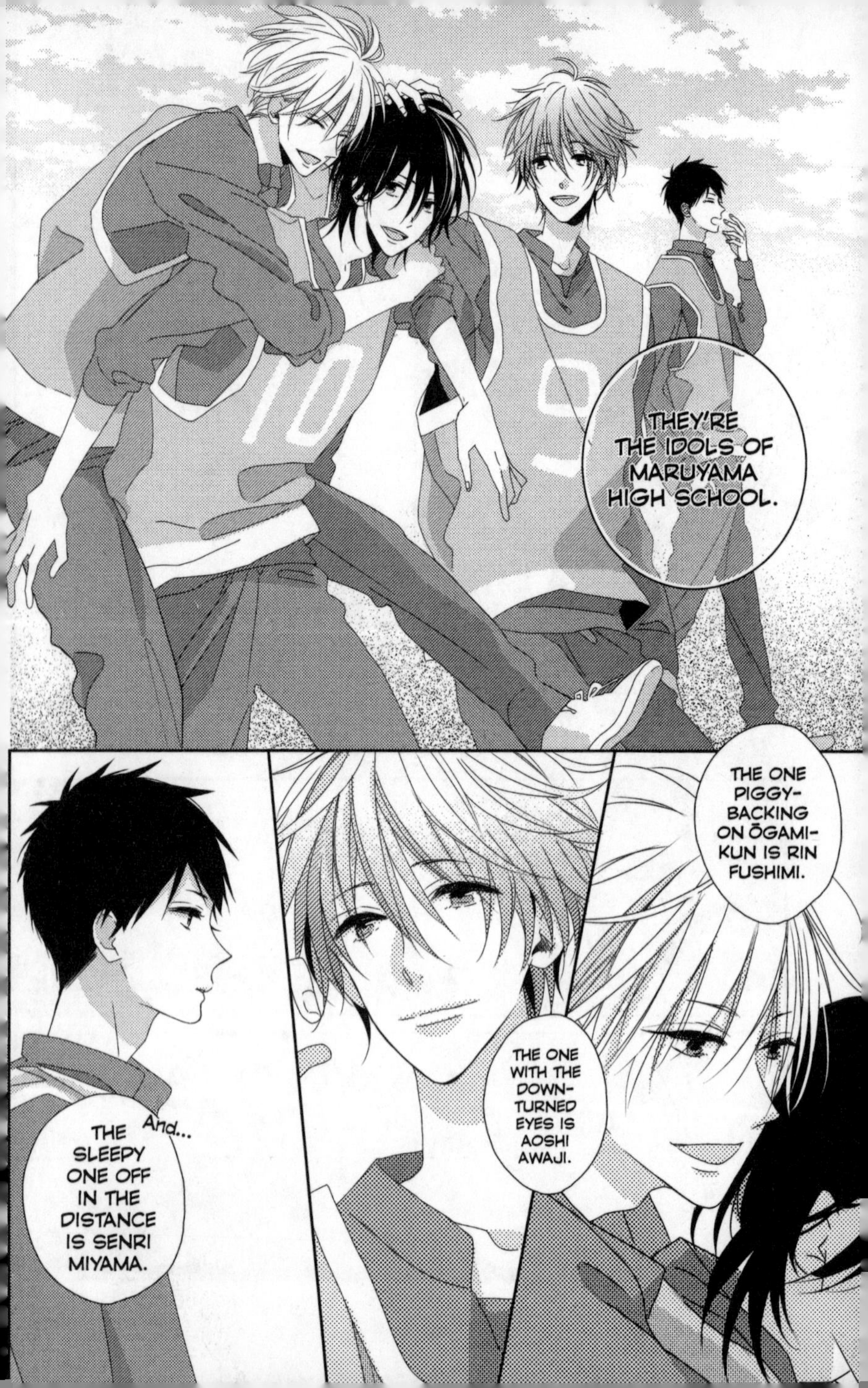
THEY'RE THE IDOLS OF MARUYAMA HIGH SCHOOL.
THE ONE PIGGY-BACKING ON ŌGAMI-KUN IS RIN FUSHIMI.
THE ONE WITH THE DOWN-TURNED EYES IS AOSHI AWAJI.
And...
THE SLEEPY ONE OFF IN THE DISTANCE IS SENRI MIYAMA.

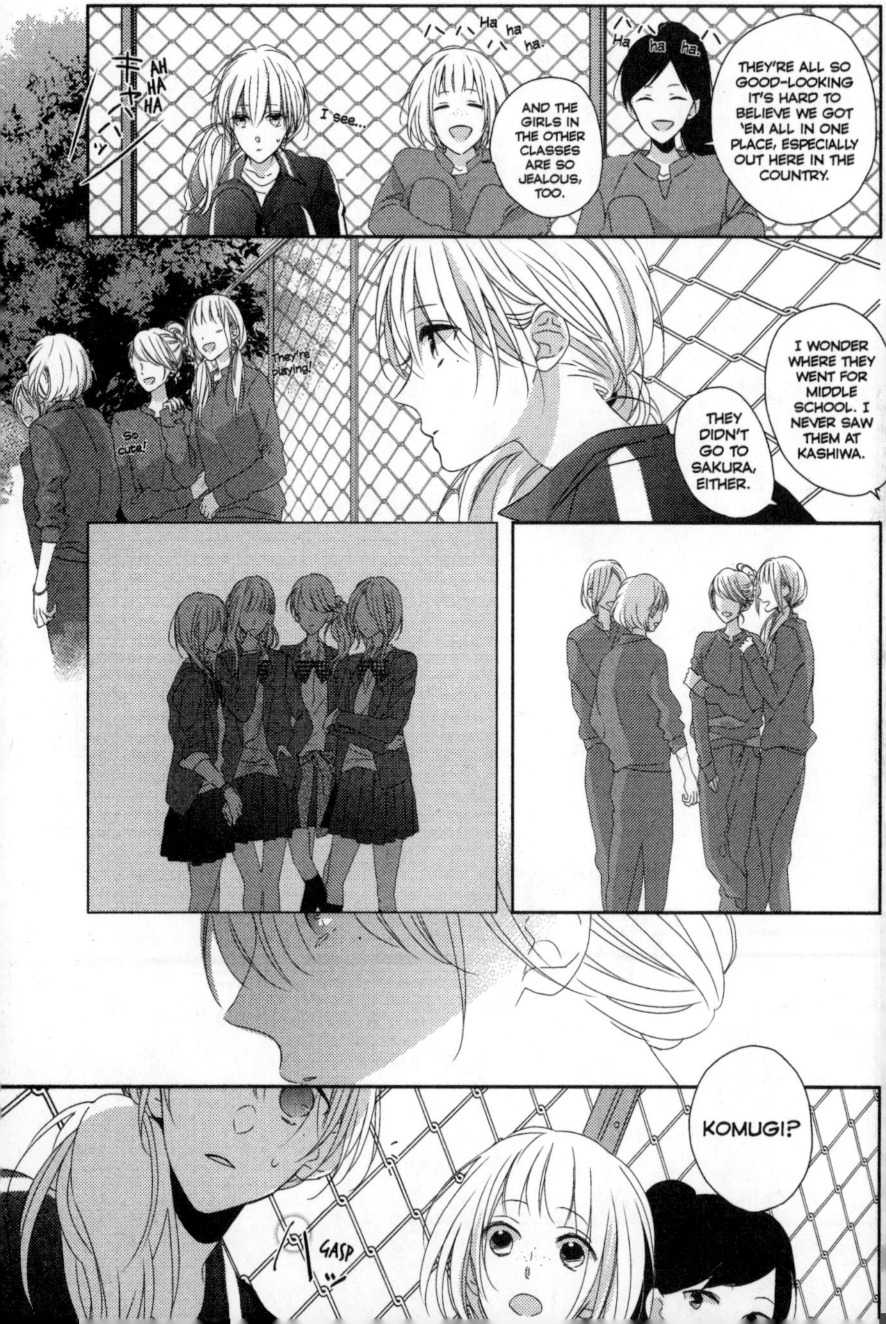
THEY'RE ALL SO GOOD-LOOKING IT'S HARD TO BELIEVE WE GOT 'EM ALL IN ONE PLACE, ESPECIALLY OUT HERE IN THE COUNTRY.
Ha ha ha.
AND THE GIRLS IN THE OTHER CLASSES ARE SO JEALOUS, TOO.
Ha ha ha.
I see...
AH HA HA
I WONDER WHERE THEY WENT FOR MIDDLE SCHOOL. I NEVER SAW THEM AT KASHIWA.
THEY DIDN'T GO TO SAKURA, EITHER.
They're playing!
So cute!
KOMUGI!?
GASP

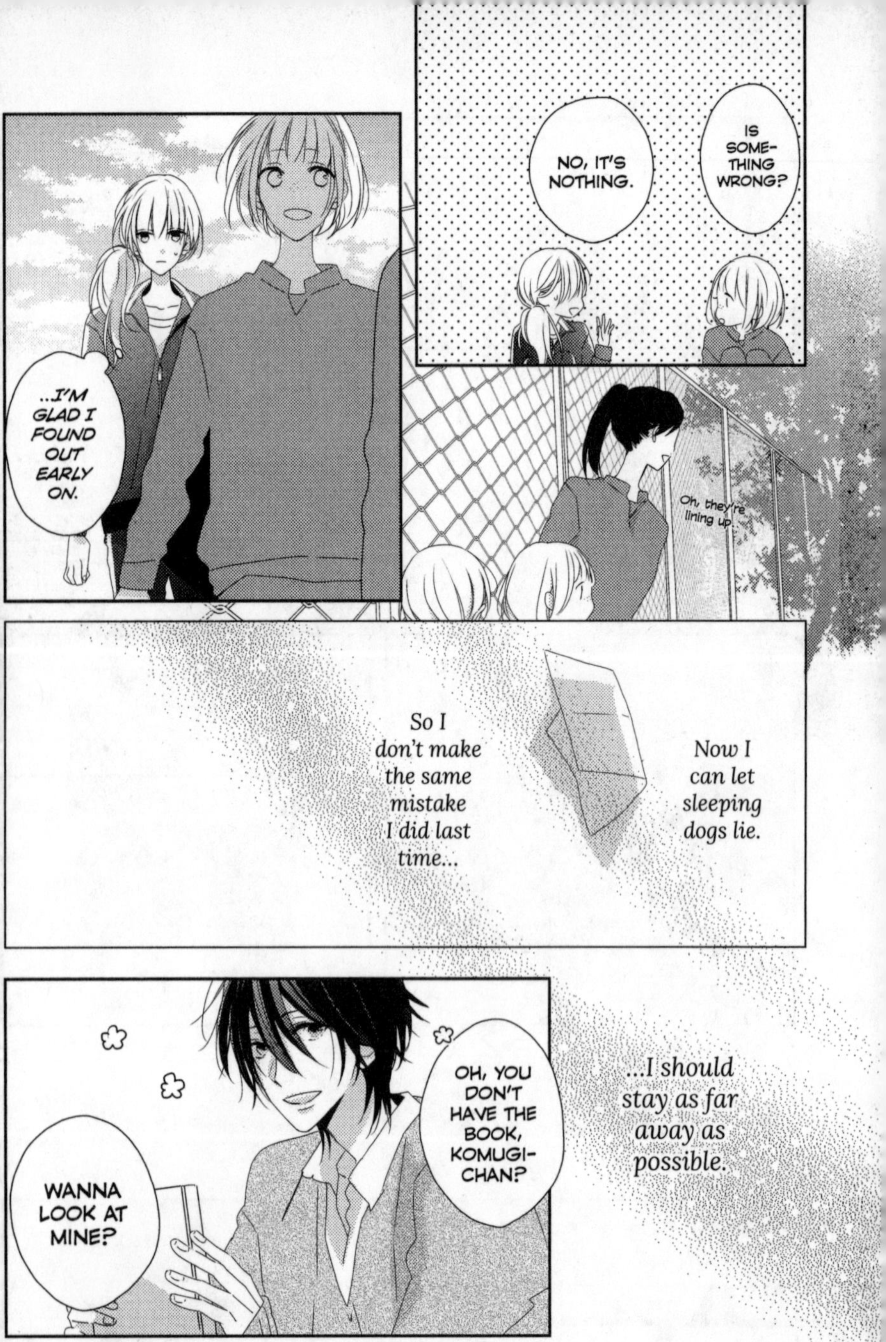
IS SOMETHING WRONG?
NO, IT'S NOTHING.
Oh, they're lining up...
...I'M GLAD I FOUND OUT EARLY ON.
Now I can let sleeping dogs lie.
So I don't make the same mistake I did last time...
...I should stay as far away as possible.
OH, YOU DON'T HAVE THE BOOK, KOMUGI-CHAN?
WANNA LOOK AT MINE?

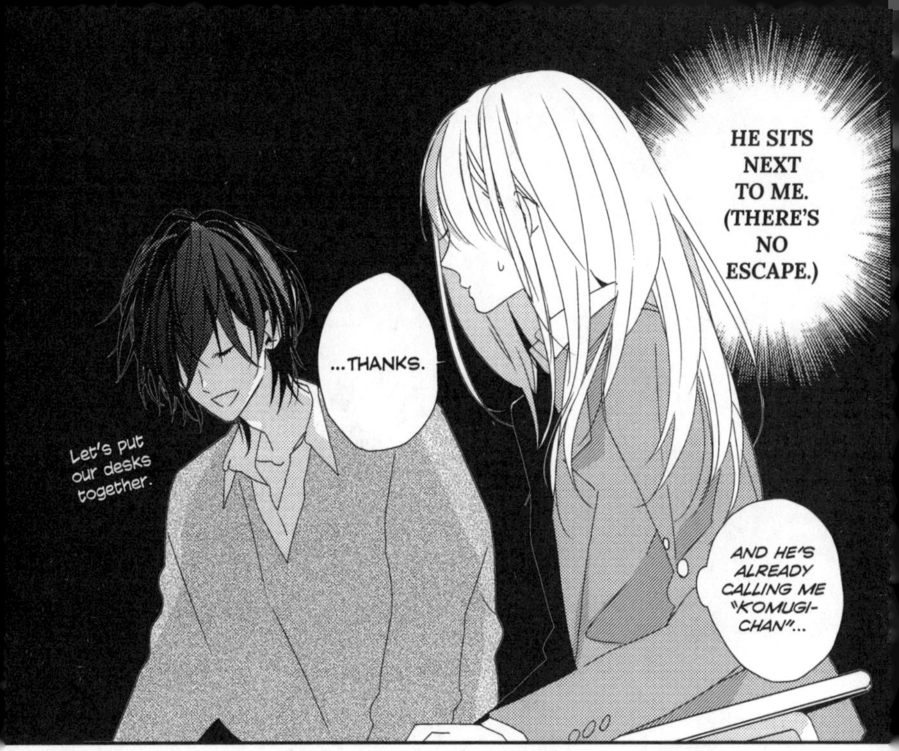
HE SITS NEXT TO ME. (THERE'S NO ESCAPE.)
...THANKS.
Let's put our desks together.
AND HE'S ALREADY CALLING ME "KOMUGI-CHAN"...

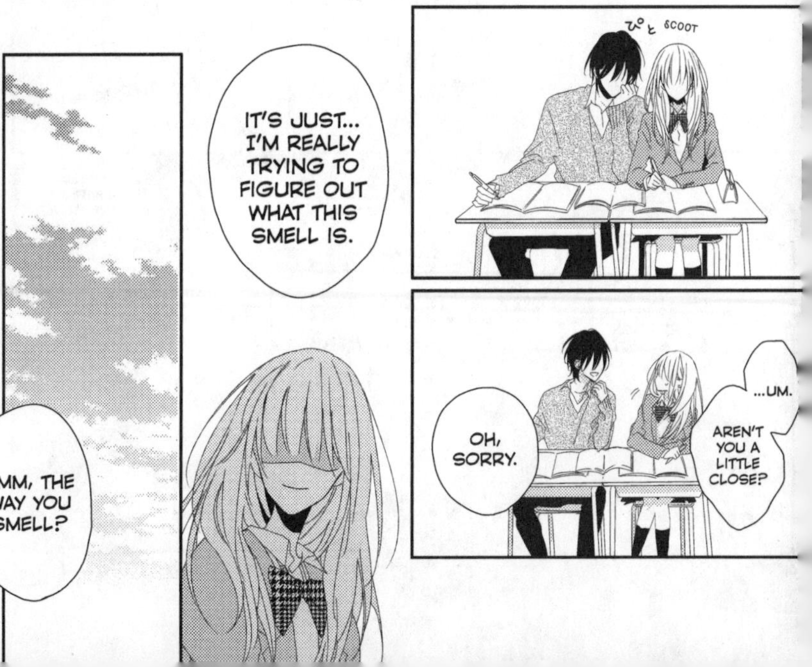
ぴと
SCOOT
...UM.
AREN'T YOU A LITTLE CLOSE?
OH, SORRY.
IT'S JUST... I'M REALLY TRYING TO FIGURE OUT WHAT THIS SMELL IS.
HMM, THE WAY YOU SMELL?

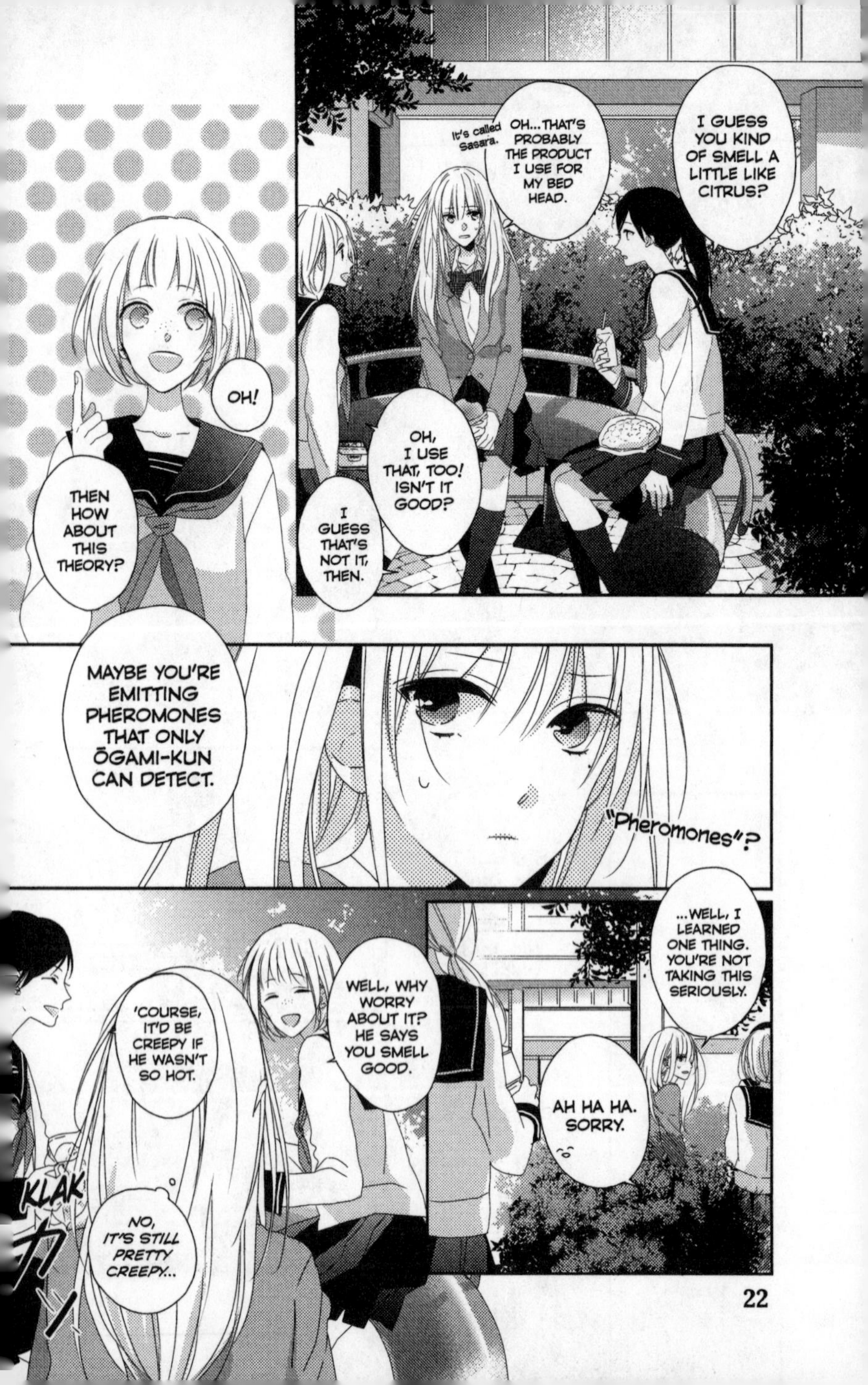
I GUESS YOU KIND OF SMELL A LITTLE LIKE CITRUS?
OH...THAT'S PROBABLY THE PRODUCT I USE FOR MY BED HEAD.
It's called Sasara.
OH, I USE THAT, TOO! ISN'T IT GOOD?
I GUESS THAT'S NOT IT, THEN.
OH!
THEN HOW ABOUT THIS THEORY?
MAYBE YOU'RE EMITTING PHEROMONES THAT ONLY ŌGAMI-KUN CAN DETECT.
"Pheromones"?
...WELL, I LEARNED ONE THING. YOU'RE NOT TAKING THIS SERIOUSLY.
AH HA HA. SORRY.
WELL, WHY WORRY ABOUT IT? HE SAYS YOU SMELL GOOD.
'COURSE, IT'D BE CREEPY IF HE WASN'T SO HOT.
NO, IT'S STILL PRETTY CREEPY...
KLAK

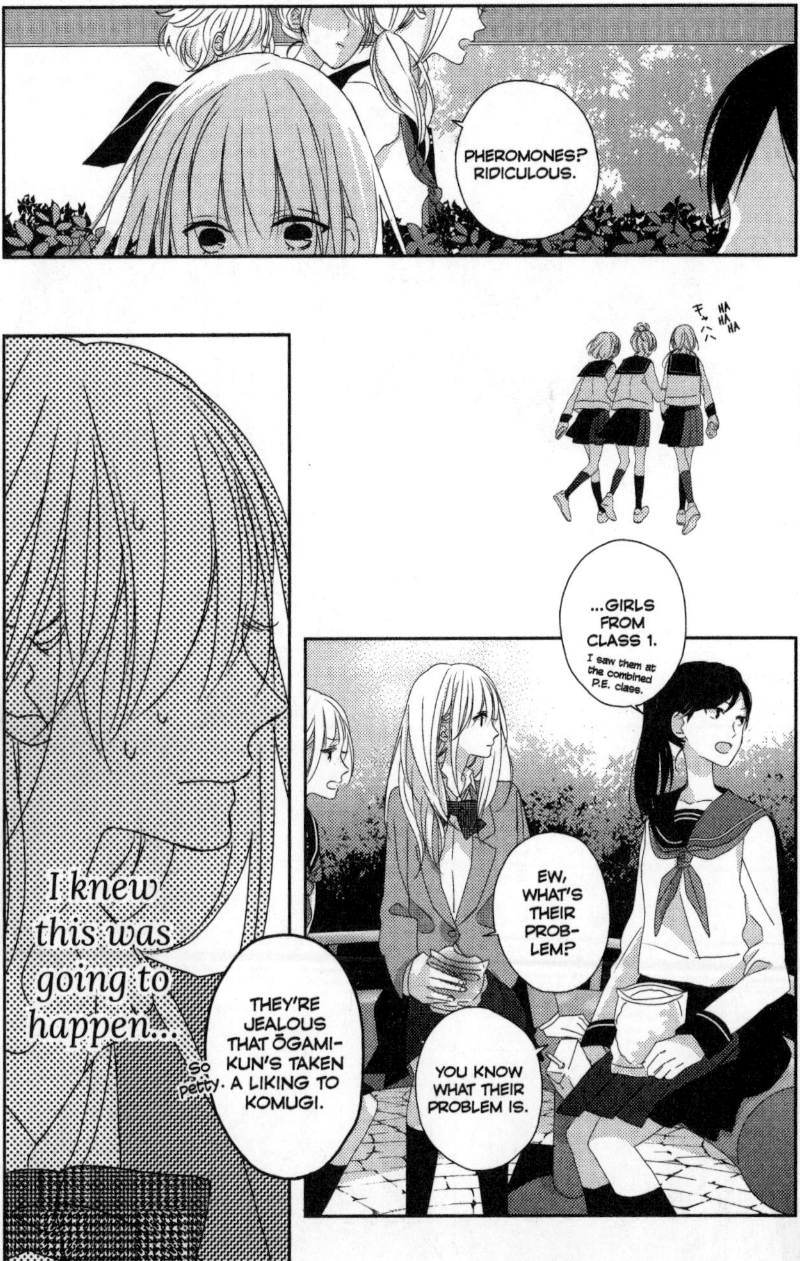
PHEROMONES? RIDICULOUS.
HA HA HA
...GIRLS FROM CLASS 1.
I saw them at the combined P.E. class.
EW, WHAT'S THEIR PROB-LEM?
YOU KNOW WHAT THEIR PROBLEM IS.
THEY'RE JEALOUS THAT ŌGAMI-KUN'S TAKEN A LIKING TO KOMUGI.
So petty.
I knew this was going to happen...

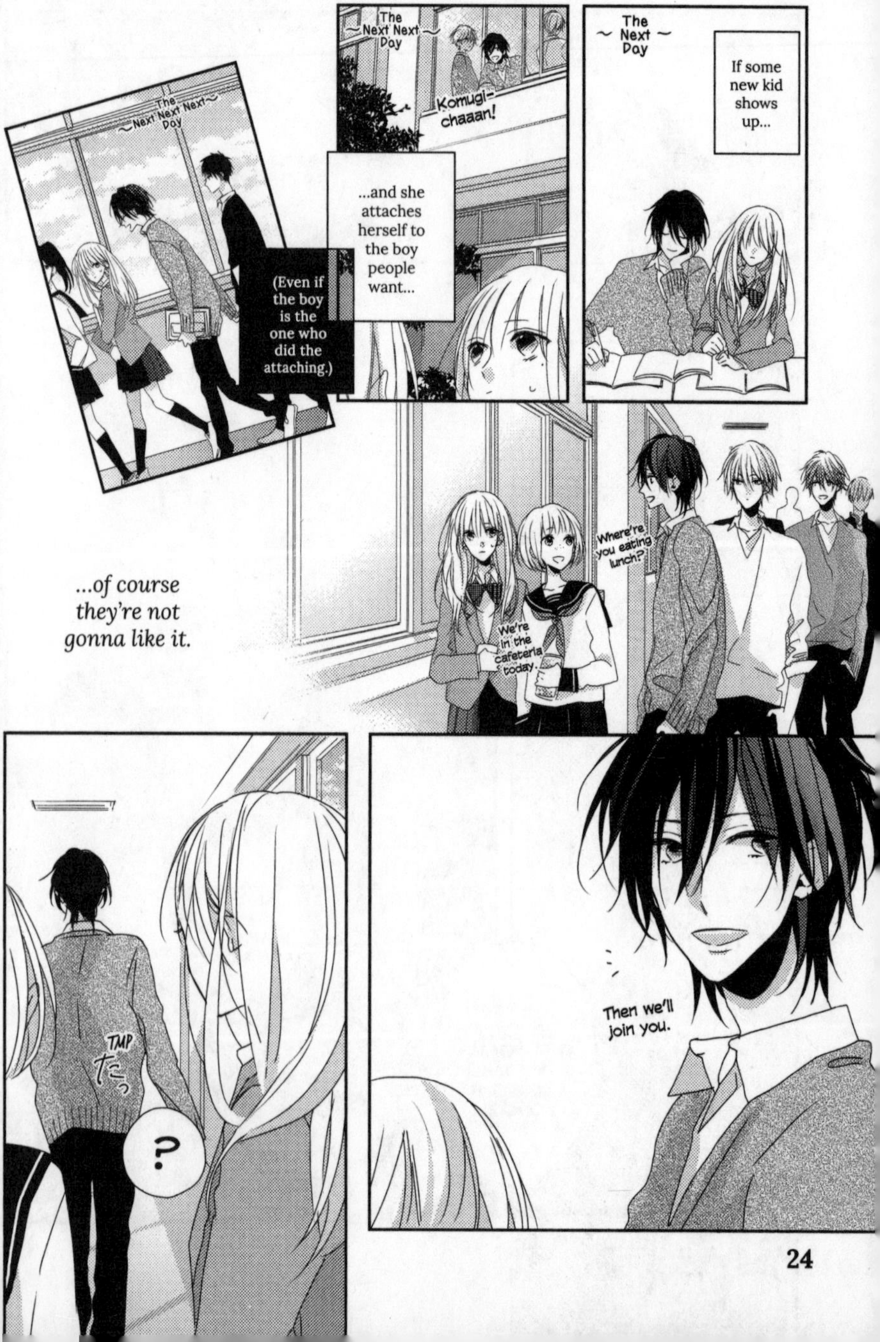
~ The Next Day ~
If some new kid shows up...
~ The Next Next Day ~
Komugi-chaaan!
...and she attaches herself to the boy people want...
~ The Next Next Next ~ Day
(Even if the boy is the one who did the attaching.)
Where're you eating lunch?
We're in the cafeteria today.
...of course they're not gonna like it.
Then we'll join you.
TMP
たっ
?

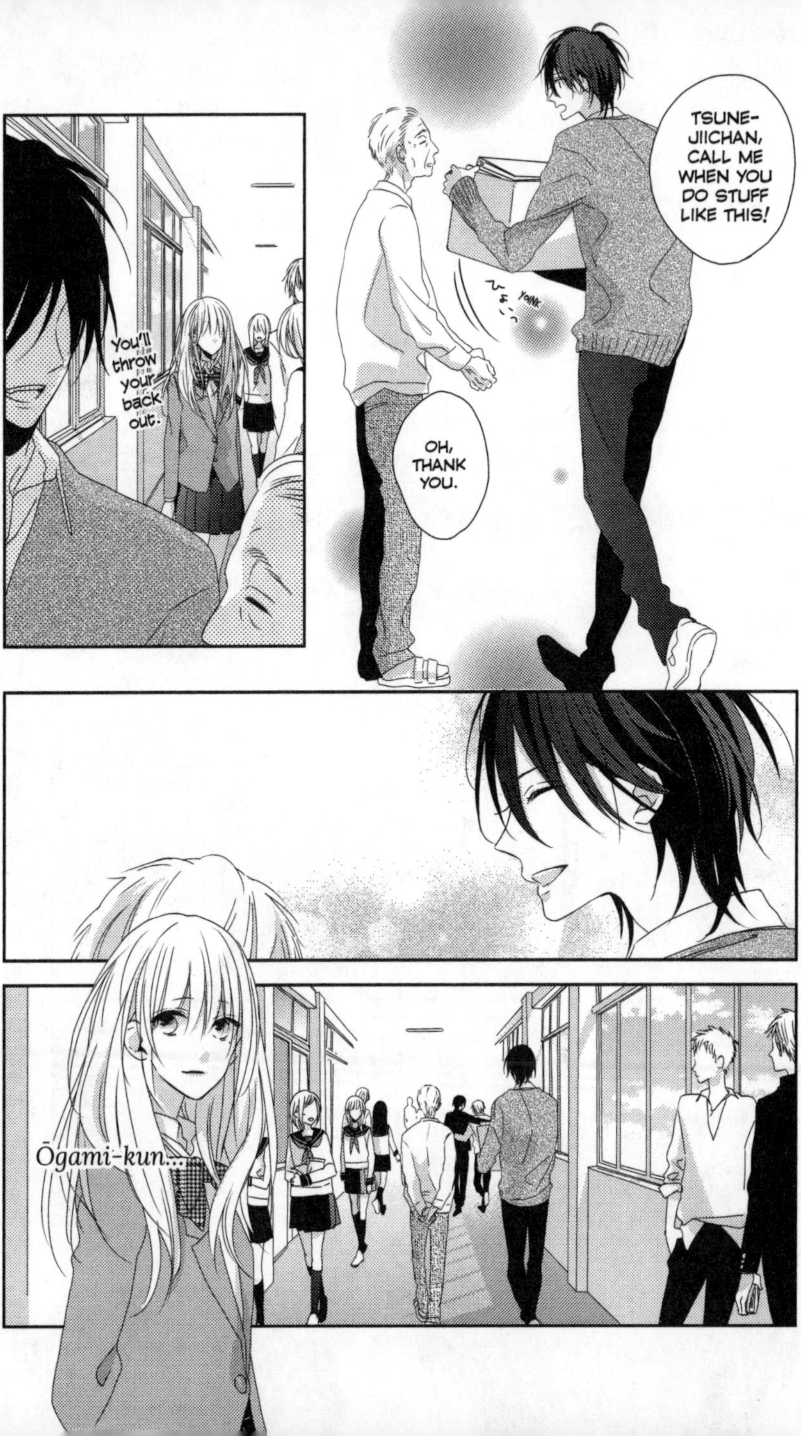
TSUNE-JIICHAN, CALL ME WHEN YOU DO STUFF LIKE THIS!
ひょいっ
YOINK
OH, THANK YOU.
You'll throw your back out.
Ōgami-kun...

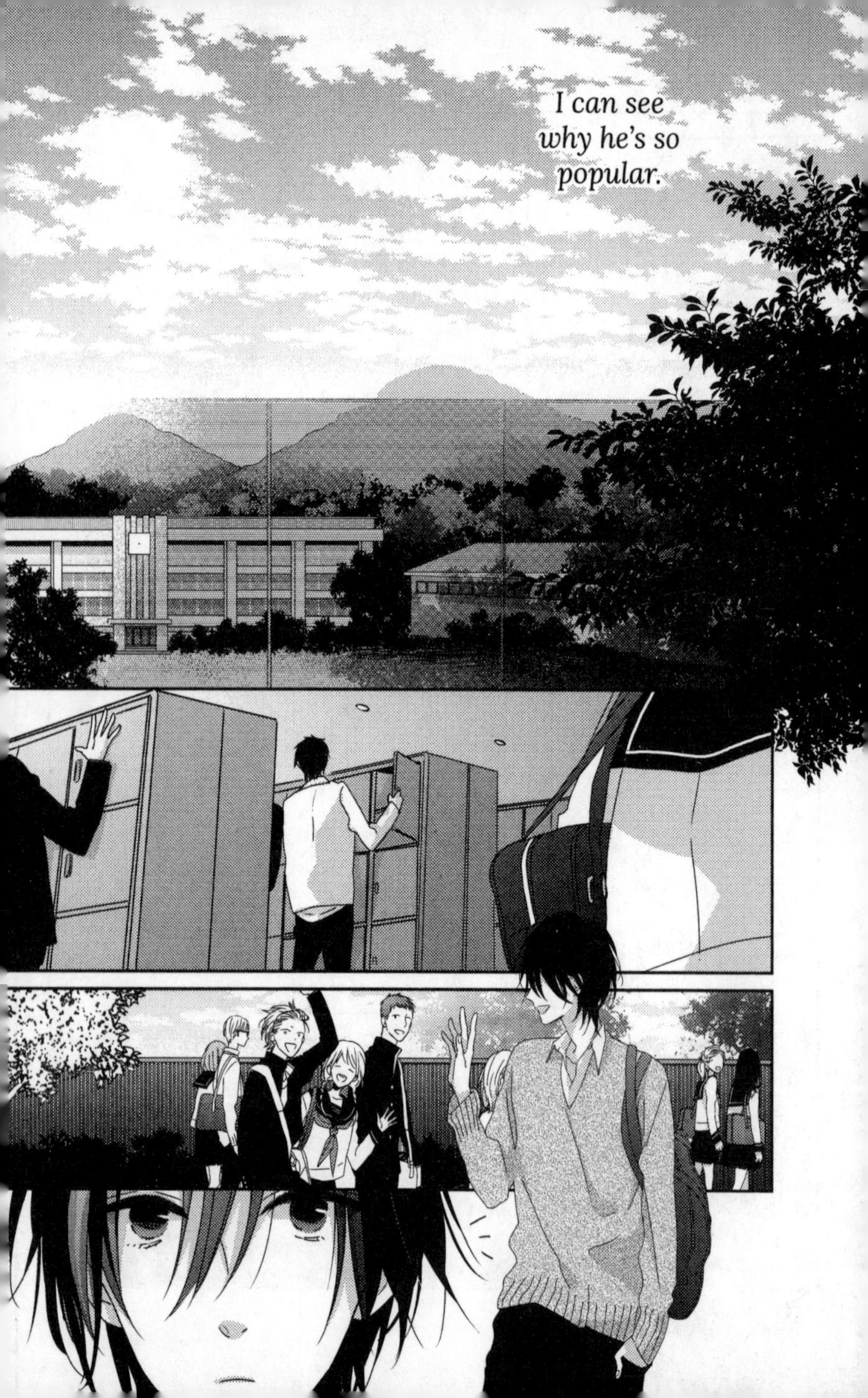
I can see why he's so popular.

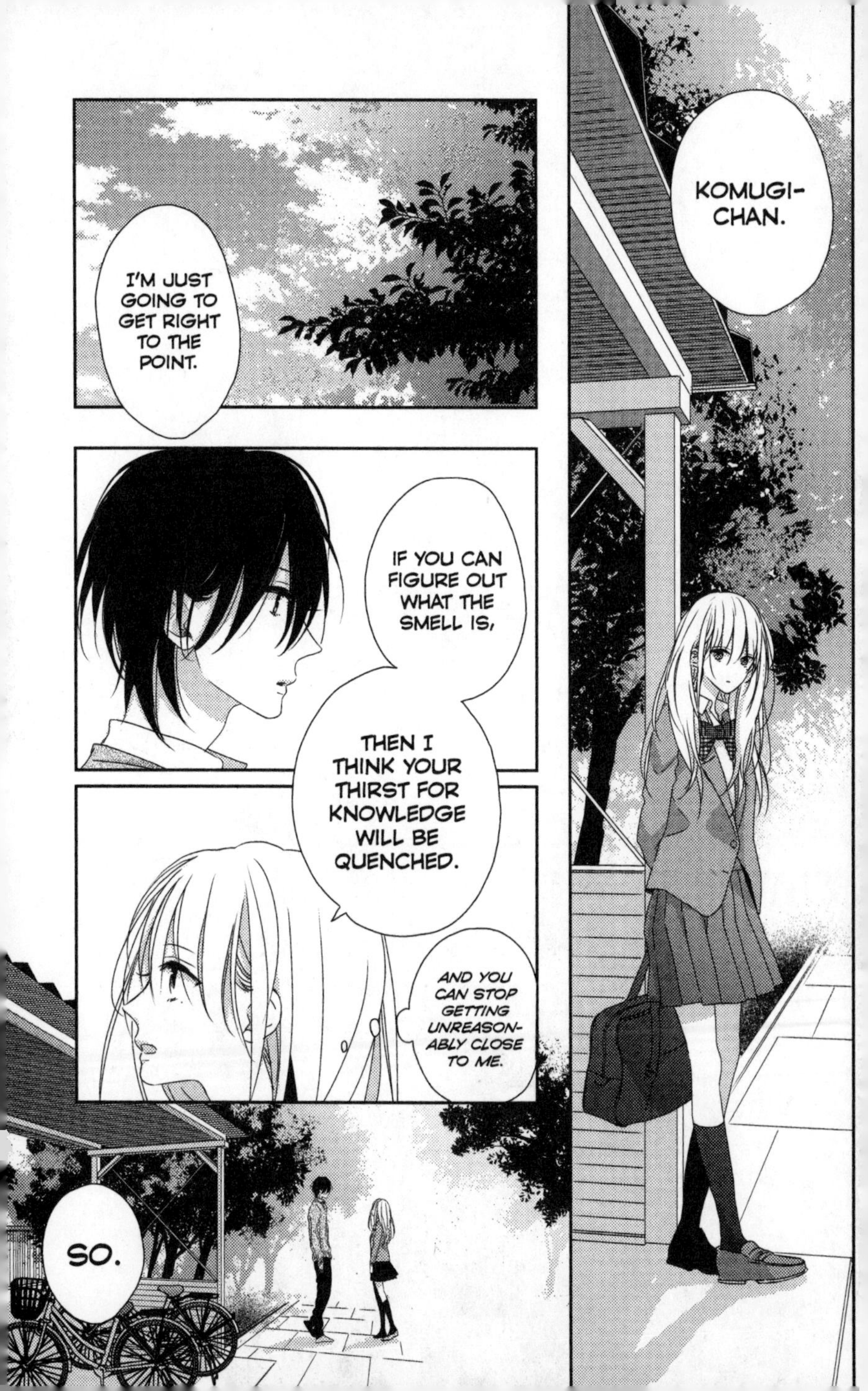
KOMUGI-CHAN.
I'M JUST GOING TO GET RIGHT TO THE POINT.
IF YOU CAN FIGURE OUT WHAT THE SMELL IS,
THEN I THINK YOUR THIRST FOR KNOWLEDGE WILL BE QUENCHED.
AND YOU CAN STOP GETTING UNREASONABLY CLOSE TO ME.
SO.

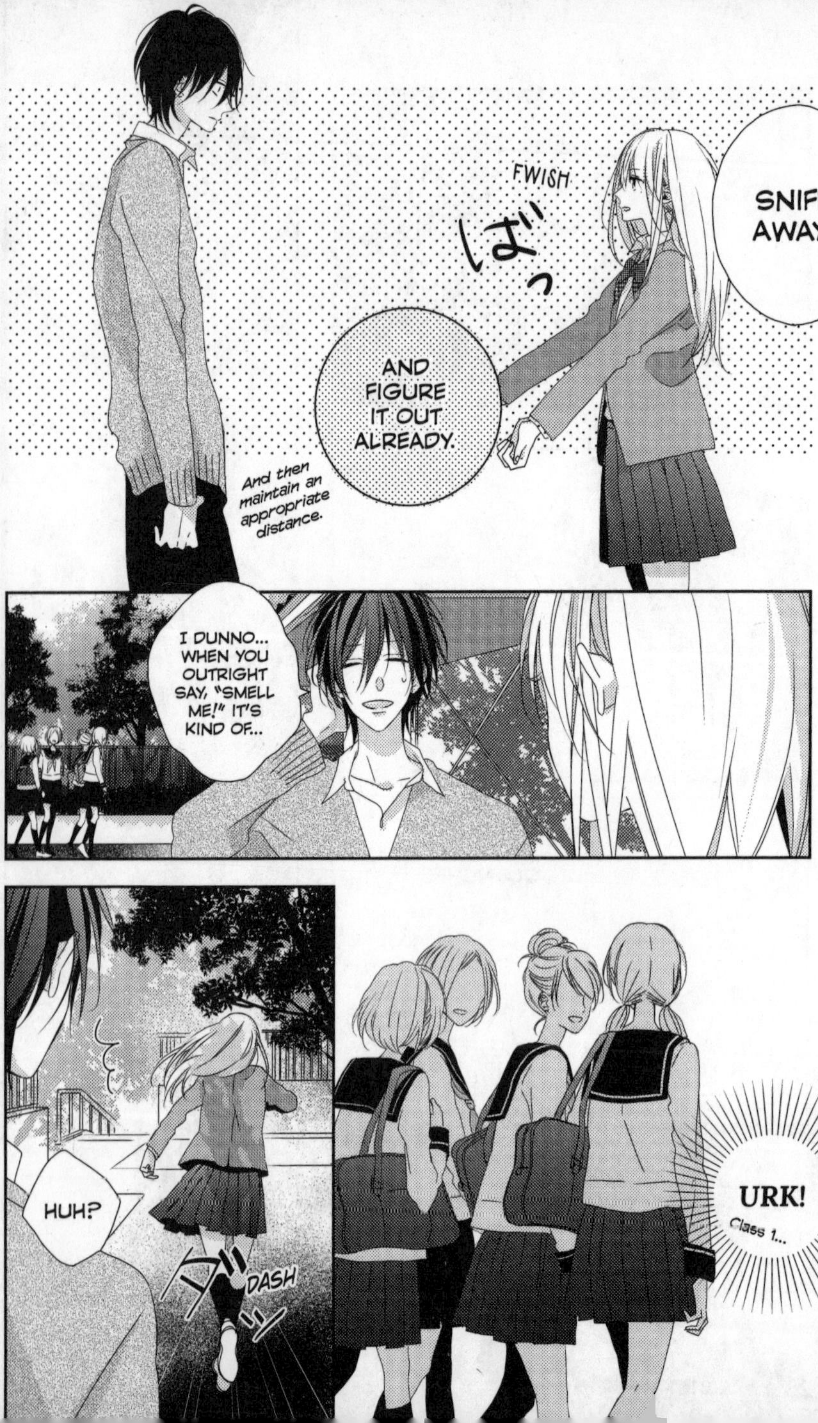
SNIFF AWAY.
FWISH
ばっ
AND FIGURE IT OUT ALREADY.
And then maintain an appropriate distance.
I DUNNO... WHEN YOU OUTRIGHT SAY, "SMELL ME!" IT'S KIND OF...
URK!
Class 1...
HUH?
DASH
ダッ

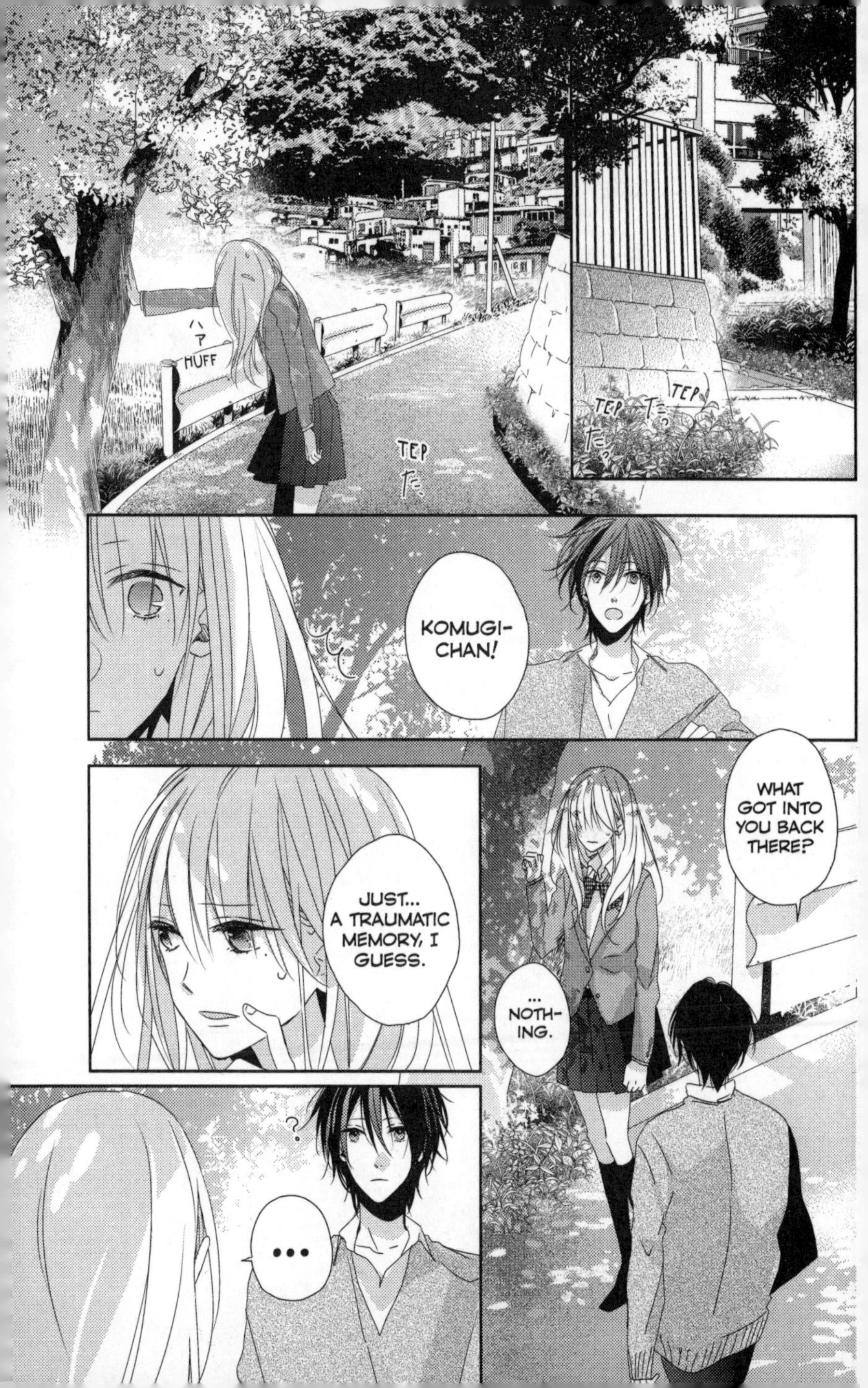
TEP
TEP
HUFF
TEP
KOMUGI-CHAN!
WHAT GOT INTO YOU BACK THERE?
... NOTHING.
JUST... A TRAUMATIC MEMORY, I GUESS.
...

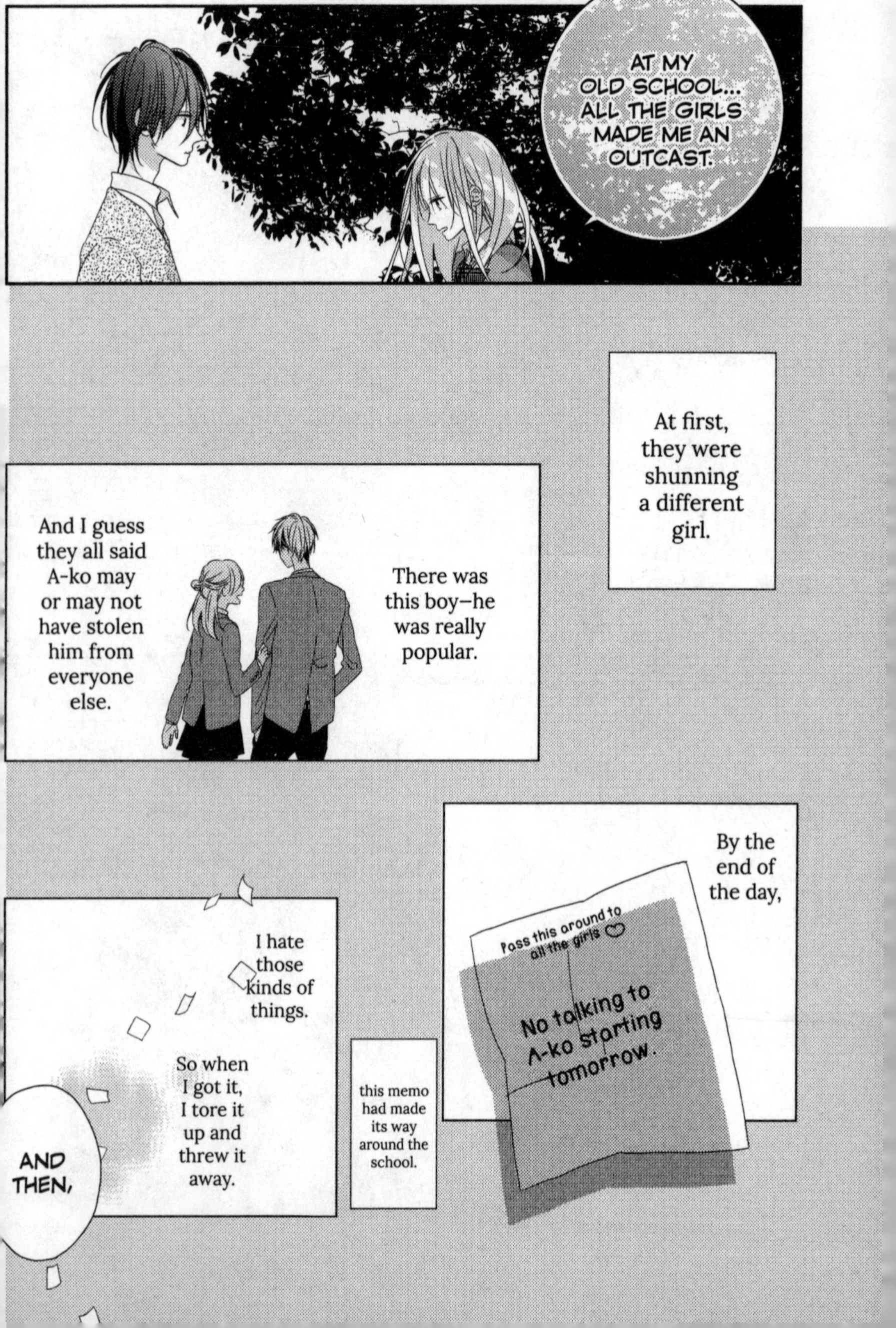
AT MY OLD SCHOOL... ALL THE GIRLS MADE ME AN OUTCAST.
At first, they were shunning a different girl.
There was this boy—he was really popular.
And I guess they all said A-ko may or may not have stolen him from everyone else.
By the end of the day,
Pass this around to all the girls ♡
No talking to A-ko starting tomorrow.
this memo had made its way around the school.
I hate those kinds of things.
So when I got it, I tore it up and threw it away.
AND THEN,

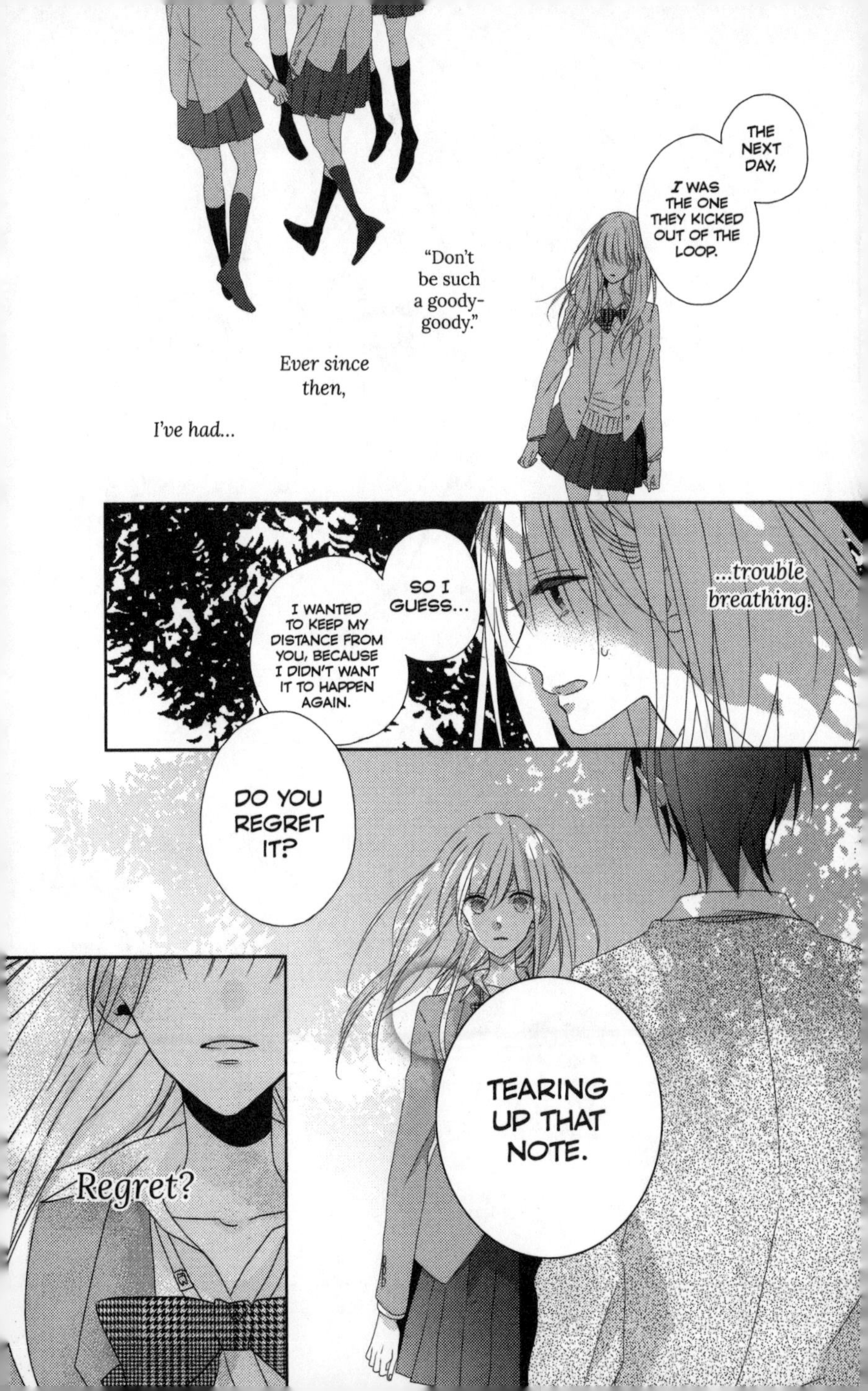
THE NEXT DAY, *I* WAS THE ONE THEY KICKED OUT OF THE LOOP.
“Don’t be such a goody-goody.”
Ever since then,
I’ve had...
...trouble breathing.
SO I GUESS...
I WANTED TO KEEP MY DISTANCE FROM YOU, BECAUSE I DIDN’T WANT IT TO HAPPEN AGAIN.
DO YOU REGRET IT?
TEARING UP THAT NOTE.
Regret?

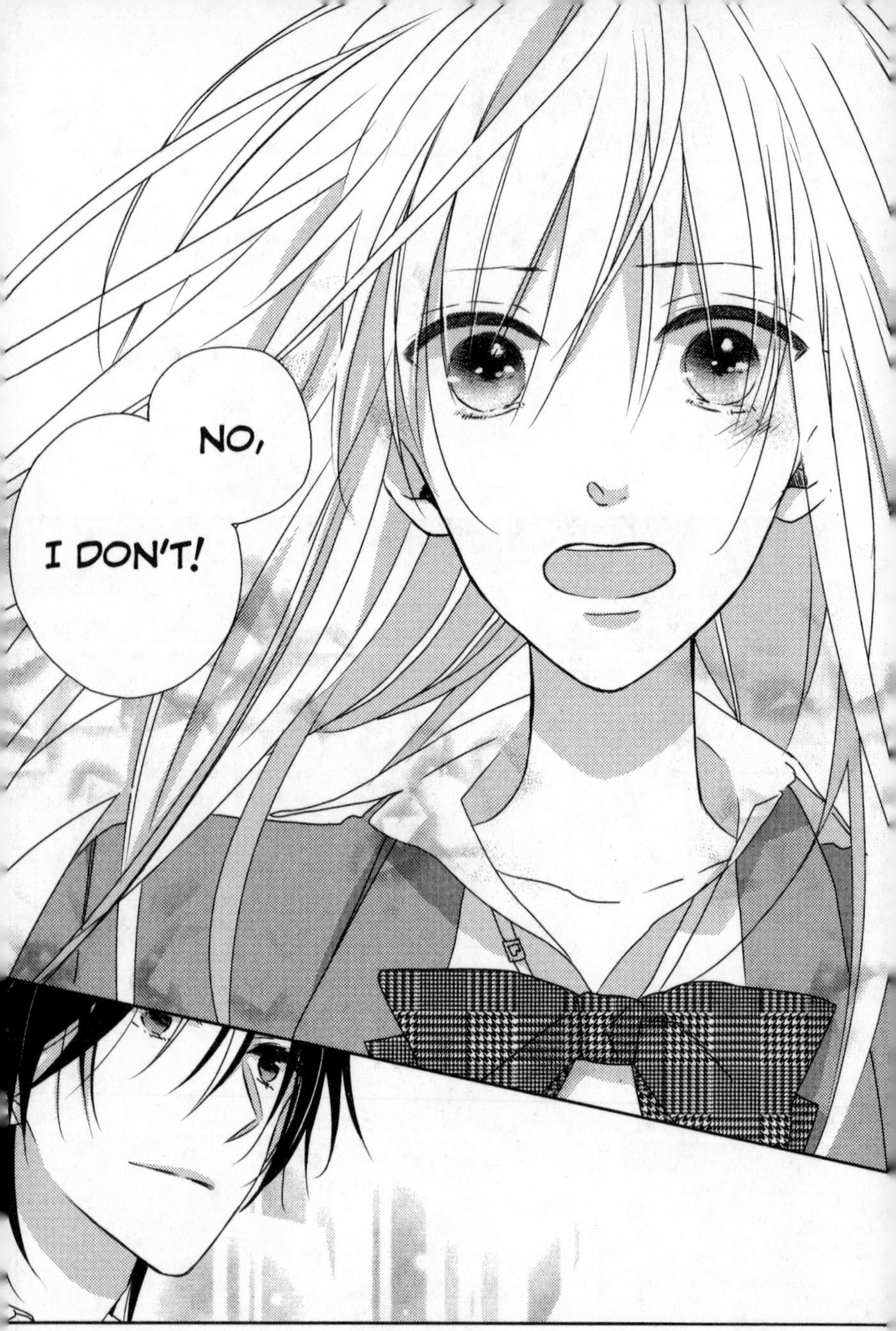
NO, I DON'T!

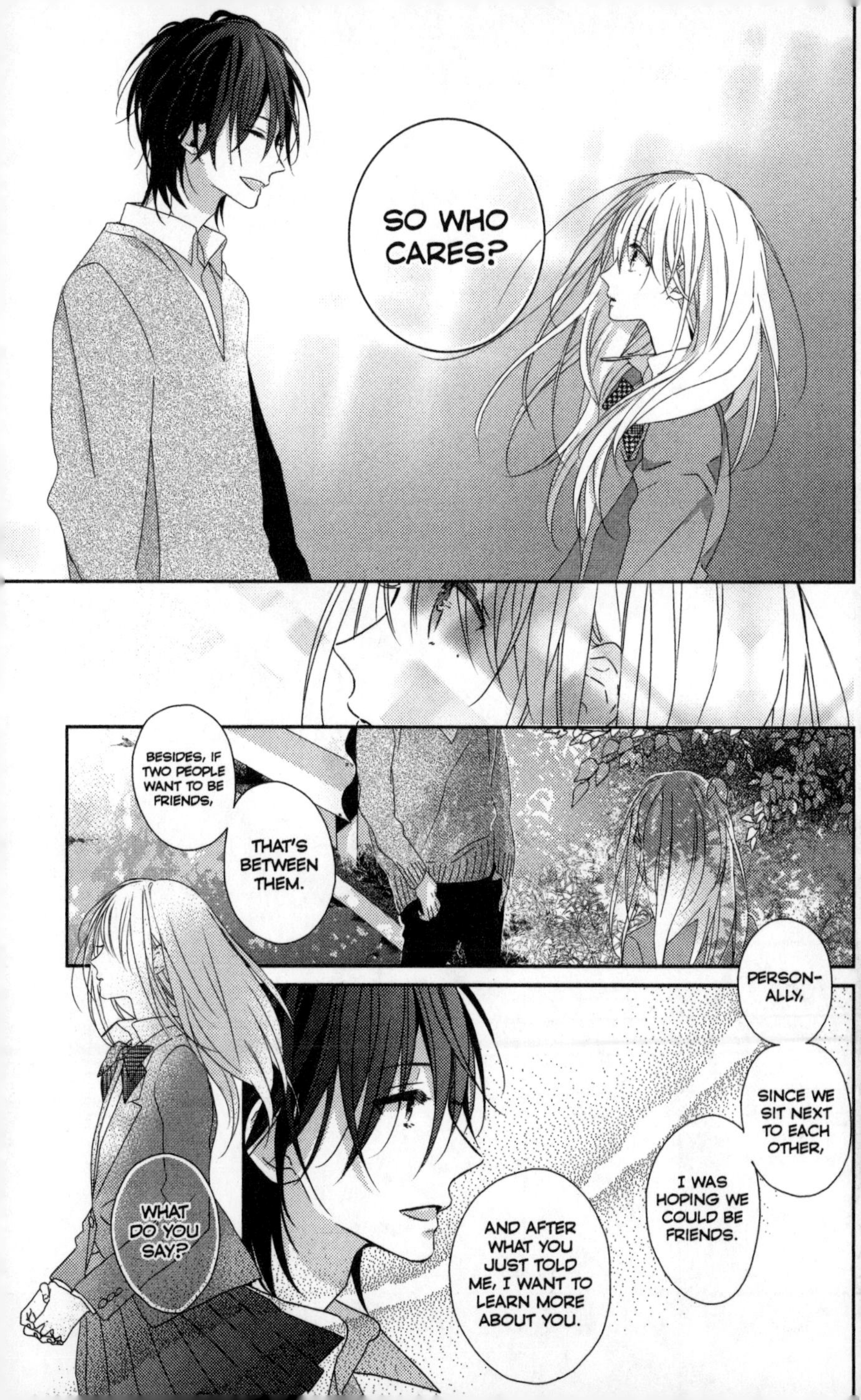
SO WHO CARES?
BESIDES, IF TWO PEOPLE WANT TO BE FRIENDS,
THAT'S BETWEEN THEM.
PERSON-ALLY,
SINCE WE SIT NEXT TO EACH OTHER,
I WAS HOPING WE COULD BE FRIENDS.
AND AFTER WHAT YOU JUST TOLD ME, I WANT TO LEARN MORE ABOUT YOU.
WHAT DO YOU SAY?

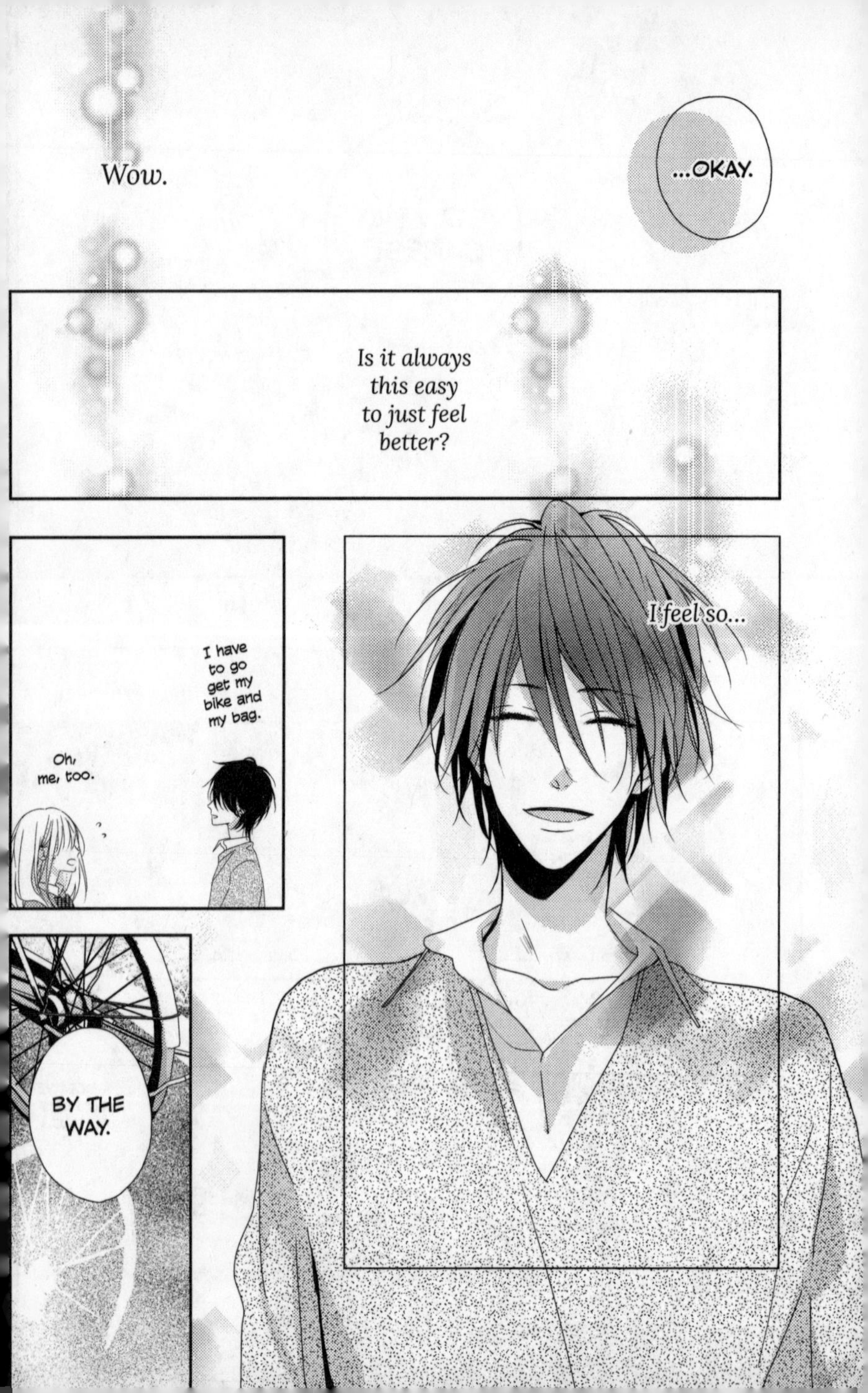
...OKAY.
Wow.
Is it always this easy to just feel better?
I feel so...
I have to go get my bike and my bag.
Oh, me, too.
BY THE WAY.

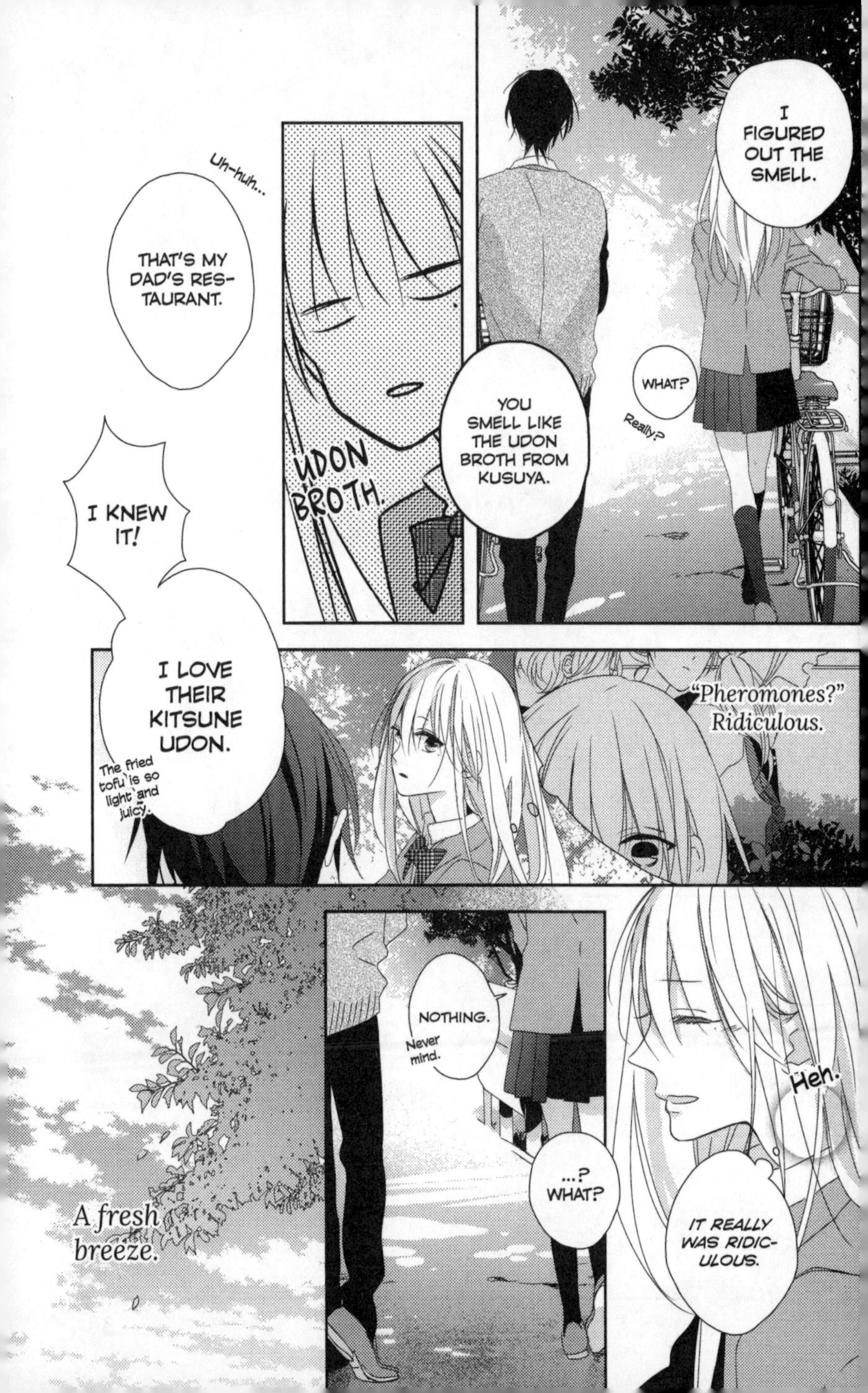
I FIGURED OUT THE SMELL.
WHAT?
Really?
YOU SMELL LIKE THE UDON BROTH FROM KUSUYA.
UDON BROTH.
Uh-huh...
THAT'S MY DAD'S RES-TAURANT.
I KNEW IT!
"Pheromones?" Ridiculous.
I LOVE THEIR KITSUNE UDON.
The fried tofu is so light and juicy.
Heh.
IT REALLY WAS RIDIC-ULOUS.
...? WHAT?
NOTHING.
Never mind.
A fresh breeze.

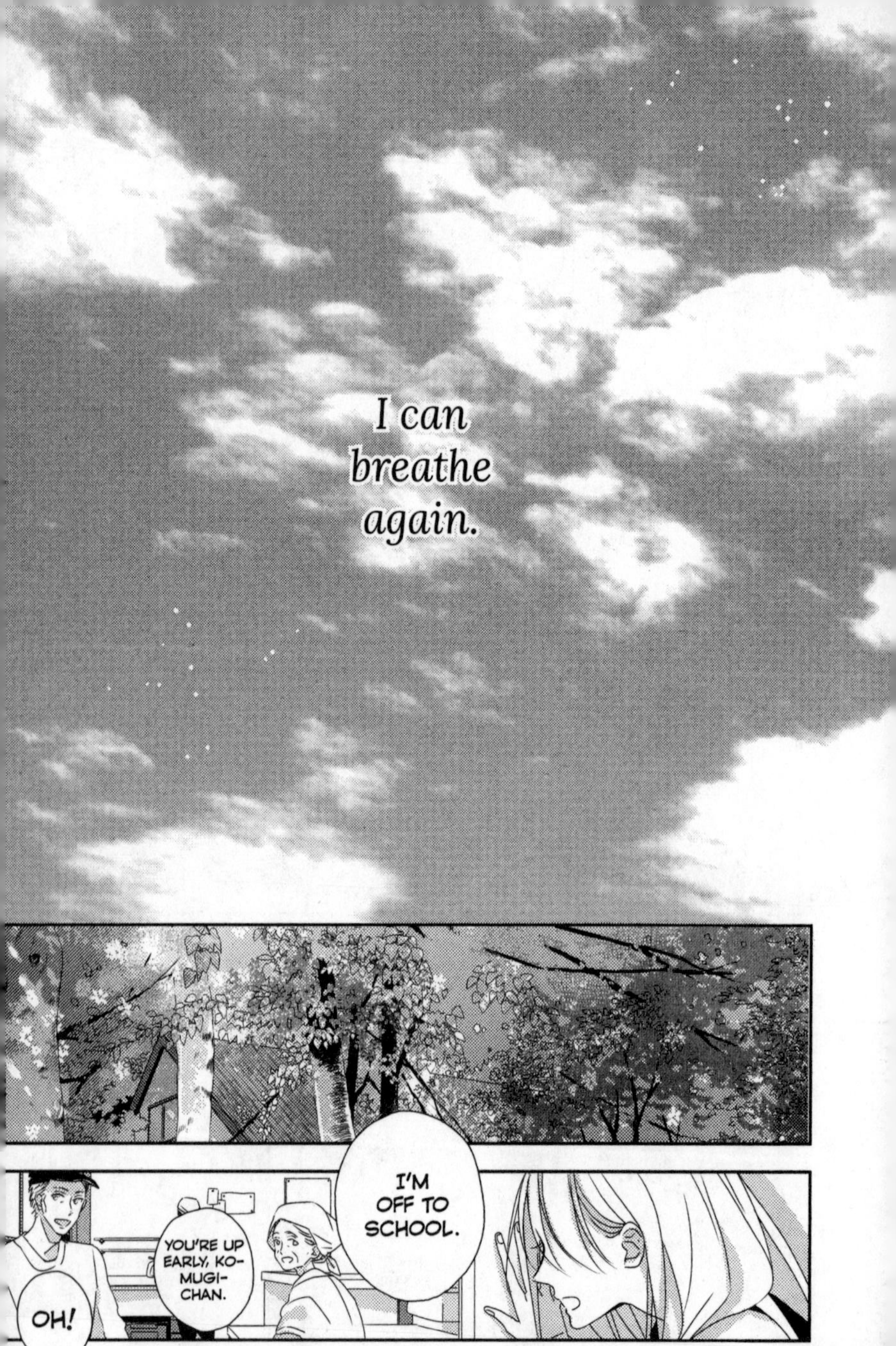
I can breathe again.
I'M OFF TO SCHOOL.
YOU'RE UP EARLY, KO-MUGI-CHAN.
OH!

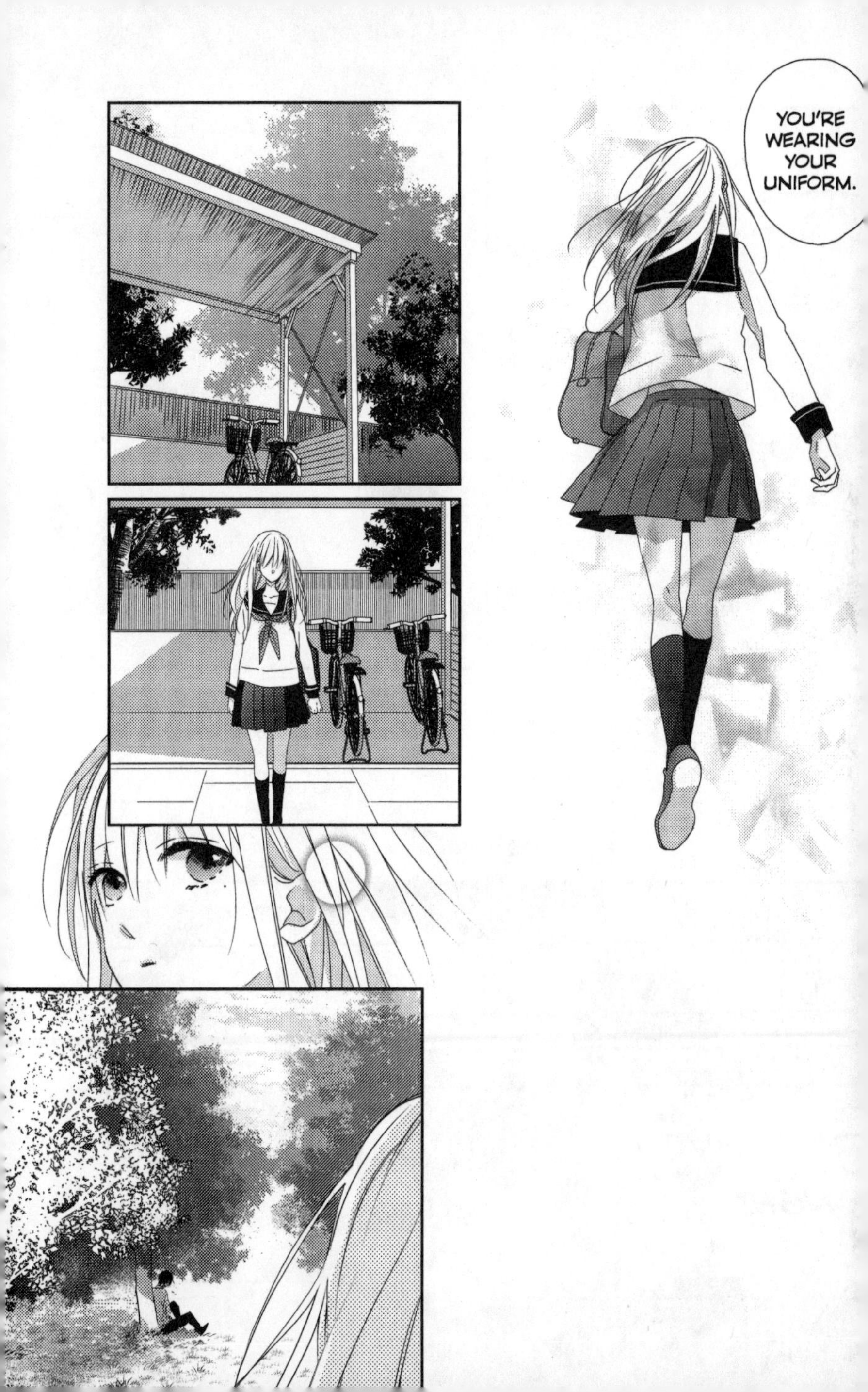
YOU'RE WEARING YOUR UNIFORM.

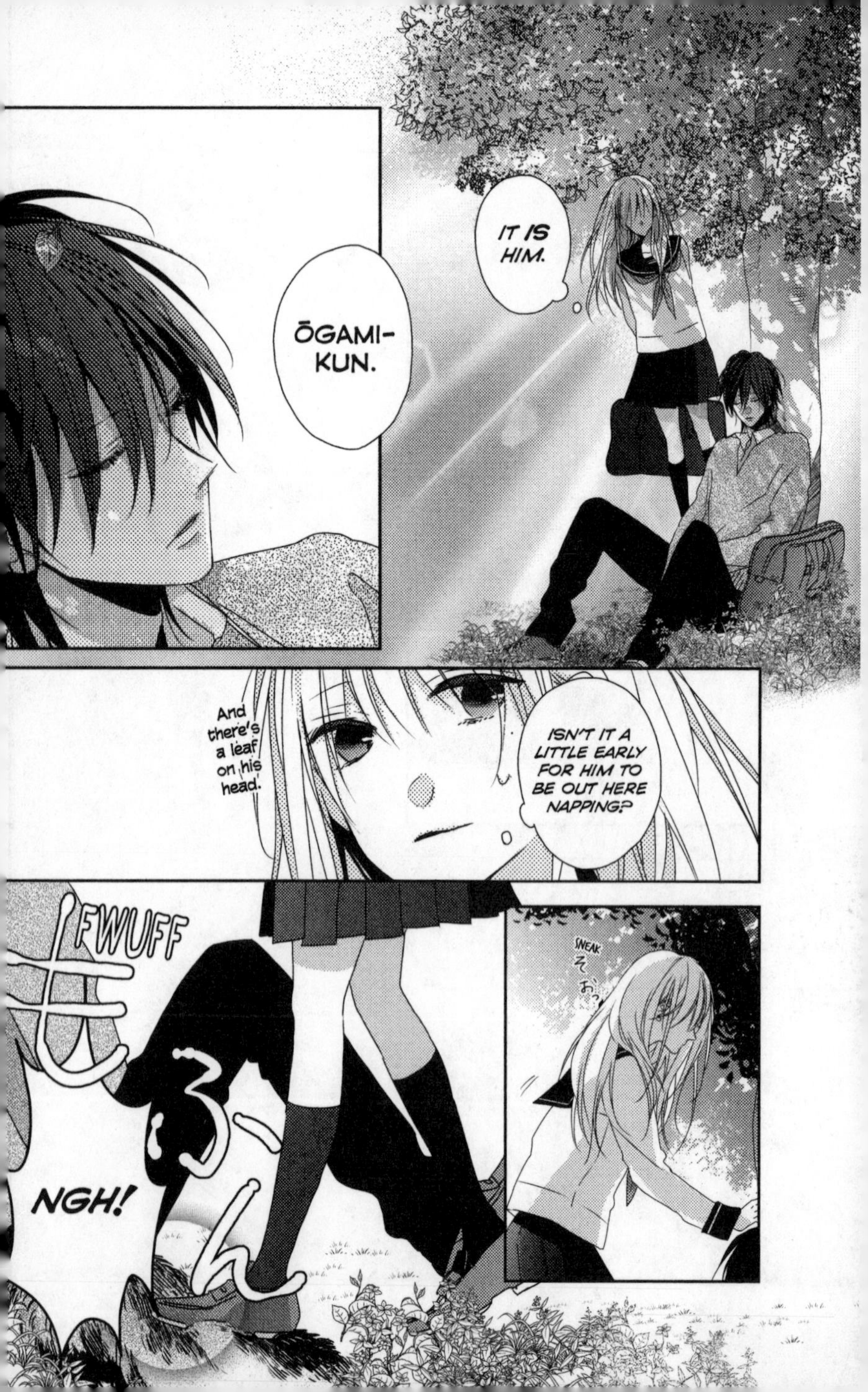
IT IS HIM.
ŌGAMI-KUN.
ISN'T IT A LITTLE EARLY FOR HIM TO BE OUT HERE NAPPING?
And there's a leaf on his head.
SNEAK
FWUFF
NGH!

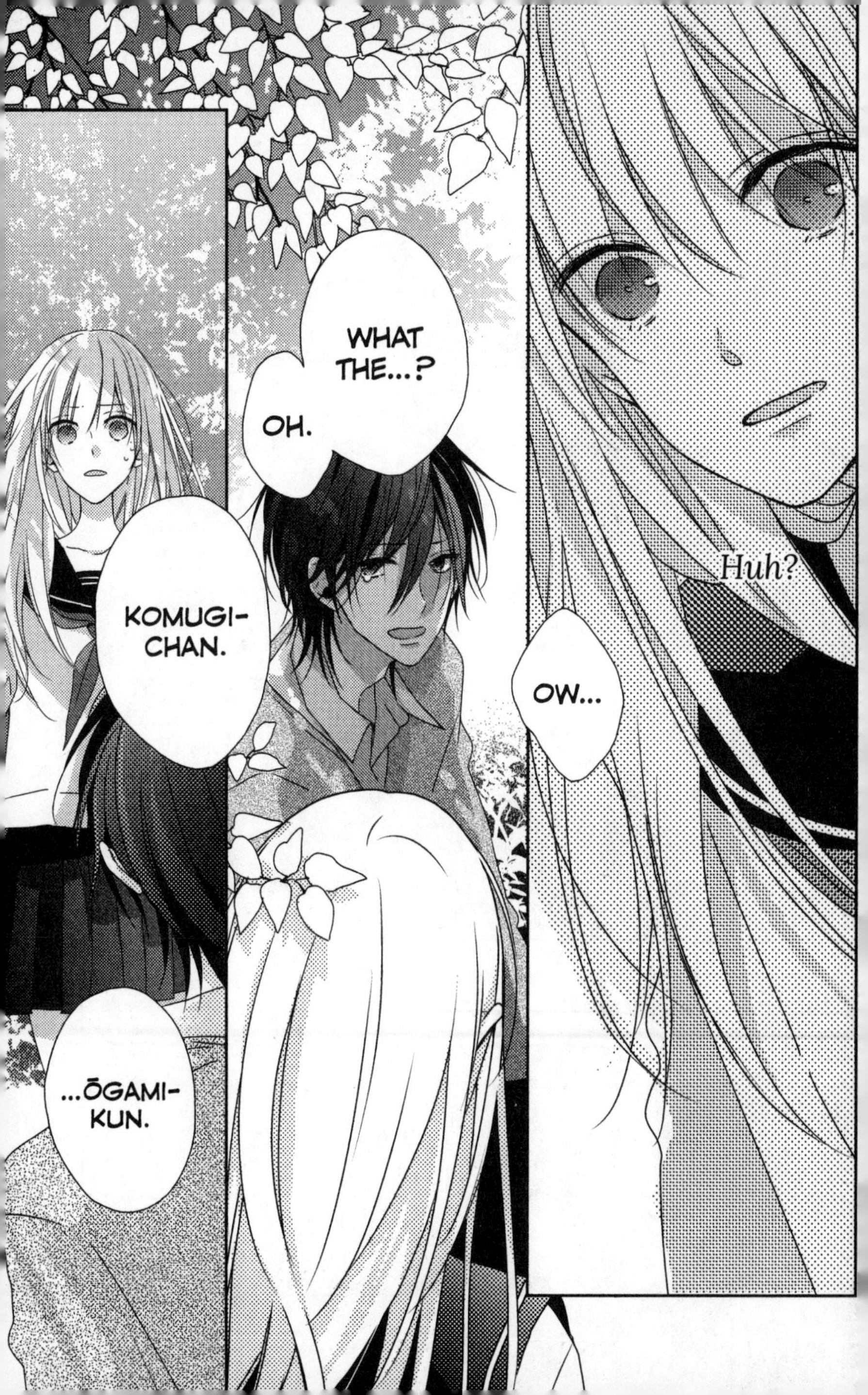
Huh?
OW...
WHAT THE...?
OH.
KOMUGI-CHAN.
...ŌGAMI-KUN.

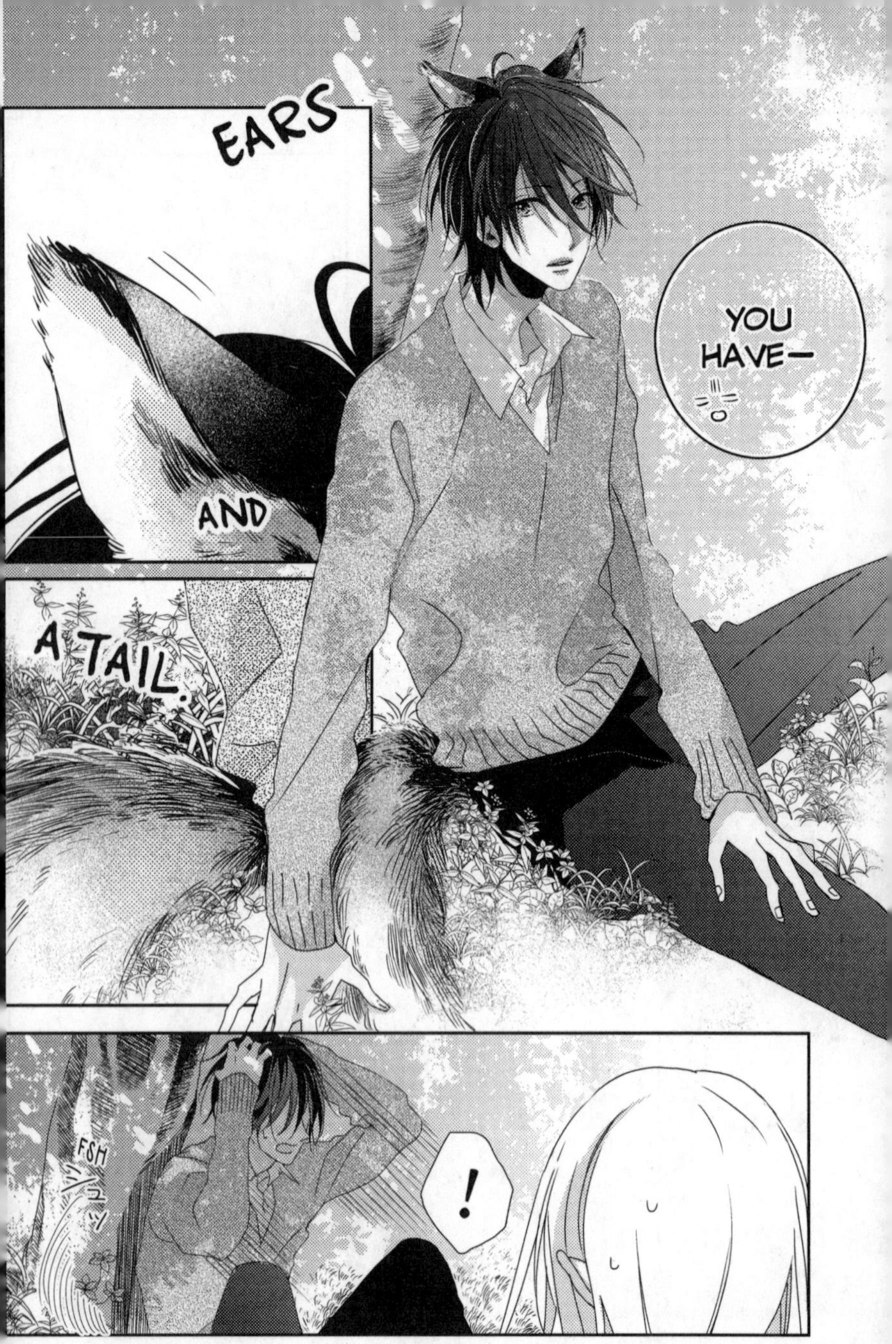
YOU HAVE—
EARS
AND
A TAIL.
!
FSH
シュッ

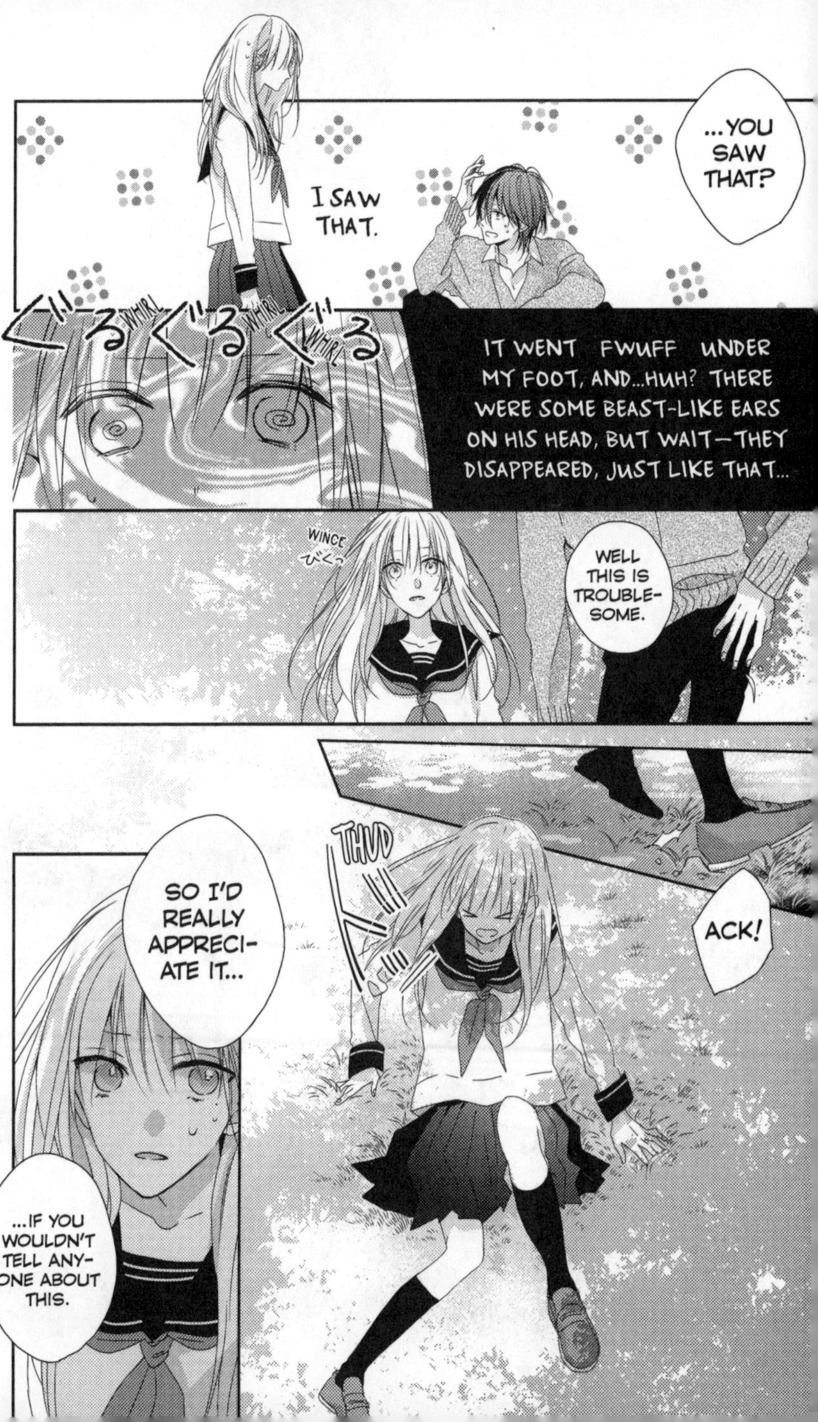
...YOU SAW THAT?
I SAW THAT.
IT WENT FWUFF UNDER MY FOOT, AND...HUH? THERE WERE SOME BEAST-LIKE EARS ON HIS HEAD, BUT WAIT—THEY DISAPPEARED, JUST LIKE THAT...
ぐるぐるぐるぐる WHIRL WHIRL WHIRL
WELL THIS IS TROUBLESOME.
WINCE びくっ
ACK!
THUD
SO I'D REALLY APPRECIATE IT...
...IF YOU WOULDN'T TELL ANYONE ABOUT THIS.

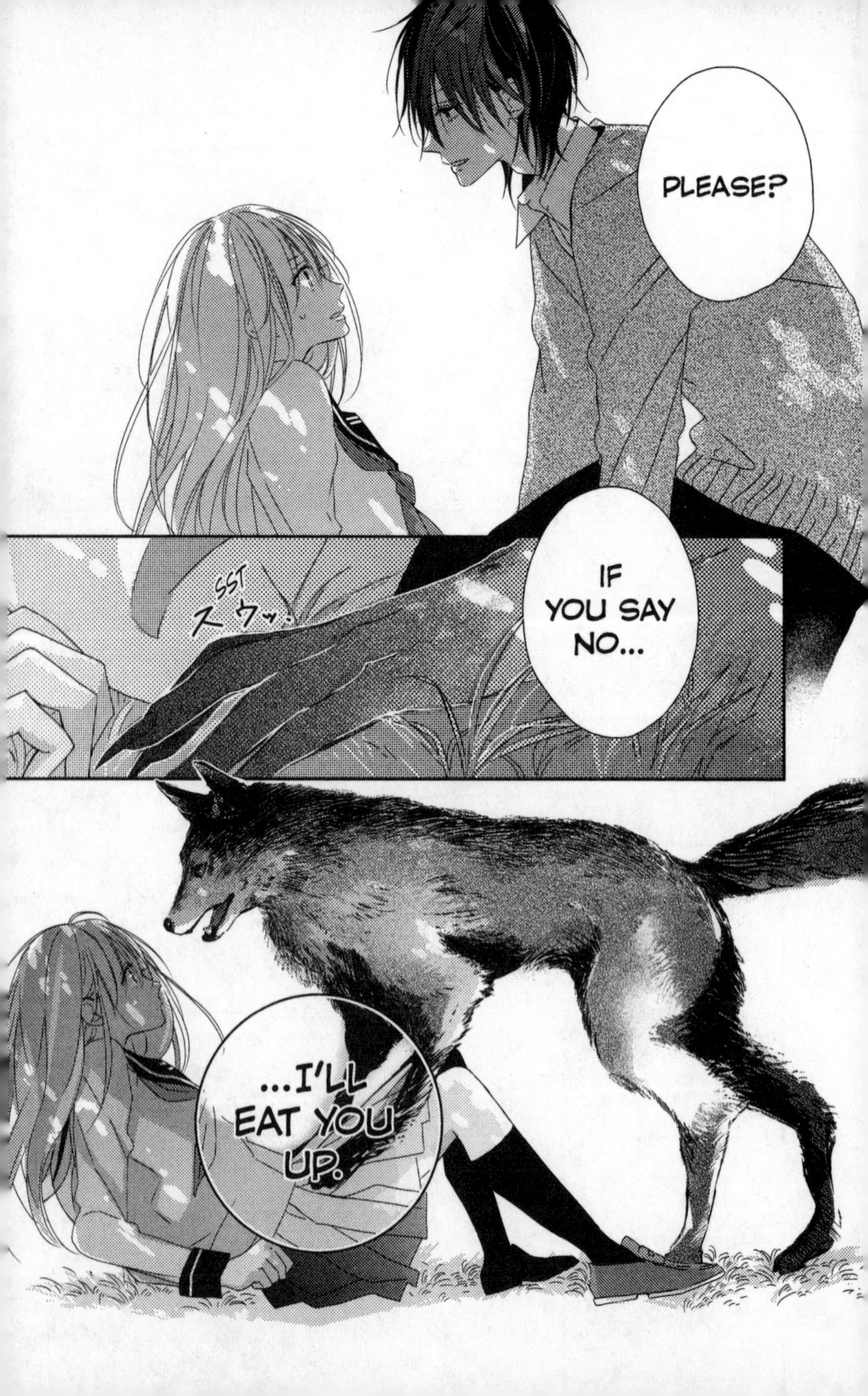
PLEASE?
IF YOU SAY NO...
SST
スウッ
...I'LL EAT YOU UP.

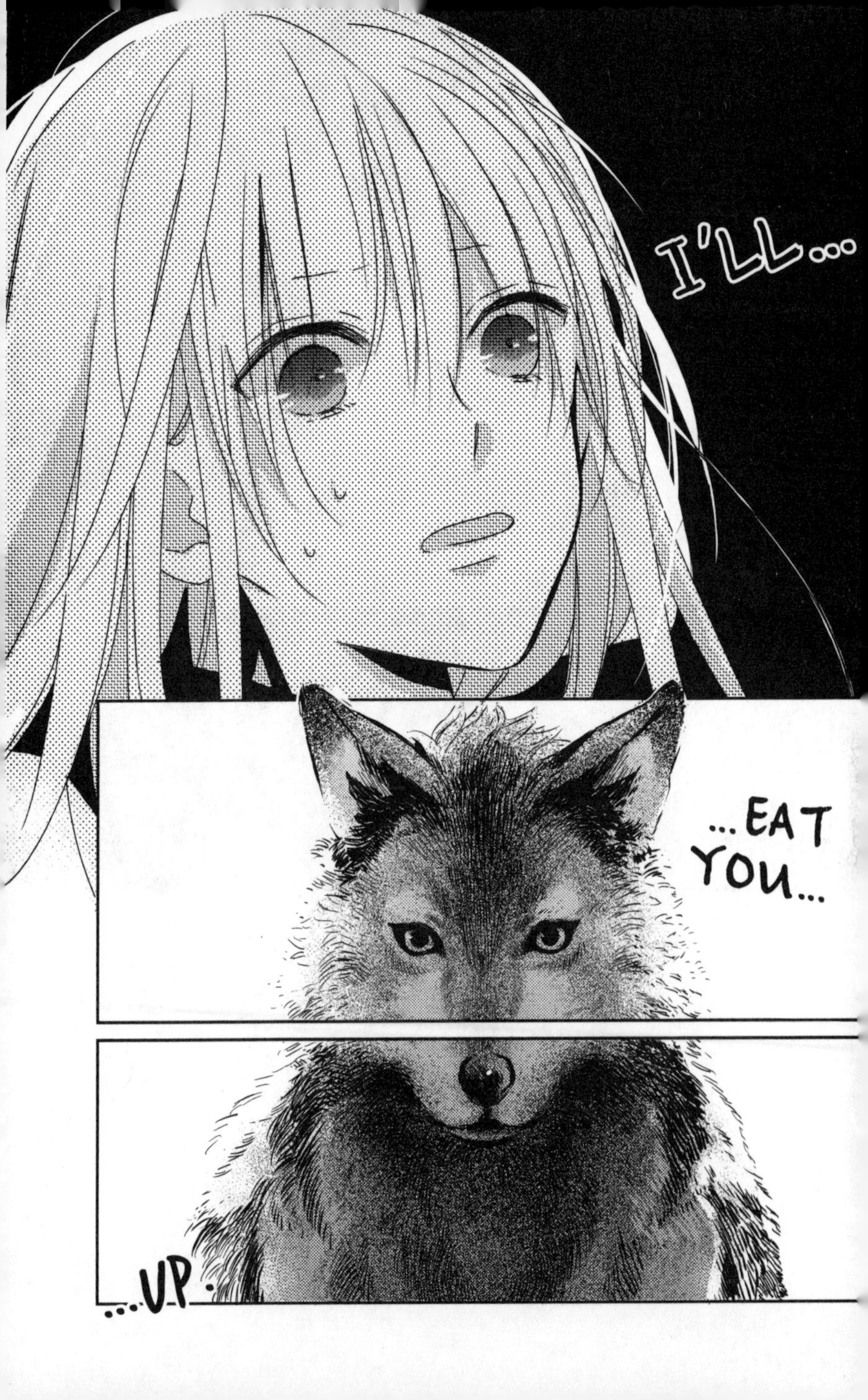
I'LL...
...EAT YOU...
...UP.

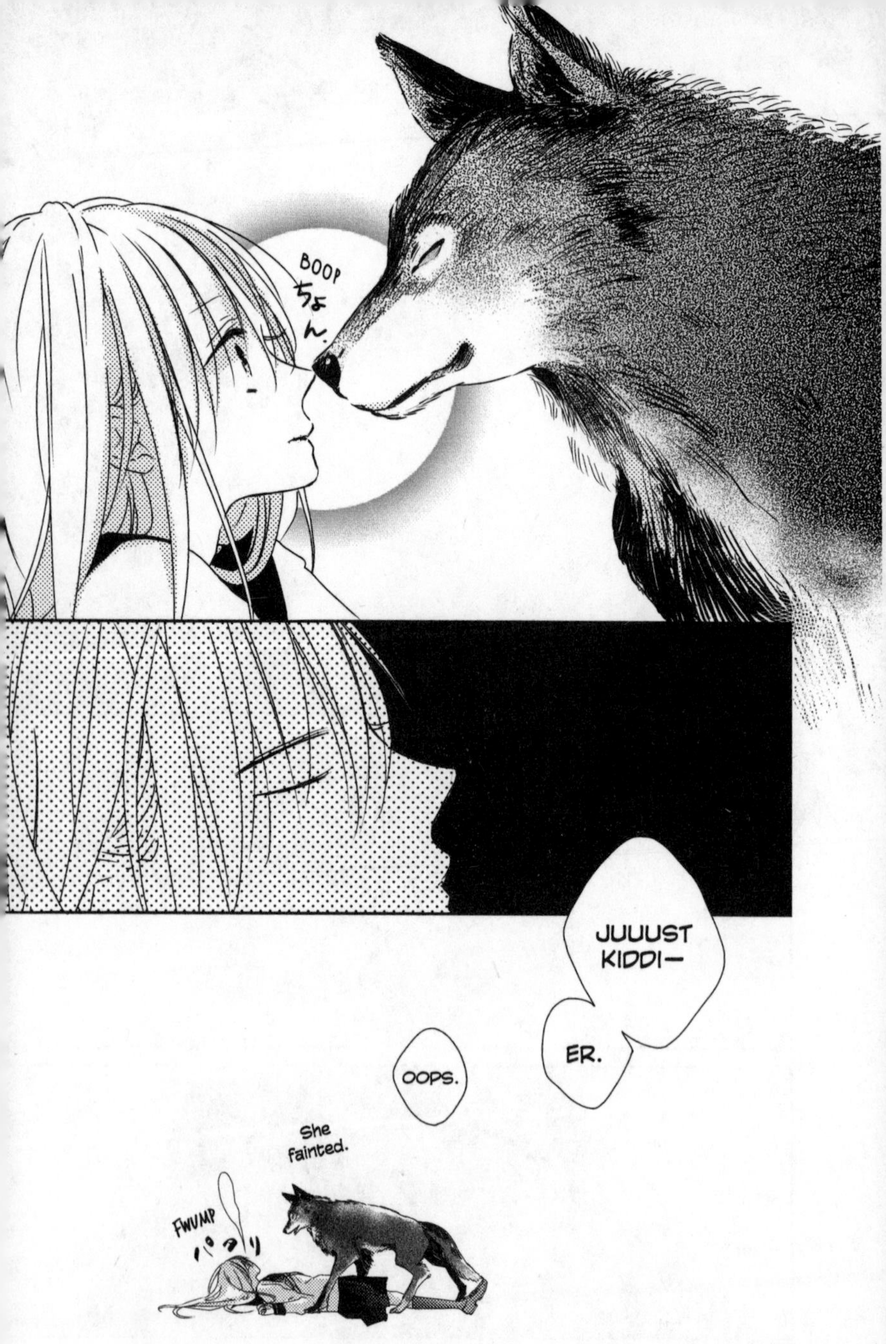
BOOP
ちょん.
JUUUST KIDDI—
ER.
OOPS.
She fainted.
FWUMP
パタリ

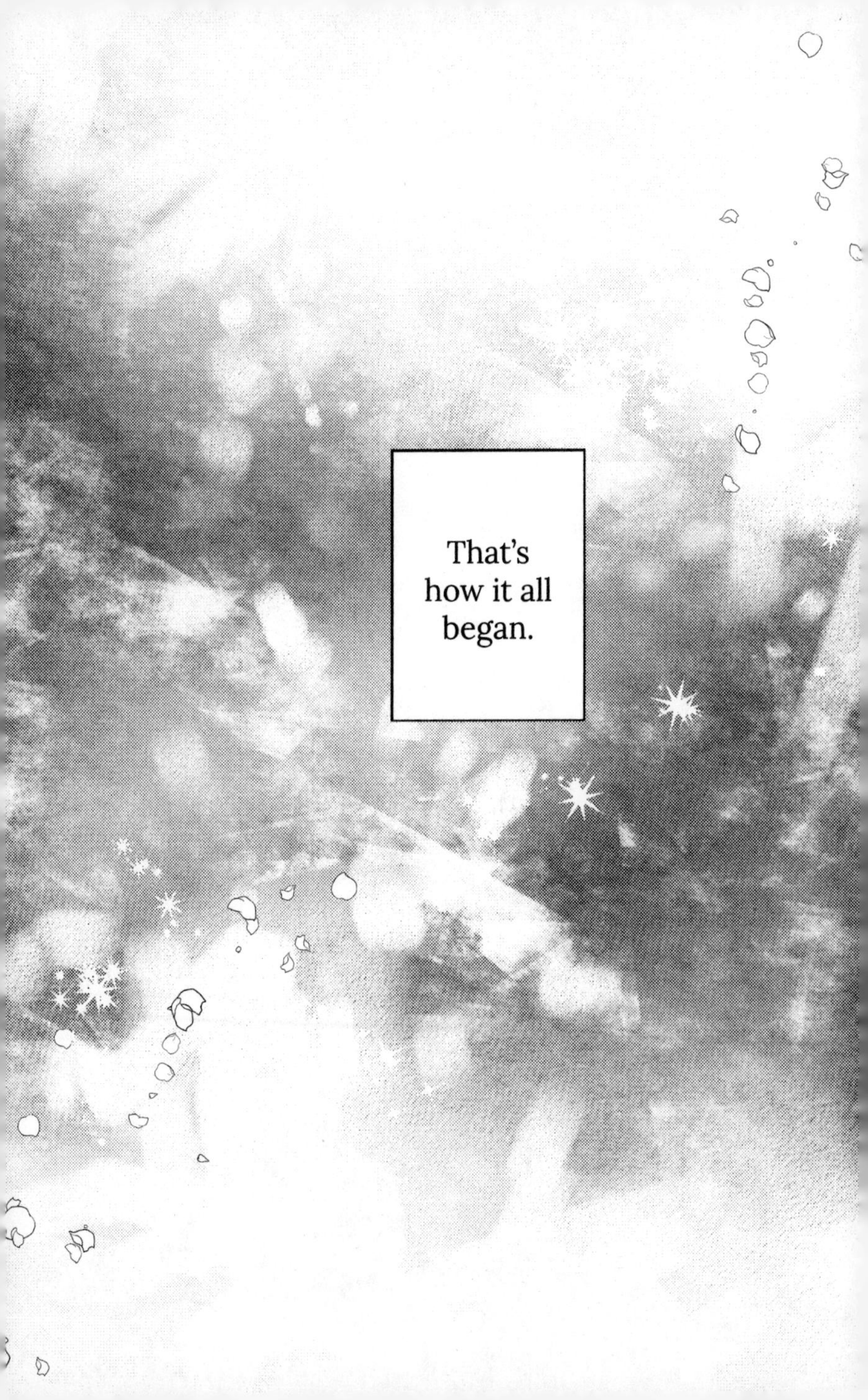
That's how it all began.

That Wolf-Boy is Mine!

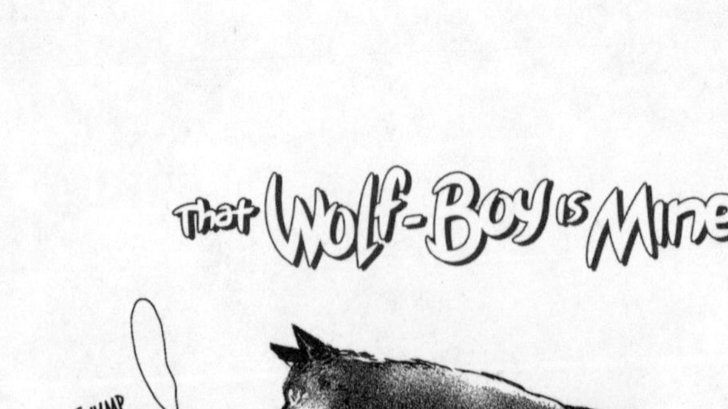
FWUMP
パタリ

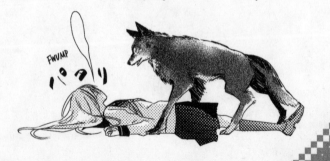

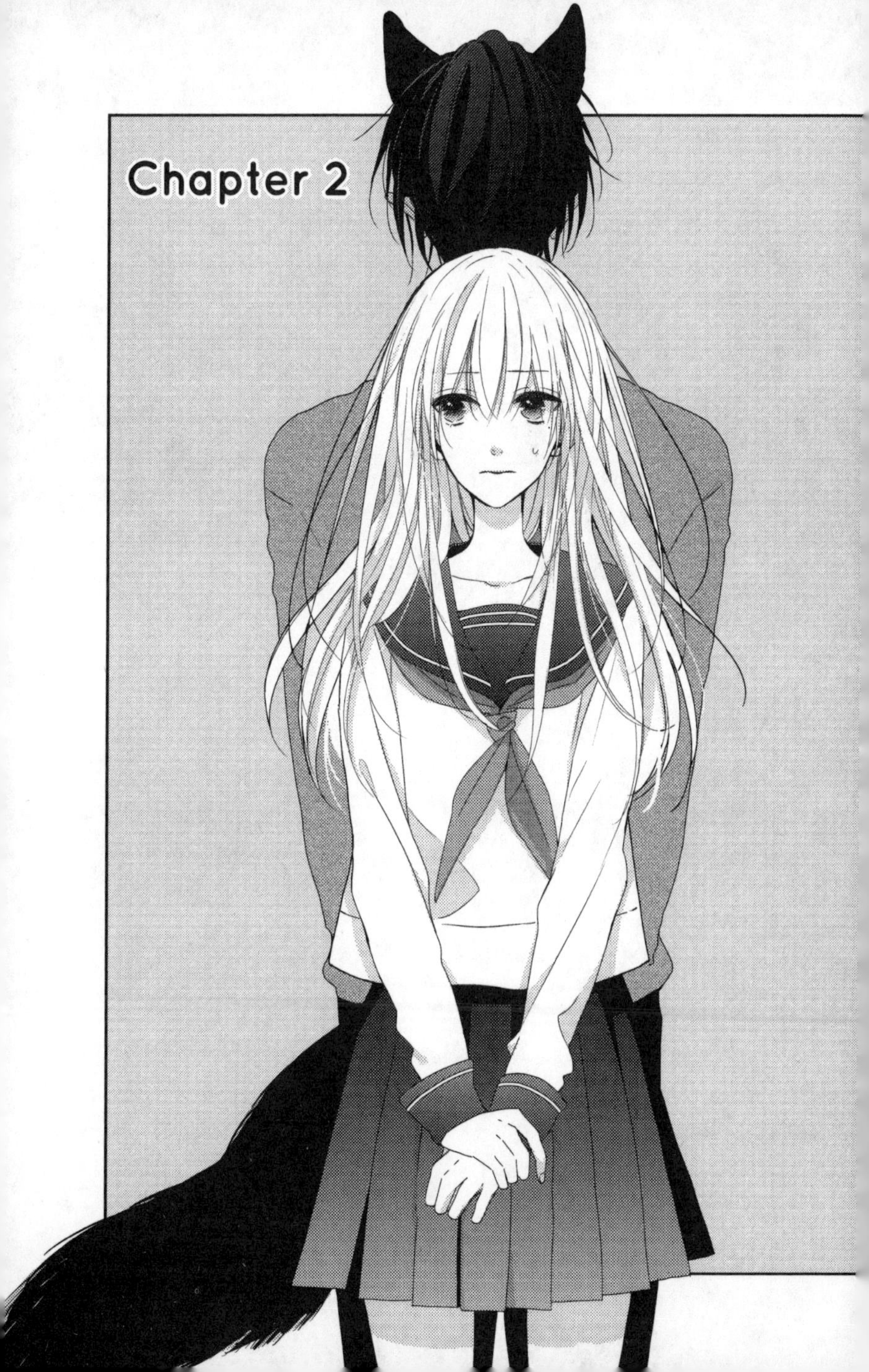
Chapter 2

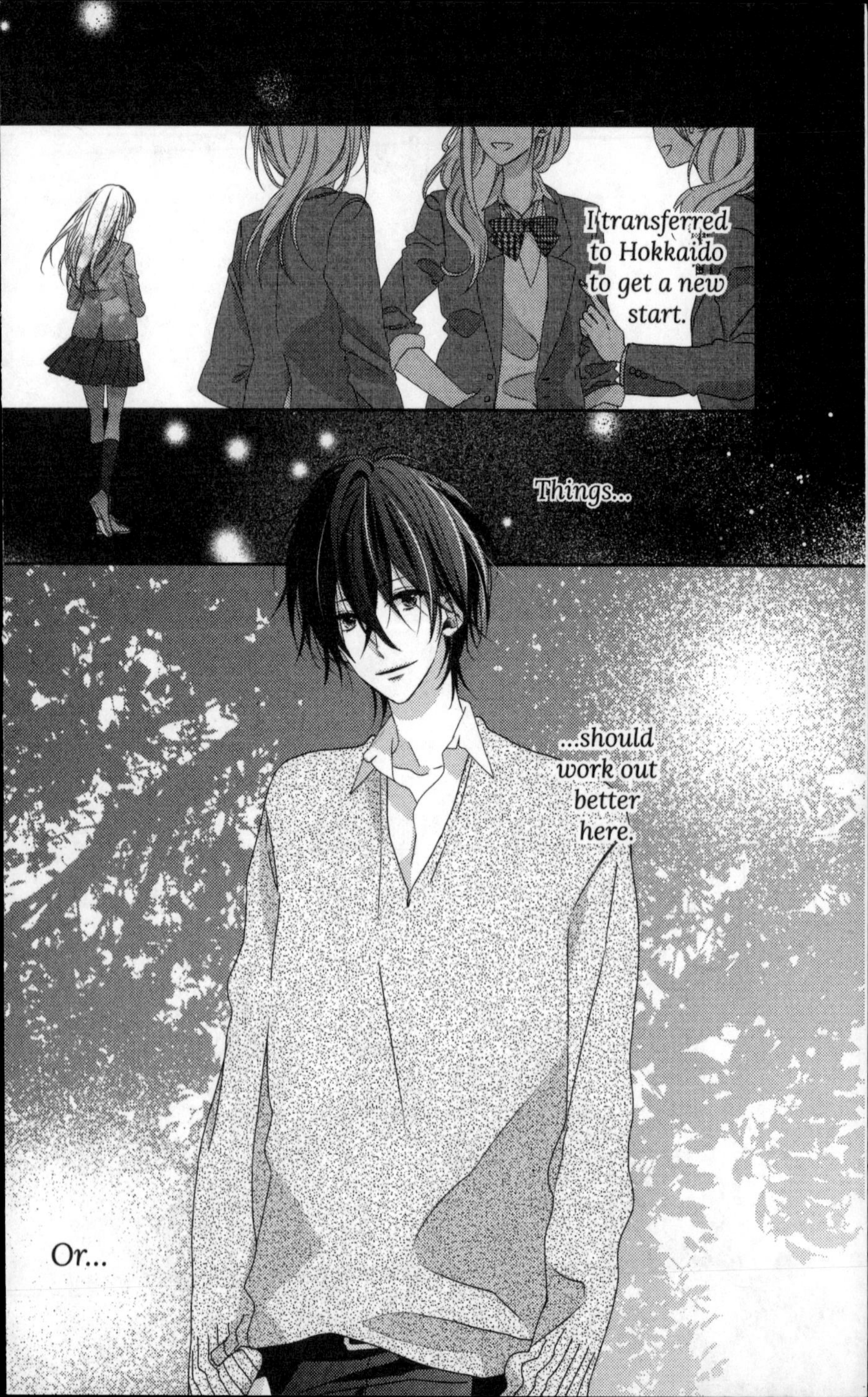
I transferred to Hokkaido to get a new start.
Things...
...should work out better here.
Or...

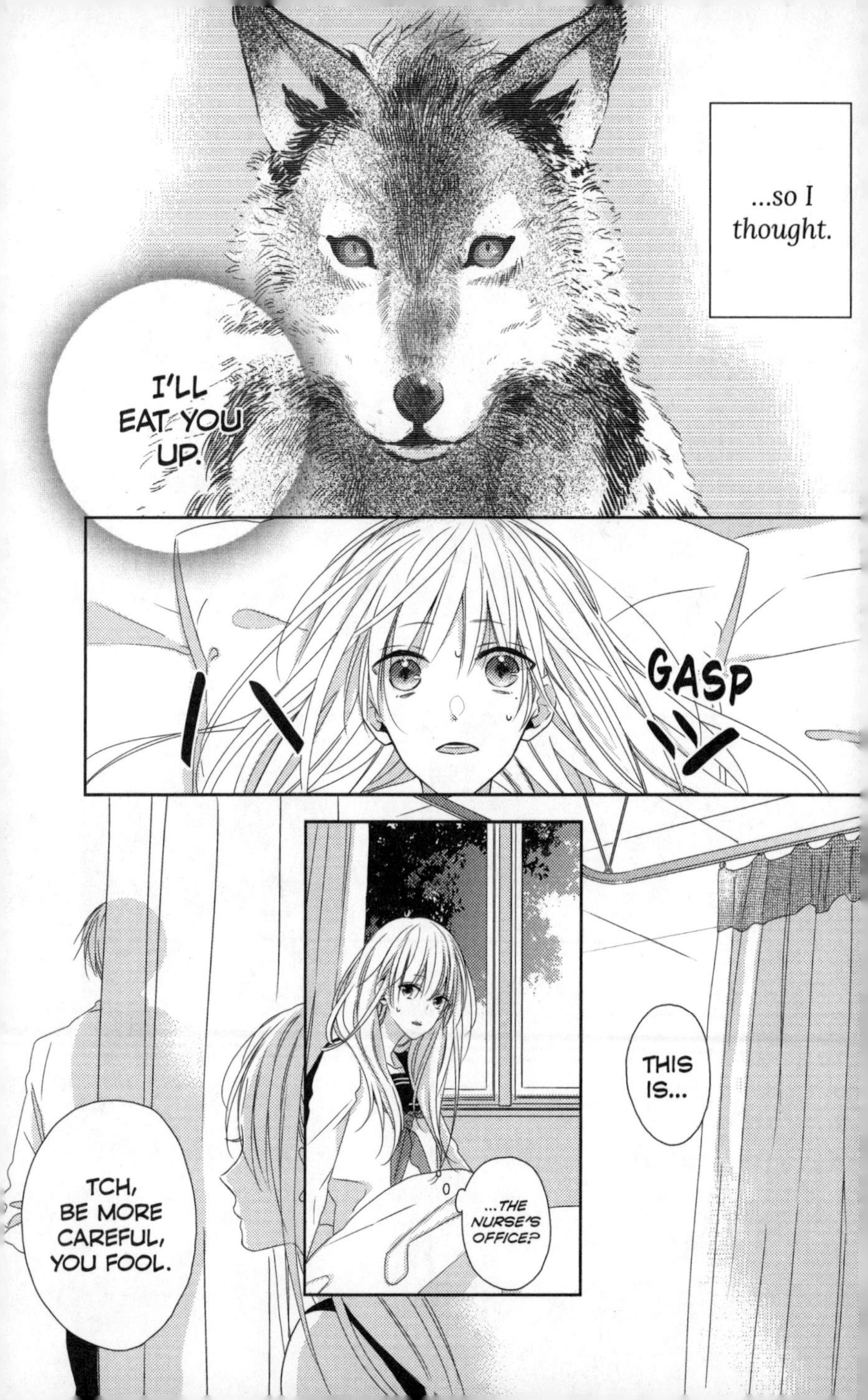
...so I thought.
I'LL EAT YOU UP.
GASP
THIS IS...
...THE NURSE'S OFFICE?
TCH, BE MORE CAREFUL, YOU FOOL.

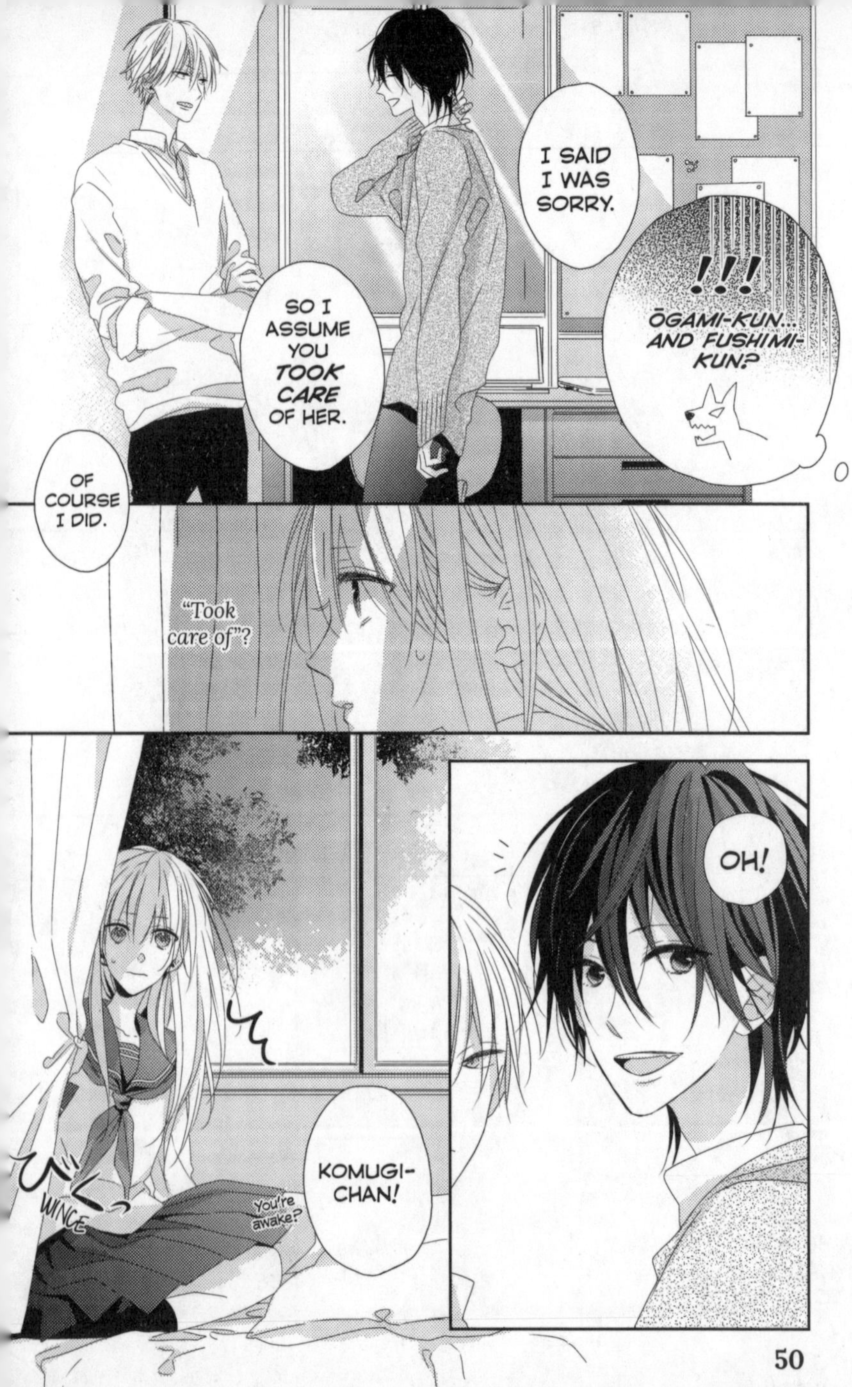
I SAID I WAS SORRY.
!!!
ŌGAMI-KUN... AND FUSHIMI-KUN?
SO I ASSUME YOU *TOOK CARE* OF HER.
OF COURSE I DID.
"Took care of"?
OH!
KOMUGI-CHAN!
You're awake?
びくっ
WINCE

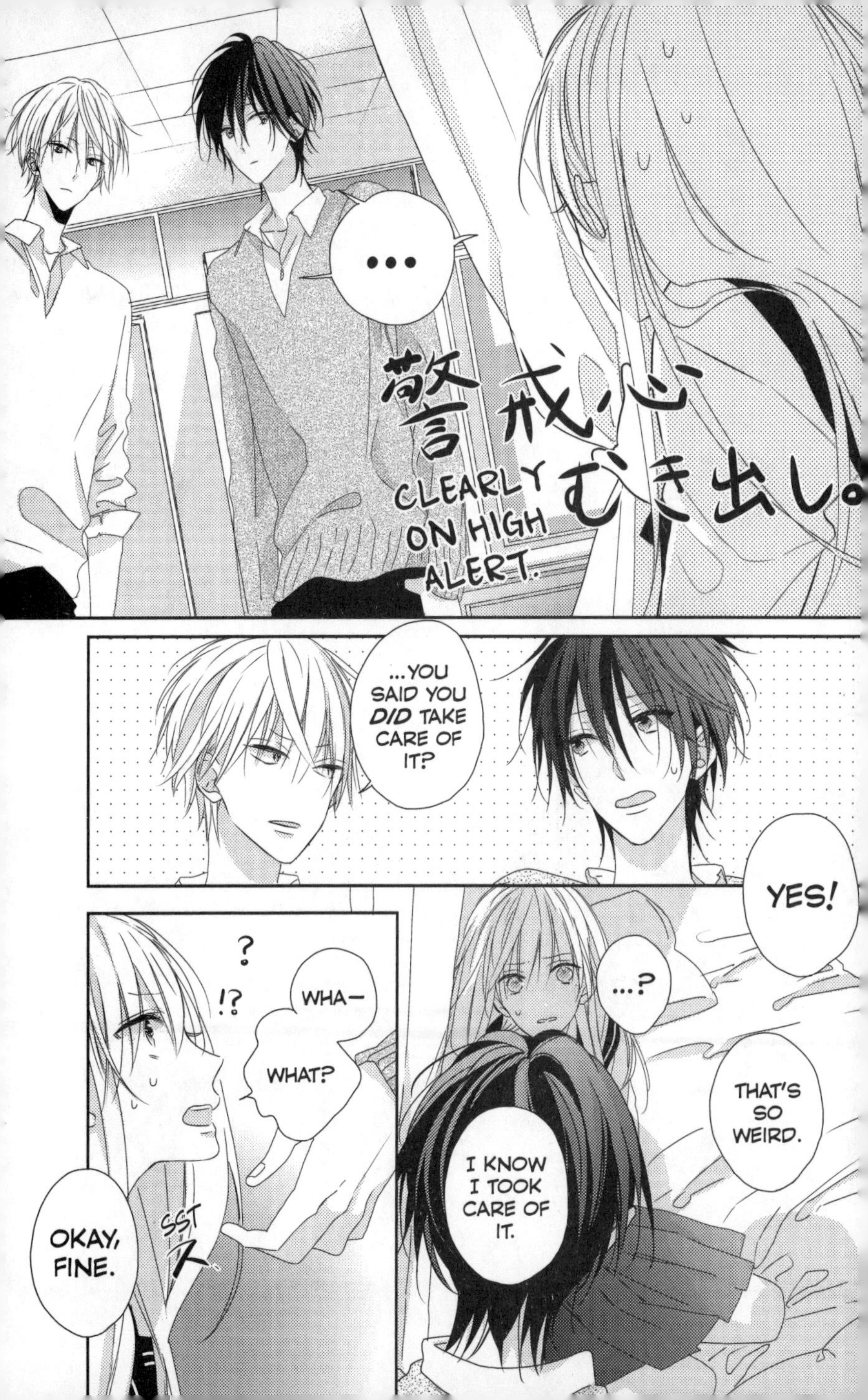
...
警戒心むき出し。
CLEARLY ON HIGH ALERT.
...YOU SAID YOU *DID* TAKE CARE OF IT?
YES!
...?
THAT'S SO WEIRD.
I KNOW I TOOK CARE OF IT.
WHA—
WHAT?
?
!?
SST
OKAY, FINE.

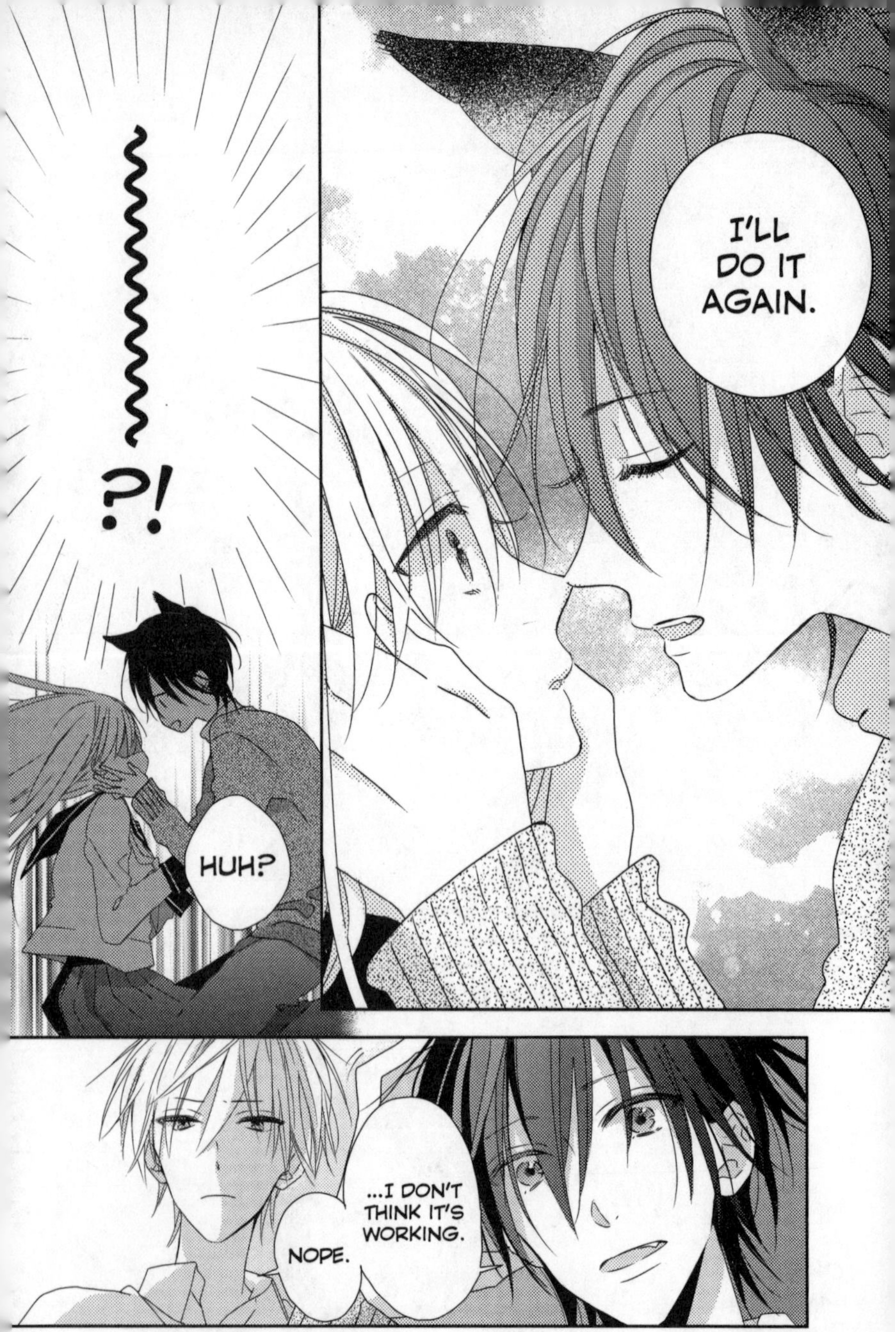
I'LL DO IT AGAIN.
~?!
HUH?
...I DON'T THINK IT'S WORKING.
NOPE.

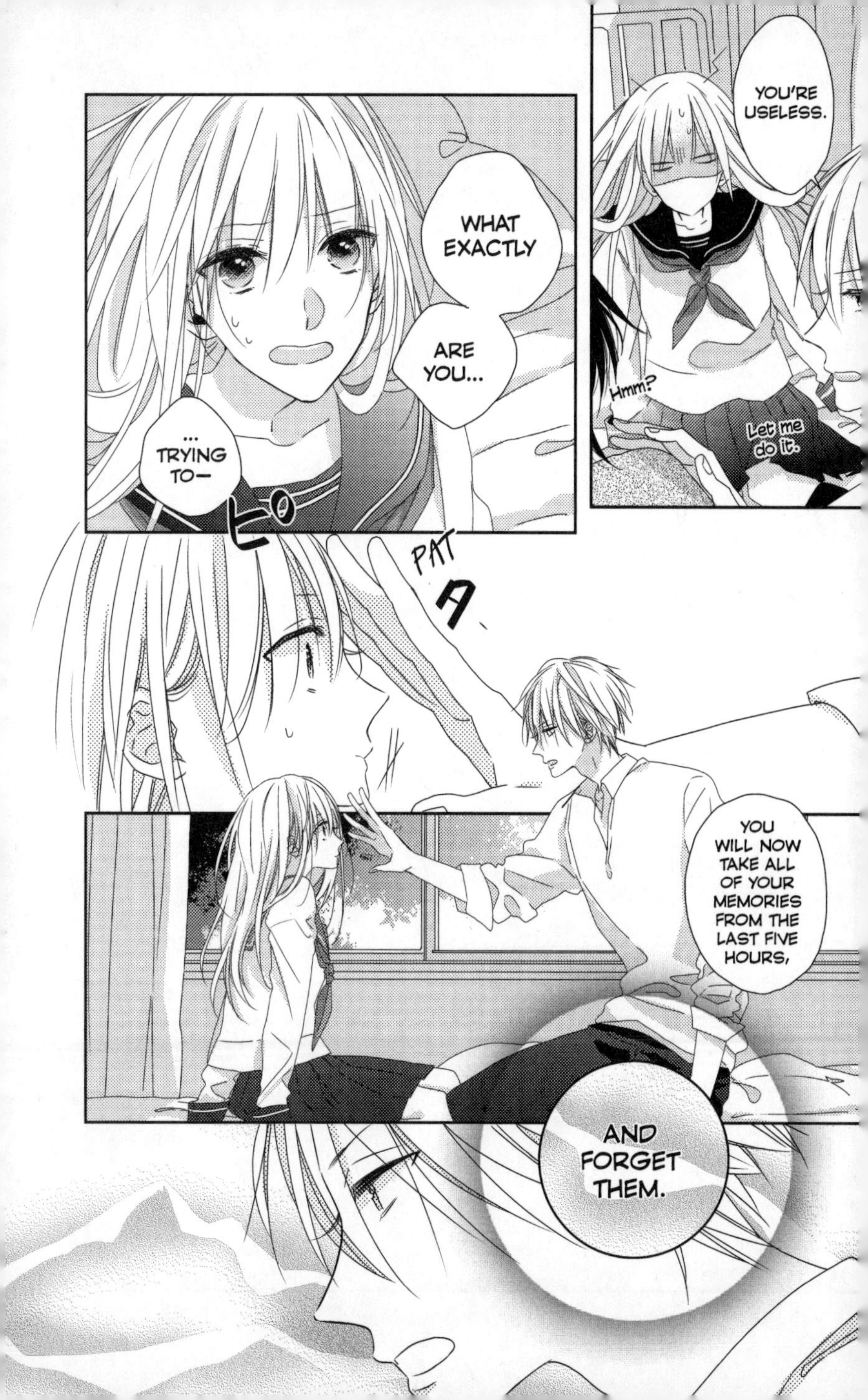
YOU'RE USELESS.
Hmm?
Let me do it.
WHAT EXACTLY
ARE YOU...
... TRYING TO—
PAT
YOU WILL NOW TAKE ALL OF YOUR MEMORIES FROM THE LAST FIVE HOURS,
AND FORGET THEM.

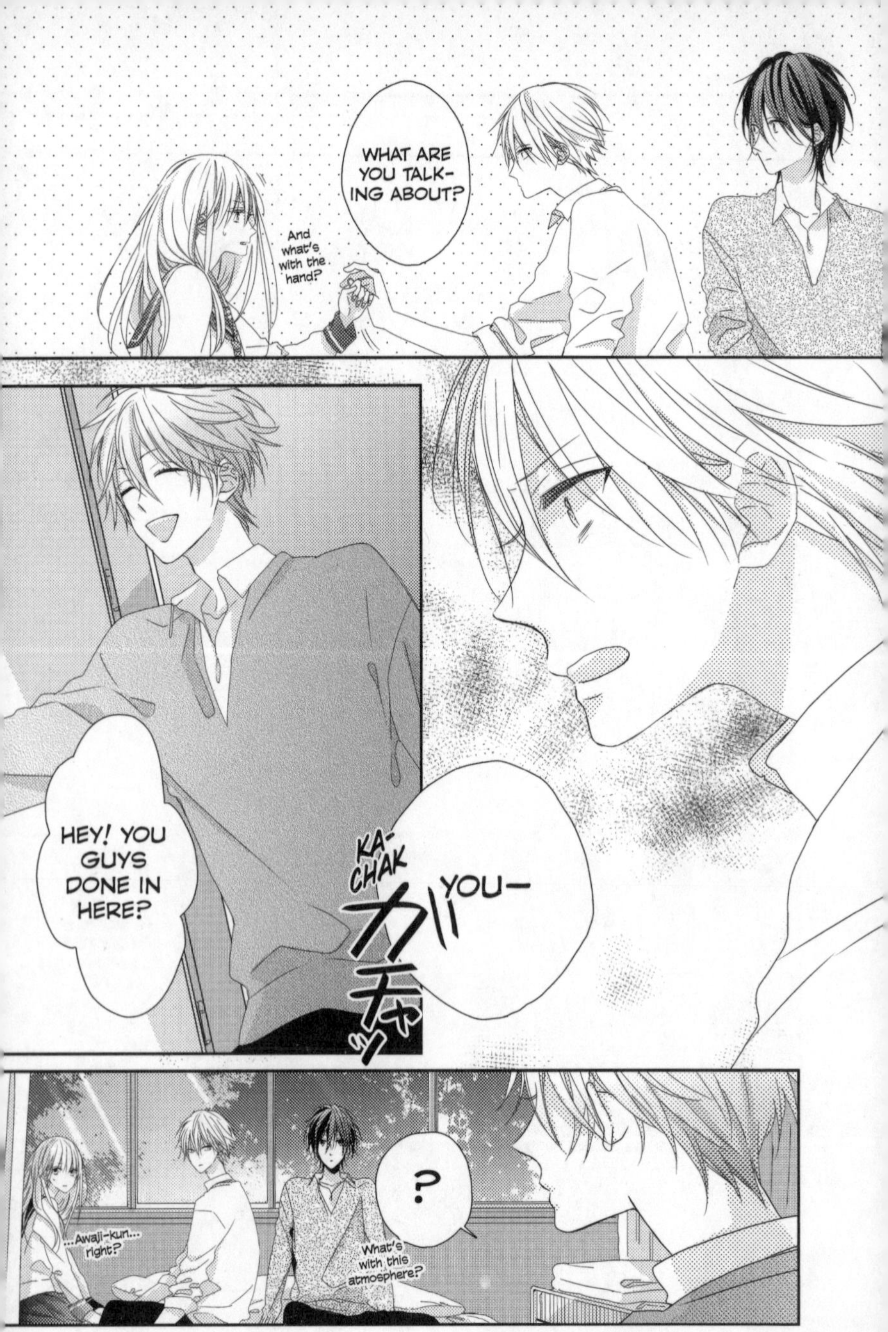
WHAT ARE YOU TALKING ABOUT?
And what's with the hand?
YOU—
KA-CHAK
HEY! YOU GUYS DONE IN HERE?
?
What's with this atmosphere?
...Awaji-kun... right?

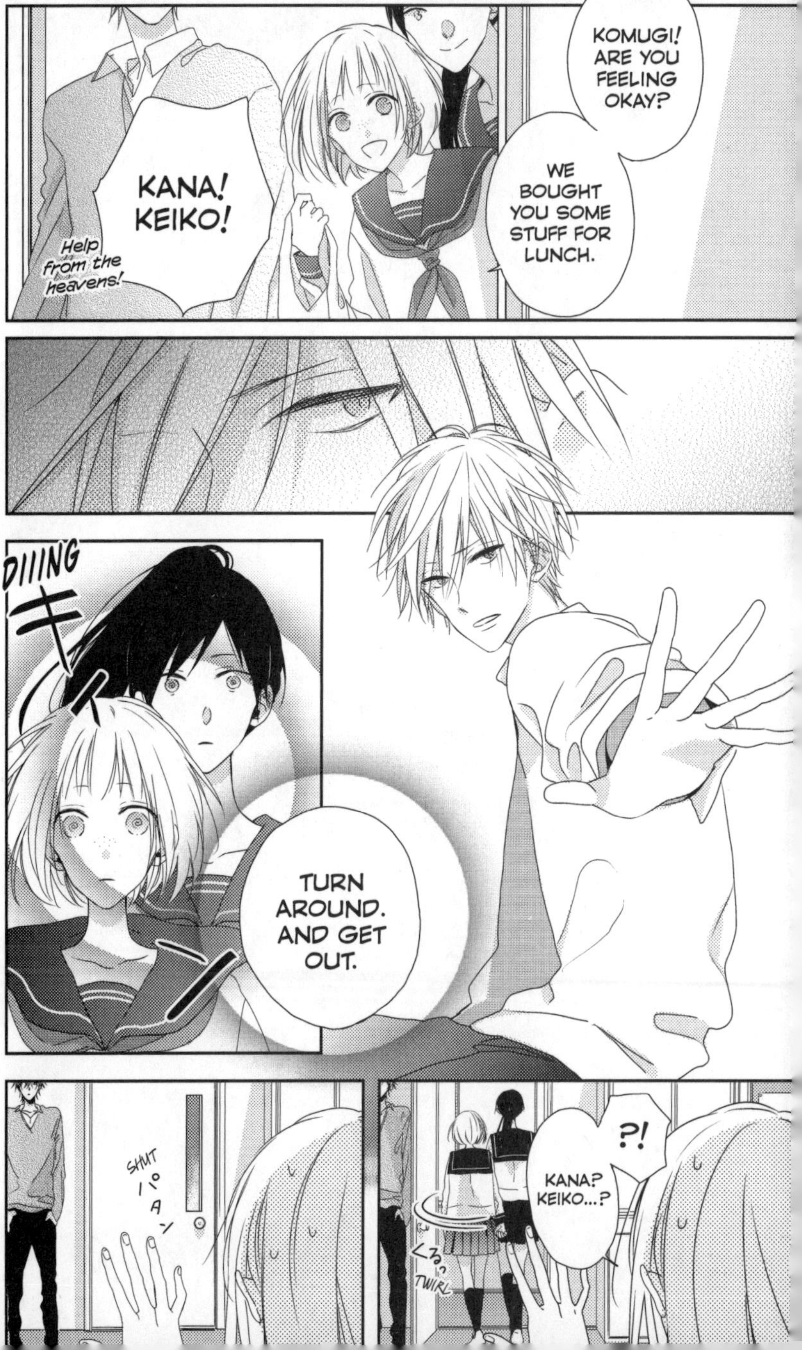
KOMUGI! ARE YOU FEELING OKAY?
WE BOUGHT YOU SOME STUFF FOR LUNCH.
KANA! KEIKO!
Help from the heavens!
TURN AROUND. AND GET OUT.
DIIING
キィ
?!
KANA? KEIKO...?
くるっ
TWIRL
SHUT
パタン

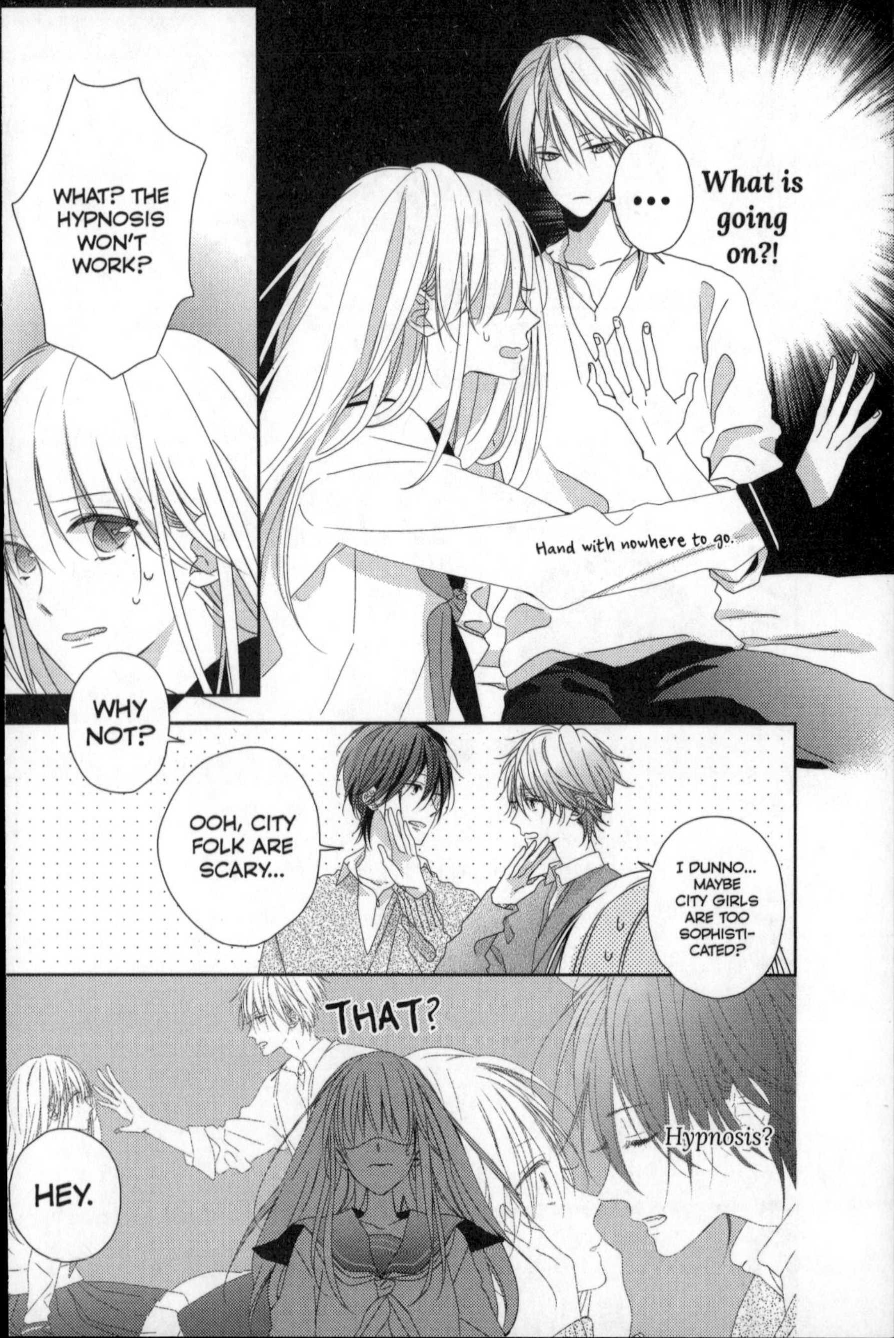
...
What is going on?!
Hand with nowhere to go.
WHAT? THE HYPNOSIS WON'T WORK?
WHY NOT?
I DUNNO... MAYBE CITY GIRLS ARE TOO SOPHISTI-CATED?
OOH, CITY FOLK ARE SCARY...
Hypnosis?
THAT?
HEY.

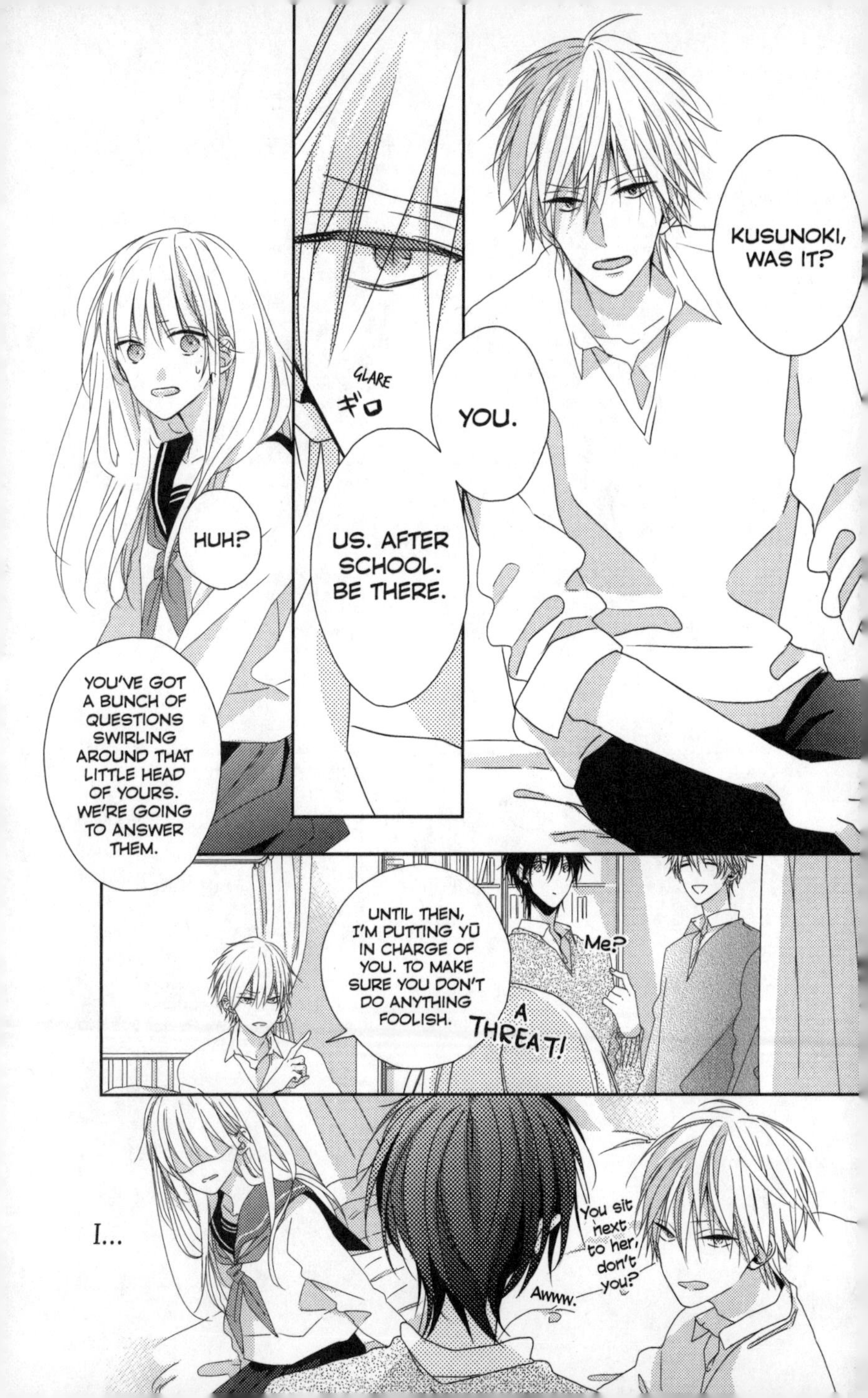
KUSUNOKI, WAS IT?
YOU.
GLARE
ギロ
US. AFTER SCHOOL. BE THERE.
HUH?
YOU'VE GOT A BUNCH OF QUESTIONS SWIRLING AROUND THAT LITTLE HEAD OF YOURS. WE'RE GOING TO ANSWER THEM.
UNTIL THEN, I'M PUTTING YŪ IN CHARGE OF YOU. TO MAKE SURE YOU DON'T DO ANYTHING FOOLISH.
Me?
A THREAT!
You sit next to her, don't you?
Awww.
I...

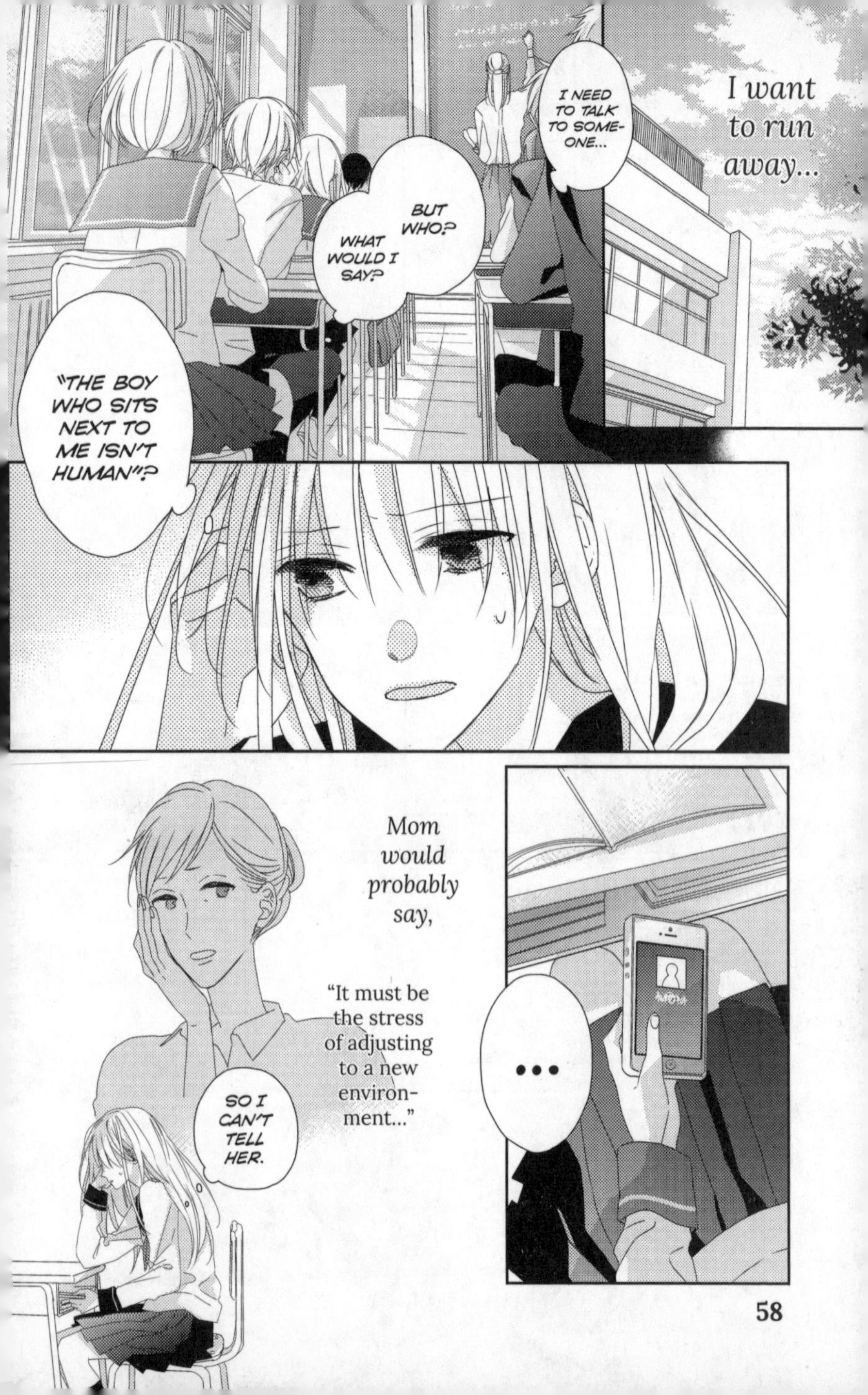
I want to run away...
I NEED TO TALK TO SOME-ONE...
BUT WHO?
WHAT WOULD I SAY?
"THE BOY WHO SITS NEXT TO ME ISN'T HUMAN"?
...
Mom would probably say,
"It must be the stress of adjusting to a new environ-ment..."
SO I CAN'T TELL HER.

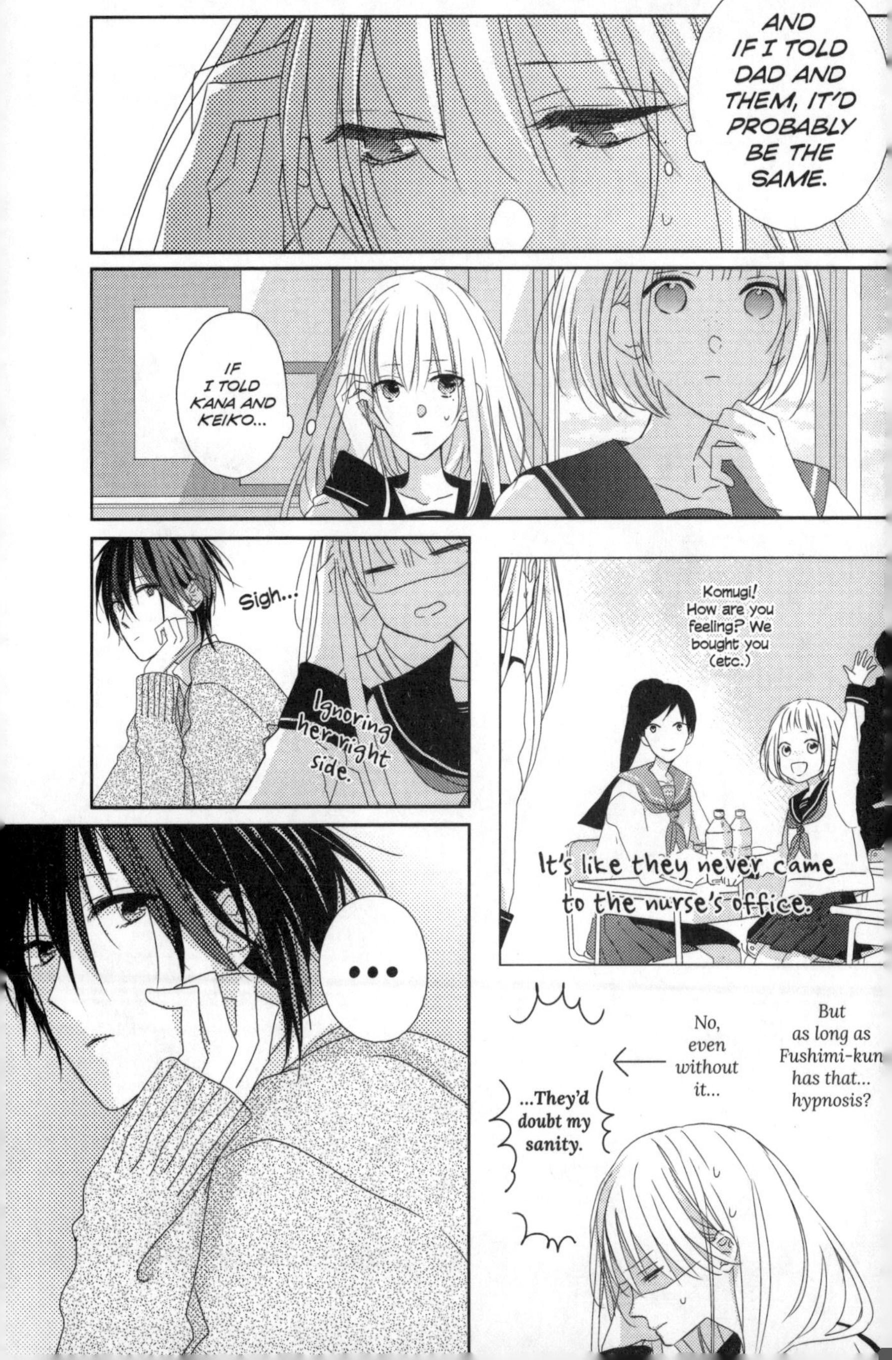
AND IF I TOLD DAD AND THEM, IT'D PROBABLY BE THE SAME.
IF I TOLD KANA AND KEIKO...
Komugi! How are you feeling? We bought you (etc.)
It's like they never came to the nurse's office.
Sigh...
Ignoring her right side.
But as long as Fushimi-kun has that... hypnosis?
No, even without it...
...They'd doubt my sanity.
...

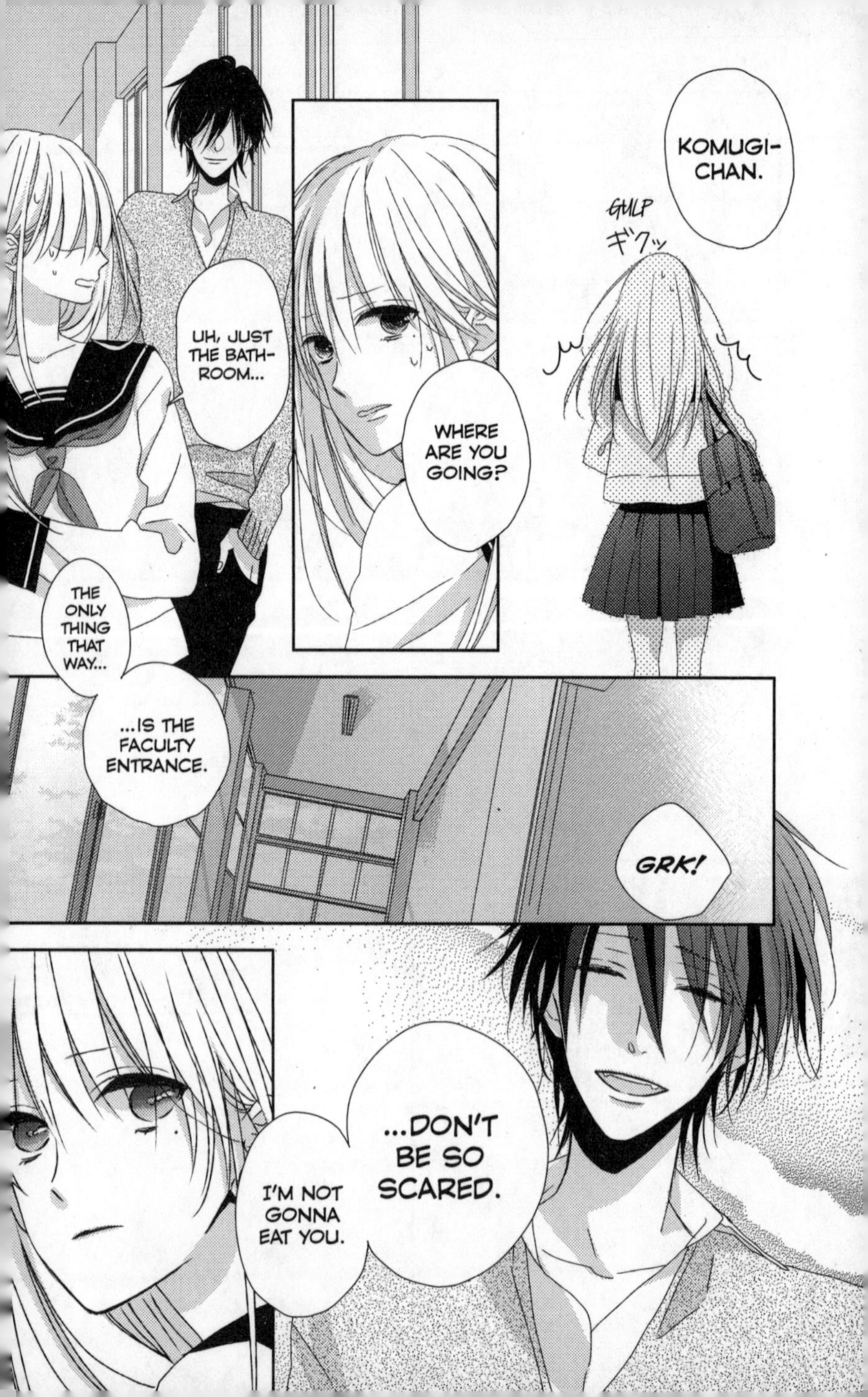
KOMUGI-CHAN.
GULP
ギクッ
WHERE ARE YOU GOING?
UH, JUST THE BATH-ROOM...
THE ONLY THING THAT WAY...
...IS THE FACULTY ENTRANCE.
GRK!
...DON'T BE SO SCARED.
I'M NOT GONNA EAT YOU.

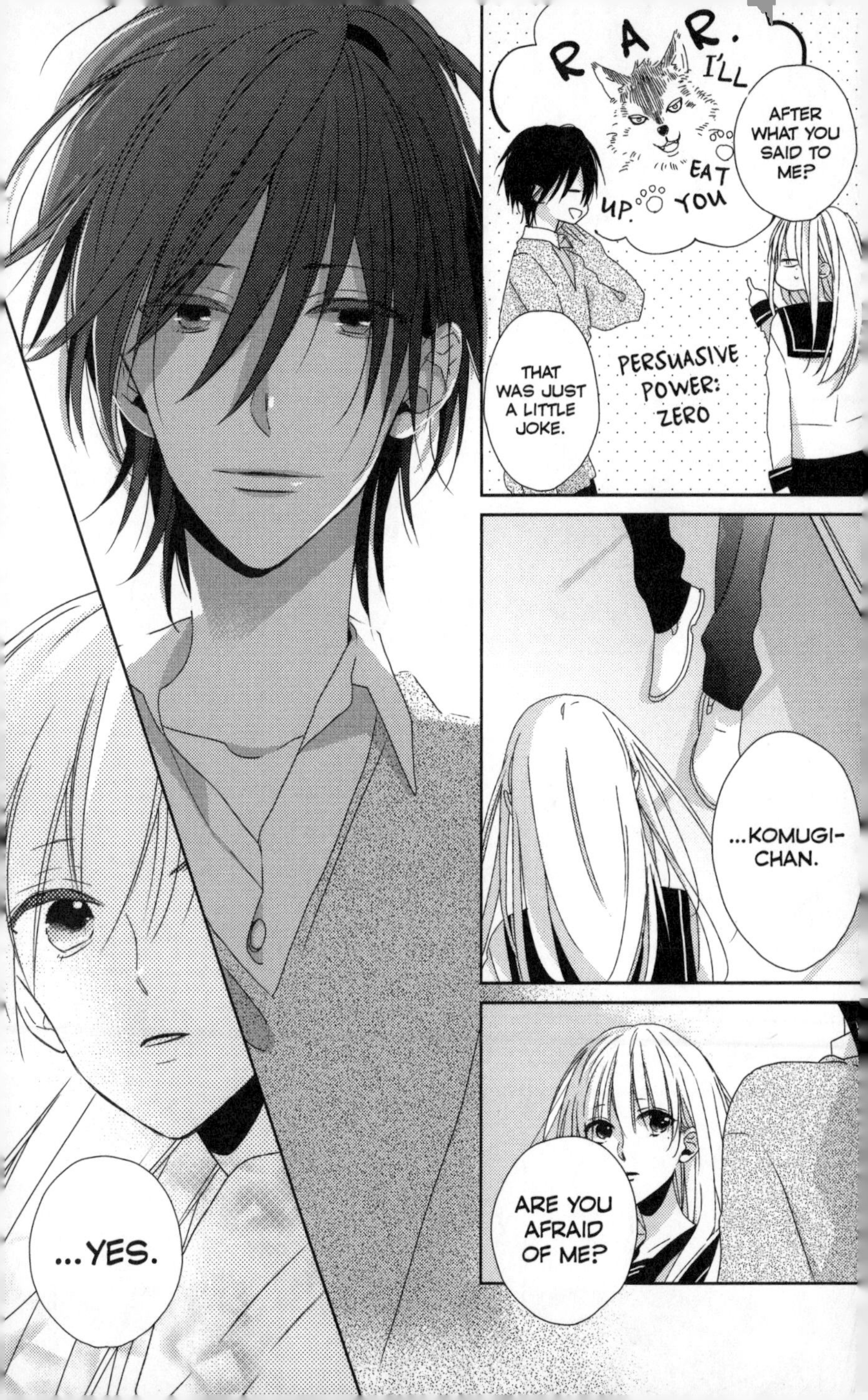

RAR. I'LL EAT YOU UP.
AFTER WHAT YOU SAID TO ME?
PERSUASIVE POWER: ZERO
THAT WAS JUST A LITTLE JOKE.
...KOMUGI-CHAN.
ARE YOU AFRAID OF ME?
...YES.

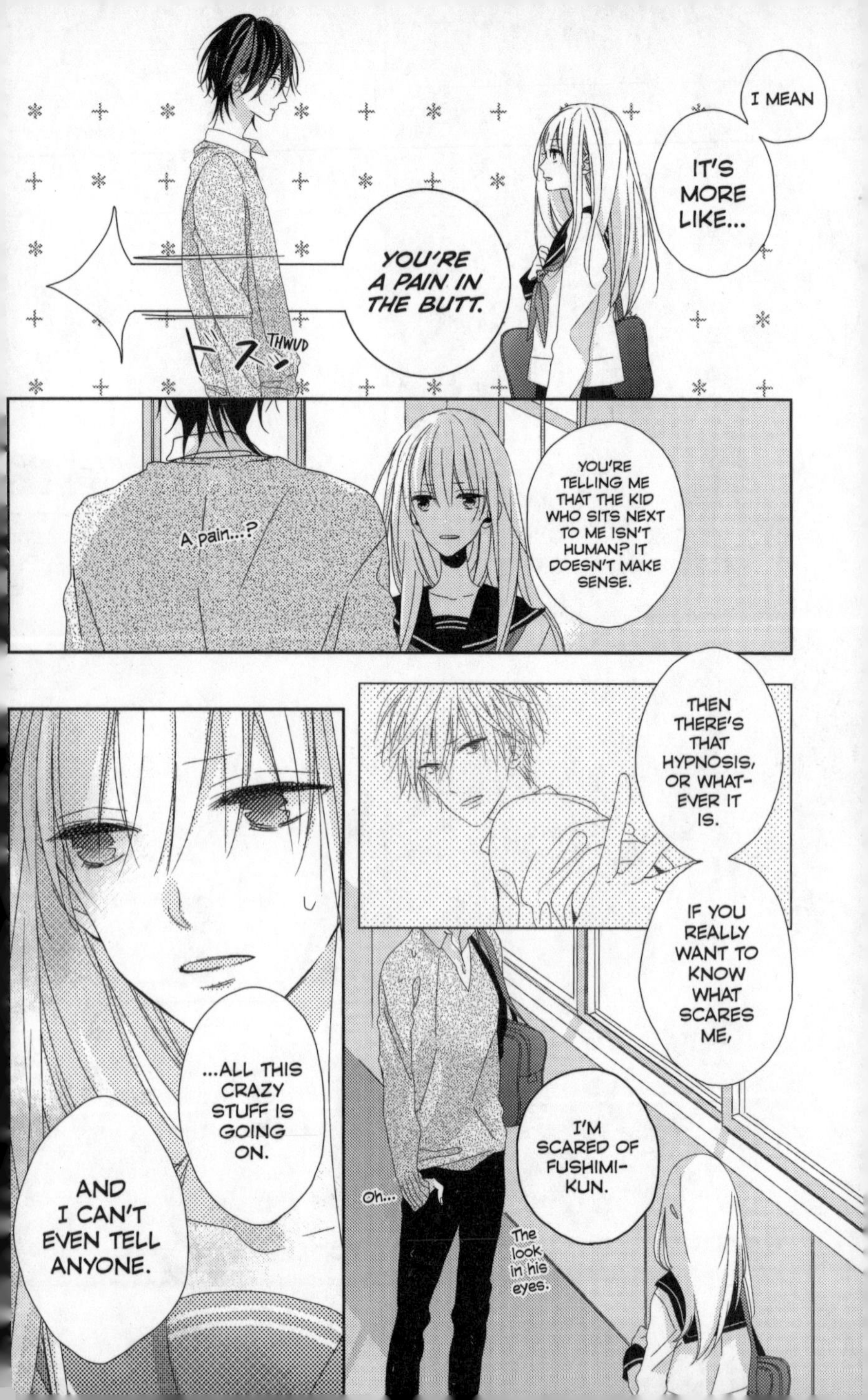
I MEAN
IT'S MORE LIKE...
YOU'RE A PAIN IN THE BUTT.
THWUD
YOU'RE TELLING ME THAT THE KID WHO SITS NEXT TO ME ISN'T HUMAN? IT DOESN'T MAKE SENSE.
A pain...?
THEN THERE'S THAT HYPNOSIS, OR WHAT-EVER IT IS.
IF YOU REALLY WANT TO KNOW WHAT SCARES ME,
I'M SCARED OF FUSHIMI-KUN.
The look in his eyes.
Oh...
...ALL THIS CRAZY STUFF IS GOING ON.
AND I CAN'T EVEN TELL ANYONE.

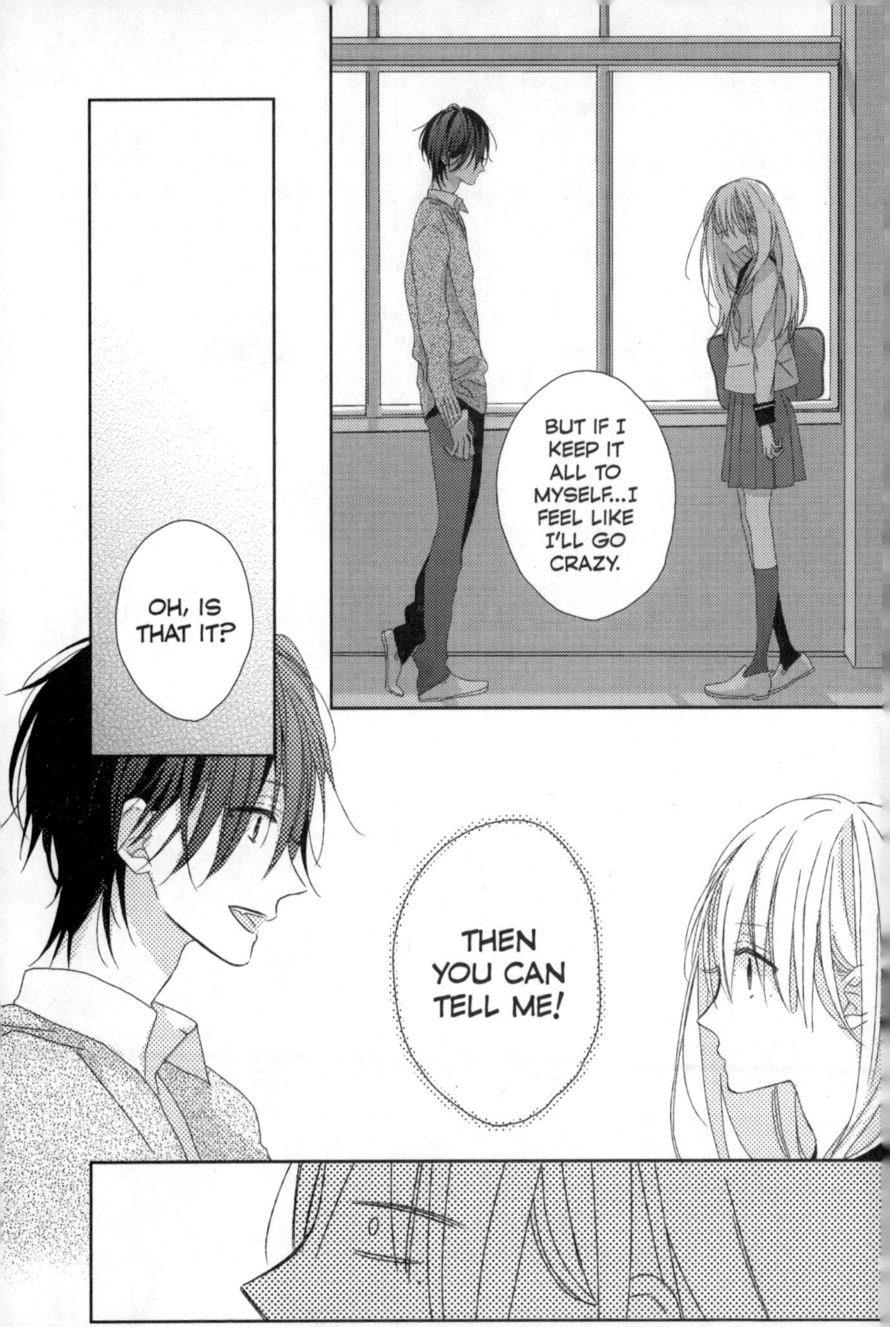
BUT IF I KEEP IT ALL TO MYSELF...I FEEL LIKE I'LL GO CRAZY.
OH, IS THAT IT?
THEN YOU CAN TELL ME!

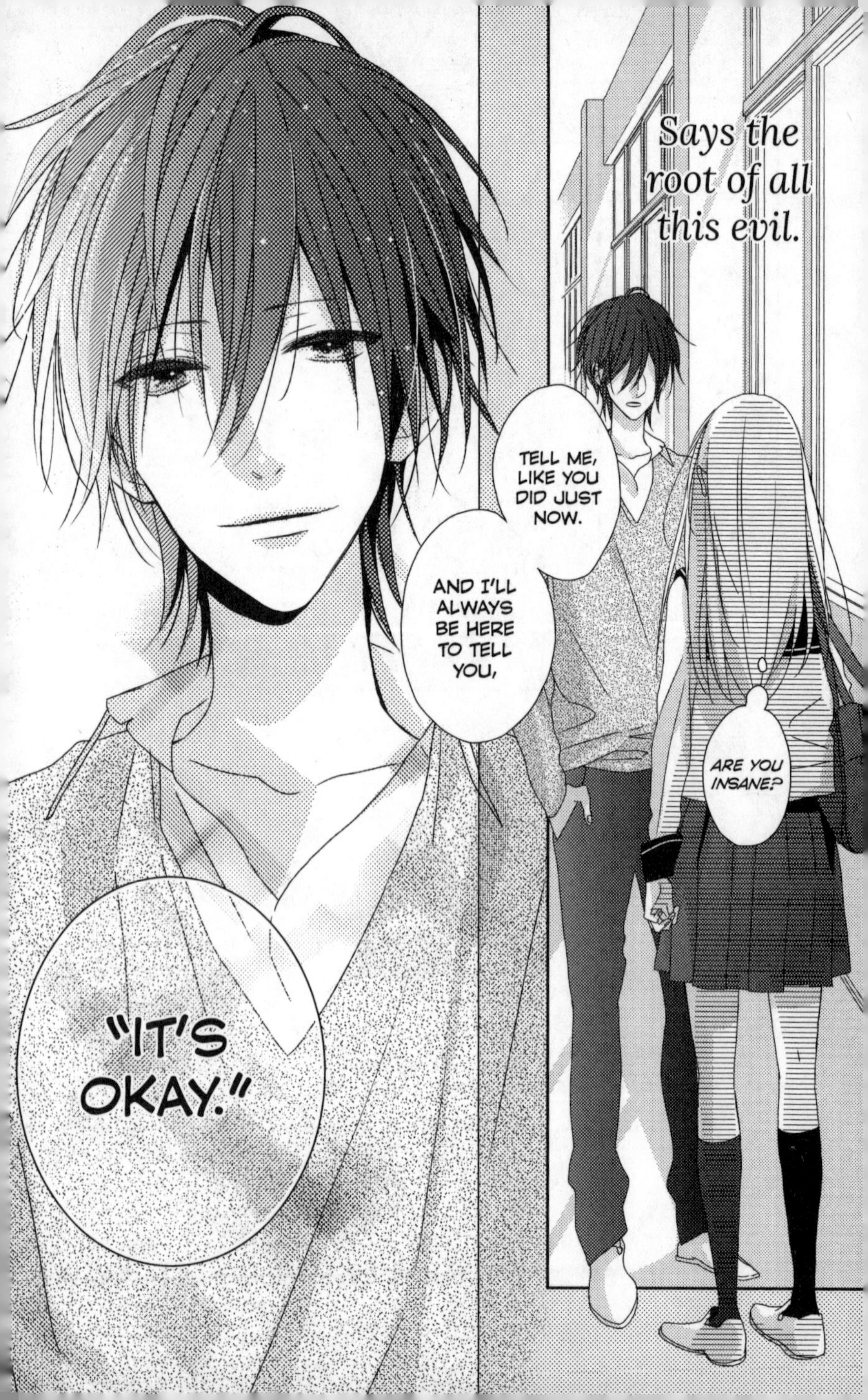
Says the root of all this evil.
TELL ME, LIKE YOU DID JUST NOW.
AND I'LL ALWAYS BE HERE TO TELL YOU,
ARE YOU INSANE?
"IT'S OKAY."

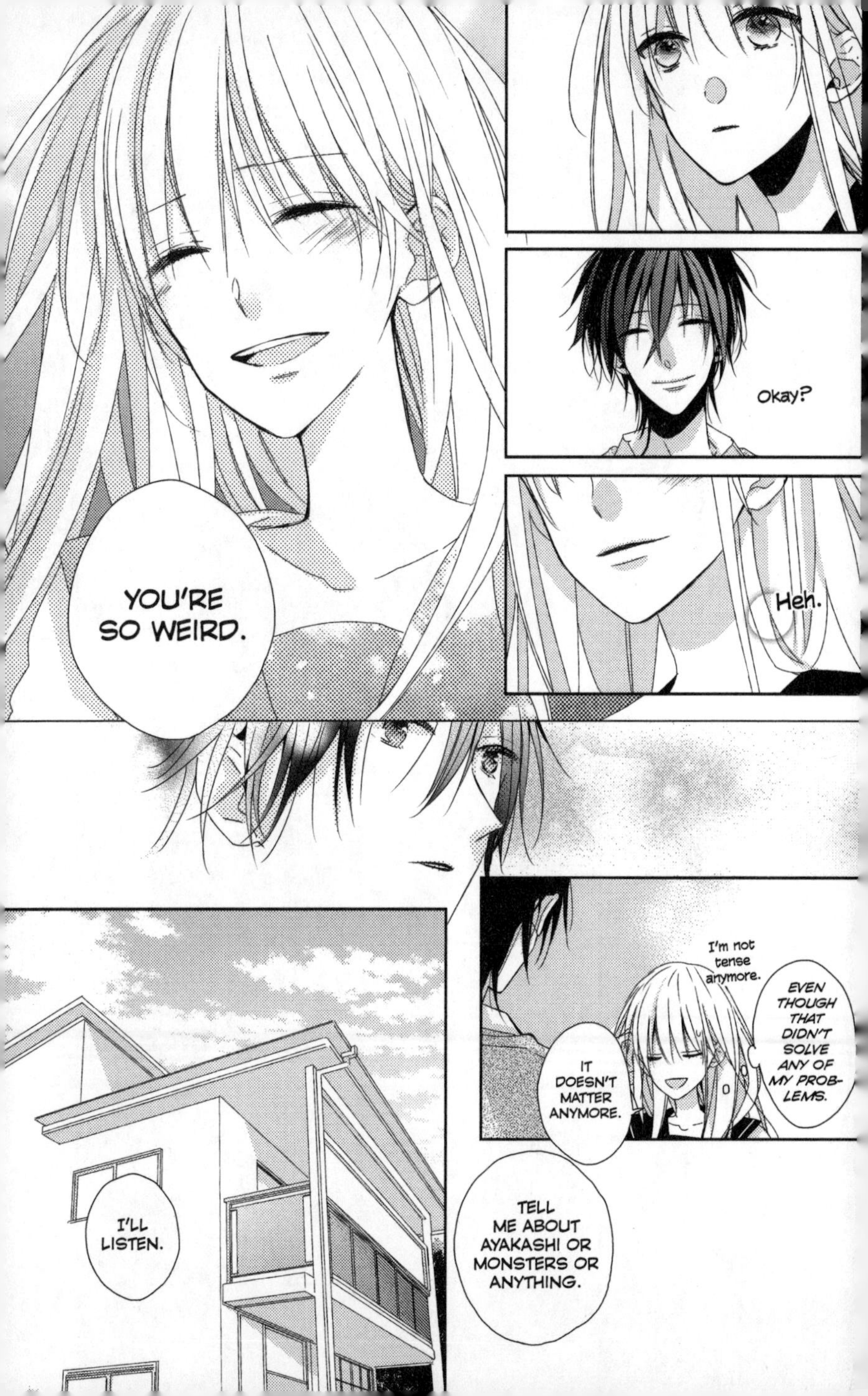
Okay?
Heh.
YOU'RE SO WEIRD.
I'm not tense anymore.
EVEN THOUGH THAT DIDN'T SOLVE ANY OF MY PROB-LEMS.
IT DOESN'T MATTER ANYMORE.
TELL ME ABOUT AYAKASHI OR MONSTERS OR ANYTHING.
I'LL LISTEN.

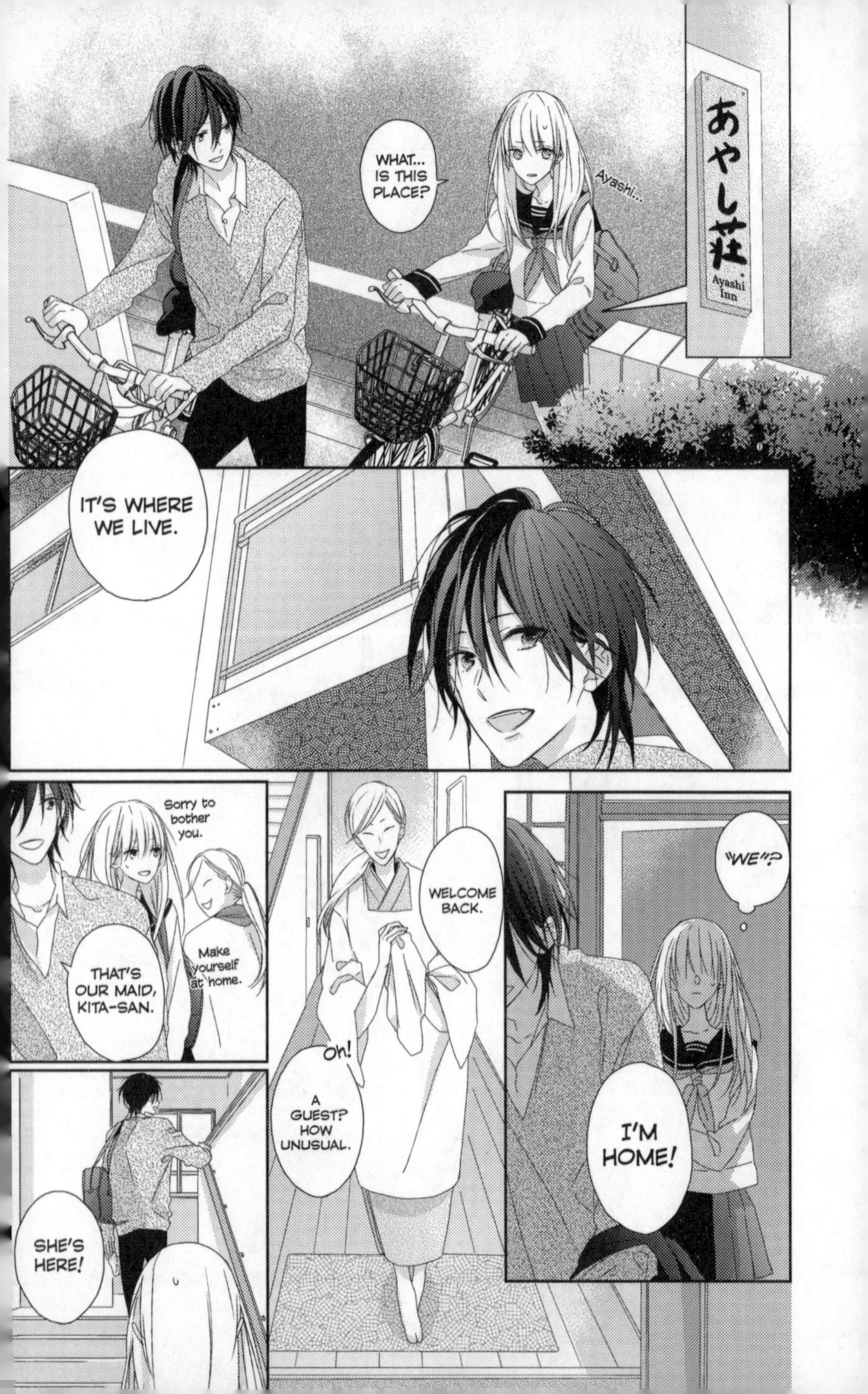
あやし荘
Ayashi Inn
Ayashi...
WHAT... IS THIS PLACE?
IT'S WHERE WE LIVE.
"WE"?
I'M HOME!
WELCOME BACK.
Oh!
A GUEST? HOW UNUSUAL.
Sorry to bother you.
Make yourself at home.
THAT'S OUR MAID, KITA-SAN.
SHE'S HERE!

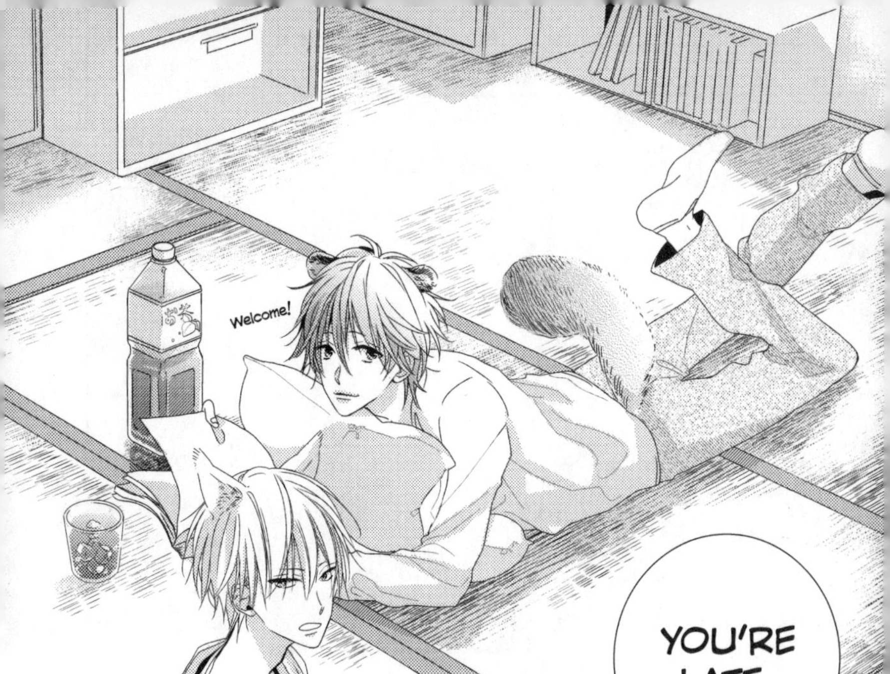
YOU'RE LATE.
Welcome!
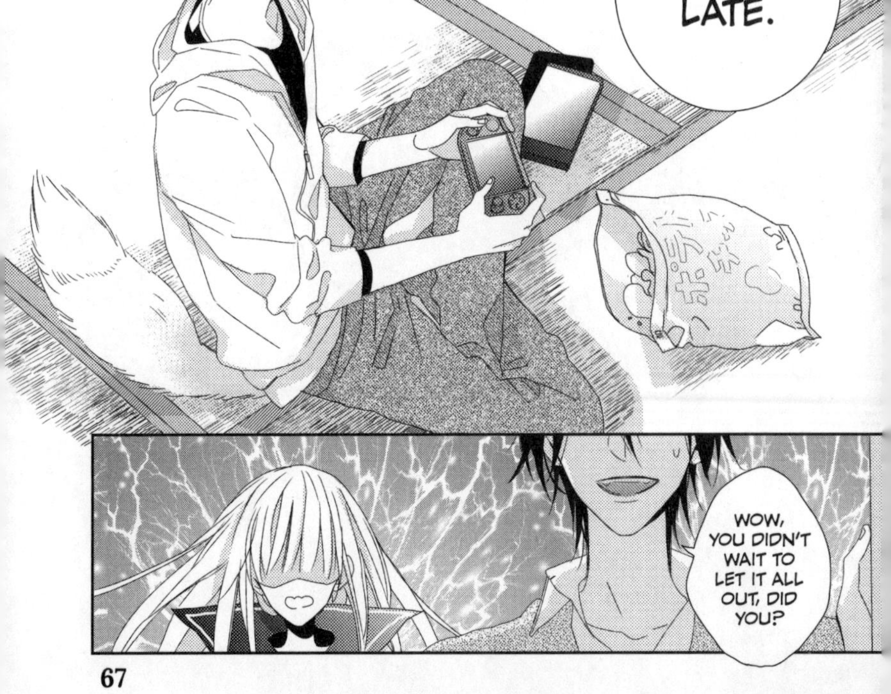
WOW, YOU DIDN'T WAIT TO LET IT ALL OUT, DID YOU?

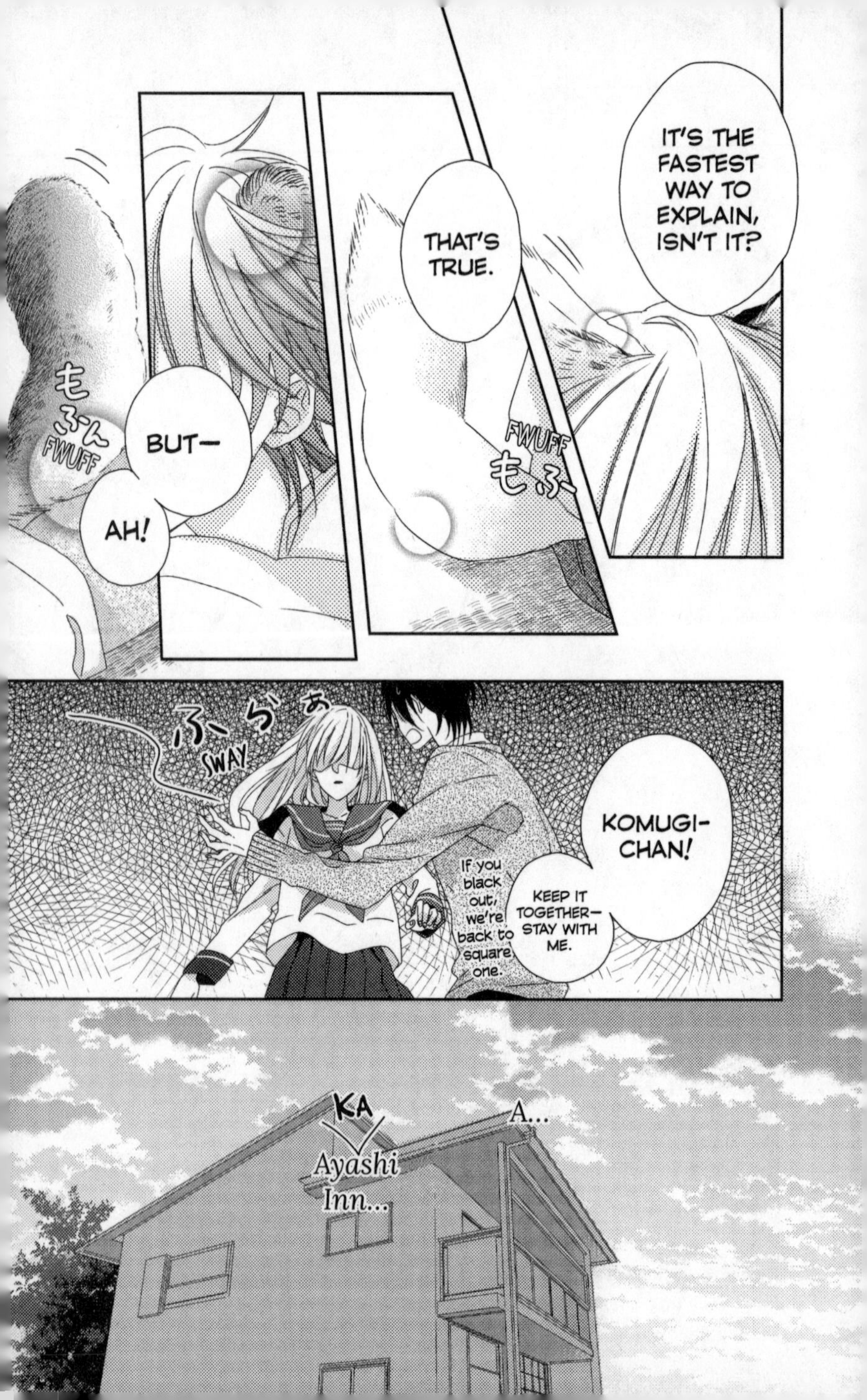
IT'S THE FASTEST WAY TO EXPLAIN, ISN'T IT?
THAT'S TRUE.
もふー
FWUFF
BUT—
AH!
もふん
FWUFF
KOMUGI-CHAN!
KEEP IT TOGETHER— STAY WITH ME.
If you black out, we're back to square one.
ふらぁ
SWAY
A...
KA
Ayashi Inn...

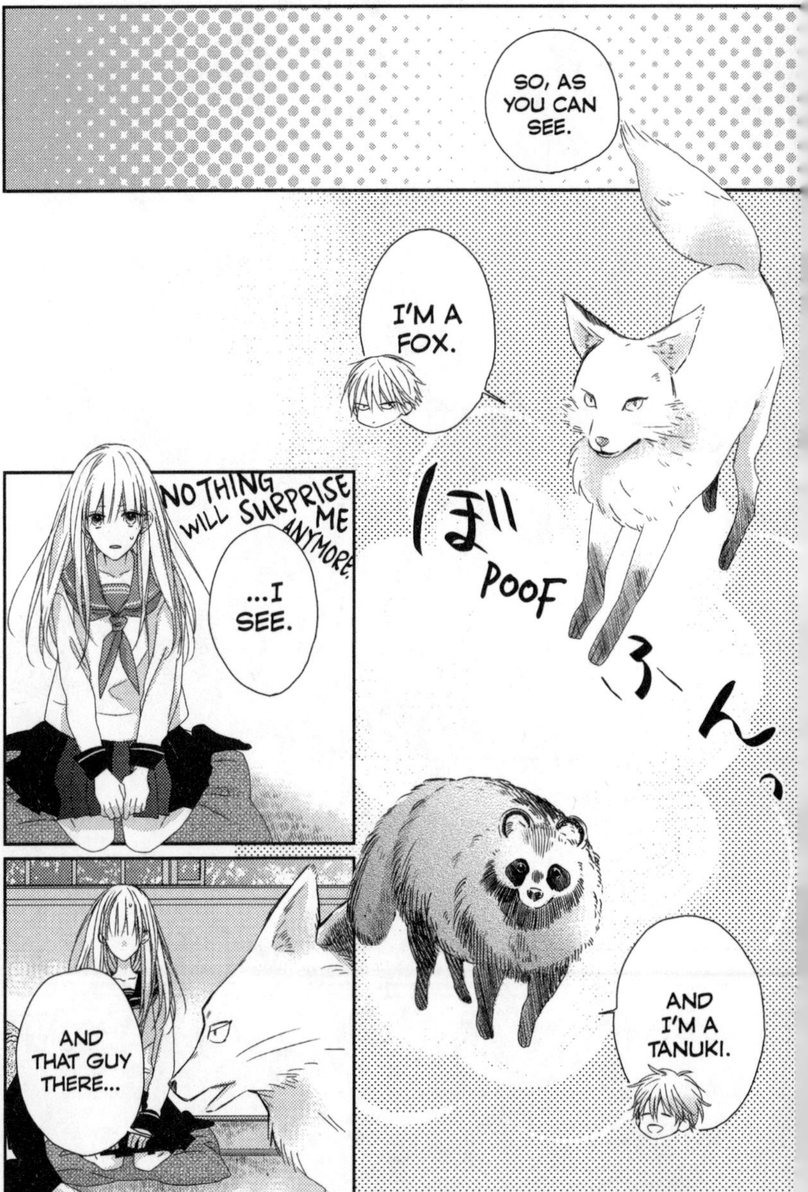
SO, AS YOU CAN SEE.
I'M A FOX.
ぼふんっ
POOF
AND I'M A TANUKI.
NOTHING WILL SURPRISE ME ANYMORE.
...I SEE.
AND THAT GUY THERE...

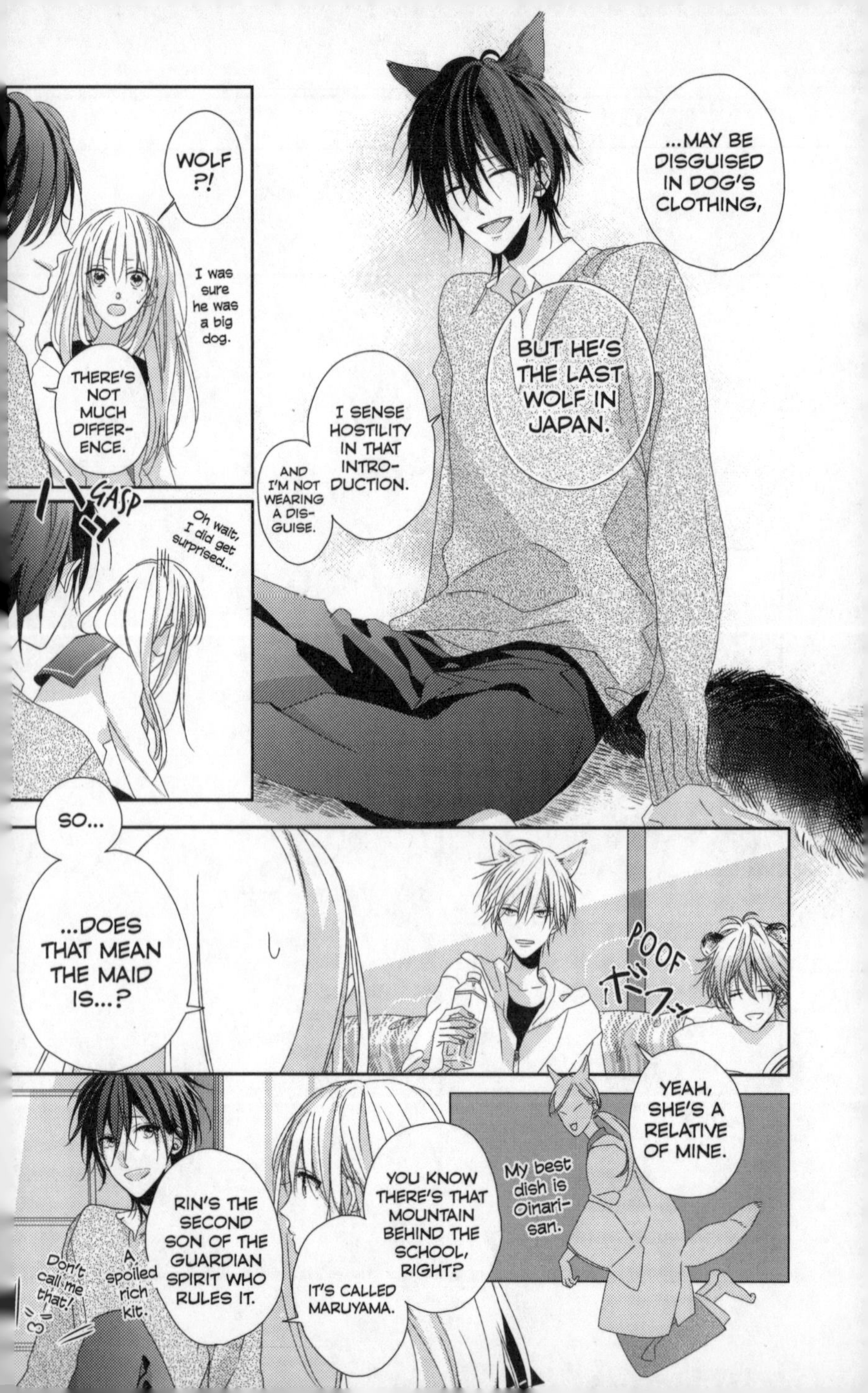
...MAY BE DISGUISED IN DOG'S CLOTHING,
BUT HE'S THE LAST WOLF IN JAPAN.
I SENSE HOSTILITY IN THAT INTRODUCTION.
AND I'M NOT WEARING A DISGUISE.
WOLF?!
I was sure he was a big dog.
THERE'S NOT MUCH DIFFERENCE.
GASP
Oh wait, I did get surprised...
SO...
...DOES THAT MEAN THE MAID IS...?
POOF
YEAH, SHE'S A RELATIVE OF MINE.
My best dish is Oinari-san.
YOU KNOW THERE'S THAT MOUNTAIN BEHIND THE SCHOOL, RIGHT?
IT'S CALLED MARUYAMA.
RIN'S THE SECOND SON OF THE GUARDIAN SPIRIT WHO RULES IT.
A spoiled rich kit.
Don't call me that!

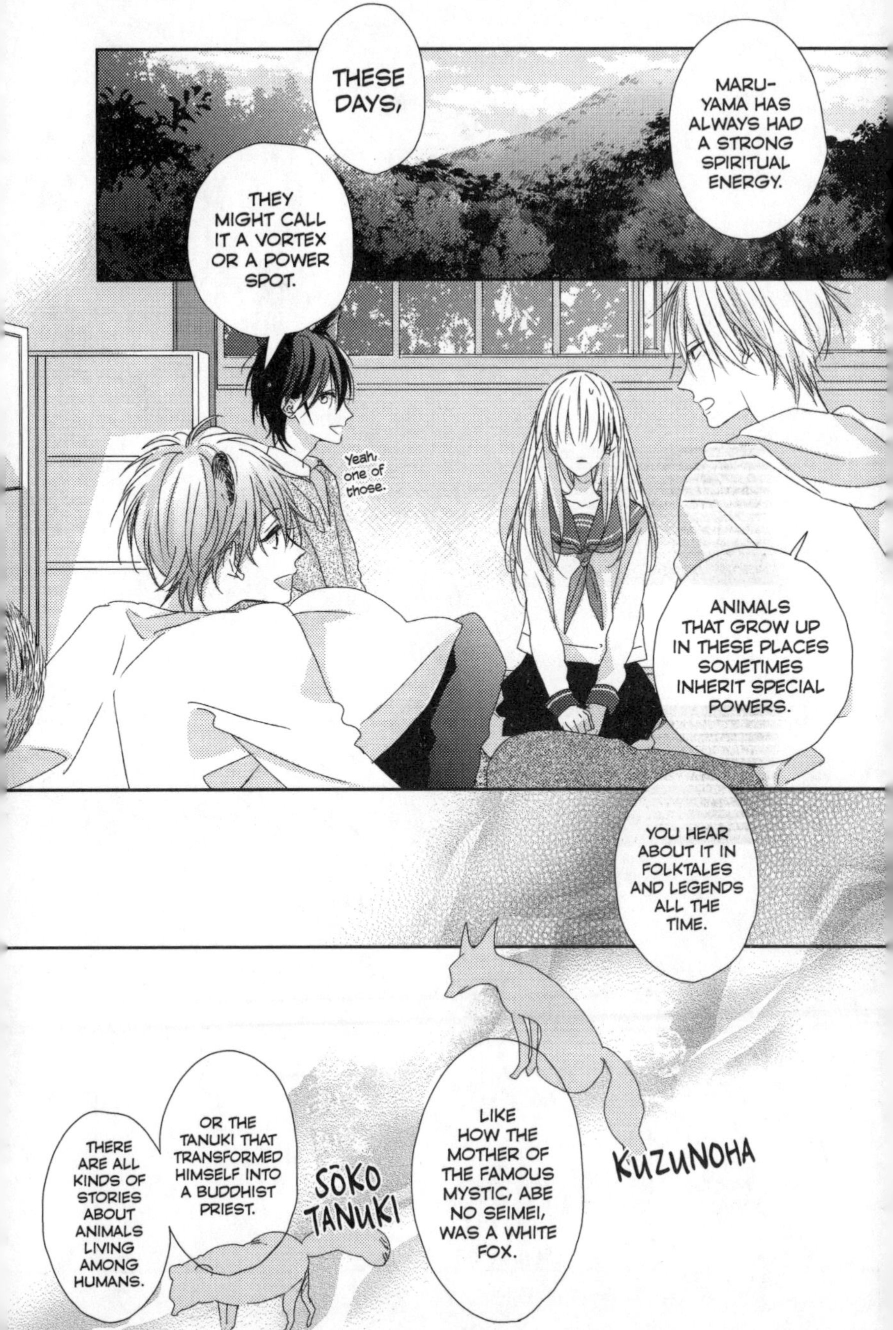

MARU-YAMA HAS ALWAYS HAD A STRONG SPIRITUAL ENERGY.
THESE DAYS,
THEY MIGHT CALL IT A VORTEX OR A POWER SPOT.
Yeah, one of those.
ANIMALS THAT GROW UP IN THESE PLACES SOMETIMES INHERIT SPECIAL POWERS.
YOU HEAR ABOUT IT IN FOLKTALES AND LEGENDS ALL THE TIME.
KUZUNOHA
LIKE HOW THE MOTHER OF THE FAMOUS MYSTIC, ABE NO SEIMEI, WAS A WHITE FOX.
SŌKO TANUKI
OR THE TANUKI THAT TRANSFORMED HIMSELF INTO A BUDDHIST PRIEST.
THERE ARE ALL KINDS OF STORIES ABOUT ANIMALS LIVING AMONG HUMANS.

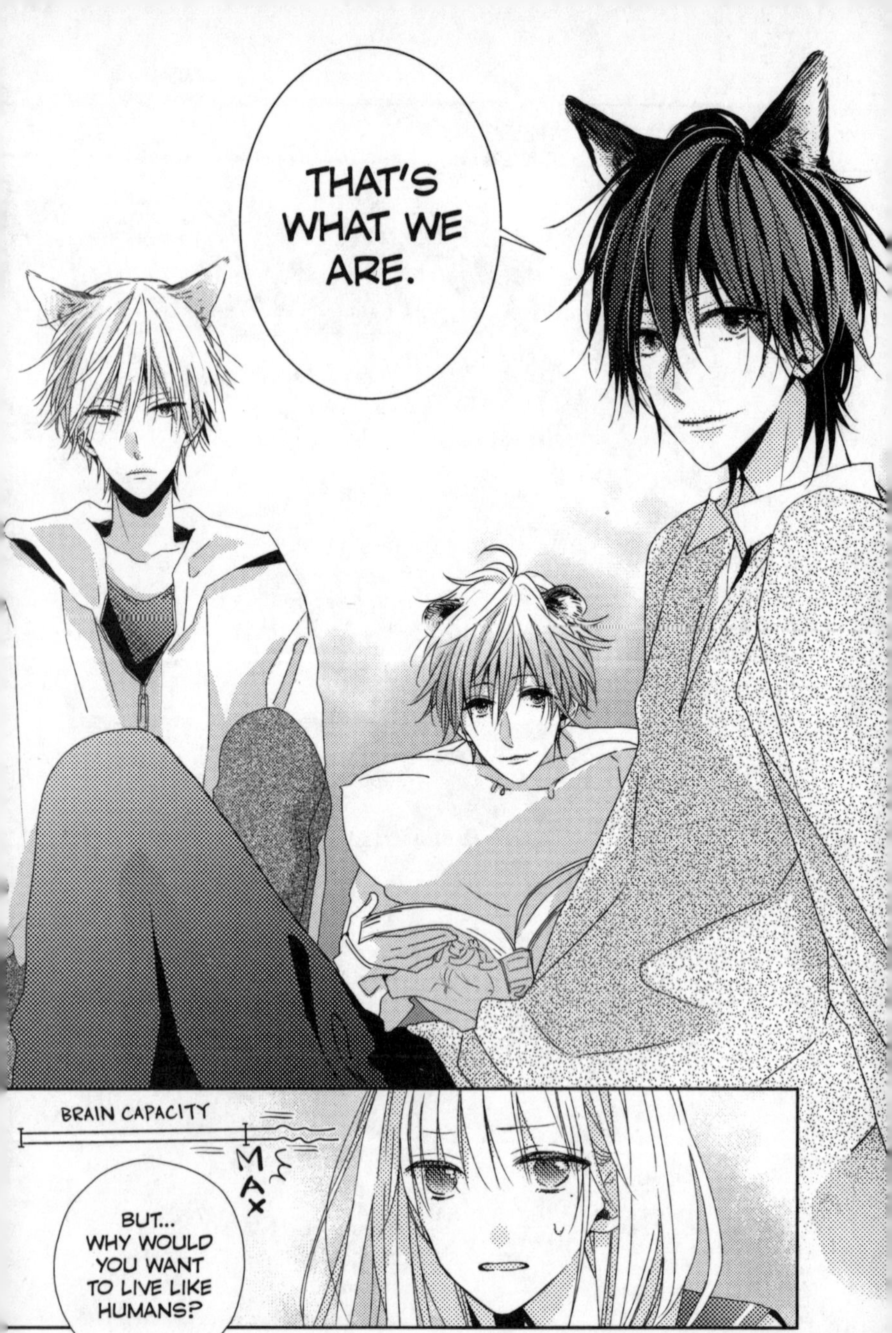
THAT'S WHAT WE ARE.
BRAIN CAPACITY
MAX
BUT... WHY WOULD YOU WANT TO LIVE LIKE HUMANS?

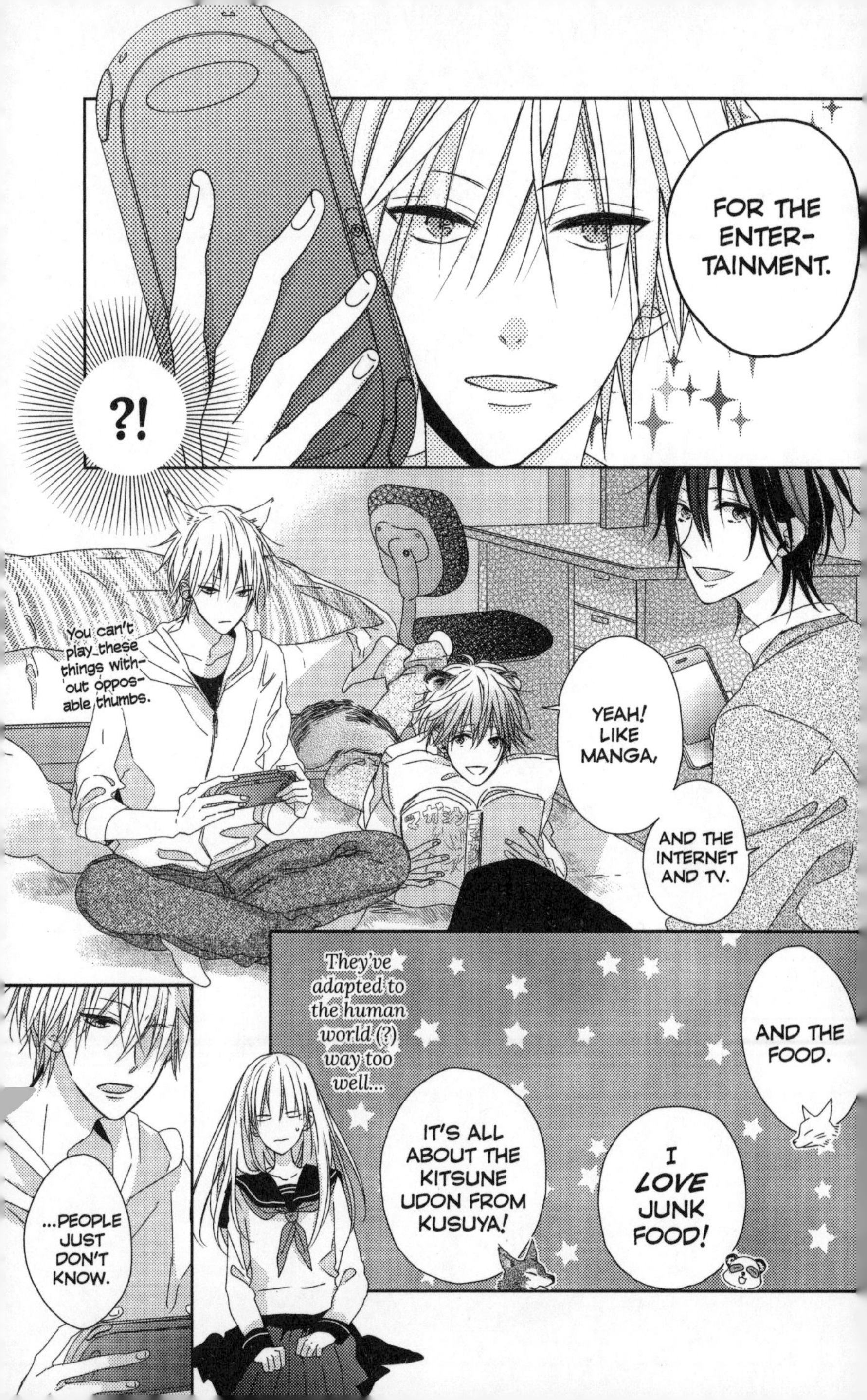
FOR THE ENTERTAINMENT.
?!
YEAH! LIKE MANGA,
AND THE INTERNET AND TV.
You can't play these things without opposable thumbs.
AND THE FOOD.
I *LOVE* JUNK FOOD!
IT'S ALL ABOUT THE KITSUNE UDON FROM KUSUYA!
They've adapted to the human world (?) way too well...
...PEOPLE JUST DON'T KNOW.

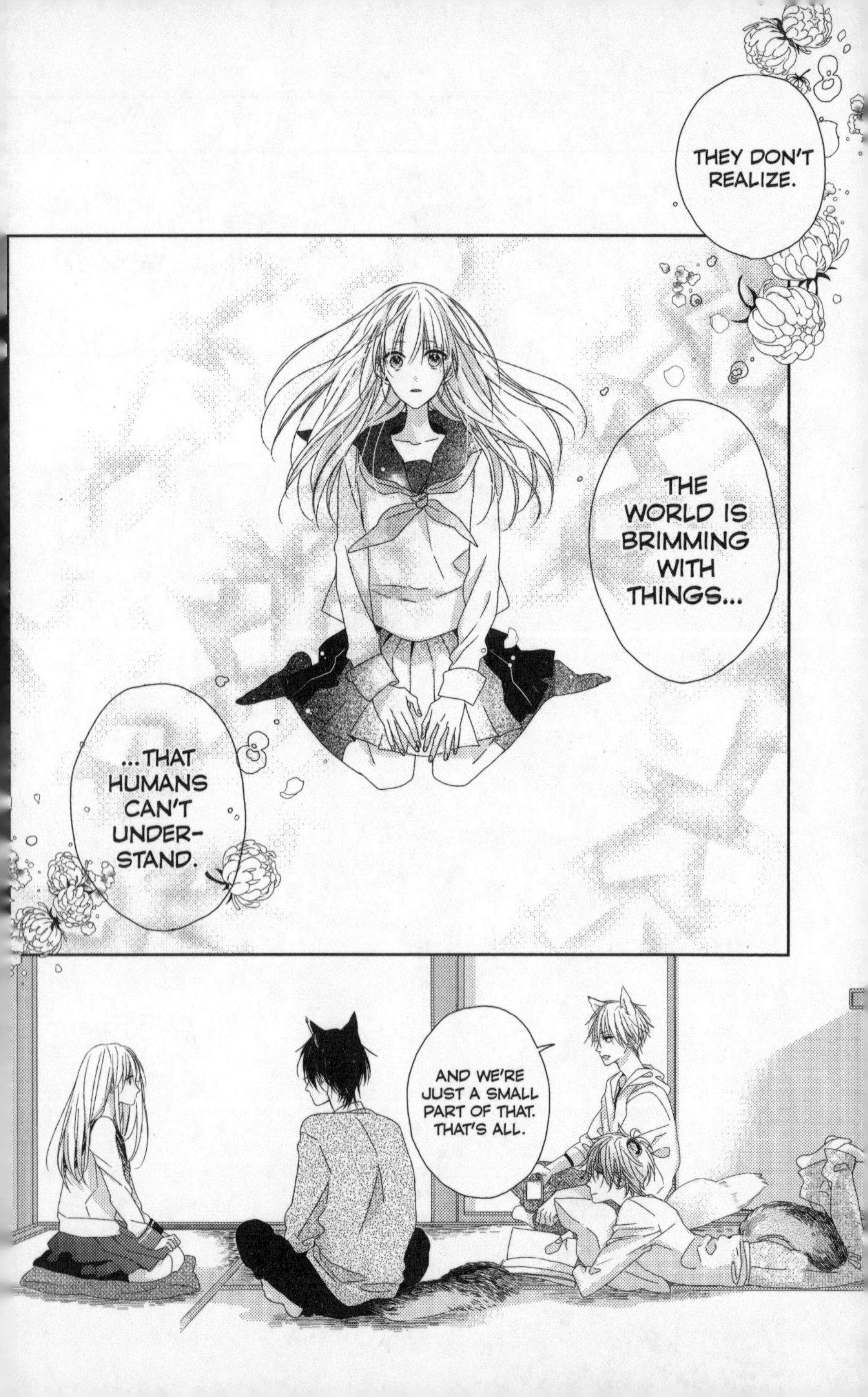
THEY DON'T REALIZE.
THE WORLD IS BRIMMING WITH THINGS...
...THAT HUMANS CAN'T UNDER-STAND.
AND WE'RE JUST A SMALL PART OF THAT. THAT'S ALL.

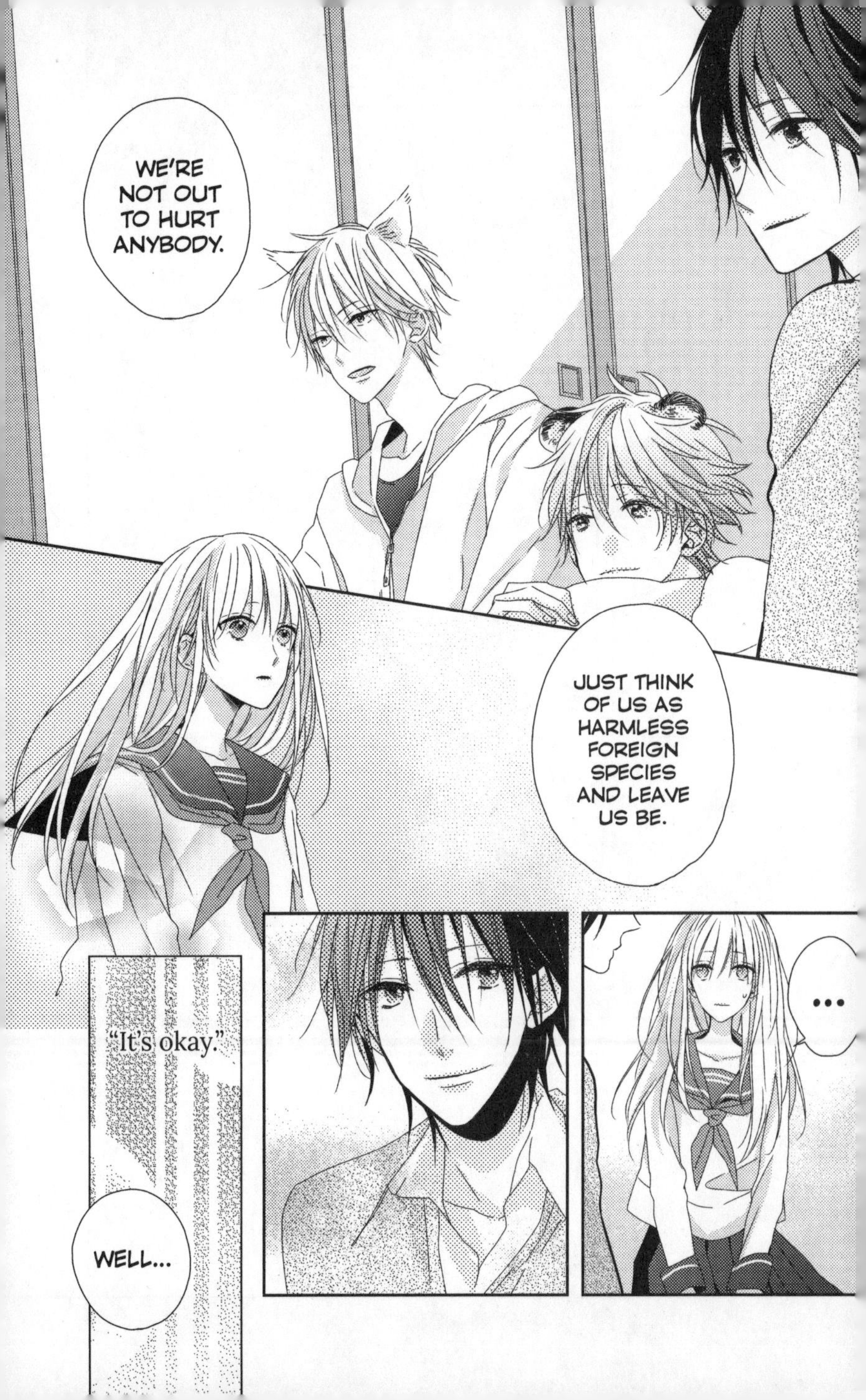
WE'RE NOT OUT TO HURT ANYBODY.
JUST THINK OF US AS HARMLESS FOREIGN SPECIES AND LEAVE US BE.
...
"It's okay."
WELL...

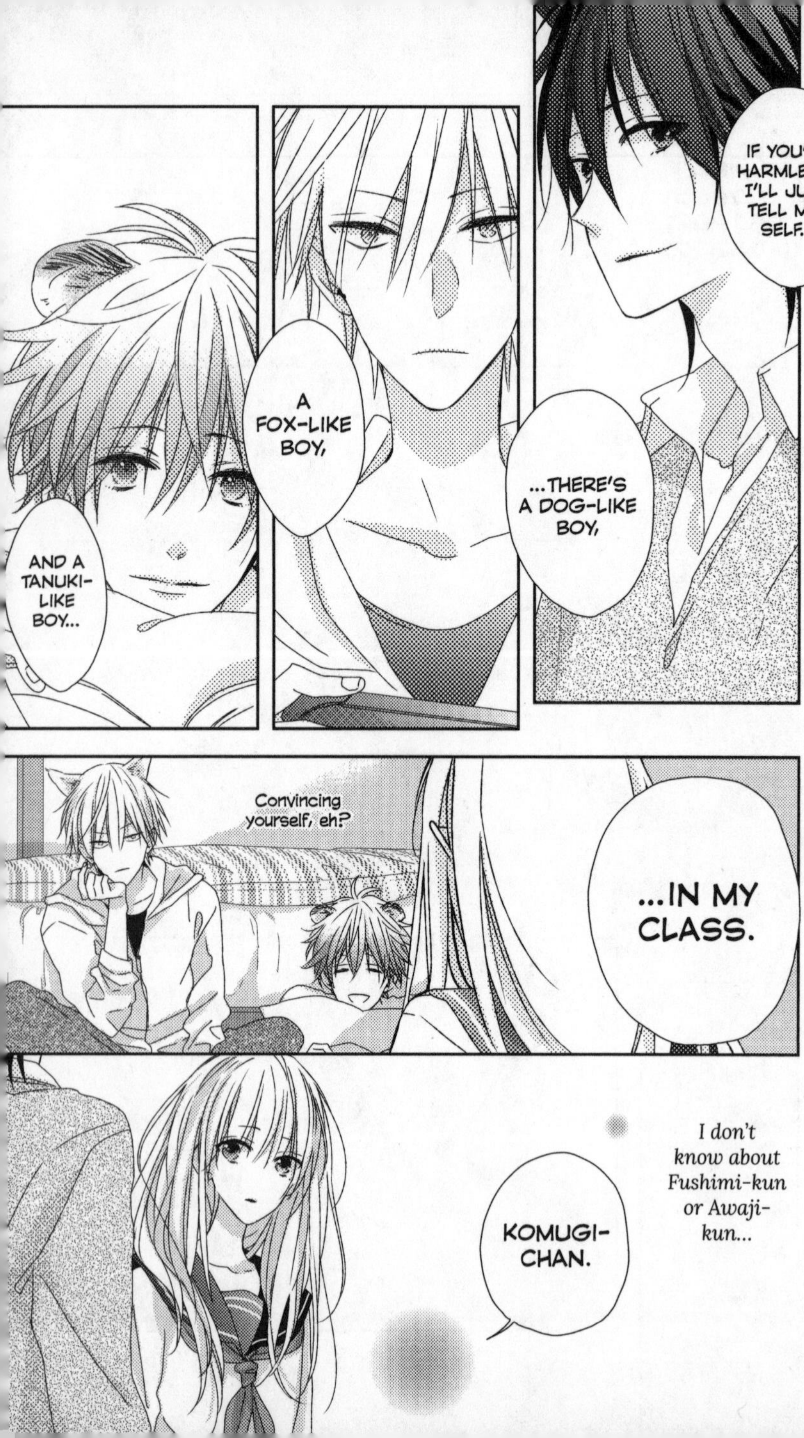
IF YOU'RE HARMLESS, I'LL JUST TELL MY-SELF...
...THERE'S A DOG-LIKE BOY,
A FOX-LIKE BOY,
AND A TANUKI-LIKE BOY...
...IN MY CLASS.
Convincing yourself, eh?
I don't know about Fushimi-kun or Awaji-kun...
KOMUGI-CHAN.

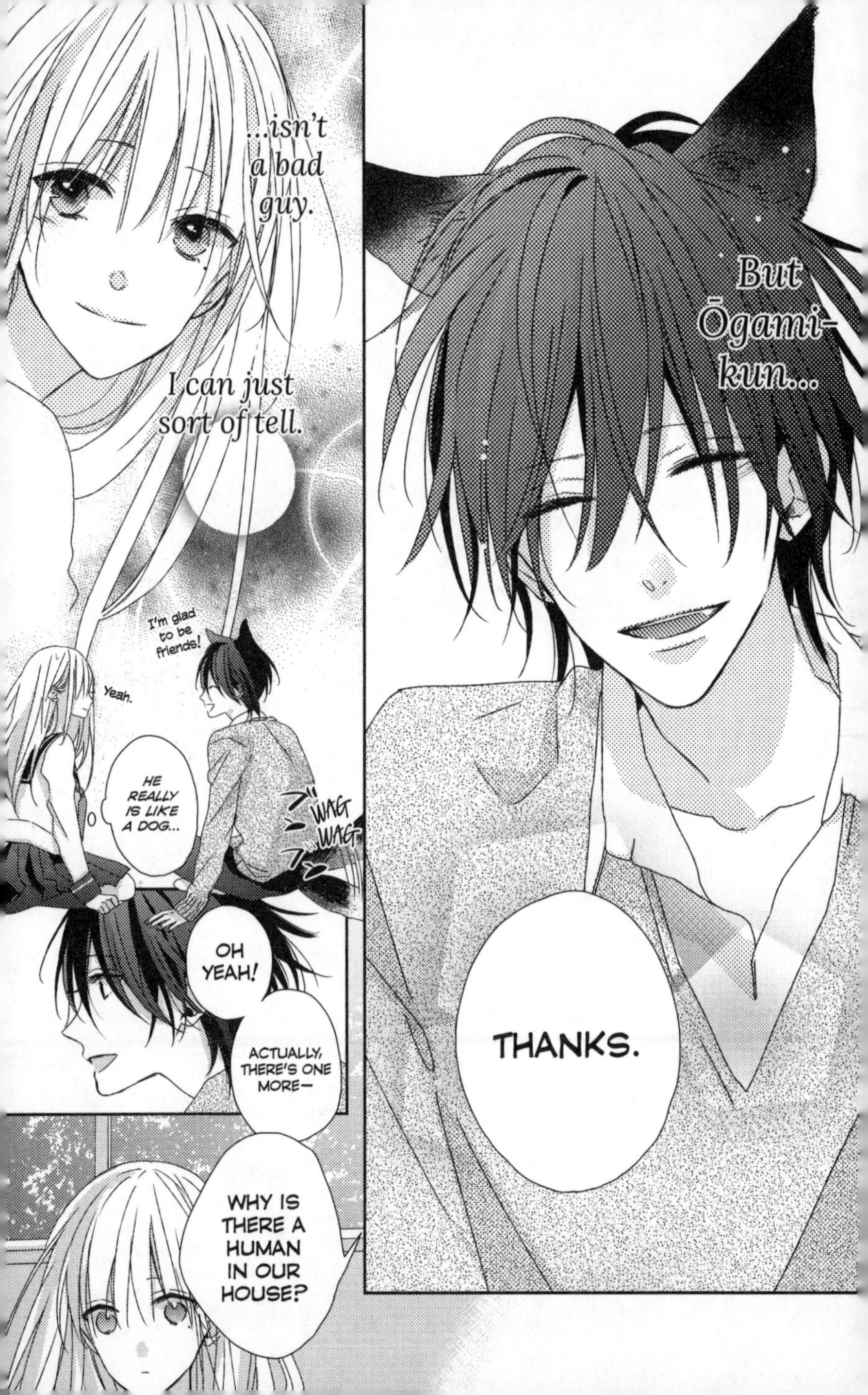
But Ōgami-kun...
THANKS.
...isn't a bad guy.
I can just sort of tell.
I'm glad to be friends!
Yeah.
HE REALLY IS LIKE A DOG...
WAG WAG
OH YEAH!
ACTUALLY, THERE'S ONE MORE—
WHY IS THERE A HUMAN IN OUR HOUSE?

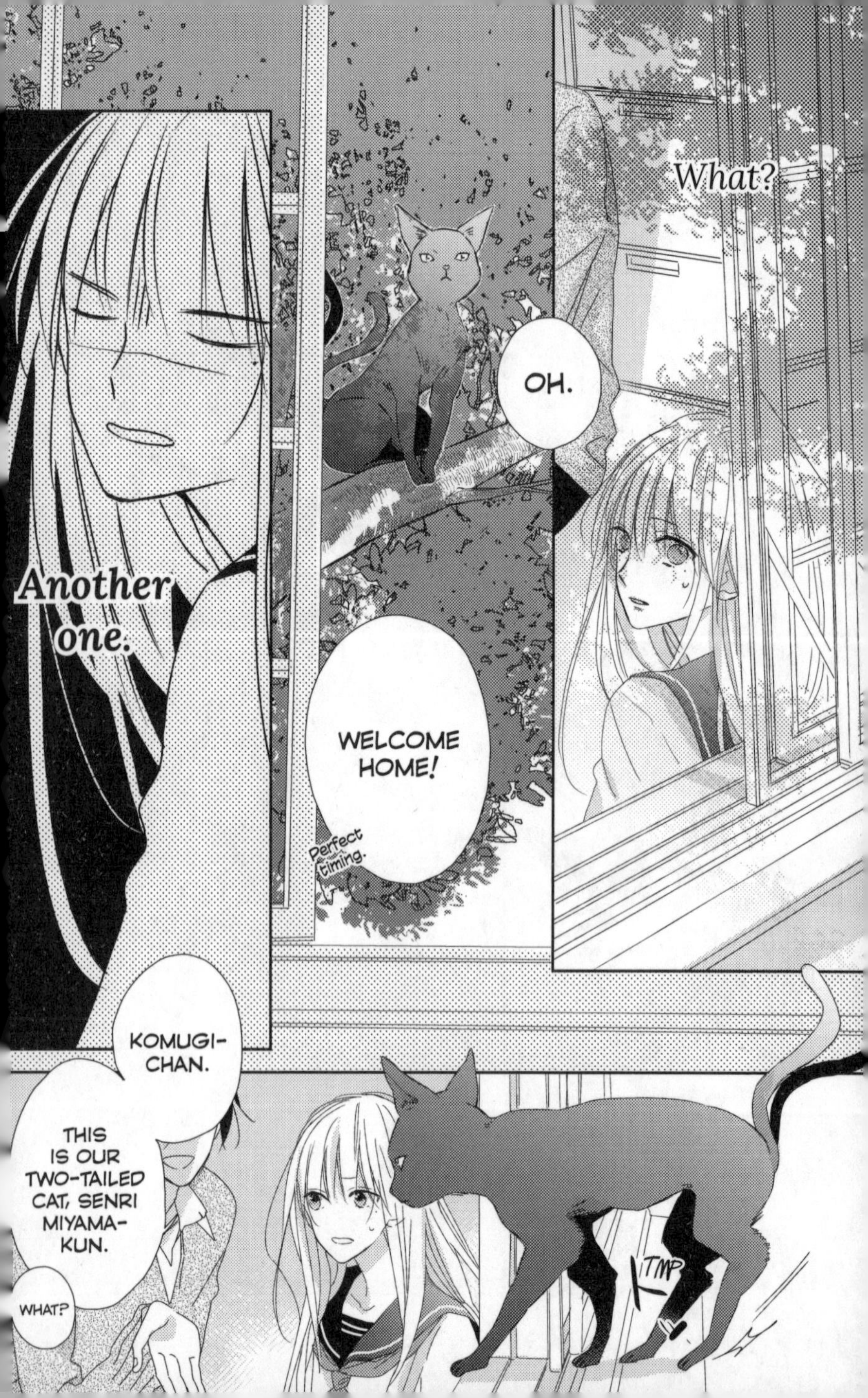
What?
OH.
WELCOME HOME!
Perfect timing.
Another one.
KOMUGI-CHAN.
THIS IS OUR TWO-TAILED CAT, SENRI MIYAMA-KUN.
TMP
WHAT?

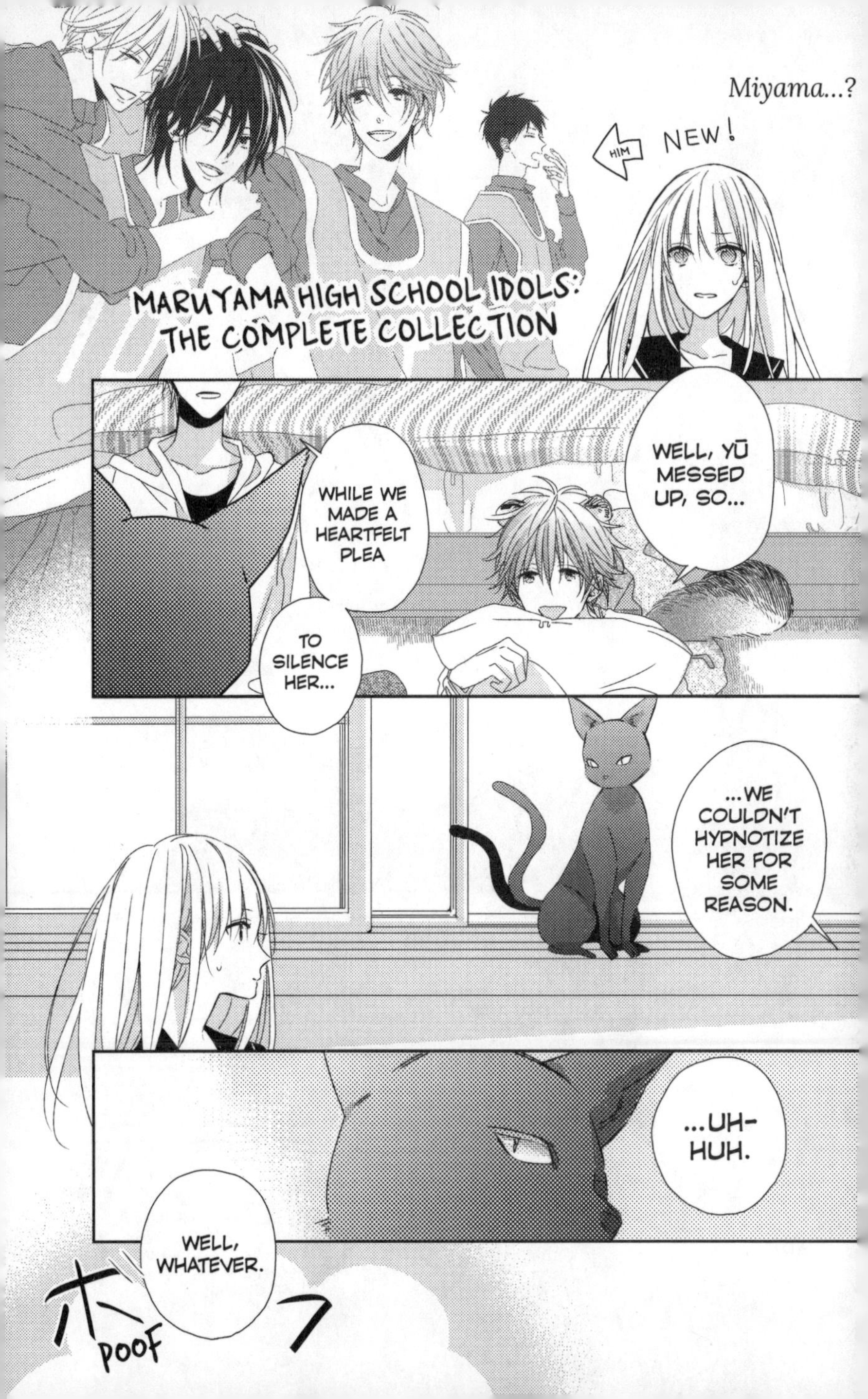
Miyama...?
NEW!
HIM
MARUYAMA HIGH SCHOOL IDOLS: THE COMPLETE COLLECTION
WELL, YŪ MESSED UP, SO...
WHILE WE MADE A HEARTFELT PLEA
TO SILENCE HER...
...WE COULDN'T HYPNOTIZE HER FOR SOME REASON.
...UH-HUH.
WELL, WHATEVER.
POOF

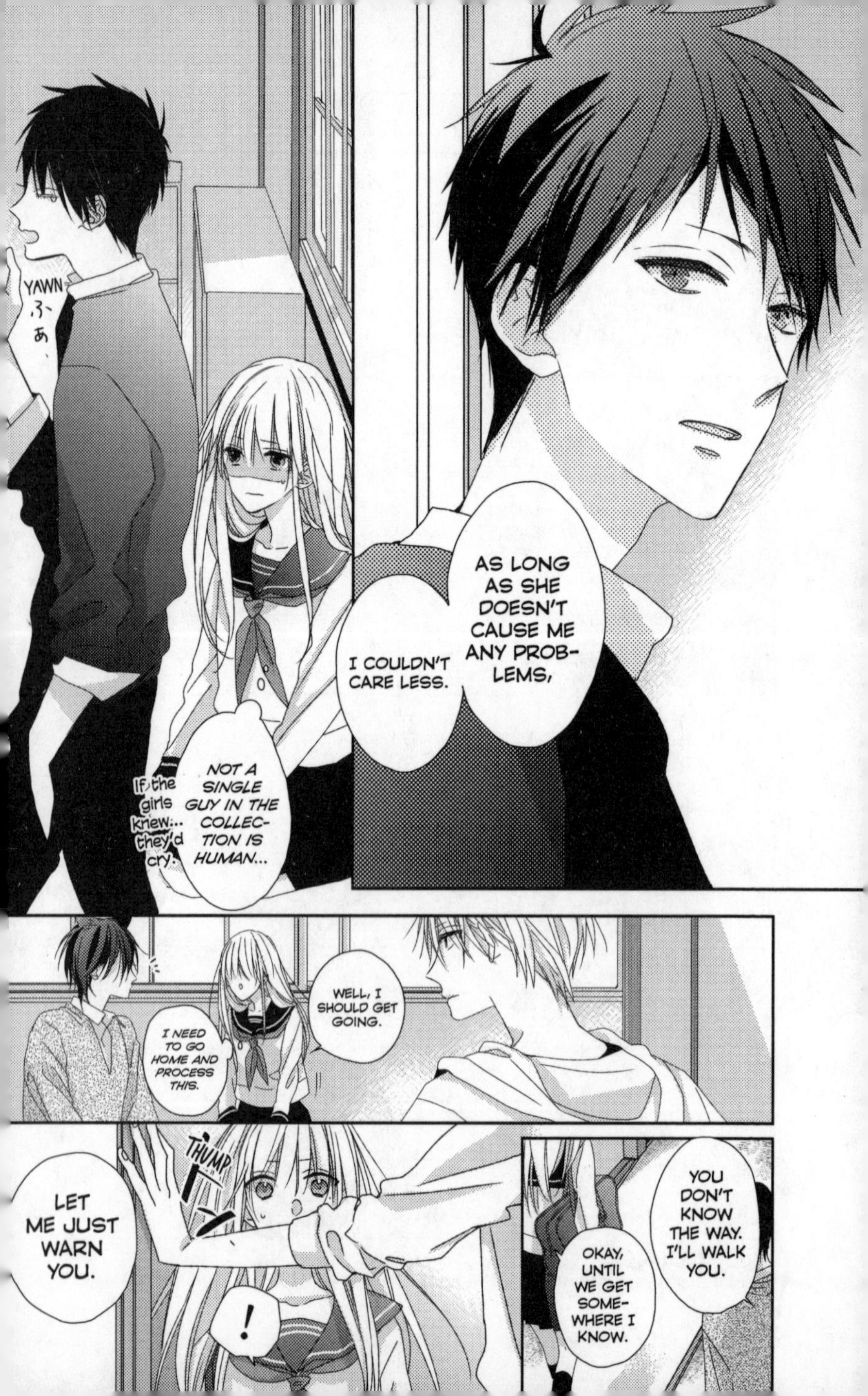
AS LONG AS SHE DOESN'T CAUSE ME ANY PROB-LEMS,
I COULDN'T CARE LESS.
YAWN
ふあ
NOT A SINGLE GUY IN THE COLLECTION IS HUMAN...
If the girls knew... they'd cry.
WELL, I SHOULD GET GOING.
I NEED TO GO HOME AND PROCESS THIS.
YOU DON'T KNOW THE WAY. I'LL WALK YOU.
OKAY, UNTIL WE GET SOME-WHERE I KNOW.
THUMP
LET ME JUST WARN YOU.
!

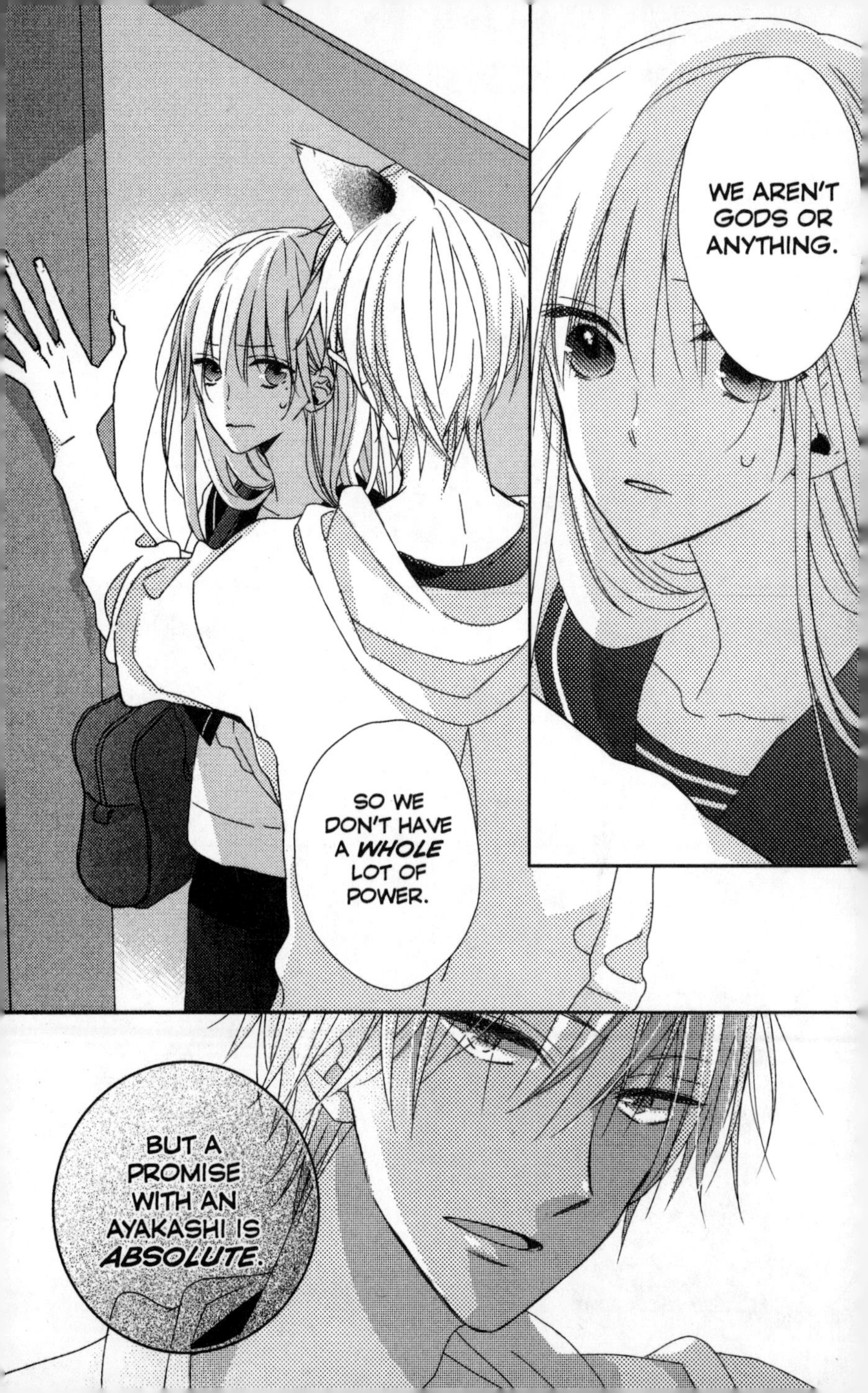
WE AREN'T GODS OR ANYTHING.
SO WE DON'T HAVE A WHOLE LOT OF POWER.
BUT A PROMISE WITH AN AYAKASHI IS ABSOLUTE.

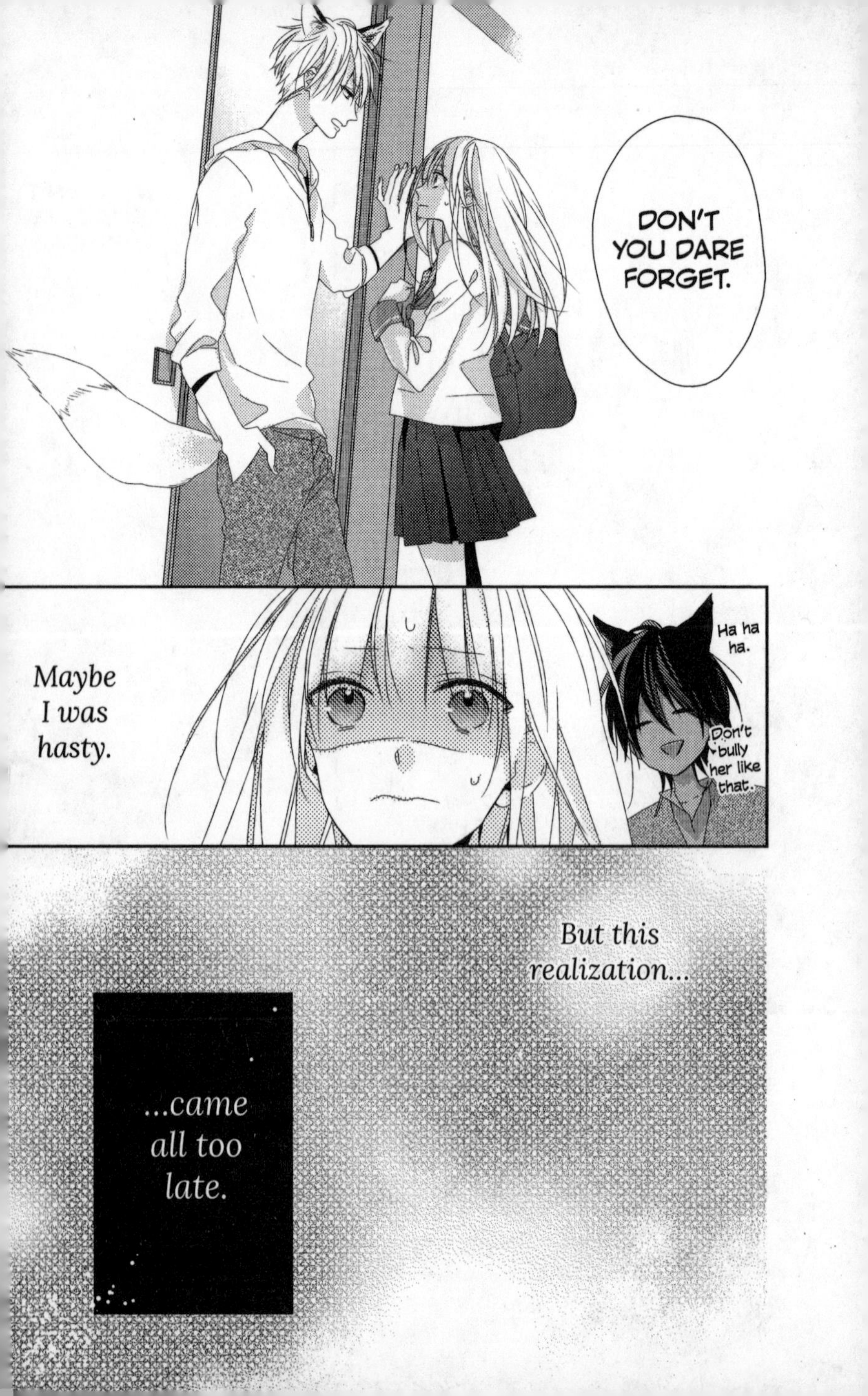
DON'T YOU DARE FORGET.
Ha ha ha.
Don't bully her like that.
Maybe I was hasty.
But this realization...
...came all too late.

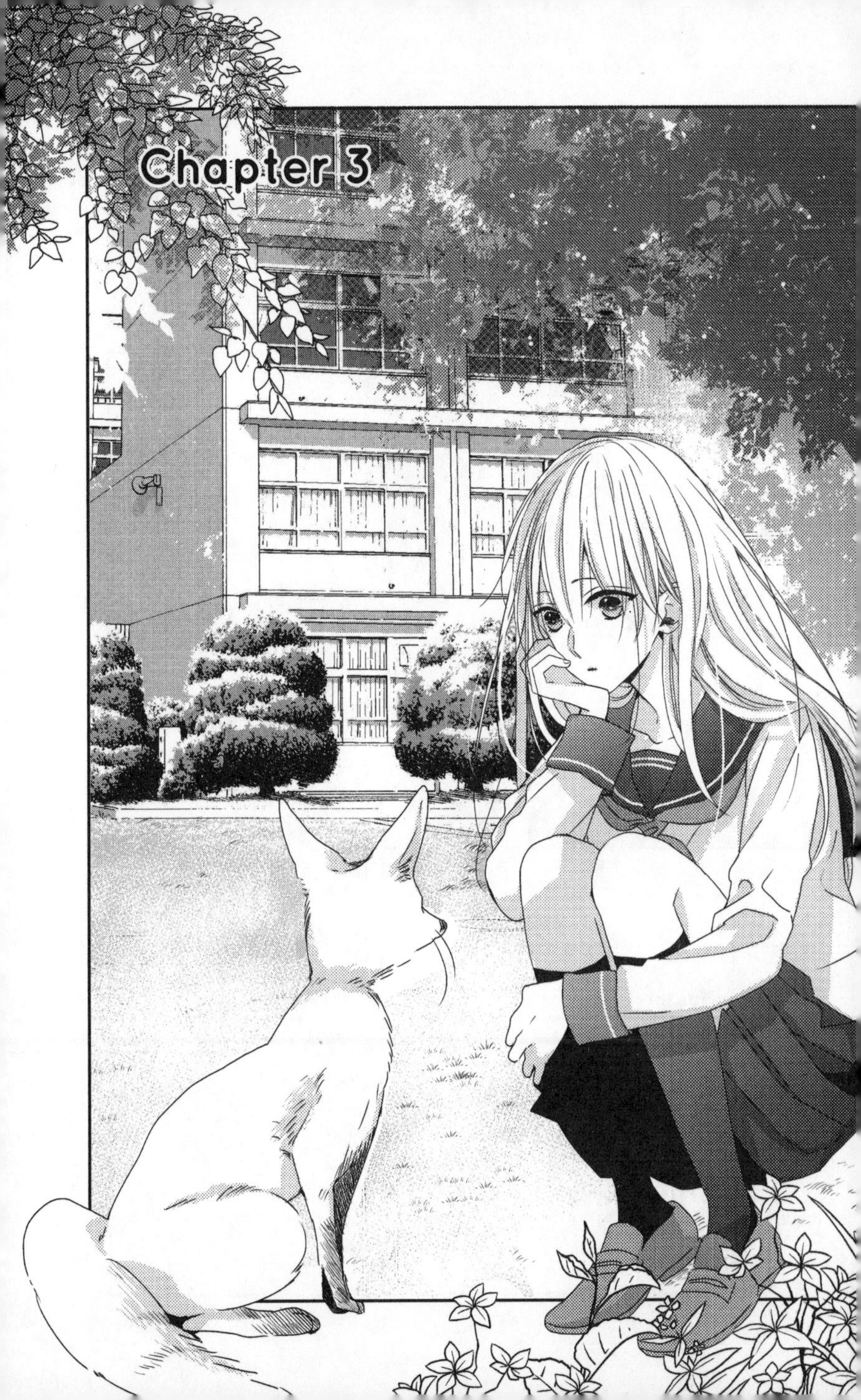
Chapter 3

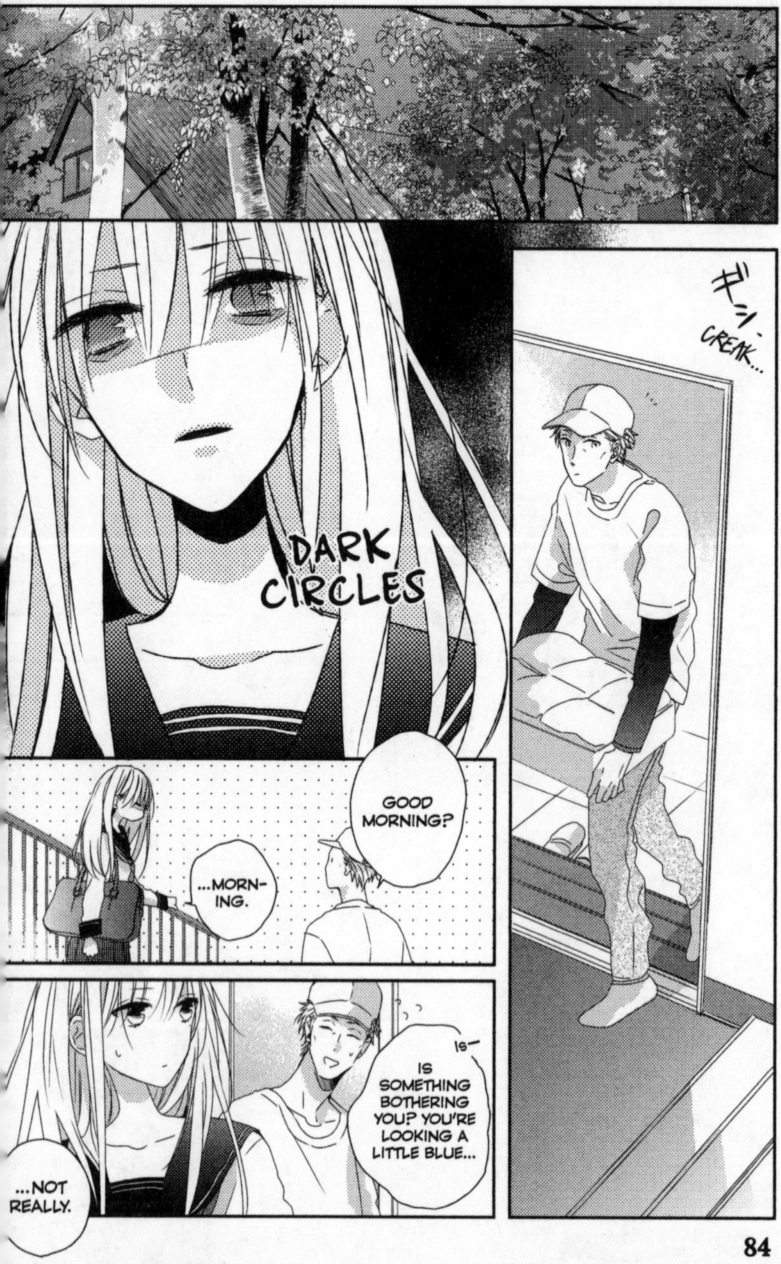
ギシ
CREAK...
DARK CIRCLES
GOOD MORNING?
...MORN-ING.
IS—
IS SOMETHING BOTHERING YOU? YOU'RE LOOKING A LITTLE BLUE...
...NOT REALLY.

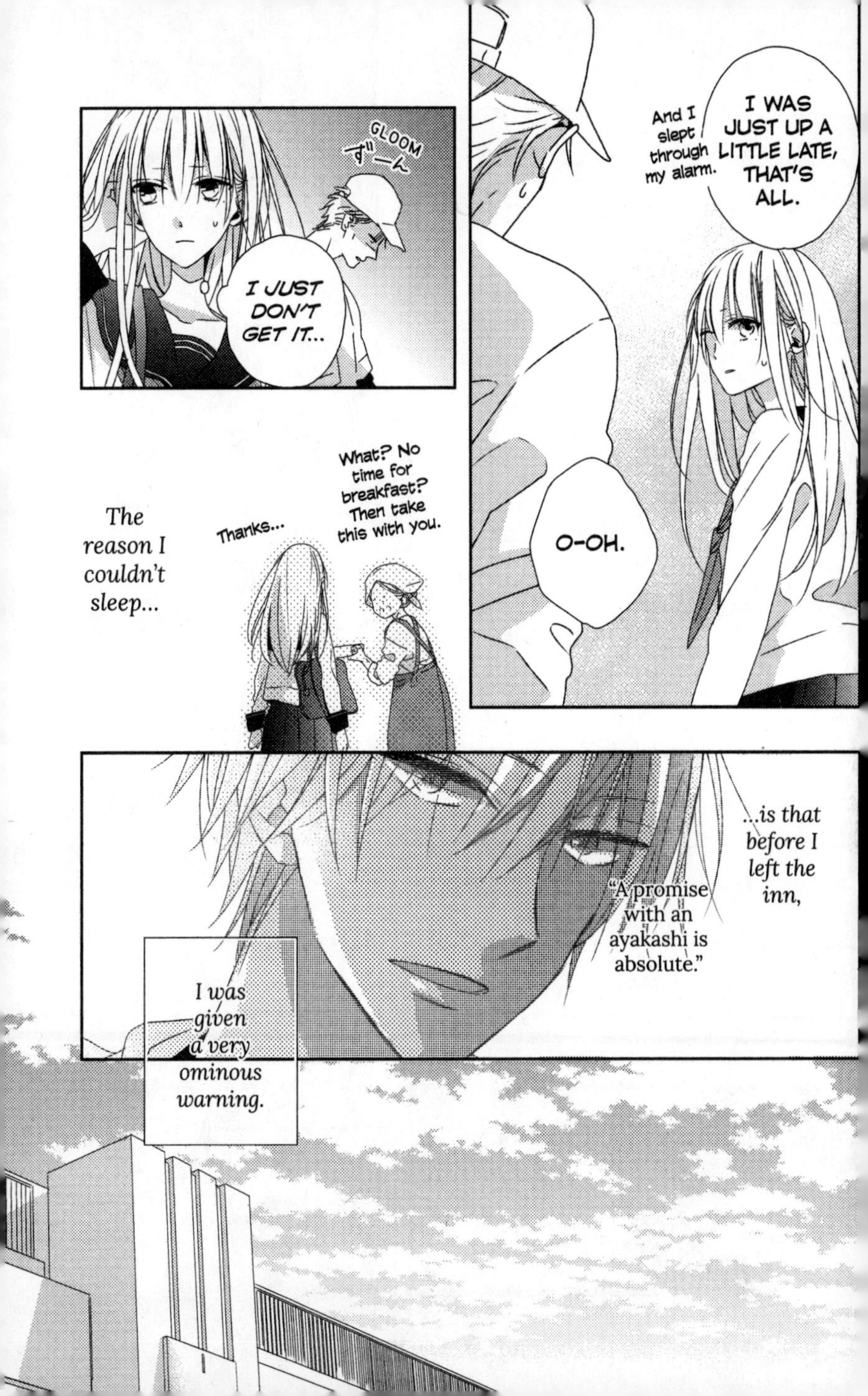
I WAS JUST UP A LITTLE LATE, THAT'S ALL.
And I slept through my alarm.
O-OH.
GLOOM
ずーん
I JUST DON'T GET IT...
What? No time for breakfast? Then take this with you.
Thanks...
The reason I couldn't sleep...
...is that before I left the inn,
"A promise with an ayakashi is absolute."
I was given a very ominous warning.

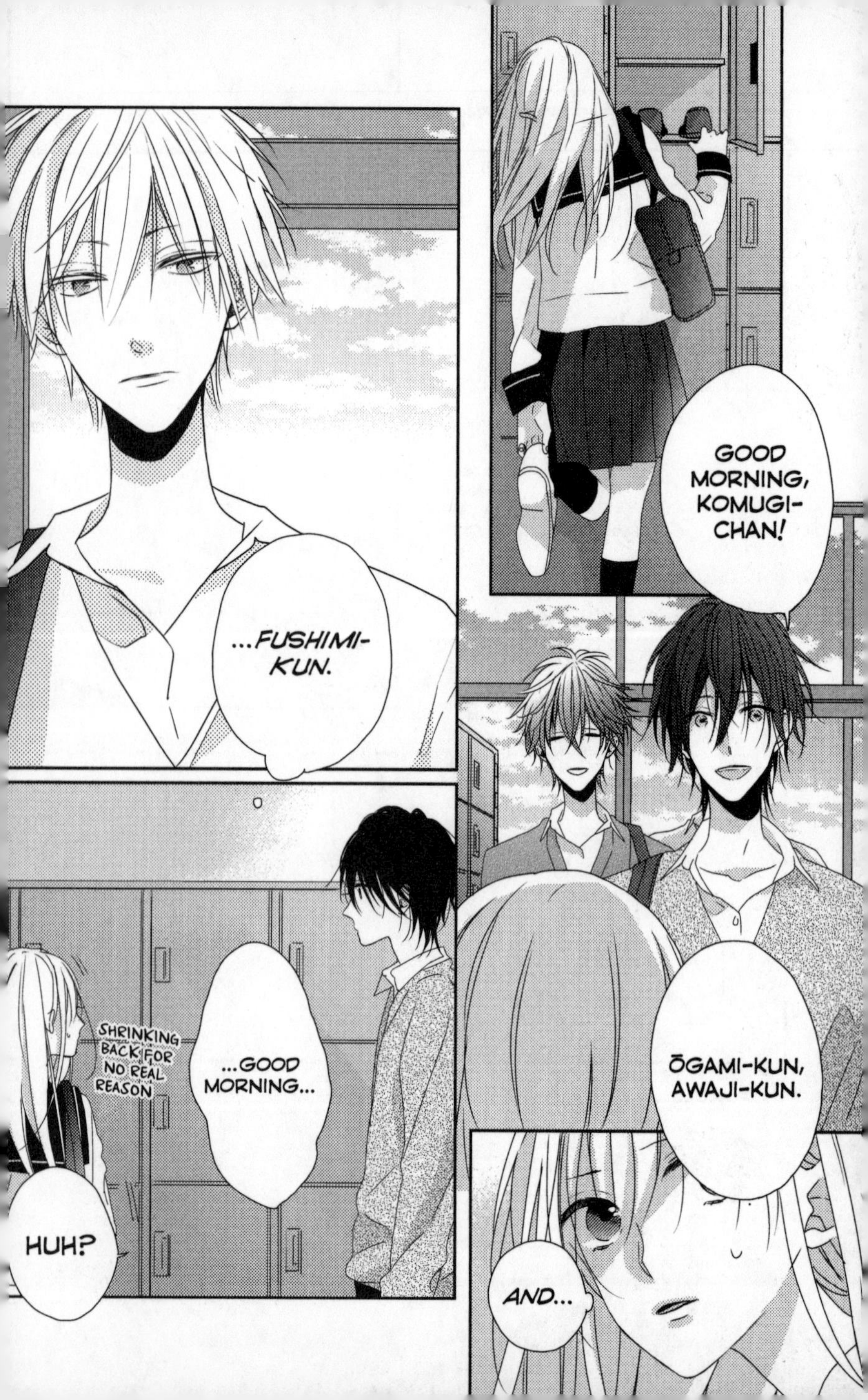
GOOD MORNING, KOMUGI-CHAN!
ŌGAMI-KUN, AWAJI-KUN.
AND...
...FUSHIMI-KUN.
...GOOD MORNING...
SHRINKING BACK FOR NO REAL REASON
HUH?

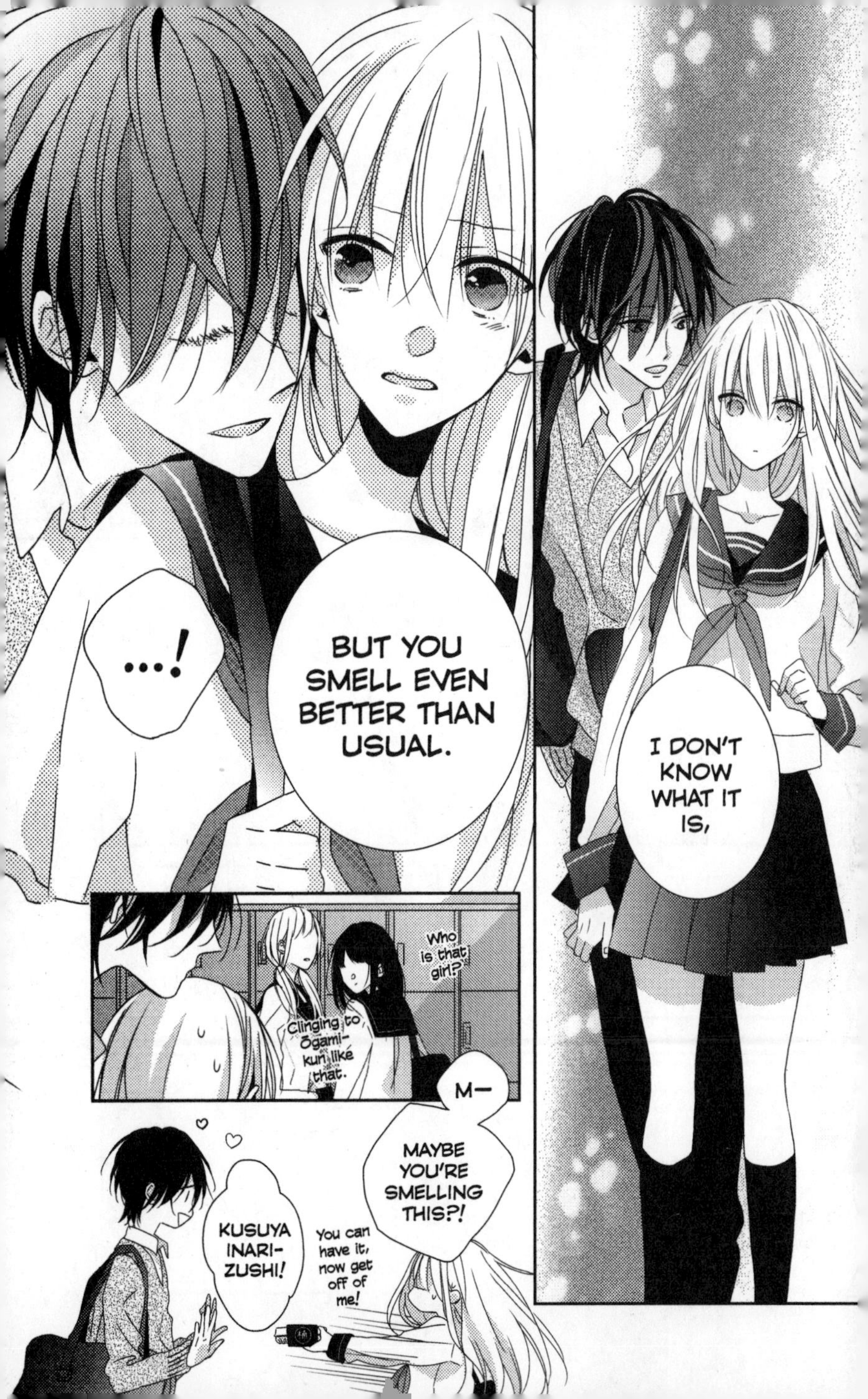
I DON'T KNOW WHAT IT IS,
BUT YOU SMELL EVEN BETTER THAN USUAL.
...!
Who is that girl?
Clinging to Ōgami-kun like that.
M—
MAYBE YOU'RE SMELLING THIS?!
You can have it, now get off of me!
KUSUYA INARI-ZUSHI!

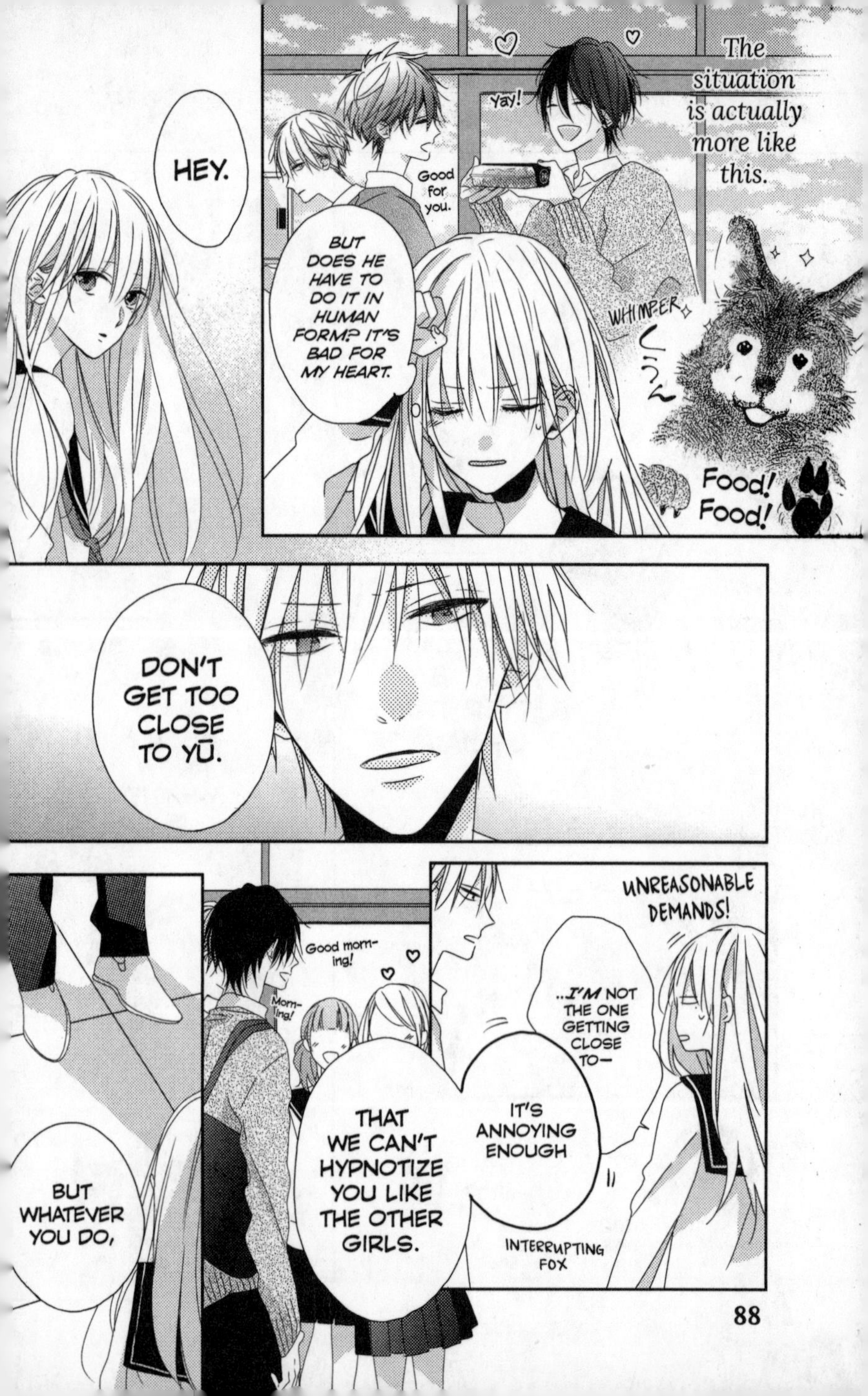
The situation is actually more like this.
Yay!
Good for you.
BUT DOES HE HAVE TO DO IT IN HUMAN FORM? IT'S BAD FOR MY HEART.
WHIMPER
Food! Food!
HEY.
DON'T GET TOO CLOSE TO YŪ.
UNREASONABLE DEMANDS!
...I'M NOT THE ONE GETTING CLOSE TO—
IT'S ANNOYING ENOUGH
INTERRUPTING FOX
Good morning!
Morning!
THAT WE CAN'T HYPNOTIZE YOU LIKE THE OTHER GIRLS.
BUT WHATEVER YOU DO,

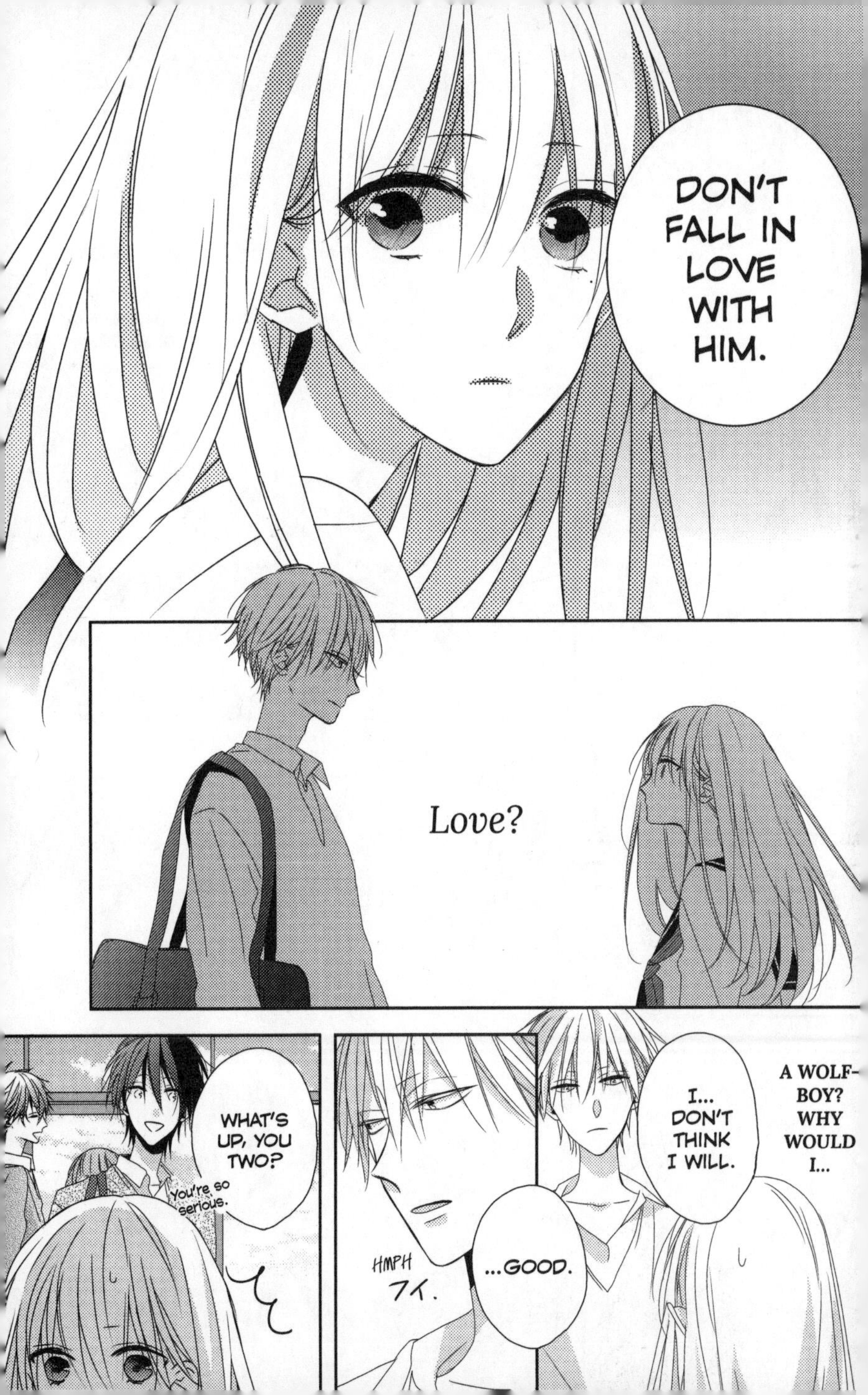
DON'T FALL IN LOVE WITH HIM.
Love?
A WOLF-BOY? WHY WOULD I...
I... DON'T THINK I WILL.
...GOOD.
HMPH フイ.
WHAT'S UP, YOU TWO?
You're so serious.

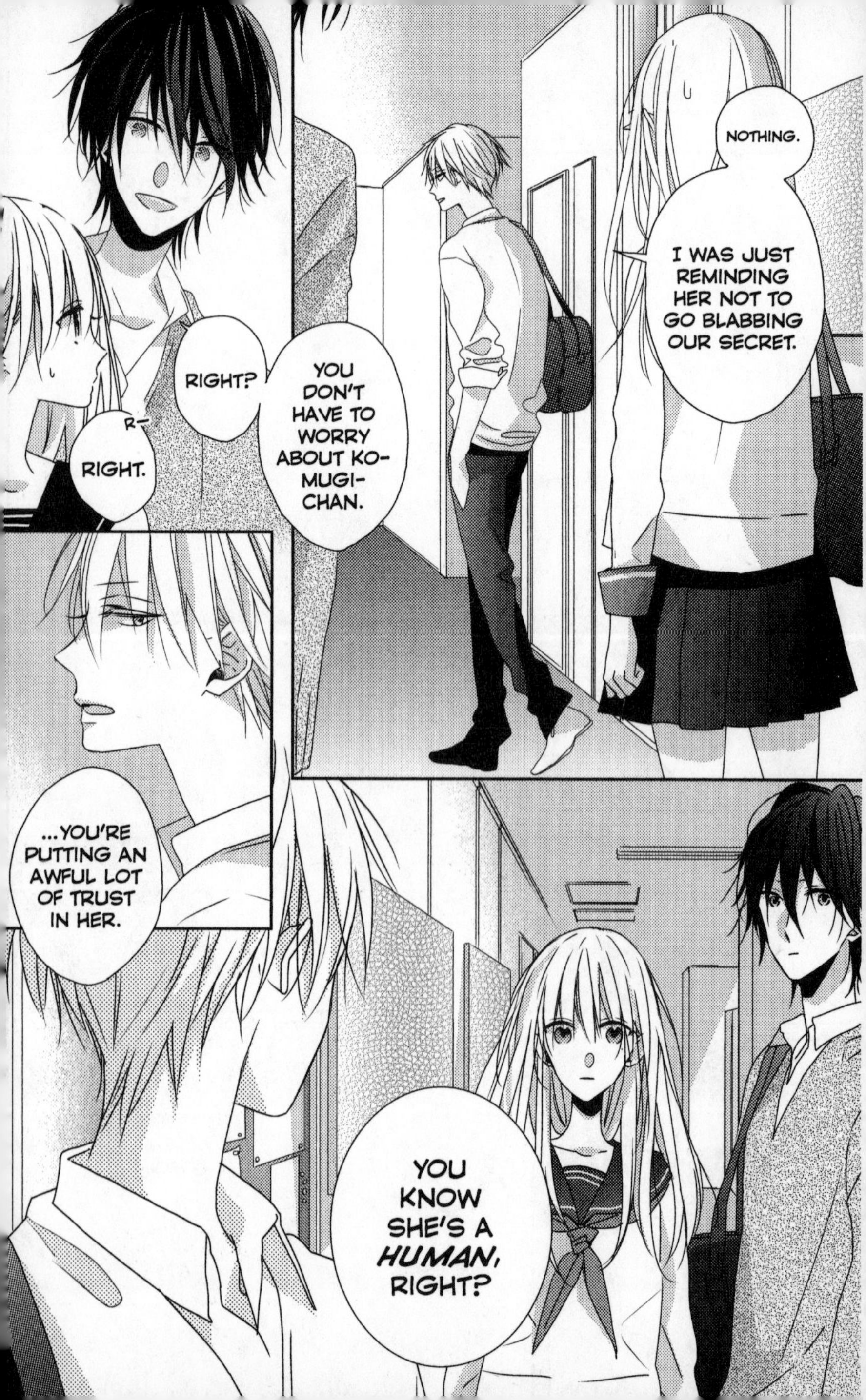
NOTHING.
I WAS JUST REMINDING HER NOT TO GO BLABBING OUR SECRET.
YOU DON'T HAVE TO WORRY ABOUT KO-MUGI-CHAN.
RIGHT?
R— RIGHT.
...YOU'RE PUTTING AN AWFUL LOT OF TRUST IN HER.
YOU KNOW SHE'S A *HUMAN*, RIGHT?

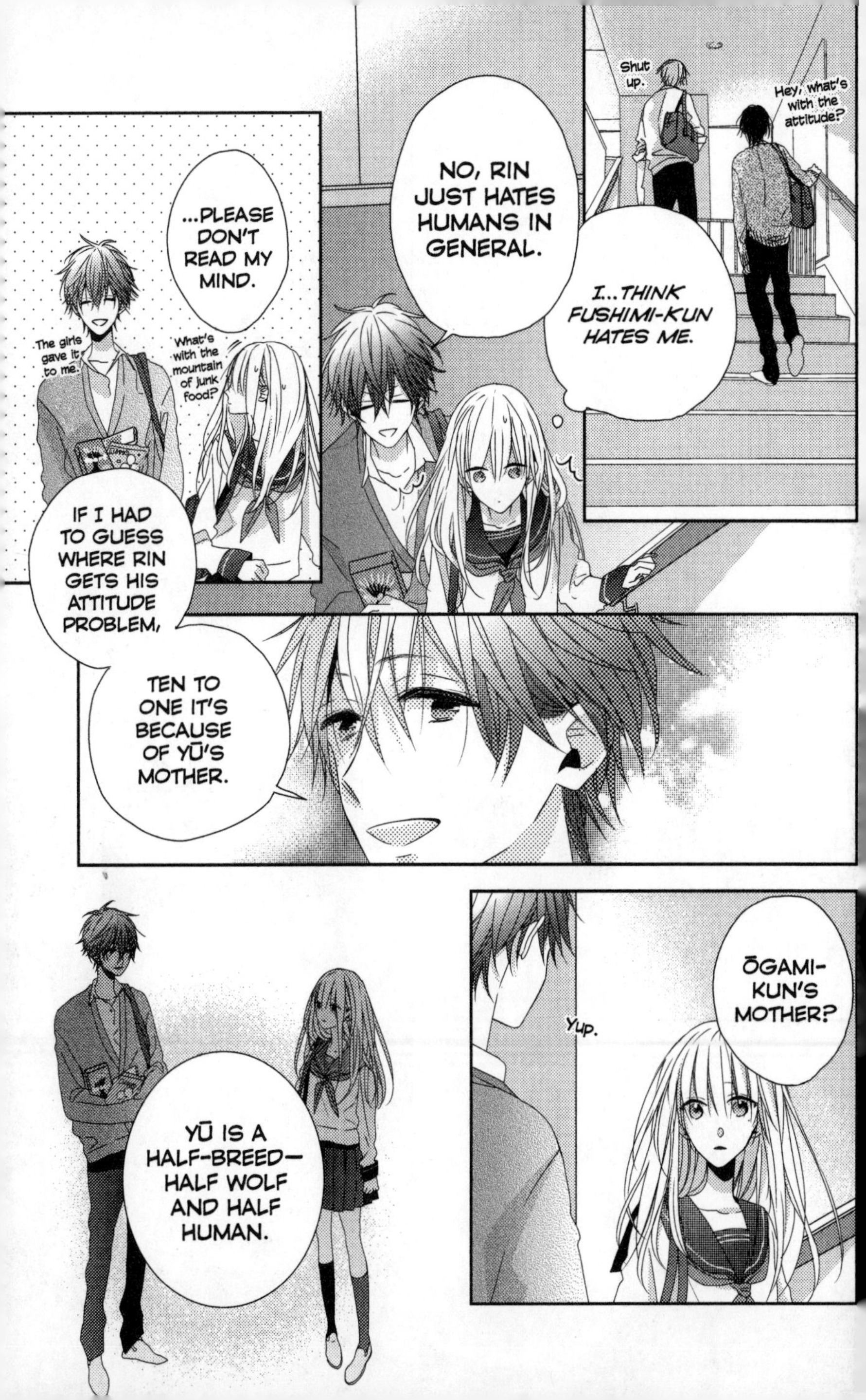
Hey, what's with the attitude?
Shut up.
I...THINK FUSHIMI-KUN HATES ME.
NO, RIN JUST HATES HUMANS IN GENERAL.
...PLEASE DON'T READ MY MIND.
What's with the mountain of junk food?
The girls gave it to me.
IF I HAD TO GUESS WHERE RIN GETS HIS ATTITUDE PROBLEM,
TEN TO ONE IT'S BECAUSE OF YŪ'S MOTHER.
ŌGAMI-KUN'S MOTHER?
Yup.
YŪ IS A HALF-BREED—HALF WOLF AND HALF HUMAN.

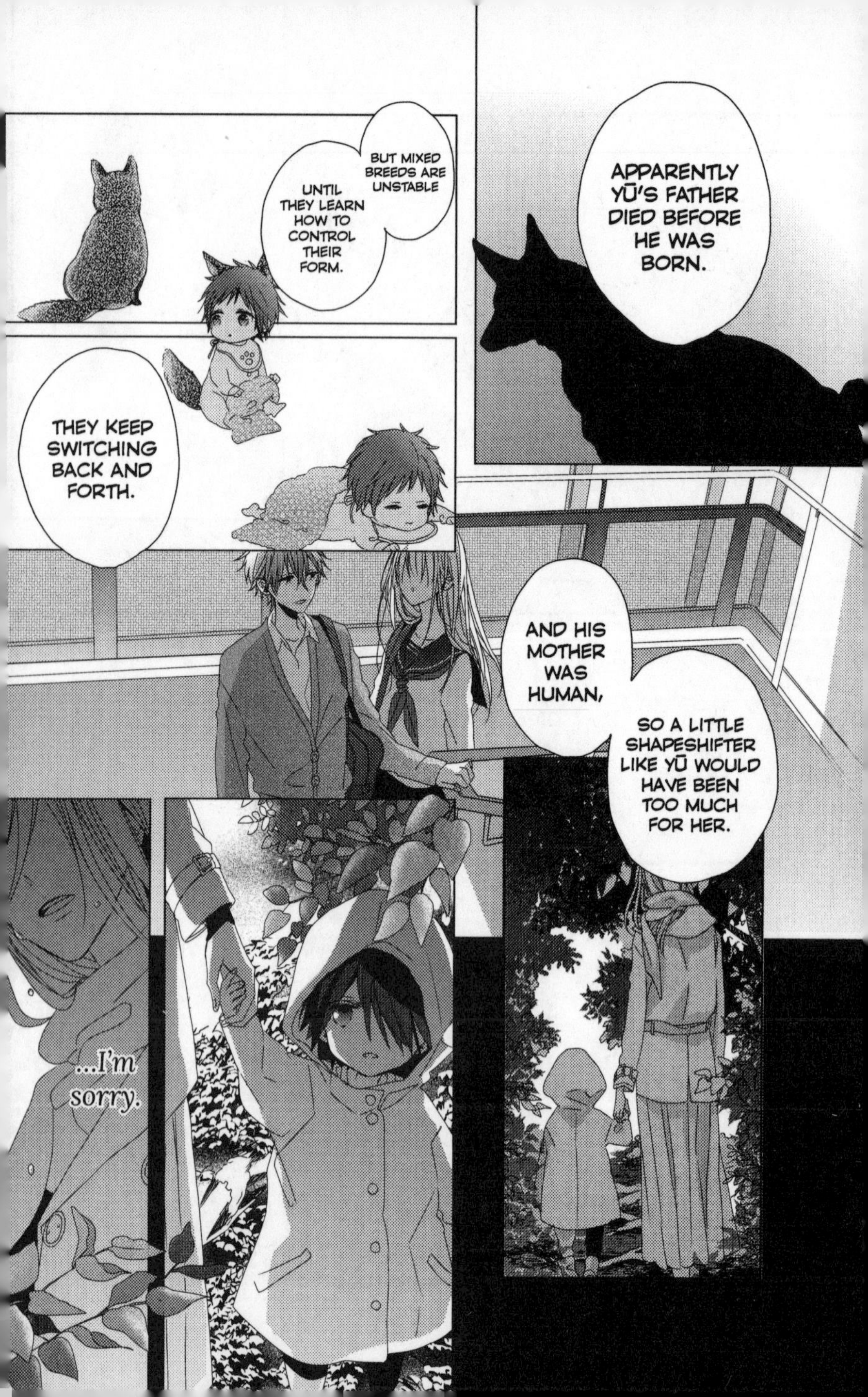
APPARENTLY YŪ'S FATHER DIED BEFORE HE WAS BORN.
BUT MIXED BREEDS ARE UNSTABLE UNTIL THEY LEARN HOW TO CONTROL THEIR FORM.
THEY KEEP SWITCHING BACK AND FORTH.
AND HIS MOTHER WAS HUMAN,
SO A LITTLE SHAPESHIFTER LIKE YŪ WOULD HAVE BEEN TOO MUCH FOR HER.
...I'm sorry.

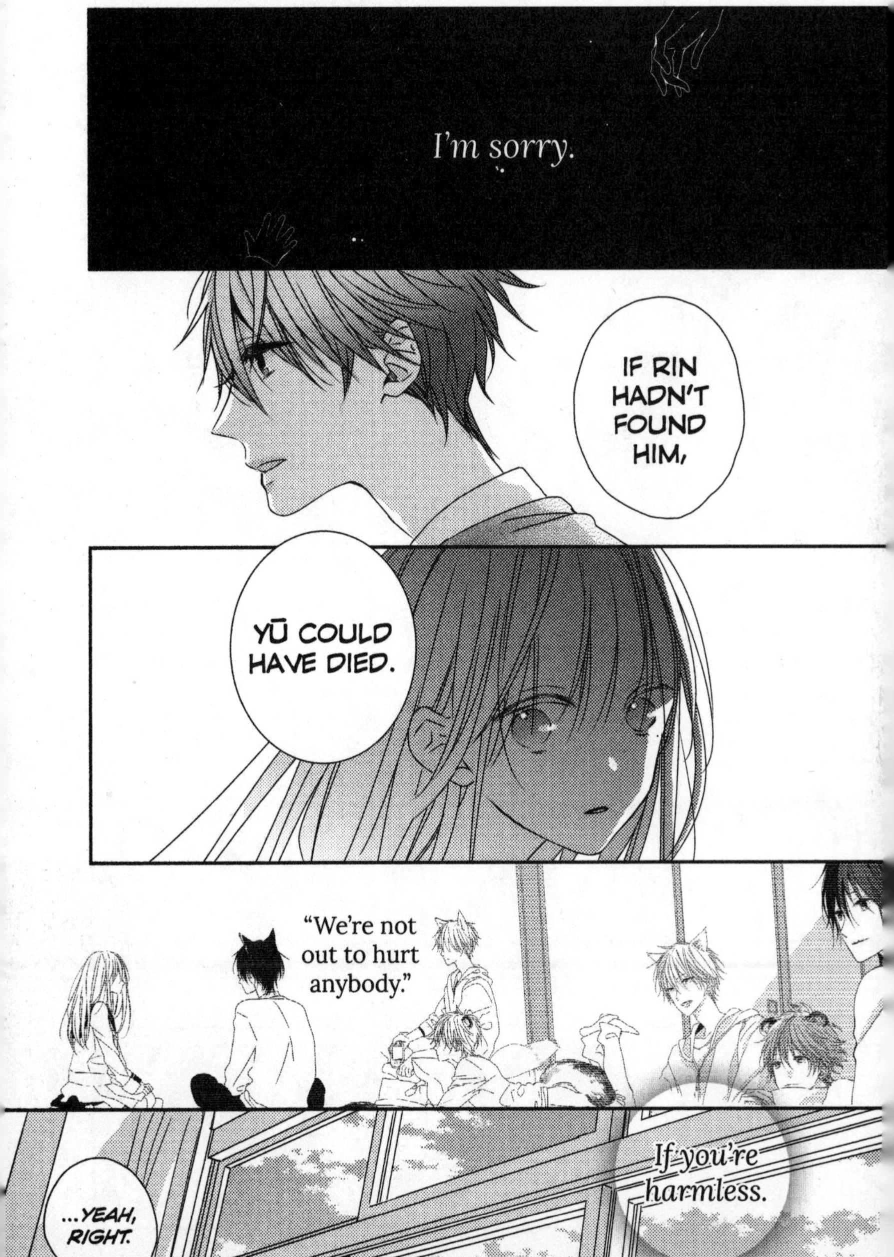
I'm sorry.
IF RIN HADN'T FOUND HIM,
YŪ COULD HAVE DIED.
"We're not out to hurt anybody."
If you're harmless.
...YEAH, RIGHT.

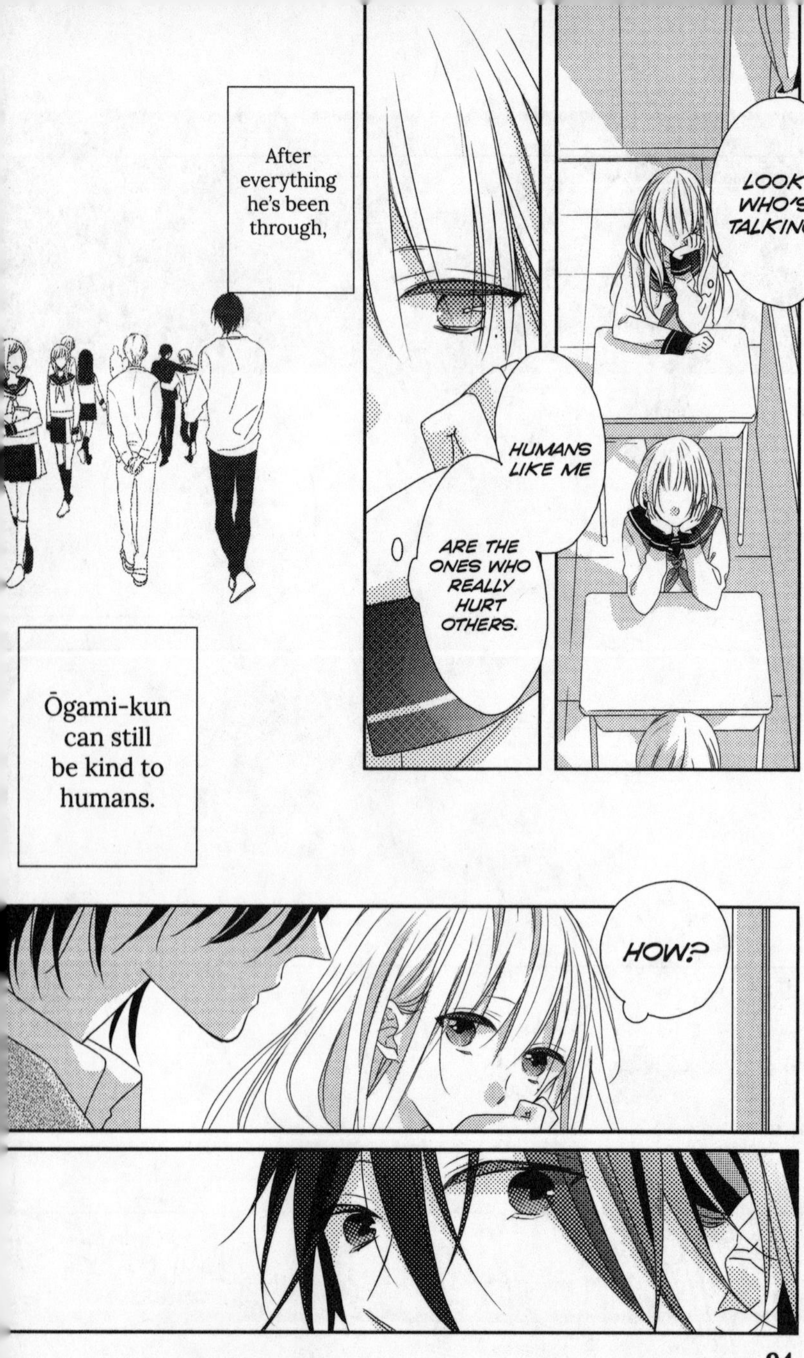
LOOK WHO'S TALKING.
HUMANS LIKE ME
ARE THE ONES WHO REALLY HURT OTHERS.
After everything he's been through,
Ōgami-kun can still be kind to humans.
HOW?

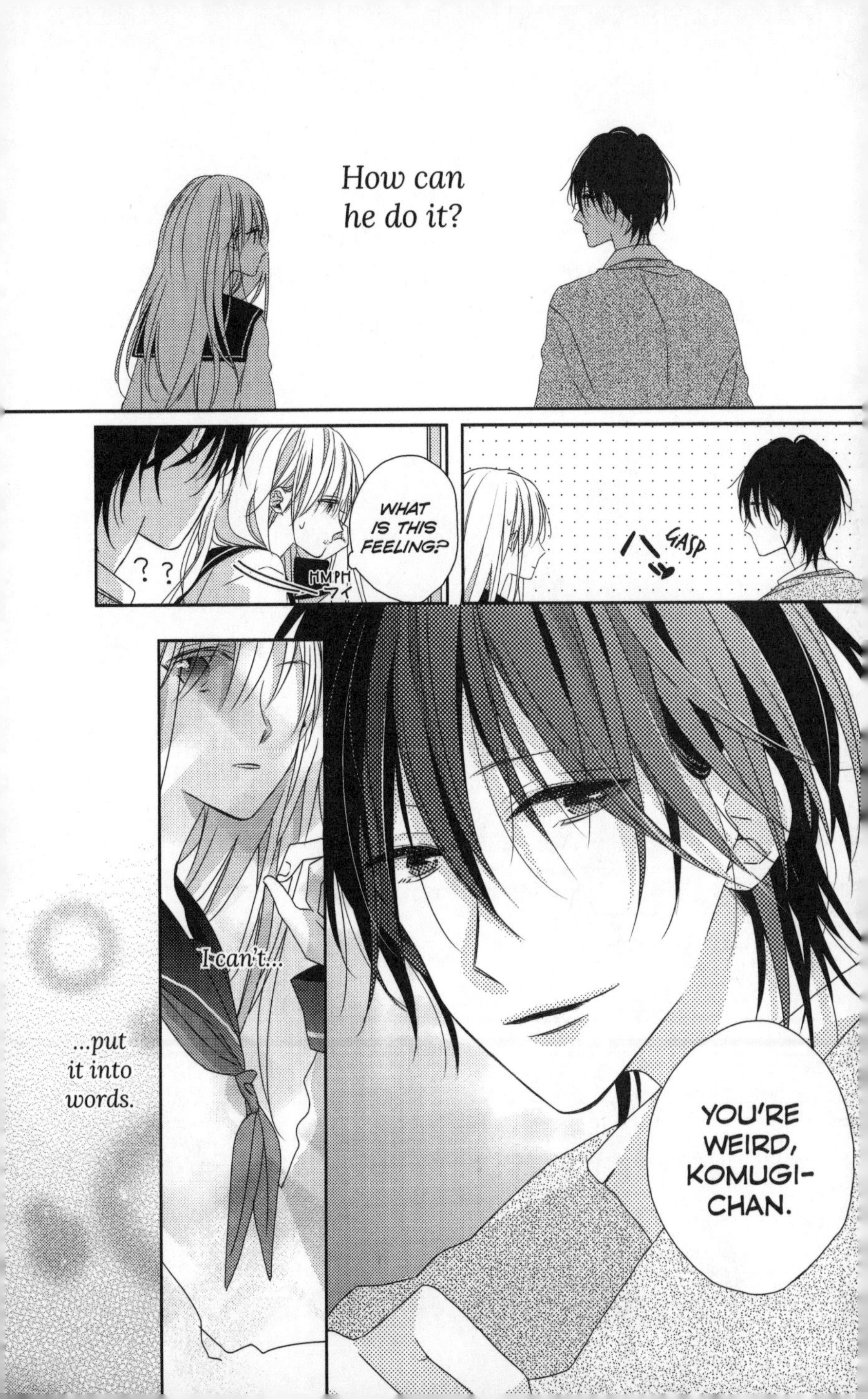
How can he do it?
GASP
WHAT IS THIS FEELING?
HMPH
? ?
YOU'RE WEIRD, KOMUGI-CHAN.
I can't...
...put it into words.

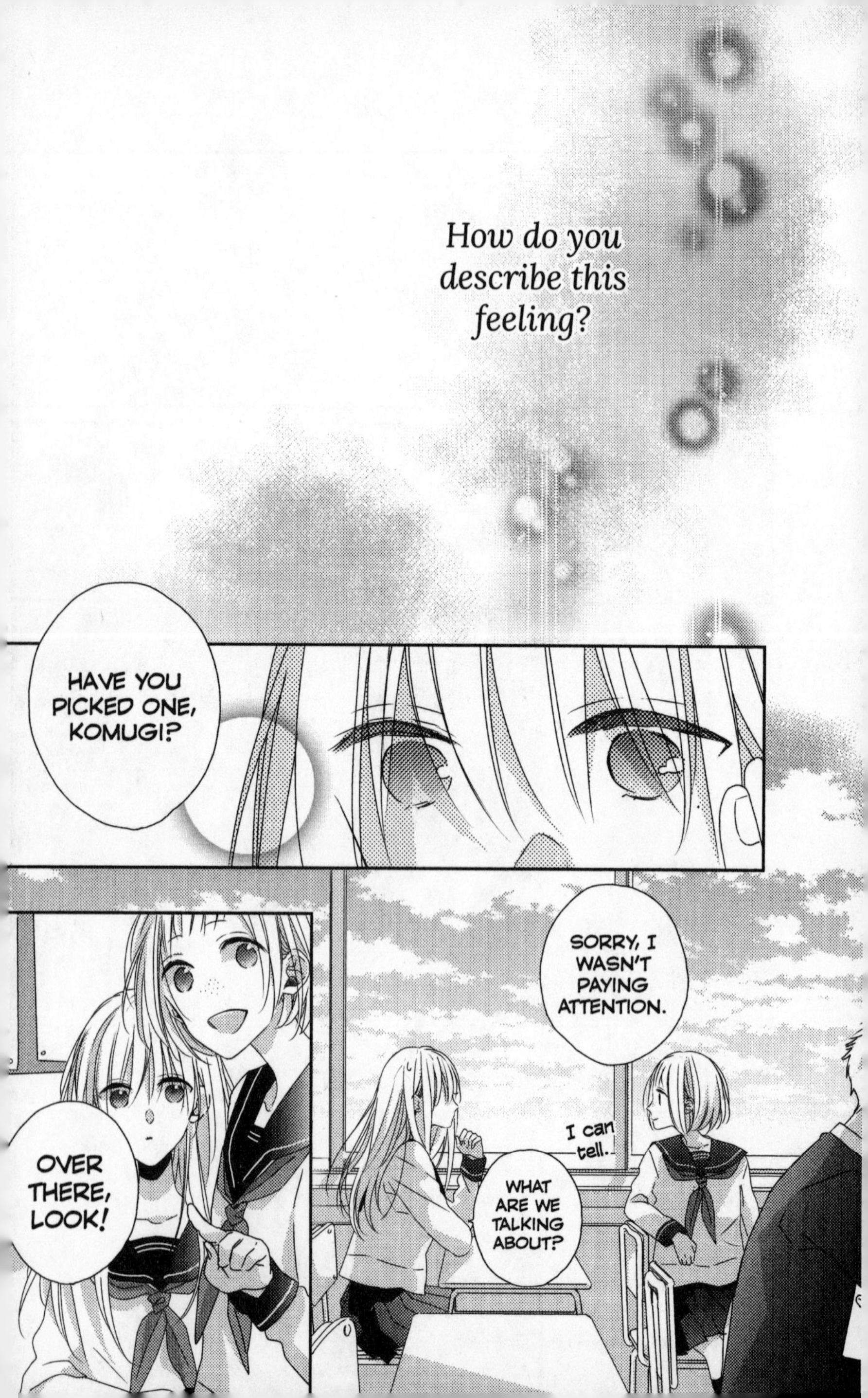
How do you describe this feeling?
HAVE YOU PICKED ONE, KOMUGI?
SORRY, I WASN'T PAYING ATTENTION.
I can tell.
WHAT ARE WE TALKING ABOUT?
OVER THERE, LOOK!

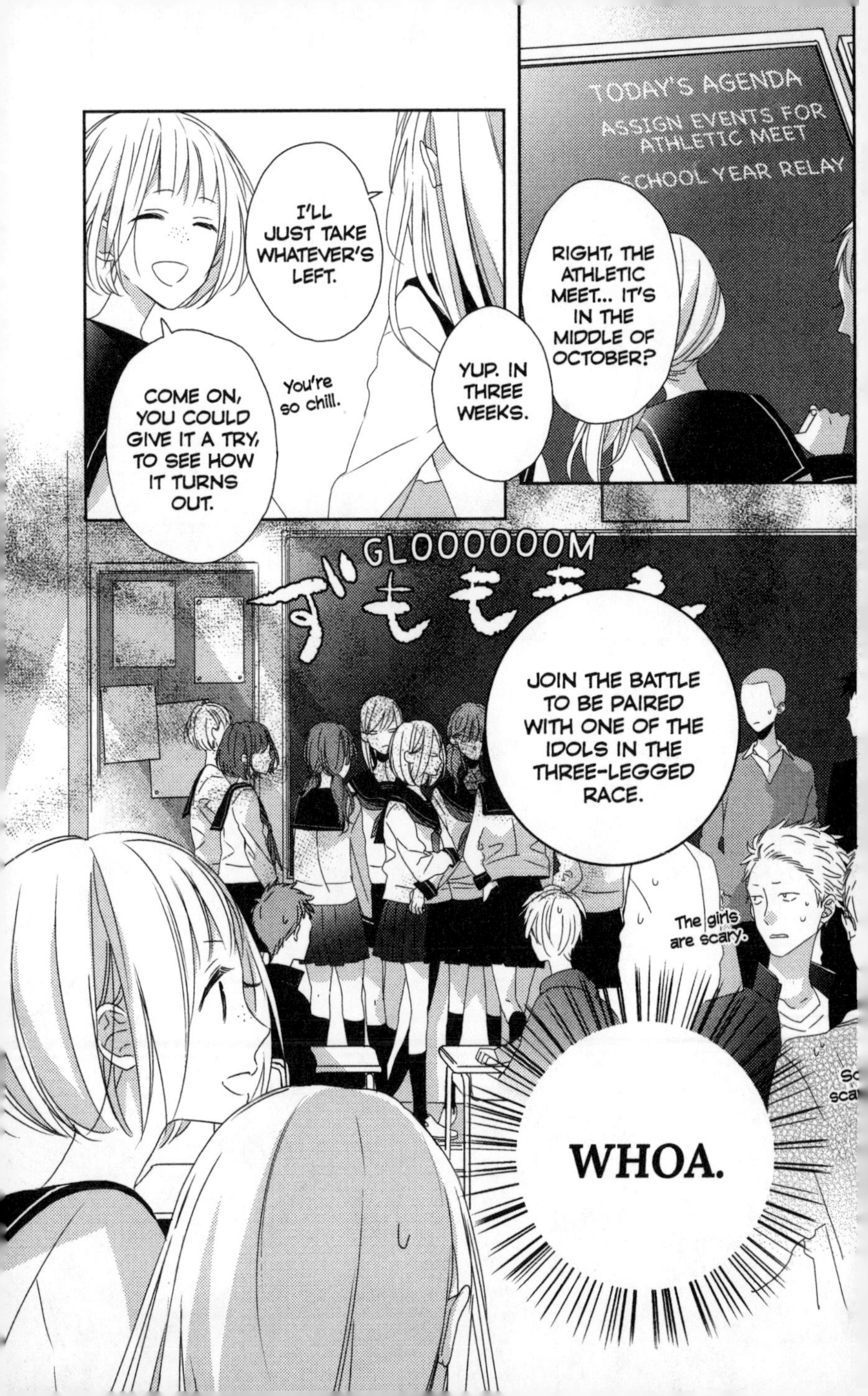
TODAY'S AGENDA
ASSIGN EVENTS FOR ATHLETIC MEET
SCHOOL YEAR RELAY
RIGHT, THE ATHLETIC MEET... IT'S IN THE MIDDLE OF OCTOBER?
YUP. IN THREE WEEKS.
I'LL JUST TAKE WHATEVER'S LEFT.
You're so chill.
COME ON, YOU COULD GIVE IT A TRY, TO SEE HOW IT TURNS OUT.
GLOOOOOOM
JOIN THE BATTLE TO BE PAIRED WITH ONE OF THE IDOLS IN THE THREE-LEGGED RACE.
The girls are scary.
WHOA.

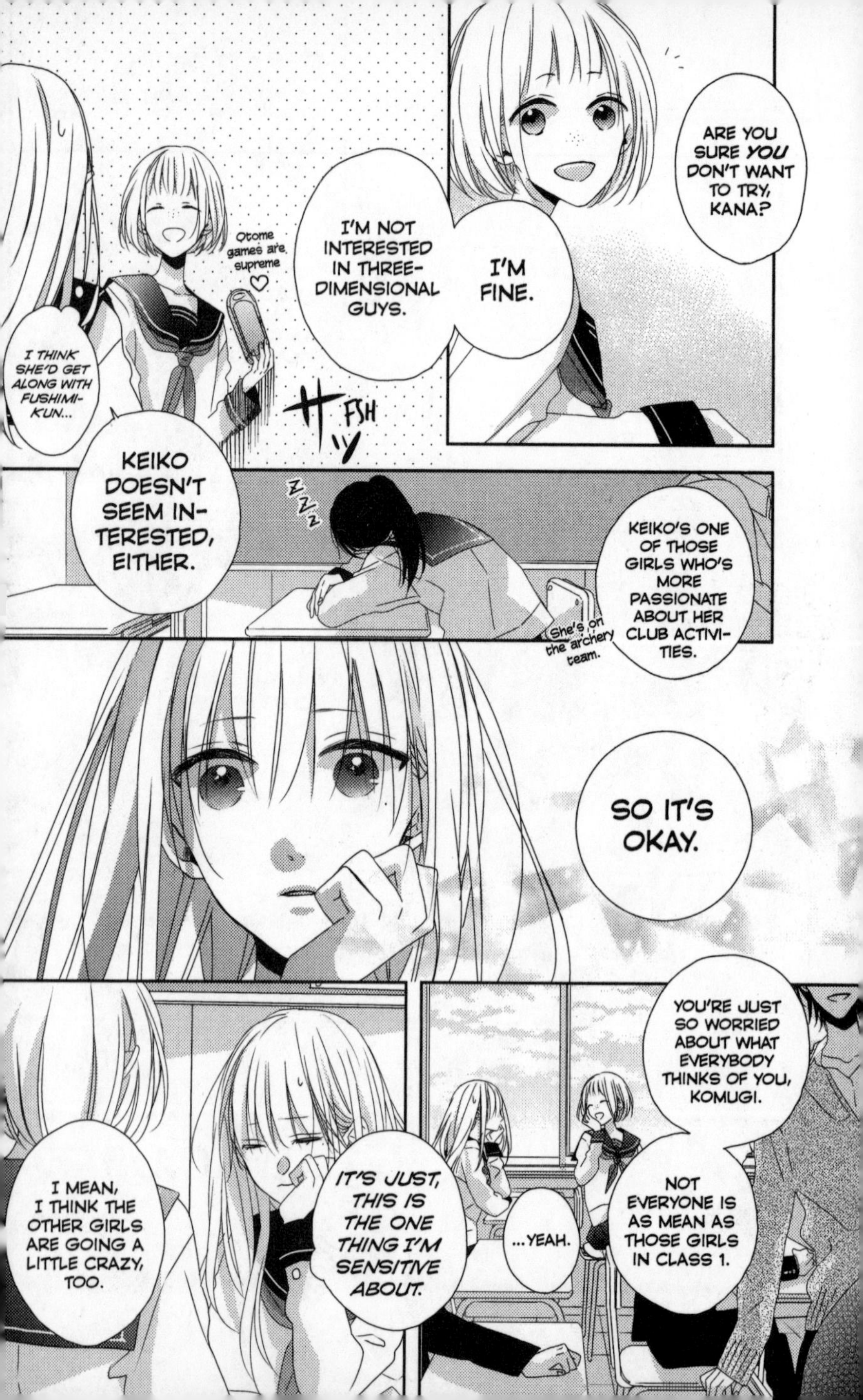
ARE YOU SURE *YOU* DON'T WANT TO TRY, KANA?
I'M FINE.
I'M NOT INTERESTED IN THREE-DIMENSIONAL GUYS.
Otome games are supreme ♡
FSH
I THINK SHE'D GET ALONG WITH FUSHIMI-KUN...
KEIKO DOESN'T SEEM IN-TERESTED, EITHER.
KEIKO'S ONE OF THOSE GIRLS WHO'S MORE PASSIONATE ABOUT HER CLUB ACTIVI-TIES.
She's on the archery team.
ZZZ
SO IT'S OKAY.
YOU'RE JUST SO WORRIED ABOUT WHAT EVERYBODY THINKS OF YOU, KOMUGI.
NOT EVERYONE IS AS MEAN AS THOSE GIRLS IN CLASS 1.
...YEAH.
IT'S JUST, THIS IS THE ONE THING I'M SENSITIVE ABOUT.
I MEAN, I THINK THE OTHER GIRLS ARE GOING A LITTLE CRAZY, TOO.

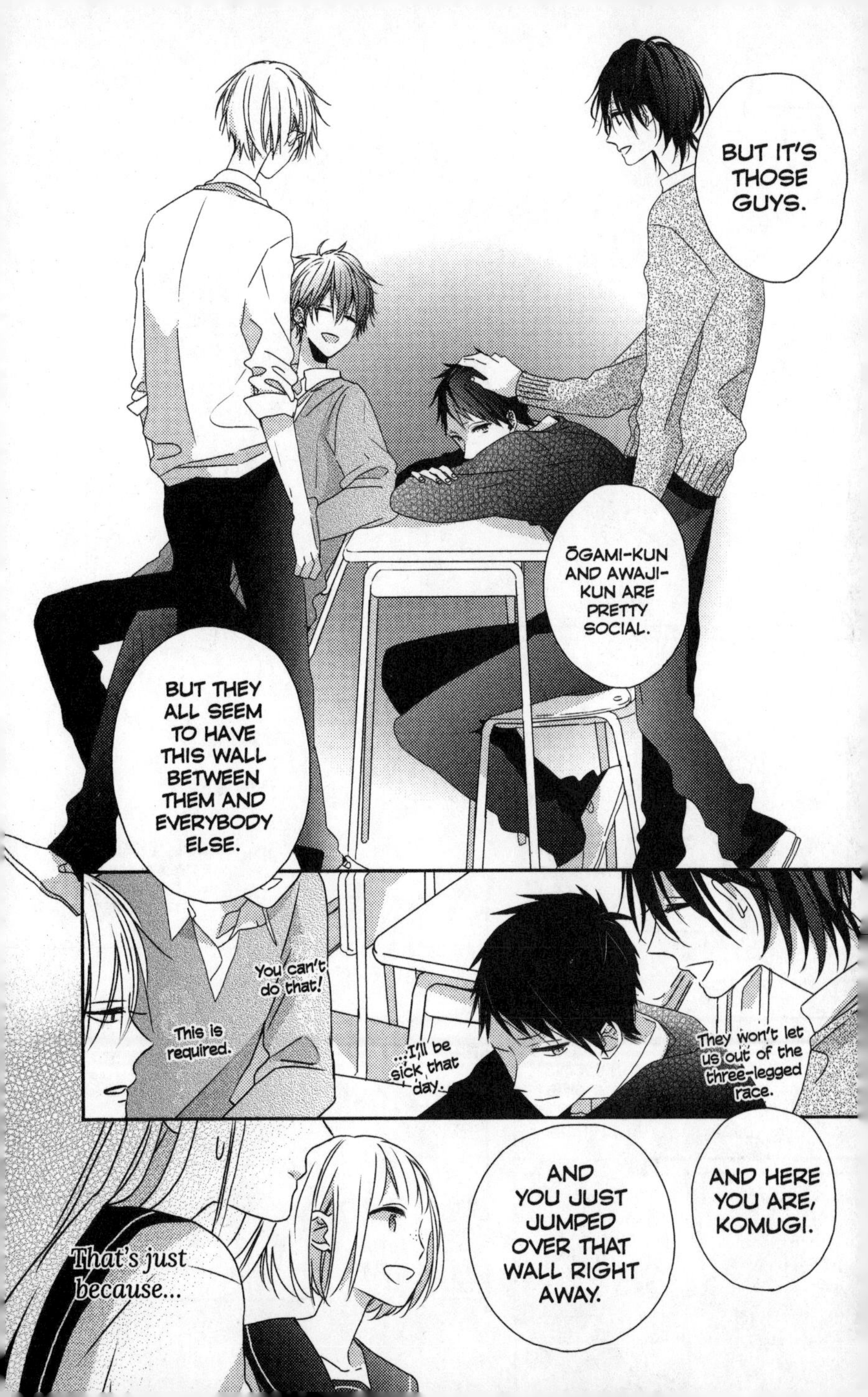
BUT IT'S THOSE GUYS.
ŌGAMI-KUN AND AWAJI-KUN ARE PRETTY SOCIAL.
BUT THEY ALL SEEM TO HAVE THIS WALL BETWEEN THEM AND EVERYBODY ELSE.
They won't let us out of the three-legged race.
...I'll be sick that day.
You can't do that!
This is required.
AND HERE YOU ARE, KOMUGI.
AND YOU JUST JUMPED OVER THAT WALL RIGHT AWAY.
That's just because...

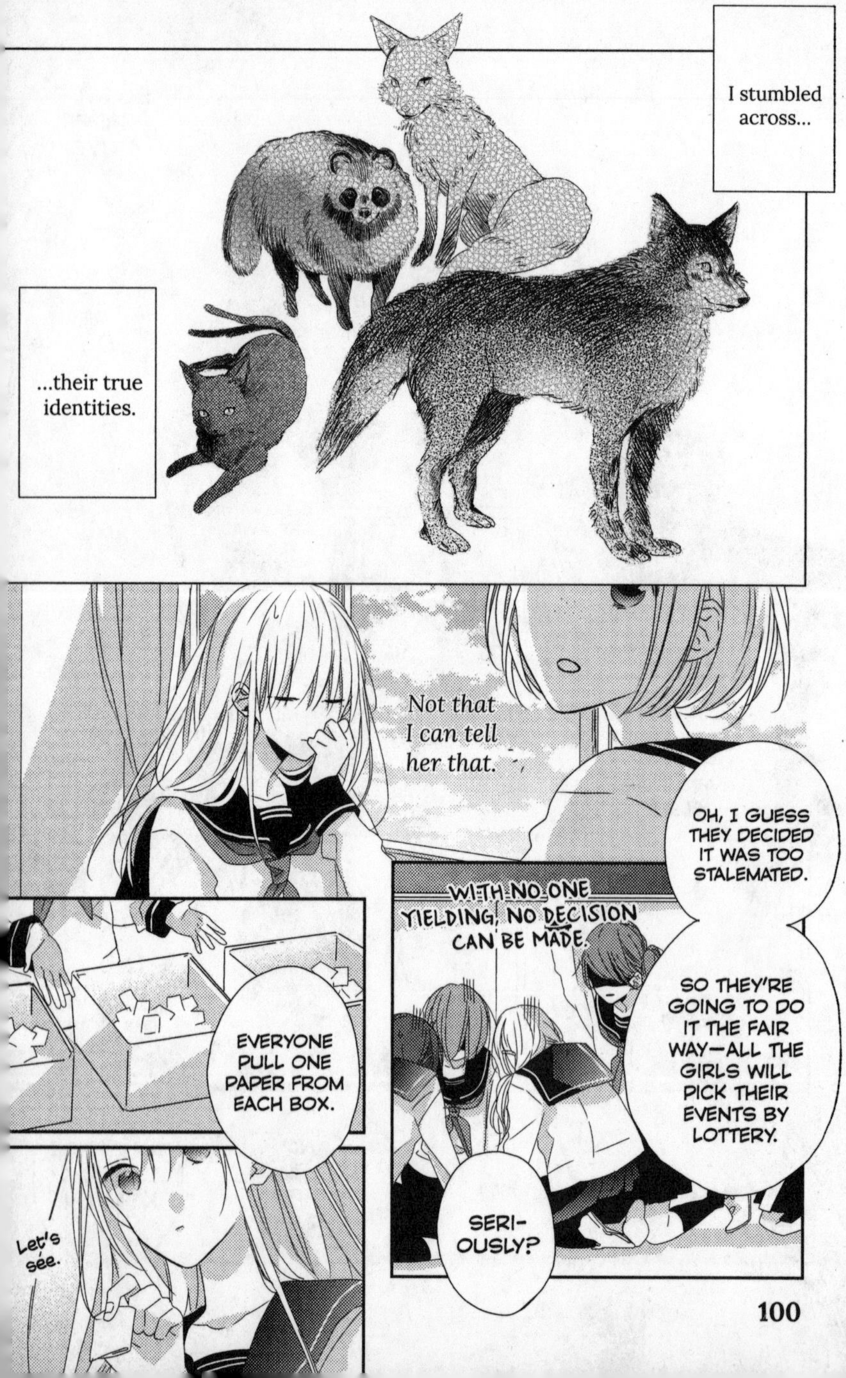
I stumbled across...
...their true identities.
Not that I can tell her that.
OH, I GUESS THEY DECIDED IT WAS TOO STALEMATED.
WITH NO ONE YIELDING, NO DECISION CAN BE MADE.
SO THEY'RE GOING TO DO IT THE FAIR WAY—ALL THE GIRLS WILL PICK THEIR EVENTS BY LOTTERY.
SERI-OUSLY?
EVERYONE PULL ONE PAPER FROM EACH BOX.
Let's see.

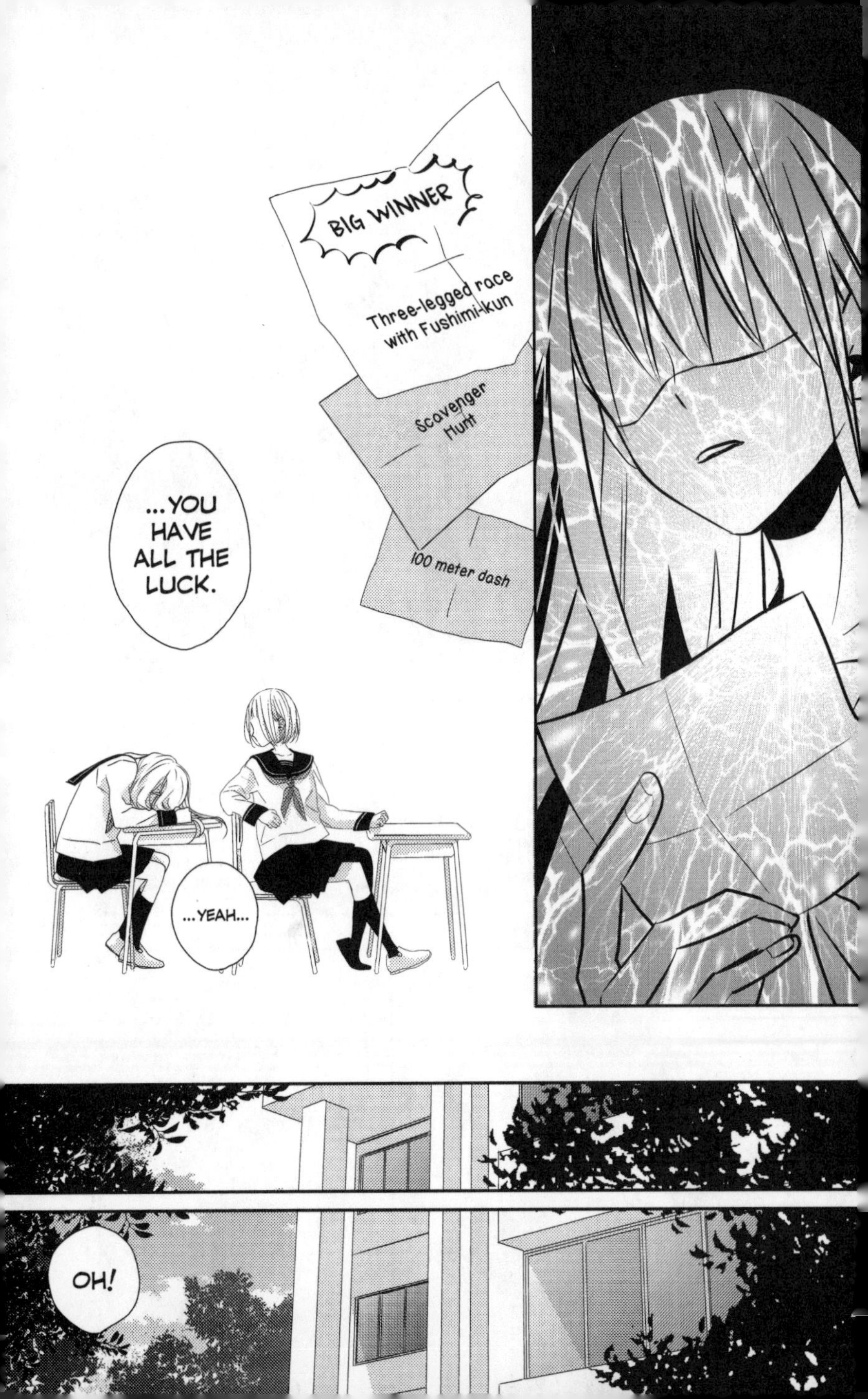
BIG WINNER
Three-legged race with Fushimi-kun
Scavenger Hunt
100 meter dash
...YOU HAVE ALL THE LUCK.
...YEAH...
OH!

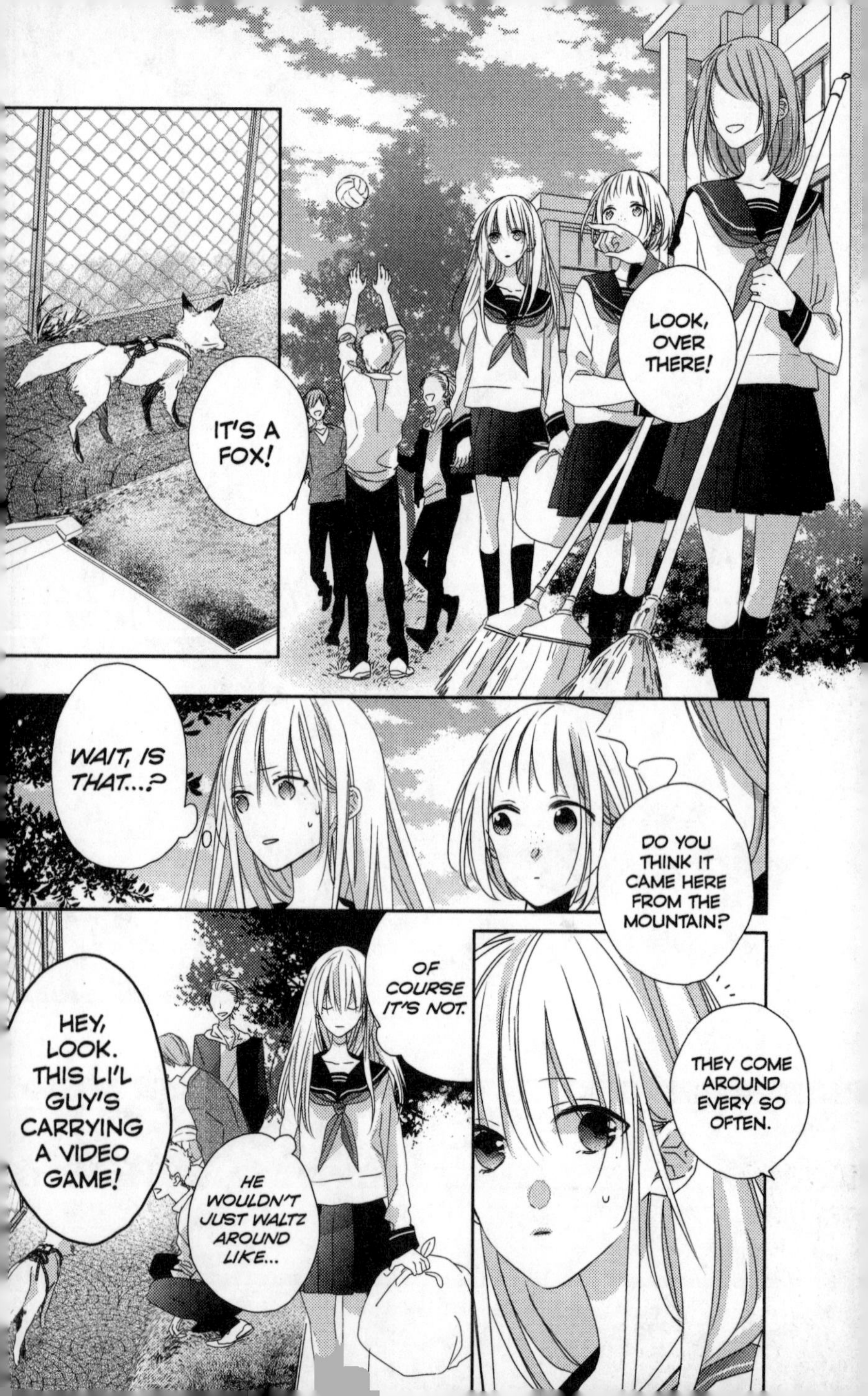
LOOK, OVER THERE!
IT'S A FOX!
DO YOU THINK IT CAME HERE FROM THE MOUNTAIN?
WAIT, IS THAT...?
...
THEY COME AROUND EVERY SO OFTEN.
OF COURSE IT'S NOT.
HE WOULDN'T JUST WALTZ AROUND LIKE...
HEY, LOOK. THIS LI'L GUY'S CARRYING A VIDEO GAME!

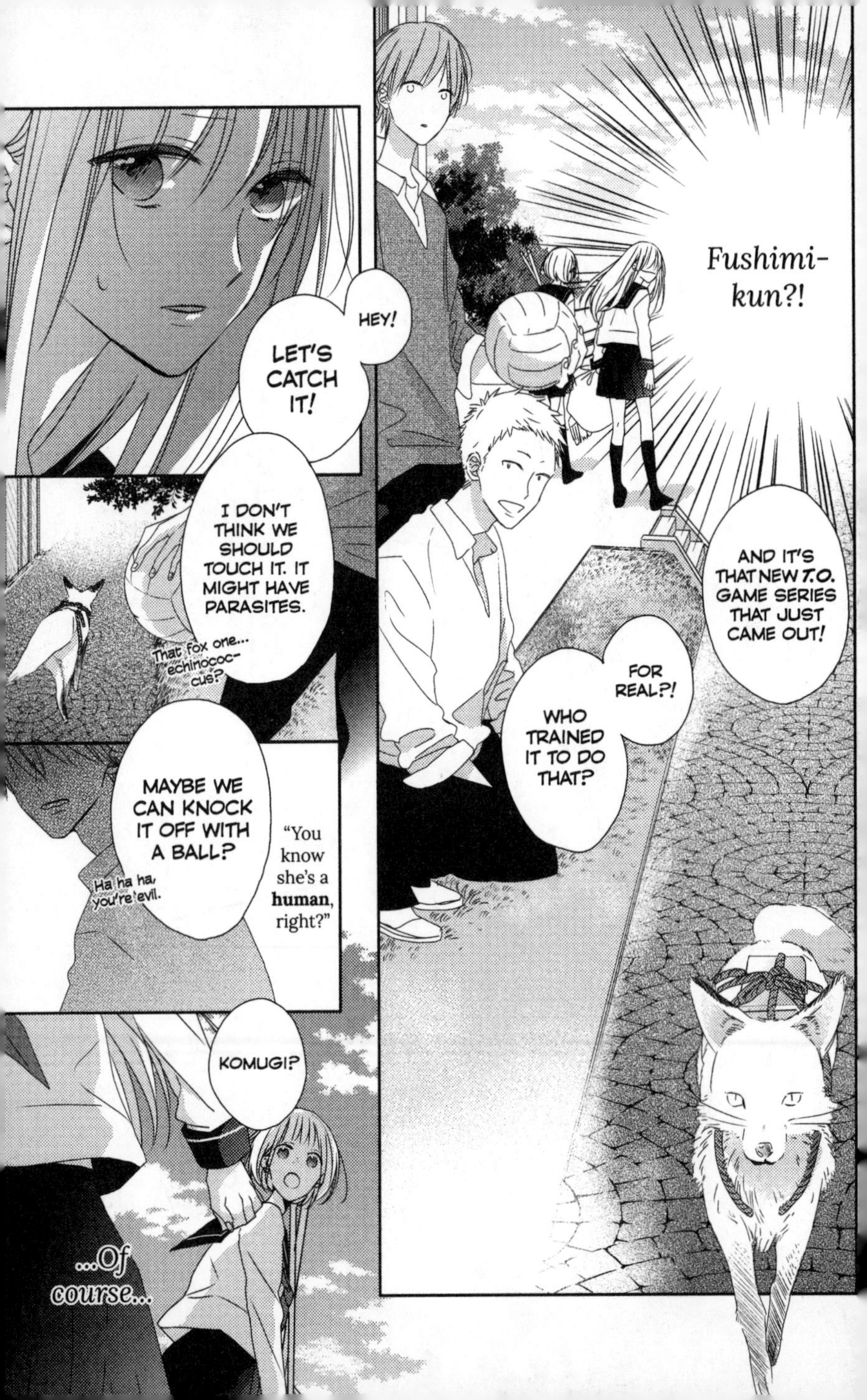
Fushimi-kun?!
AND IT'S THAT NEW *T.O.* GAME SERIES THAT JUST CAME OUT!
FOR REAL?!
WHO TRAINED IT TO DO THAT?
HEY!
LET'S CATCH IT!
I DON'T THINK WE SHOULD TOUCH IT. IT MIGHT HAVE PARASITES.
That fox one... echinococcus?
MAYBE WE CAN KNOCK IT OFF WITH A BALL?
Ha ha ha, you're evil.
"You know she's a **human**, right?"
KOMUGI?
...Of course...

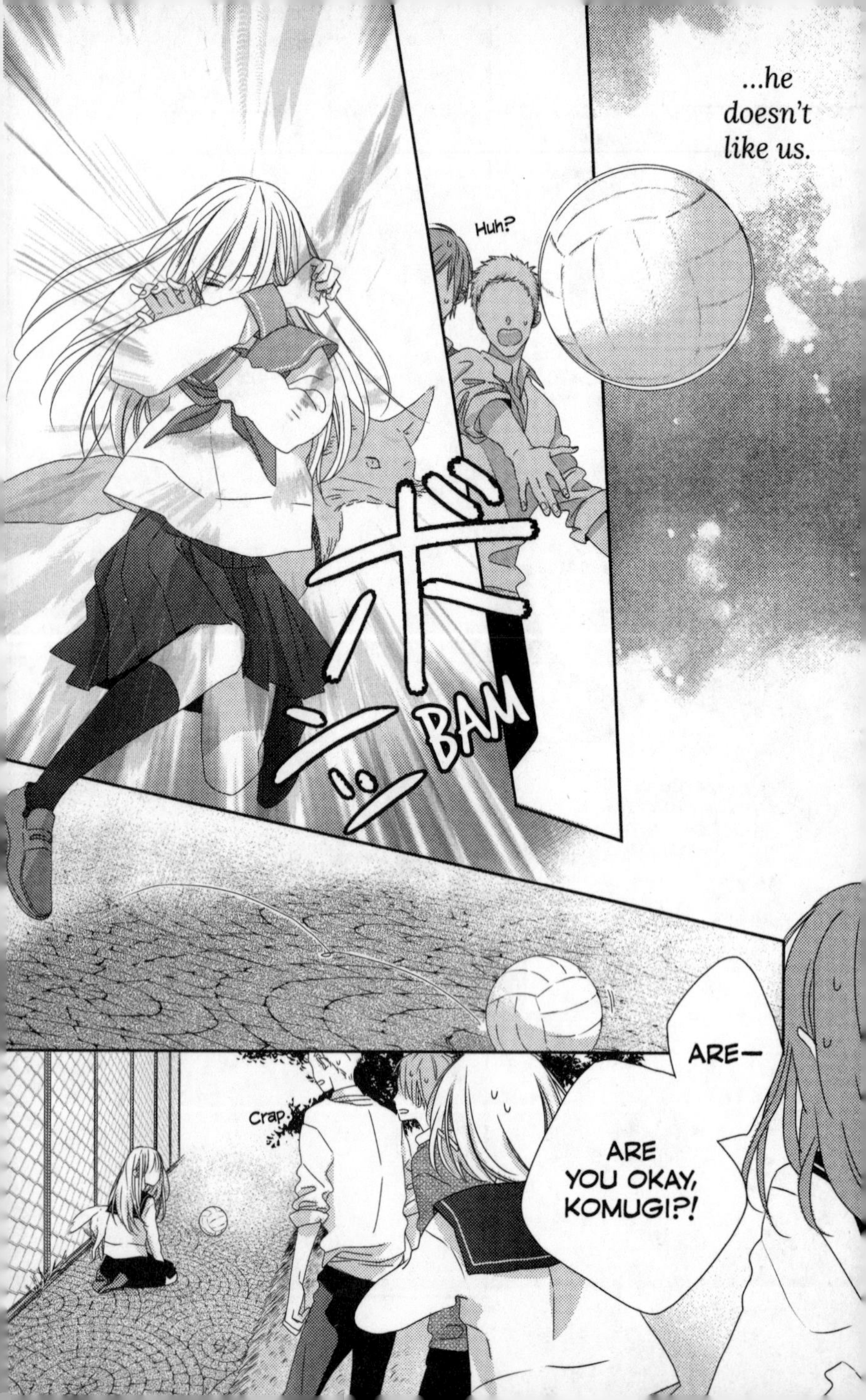
...he doesn't like us.
Huh?
BAM
ARE—
ARE YOU OKAY, KOMUGI?!
Crap.

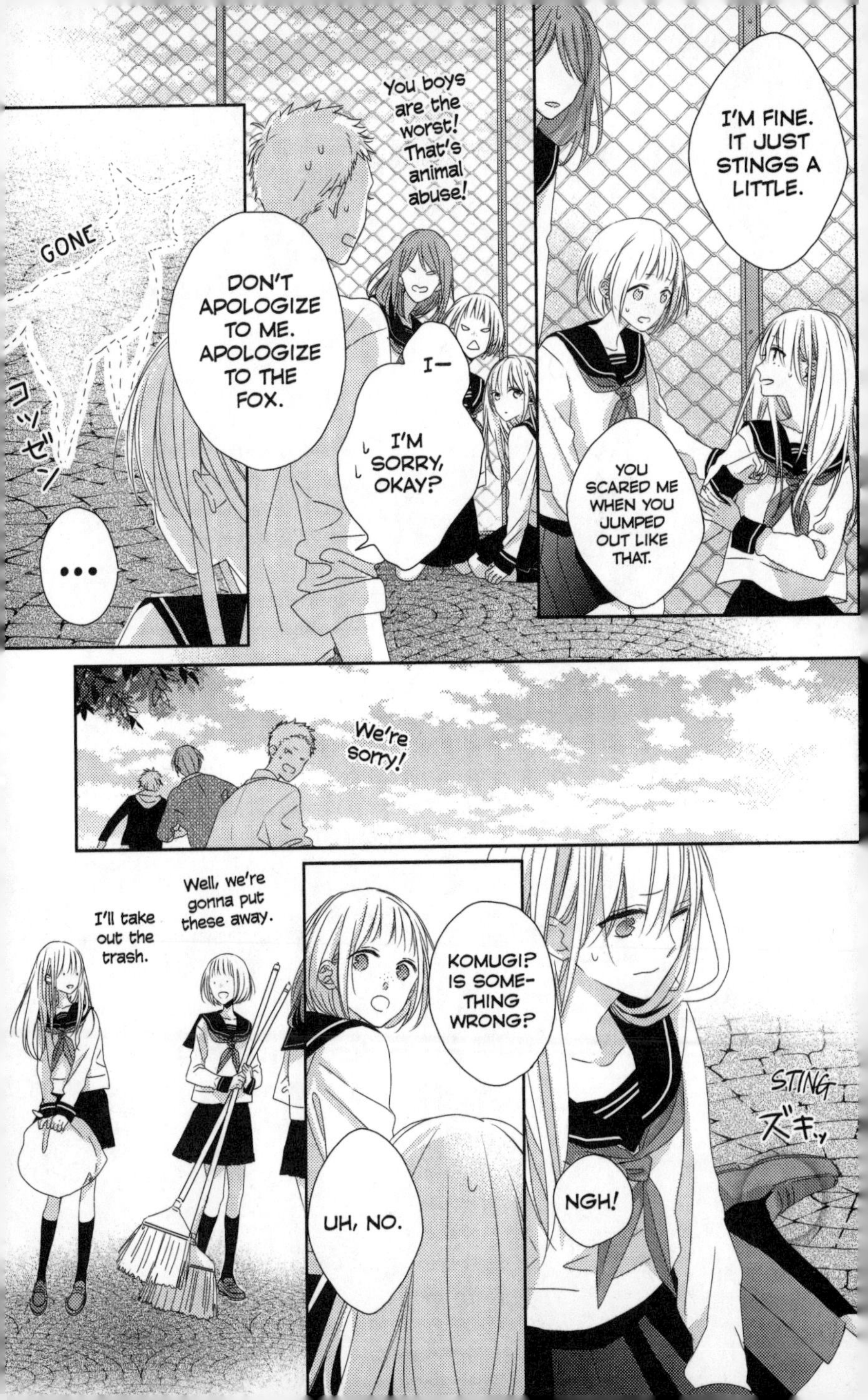
I'M FINE. IT JUST STINGS A LITTLE.
YOU SCARED ME WHEN YOU JUMPED OUT LIKE THAT.
You boys are the worst! That's animal abuse!
I—
I'M SORRY, OKAY?
DON'T APOLOGIZE TO ME. APOLOGIZE TO THE FOX.
GONE
コッゼン
...
We're sorry!
KOMUGI? IS SOME-THING WRONG?
STING
ズキッ
NGH!
UH, NO.
Well, we're gonna put these away.
I'll take out the trash.

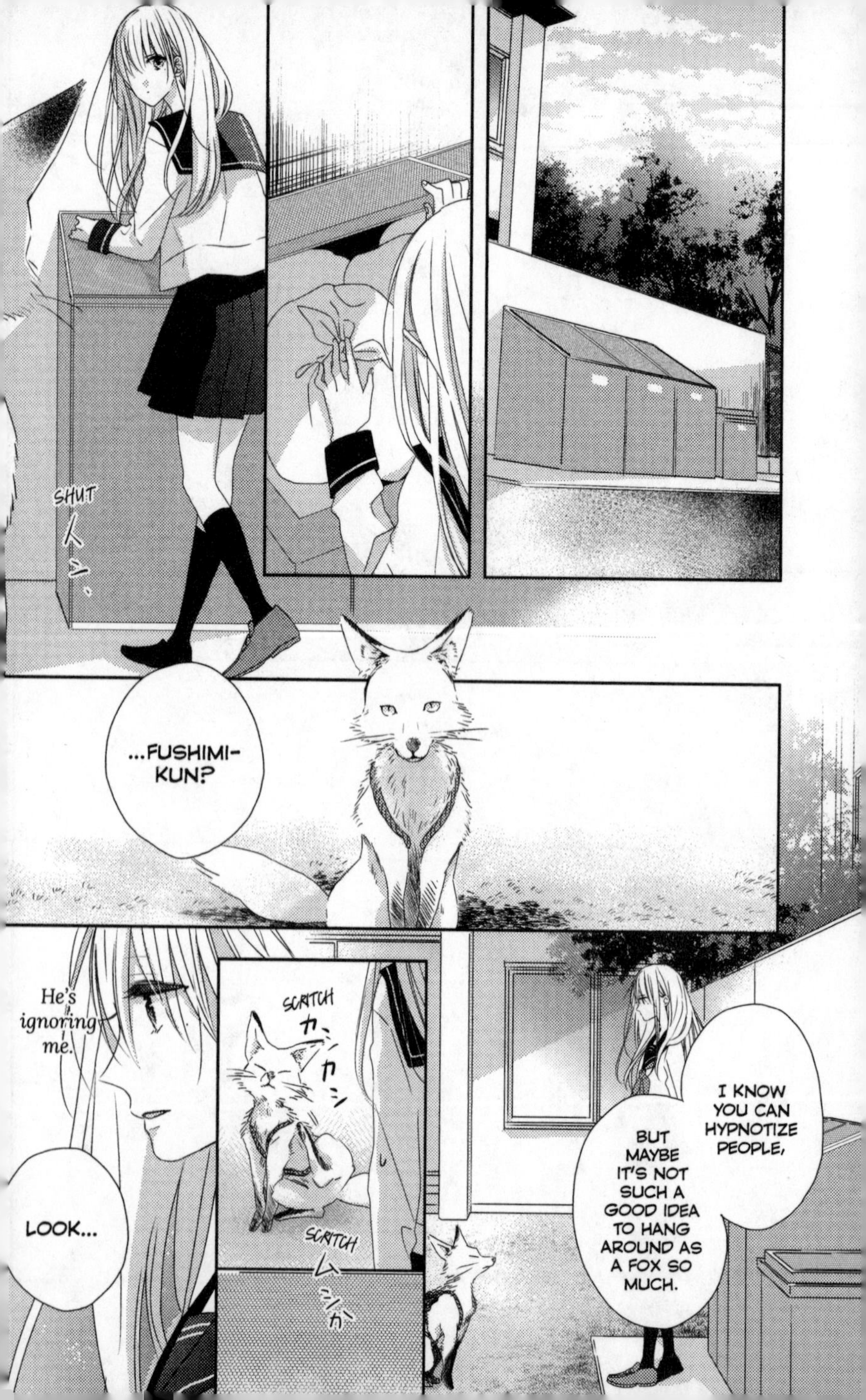
SHUT
...FUSHIMI-KUN?
I KNOW YOU CAN HYPNOTIZE PEOPLE,
BUT MAYBE IT'S NOT SUCH A GOOD IDEA TO HANG AROUND AS A FOX SO MUCH.
SCRITCH
カシカシ
SCRITCH
He's ignoring me.
LOOK...

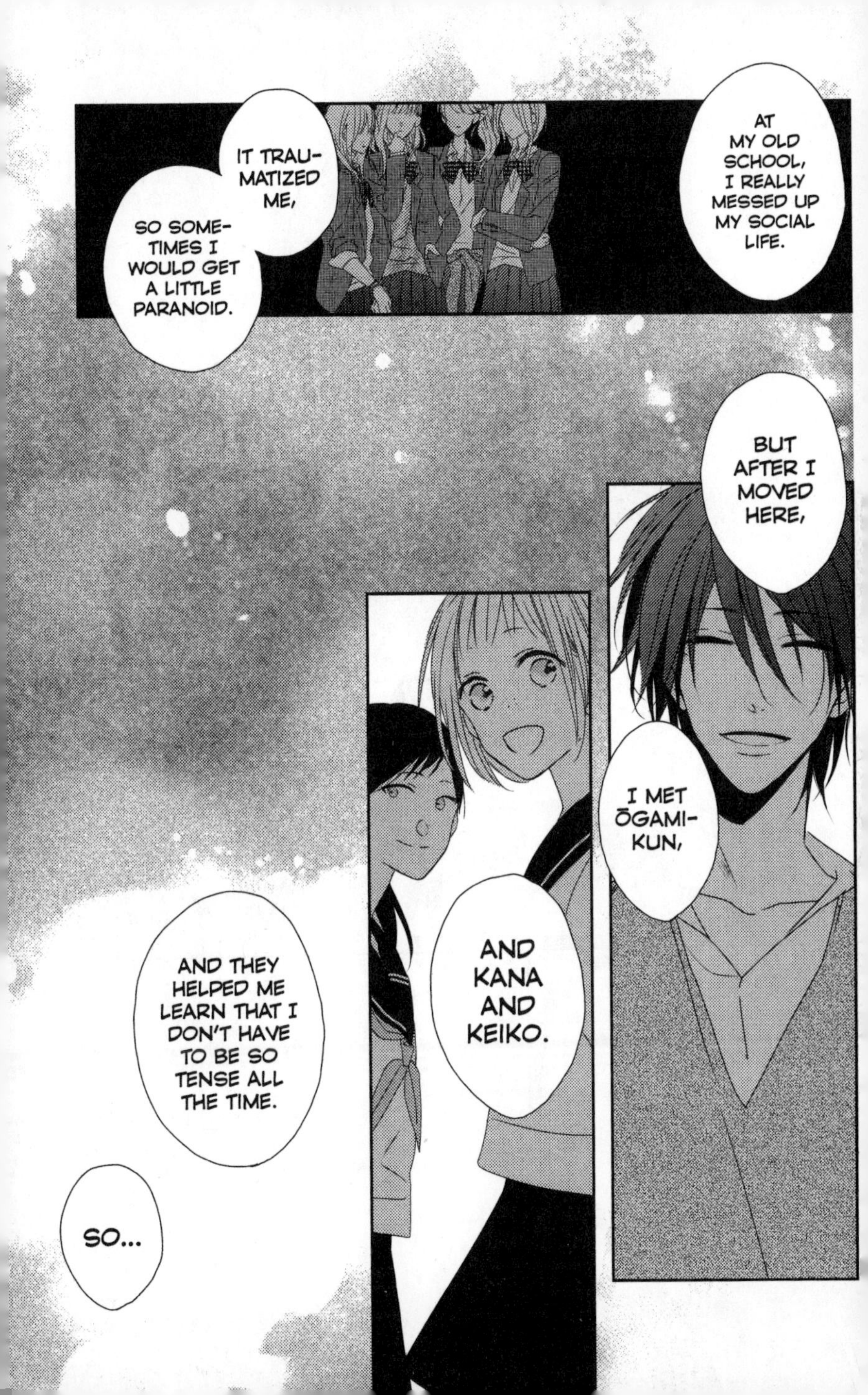
AT MY OLD SCHOOL, I REALLY MESSED UP MY SOCIAL LIFE.
IT TRAU-MATIZED ME,
SO SOME-TIMES I WOULD GET A LITTLE PARANOID.
BUT AFTER I MOVED HERE,
I MET ŌGAMI-KUN,
AND KANA AND KEIKO.
AND THEY HELPED ME LEARN THAT I DON'T HAVE TO BE SO TENSE ALL THE TIME.
SO...

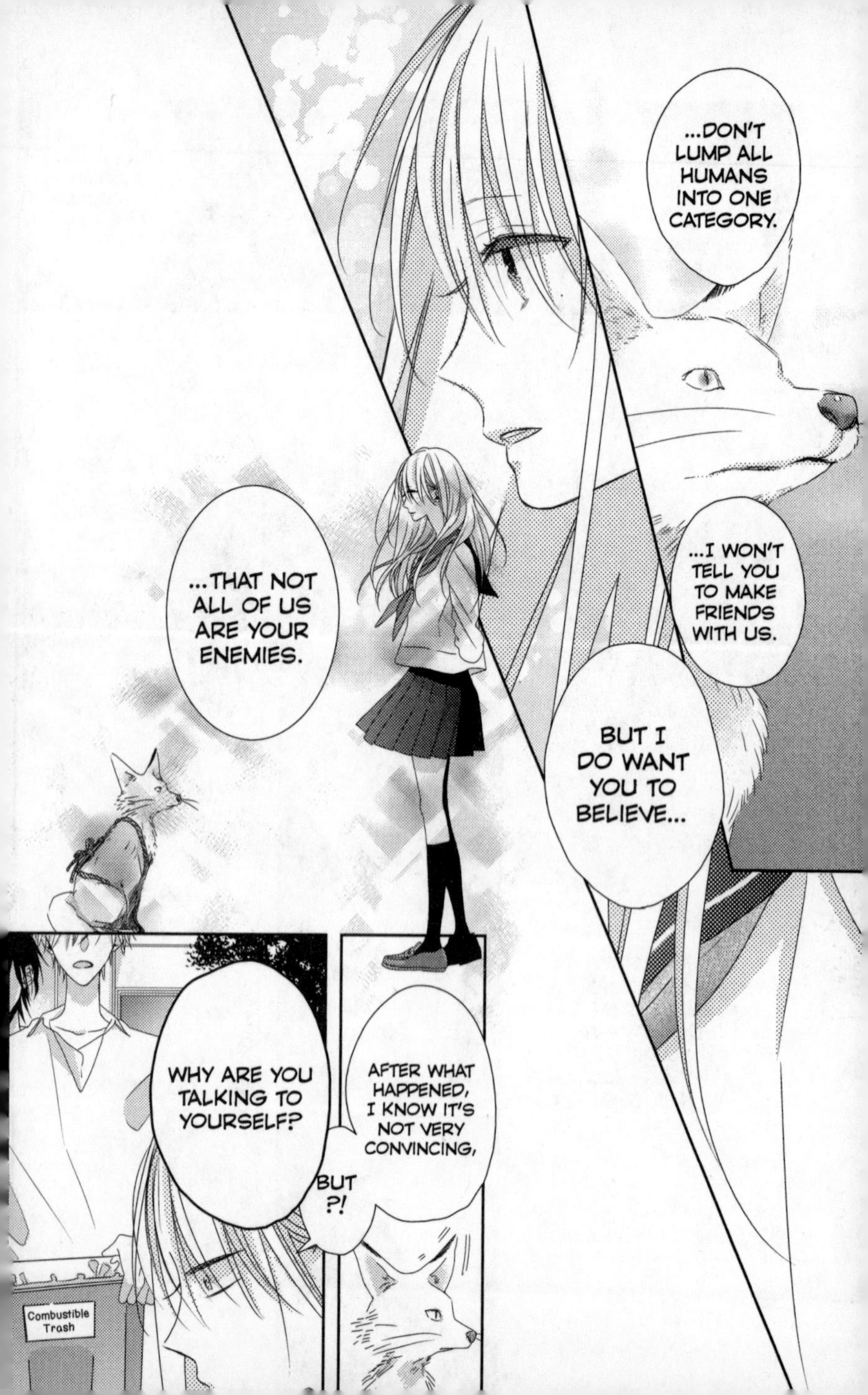
...DON'T LUMP ALL HUMANS INTO ONE CATEGORY.
...I WON'T TELL YOU TO MAKE FRIENDS WITH US.
BUT I DO WANT YOU TO BELIEVE...
...THAT NOT ALL OF US ARE YOUR ENEMIES.
AFTER WHAT HAPPENED, I KNOW IT'S NOT VERY CONVINCING,
BUT ?!
WHY ARE YOU TALKING TO YOURSELF?
Combustible Trash

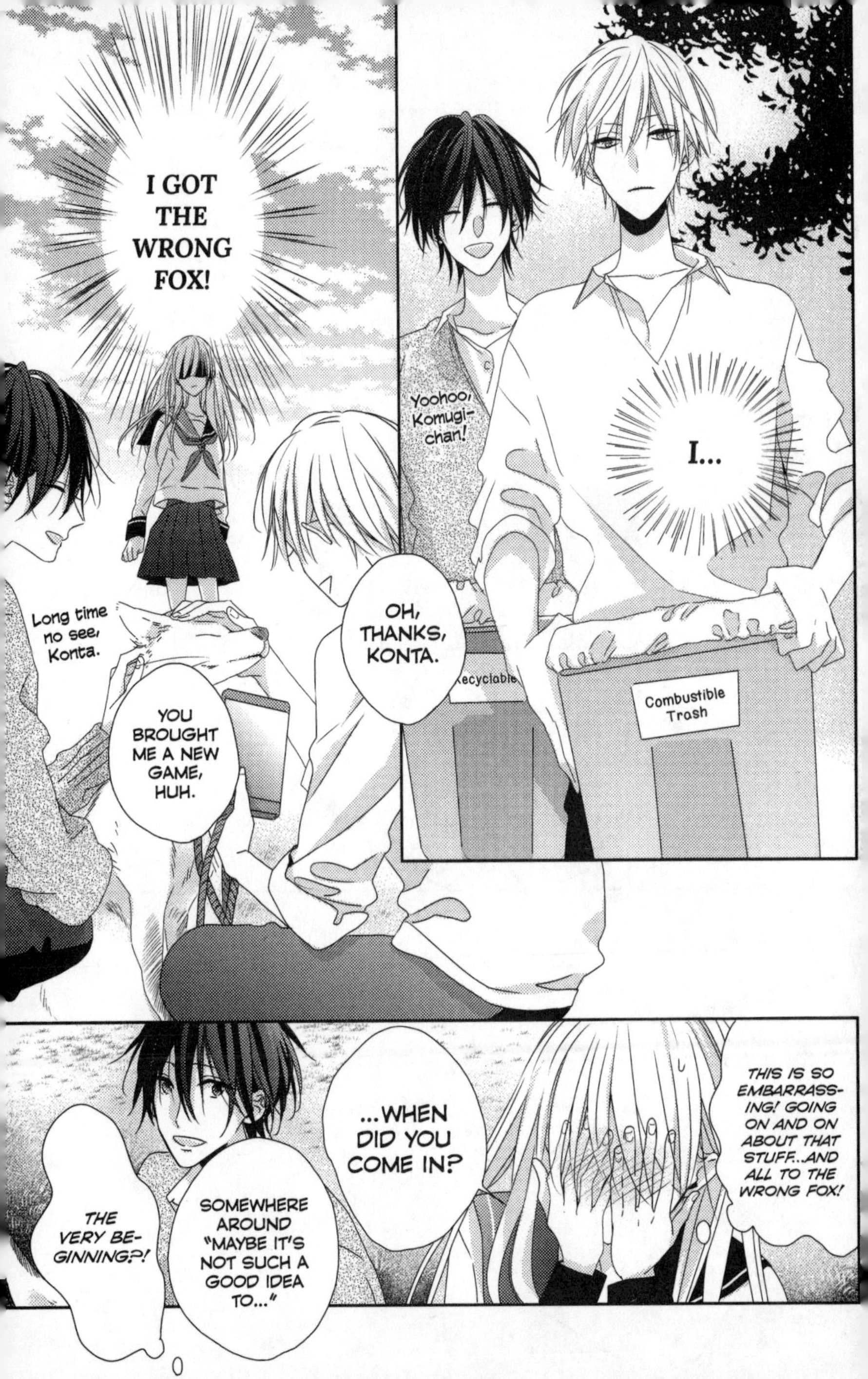
Yoohoo, Komugi-chan!
I...
Recyclable
Combustible Trash
I GOT THE WRONG FOX!
OH, THANKS, KONTA.
Long time no see, Konta.
YOU BROUGHT ME A NEW GAME, HUH.
THIS IS SO EMBARRASS-ING! GOING ON AND ON ABOUT THAT STUFF...AND ALL TO THE WRONG FOX!
...WHEN DID YOU COME IN?
SOMEWHERE AROUND "MAYBE IT'S NOT SUCH A GOOD IDEA TO..."
THE VERY BE-GINNING?!

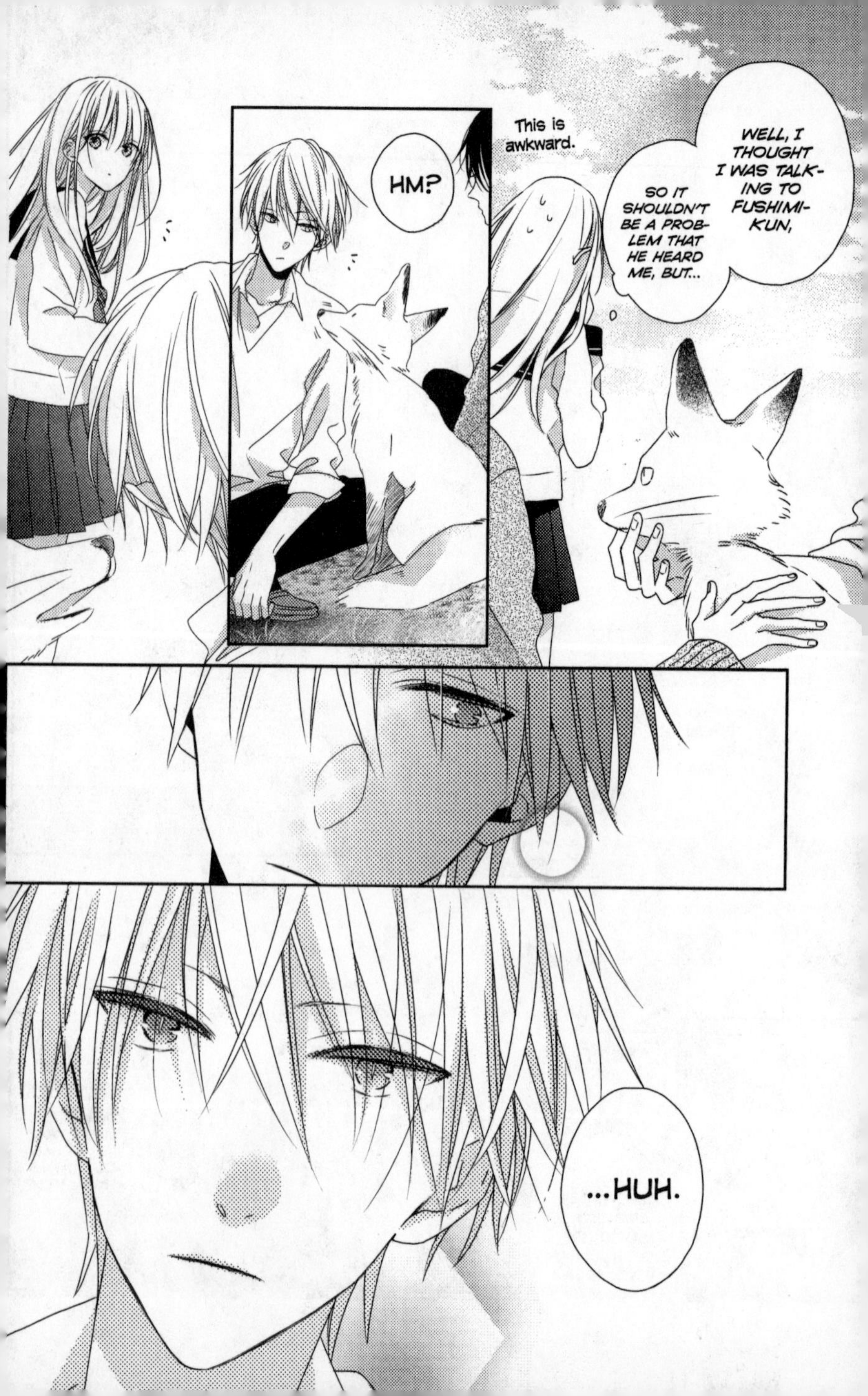
WELL, I THOUGHT I WAS TALKING TO FUSHIMI-KUN,
SO IT SHOULDN'T BE A PROBLEM THAT HE HEARD ME, BUT...
This is awkward.
HM?
...HUH.

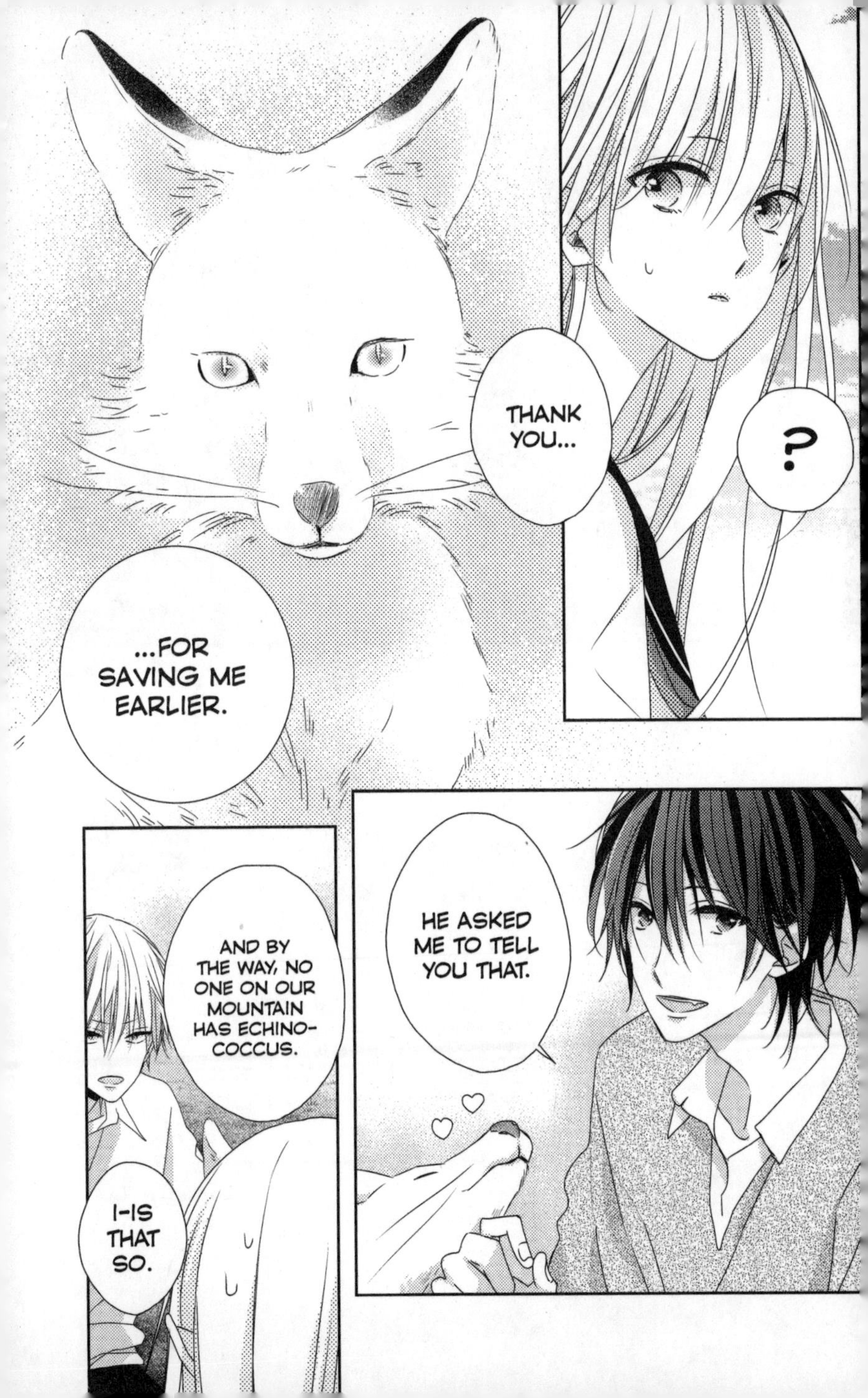
THANK YOU...
?
...FOR SAVING ME EARLIER.
HE ASKED ME TO TELL YOU THAT.
AND BY THE WAY, NO ONE ON OUR MOUNTAIN HAS ECHINO-COCCUS.
I-IS THAT SO.

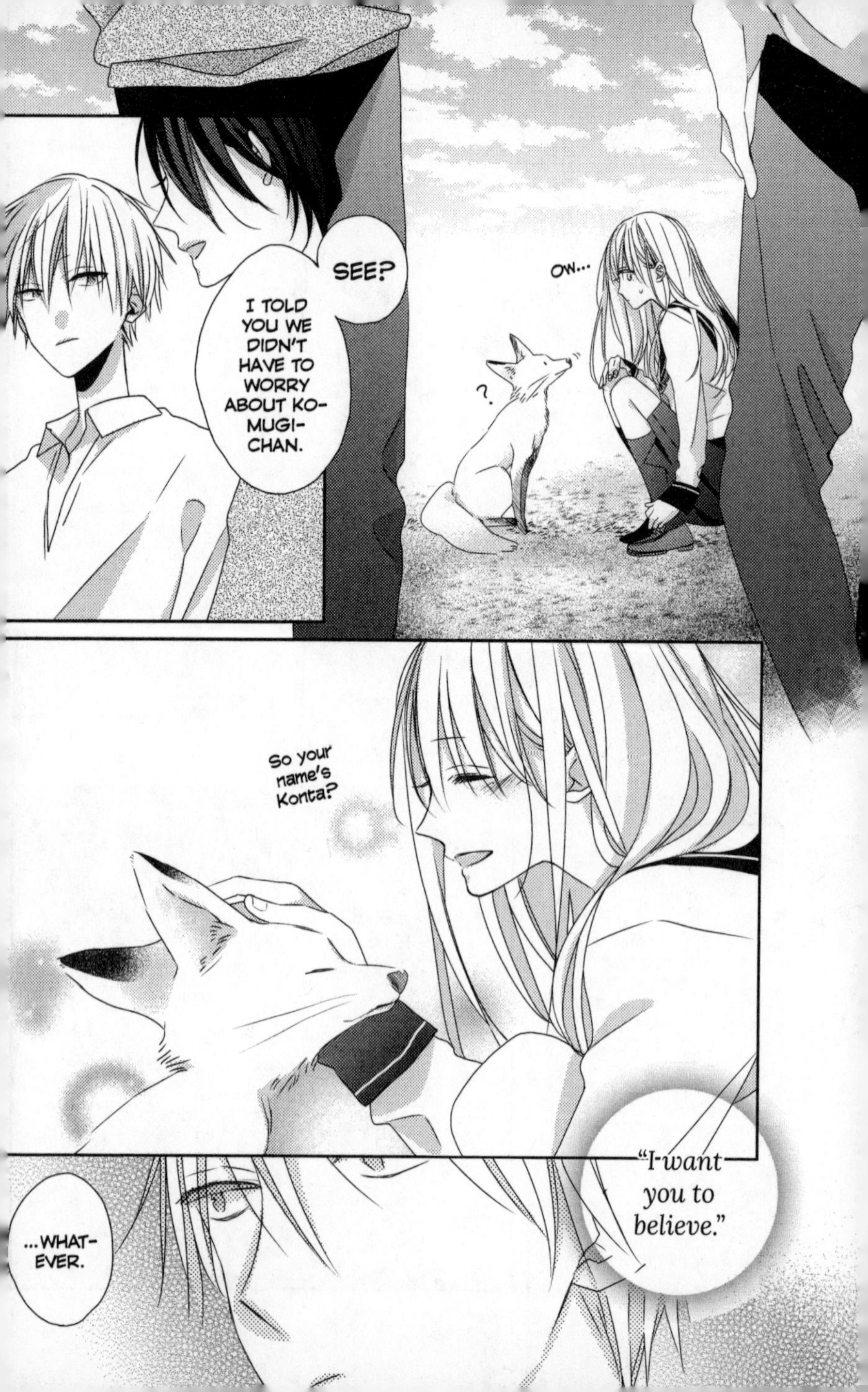
OW...
?
SEE?
I TOLD YOU WE DIDN'T HAVE TO WORRY ABOUT KO-MUGI-CHAN.
So your name's Konta?
"I want you to believe."
...WHAT-EVER.

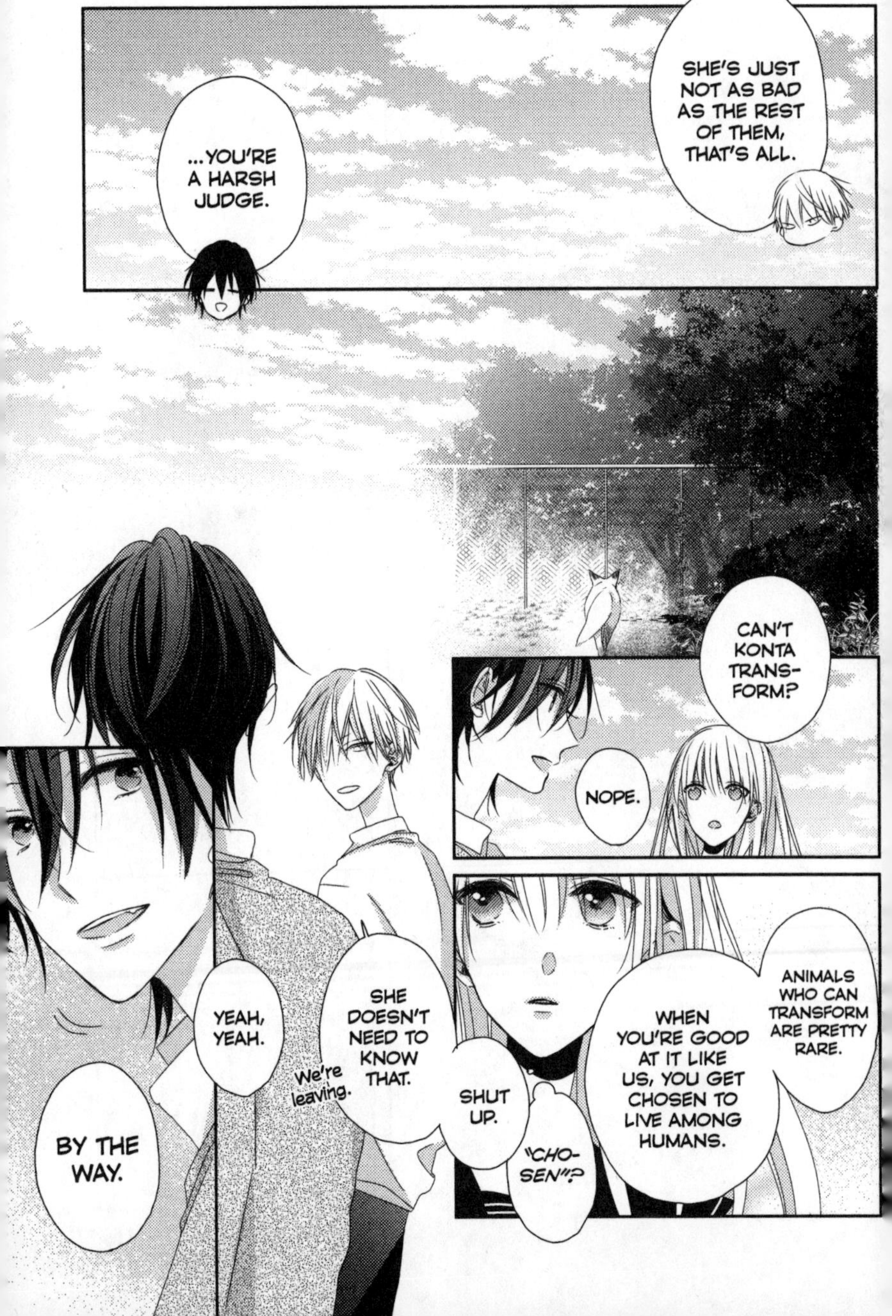
SHE'S JUST NOT AS BAD AS THE REST OF THEM, THAT'S ALL.
...YOU'RE A HARSH JUDGE.
CAN'T KONTA TRANS-FORM?
NOPE.
ANIMALS WHO CAN TRANSFORM ARE PRETTY RARE.
WHEN YOU'RE GOOD AT IT LIKE US, YOU GET CHOSEN TO LIVE AMONG HUMANS.
"CHO-SEN"?
SHUT UP.
SHE DOESN'T NEED TO KNOW THAT.
We're leaving.
YEAH, YEAH.
BY THE WAY.

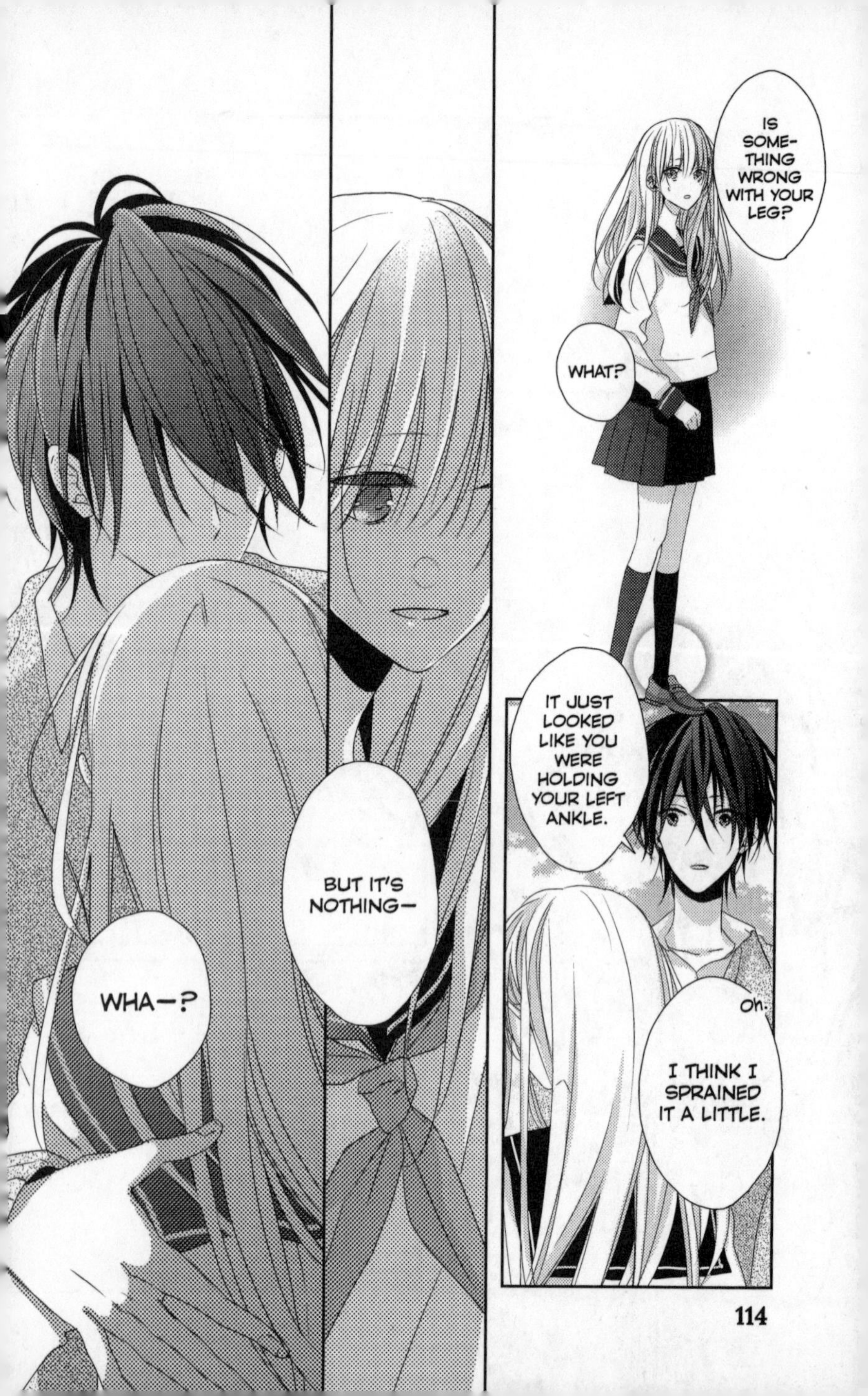
IS SOMETHING WRONG WITH YOUR LEG?
WHAT?
IT JUST LOOKED LIKE YOU WERE HOLDING YOUR LEFT ANKLE.
Oh.
I THINK I SPRAINED IT A LITTLE.
BUT IT'S NOTHING—
WHA—?

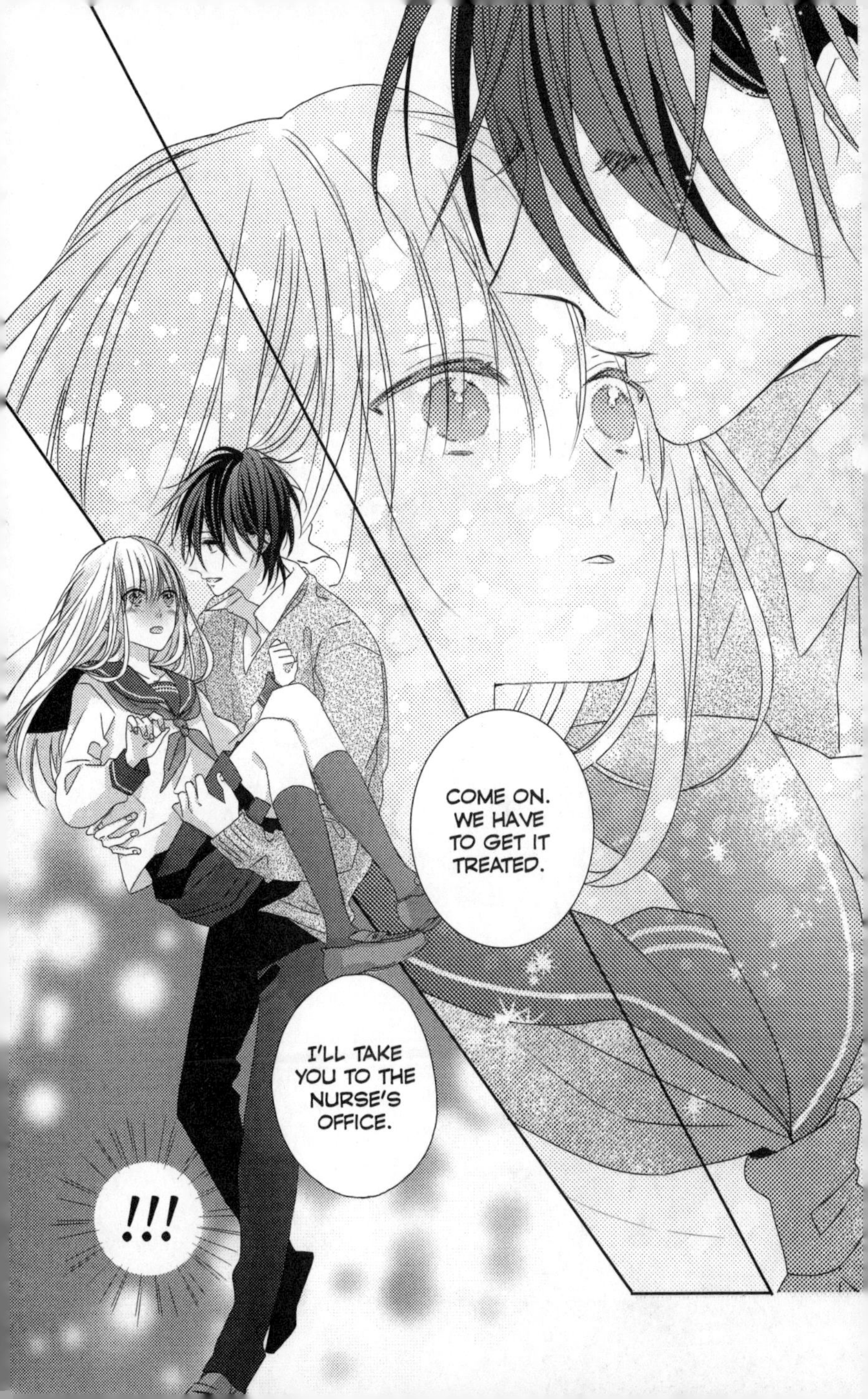
COME ON. WE HAVE TO GET IT TREATED.
I'LL TAKE YOU TO THE NURSE'S OFFICE.
!!!

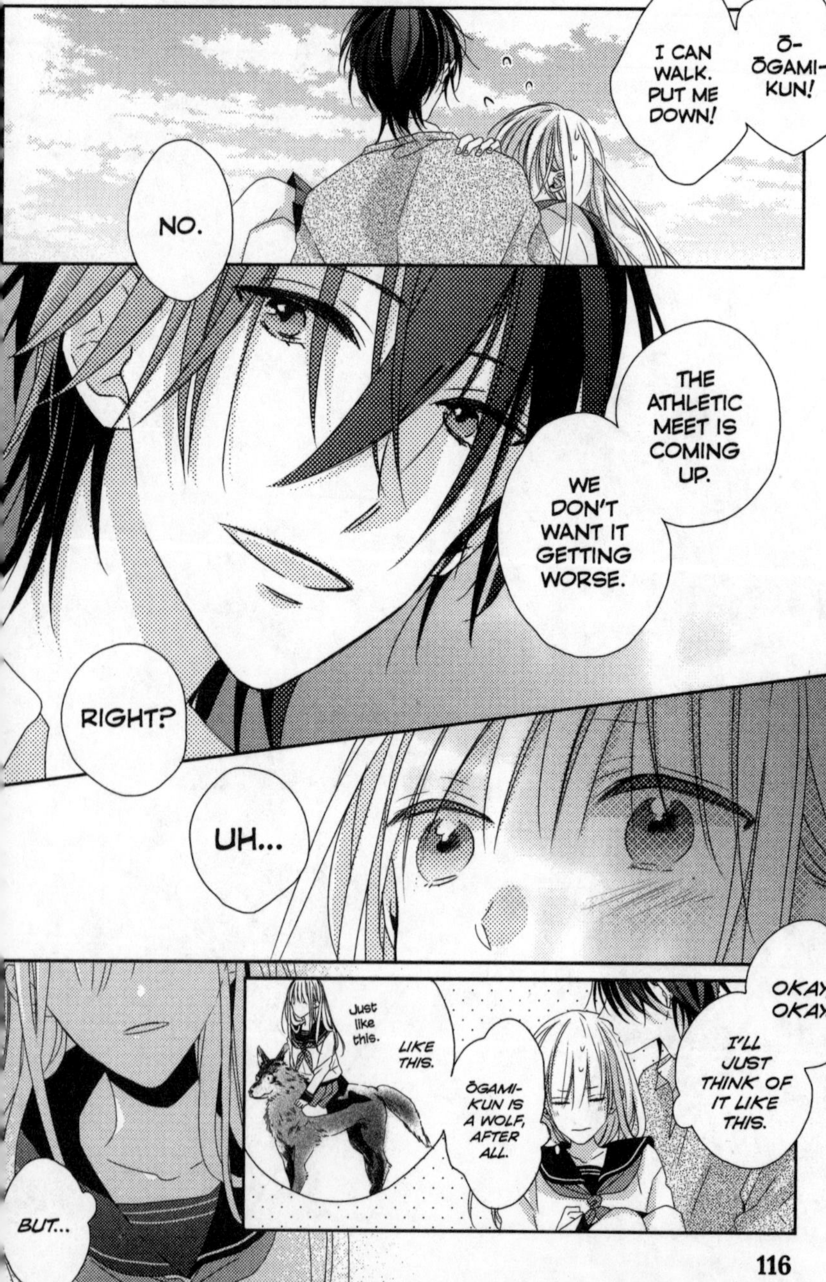
Ō-ŌGAMI-KUN!
I CAN WALK. PUT ME DOWN!
NO.
THE ATHLETIC MEET IS COMING UP.
WE DON'T WANT IT GETTING WORSE.
RIGHT?
UH...
OKAY, OKAY.
I'LL JUST THINK OF IT LIKE THIS.
ŌGAMI-KUN IS A WOLF, AFTER ALL.
LIKE THIS.
Just like this.
BUT...

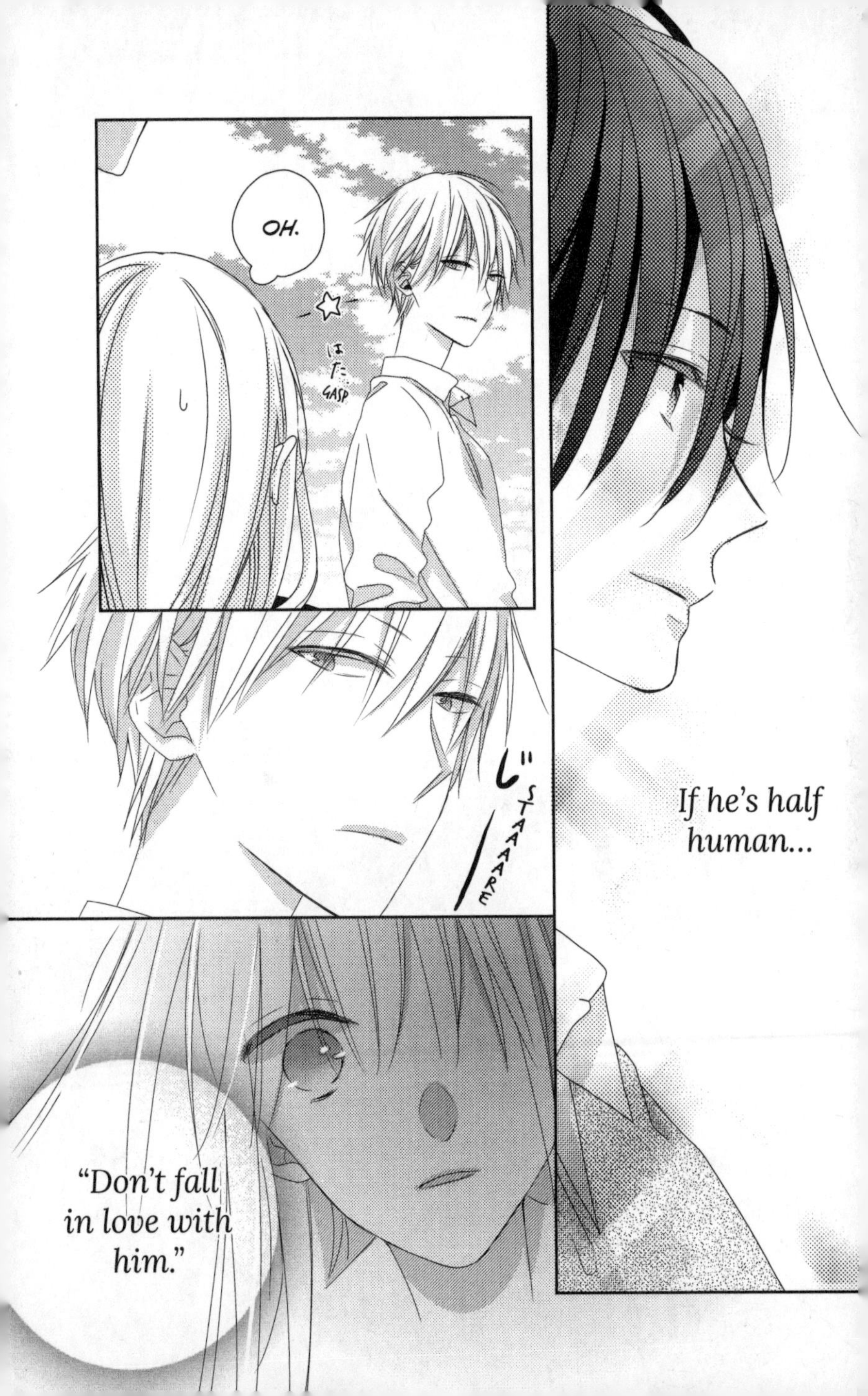
If he's half human...
OH.
はっ
GASP
じー
STAAAARE
"Don't fall in love with him."

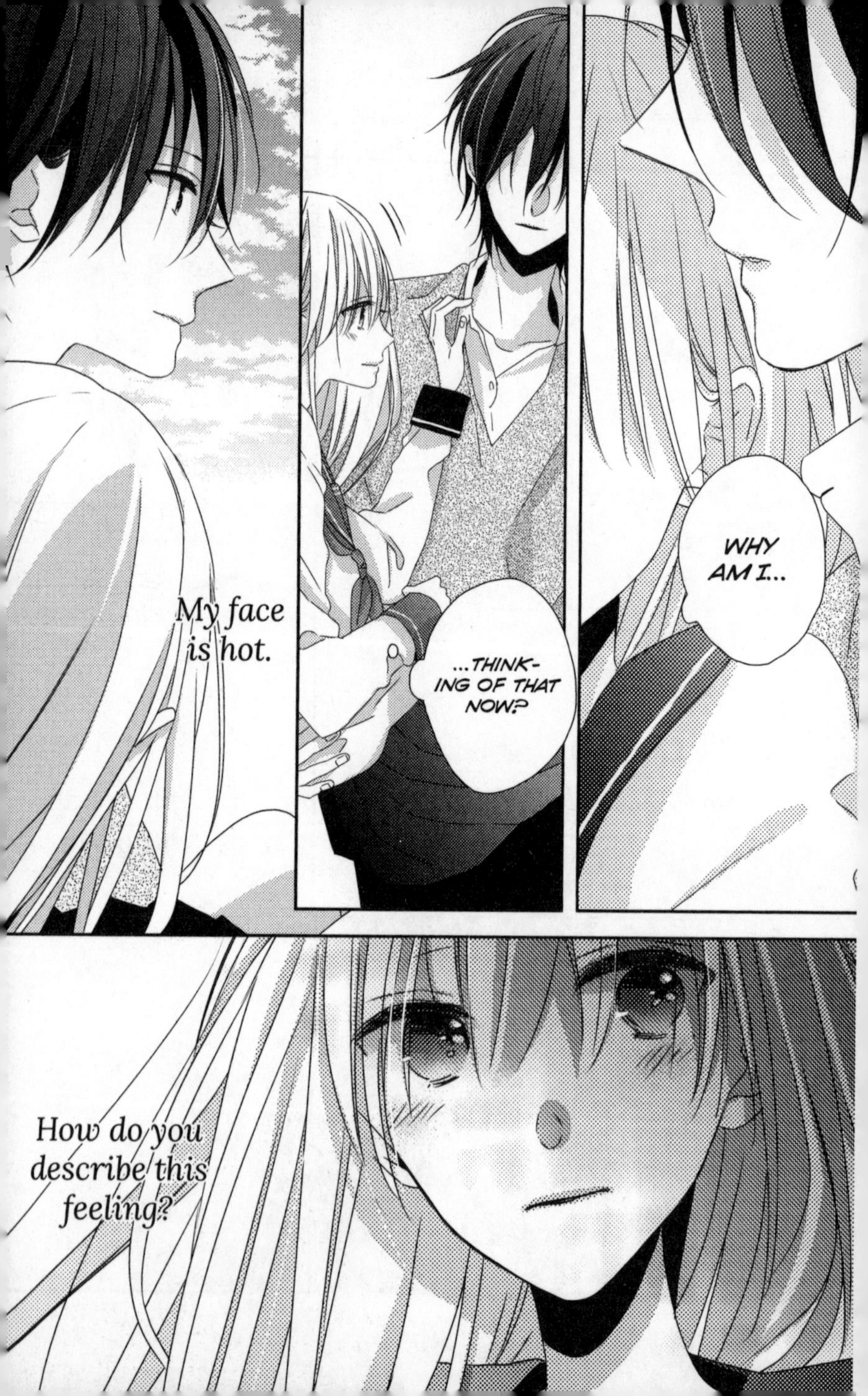
WHY AM I...
...THINKING OF THAT NOW?
My face is hot.
How do you describe this feeling?

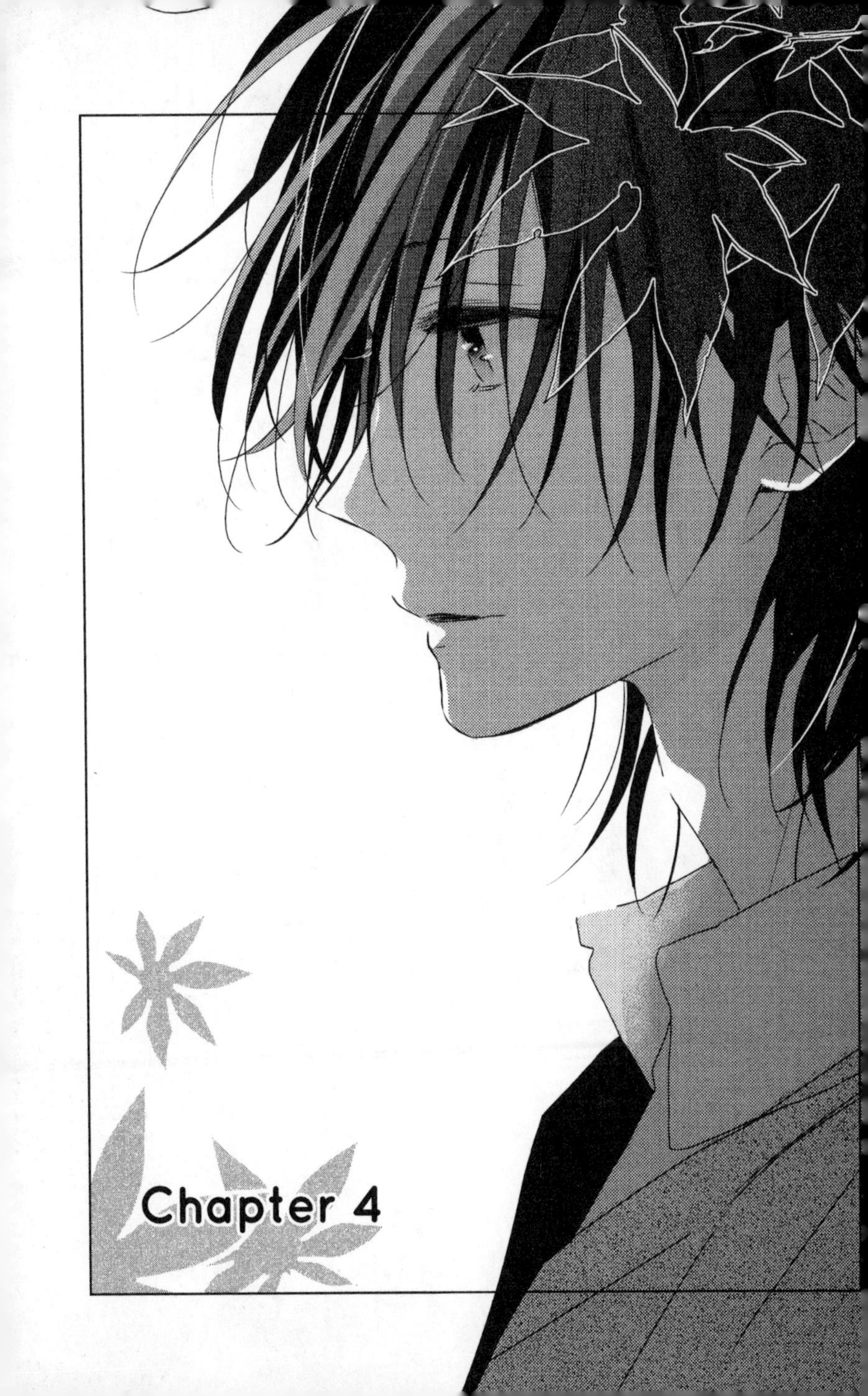
Chapter 4

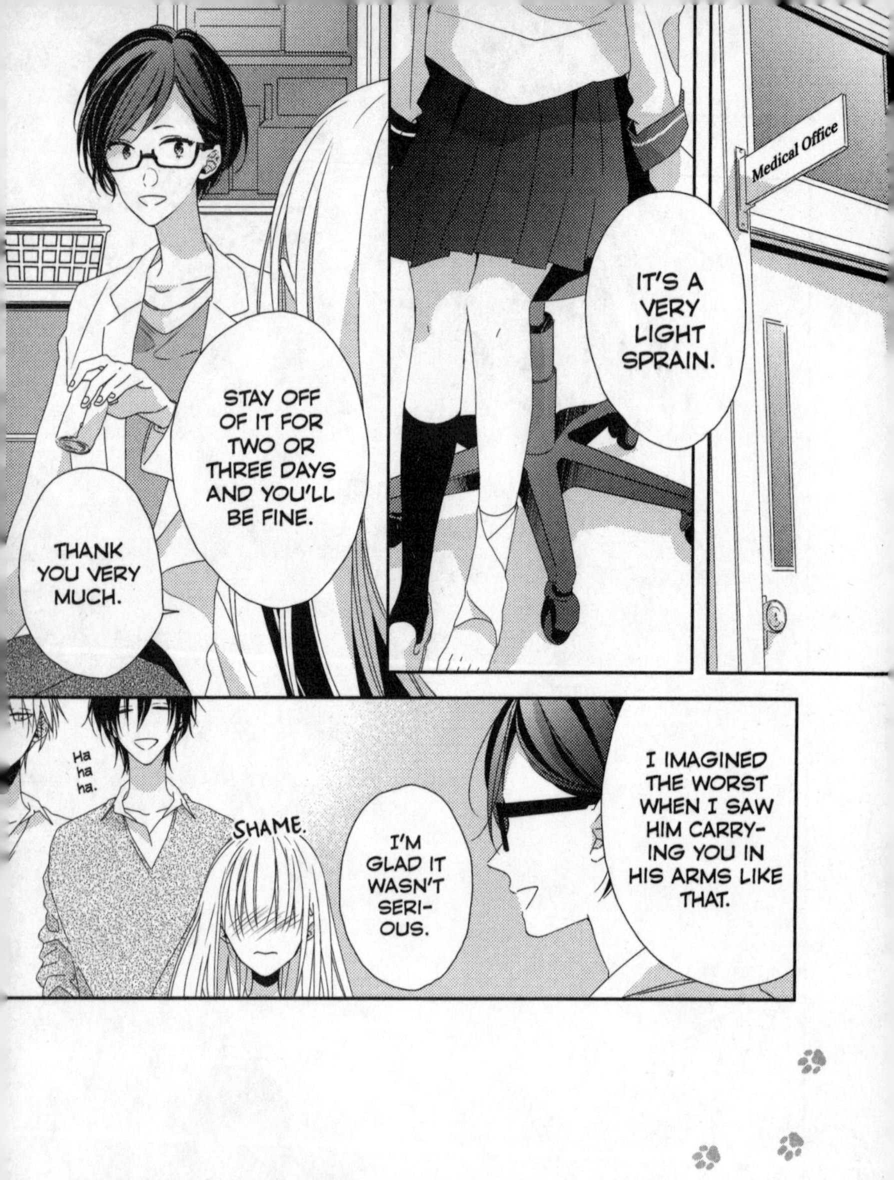
Medical Office
IT'S A VERY LIGHT SPRAIN.
STAY OFF OF IT FOR TWO OR THREE DAYS AND YOU'LL BE FINE.
THANK YOU VERY MUCH.
I IMAGINED THE WORST WHEN I SAW HIM CARRYING YOU IN HIS ARMS LIKE THAT.
I'M GLAD IT WASN'T SERIOUS.
SHAME.
Ha ha ha.

That Wolf-Boy is Mine!

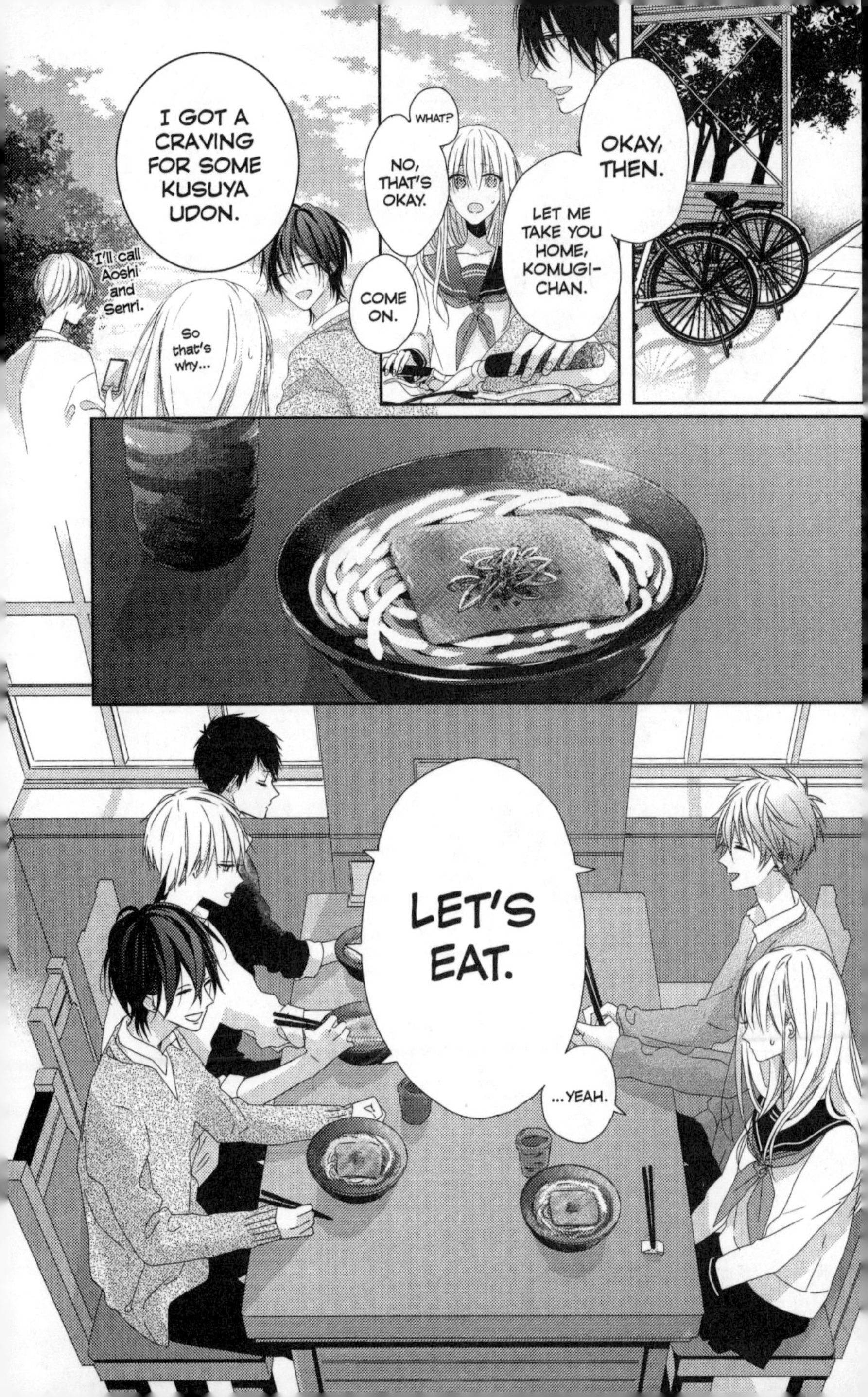
OKAY, THEN.
LET ME TAKE YOU HOME, KOMUGI-CHAN.
WHAT?
NO, THAT'S OKAY.
COME ON.
I GOT A CRAVING FOR SOME KUSUYA UDON.
So that's why...
I'll call Aoshi and Senri.
LET'S EAT.
...YEAH.

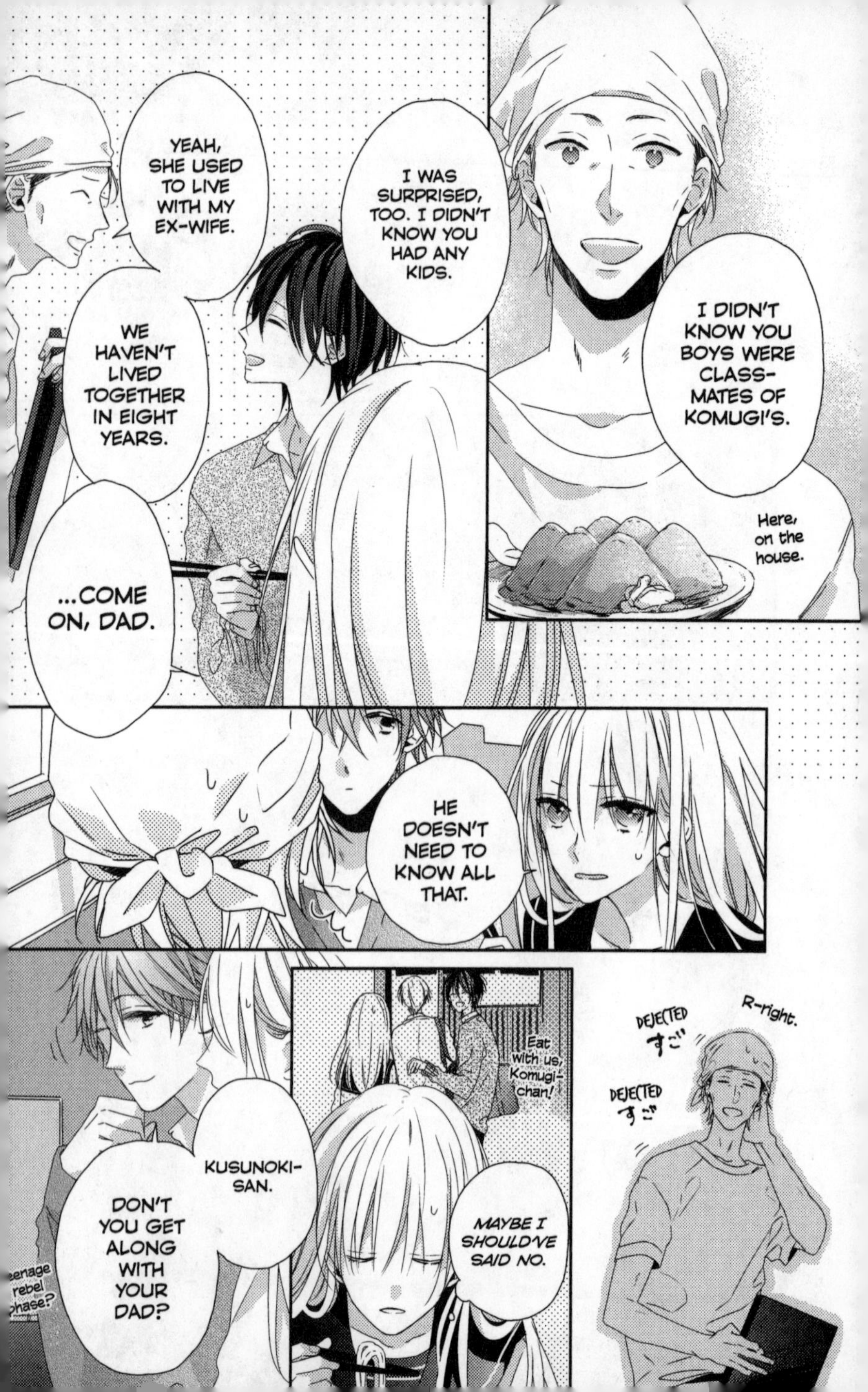
I DIDN'T KNOW YOU BOYS WERE CLASS-MATES OF KOMUGI'S.
Here, on the house.
I WAS SURPRISED, TOO. I DIDN'T KNOW YOU HAD ANY KIDS.
YEAH, SHE USED TO LIVE WITH MY EX-WIFE.
WE HAVEN'T LIVED TOGETHER IN EIGHT YEARS.
...COME ON, DAD.
HE DOESN'T NEED TO KNOW ALL THAT.
R-right.
DEJECTED すご
DEJECTED すご
Eat with us, Komugi-chan!
MAYBE I SHOULD'VE SAID NO.
KUSUNOKI-SAN.
DON'T YOU GET ALONG WITH YOUR DAD?
eenage rebel phase?

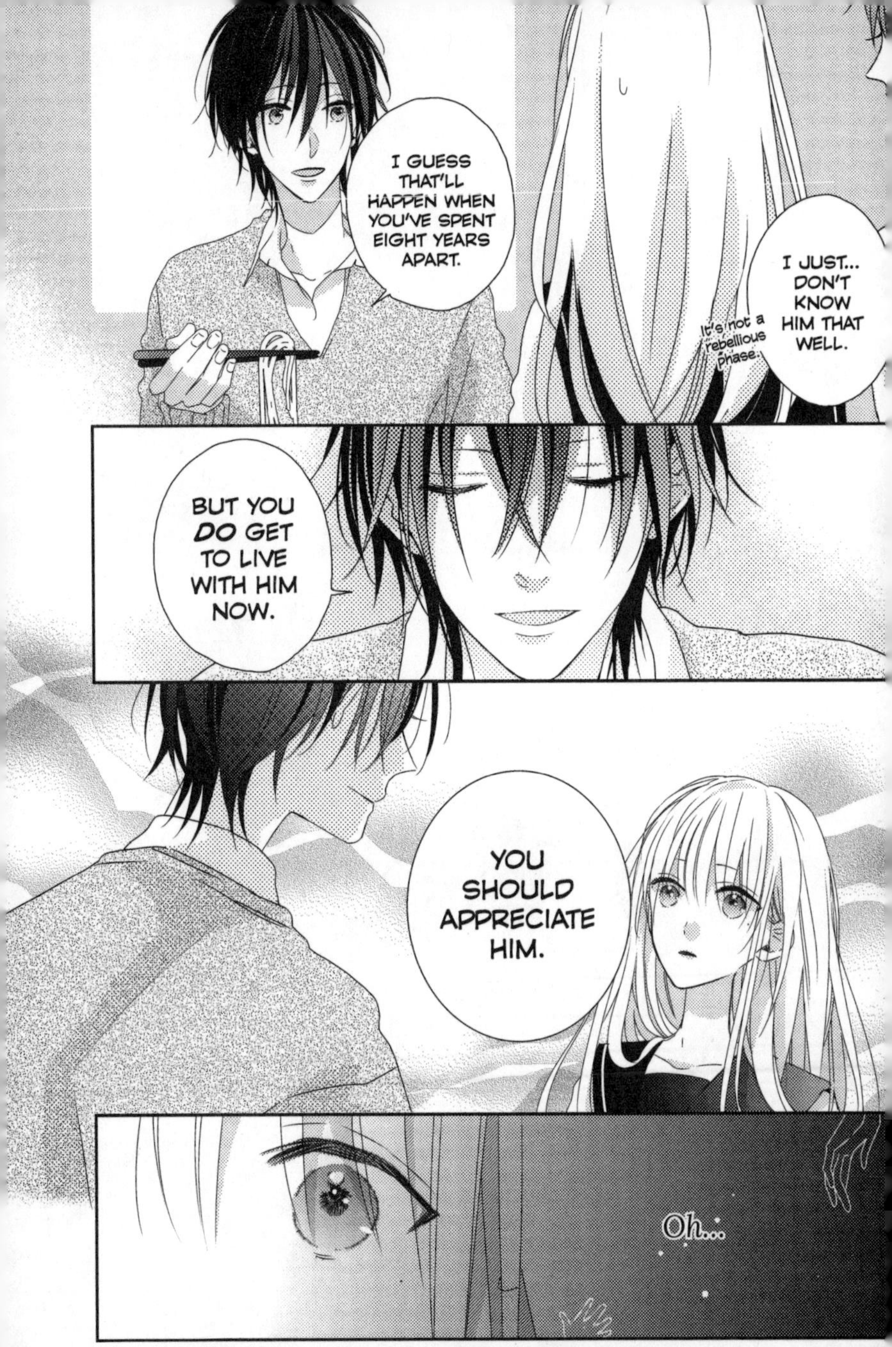
I JUST... DON'T KNOW HIM THAT WELL.
It's not a rebellious phase.
I GUESS THAT'LL HAPPEN WHEN YOU'VE SPENT EIGHT YEARS APART.
BUT YOU *DO* GET TO LIVE WITH HIM NOW.
YOU SHOULD APPRECIATE HIM.
Oh...

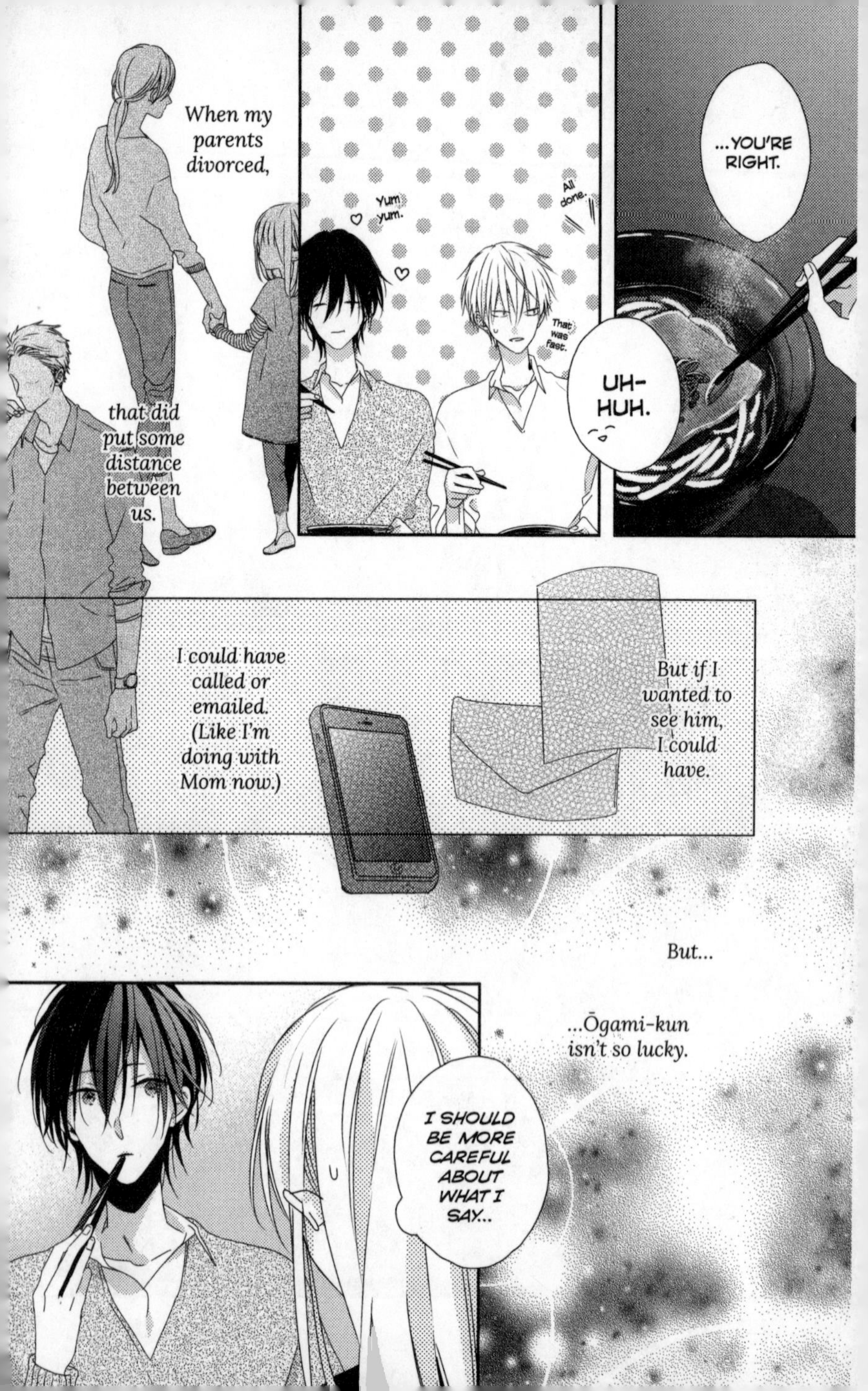
...YOU'RE RIGHT.
UH-HUH.
All done.
That was fast.
Yum yum.
When my parents divorced,
that did put some distance between us.
But if I wanted to see him, I could have.
I could have called or emailed. (Like I'm doing with Mom now.)
But...
...Ōgami-kun isn't so lucky.
I SHOULD BE MORE CAREFUL ABOUT WHAT I SAY...

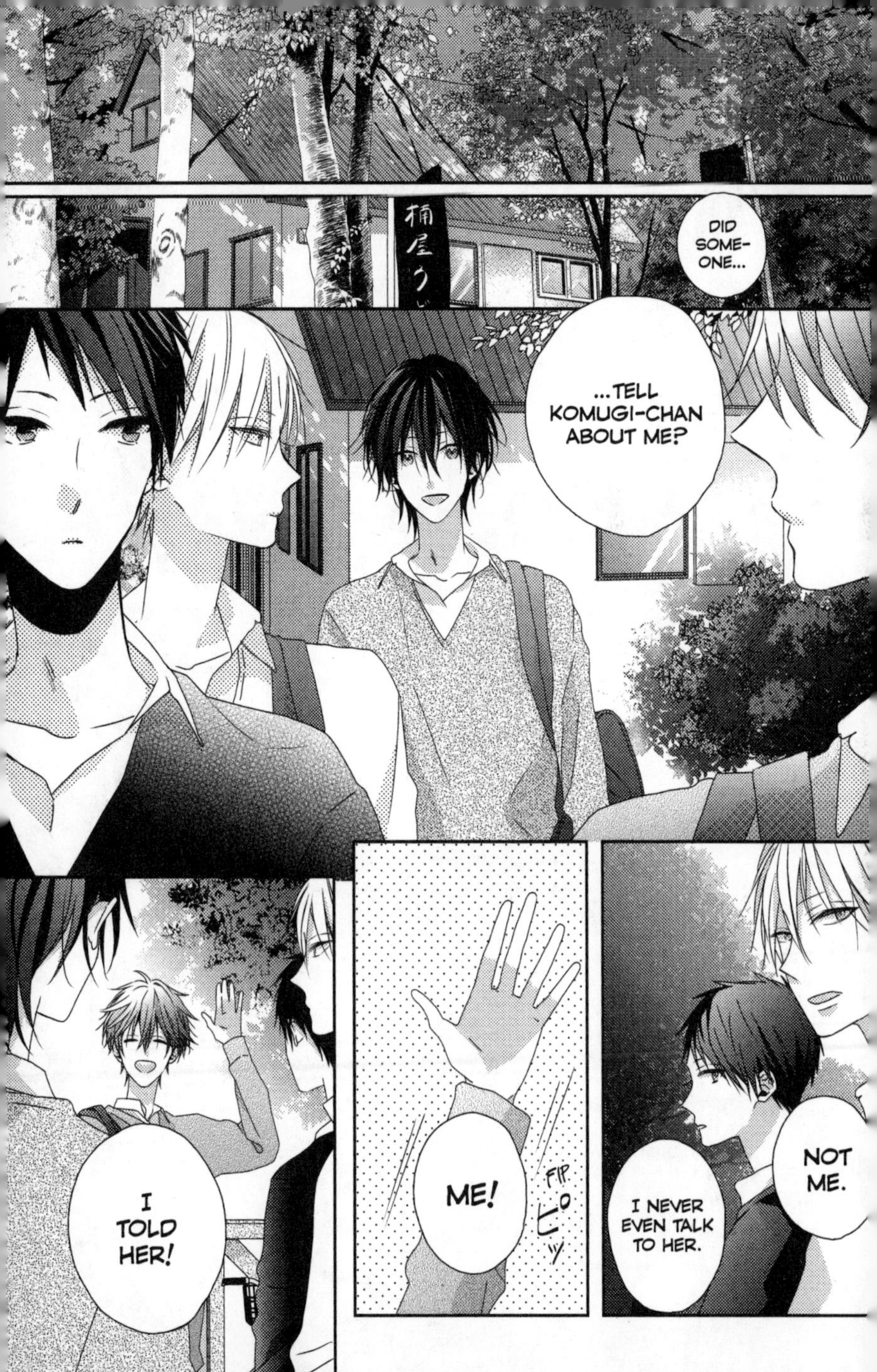
DID SOME-ONE...
...TELL KOMUGI-CHAN ABOUT ME?
NOT ME.
I NEVER EVEN TALK TO HER.
FIP
ピッ
ME!
I TOLD HER!

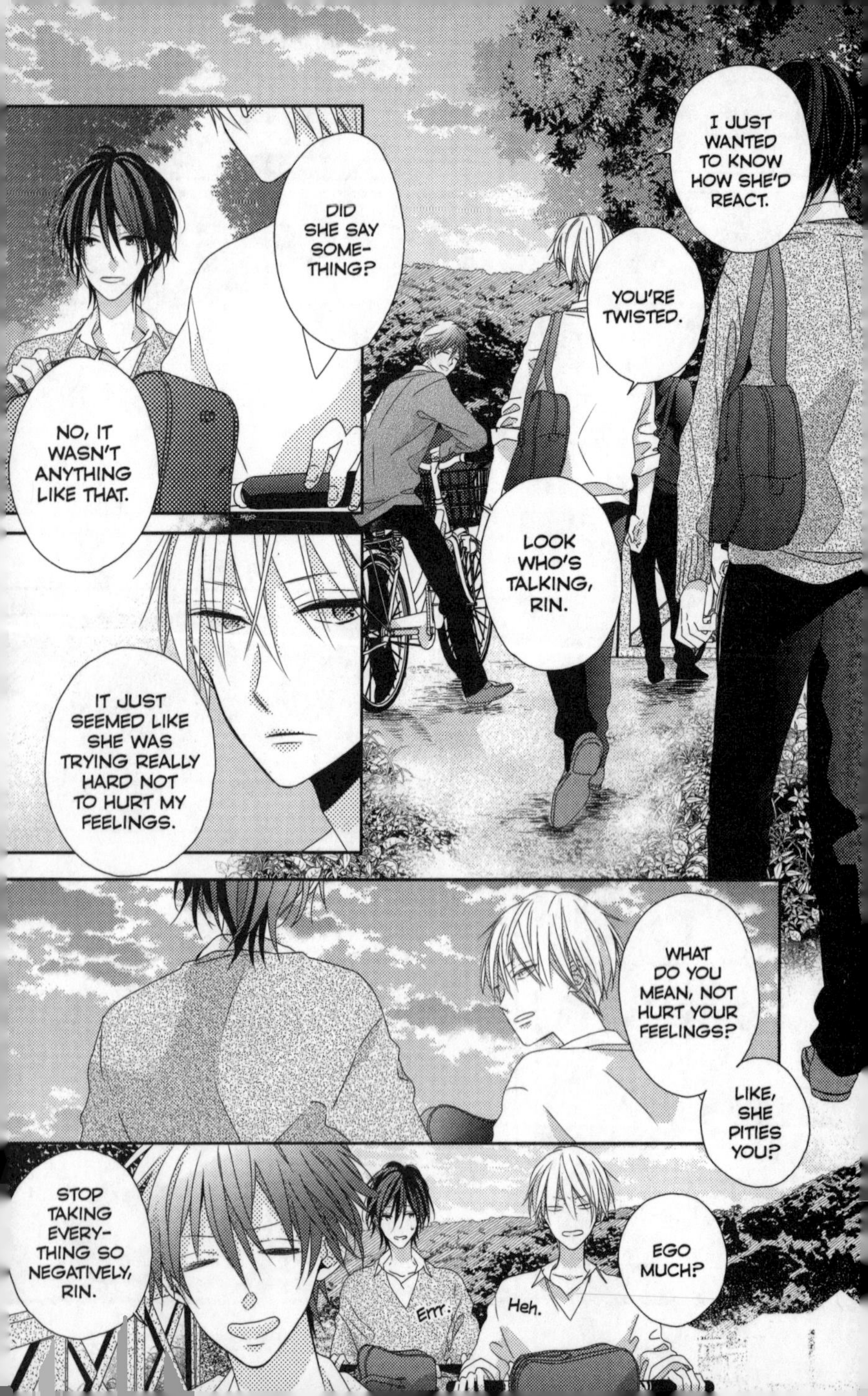
I JUST WANTED TO KNOW HOW SHE'D REACT.
YOU'RE TWISTED.
LOOK WHO'S TALKING, RIN.
DID SHE SAY SOME-THING?
NO, IT WASN'T ANYTHING LIKE THAT.
IT JUST SEEMED LIKE SHE WAS TRYING REALLY HARD NOT TO HURT MY FEELINGS.
WHAT DO YOU MEAN, NOT HURT YOUR FEELINGS?
LIKE, SHE PITIES YOU?
EGO MUCH?
Heh.
Errr.
STOP TAKING EVERY-THING SO NEGATIVELY, RIN.

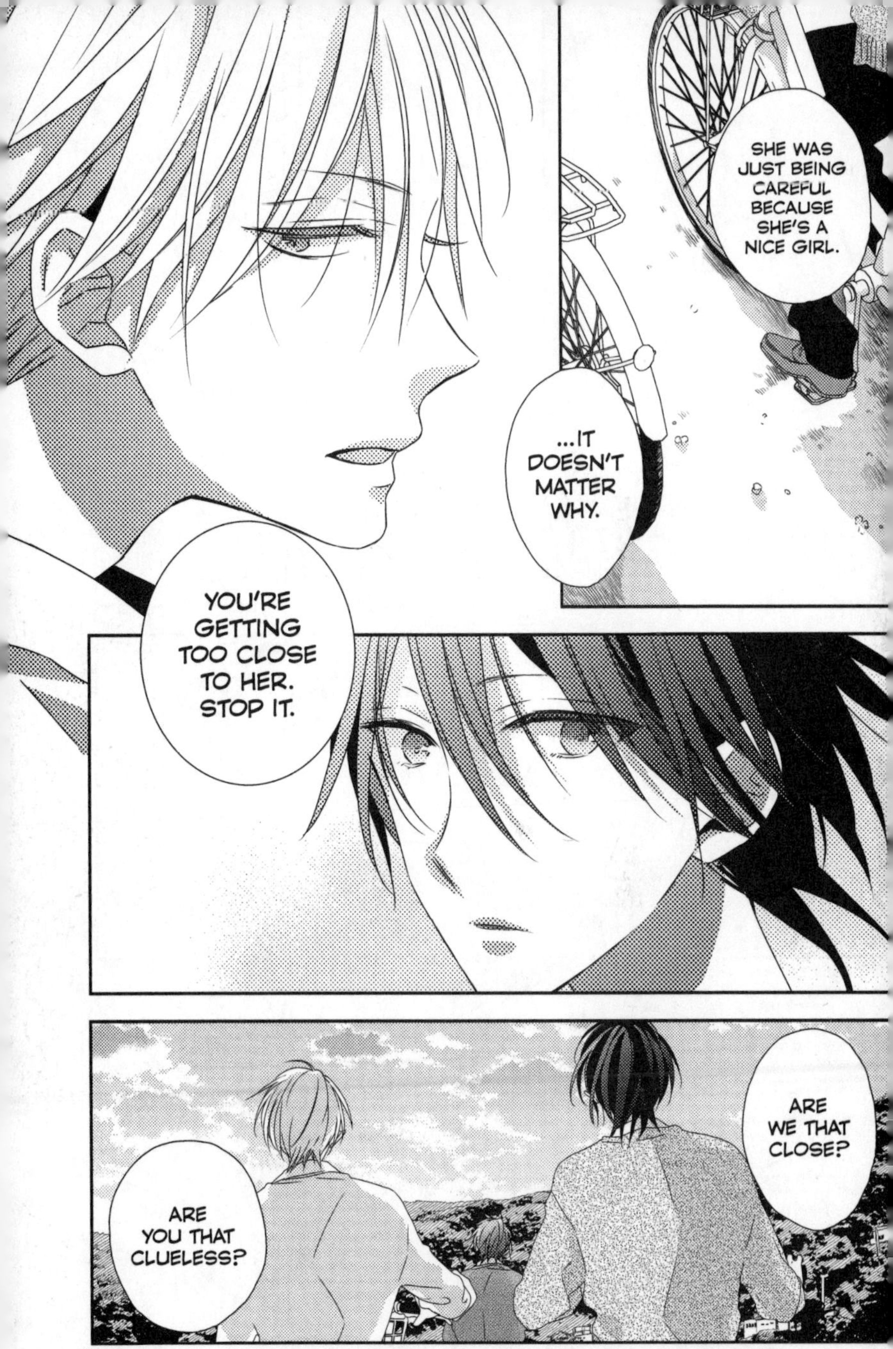
SHE WAS JUST BEING CAREFUL BECAUSE SHE'S A NICE GIRL.
...IT DOESN'T MATTER WHY.
YOU'RE GETTING TOO CLOSE TO HER. STOP IT.
ARE WE THAT CLOSE?
ARE YOU THAT CLUELESS?

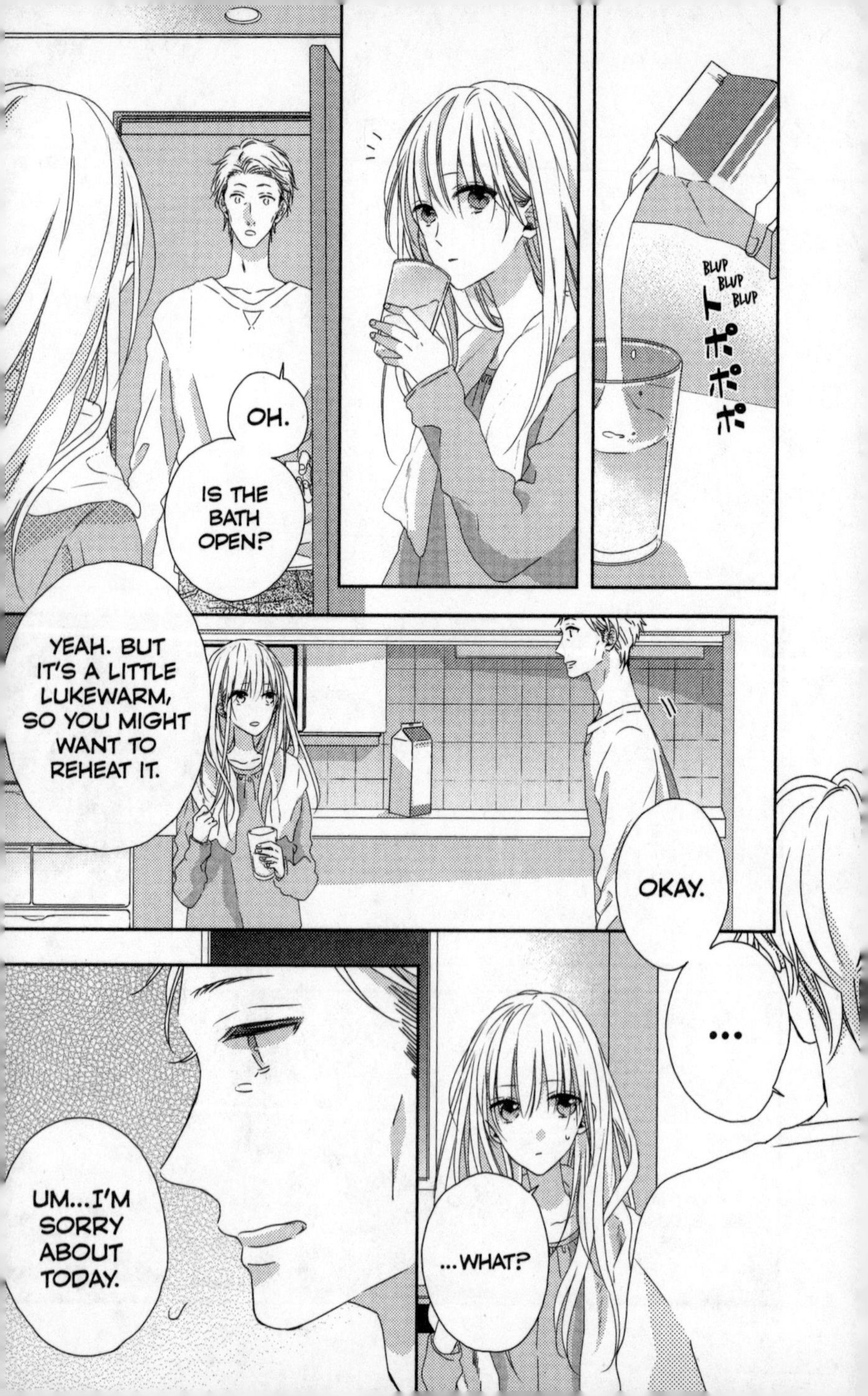
BLUP BLUP BLUP
トポポポ
OH.
IS THE BATH OPEN?
YEAH. BUT IT'S A LITTLE LUKEWARM, SO YOU MIGHT WANT TO REHEAT IT.
OKAY.
...
...WHAT?
UM...I'M SORRY ABOUT TODAY.

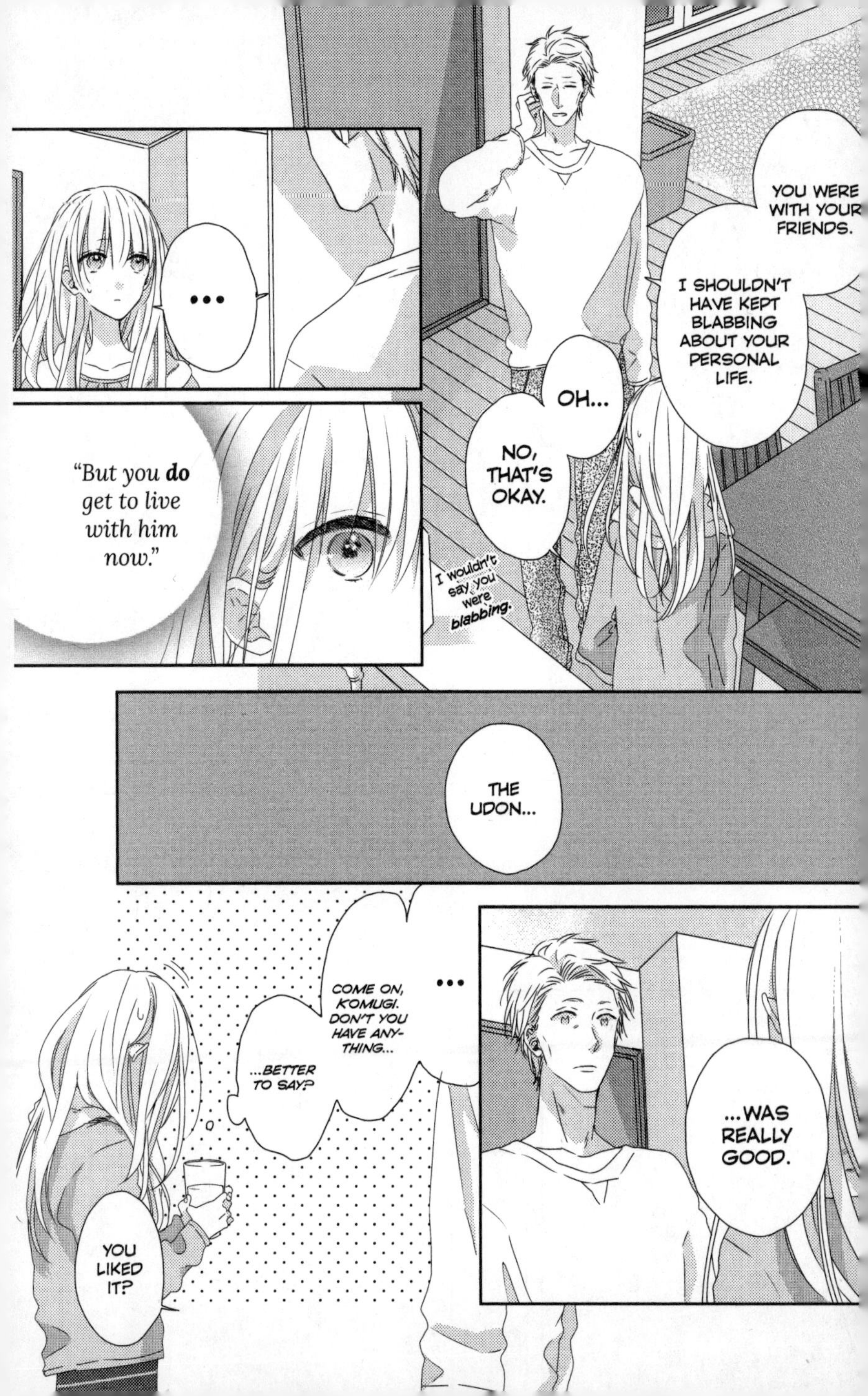
YOU WERE WITH YOUR FRIENDS.
I SHOULDN'T HAVE KEPT BLABBING ABOUT YOUR PERSONAL LIFE.
OH...
NO, THAT'S OKAY.
I wouldn't say you were *blabbing*.
...
“But you **do** get to live with him now.”
THE UDON...
...WAS REALLY GOOD.
...
COME ON, KOMUGI. DON'T YOU HAVE ANYTHING...
...BETTER TO SAY?
YOU LIKED IT?

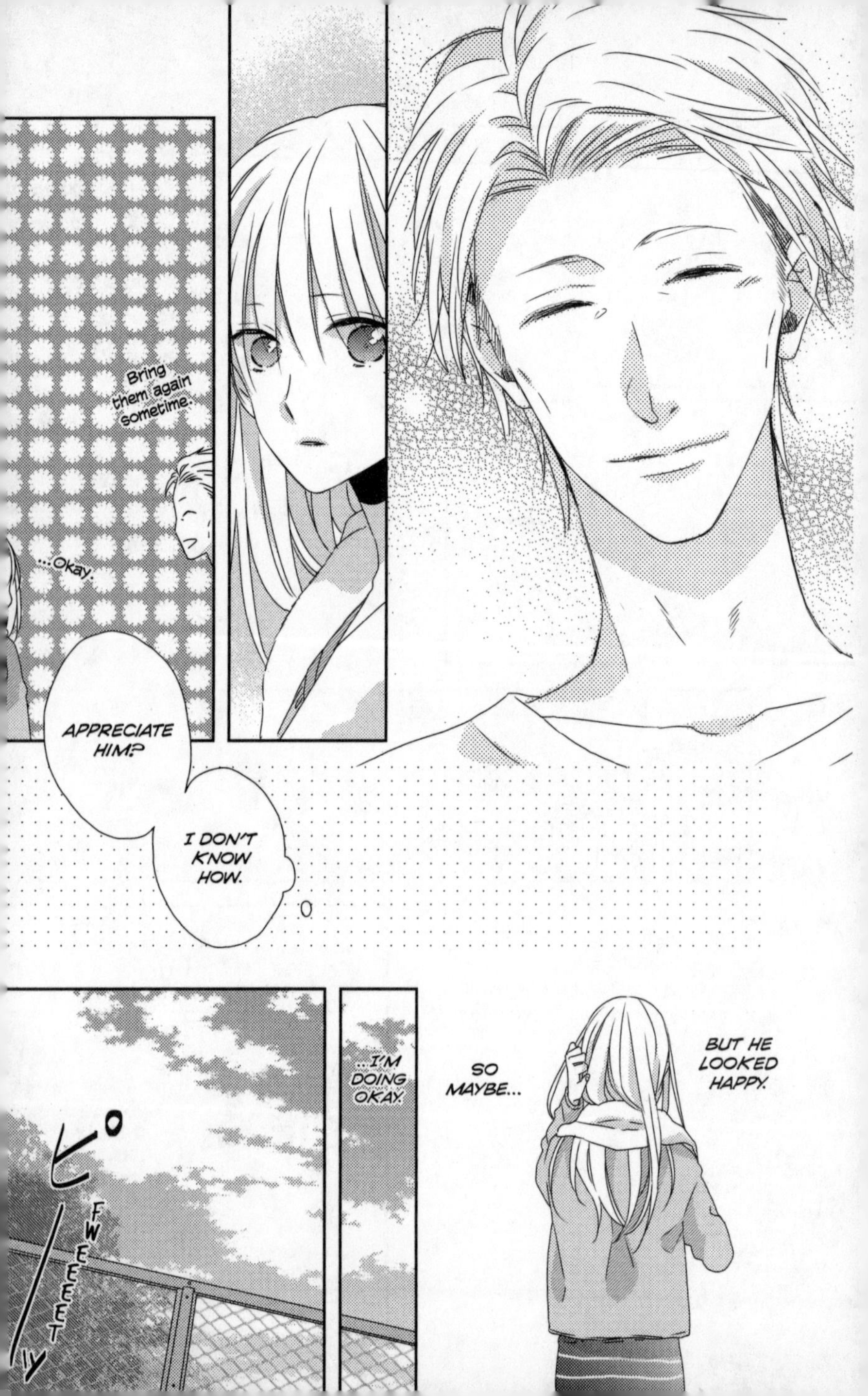
Bring them again sometime.
...Okay.
APPRECIATE HIM?
I DON'T KNOW HOW.
BUT HE LOOKED HAPPY.
SO MAYBE...
...I'M DOING OKAY.
FWEEEETT

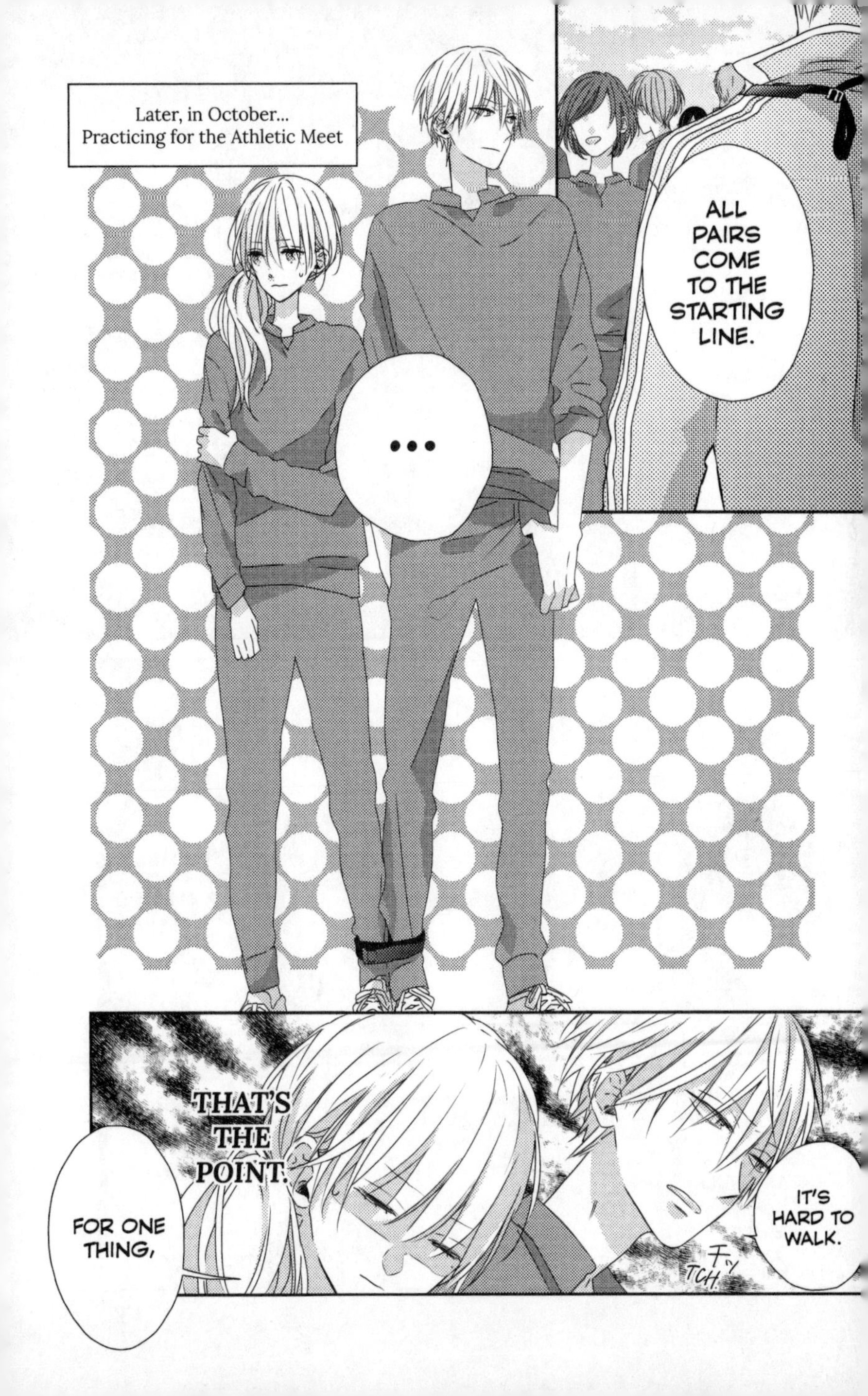
Later, in October...
Practicing for the Athletic Meet
ALL PAIRS COME TO THE STARTING LINE.
...
IT'S HARD TO WALK.
チッ TCH.
THAT'S THE POINT.
FOR ONE THING,

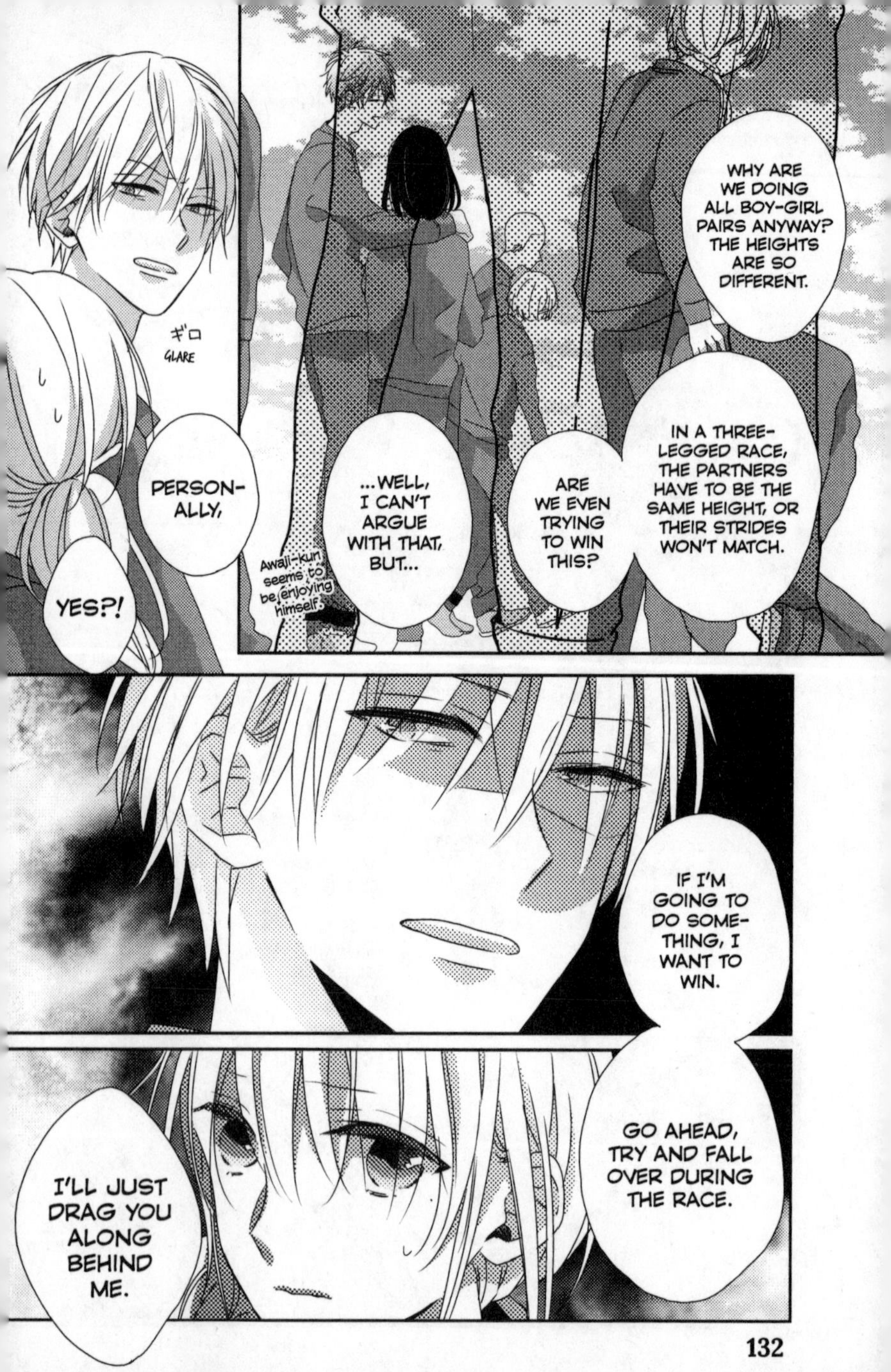
WHY ARE WE DOING ALL BOY-GIRL PAIRS ANYWAY? THE HEIGHTS ARE SO DIFFERENT.
IN A THREE-LEGGED RACE, THE PARTNERS HAVE TO BE THE SAME HEIGHT, OR THEIR STRIDES WON'T MATCH.
ARE WE EVEN TRYING TO WIN THIS?
...WELL, I CAN'T ARGUE WITH THAT, BUT...
Awaji-kun seems to be enjoying himself.
ギロ
GLARE
PERSON-ALLY,
YES?!
IF I'M GOING TO DO SOME-THING, I WANT TO WIN.
GO AHEAD, TRY AND FALL OVER DURING THE RACE.
I'LL JUST DRAG YOU ALONG BEHIND ME.

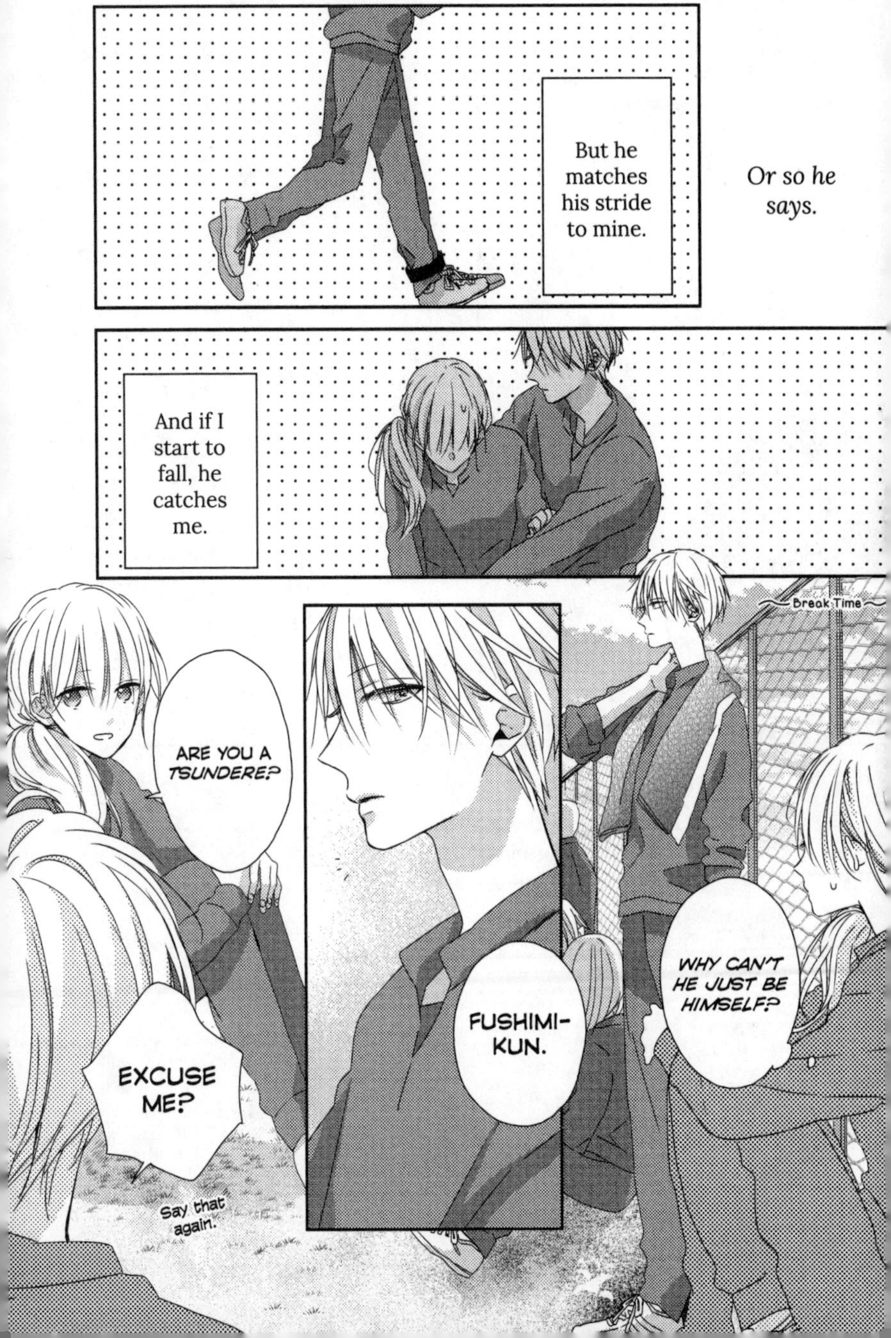
Or so he says.
But he matches his stride to mine.
And if I start to fall, he catches me.
~Break Time~
WHY CAN'T HE JUST BE HIMSELF?
FUSHIMI-KUN.
ARE YOU A TSUNDERE?
EXCUSE ME?
Say that again.

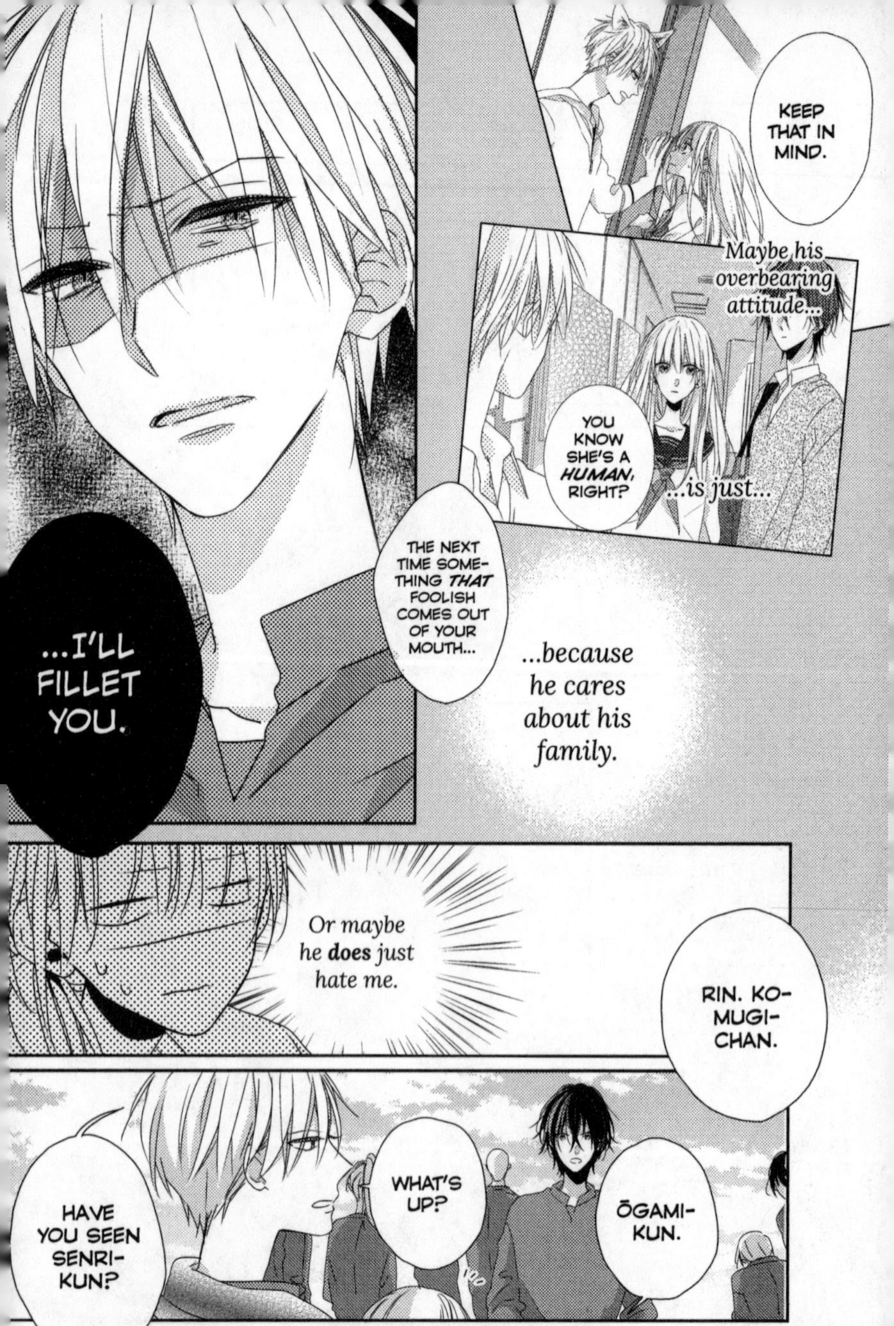
KEEP THAT IN MIND.
Maybe his overbearing attitude...
YOU KNOW SHE'S A *HUMAN*, RIGHT?
...is just...
THE NEXT TIME SOME-THING *THAT* FOOLISH COMES OUT OF YOUR MOUTH...
...I'LL FILLET YOU.
...because he cares about his family.
Or maybe he **does** just hate me.
RIN. KOMUGI-CHAN.
ŌGAMI-KUN.
WHAT'S UP?
HAVE YOU SEEN SENRI-KUN?

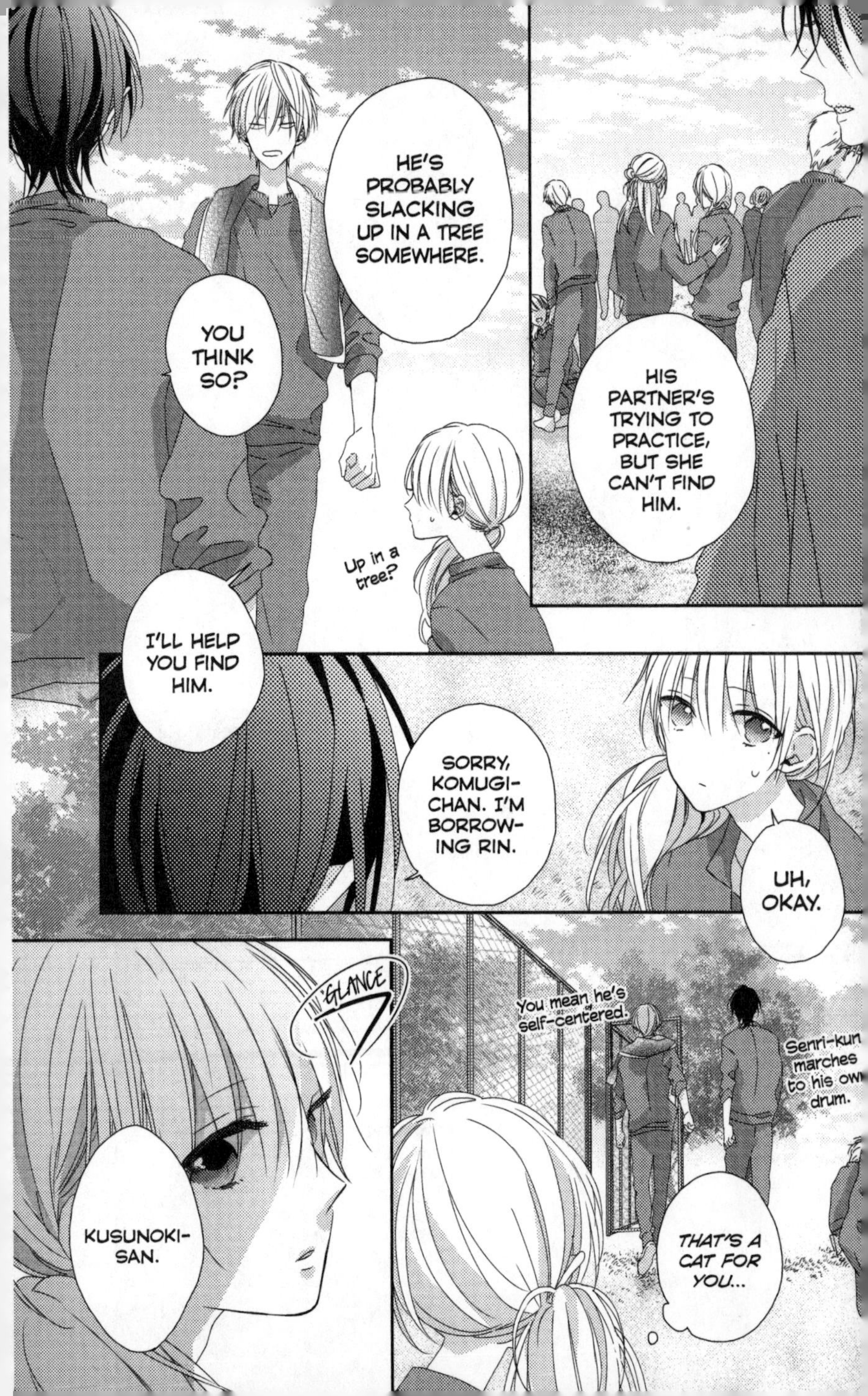
HIS PARTNER'S TRYING TO PRACTICE, BUT SHE CAN'T FIND HIM.
HE'S PROBABLY SLACKING UP IN A TREE SOMEWHERE.
YOU THINK SO?
Up in a tree?
I'LL HELP YOU FIND HIM.
UH, OKAY.
SORRY, KOMUGI-CHAN. I'M BORROWING RIN.
Senri-kun marches to his ow drum.
You mean he's self-centered.
THAT'S A CAT FOR YOU...
GLANCE
KUSUNOKI-SAN.

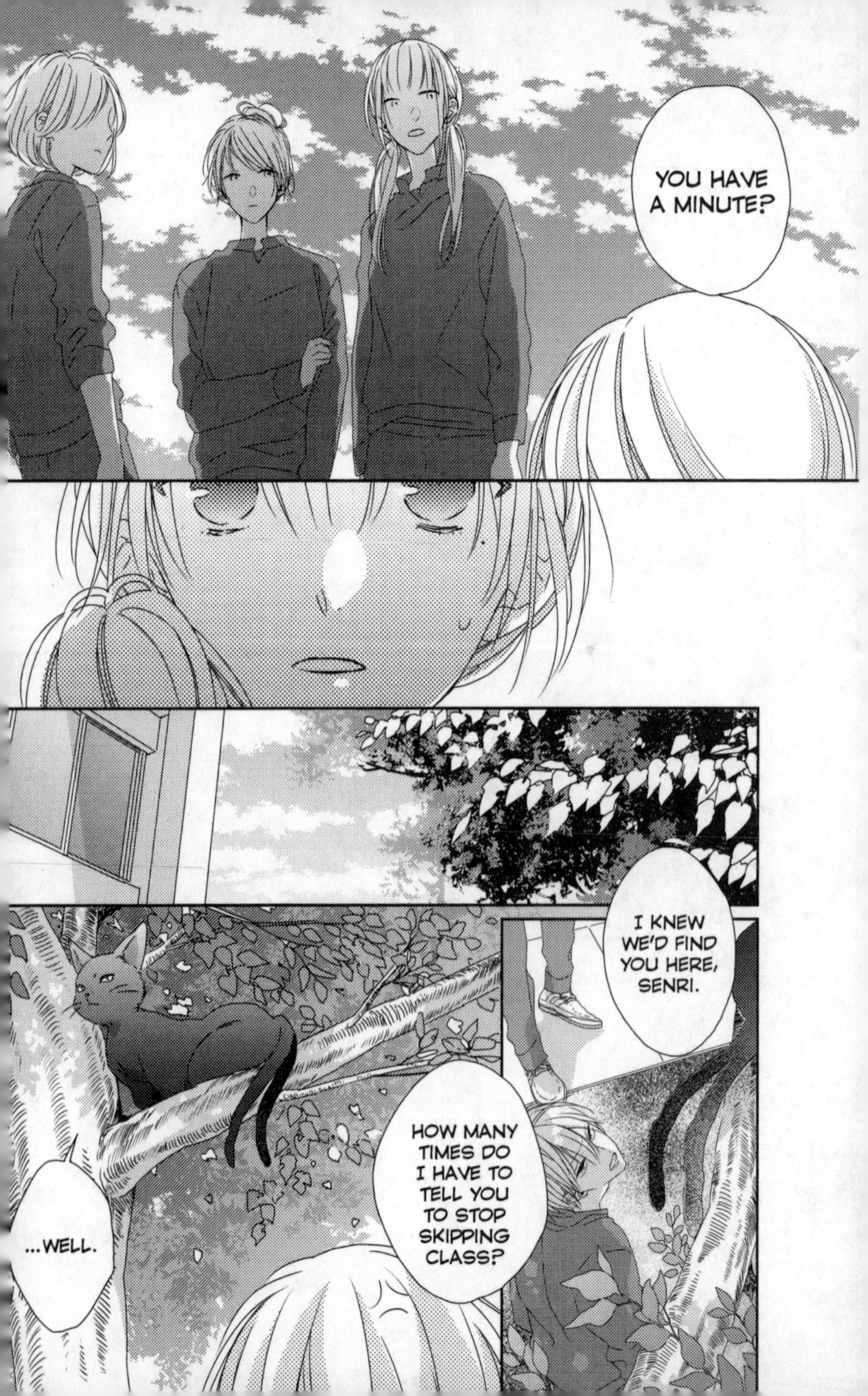
YOU HAVE A MINUTE?
I KNEW WE'D FIND YOU HERE, SENRI.
HOW MANY TIMES DO I HAVE TO TELL YOU TO STOP SKIPPING CLASS?
...WELL.

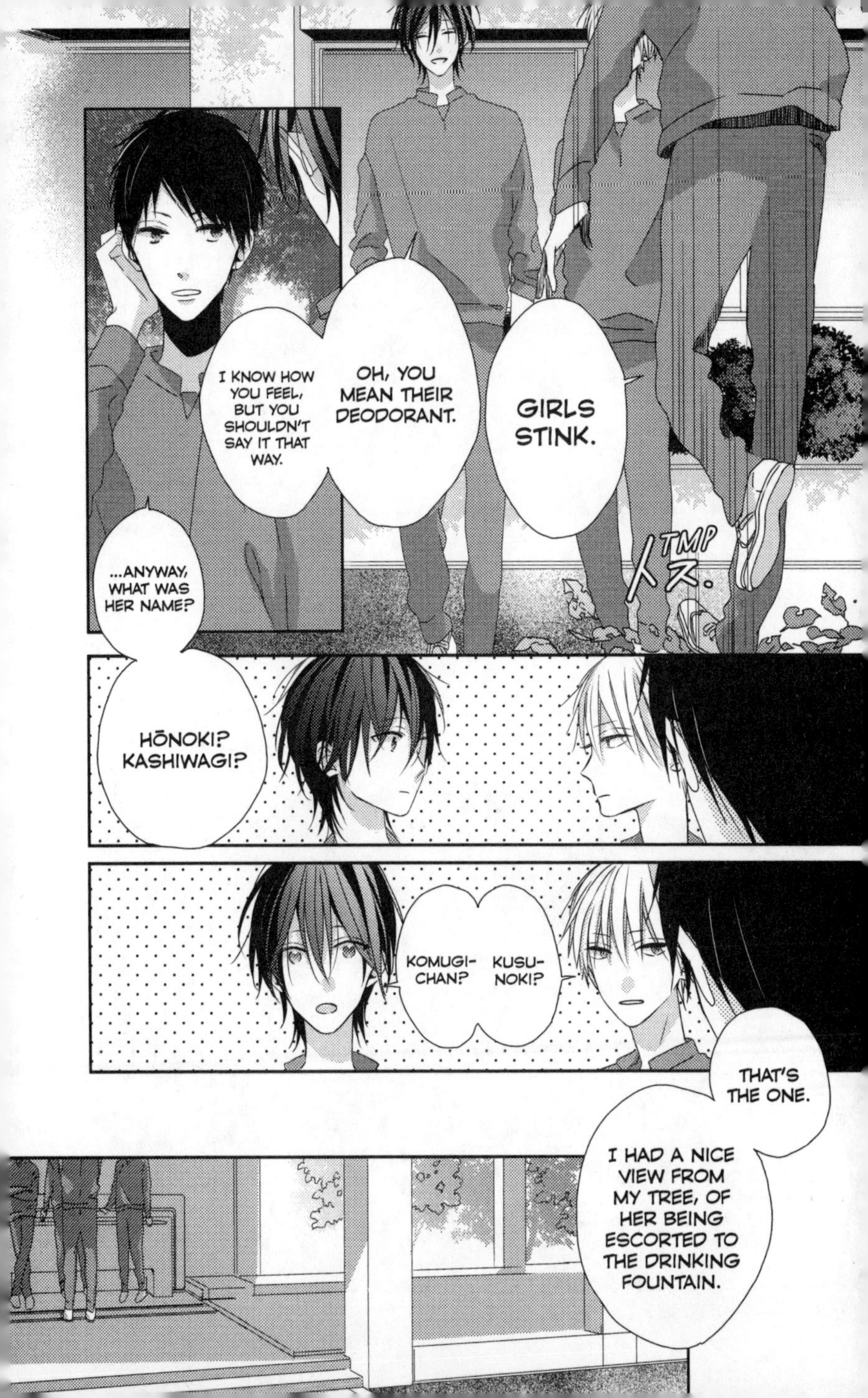
GIRLS STINK.
OH, YOU MEAN THEIR DEODORANT.
I KNOW HOW YOU FEEL, BUT YOU SHOULDN'T SAY IT THAT WAY.
TMP トス。
...ANYWAY, WHAT WAS HER NAME?
HŌNOKI? KASHIWAGI?
KUSU-NOKI?
KOMUGI-CHAN?
THAT'S THE ONE.
I HAD A NICE VIEW FROM MY TREE, OF HER BEING ESCORTED TO THE DRINKING FOUNTAIN.

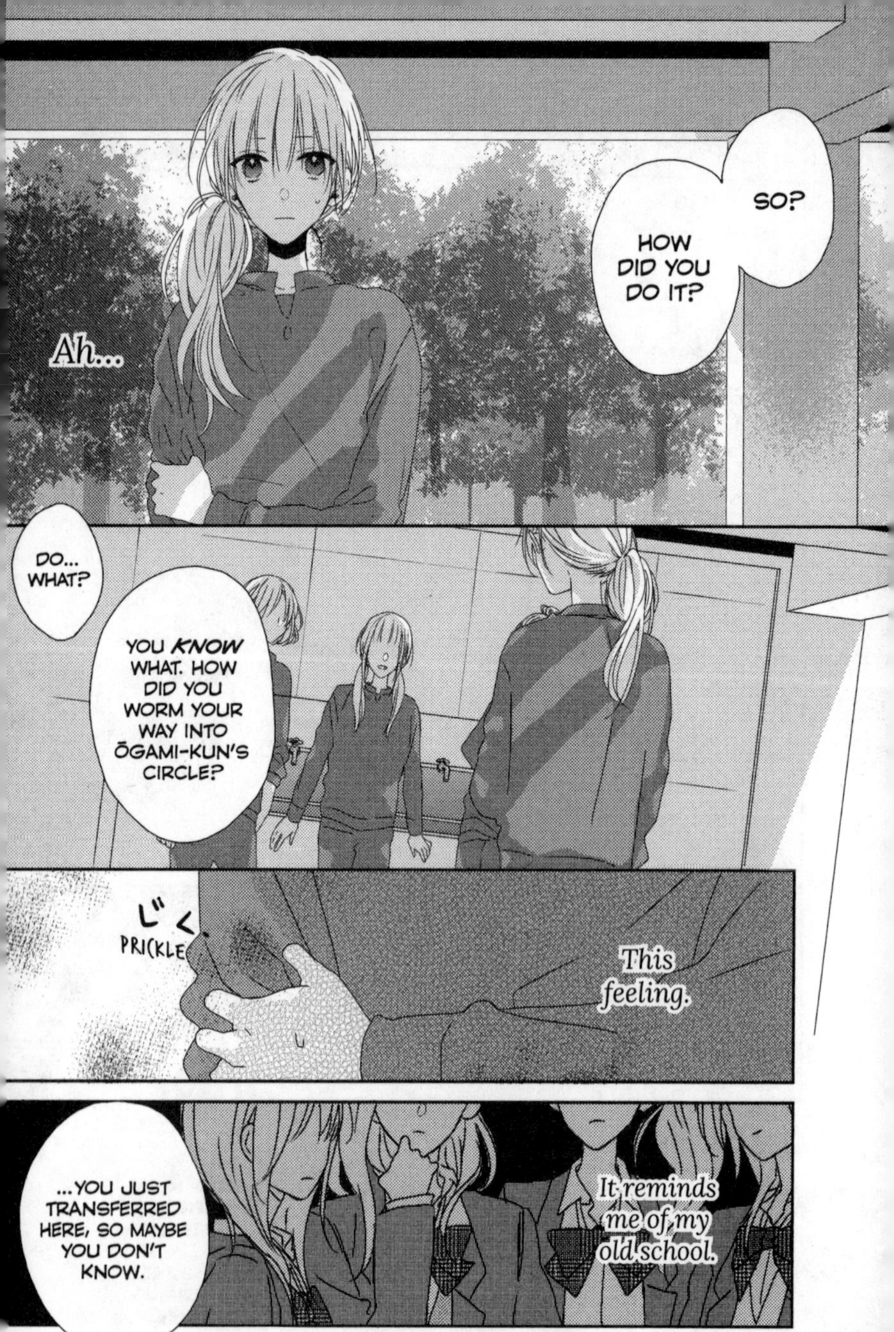
SO? HOW DID YOU DO IT?
Ah...
DO... WHAT?
YOU *KNOW* WHAT. HOW DID YOU WORM YOUR WAY INTO ŌGAMI-KUN'S CIRCLE?
This feeling.
じく
PRICKLE
It reminds me of my old school.
...YOU JUST TRANSFERRED HERE, SO MAYBE YOU DON'T KNOW.

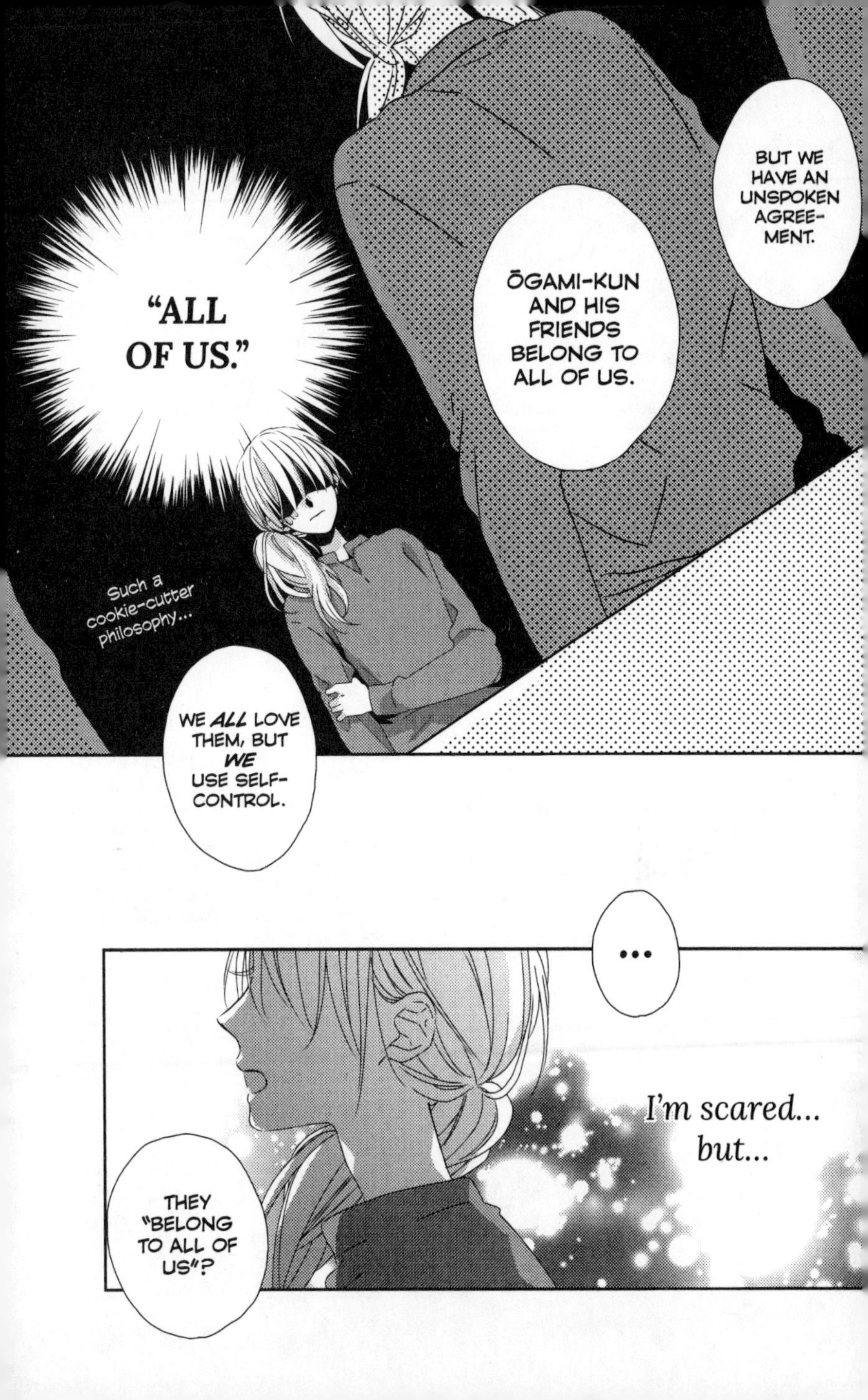
BUT WE HAVE AN UNSPOKEN AGREEMENT.
ŌGAMI-KUN AND HIS FRIENDS BELONG TO ALL OF US.
"ALL OF US."
Such a cookie-cutter philosophy...
WE ALL LOVE THEM, BUT WE USE SELF-CONTROL.
...
I'm scared... but...
THEY "BELONG TO ALL OF US"?

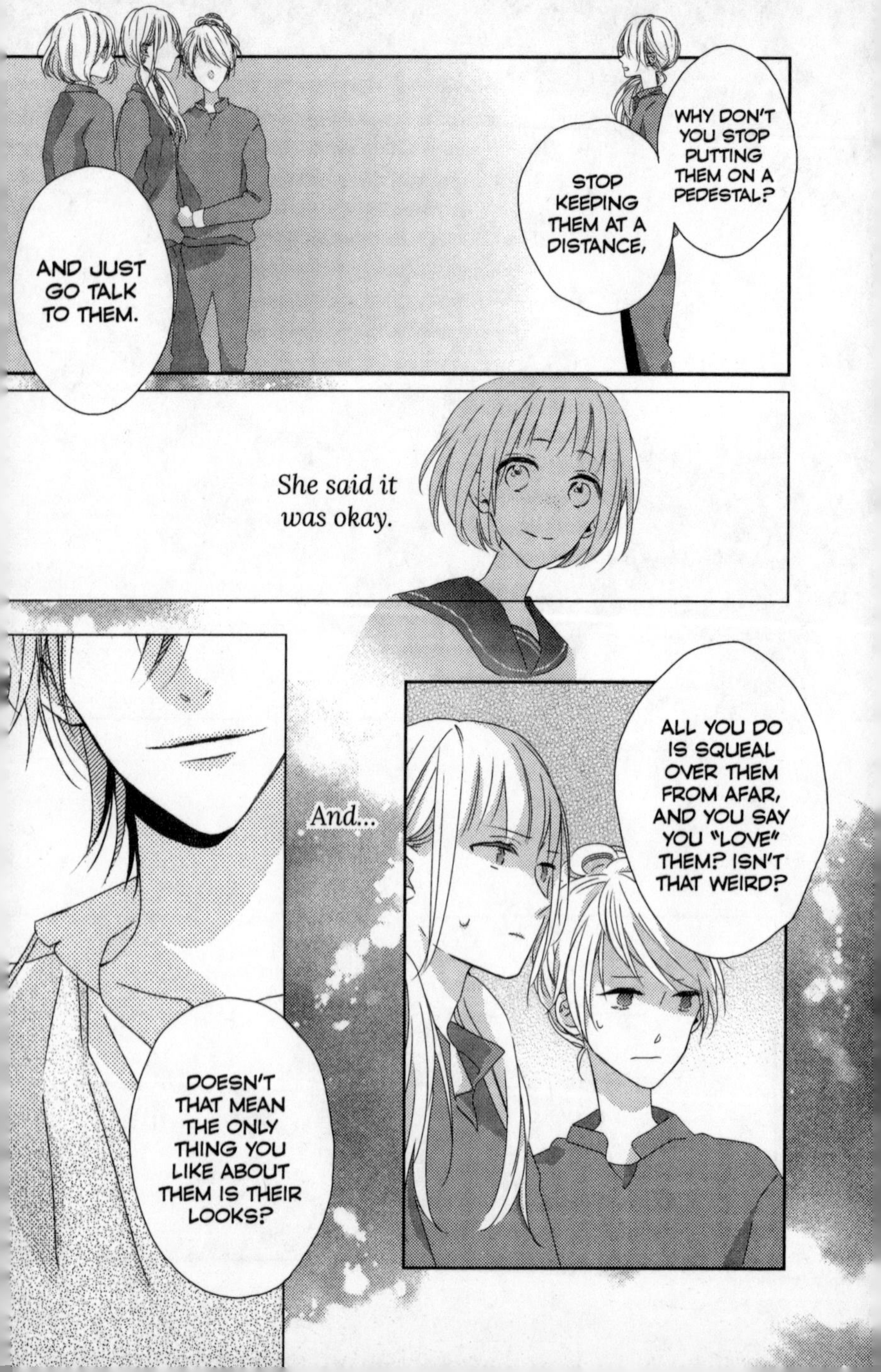
WHY DON'T YOU STOP PUTTING THEM ON A PEDESTAL?
STOP KEEPING THEM AT A DISTANCE,
AND JUST GO TALK TO THEM.
She said it was okay.
ALL YOU DO IS SQUEAL OVER THEM FROM AFAR, AND YOU SAY YOU "LOVE" THEM? ISN'T THAT WEIRD?
And...
DOESN'T THAT MEAN THE ONLY THING YOU LIKE ABOUT THEM IS THEIR LOOKS?

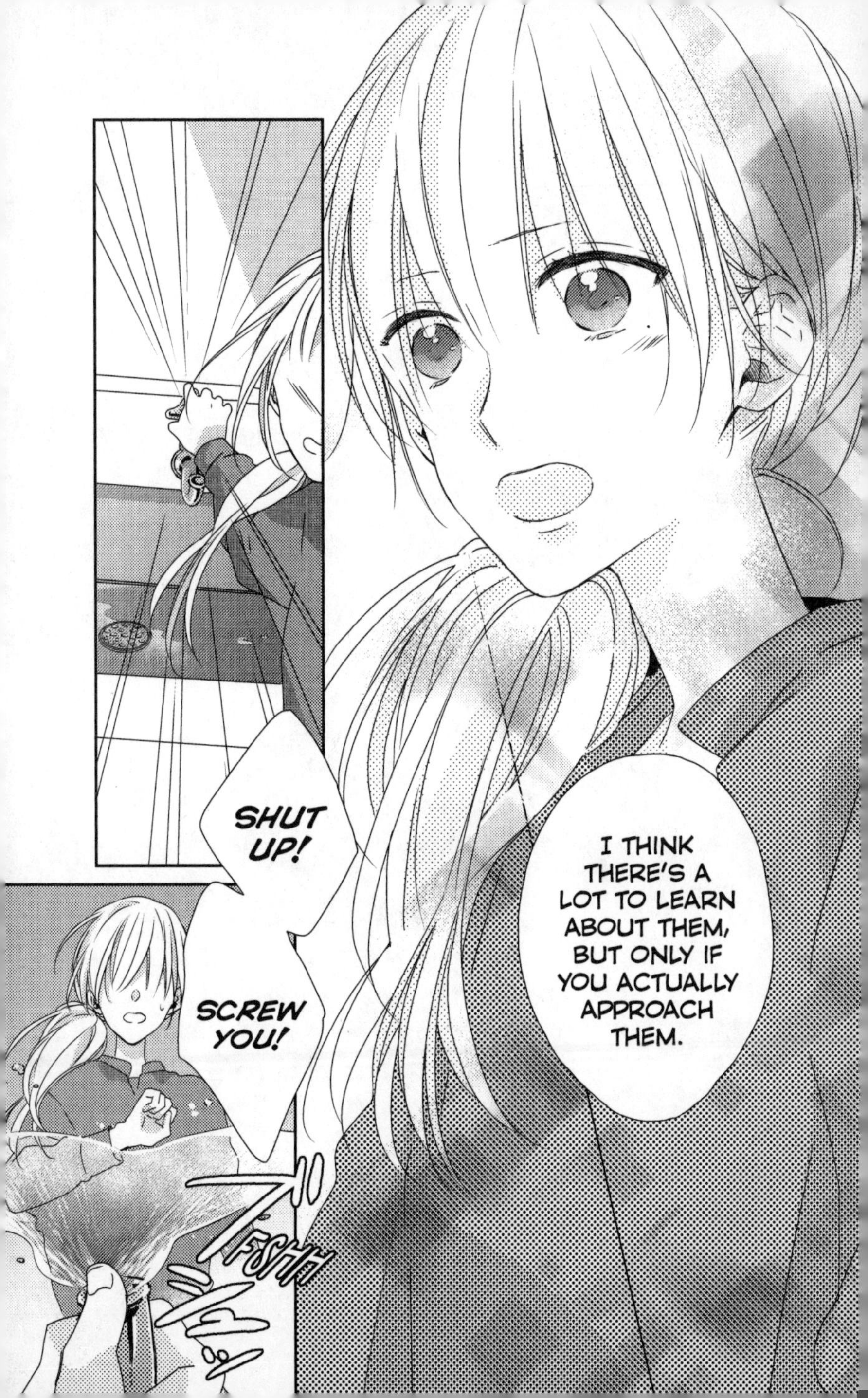
I THINK THERE'S A LOT TO LEARN ABOUT THEM, BUT ONLY IF YOU ACTUALLY APPROACH THEM.
SHUT UP!
SCREW YOU!
FSHH

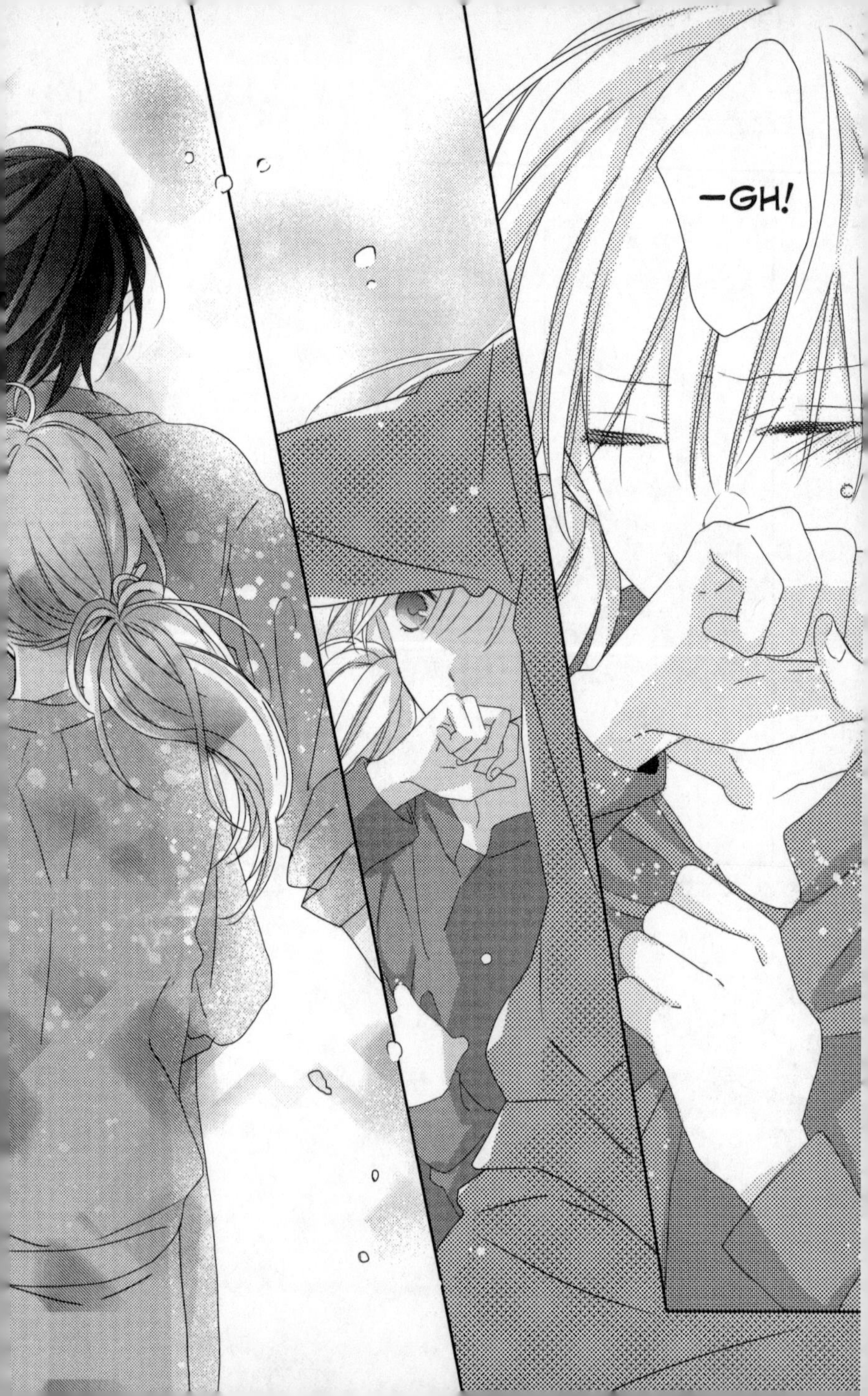
-GH!

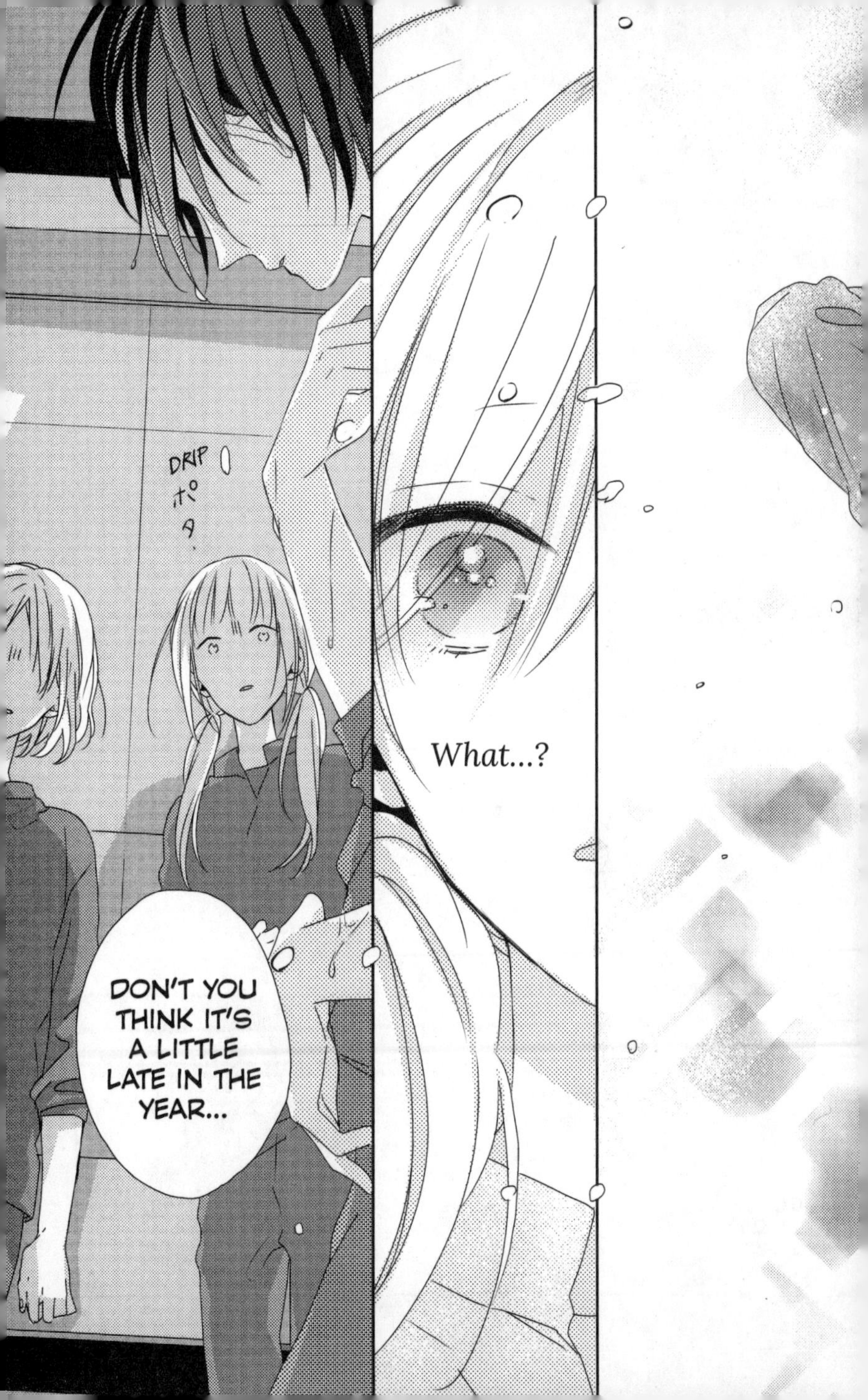
What...?
DRIP ポタ
DON'T YOU THINK IT'S A LITTLE LATE IN THE YEAR...

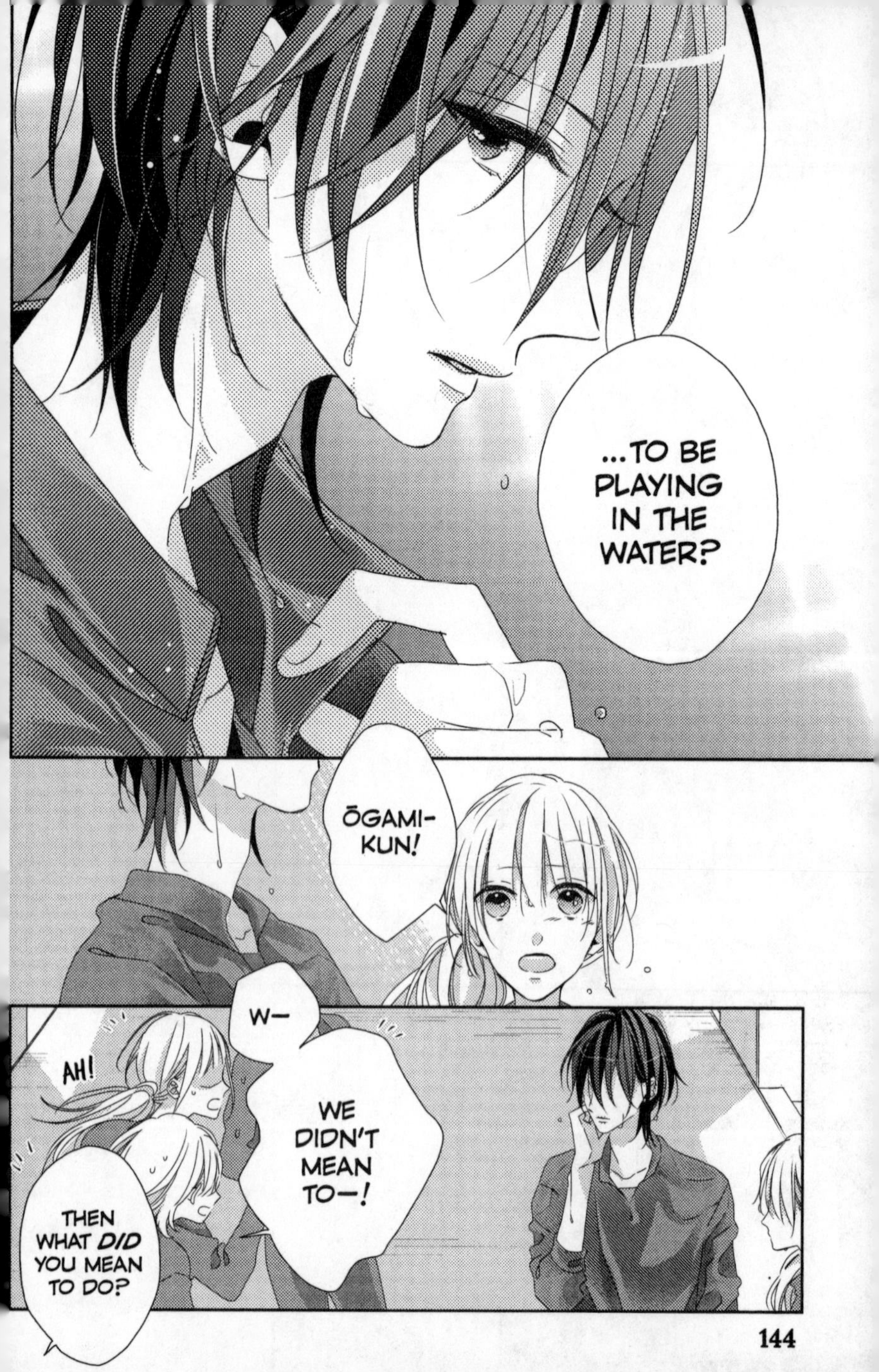
...TO BE PLAYING IN THE WATER?
ŌGAMI-KUN!
W—
WE DIDN'T MEAN TO—!
AH!
THEN WHAT *DID* YOU MEAN TO DO?

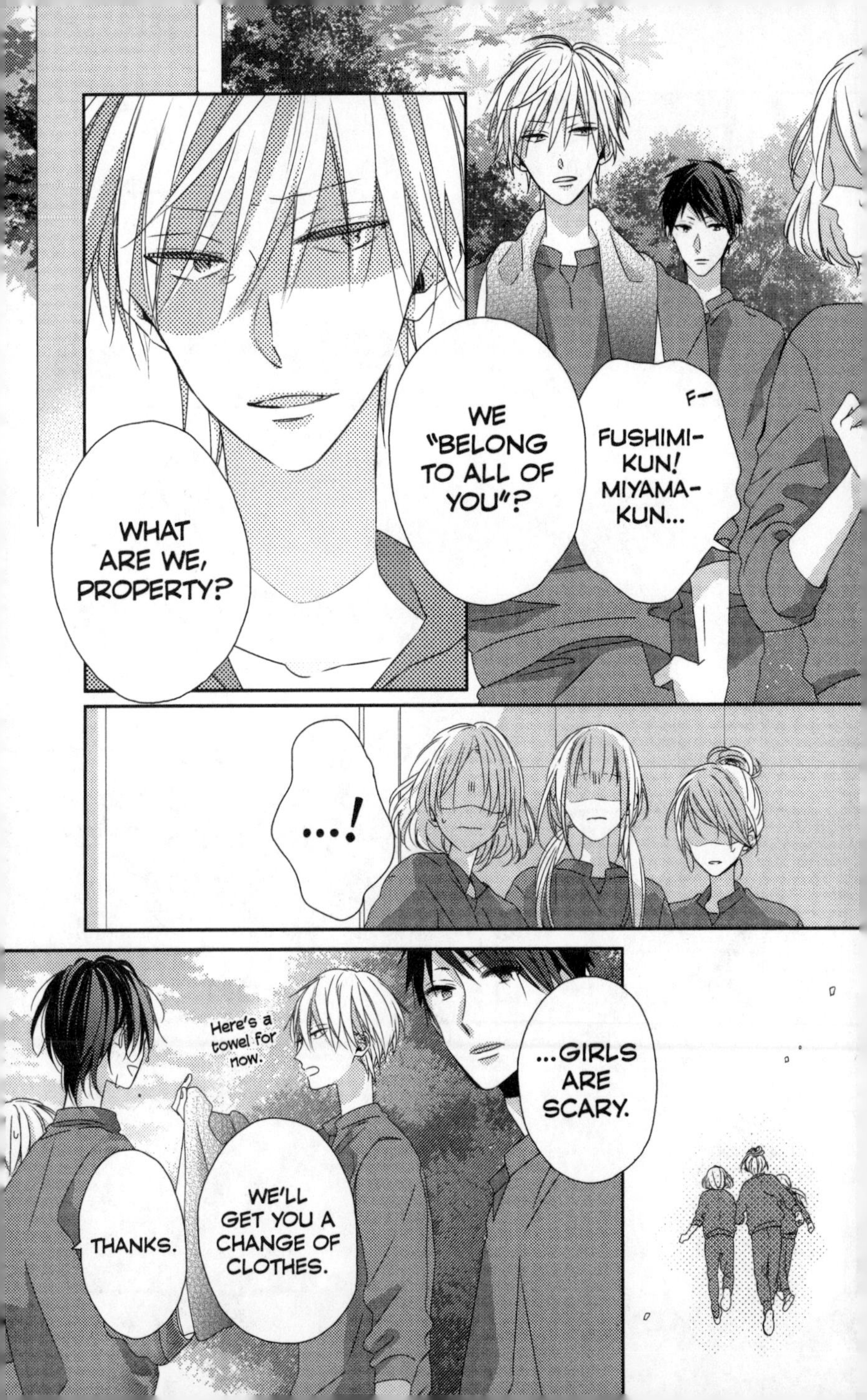
F— FUSHIMI-KUN! MIYAMA-KUN...
WE "BELONG TO ALL OF YOU"?
WHAT ARE WE, PROPERTY?
...!
...GIRLS ARE SCARY.
Here's a towel for now.
WE'LL GET YOU A CHANGE OF CLOTHES.
THANKS.

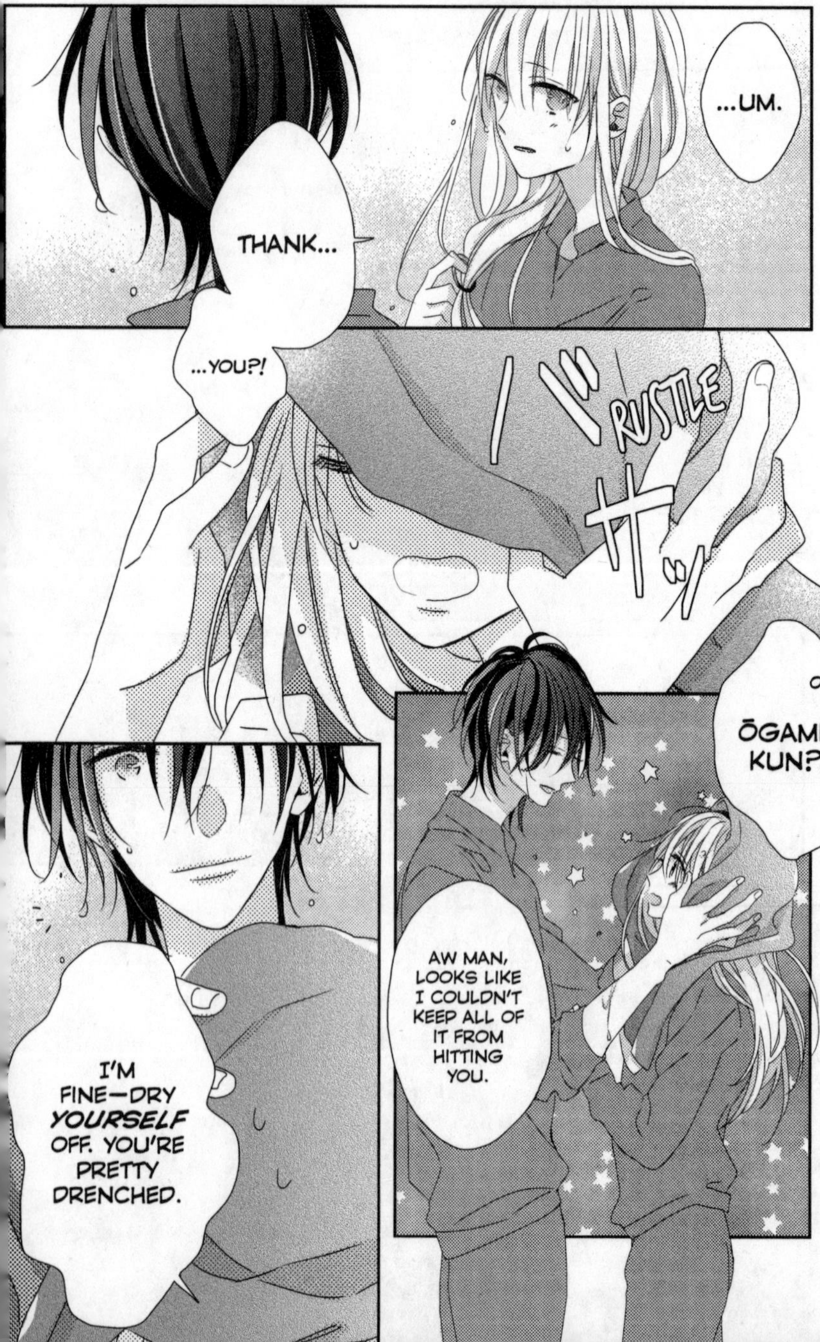
...UM.
THANK...
...YOU?!
RUSTLE
O- ŌGAMI-KUN?!
AW MAN, LOOKS LIKE I COULDN'T KEEP ALL OF IT FROM HITTING YOU.
I'M FINE—DRY *YOURSELF* OFF. YOU'RE PRETTY DRENCHED.

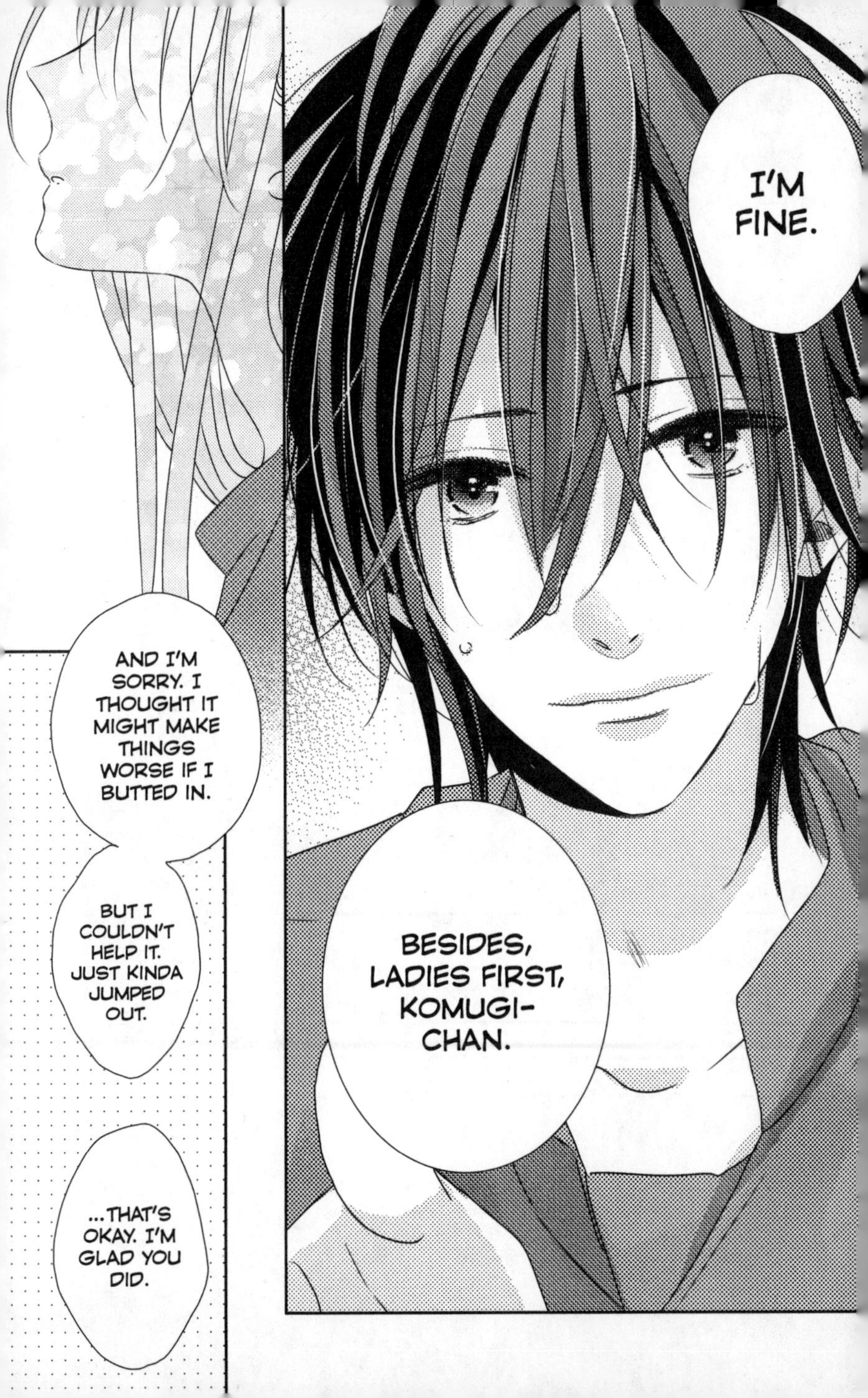
I'M FINE.
BESIDES, LADIES FIRST, KOMUGI-CHAN.
AND I'M SORRY. I THOUGHT IT MIGHT MAKE THINGS WORSE IF I BUTTED IN.
BUT I COULDN'T HELP IT. JUST KINDA JUMPED OUT.
...THAT'S OKAY. I'M GLAD YOU DID.

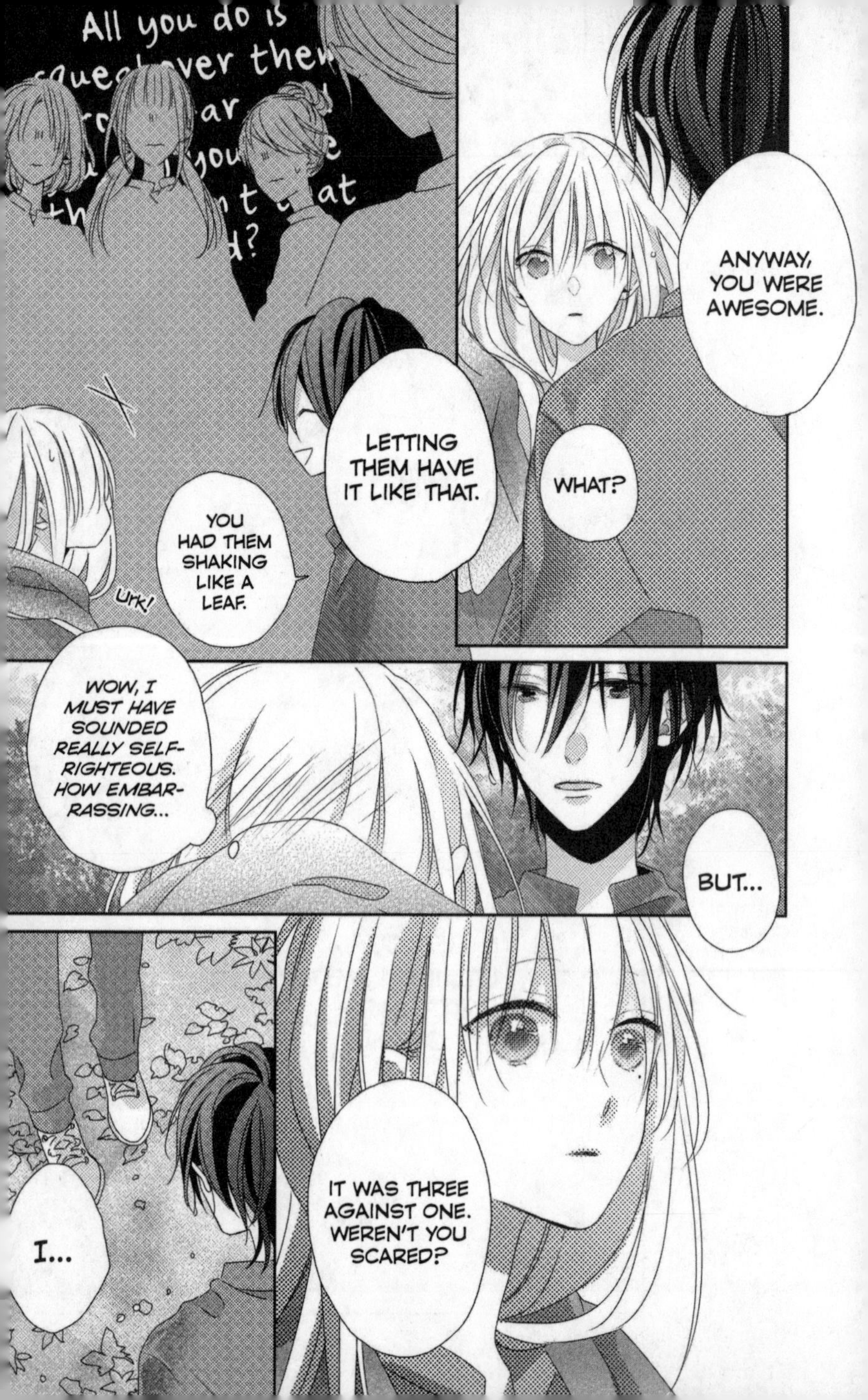
ANYWAY, YOU WERE AWESOME.
WHAT?
All you do is
LETTING THEM HAVE IT LIKE THAT.
YOU HAD THEM SHAKING LIKE A LEAF.
Urk!
WOW, I MUST HAVE SOUNDED REALLY SELF-RIGHTEOUS. HOW EMBARRASSING...
BUT...
IT WAS THREE AGAINST ONE. WEREN'T YOU SCARED?
I...

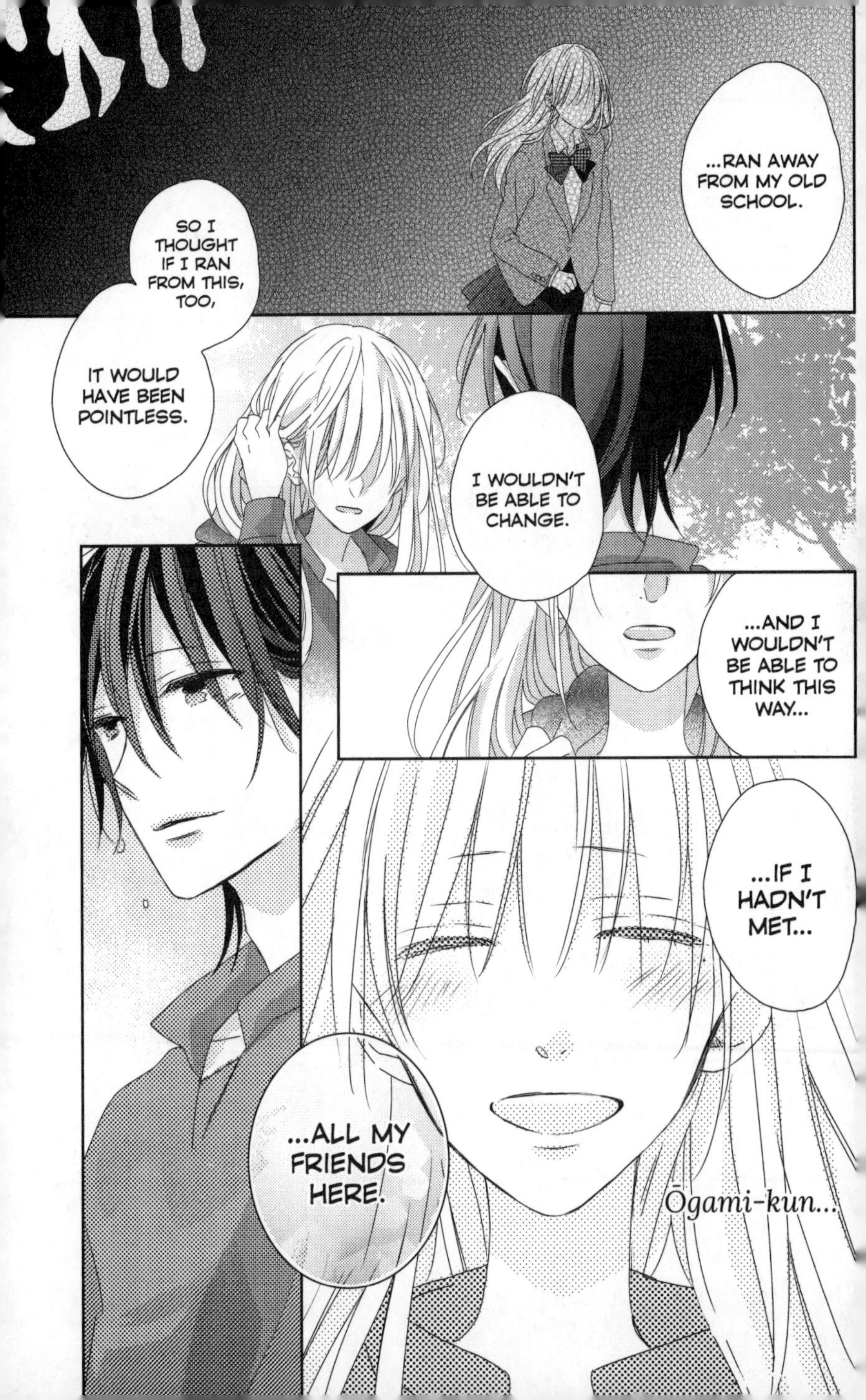
...RAN AWAY FROM MY OLD SCHOOL.
SO I THOUGHT IF I RAN FROM THIS, TOO,
IT WOULD HAVE BEEN POINTLESS.
I WOULDN'T BE ABLE TO CHANGE.
...AND I WOULDN'T BE ABLE TO THINK THIS WAY...
...IF I HADN'T MET...
...ALL MY FRIENDS HERE.
Ōgami-kun...

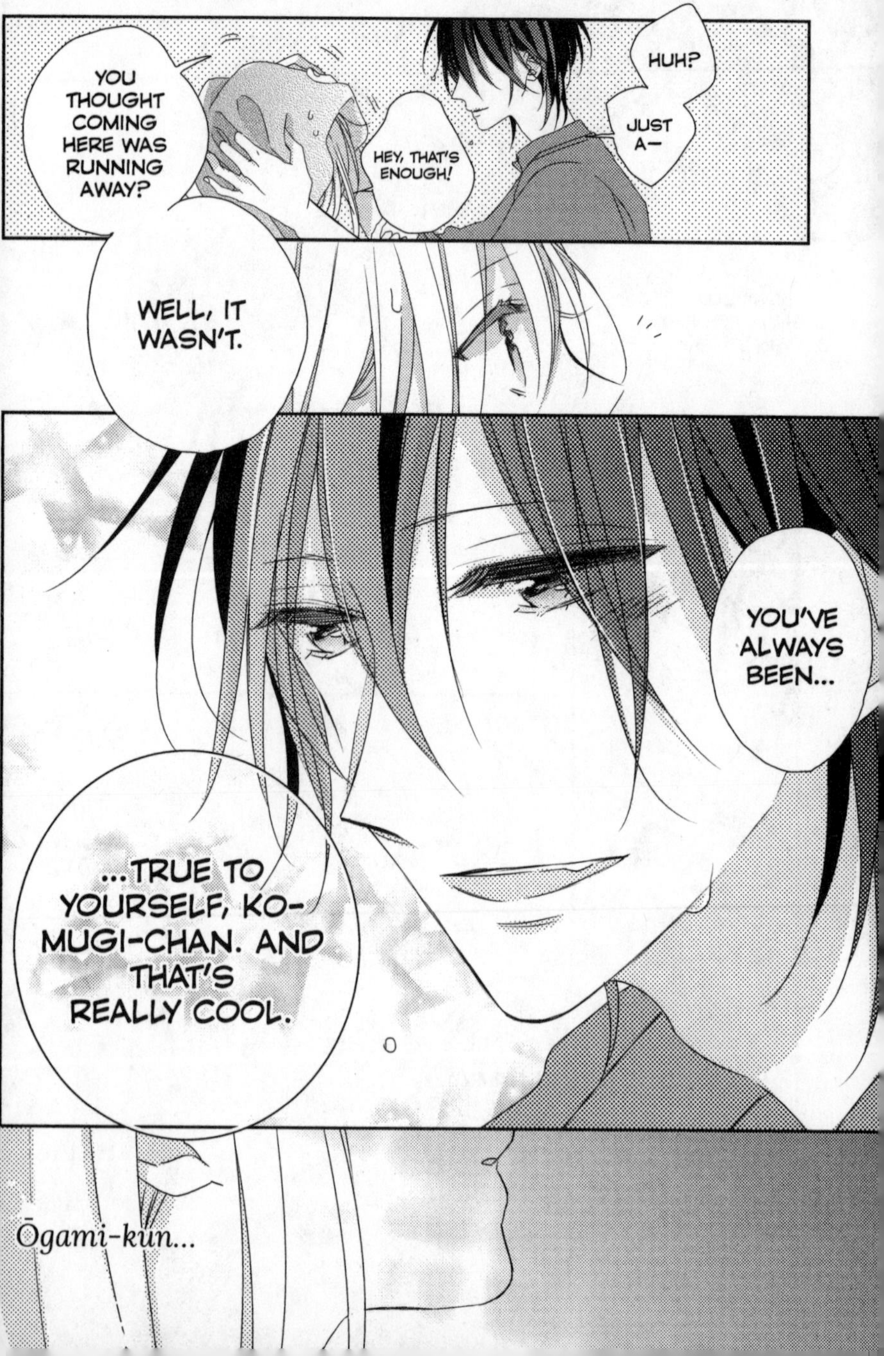
HUH?
JUST A—
HEY, THAT'S ENOUGH!
YOU THOUGHT COMING HERE WAS RUNNING AWAY?
WELL, IT WASN'T.
YOU'VE ALWAYS BEEN...
...TRUE TO YOURSELF, KO-MUGI-CHAN. AND THAT'S REALLY COOL.
Ōgami-kun...

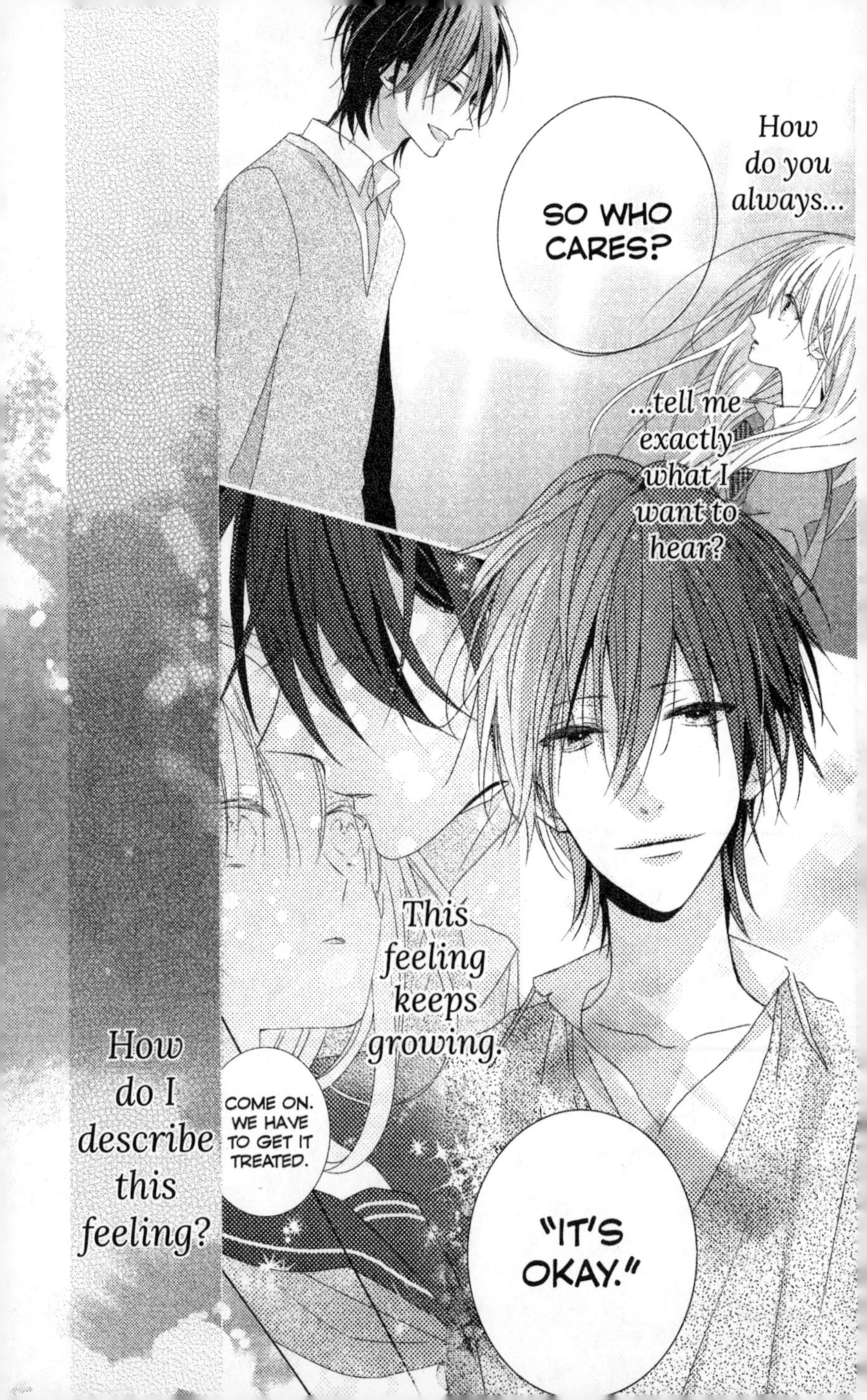
How do you always...
SO WHO CARES?
...tell me exactly what I want to hear?
This feeling keeps growing.
"IT'S OKAY."
COME ON. WE HAVE TO GET IT TREATED.
How do I describe this feeling?

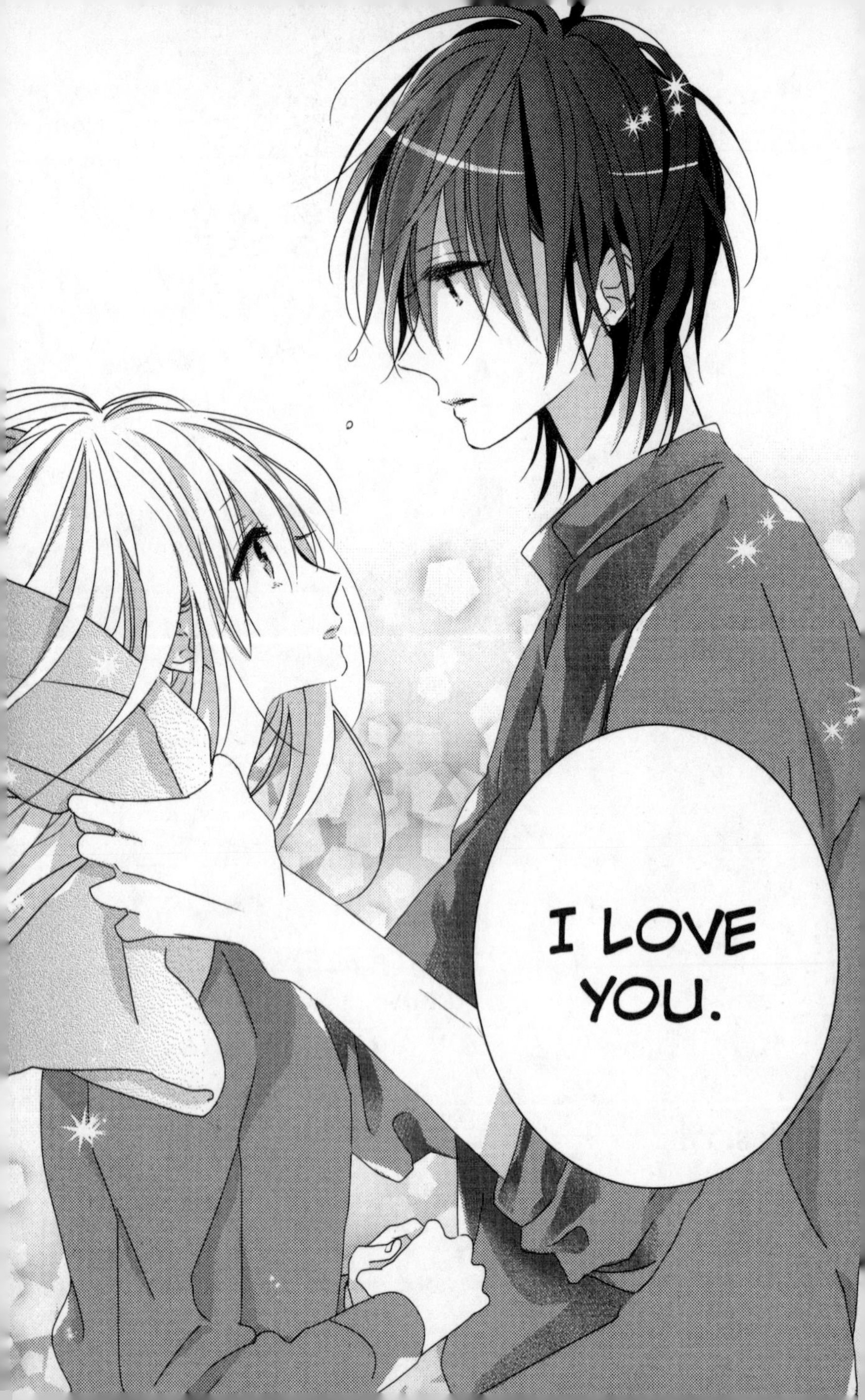
I LOVE YOU.

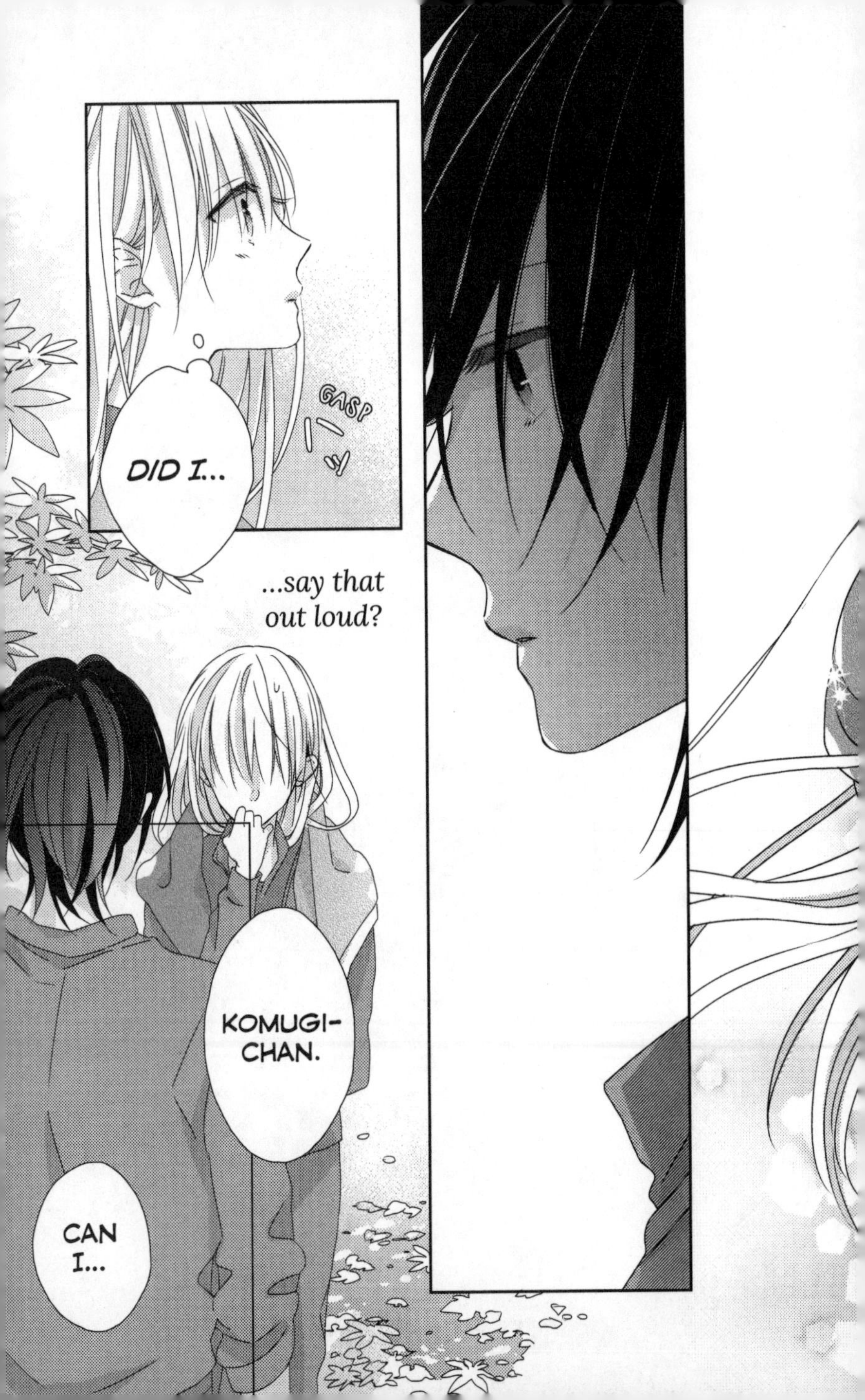
GASP
DID I...
...say that out loud?
KOMUGI-CHAN.
CAN I...

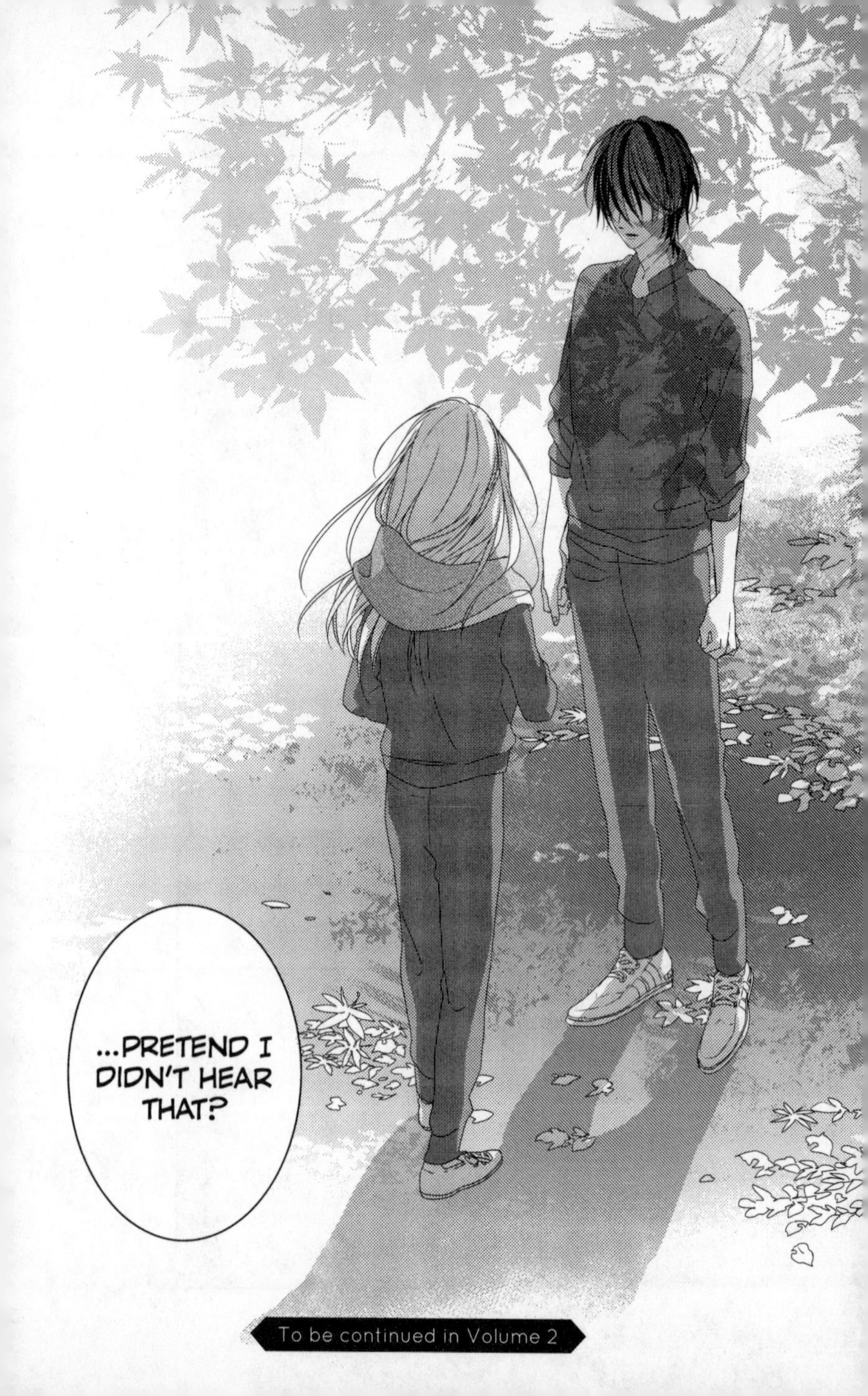
...PRETEND I DIDN'T HEAR THAT?
To be continued in Volume 2

That Wolf-Boy is Mine!

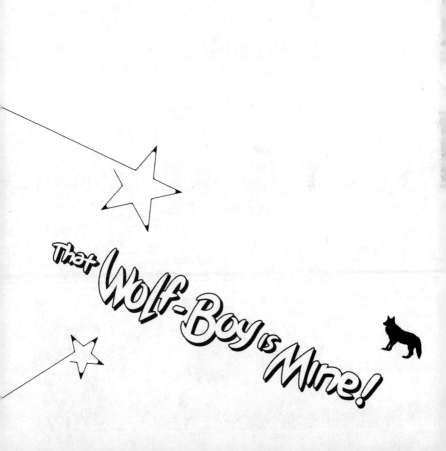

That Wolf-Boy is Mine! Volume 1 Bonus Pages

At Ōgami-kun and his friends' temporary residence,

Ayashi Inn,

Kita-san the kita-kitsune* (cop-out name)...

...is the live-in maid.

*Japanese for Red fox

(Cleaning the Bath)

But when there's no school, the boys take turns doing the chores.

SQUIK SQUIK

	Meals	Cleaning	Laundry	Of
First Sunday	Yū	Aoshi	Rin	S
Second	Senri	Yū	Aoshi	R
Third	Rin	Senri	Yū	Ao
			Senri	Yū

FIP

HEY, HEY.

Z z z

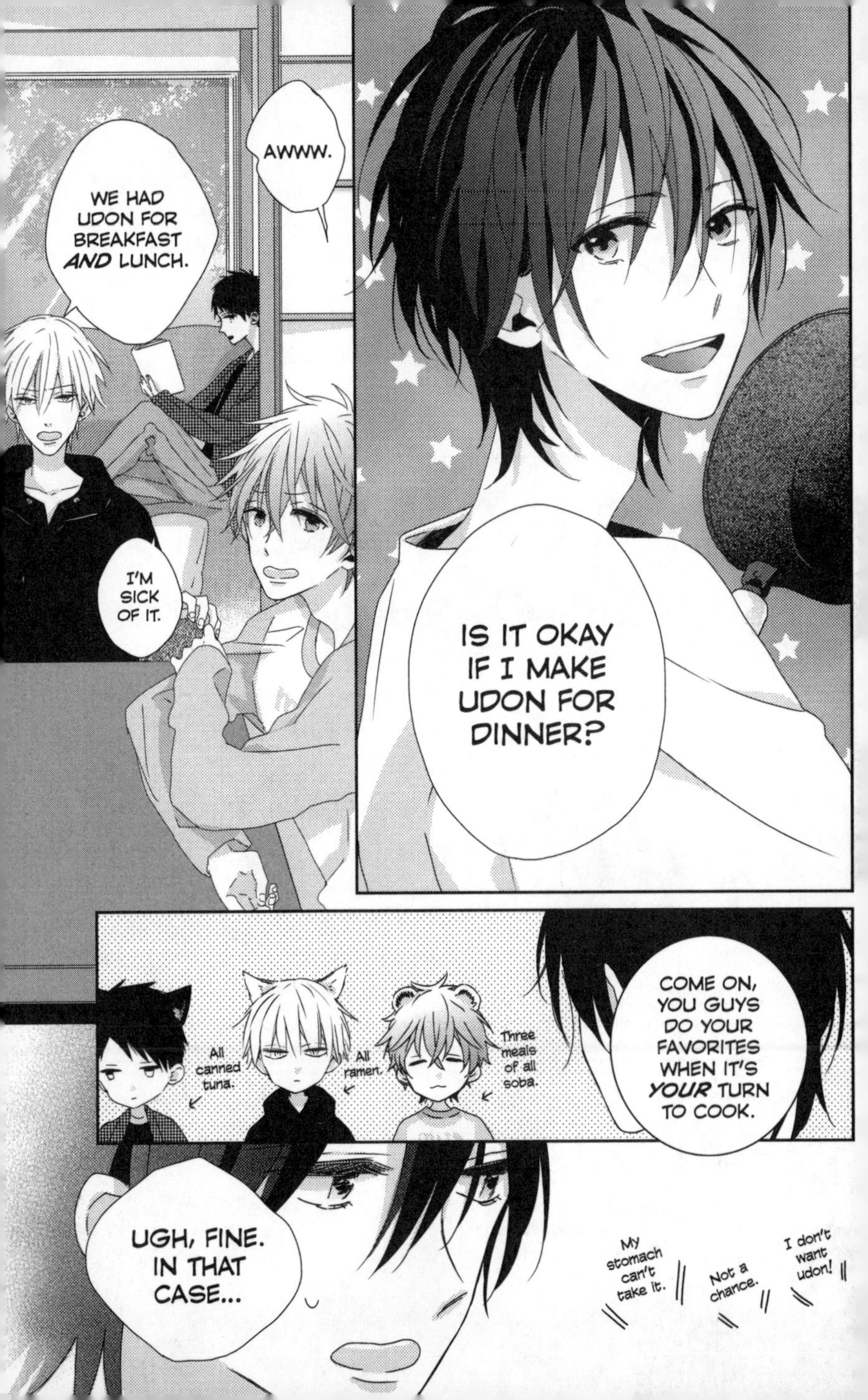
IS IT OKAY IF I MAKE UDON FOR DINNER?
AWWW.
WE HAD UDON FOR BREAKFAST *AND* LUNCH.
I'M SICK OF IT.
COME ON, YOU GUYS DO YOUR FAVORITES WHEN IT'S *YOUR* TURN TO COOK.
Three meals of all soba.
All ramen.
All canned tuna.
I don't want udon!
Not a chance.
My stomach can't take it.
UGH, FINE. IN THAT CASE...

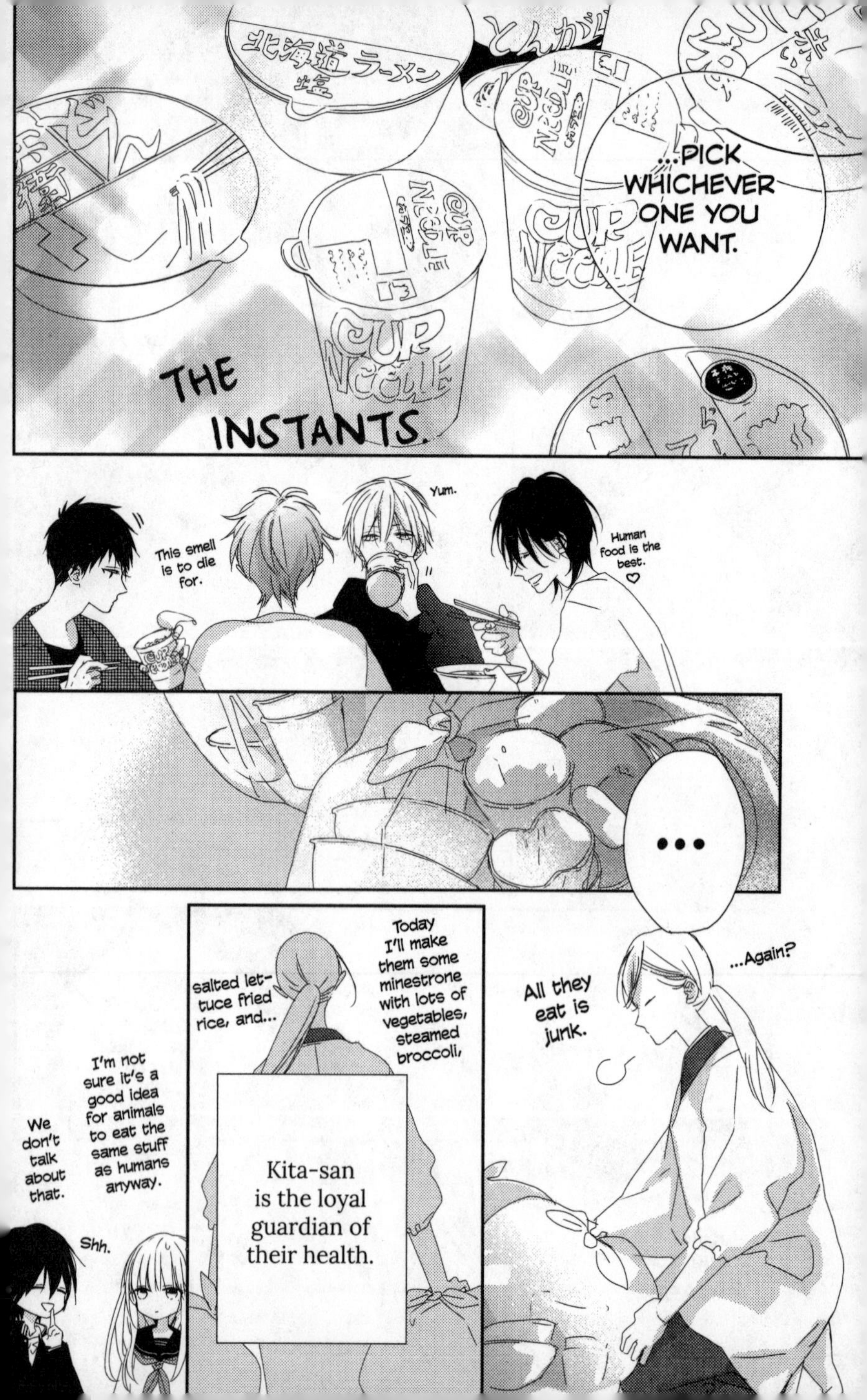

...PICK WHICHEVER ONE YOU WANT.
北海道ラーメン
塩
CUP NOODLE
THE INSTANTS.
Human food is the best. ♡
Yum.
This smell is to die for.
...
...Again?
All they eat is junk.
Today I'll make them some minestrone with lots of vegetables, steamed broccoli,
salted let-tuce fried rice, and...
Kita-san is the loyal guardian of their health.
I'm not sure it's a good idea for animals to eat the same stuff as humans anyway.
We don't talk about that.
Shh.

Afterword

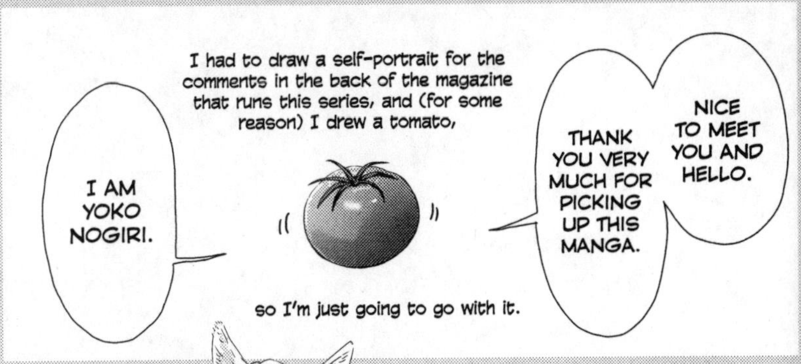
NICE TO MEET YOU AND HELLO.
THANK YOU VERY MUCH FOR PICKING UP THIS MANGA.
I had to draw a self-portrait for the comments in the back of the magazine that runs this series, and (for some reason) I drew a tomato,
I AM YOKO NOGIRI.
so I'm just going to go with it.

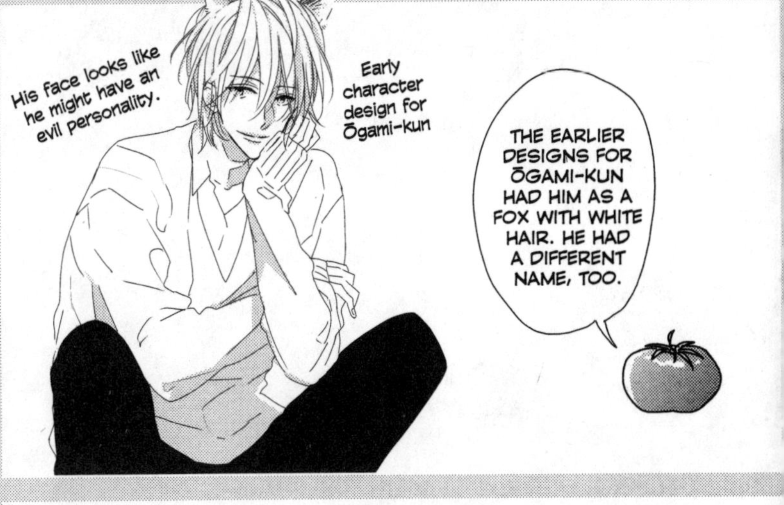
THE EARLIER DESIGNS FOR ŌGAMI-KUN HAD HIM AS A FOX WITH WHITE HAIR. HE HAD A DIFFERENT NAME, TOO.
Early character design for Ōgami-kun
His face looks like he might have an evil personality.

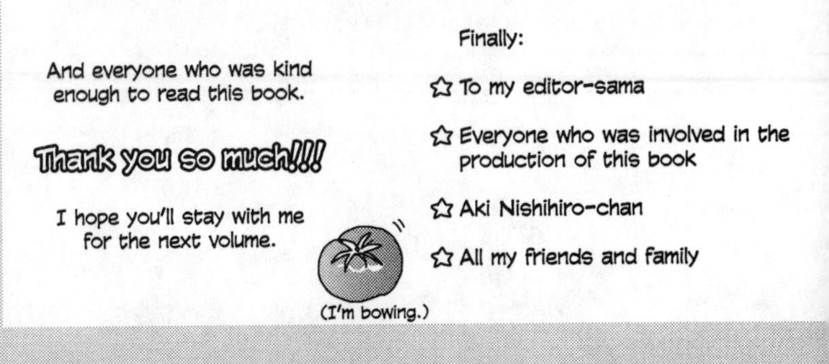
Finally:
☆ To my editor-sama
☆ Everyone who was involved in the production of this book
☆ Aki Nishihiro-chan
☆ All my friends and family
And everyone who was kind enough to read this book.
Thank you so much!!!
I hope you'll stay with me for the next volume.
(I'm bowing.)

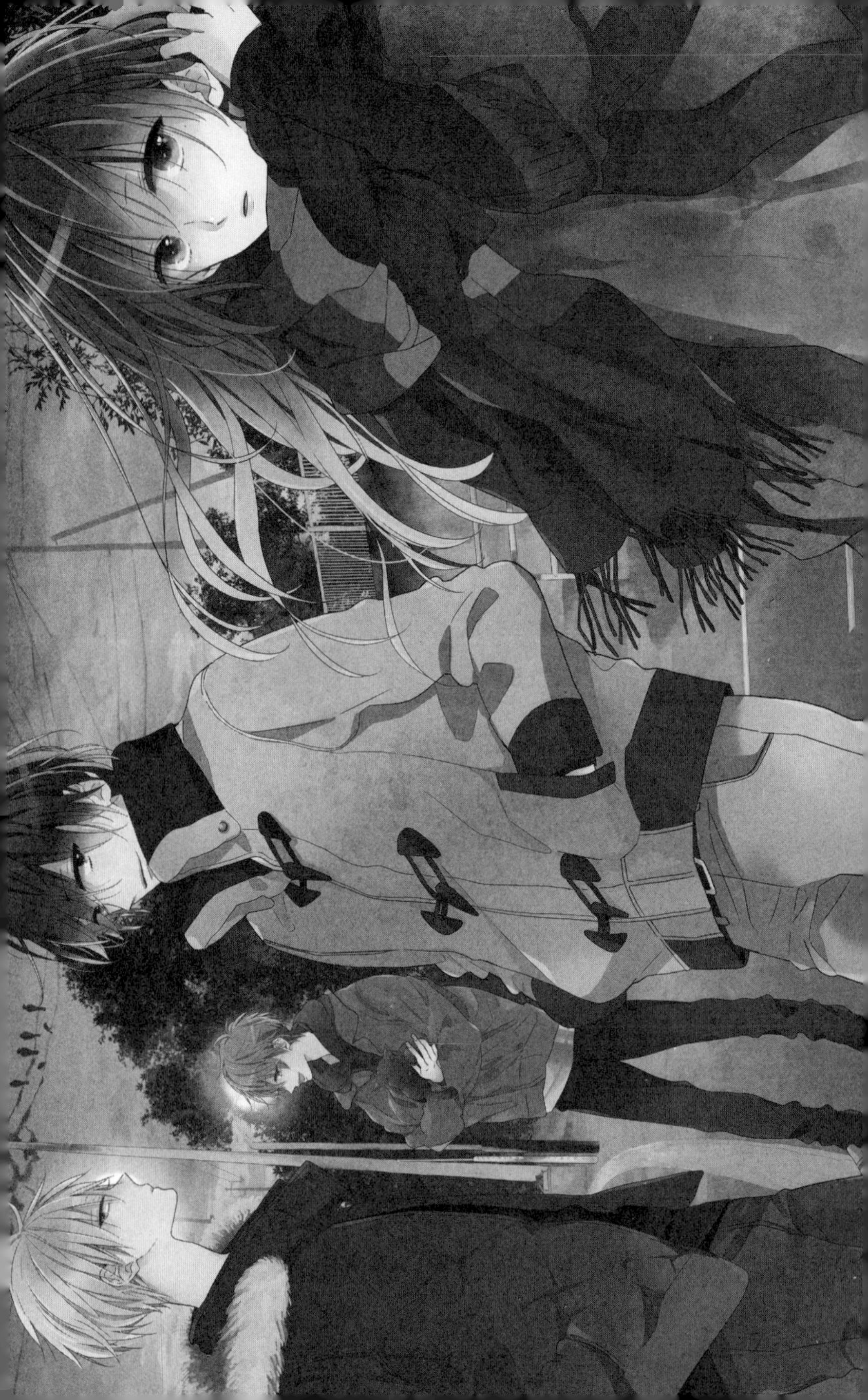

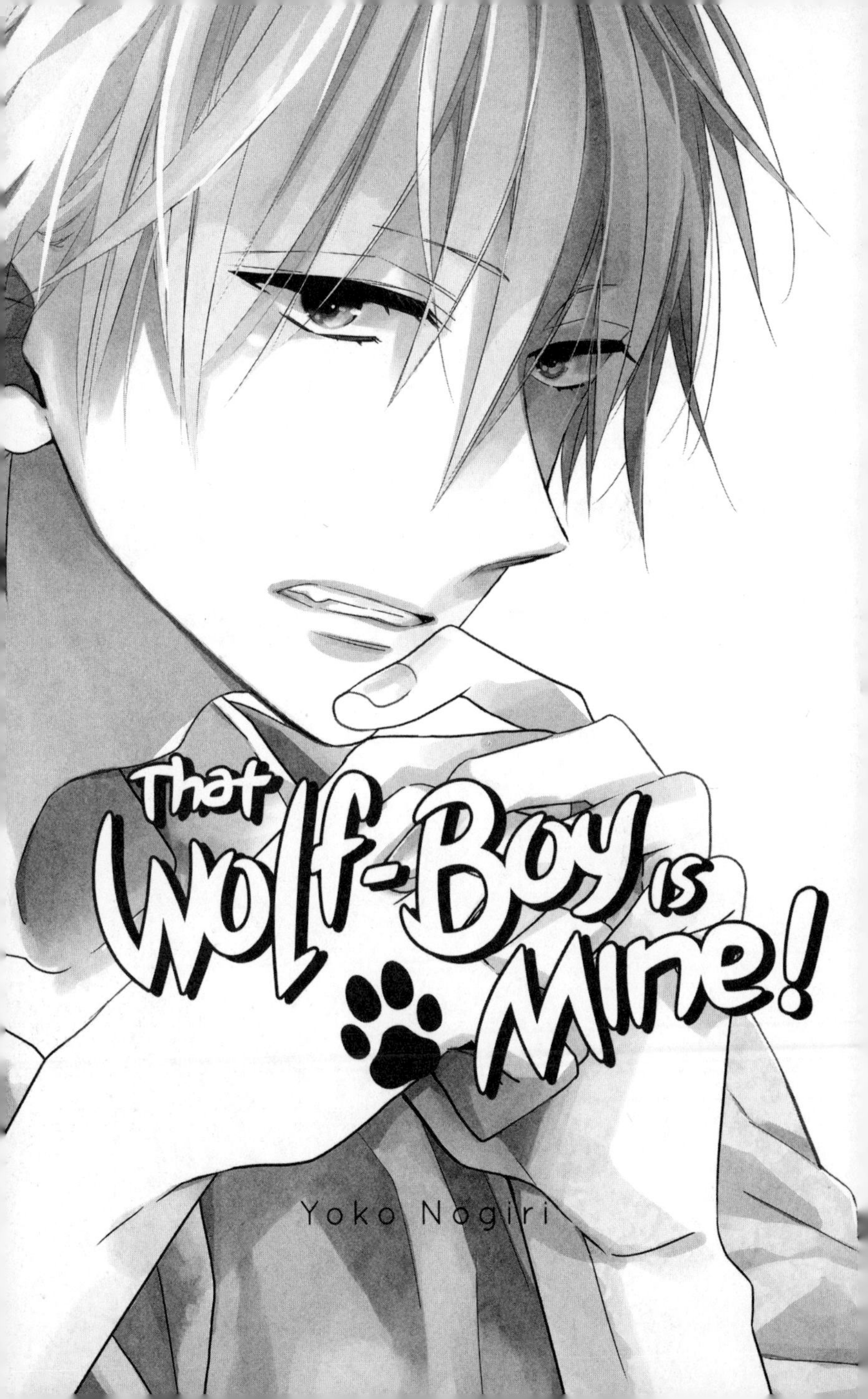
That Wolf-Boy is Mine!
Yoko Nogiri

That Wolf-Boy is Mine!

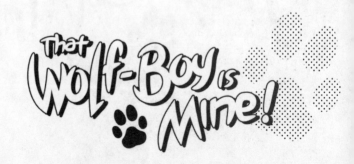

Chapter 5

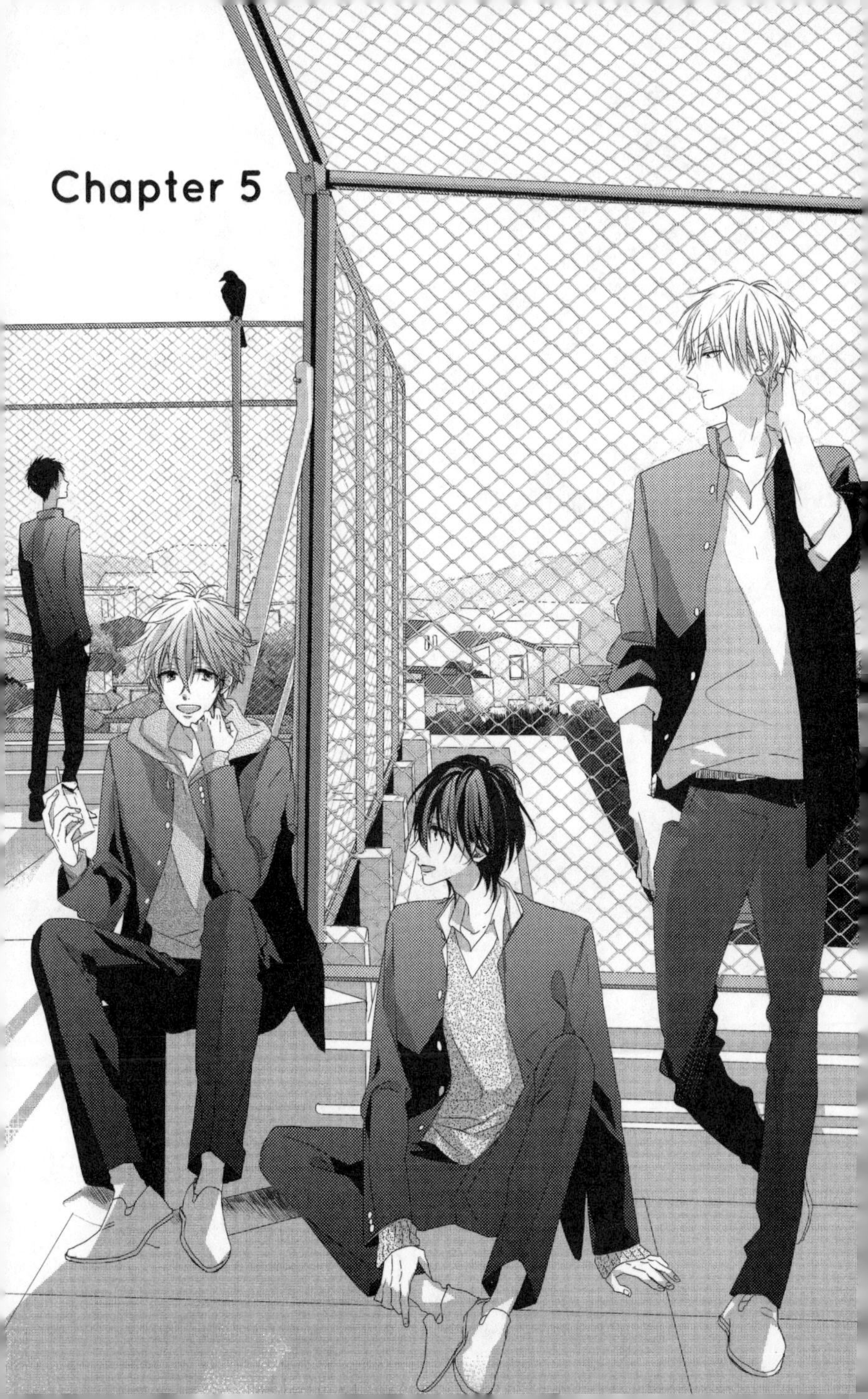

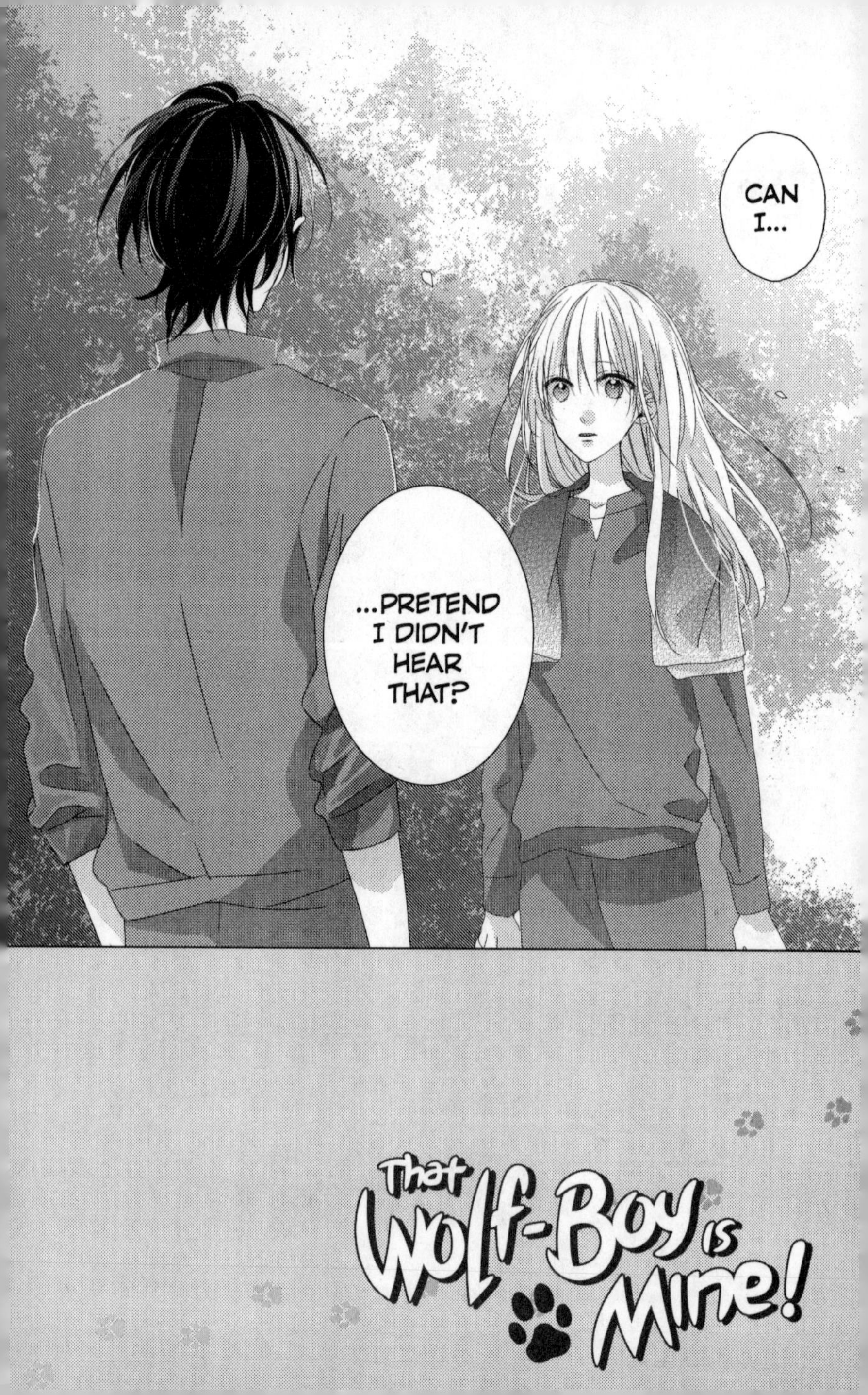
CAN I...
...PRETEND I DIDN'T HEAR THAT?

That Wolf-Boy is Mine!

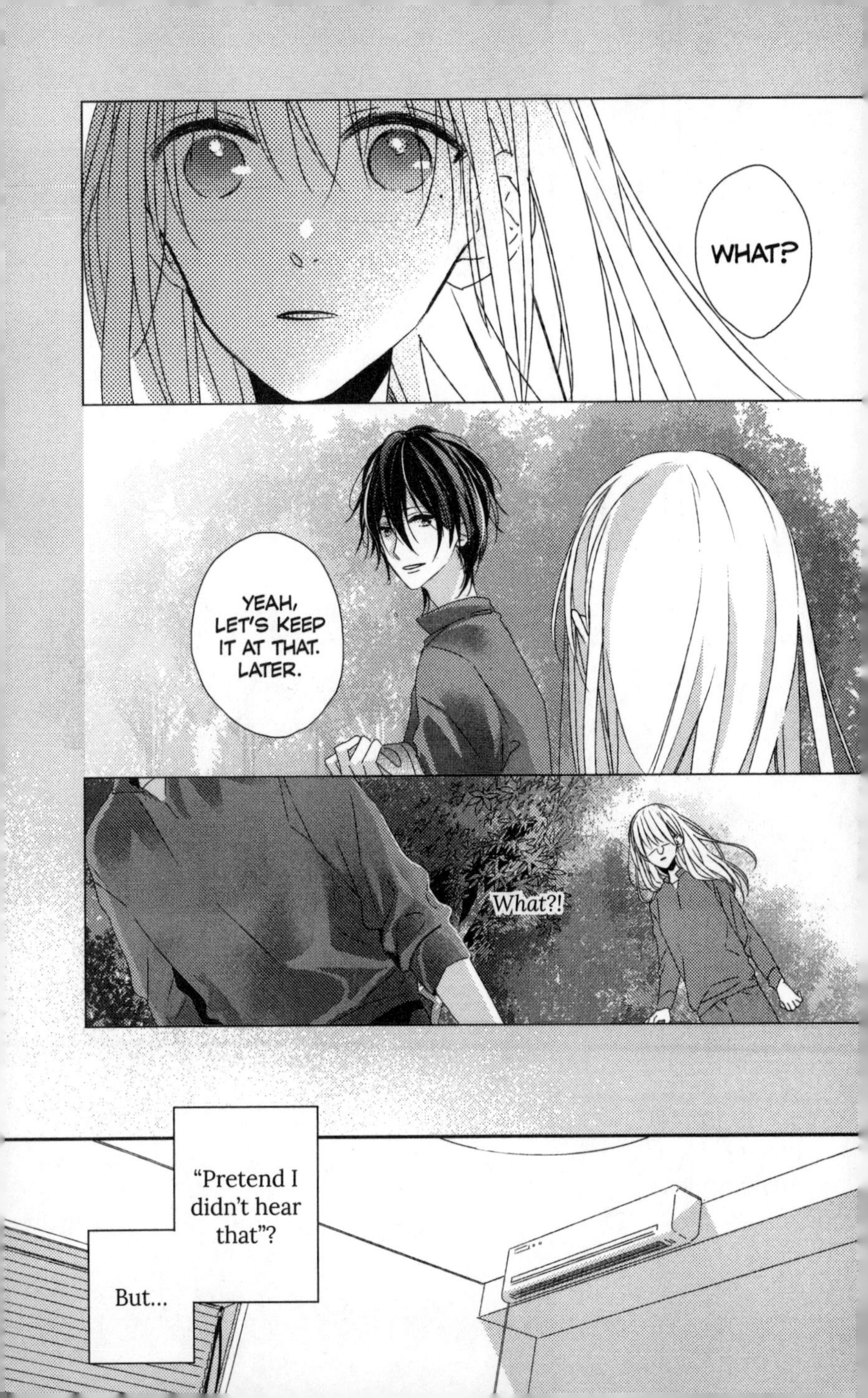
WHAT?
YEAH, LET'S KEEP IT AT THAT. LATER.
What?!
"Pretend I didn't hear that"?
But...

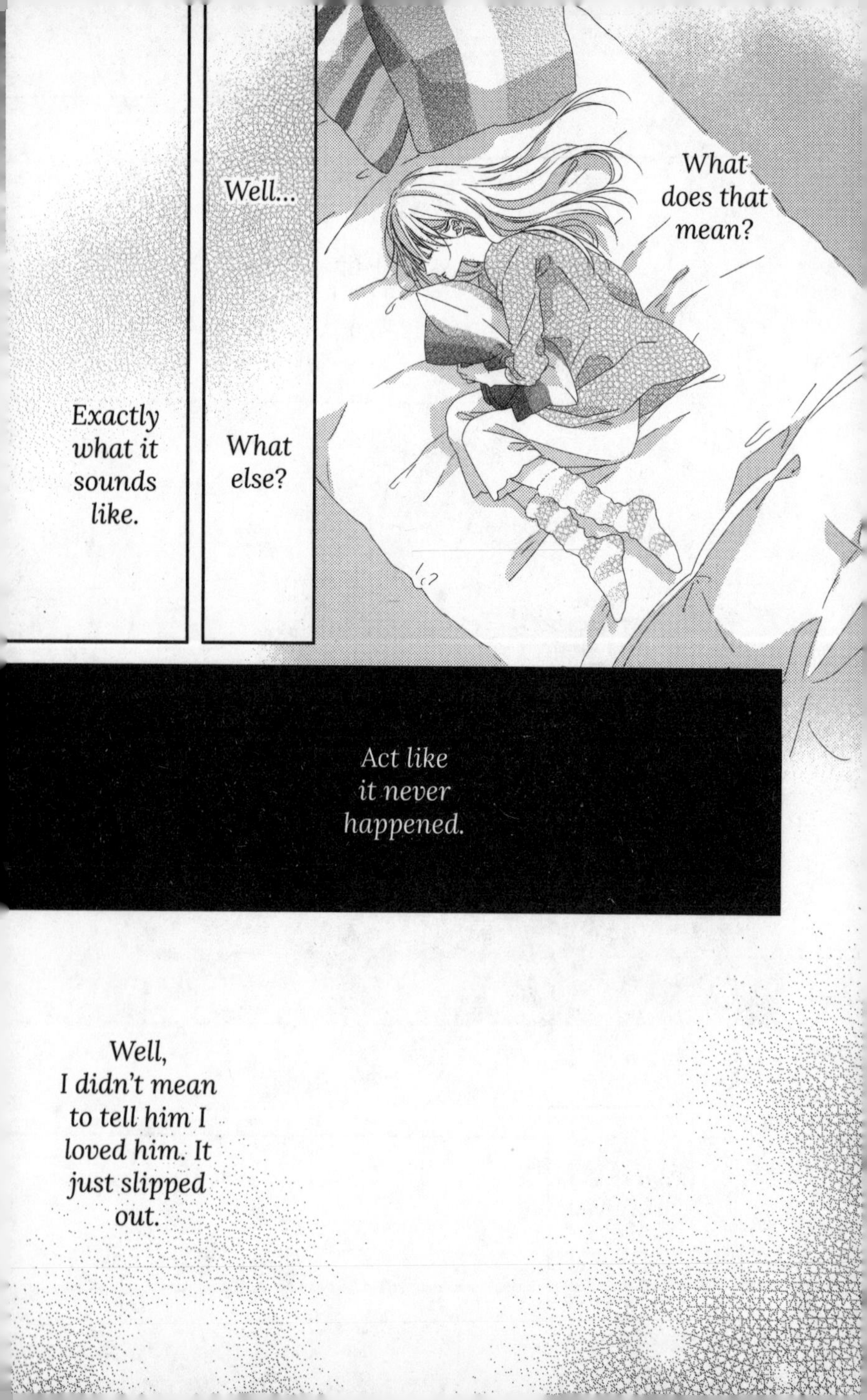
What does that mean?
Well...
What else?
Exactly what it sounds like.
Act like it never happened.
Well, I didn't mean to tell him I loved him. It just slipped out.

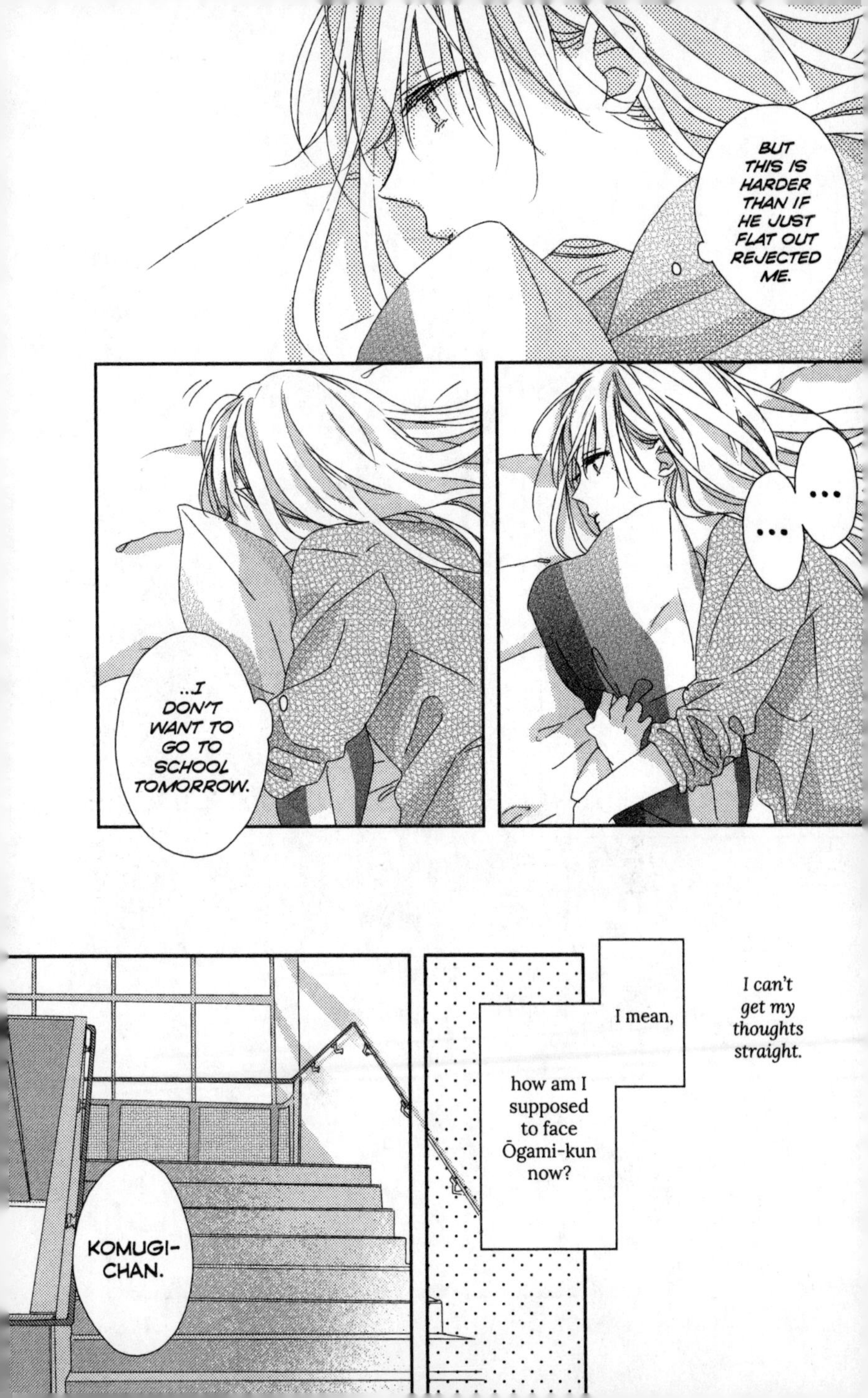
BUT THIS IS HARDER THAN IF HE JUST FLAT OUT REJECTED ME.
... ...
...I DON'T WANT TO GO TO SCHOOL TOMORROW.
I can't get my thoughts straight.
I mean,
how am I supposed to face Ōgami-kun now?
KOMUGI-CHAN.

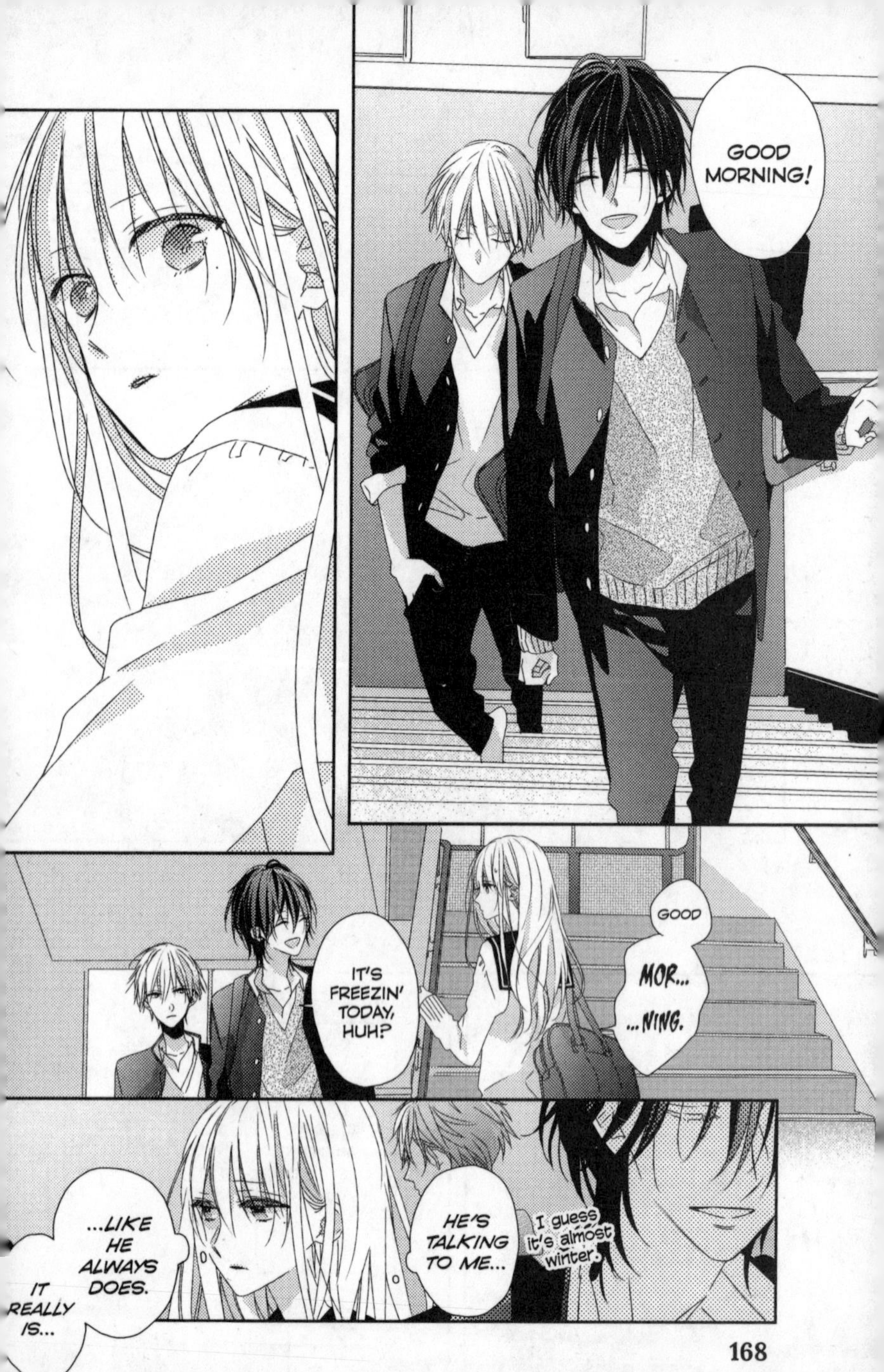
GOOD MORNING!
GOOD
MOR...
...NING.
IT'S FREEZIN' TODAY, HUH?
I guess it's almost winter.
HE'S TALKING TO ME...
...LIKE HE ALWAYS DOES.
IT REALLY IS...

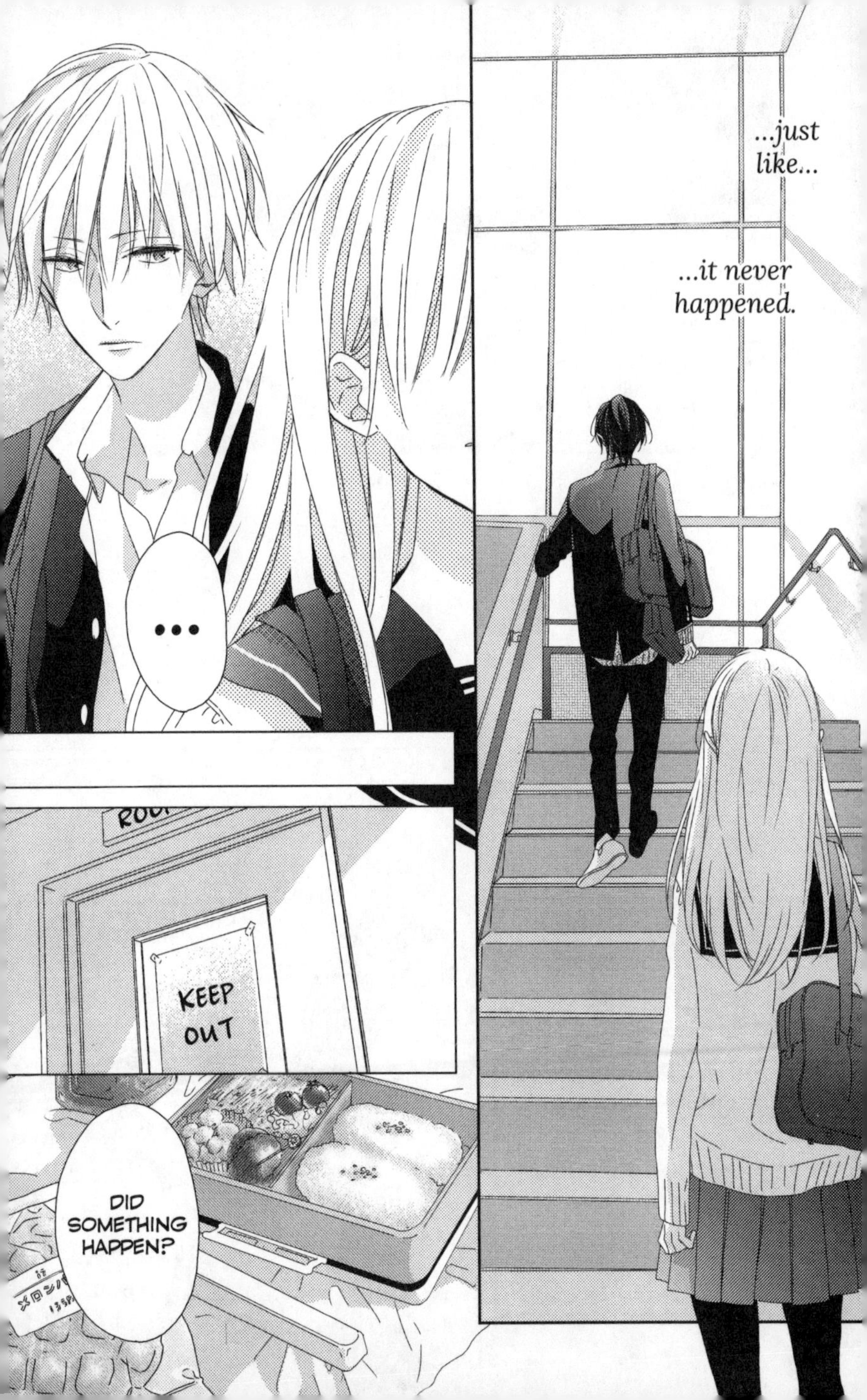
...just like...
...it never happened.
...
KEEP OUT
DID SOMETHING HAPPEN?

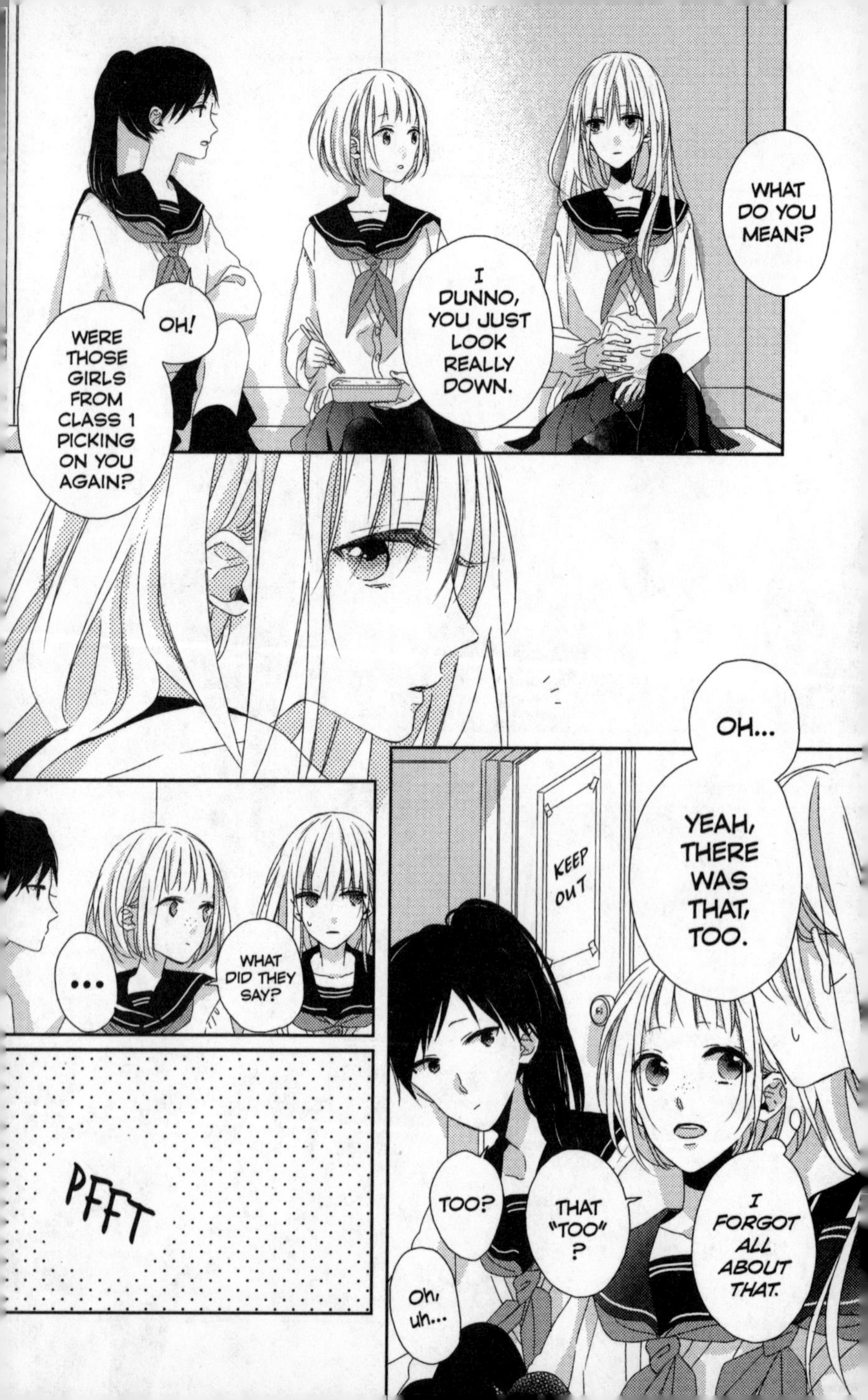
WHAT DO YOU MEAN?
I DUNNO, YOU JUST LOOK REALLY DOWN.
OH!
WERE THOSE GIRLS FROM CLASS 1 PICKING ON YOU AGAIN?
OH...
YEAH, THERE WAS THAT, TOO.
KEEP OUT
I FORGOT ALL ABOUT THAT.
THAT "TOO"?
TOO?
Oh, uh...
WHAT DID THEY SAY?
...
PFFT

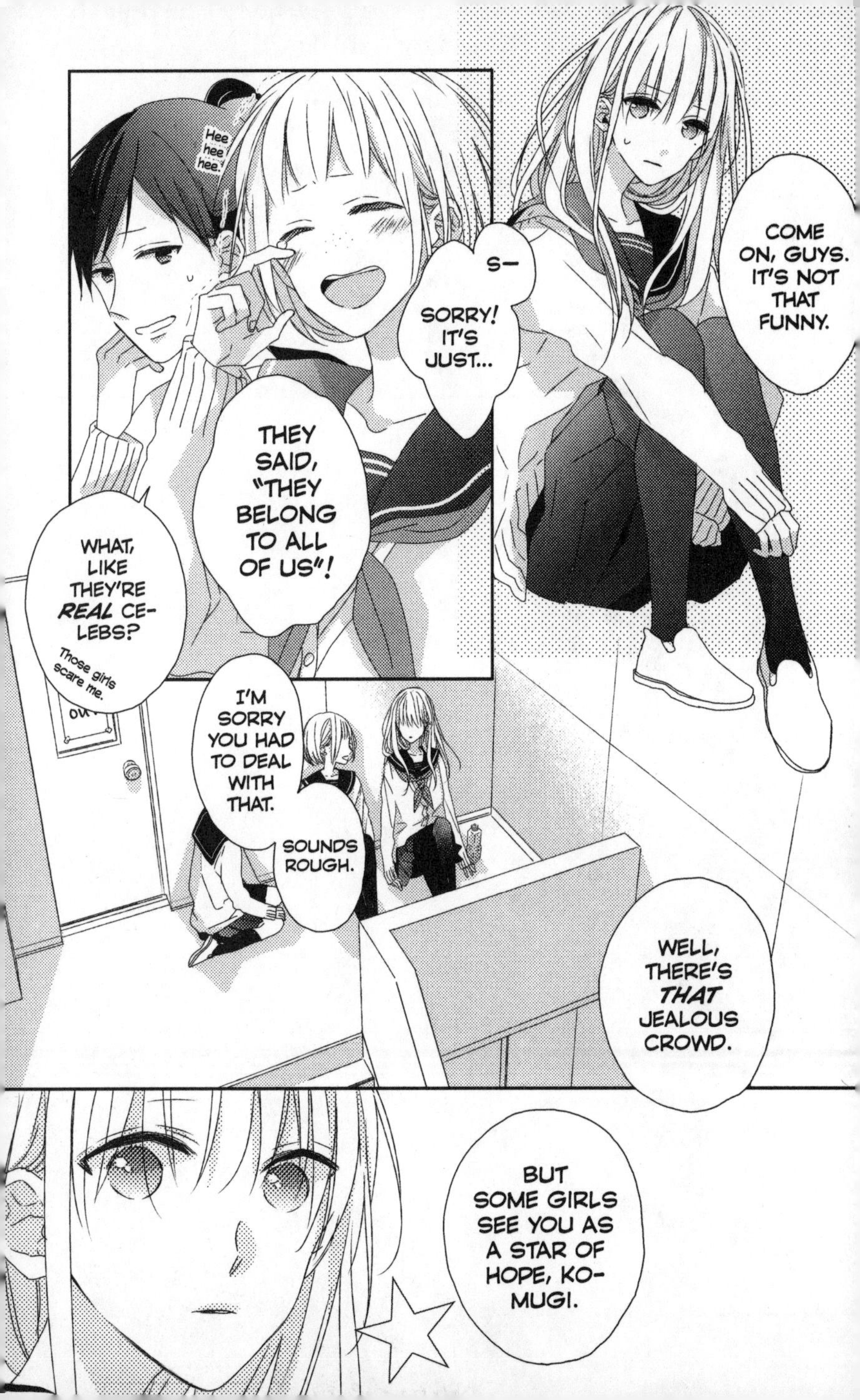
COME ON, GUYS. IT'S NOT THAT FUNNY.
Hee hee hee.
S—
SORRY! IT'S JUST...
THEY SAID, "THEY BELONG TO ALL OF US"!
WHAT, LIKE THEY'RE *REAL* CE-LEBS?
Those girls scare me.
I'M SORRY YOU HAD TO DEAL WITH THAT.
SOUNDS ROUGH.
WELL, THERE'S *THAT* JEALOUS CROWD.
BUT SOME GIRLS SEE YOU AS A STAR OF HOPE, KO-MUGI.

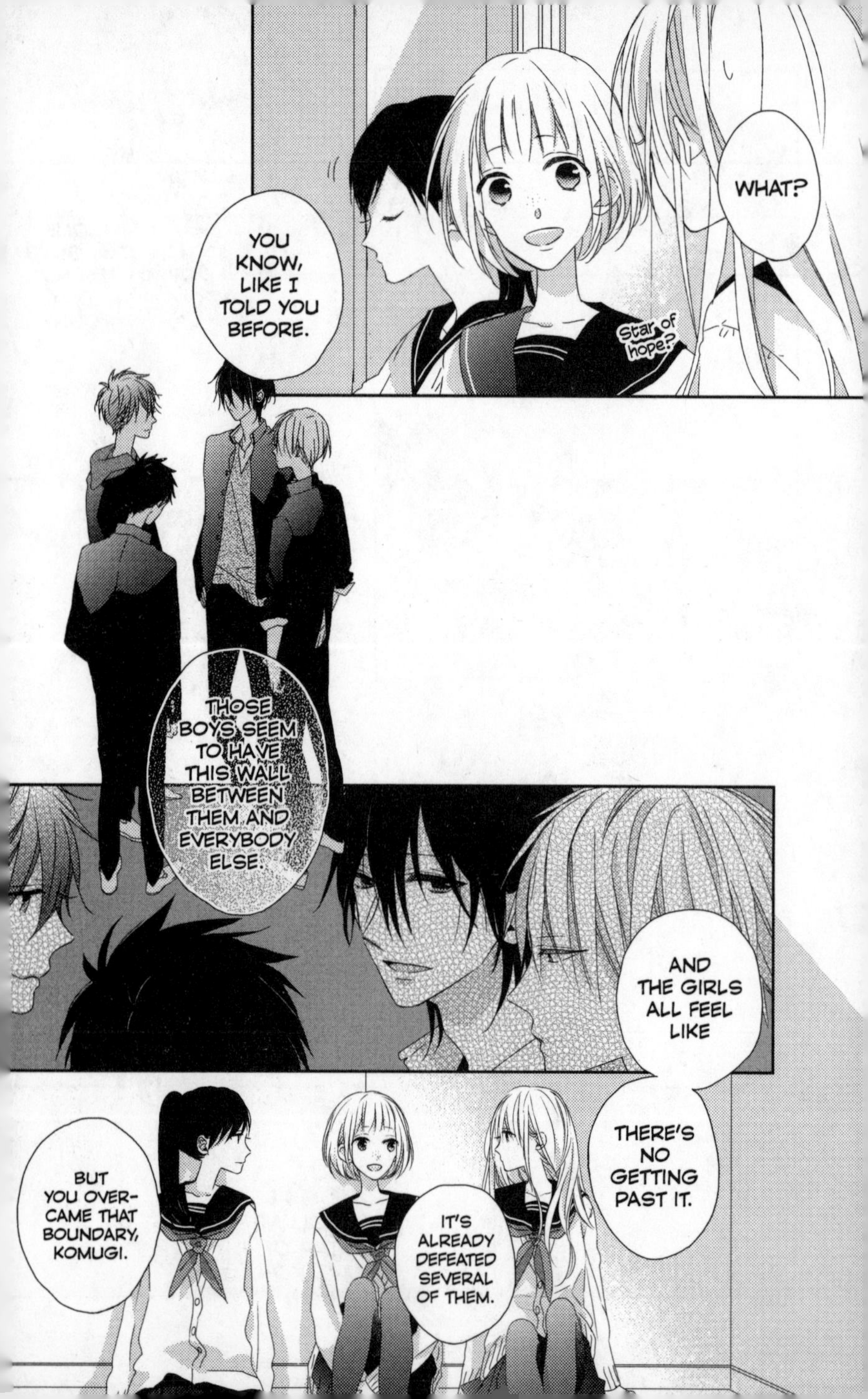
WHAT?
Star of hope?
YOU KNOW, LIKE I TOLD YOU BEFORE.
THOSE BOYS SEEM TO HAVE THIS WALL BETWEEN THEM AND EVERYBODY ELSE.
AND THE GIRLS ALL FEEL LIKE
THERE'S NO GETTING PAST IT.
IT'S ALREADY DEFEATED SEVERAL OF THEM.
BUT YOU OVER-CAME THAT BOUNDARY, KOMUGI.

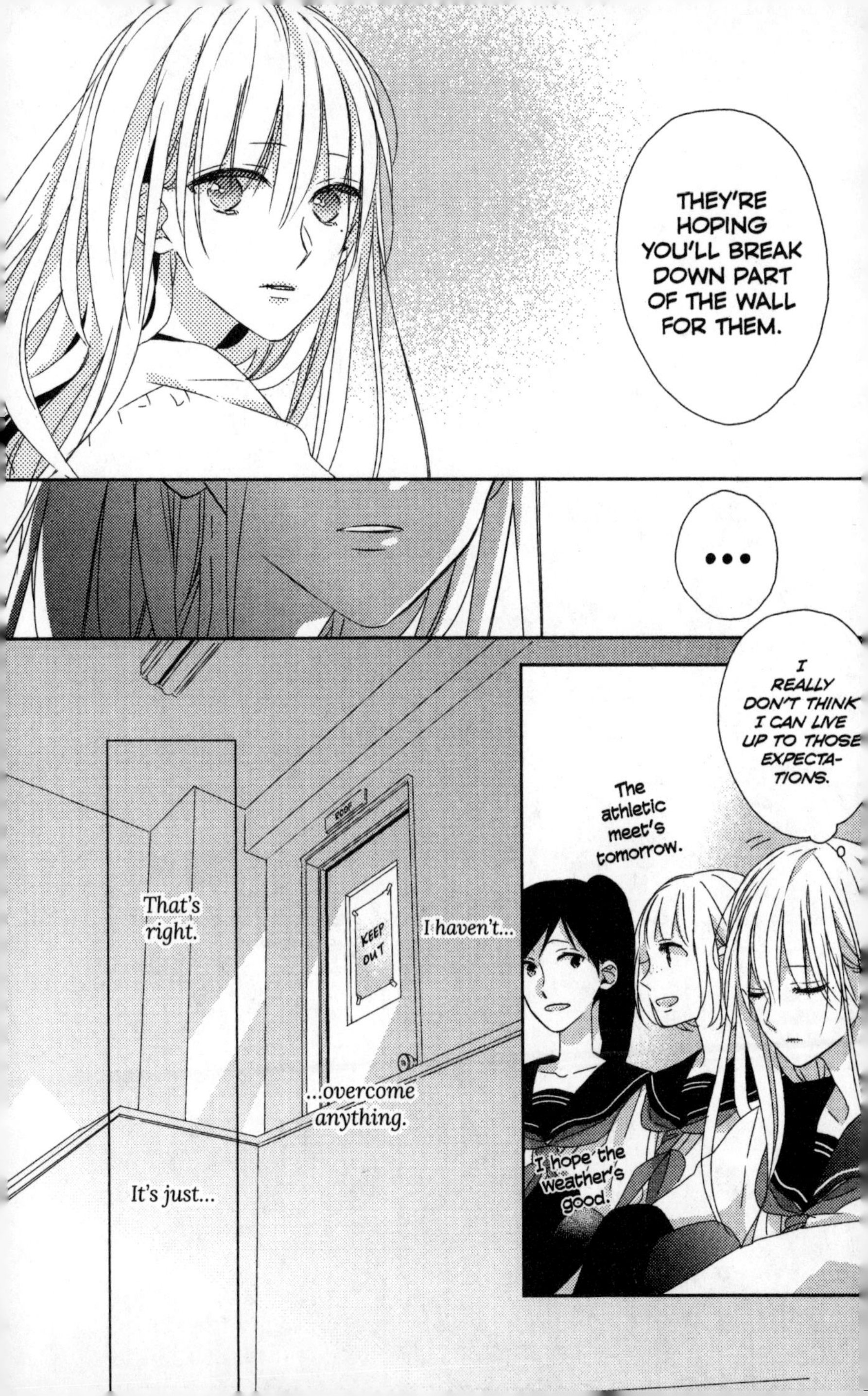
THEY'RE HOPING YOU'LL BREAK DOWN PART OF THE WALL FOR THEM.
...
I REALLY DON'T THINK I CAN LIVE UP TO THOSE EXPECTATIONS.
The athletic meet's tomorrow.
I hope the weather's good.
That's right.
I haven't...
...overcome anything.
It's just...
KEEP OUT

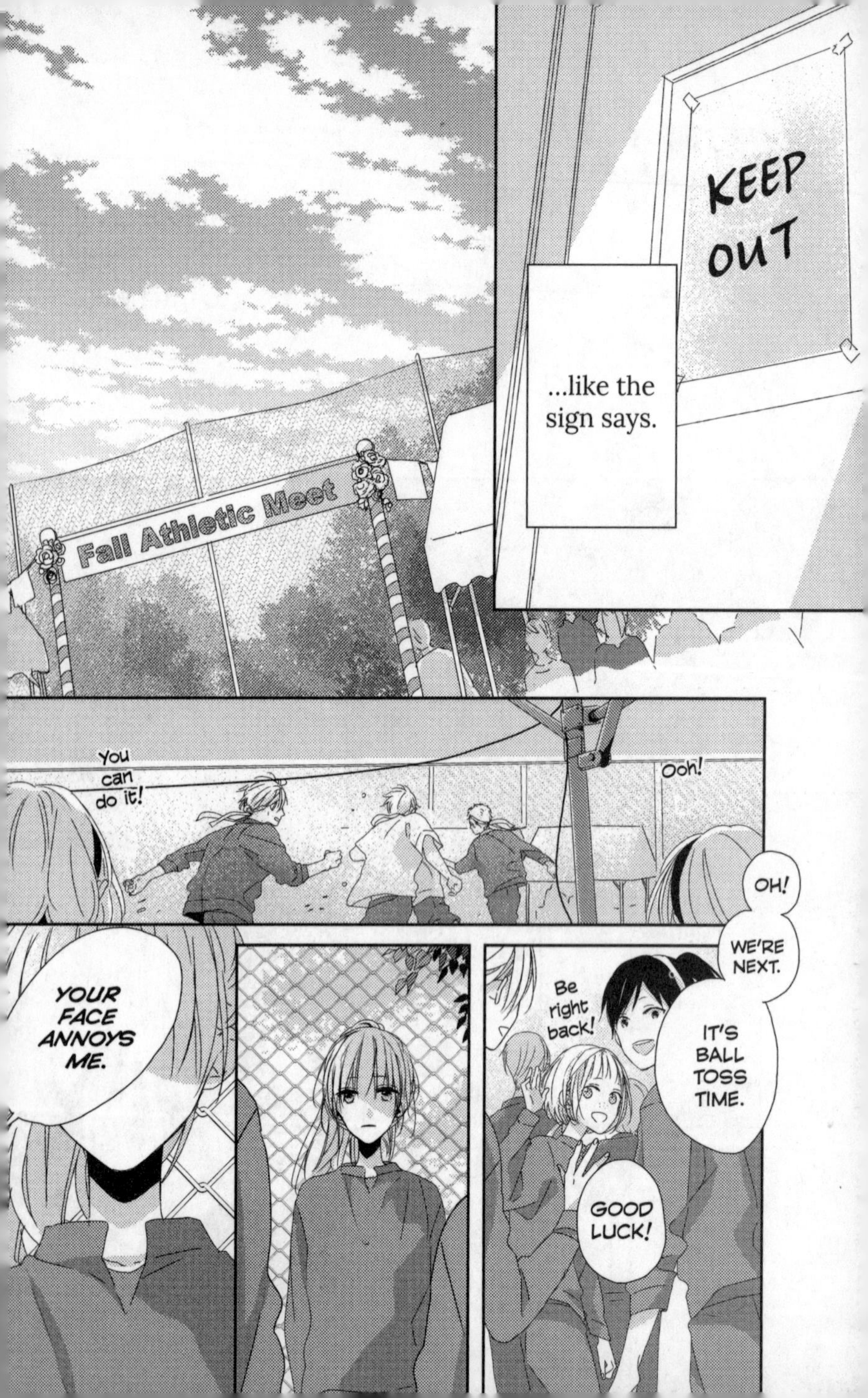
KEEP OUT
...like the sign says.
Fall Athletic Meet
Ooh!
You can do it!
OH!
WE'RE NEXT.
IT'S BALL TOSS TIME.
Be right back!
GOOD LUCK!
YOUR FACE ANNOYS ME.

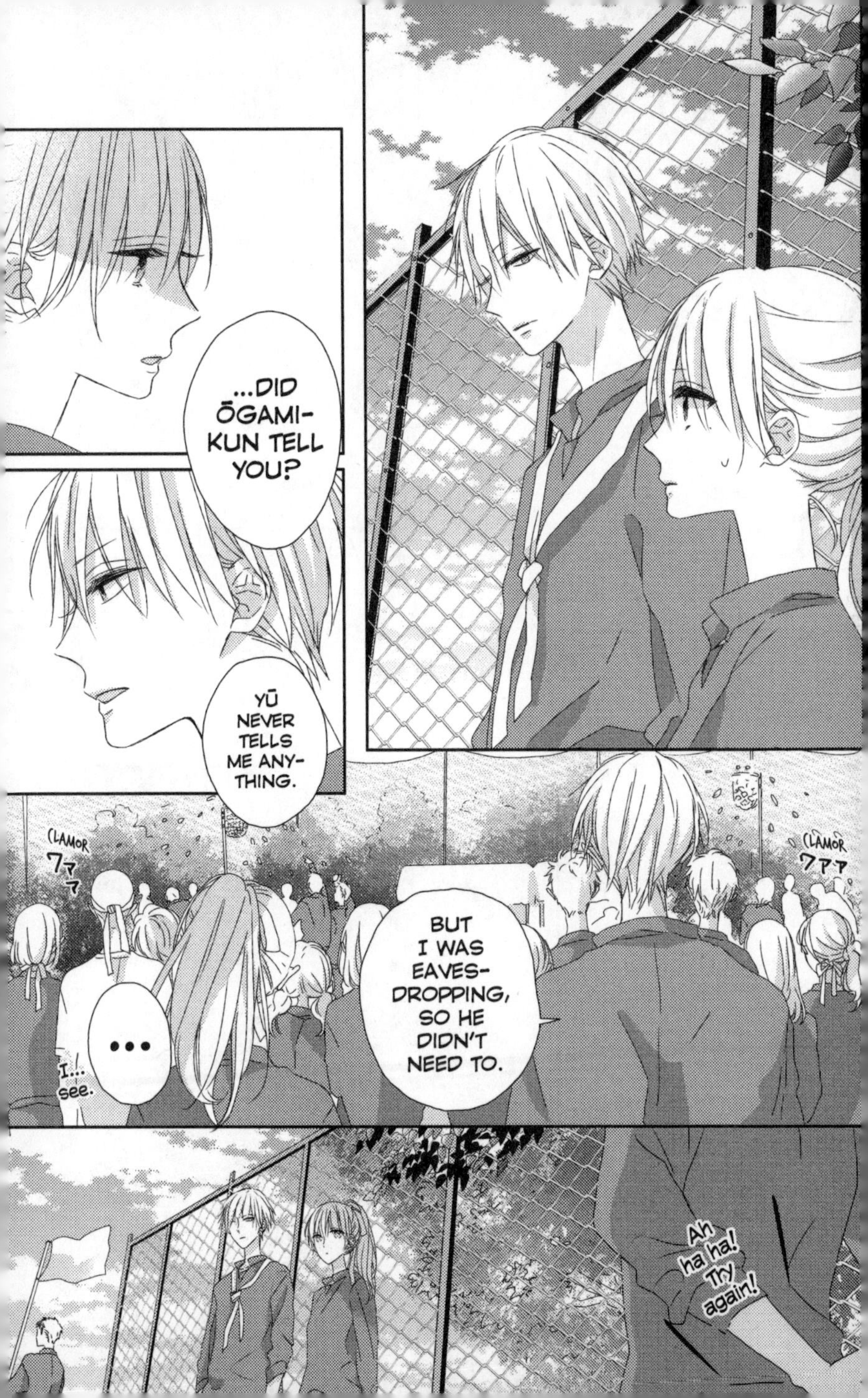
...DID ŌGAMI-KUN TELL YOU?
YŪ NEVER TELLS ME ANYTHING.
CLAMOR ワァァ
BUT I WAS EAVES-DROPPING, SO HE DIDN'T NEED TO.
CLAMOR ワァァ
...
I... see.
Ah ha ha! Try again!

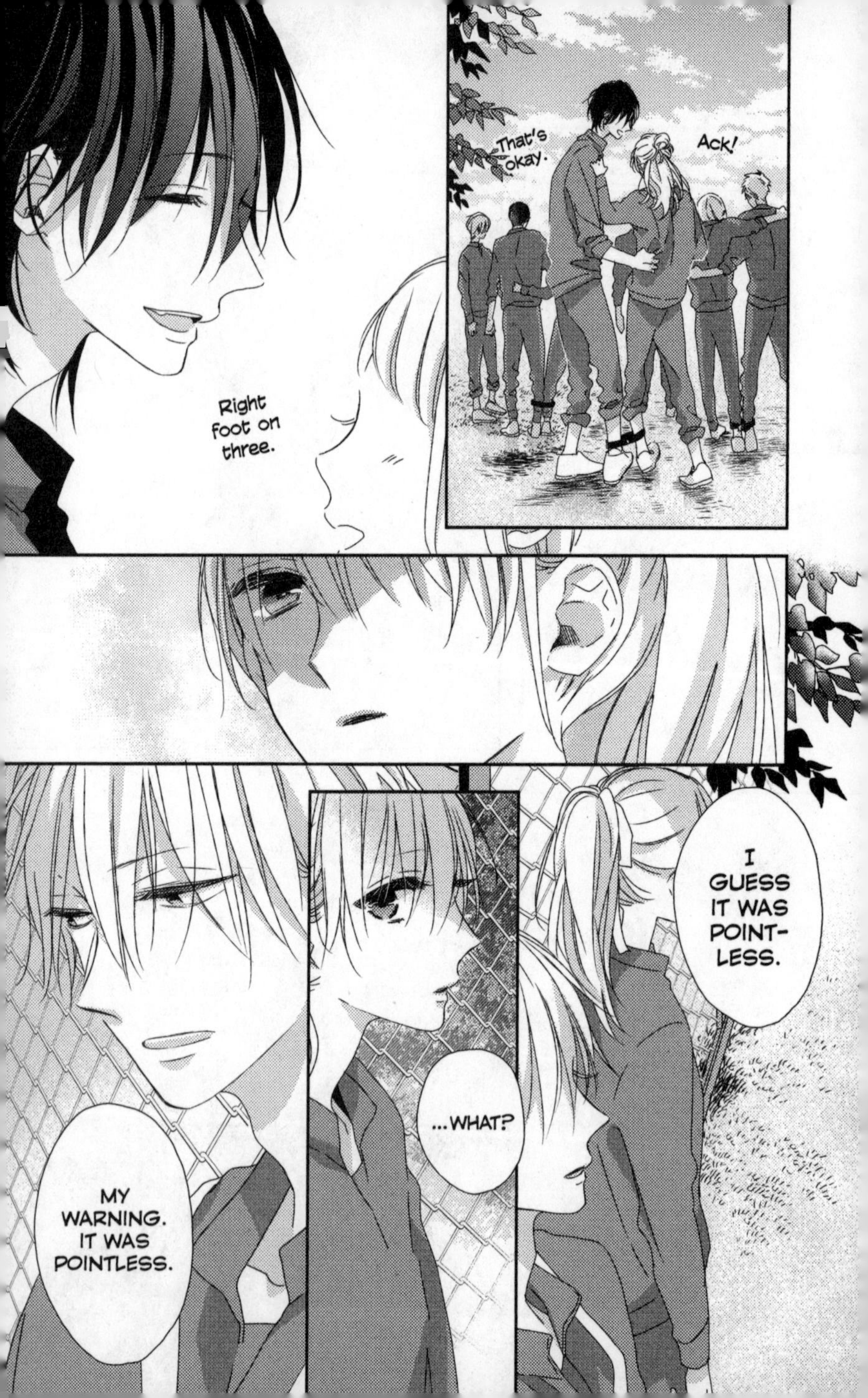
Ack!
That's okay.
Right foot on three.
I GUESS IT WAS POINTLESS.
...WHAT?
MY WARNING. IT WAS POINTLESS.

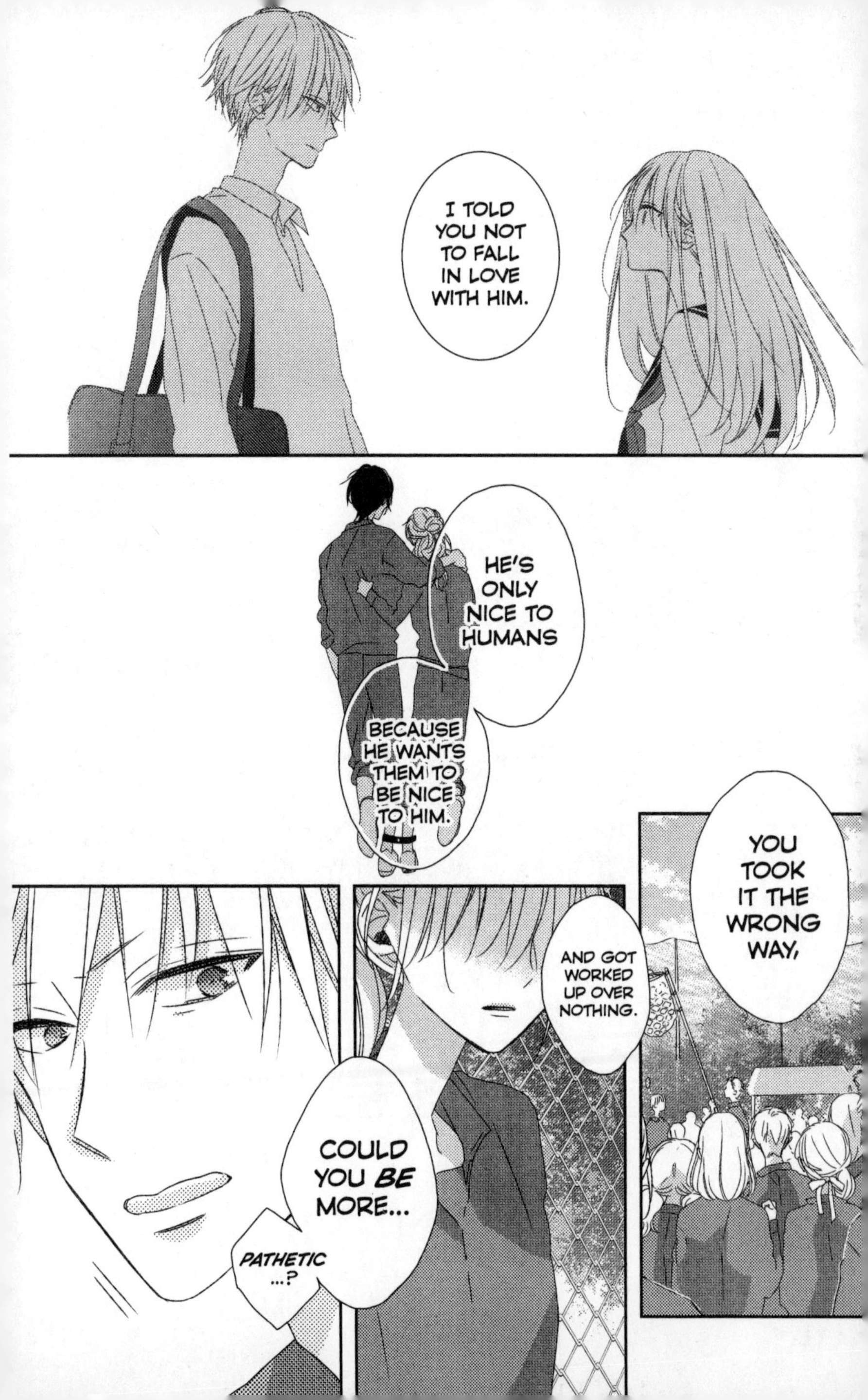
I TOLD YOU NOT TO FALL IN LOVE WITH HIM.
HE'S ONLY NICE TO HUMANS
BECAUSE HE WANTS THEM TO BE NICE TO HIM.
YOU TOOK IT THE WRONG WAY,
AND GOT WORKED UP OVER NOTHING.
COULD YOU *BE* MORE...
PATHETIC ...?

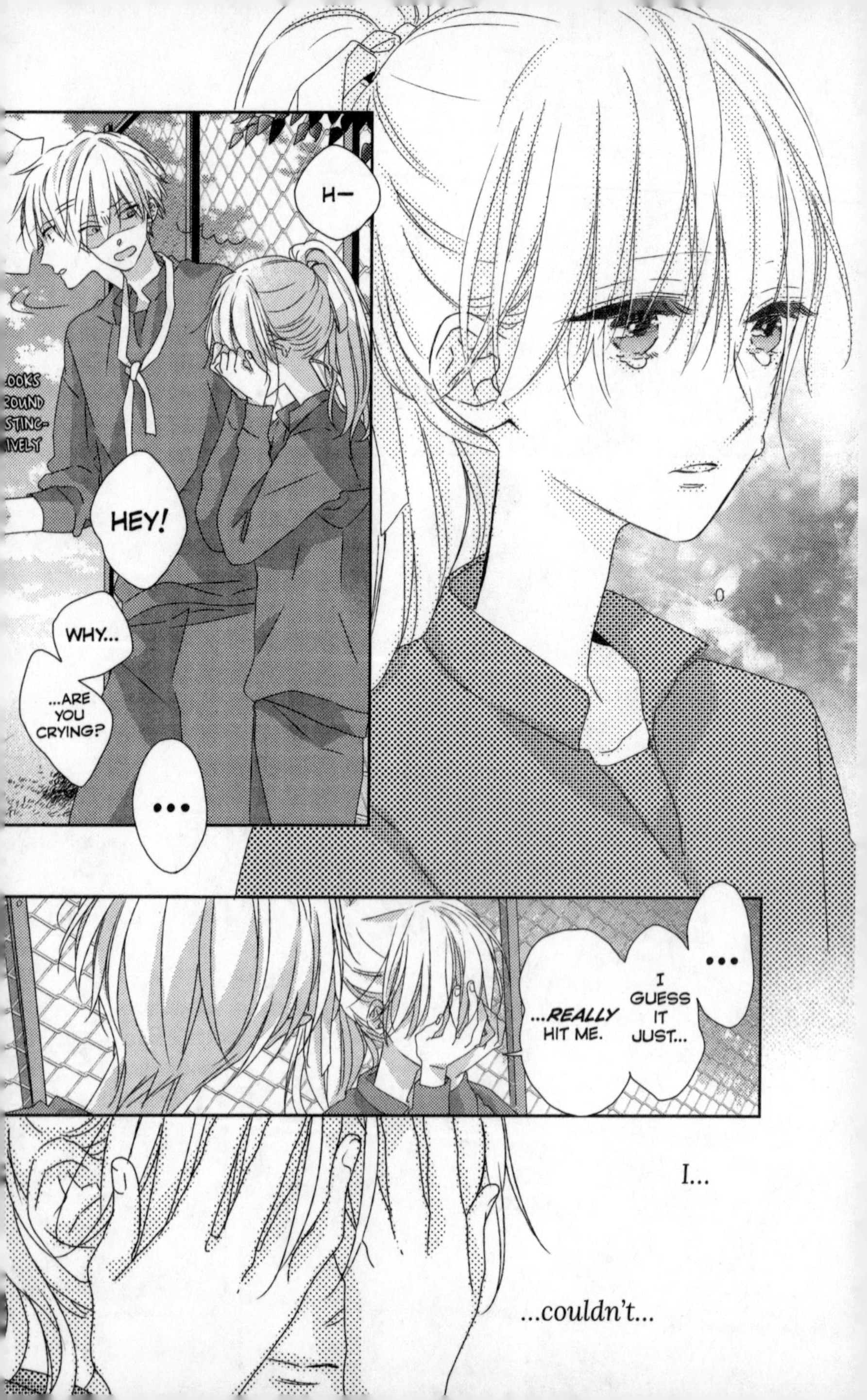
H–
HEY!
WHY...
...ARE YOU CRYING?
...
...
I GUESS IT JUST...
...*REALLY* HIT ME.
I...
...couldn't...

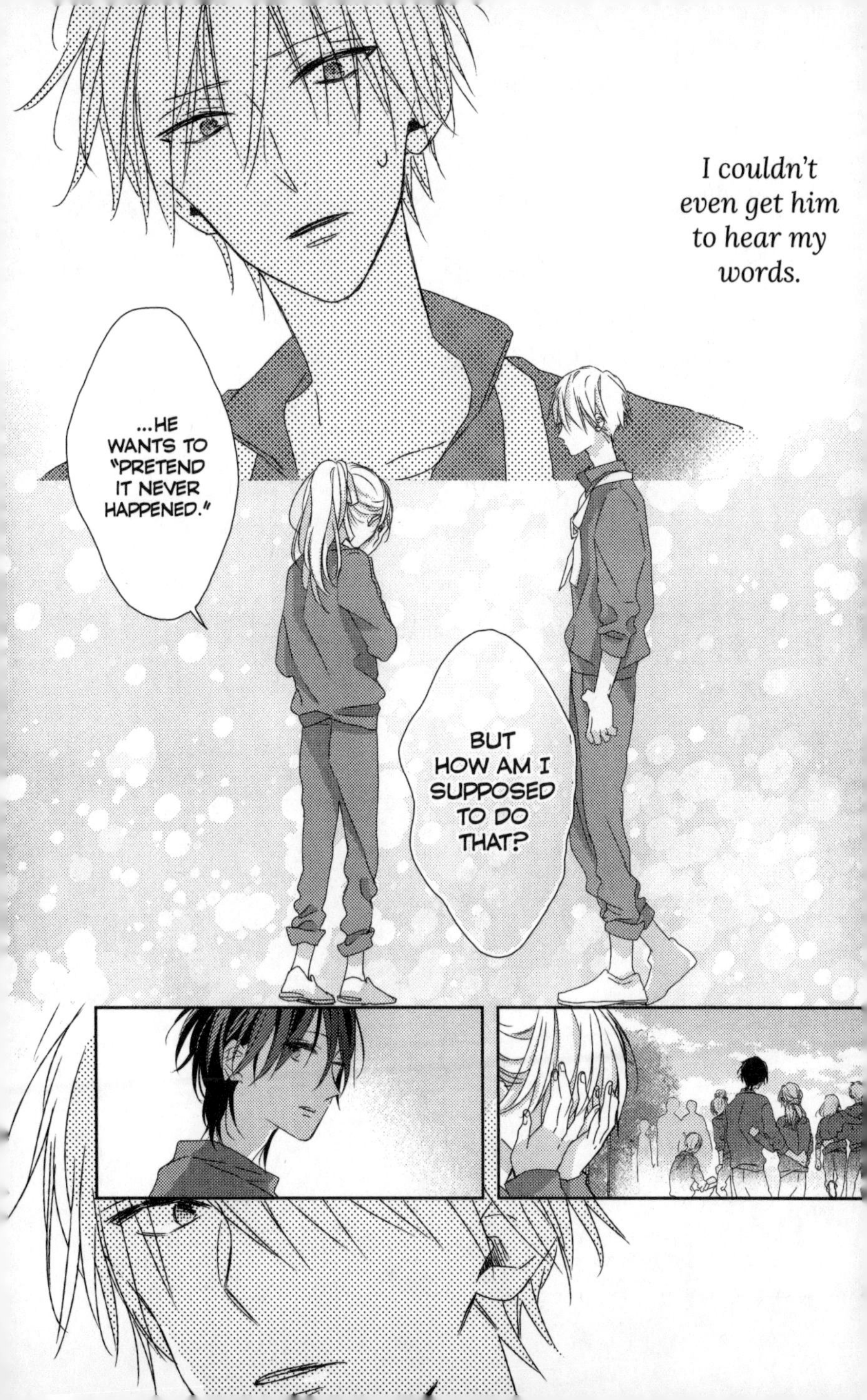
I couldn't even get him to hear my words.
...HE WANTS TO "PRETEND IT NEVER HAPPENED."
BUT HOW AM I SUPPOSED TO DO THAT?

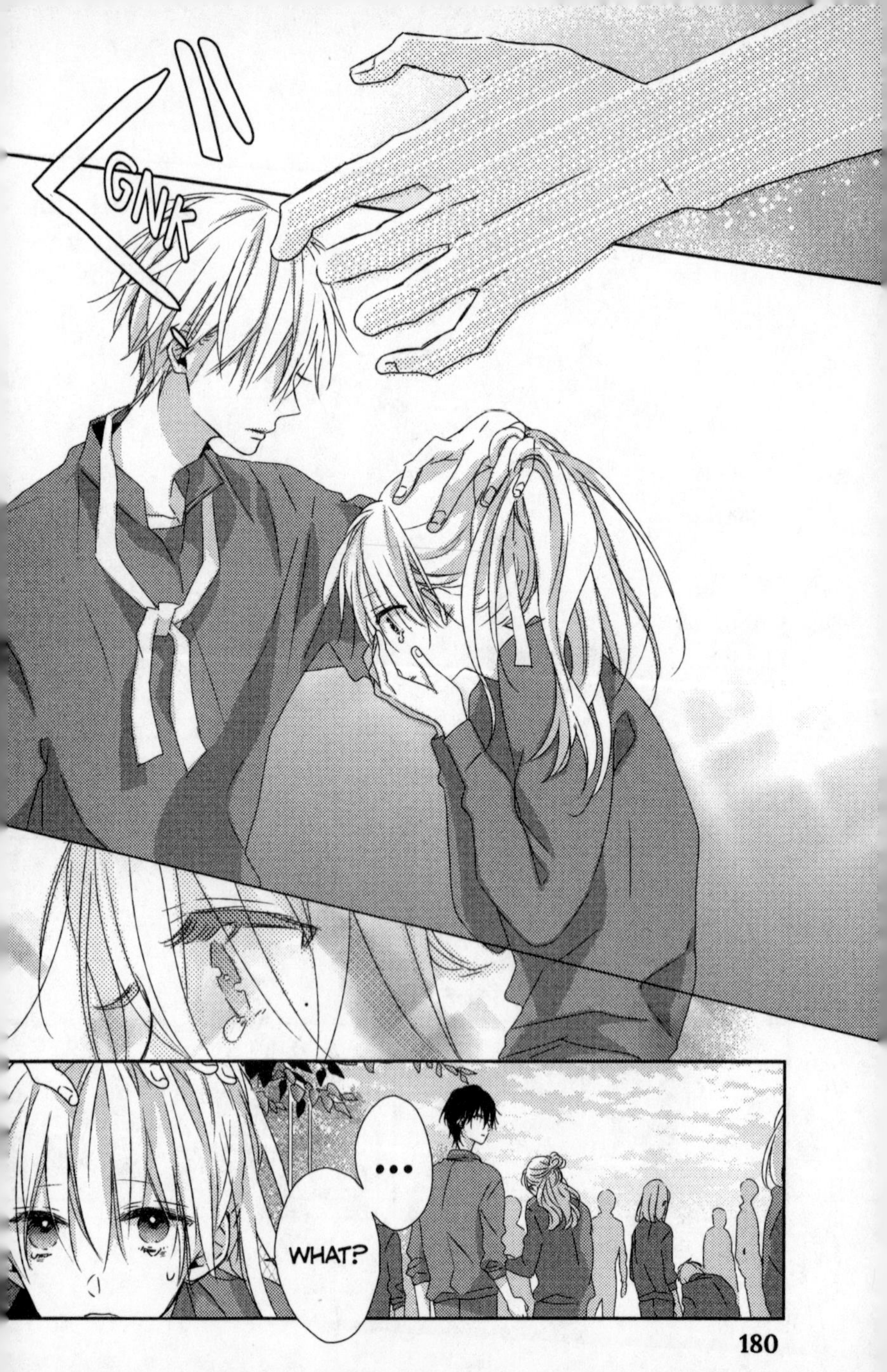
GNK
...
WHAT?

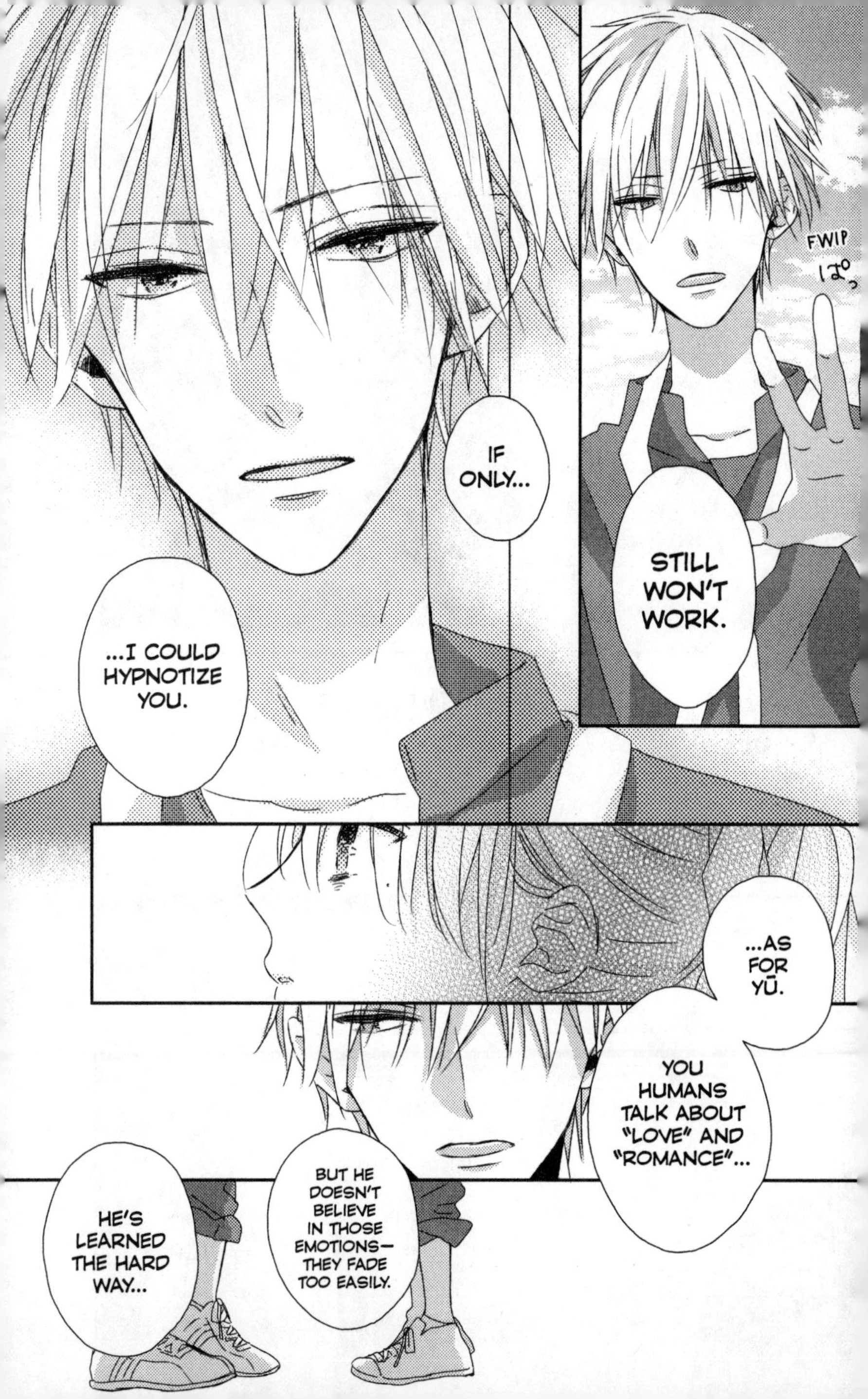
FWIP
ぱっ
STILL WON'T WORK.
IF ONLY...
...I COULD HYPNOTIZE YOU.
...AS FOR YŪ.
YOU HUMANS TALK ABOUT "LOVE" AND "ROMANCE"...
BUT HE DOESN'T BELIEVE IN THOSE EMOTIONS—THEY FADE TOO EASILY.
HE'S LEARNED THE HARD WAY...

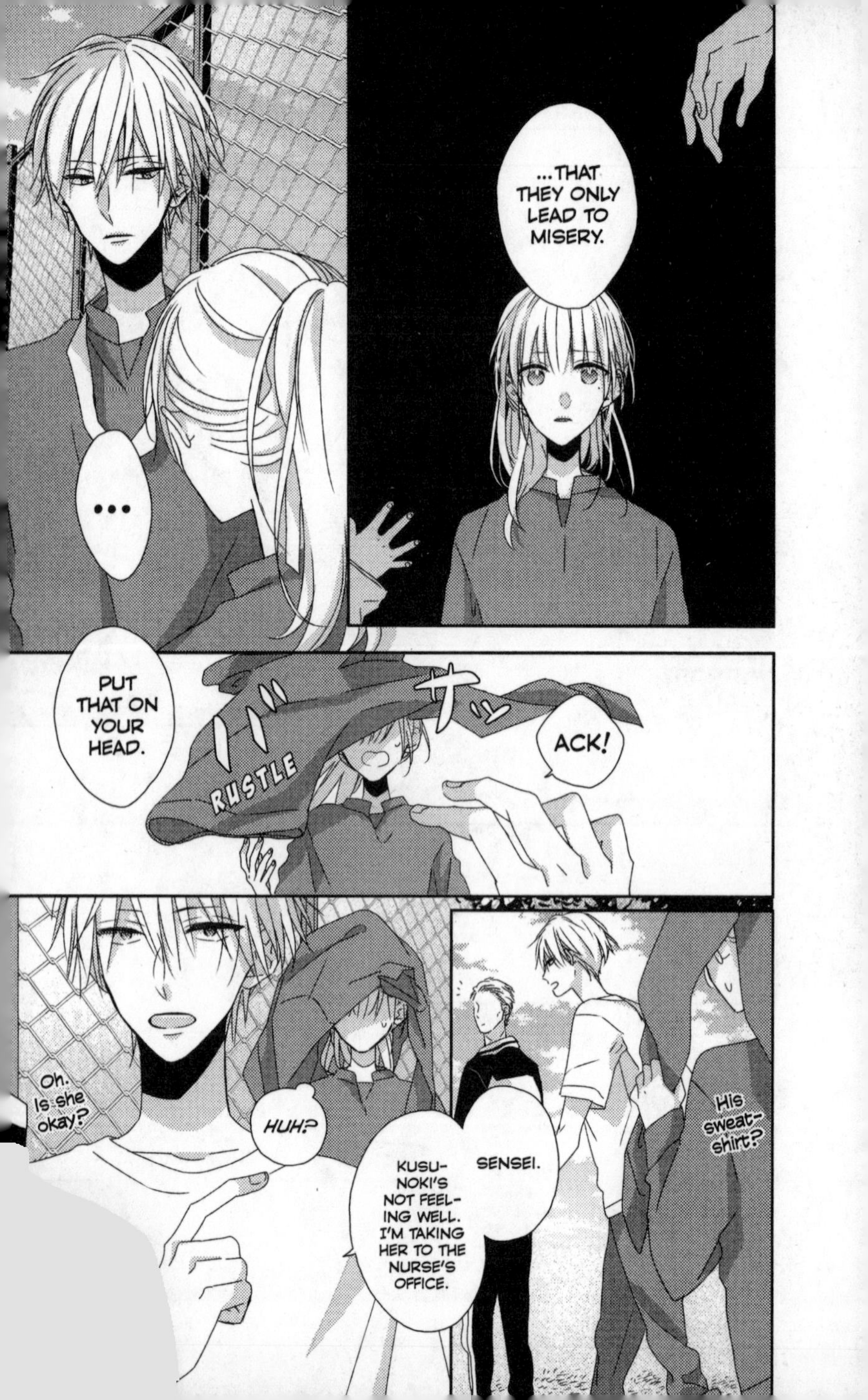
...THAT THEY ONLY LEAD TO MISERY.
...
PUT THAT ON YOUR HEAD.
RUSTLE
ACK!
His sweat-shirt?
SENSEI.
KUSU-NOKI'S NOT FEEL-ING WELL. I'M TAKING HER TO THE NURSE'S OFFICE.
HUH?
Oh. Is she okay?

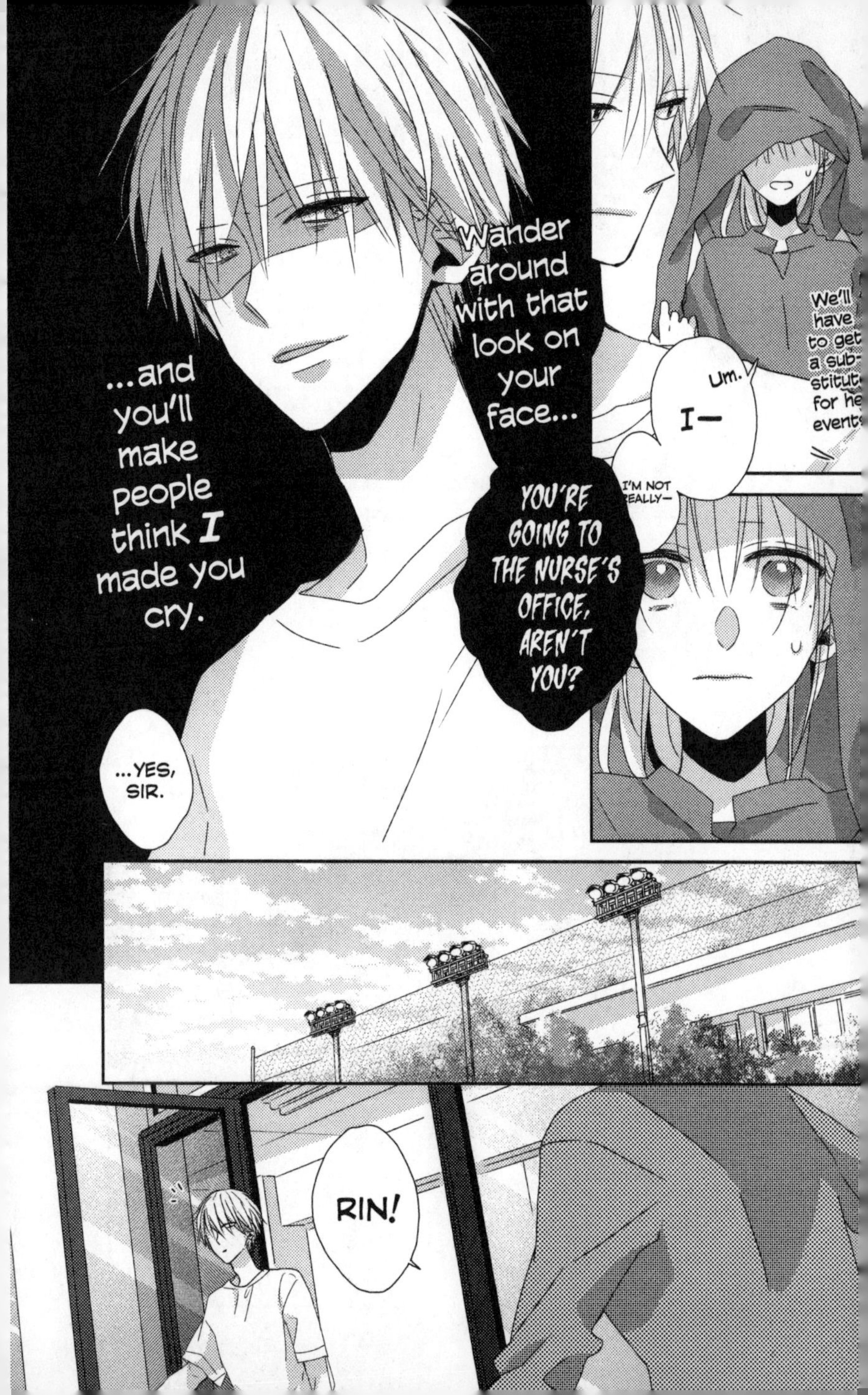
We'll have to get a sub- stitut for he event
Um. I—
I'M NOT REALLY—
Wander around with that look on your face...
...and you'll make people think I made you cry.
YOU'RE GOING TO THE NURSE'S OFFICE, AREN'T YOU?
...YES, SIR.
RIN!

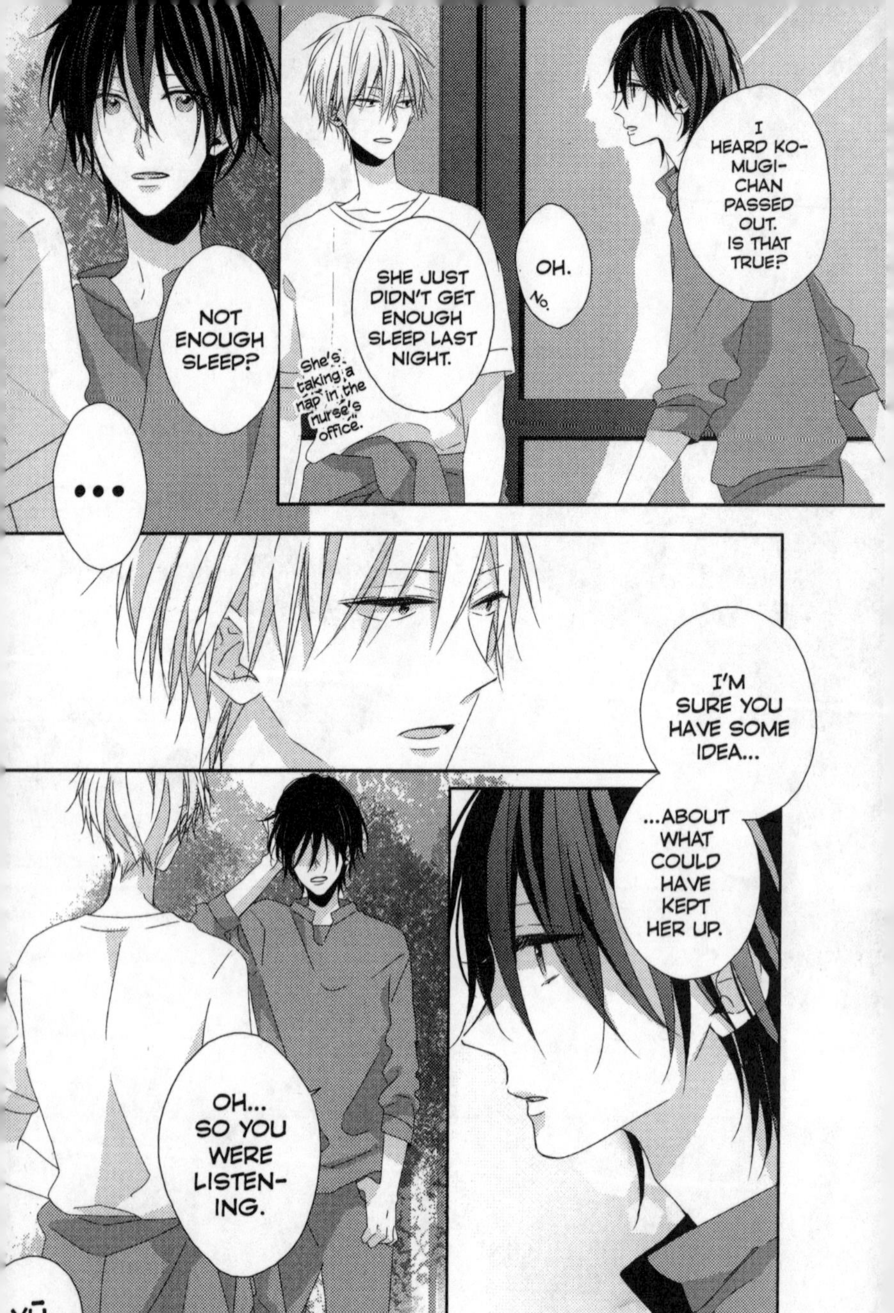
I HEARD KO-MUGI-CHAN PASSED OUT. IS THAT TRUE?
OH.
No.
SHE JUST DIDN'T GET ENOUGH SLEEP LAST NIGHT.
She's taking a nap in the nurse's office.
NOT ENOUGH SLEEP?
...
I'M SURE YOU HAVE SOME IDEA...
...ABOUT WHAT COULD HAVE KEPT HER UP.
OH... SO YOU WERE LISTEN-ING.
YŪ.

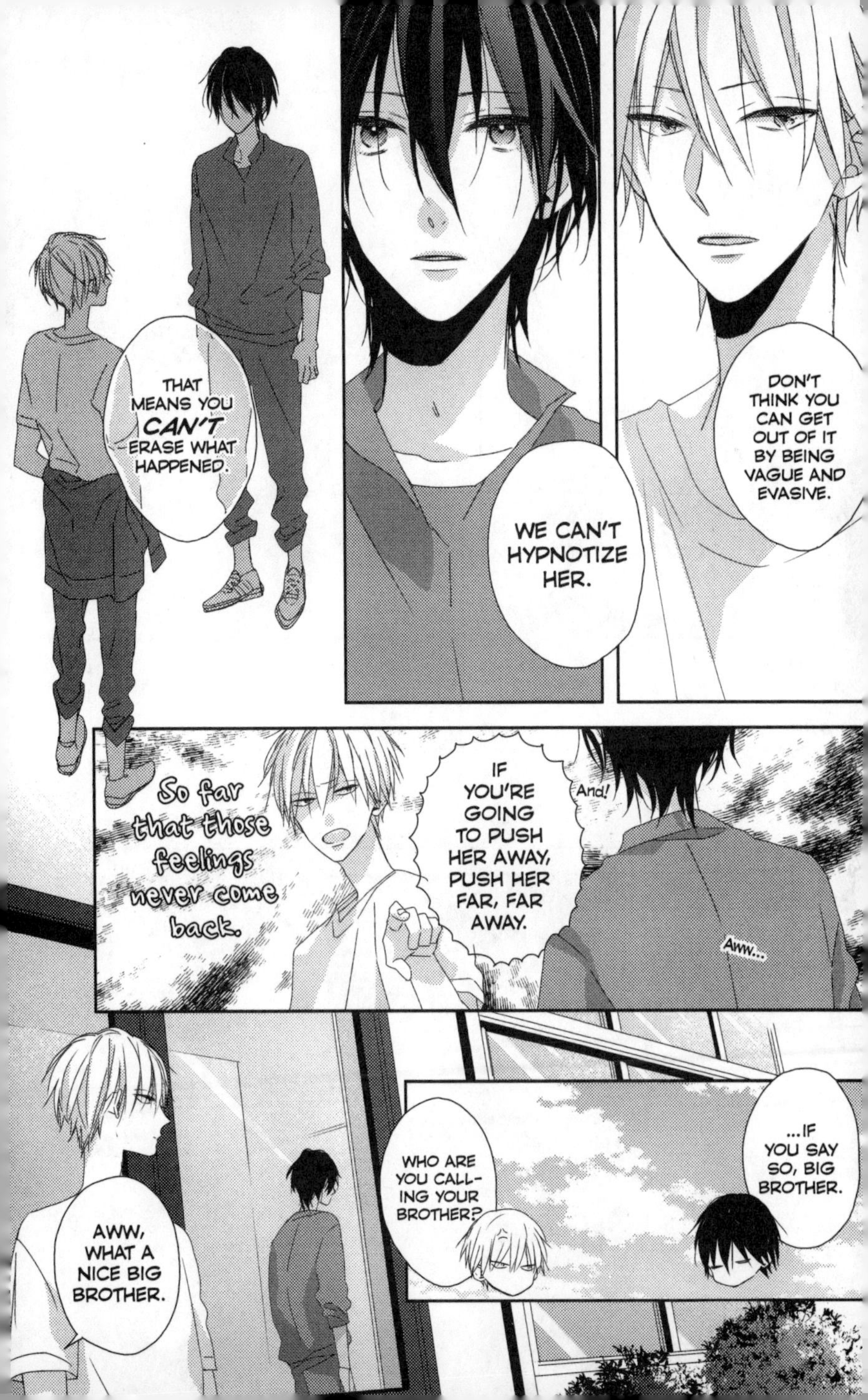
DON'T THINK YOU CAN GET OUT OF IT BY BEING VAGUE AND EVASIVE.
WE CAN'T HYPNOTIZE HER.
THAT MEANS YOU CAN'T ERASE WHAT HAPPENED.
And!
IF YOU'RE GOING TO PUSH HER AWAY, PUSH HER FAR, FAR AWAY.
So far that those feelings never come back.
Aww...
...IF YOU SAY SO, BIG BROTHER.
WHO ARE YOU CALLING YOUR BROTHER?
AWW, WHAT A NICE BIG BROTHER.

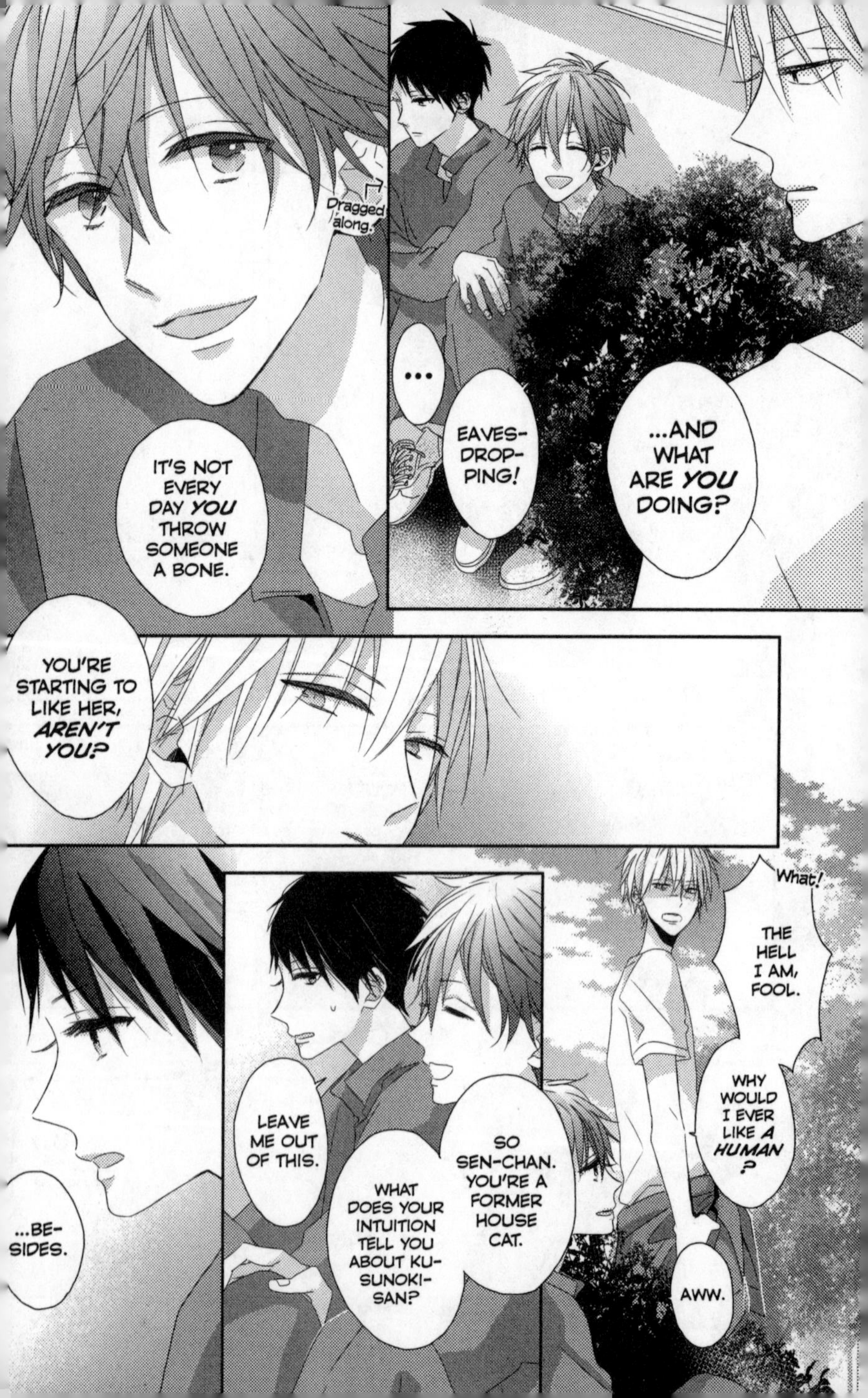
...AND WHAT ARE YOU DOING?
EAVES-DROPPING!
...
Dragged along.
IT'S NOT EVERY DAY YOU THROW SOMEONE A BONE.
YOU'RE STARTING TO LIKE HER, AREN'T YOU?
What!
THE HELL I AM, FOOL.
WHY WOULD I EVER LIKE A HUMAN?
AWW.
SO SEN-CHAN. YOU'RE A FORMER HOUSE CAT.
LEAVE ME OUT OF THIS.
WHAT DOES YOUR INTUITION TELL YOU ABOUT KU-SUNOKI-SAN?
...BE-SIDES.

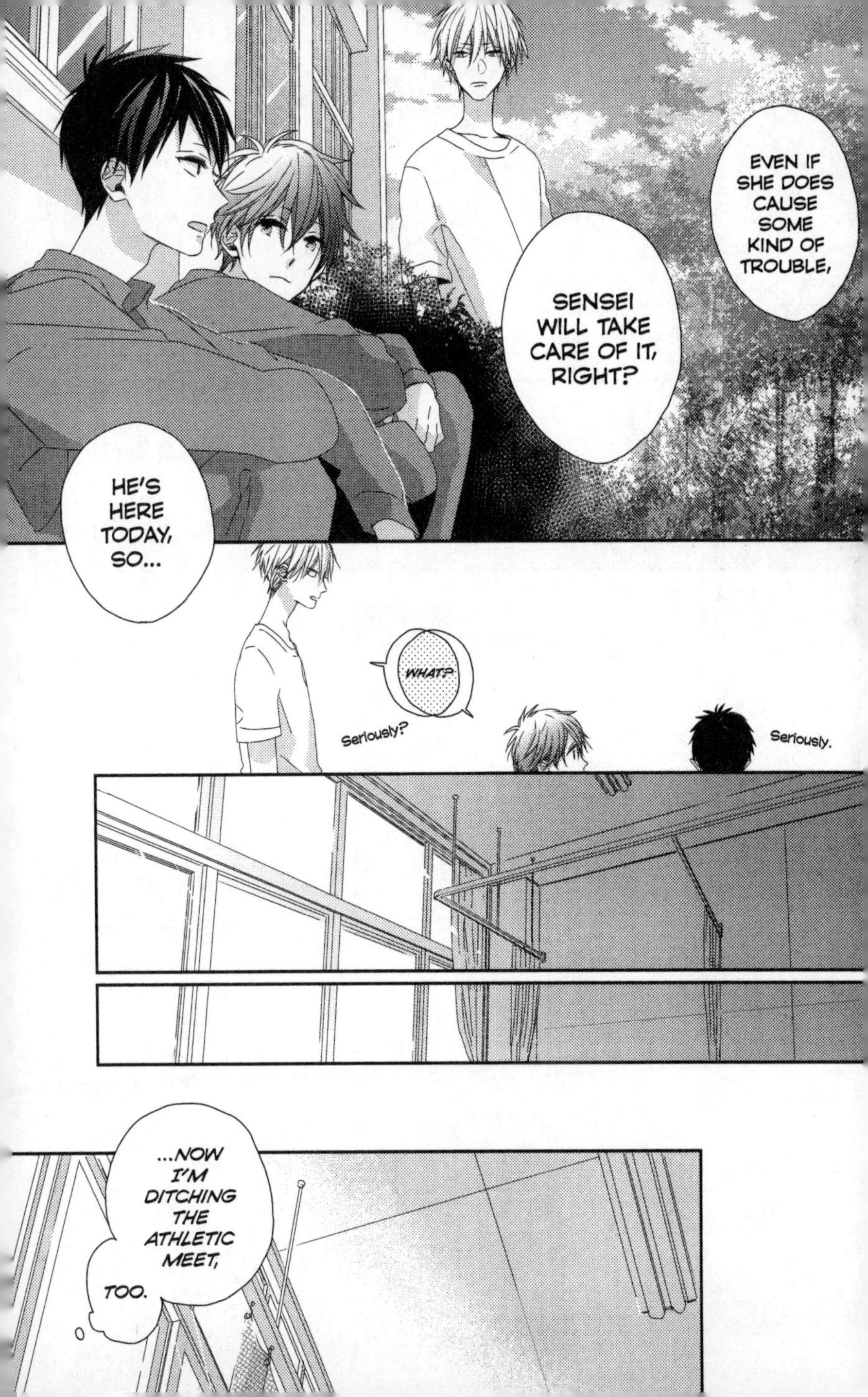
EVEN IF SHE DOES CAUSE SOME KIND OF TROUBLE,
SENSEI WILL TAKE CARE OF IT, RIGHT?
HE'S HERE TODAY, SO...
WHAT?
Seriously.
Seriously?
...NOW I'M DITCHING THE ATHLETIC MEET,
TOO.

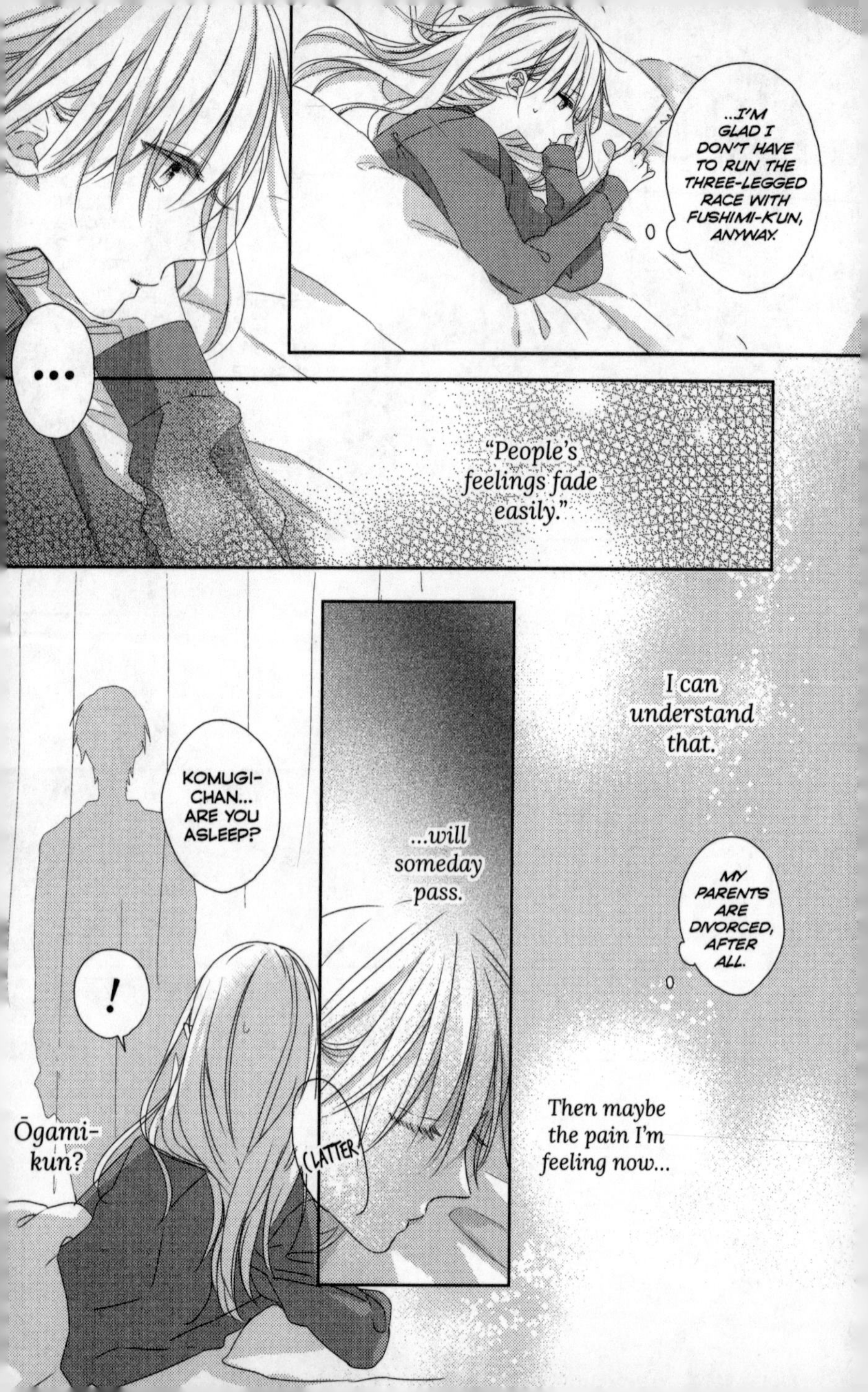

...I'M GLAD I DON'T HAVE TO RUN THE THREE-LEGGED RACE WITH FUSHIMI-KUN, ANYWAY.
...
"People's feelings fade easily."
I can understand that.
MY PARENTS ARE DIVORCED, AFTER ALL.
Then maybe the pain I'm feeling now...
...will someday pass.
CLATTER
KOMUGI-CHAN... ARE YOU ASLEEP?
!
Ōgami-kun?

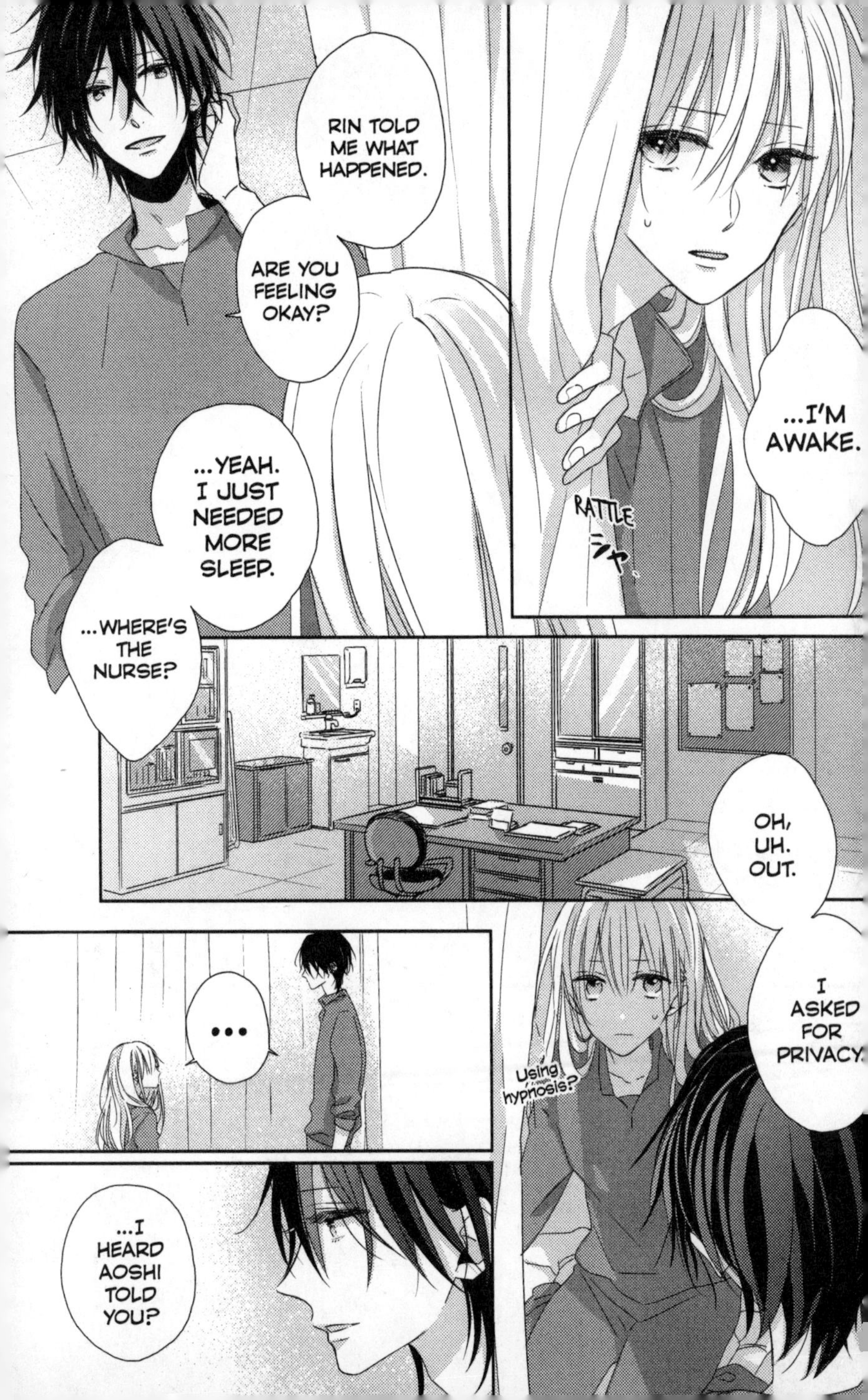
...I'M AWAKE.
RATTLE
RIN TOLD ME WHAT HAPPENED.
ARE YOU FEELING OKAY?
...YEAH. I JUST NEEDED MORE SLEEP.
...WHERE'S THE NURSE?
OH, UH. OUT.
I ASKED FOR PRIVACY.
Using hypnosis?
...
...I HEARD AOSHI TOLD YOU?

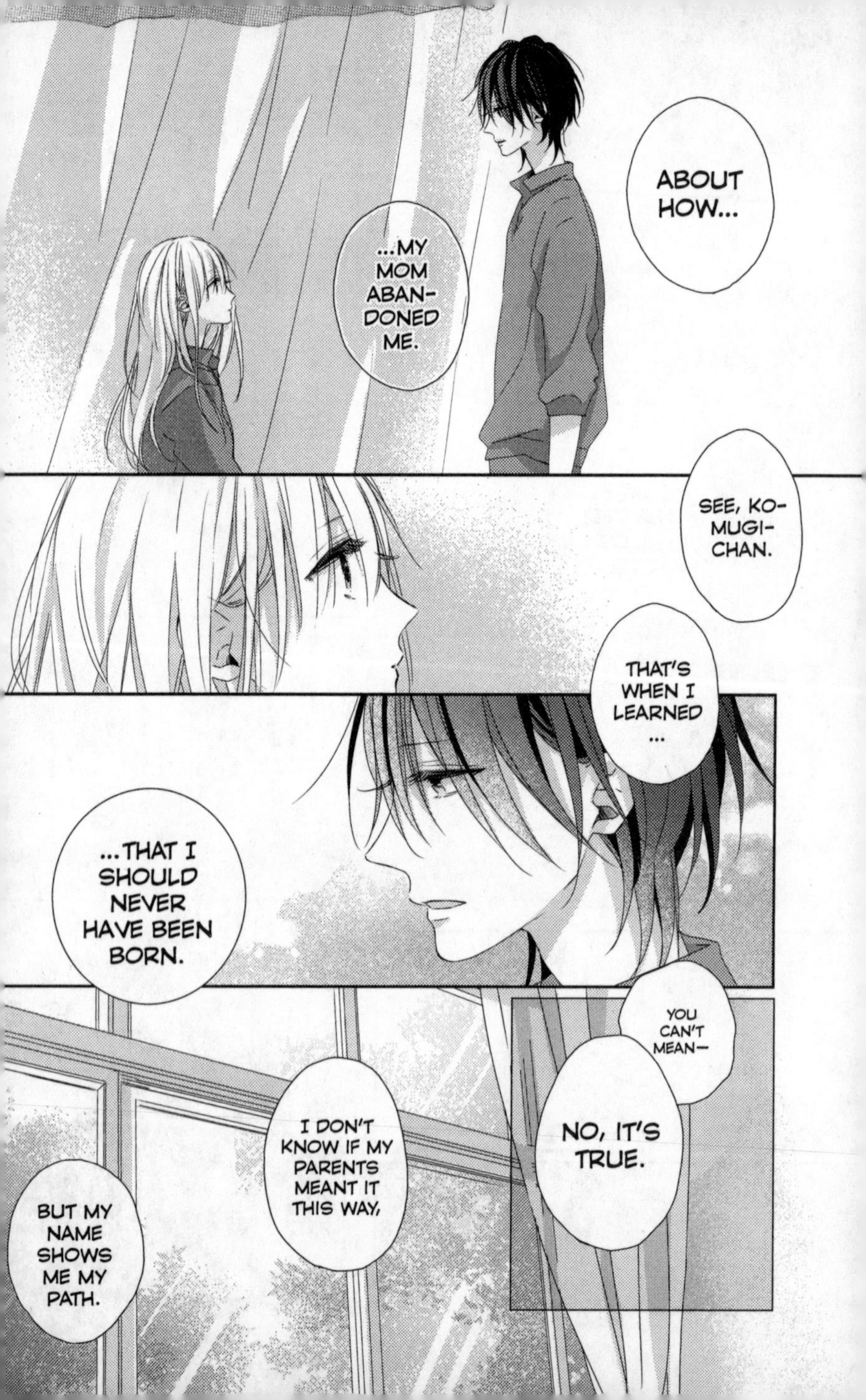
ABOUT HOW...
...MY MOM ABANDONED ME.
SEE, KOMUGI-CHAN.
THAT'S WHEN I LEARNED...
...THAT I SHOULD NEVER HAVE BEEN BORN.
YOU CAN'T MEAN—
NO, IT'S TRUE.
I DON'T KNOW IF MY PARENTS MEANT IT THIS WAY,
BUT MY NAME SHOWS ME MY PATH.

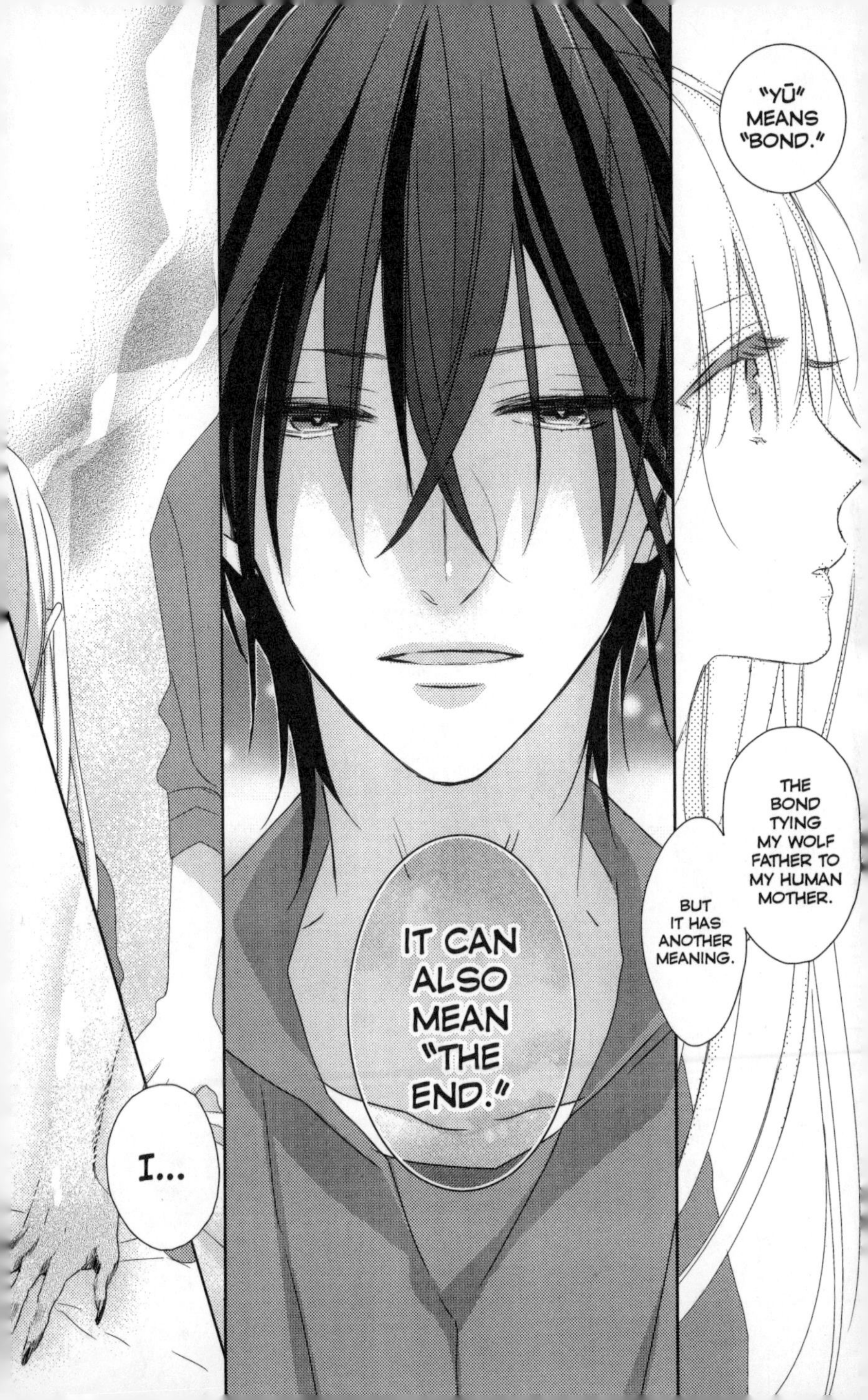
"YŪ" MEANS "BOND."
THE BOND TYING MY WOLF FATHER TO MY HUMAN MOTHER.
BUT IT HAS ANOTHER MEANING.
IT CAN ALSO MEAN "THE END."
I...

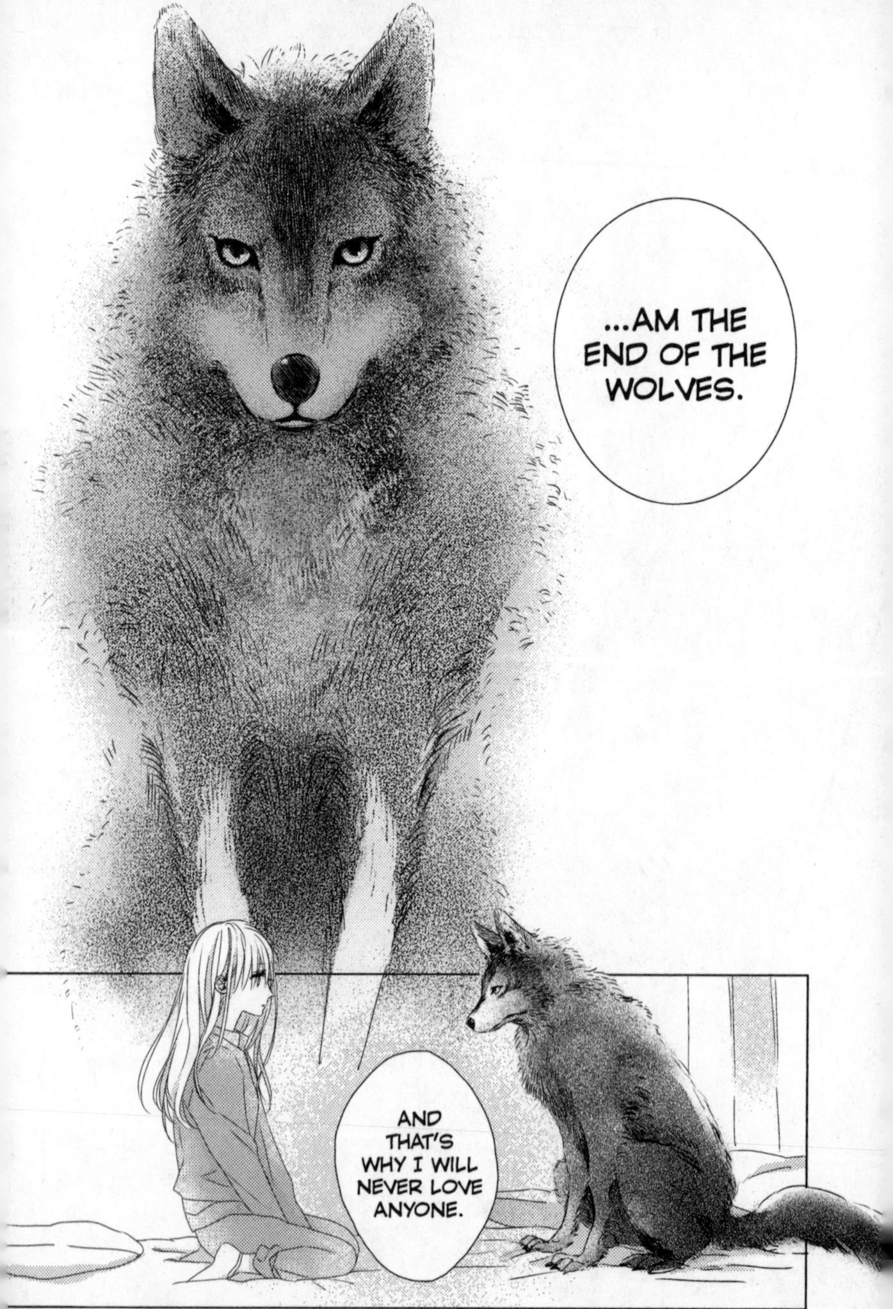
...AM THE END OF THE WOLVES.
AND THAT'S WHY I WILL NEVER LOVE ANYONE.

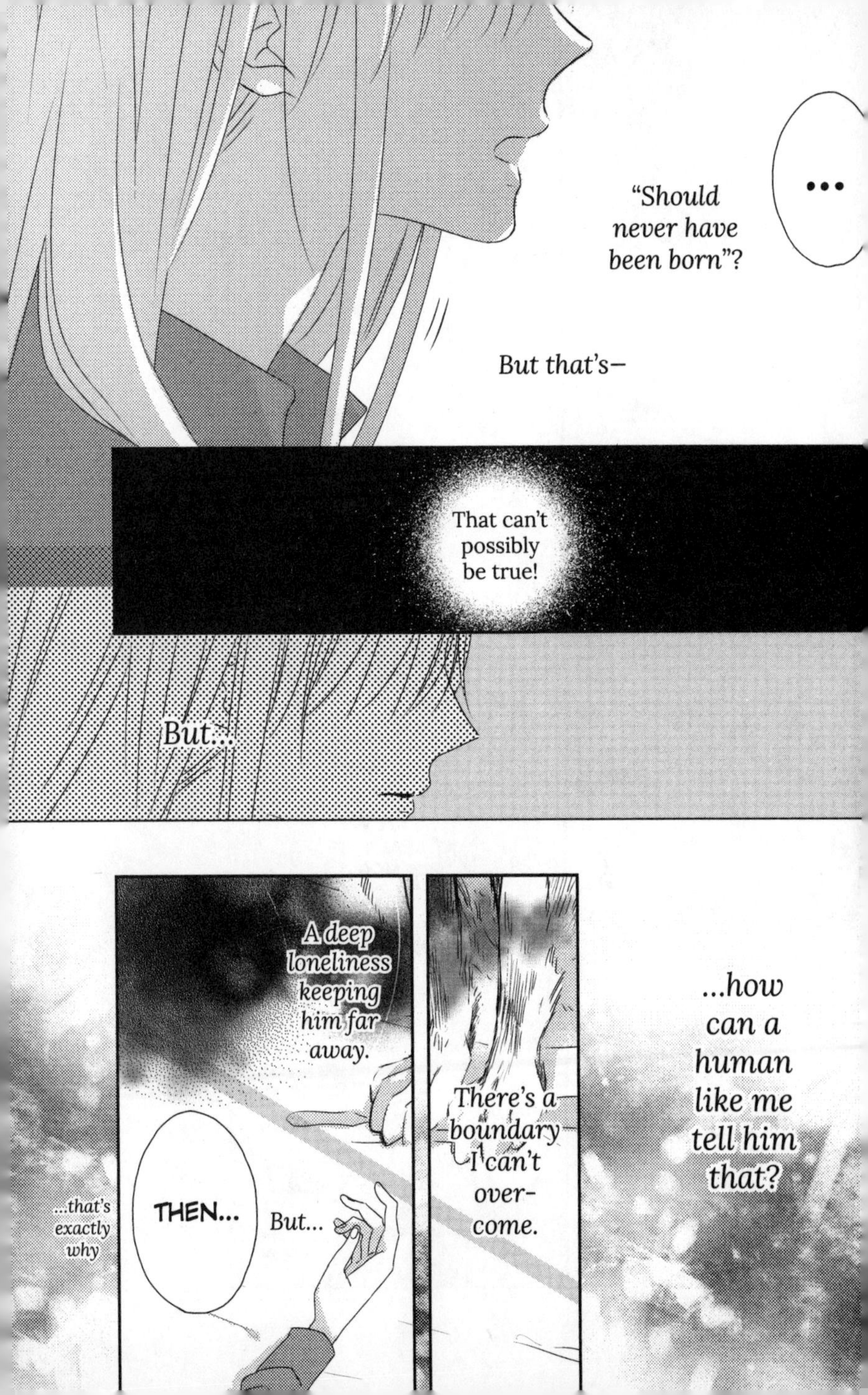
...
"Should never have been born"?
But that's–
That can't possibly be true!
But...
...how can a human like me tell him that?
There's a boundary I can't overcome.
A deep loneliness keeping him far away.
But...
THEN...
...that's exactly why

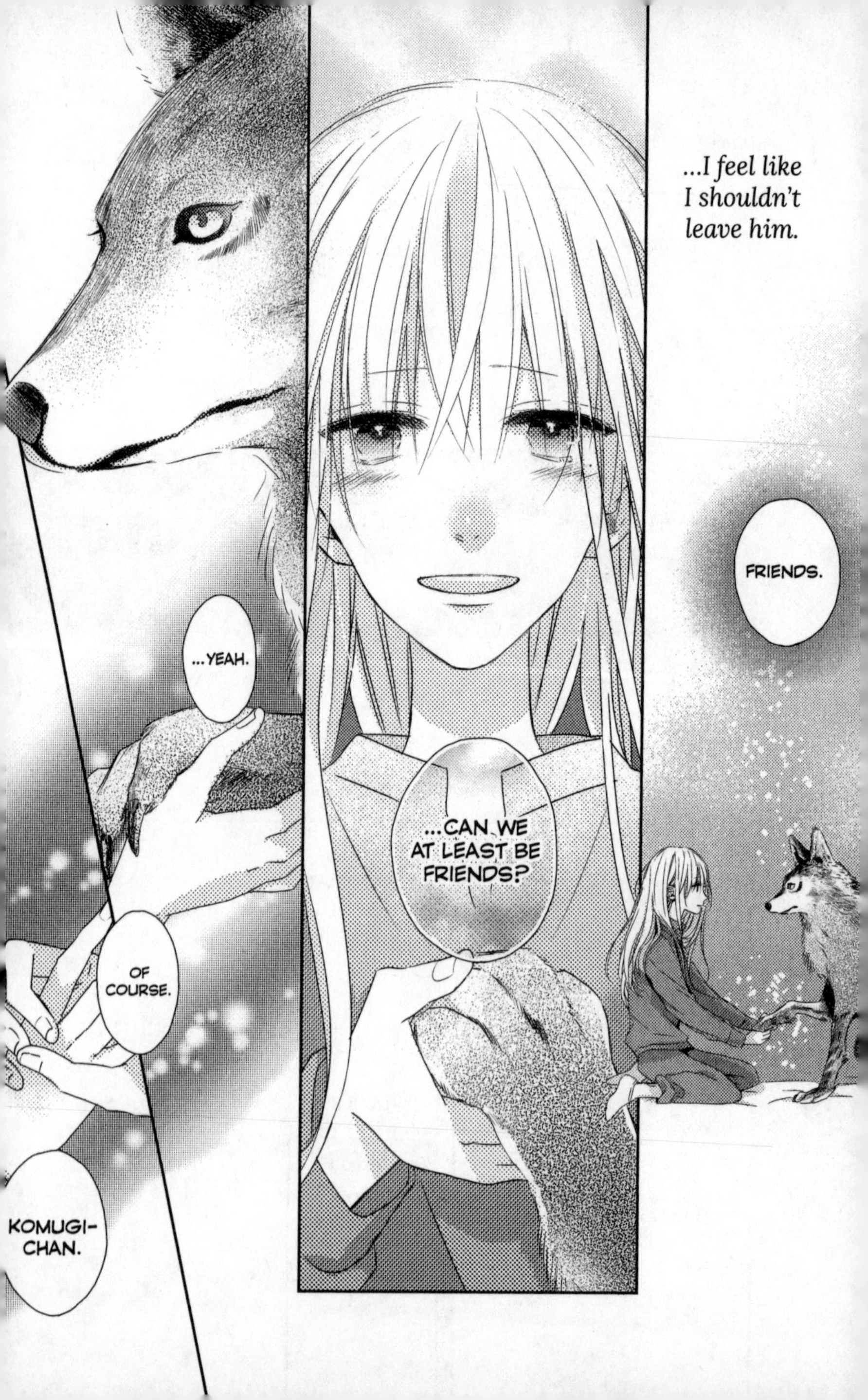
...I feel like I shouldn't leave him.
FRIENDS.
...CAN WE AT LEAST BE FRIENDS?
...YEAH.
OF COURSE.
KOMUGI-CHAN.

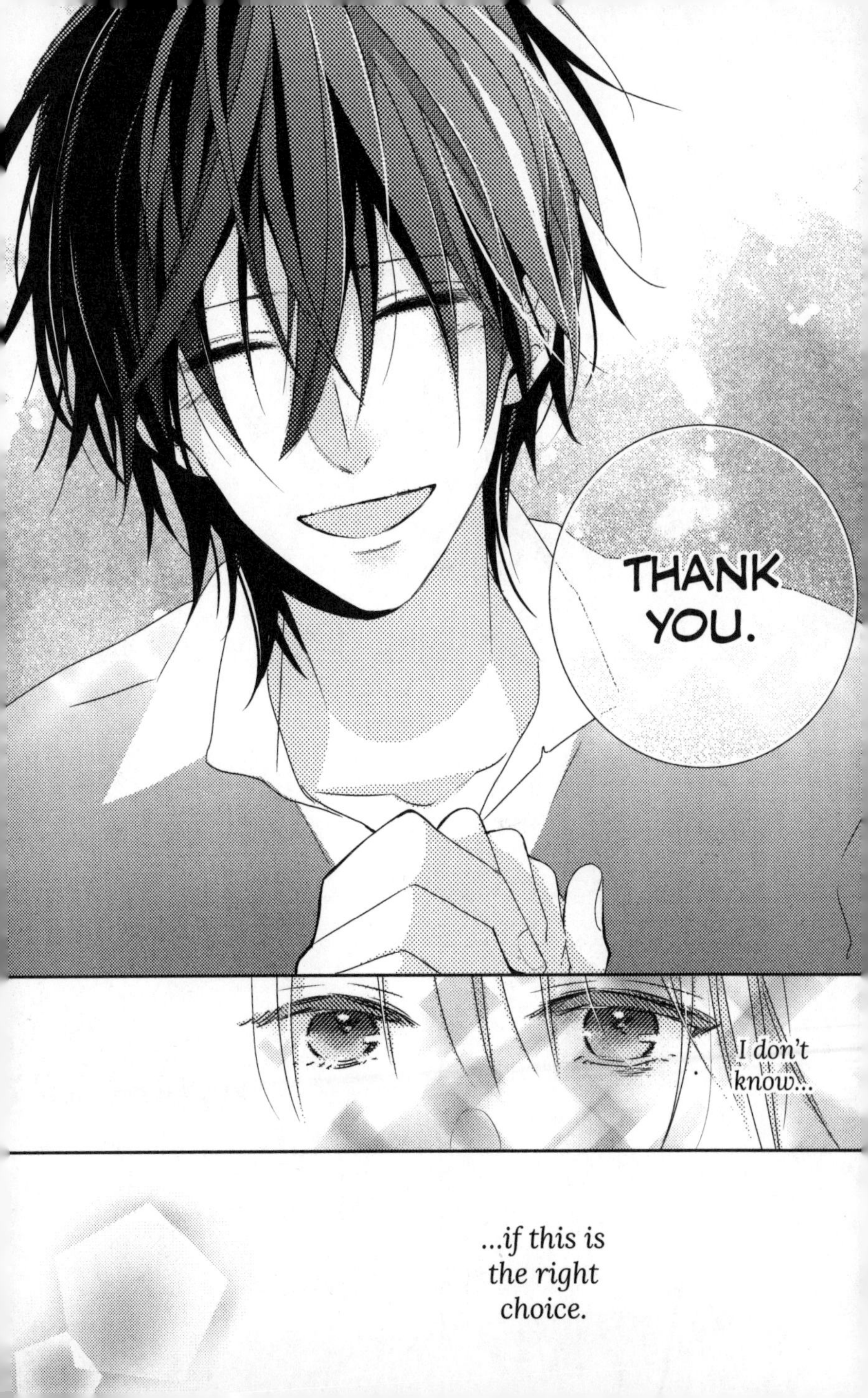
THANK YOU.
I don't know...
...if this is the right choice.

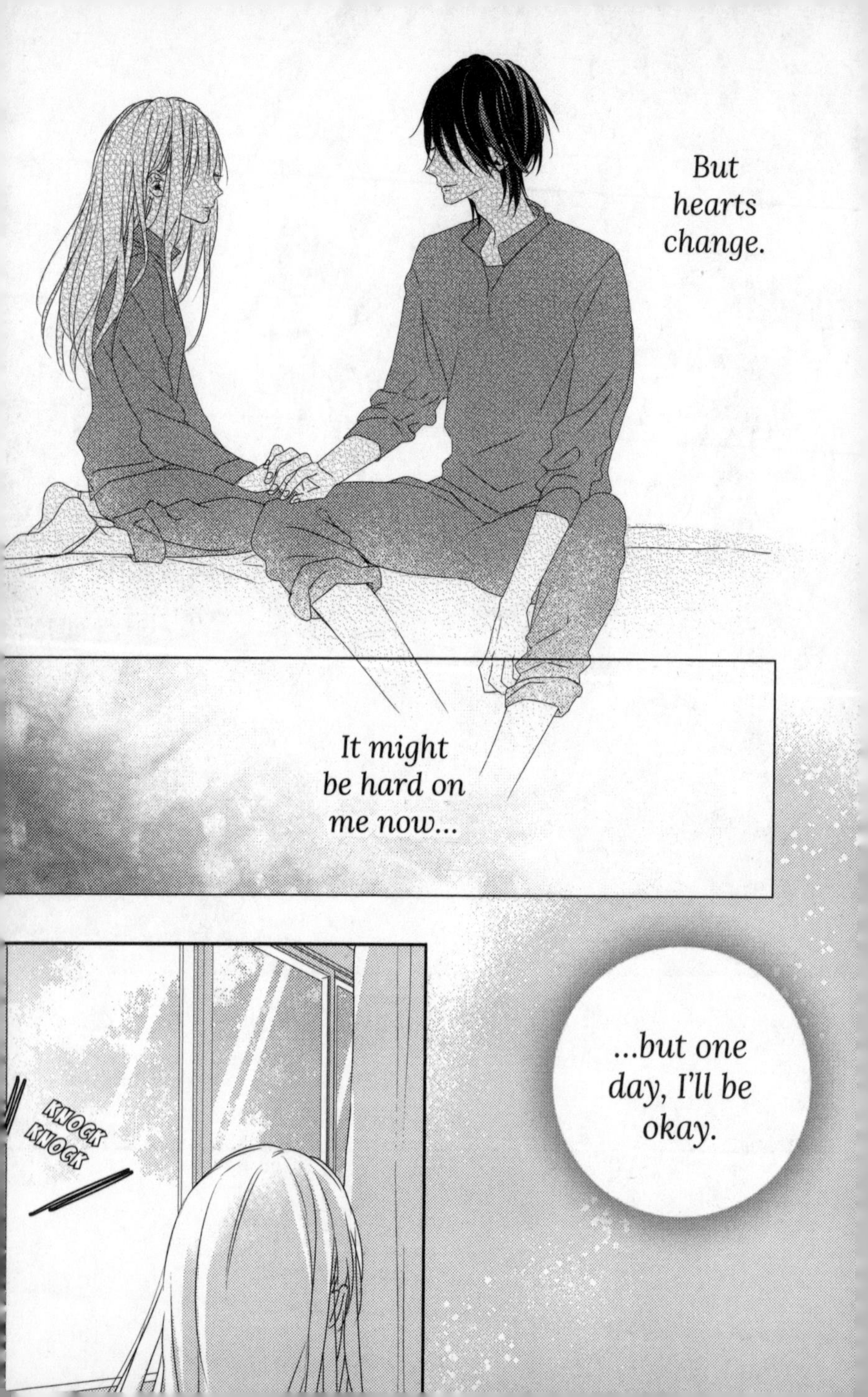
But hearts change.
It might be hard on me now...
...but one day, I'll be okay.
KNOCK KNOCK

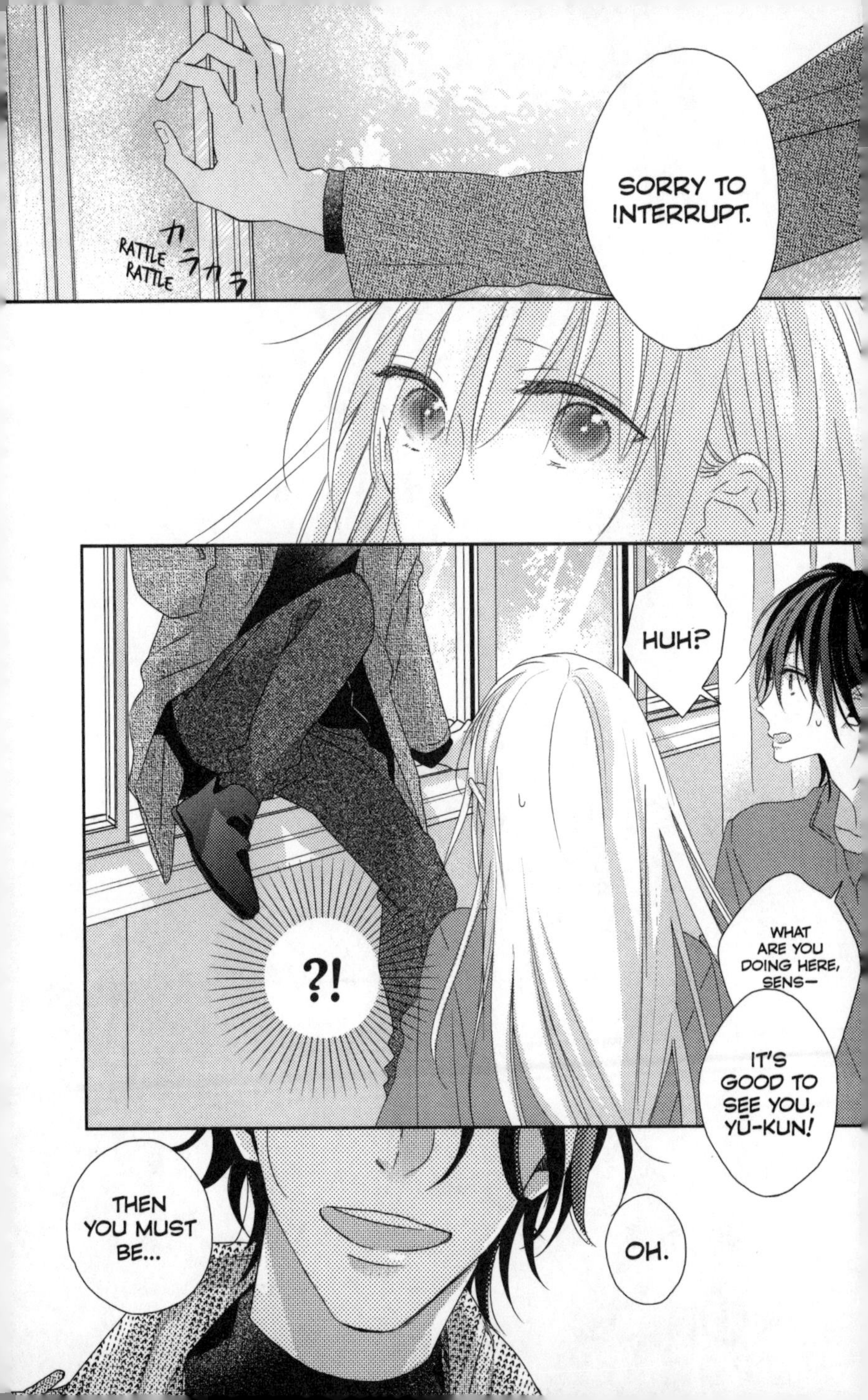

SORRY TO INTERRUPT.
カラカラ
RATTLE RATTLE
HUH?
WHAT ARE YOU DOING HERE, SENS—
IT'S GOOD TO SEE YOU, YŪ-KUN!
?!
OH.
THEN YOU MUST BE...

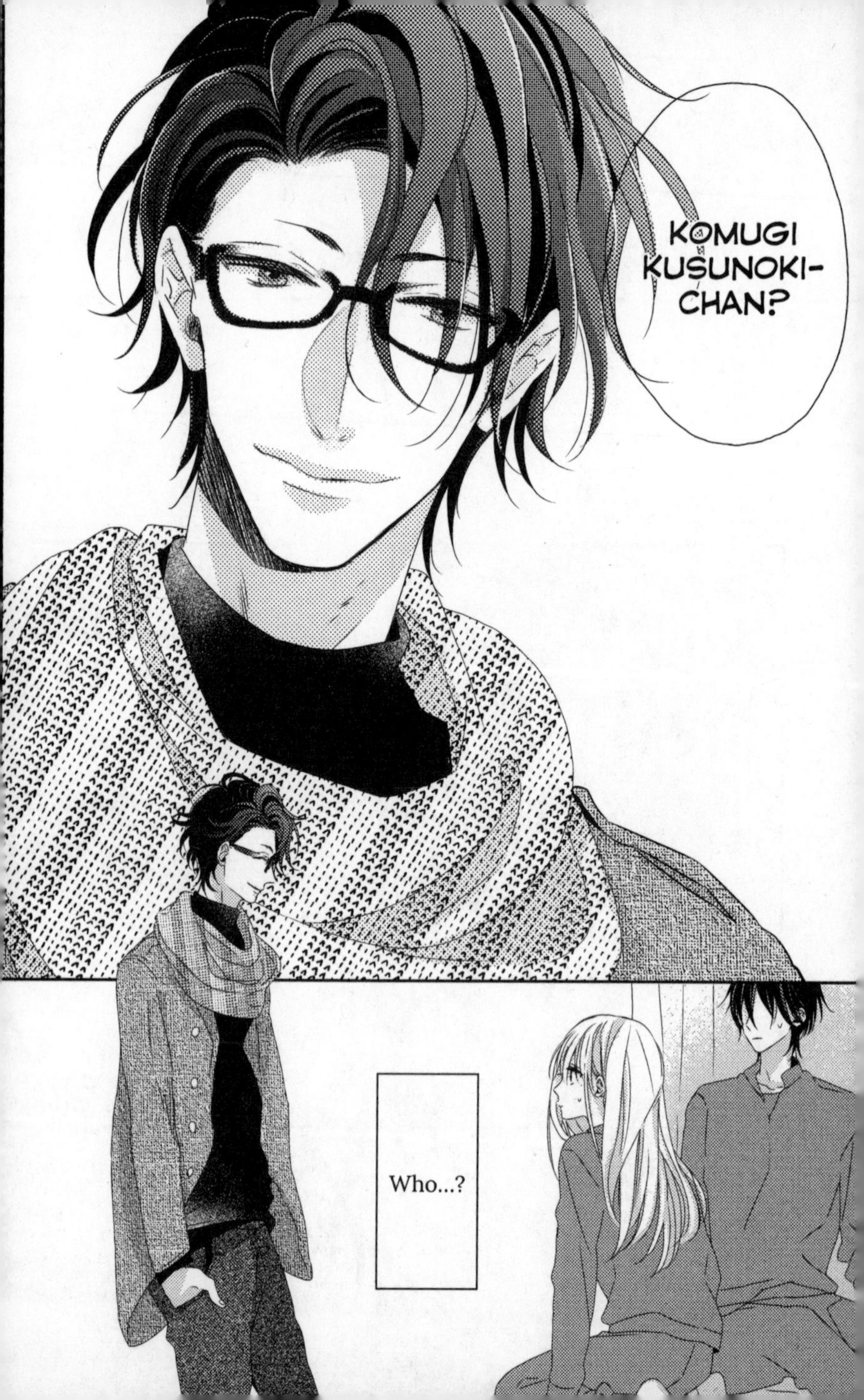
KOMUGI KUSUNOKI-CHAN?
Who...?

Chapter 6

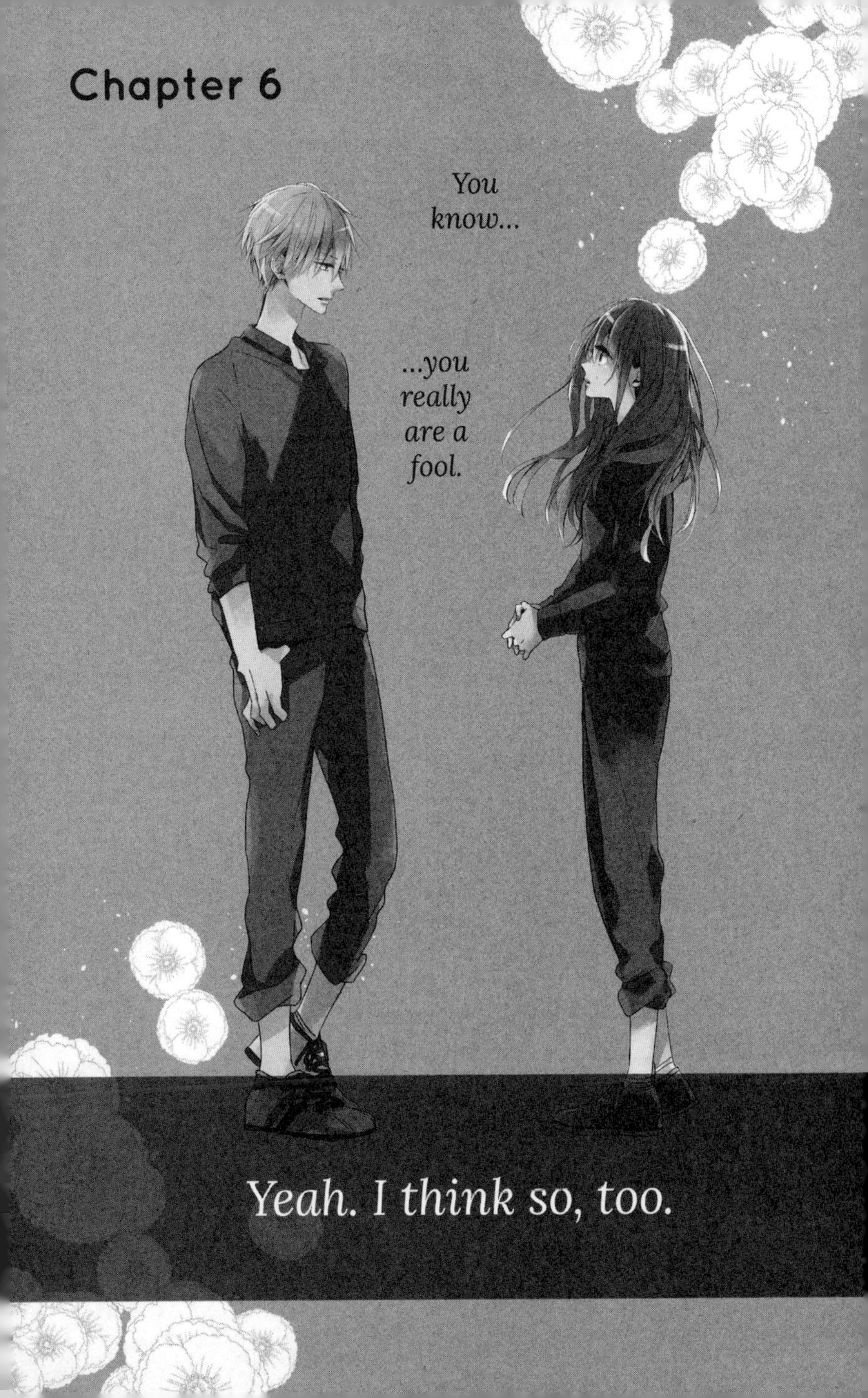
You know...
...you really are a fool.
Yeah. I think so, too.

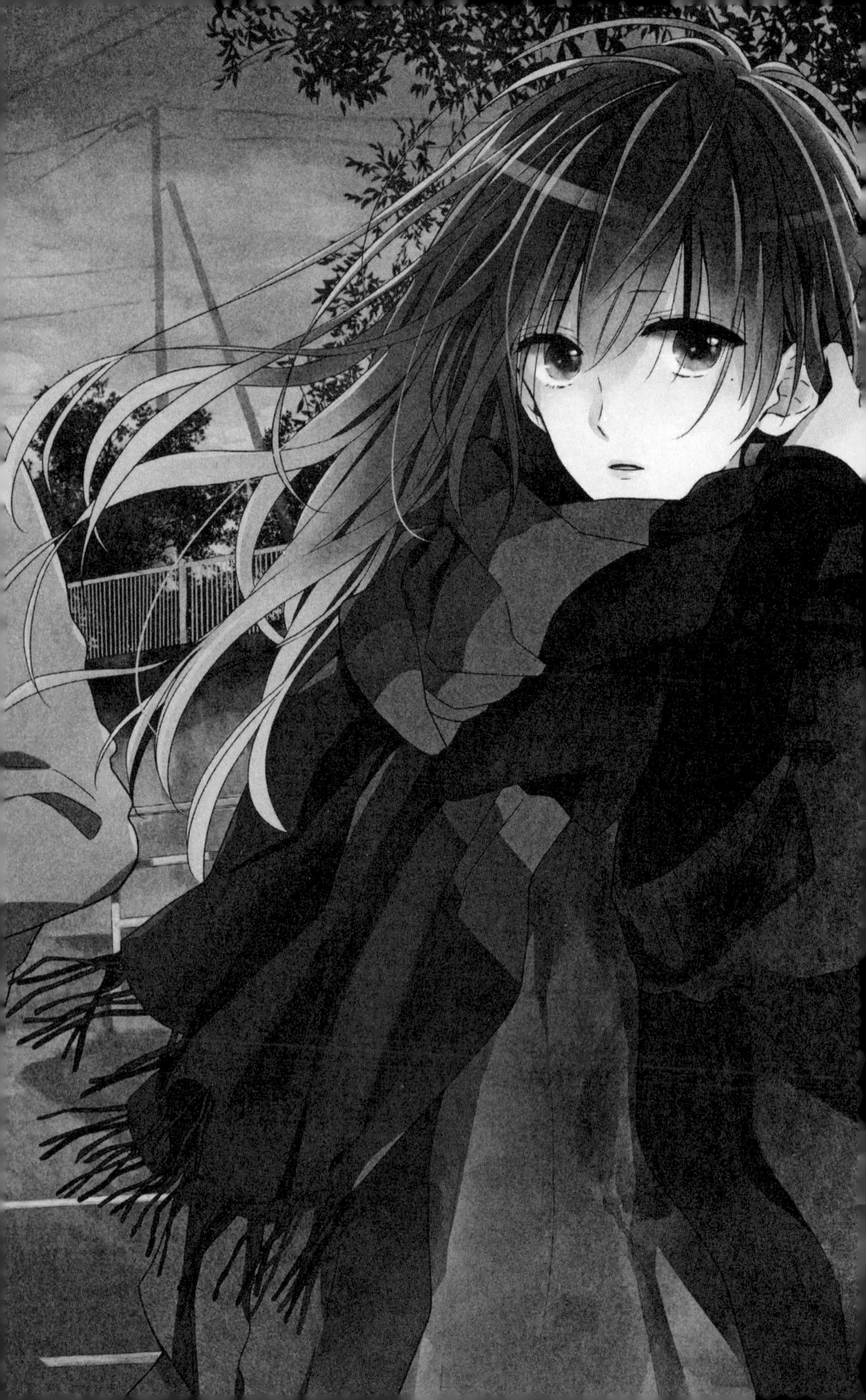

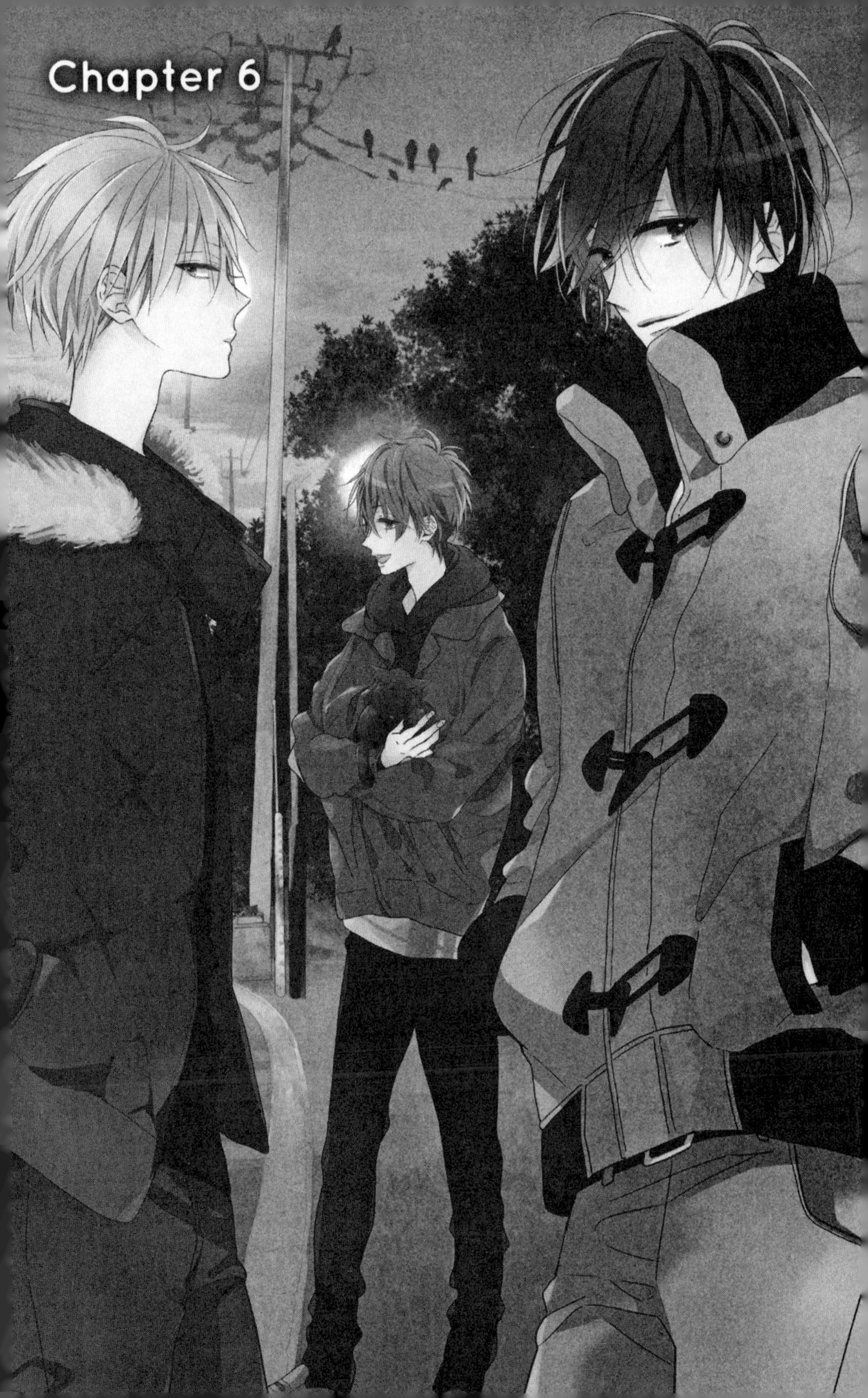
Chapter 6

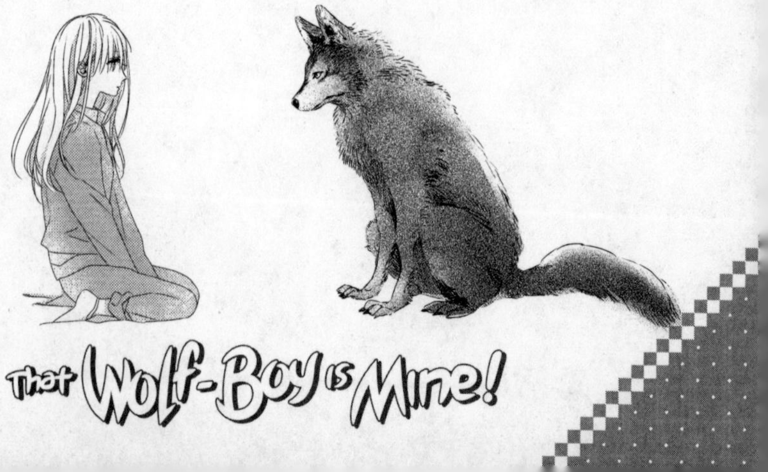

That Wolf-Boy is Mine!

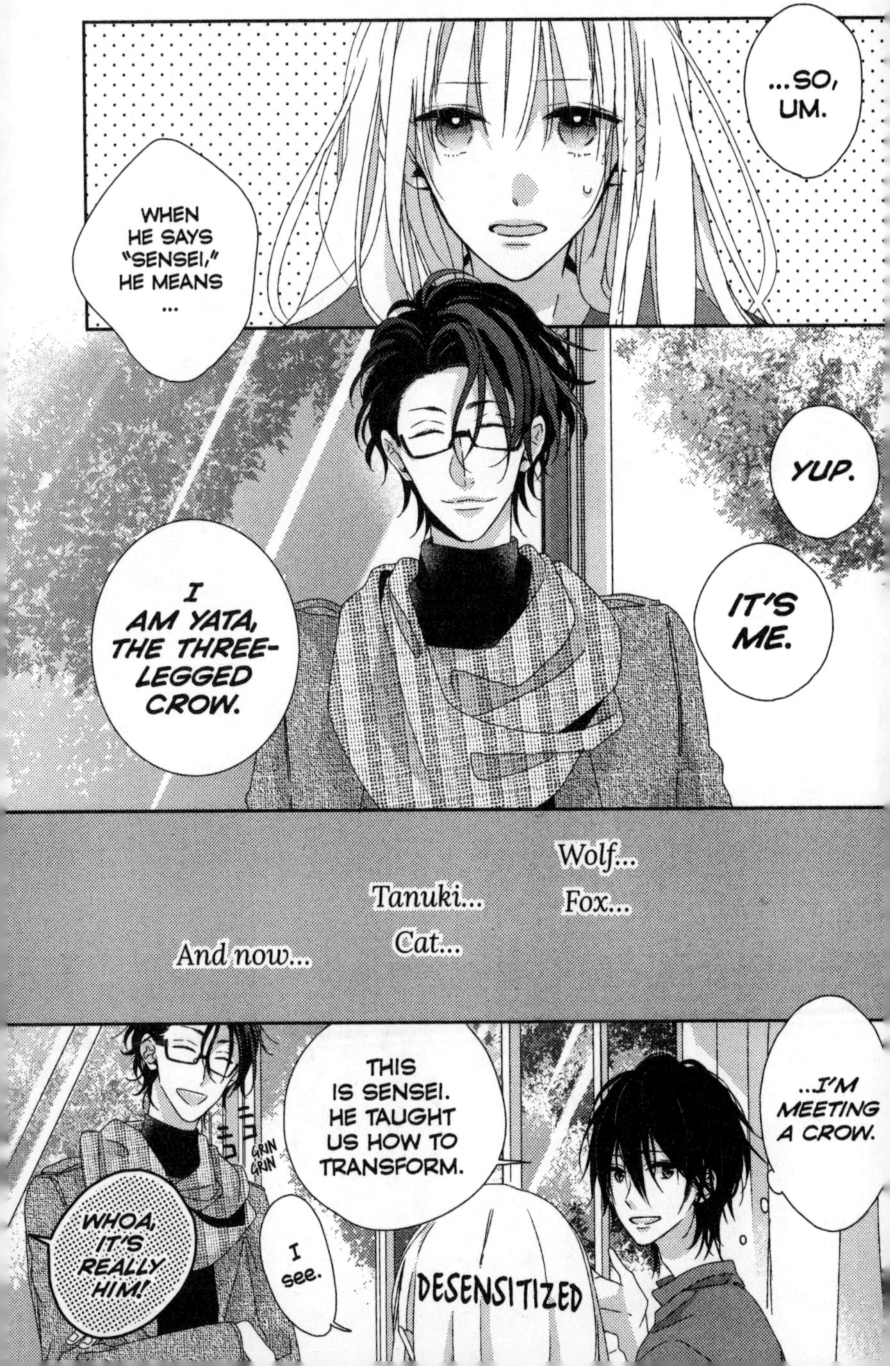
...SO, UM.
WHEN HE SAYS "SENSEI," HE MEANS ...
YUP.
IT'S ME.
I AM YATA, THE THREE-LEGGED CROW.
Wolf...
Fox...
Tanuki...
Cat...
And now...
...I'M MEETING A CROW.
THIS IS SENSEI. HE TAUGHT US HOW TO TRANSFORM.
DESENSITIZED
I see.
GRIN GRIN
WHOA, IT'S REALLY HIM!

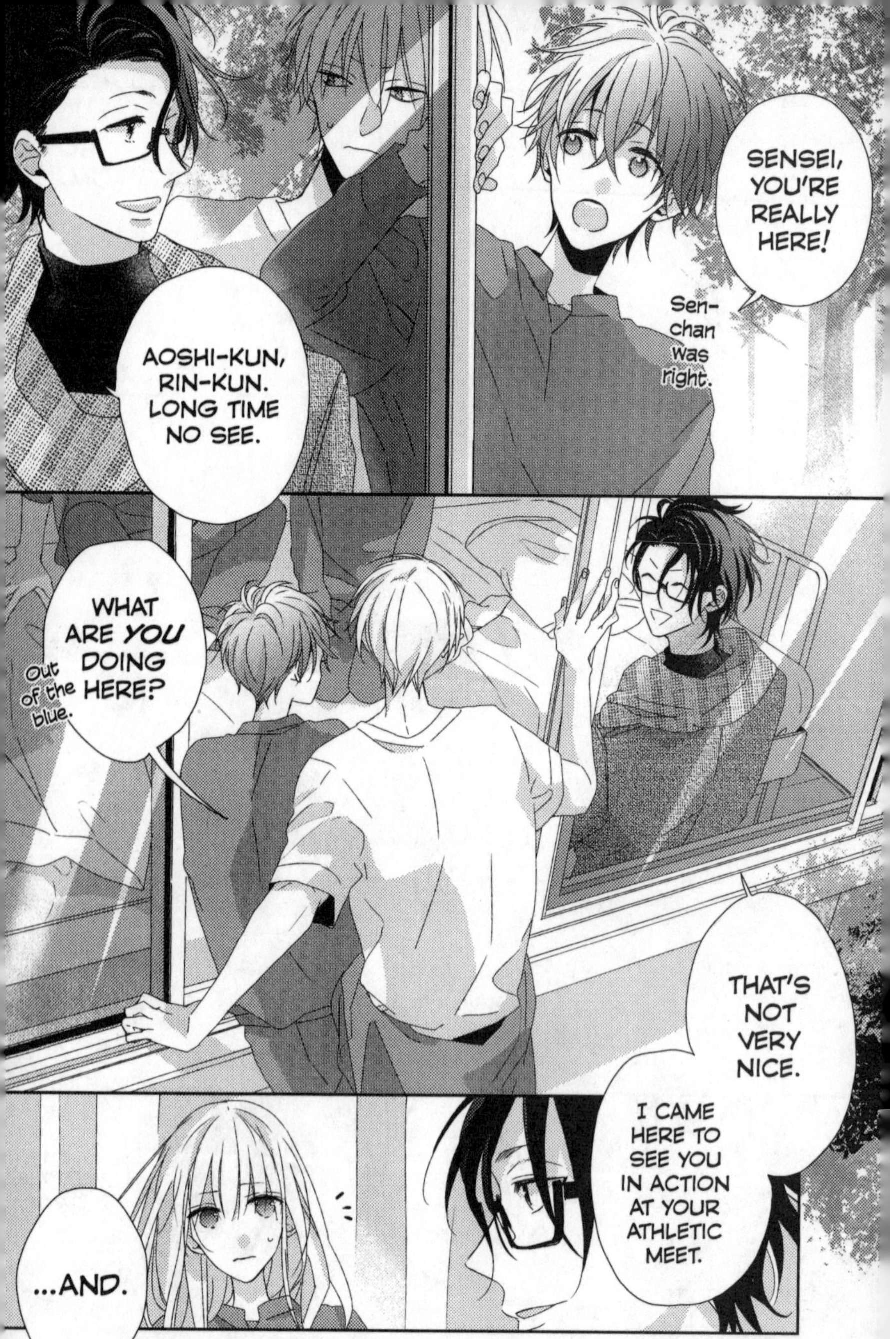
SENSEI, YOU'RE REALLY HERE!
Sen-chan was right.
AOSHI-KUN, RIN-KUN. LONG TIME NO SEE.
WHAT ARE *YOU* DOING HERE?
Out of the blue.
THAT'S NOT VERY NICE.
I CAME HERE TO SEE YOU IN ACTION AT YOUR ATHLETIC MEET.
...AND.

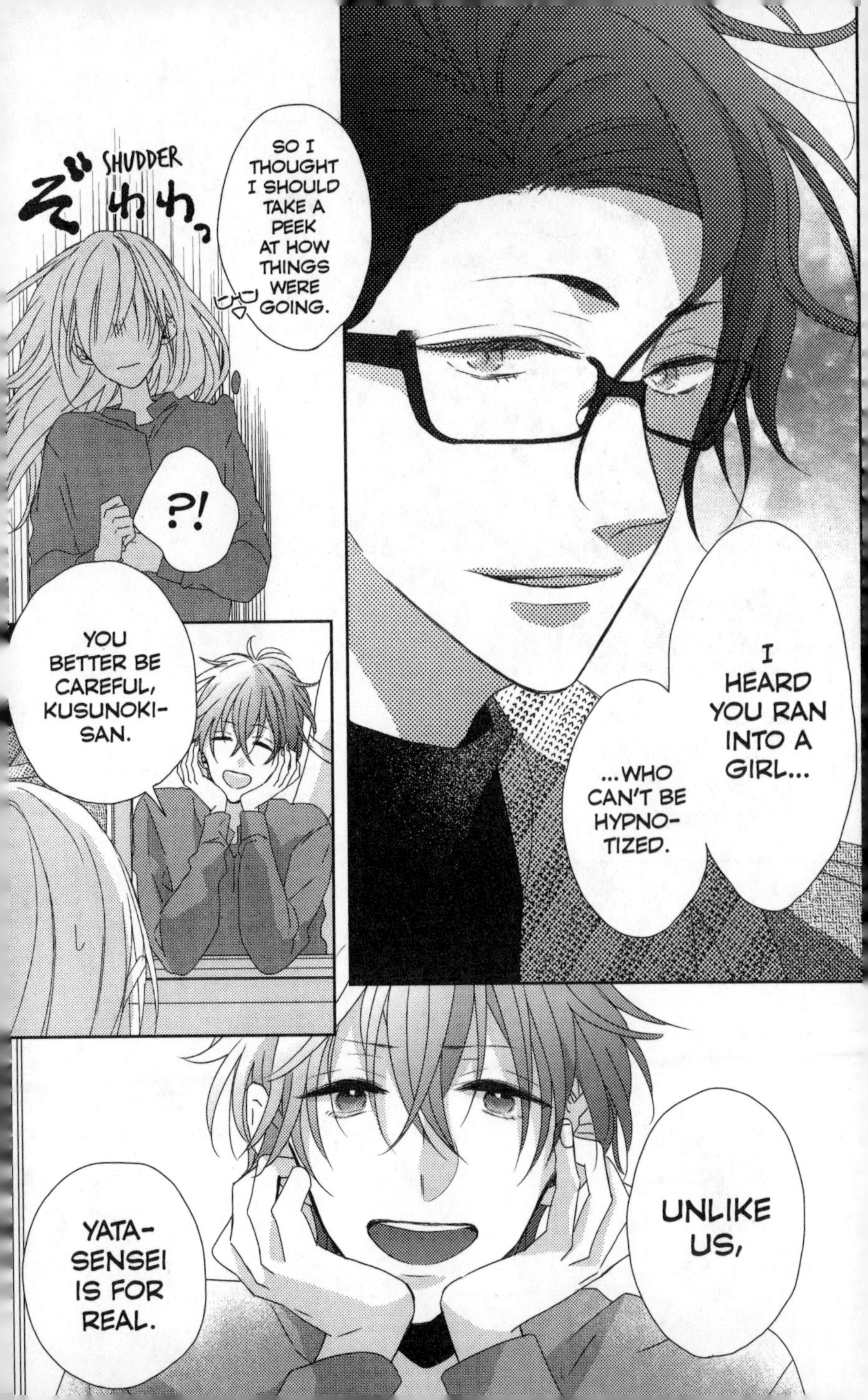
SO I THOUGHT I SHOULD TAKE A PEEK AT HOW THINGS WERE GOING.
I HEARD YOU RAN INTO A GIRL...
...WHO CAN'T BE HYPNOTIZED.
ぞわわっ
SHUDDER
?!
YOU BETTER BE CAREFUL, KUSUNOKI-SAN.
UNLIKE US,
YATA-SENSEI IS FOR REAL.

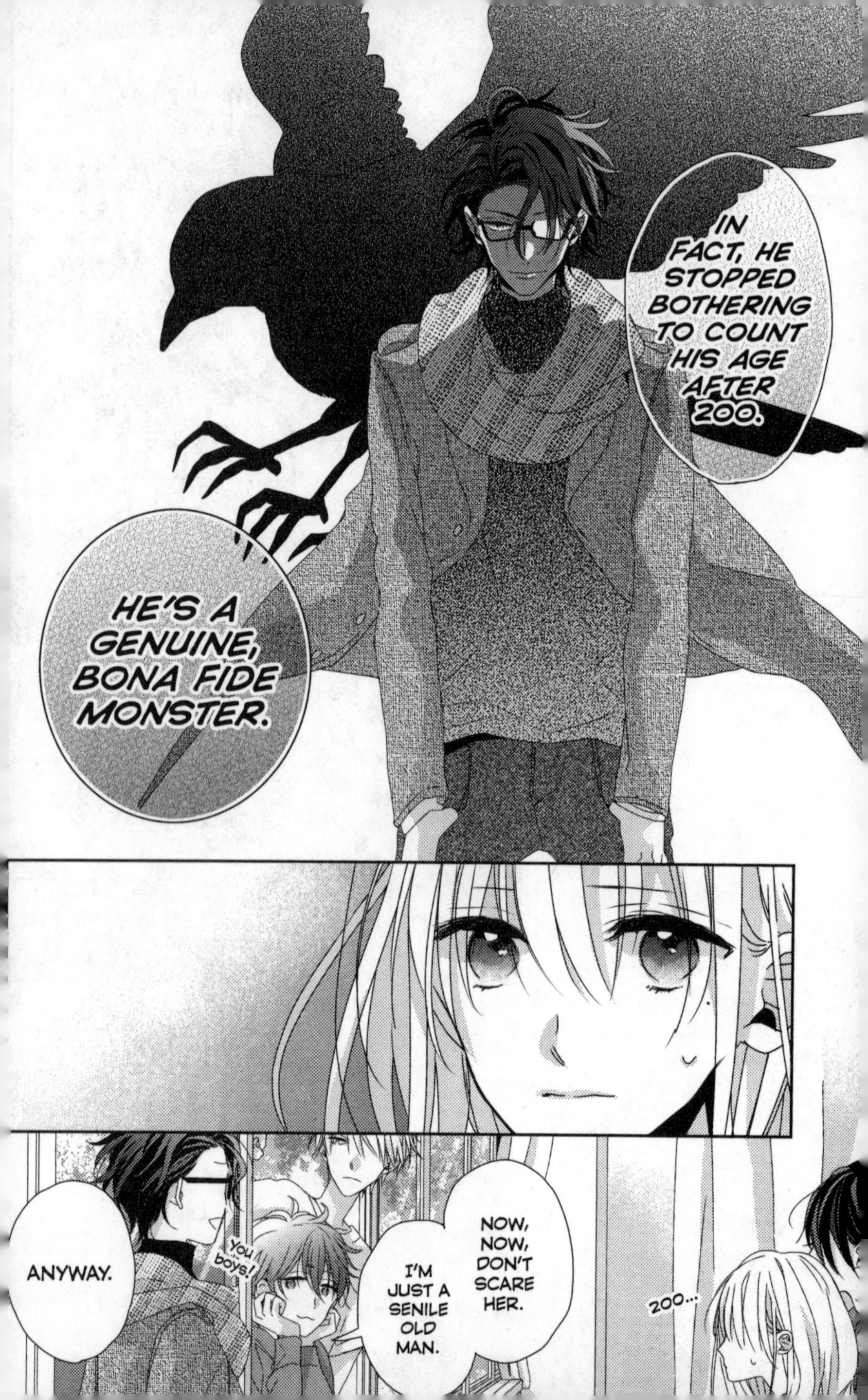
IN FACT, HE STOPPED BOTHERING TO COUNT HIS AGE AFTER 200.
HE'S A GENUINE, BONA FIDE MONSTER.
200...
NOW, NOW, DON'T SCARE HER.
I'M JUST A SENILE OLD MAN.
You boys!
ANYWAY.

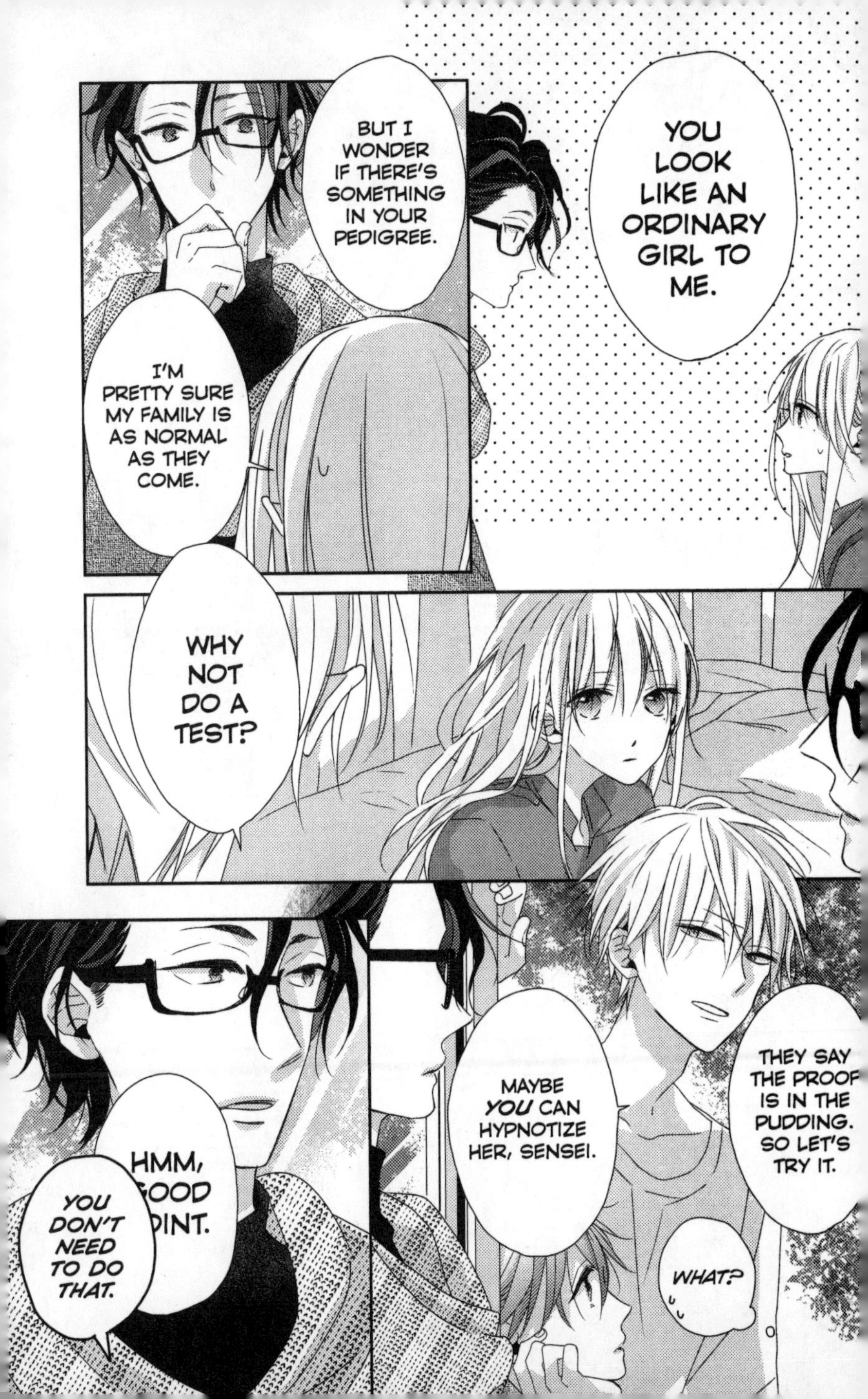
YOU LOOK LIKE AN ORDINARY GIRL TO ME.
BUT I WONDER IF THERE'S SOMETHING IN YOUR PEDIGREE.
I'M PRETTY SURE MY FAMILY IS AS NORMAL AS THEY COME.
WHY NOT DO A TEST?
THEY SAY THE PROOF IS IN THE PUDDING. SO LET'S TRY IT.
MAYBE *YOU* CAN HYPNOTIZE HER, SENSEI.
WHAT?
HMM, OOD INT.
YOU DON'T NEED TO DO THAT.

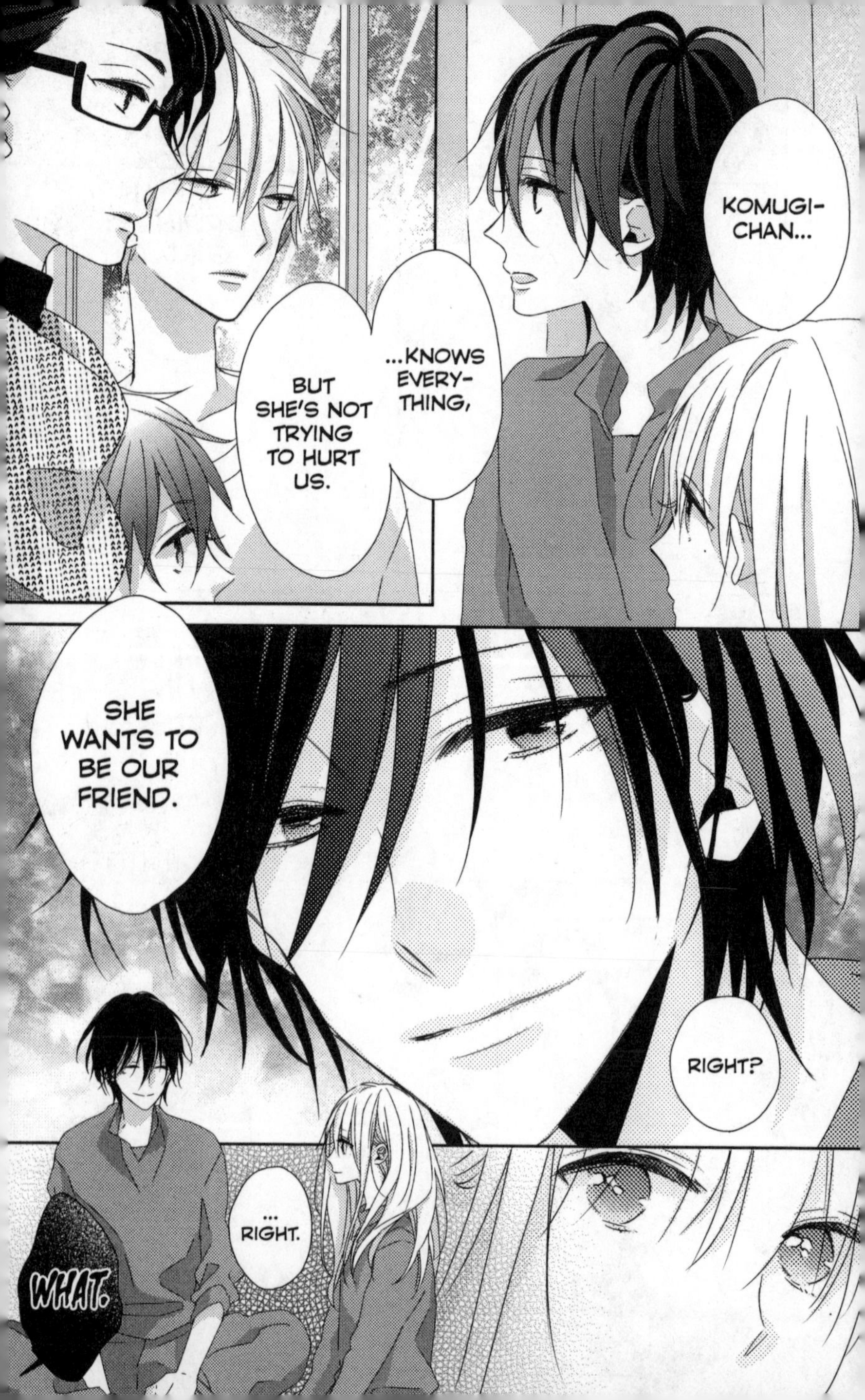
KOMUGI-CHAN...
...KNOWS EVERY-THING,
BUT SHE'S NOT TRYING TO HURT US.
SHE WANTS TO BE OUR FRIEND.
RIGHT?
...RIGHT.
WHAT.

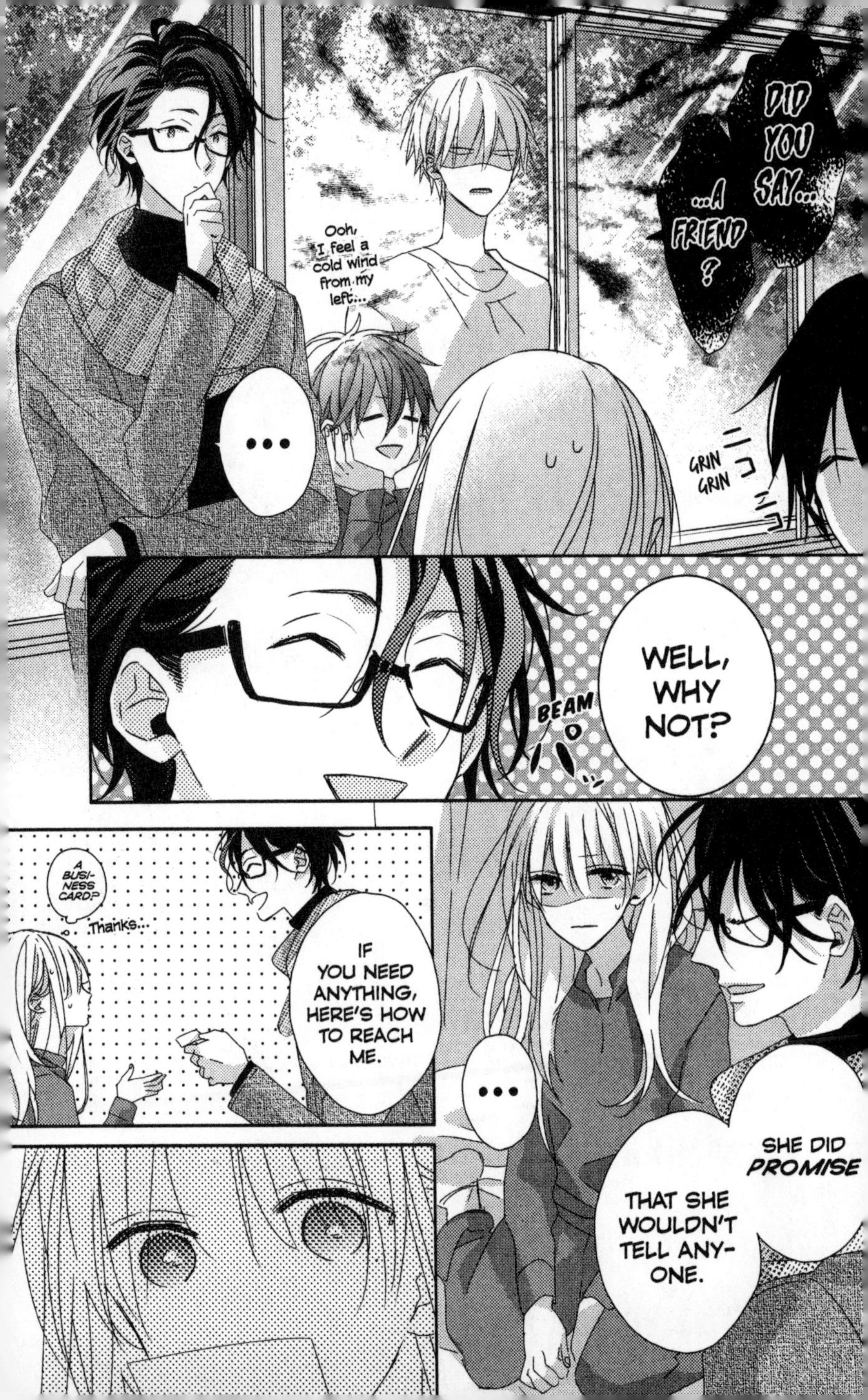
DID YOU SAY...
...A FRIEND?
GRIN GRIN
Ooh, I feel a cold wind from my left...
...
WELL, WHY NOT?
BEAM
SHE DID PROMISE
THAT SHE WOULDN'T TELL ANY-ONE.
...
IF YOU NEED ANYTHING, HERE'S HOW TO REACH ME.
A BUSI-NESS CARD?
Thanks...

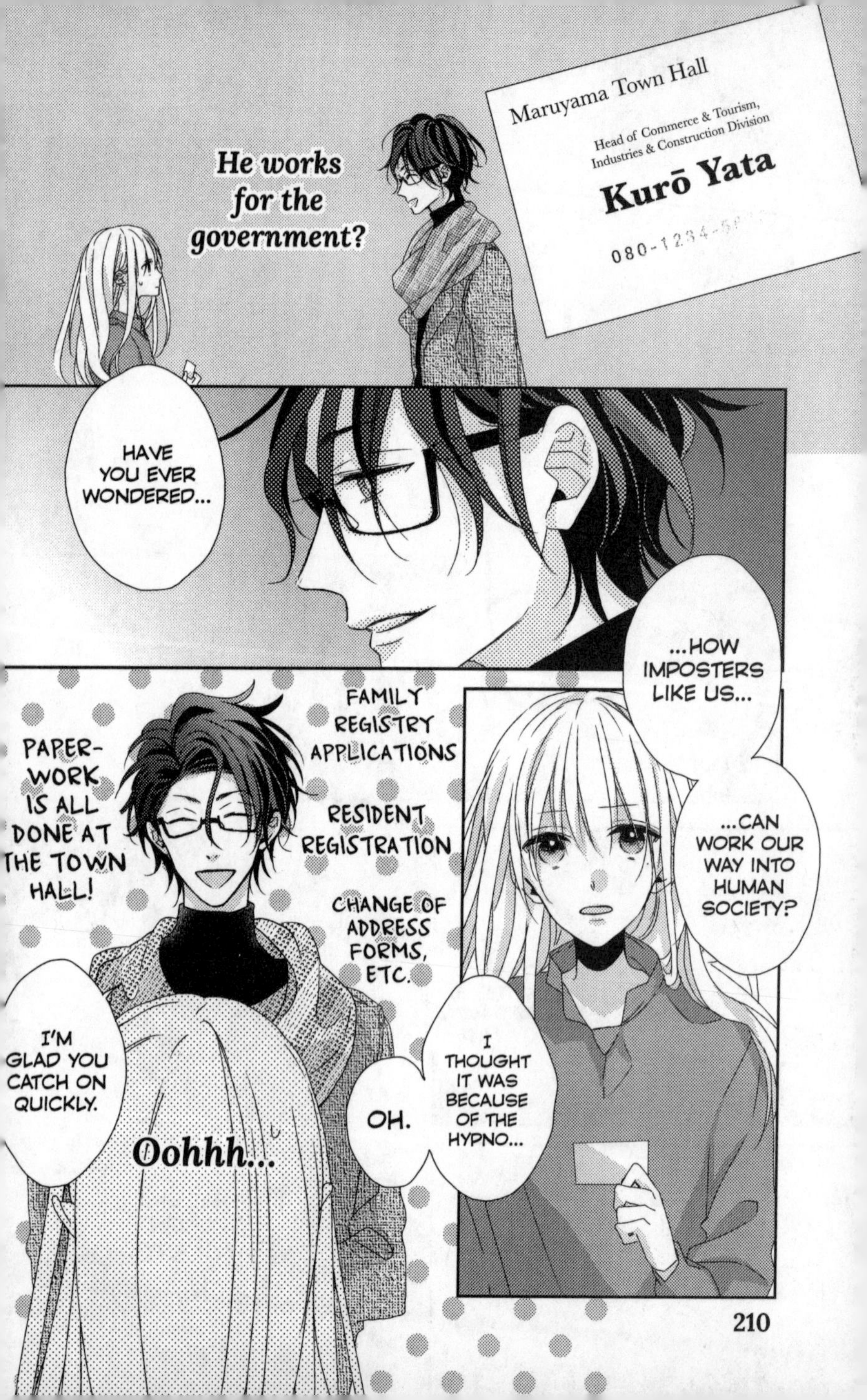
Maruyama Town Hall
Head of Commerce & Tourism, Industries & Construction Division
Kurō Yata
He works for the government?
HAVE YOU EVER WONDERED...
...HOW IMPOSTERS LIKE US...
...CAN WORK OUR WAY INTO HUMAN SOCIETY?
I THOUGHT IT WAS BECAUSE OF THE HYPNO...
OH.
FAMILY REGISTRY APPLICATIONS
RESIDENT REGISTRATION
CHANGE OF ADDRESS FORMS, ETC.
PAPERWORK IS ALL DONE AT THE TOWN HALL!
I'M GLAD YOU CATCH ON QUICKLY.
Oohhh...

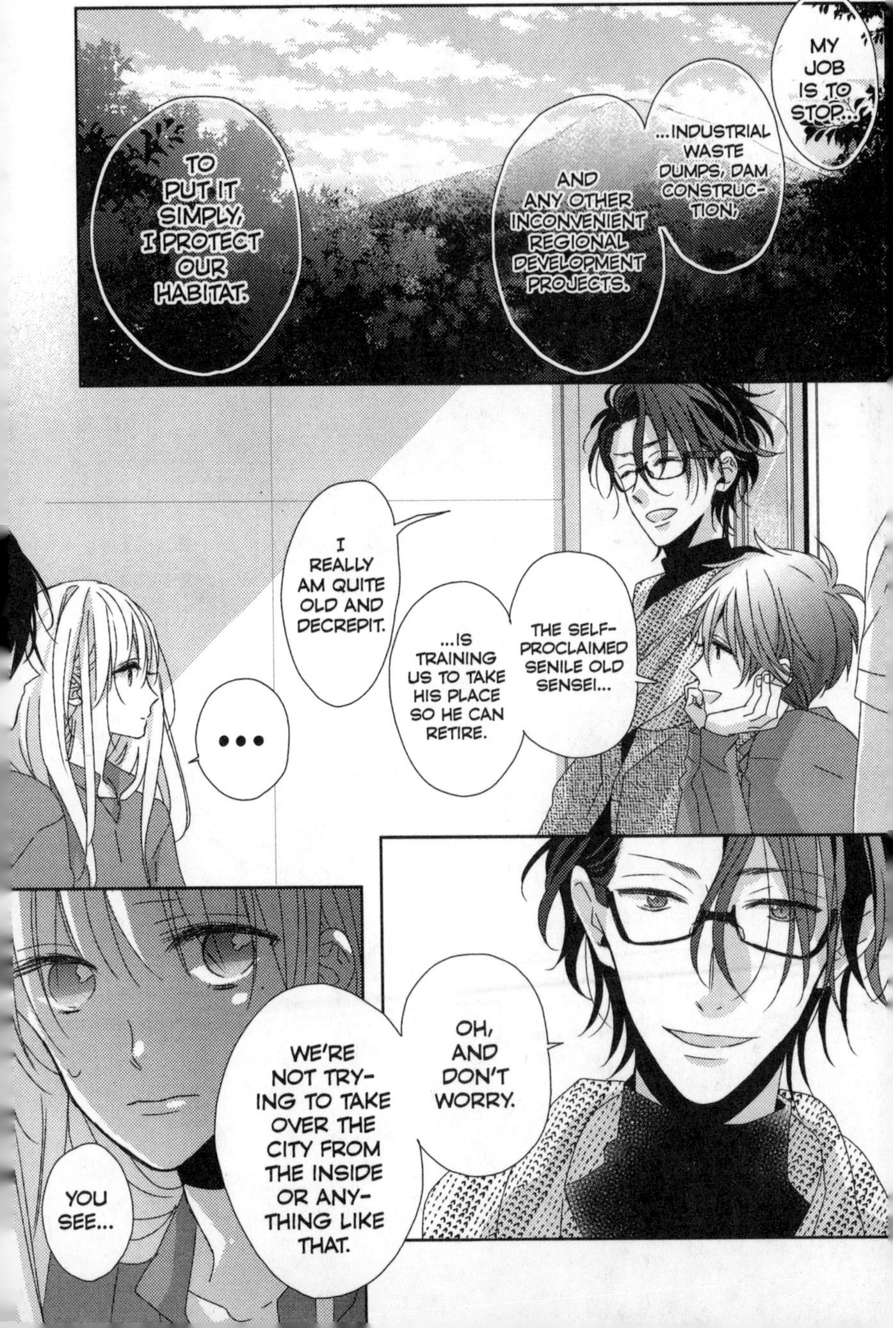
MY JOB IS TO STOP...
...INDUSTRIAL WASTE DUMPS, DAM CONSTRUCTION,
AND ANY OTHER INCONVENIENT REGIONAL DEVELOPMENT PROJECTS.
TO PUT IT SIMPLY, I PROTECT OUR HABITAT.
THE SELF-PROCLAIMED SENILE OLD SENSEI...
...IS TRAINING US TO TAKE HIS PLACE SO HE CAN RETIRE.
I REALLY AM QUITE OLD AND DECREPIT.
...
OH, AND DON'T WORRY.
WE'RE NOT TRYING TO TAKE OVER THE CITY FROM THE INSIDE OR ANYTHING LIKE THAT.
YOU SEE...

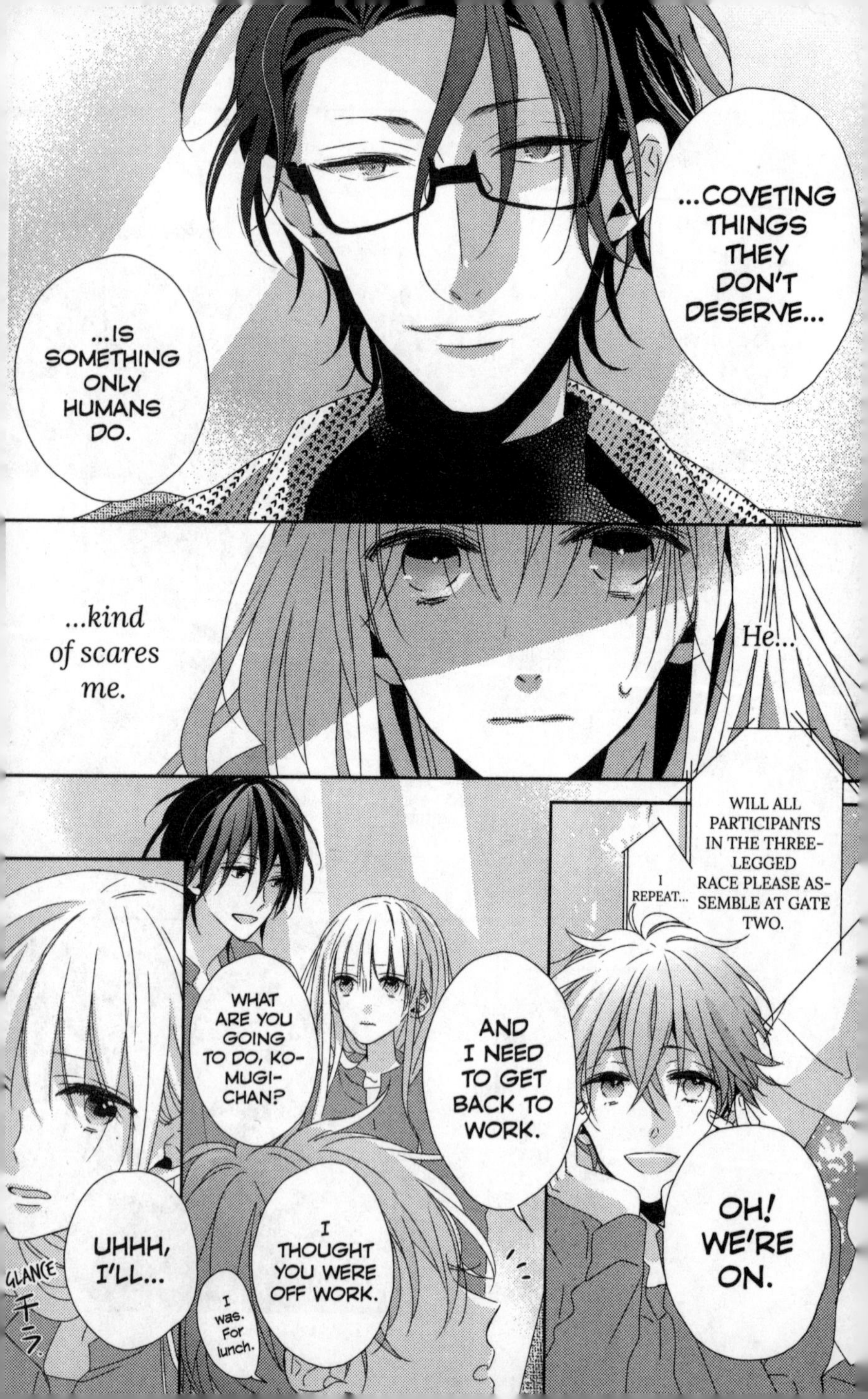
...COVETING THINGS THEY DON'T DESERVE...
...IS SOMETHING ONLY HUMANS DO.
He...
...kind of scares me.
WILL ALL PARTICIPANTS IN THE THREE-LEGGED RACE PLEASE ASSEMBLE AT GATE TWO.
I REPEAT...
OH! WE'RE ON.
AND I NEED TO GET BACK TO WORK.
I THOUGHT YOU WERE OFF WORK.
I was. For lunch.
WHAT ARE YOU GOING TO DO, KO-MUGI-CHAN?
UHHH, I'LL...
GLANCE
チラ

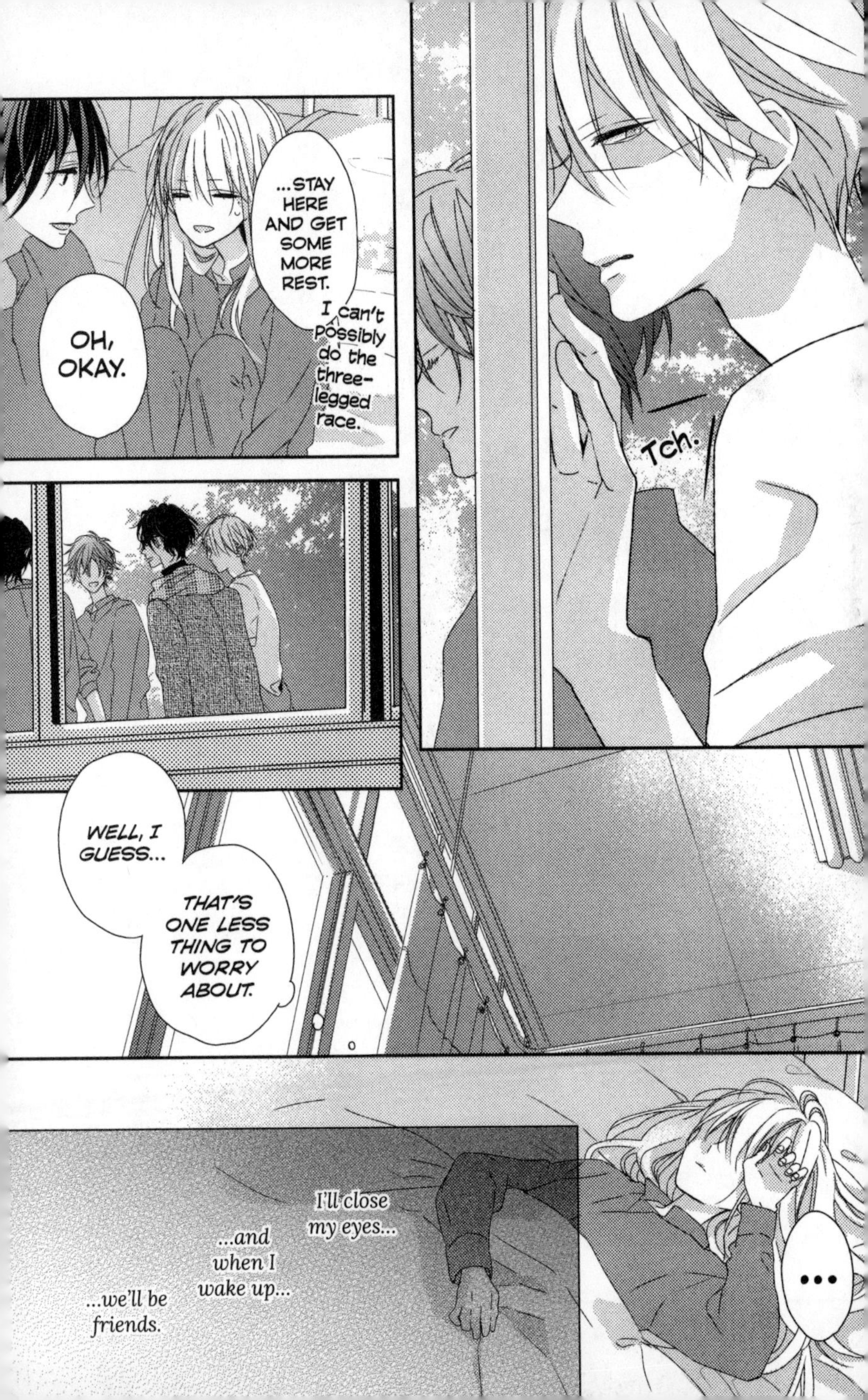
Tch.
...STAY HERE AND GET SOME MORE REST.
I can't possibly do the three-legged race.
OH, OKAY.
WELL, I GUESS...
THAT'S ONE LESS THING TO WORRY ABOUT.
...
I'll close my eyes...
...and when I wake up...
...we'll be friends.

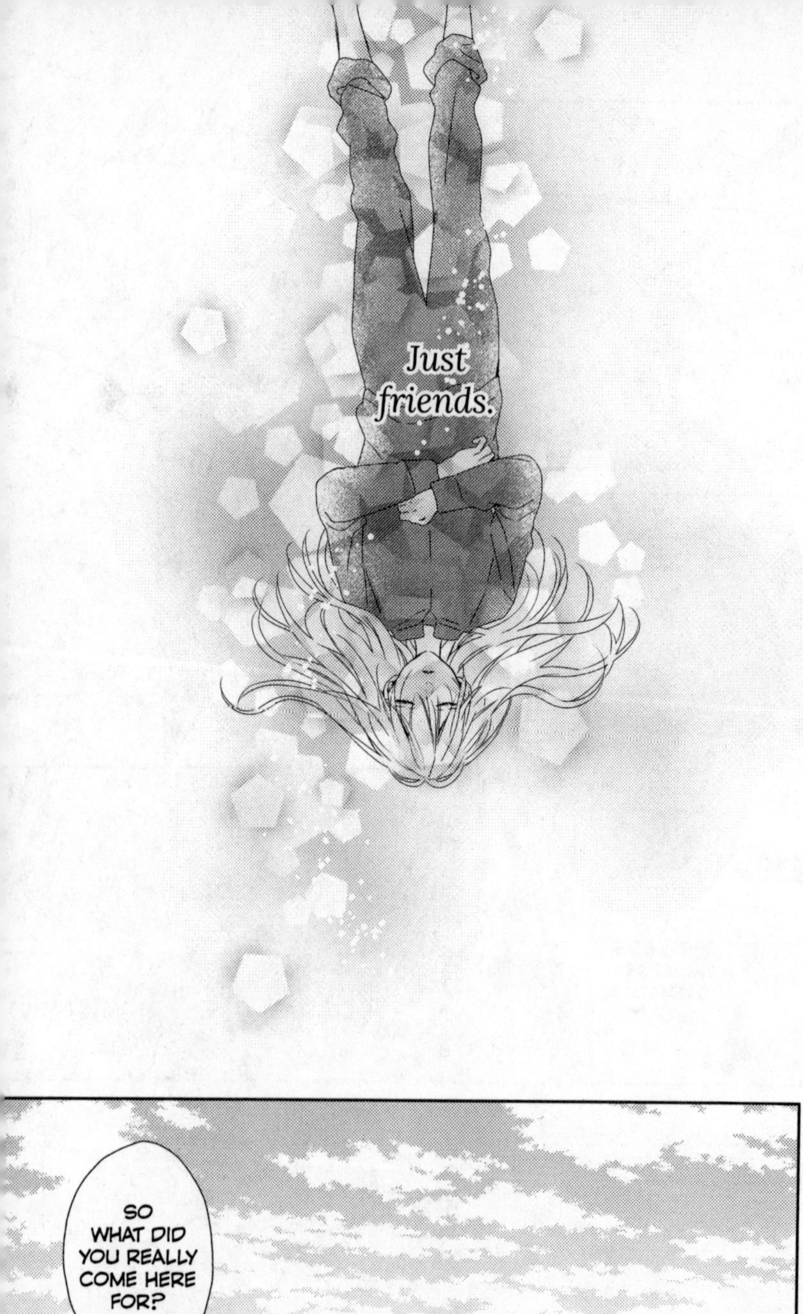
Just friends.
SO WHAT DID YOU REALLY COME HERE FOR?

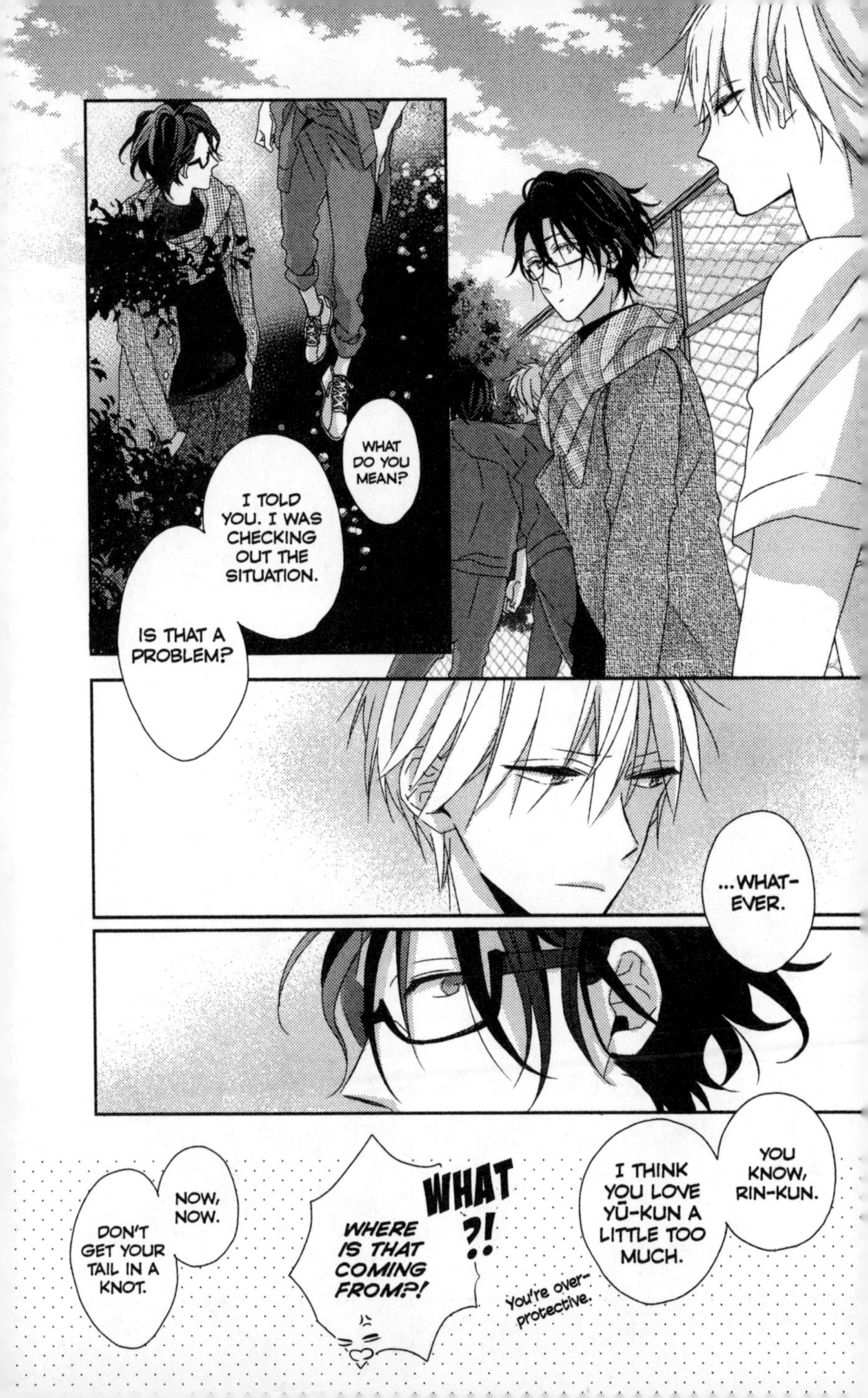
WHAT DO YOU MEAN?
I TOLD YOU. I WAS CHECKING OUT THE SITUATION.
IS THAT A PROBLEM?
...WHAT-EVER.
YOU KNOW, RIN-KUN.
I THINK YOU LOVE YŪ-KUN A LITTLE TOO MUCH.
You're over-protective.
WHAT ?!
WHERE IS THAT COMING FROM?!
NOW, NOW.
DON'T GET YOUR TAIL IN A KNOT.

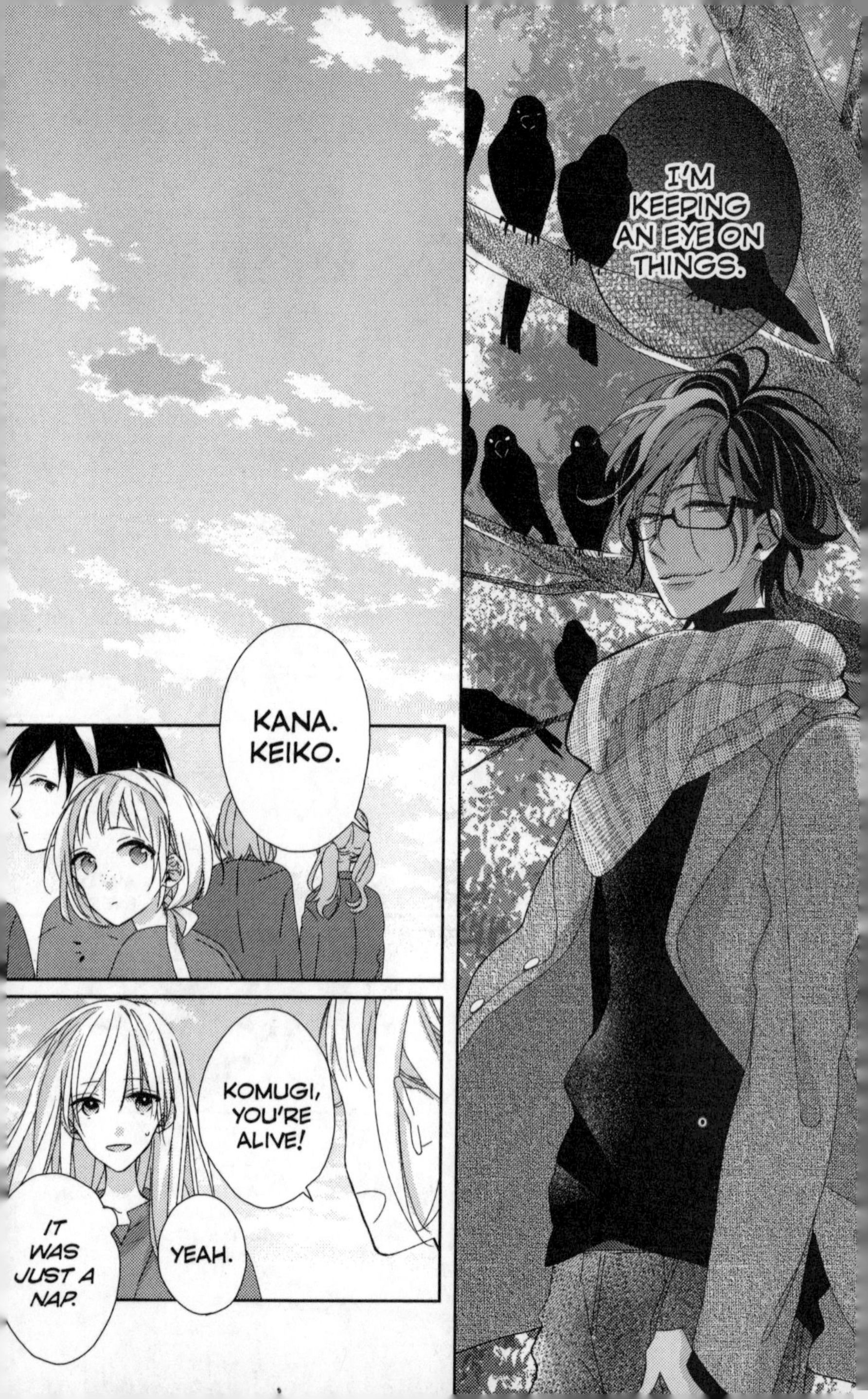
I'M KEEPING AN EYE ON THINGS.
KANA. KEIKO.
KOMUGI, YOU'RE ALIVE!
YEAH.
IT WAS JUST A NAP.

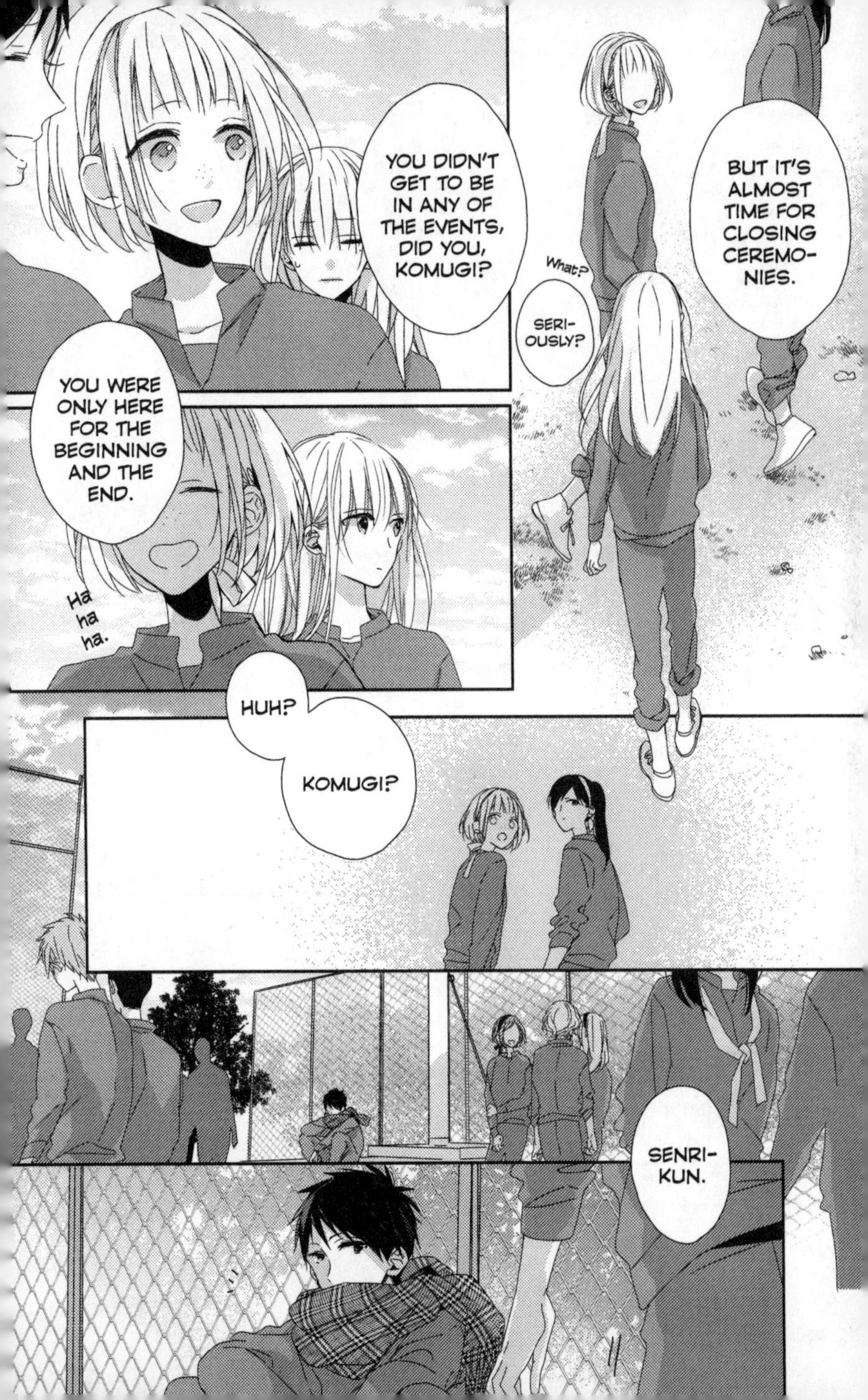
BUT IT'S ALMOST TIME FOR CLOSING CEREMONIES.
What?
SERIOUSLY?
YOU DIDN'T GET TO BE IN ANY OF THE EVENTS, DID YOU, KOMUGI?
YOU WERE ONLY HERE FOR THE BEGINNING AND THE END.
Ha ha ha.
HUH?
KOMUGI?
SENRI-KUN.

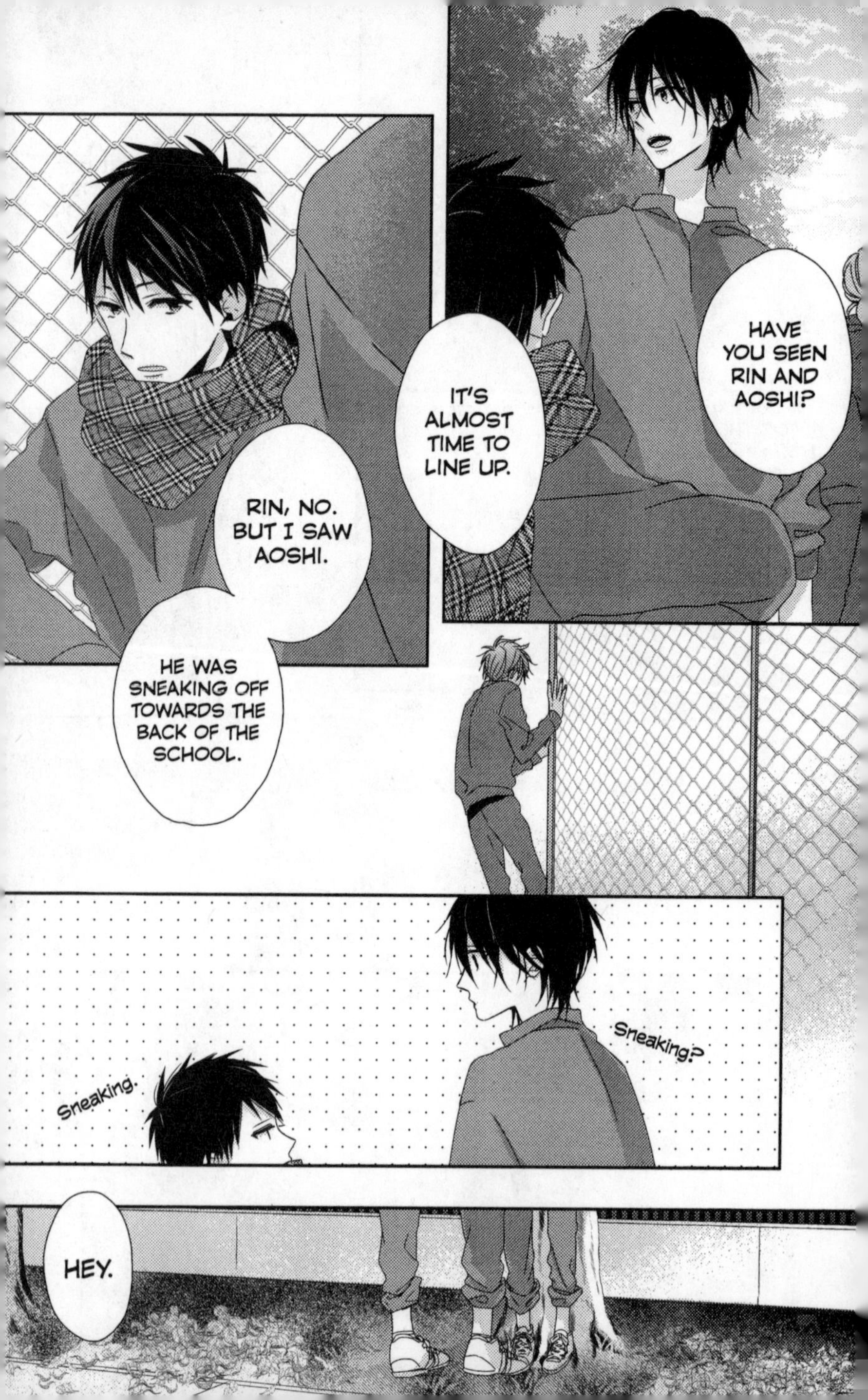
HAVE YOU SEEN RIN AND AOSHI?
IT'S ALMOST TIME TO LINE UP.
RIN, NO. BUT I SAW AOSHI.
HE WAS SNEAKING OFF TOWARDS THE BACK OF THE SCHOOL.
Sneaking?
Sneaking.
HEY.

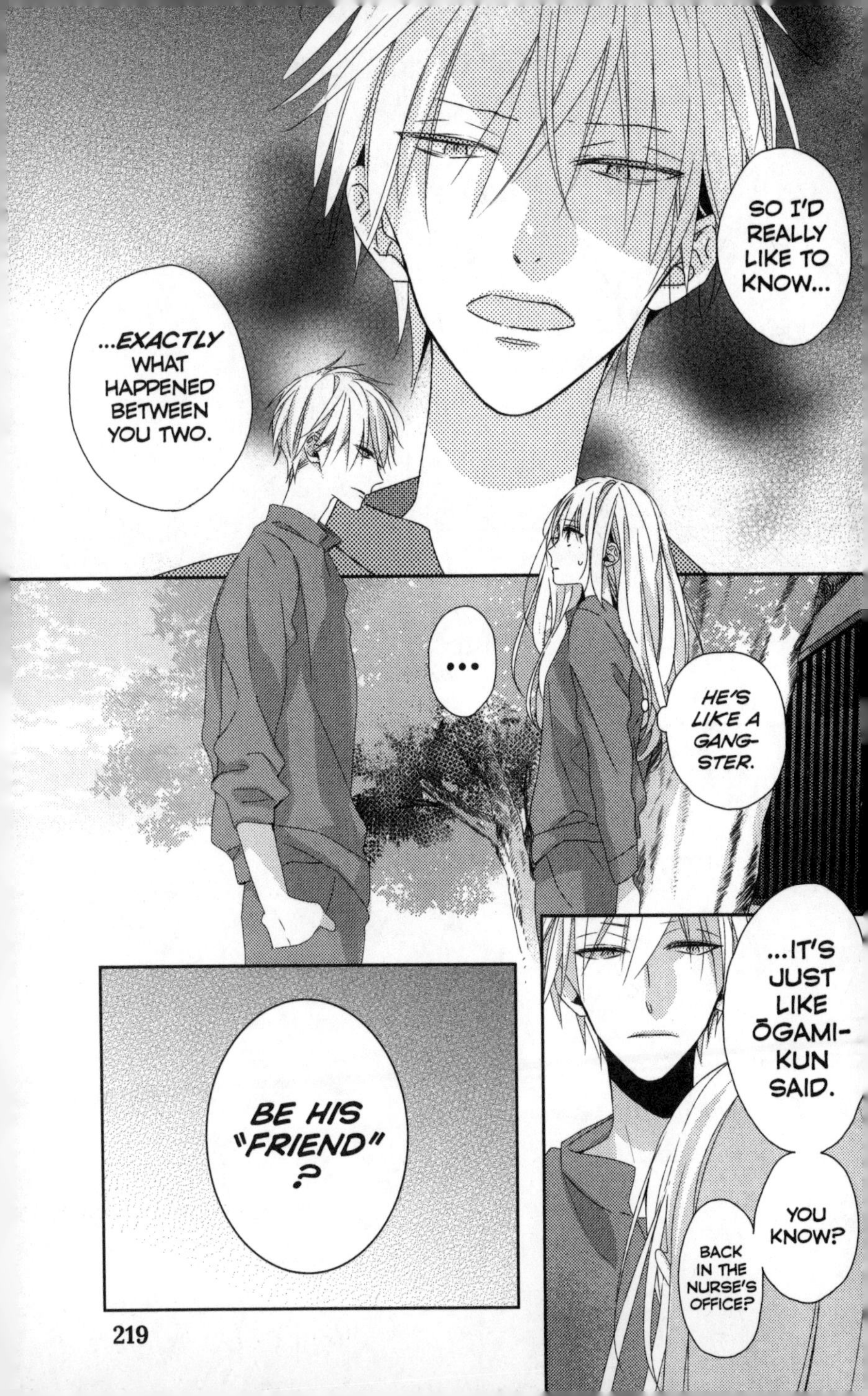
SO I'D REALLY LIKE TO KNOW...
...*EXACTLY* WHAT HAPPENED BETWEEN YOU TWO.
...
HE'S LIKE A GANG-STER.
...IT'S JUST LIKE ŌGAMI-KUN SAID.
YOU KNOW?
BACK IN THE NURSE'S OFFICE?
BE HIS "FRIEND"?

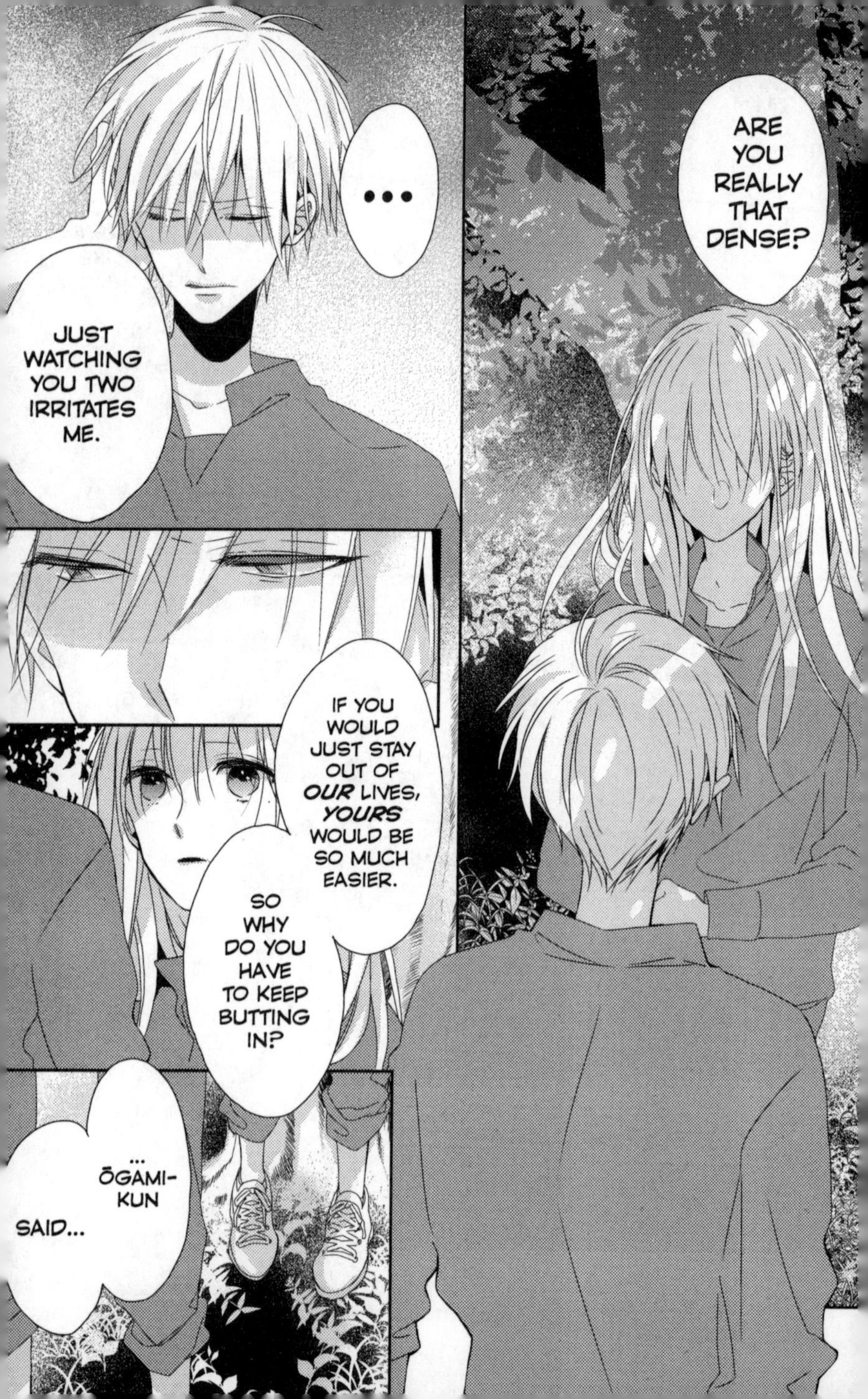
ARE YOU REALLY THAT DENSE?
...
JUST WATCHING YOU TWO IRRITATES ME.
IF YOU WOULD JUST STAY OUT OF OUR LIVES, YOURS WOULD BE SO MUCH EASIER.
SO WHY DO YOU HAVE TO KEEP BUTTING IN?
... ŌGAMI-KUN SAID...

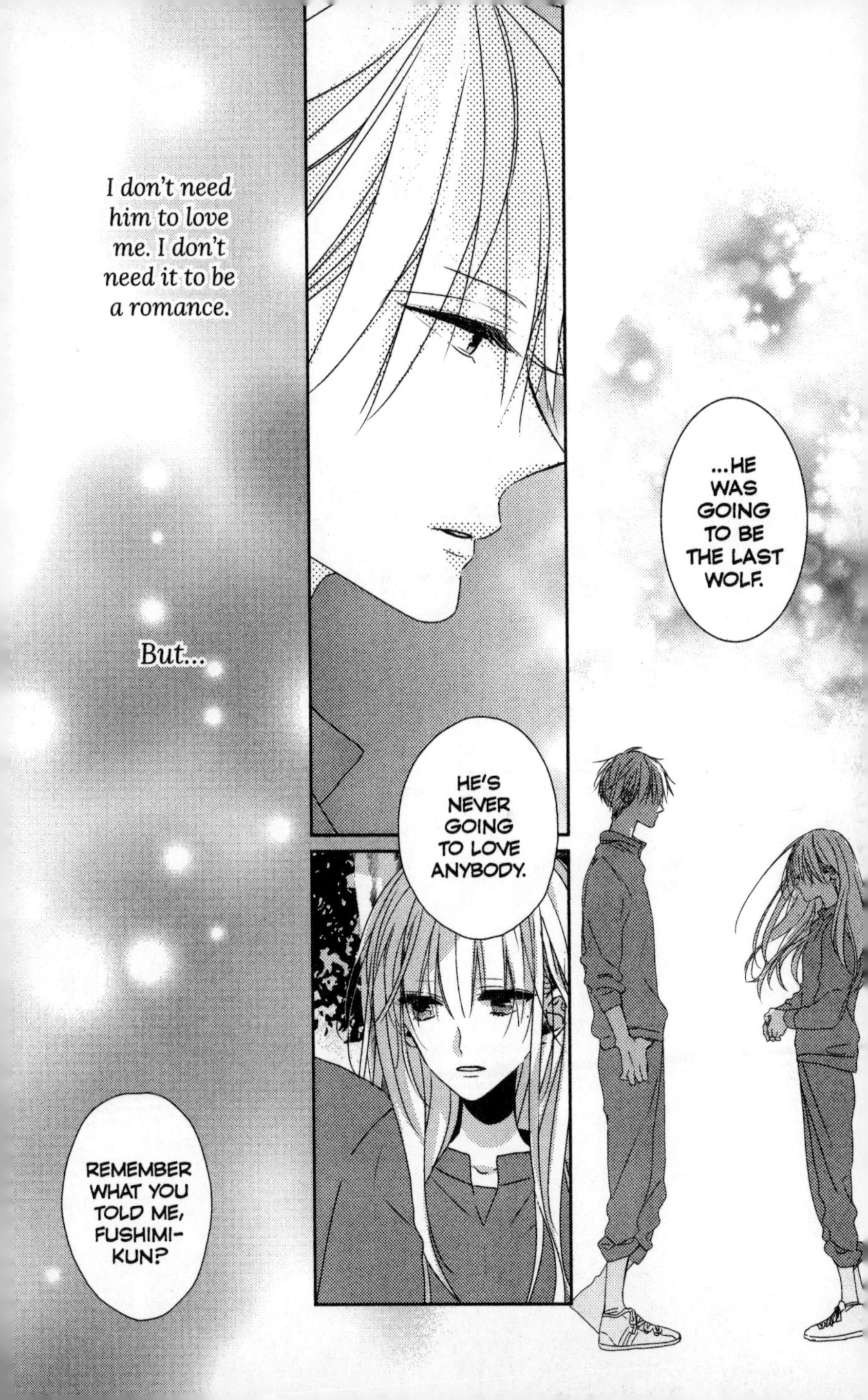
...HE WAS GOING TO BE THE LAST WOLF.
HE'S NEVER GOING TO LOVE ANYBODY.
I don't need him to love me. I don't need it to be a romance.
But...
REMEMBER WHAT YOU TOLD ME, FUSHIMI-KUN?

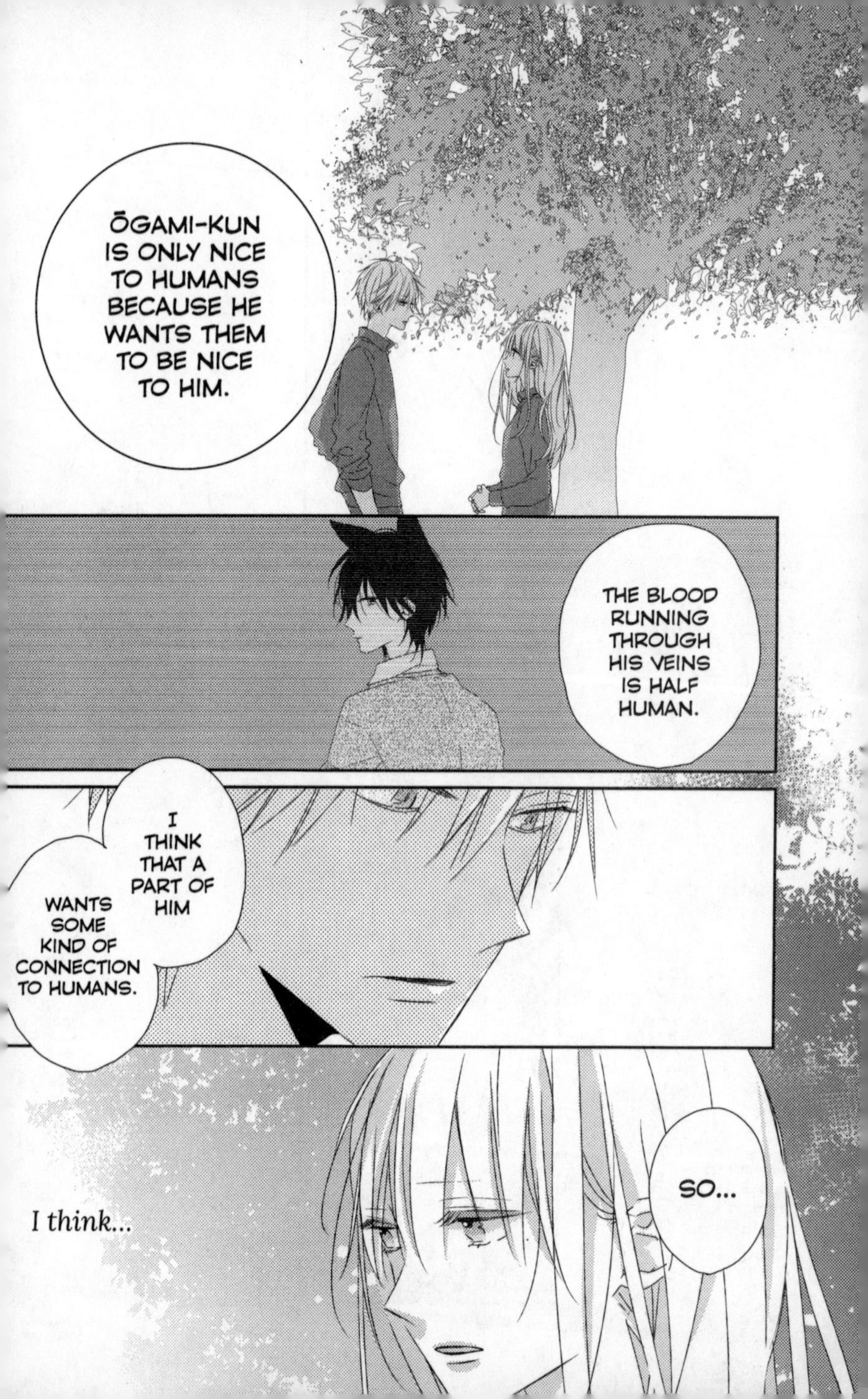
ŌGAMI-KUN IS ONLY NICE TO HUMANS BECAUSE HE WANTS THEM TO BE NICE TO HIM.
THE BLOOD RUNNING THROUGH HIS VEINS IS HALF HUMAN.
I THINK THAT A PART OF HIM
WANTS SOME KIND OF CONNECTION TO HUMANS.
SO...
I think...

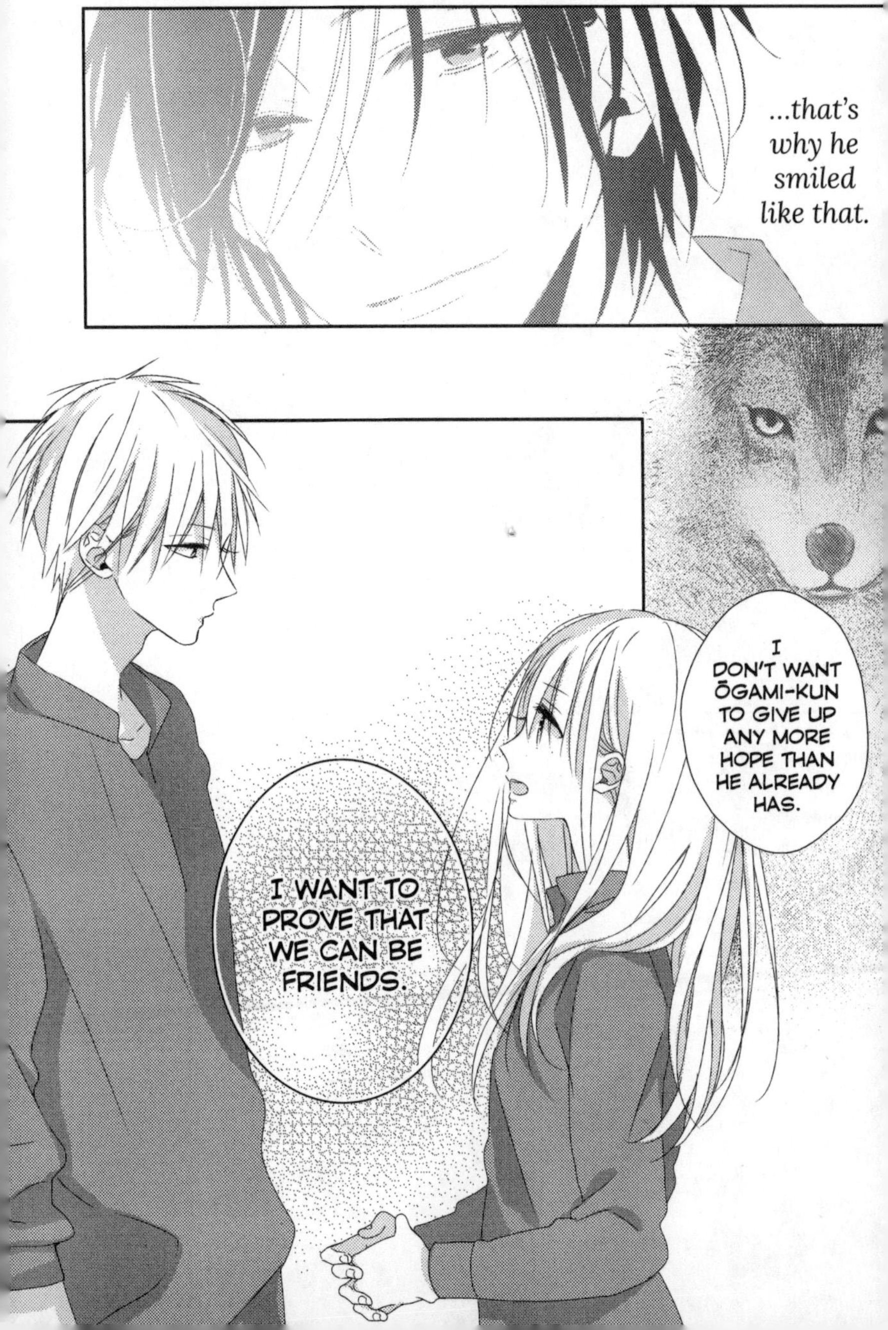
...that's why he smiled like that.
I DON'T WANT ŌGAMI-KUN TO GIVE UP ANY MORE HOPE THAN HE ALREADY HAS.
I WANT TO PROVE THAT WE CAN BE FRIENDS.

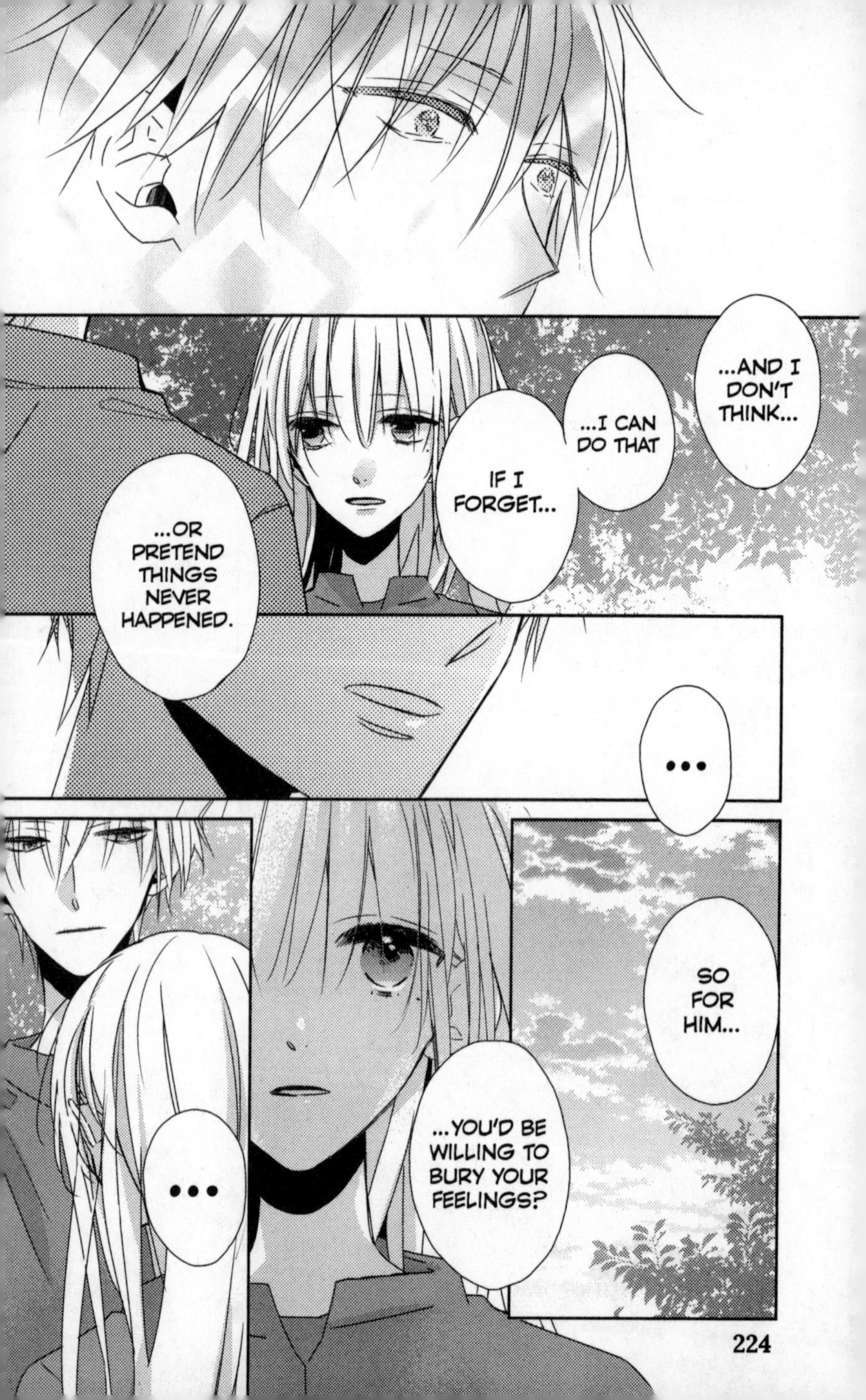
...AND I DON'T THINK...
...I CAN DO THAT
IF I FORGET...
...OR PRETEND THINGS NEVER HAPPENED.
...
SO FOR HIM...
...YOU'D BE WILLING TO BURY YOUR FEELINGS?
...

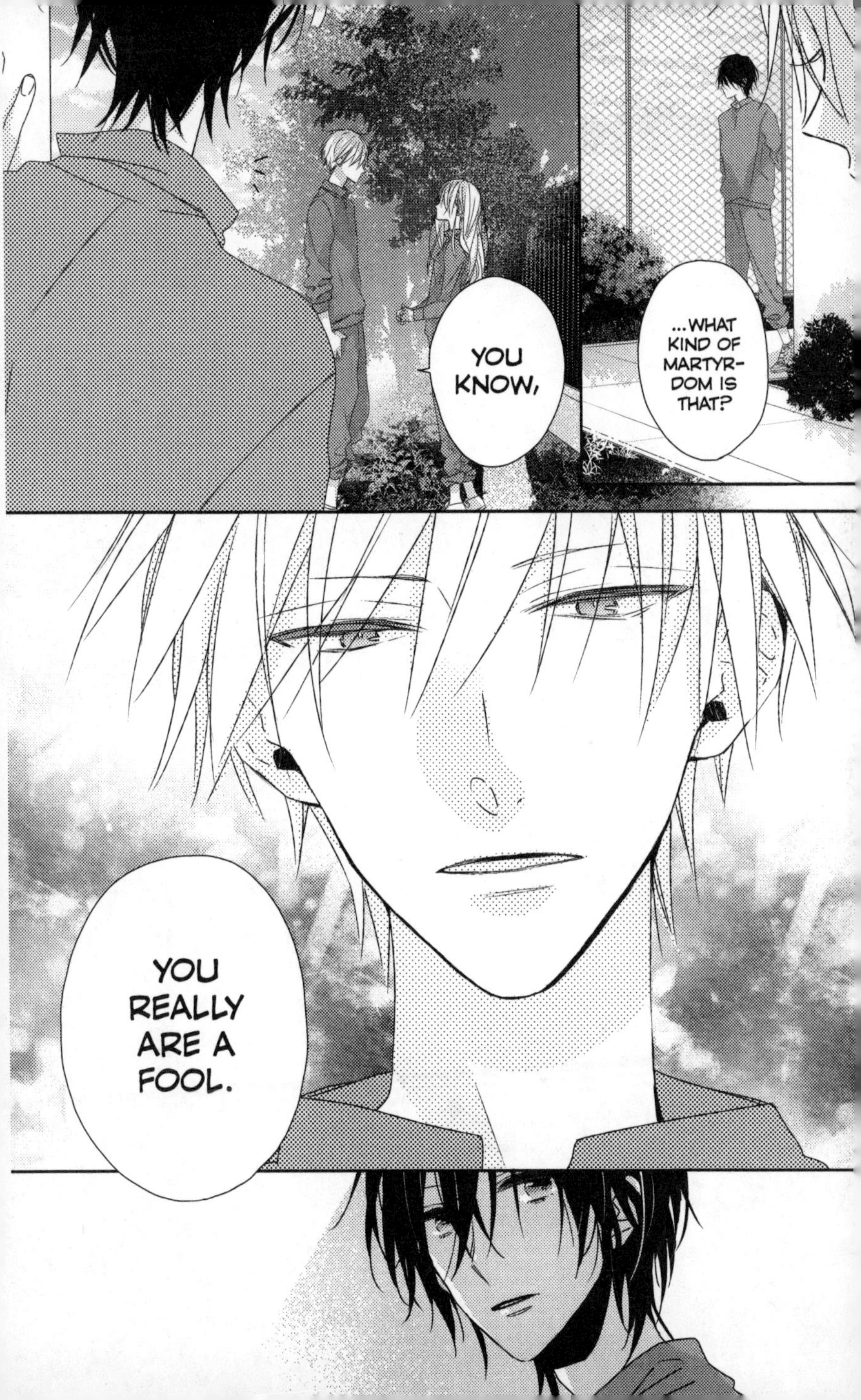
...WHAT KIND OF MARTYR-DOM IS THAT?
YOU KNOW,
YOU REALLY ARE A FOOL.

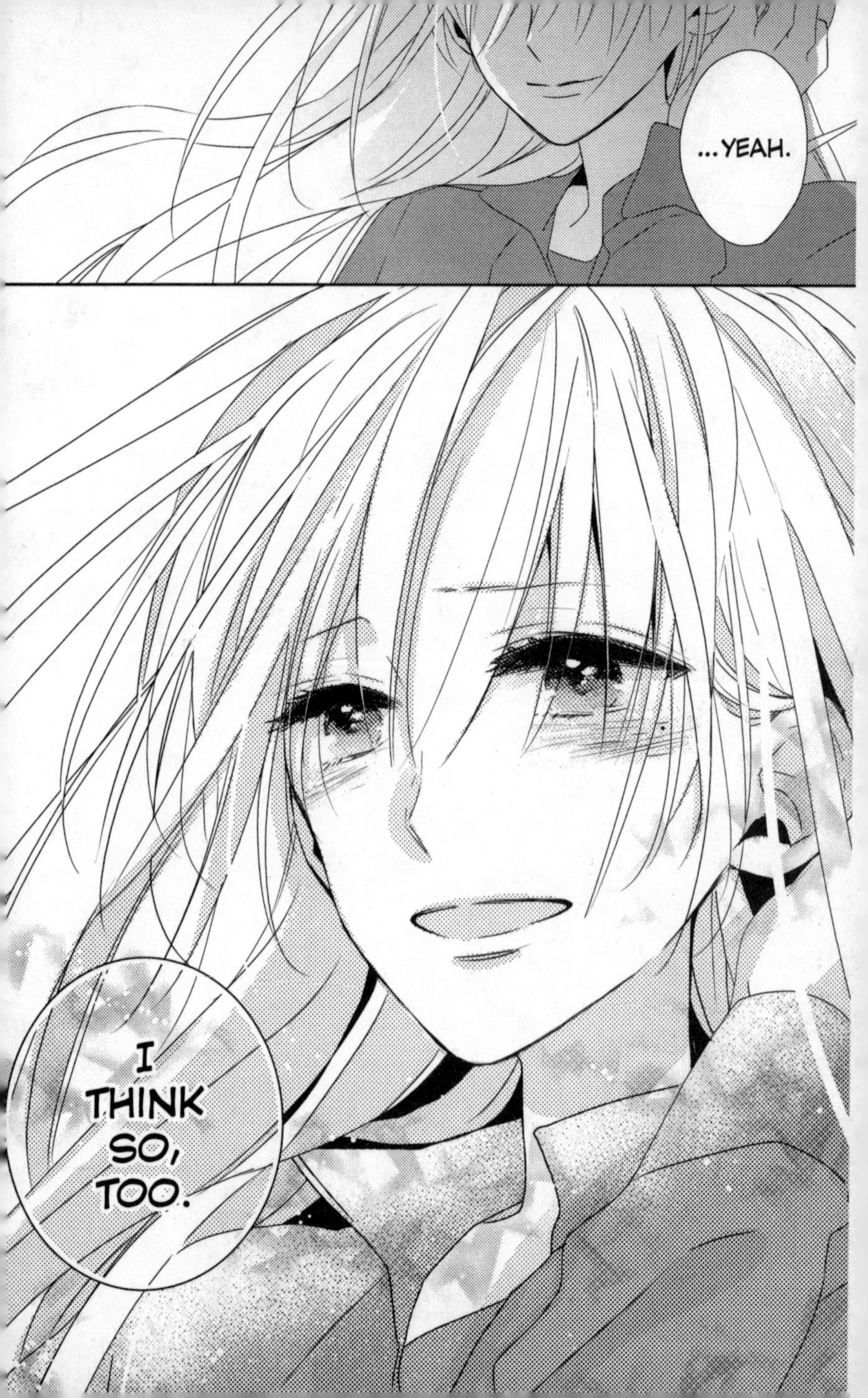
...YEAH.
I THINK SO, TOO.

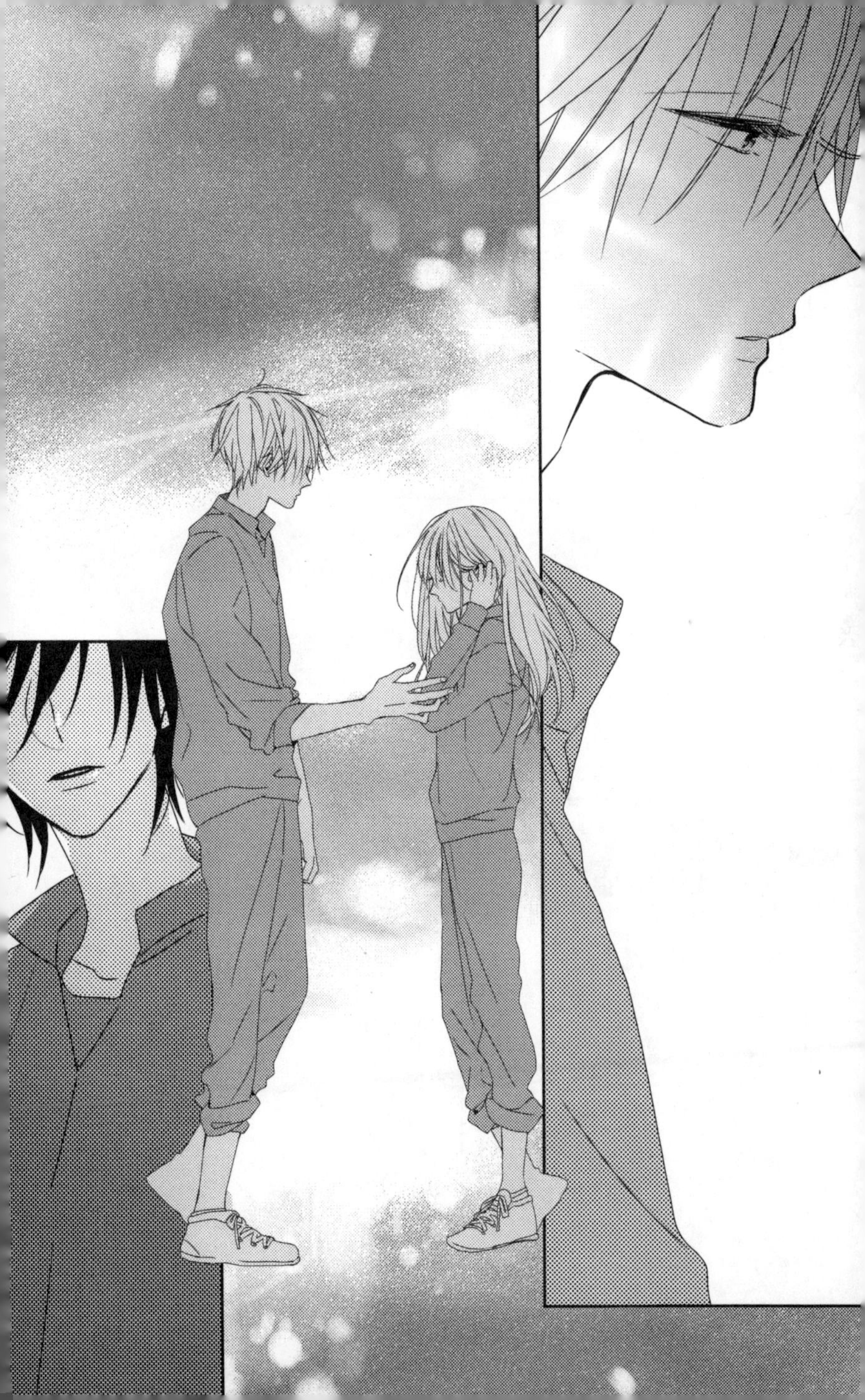

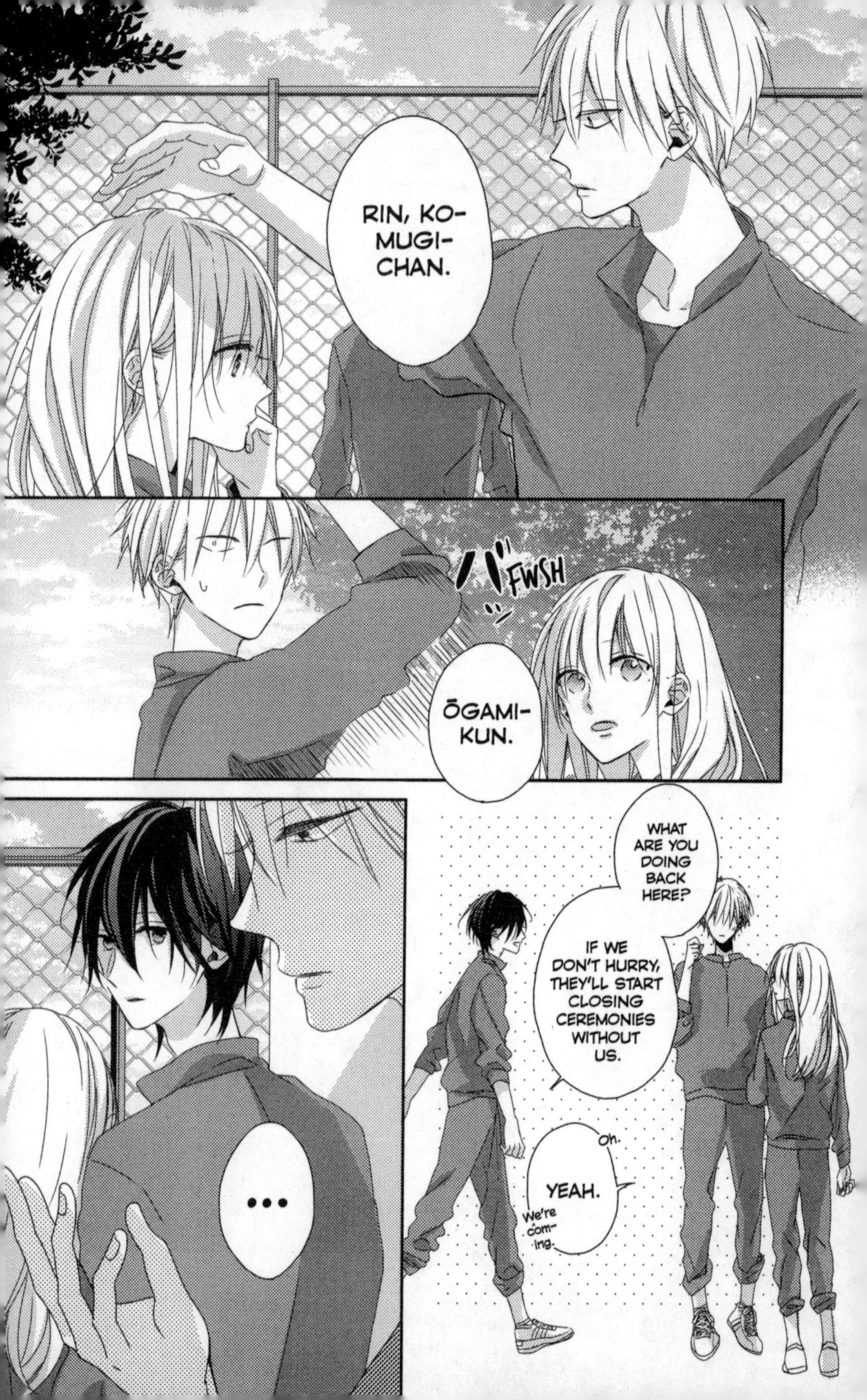
RIN, KO-MUGI-CHAN.
FWSH
ŌGAMI-KUN.
WHAT ARE YOU DOING BACK HERE?
IF WE DON'T HURRY, THEY'LL START CLOSING CEREMONIES WITHOUT US.
Oh.
YEAH.
We're com-ing.
...

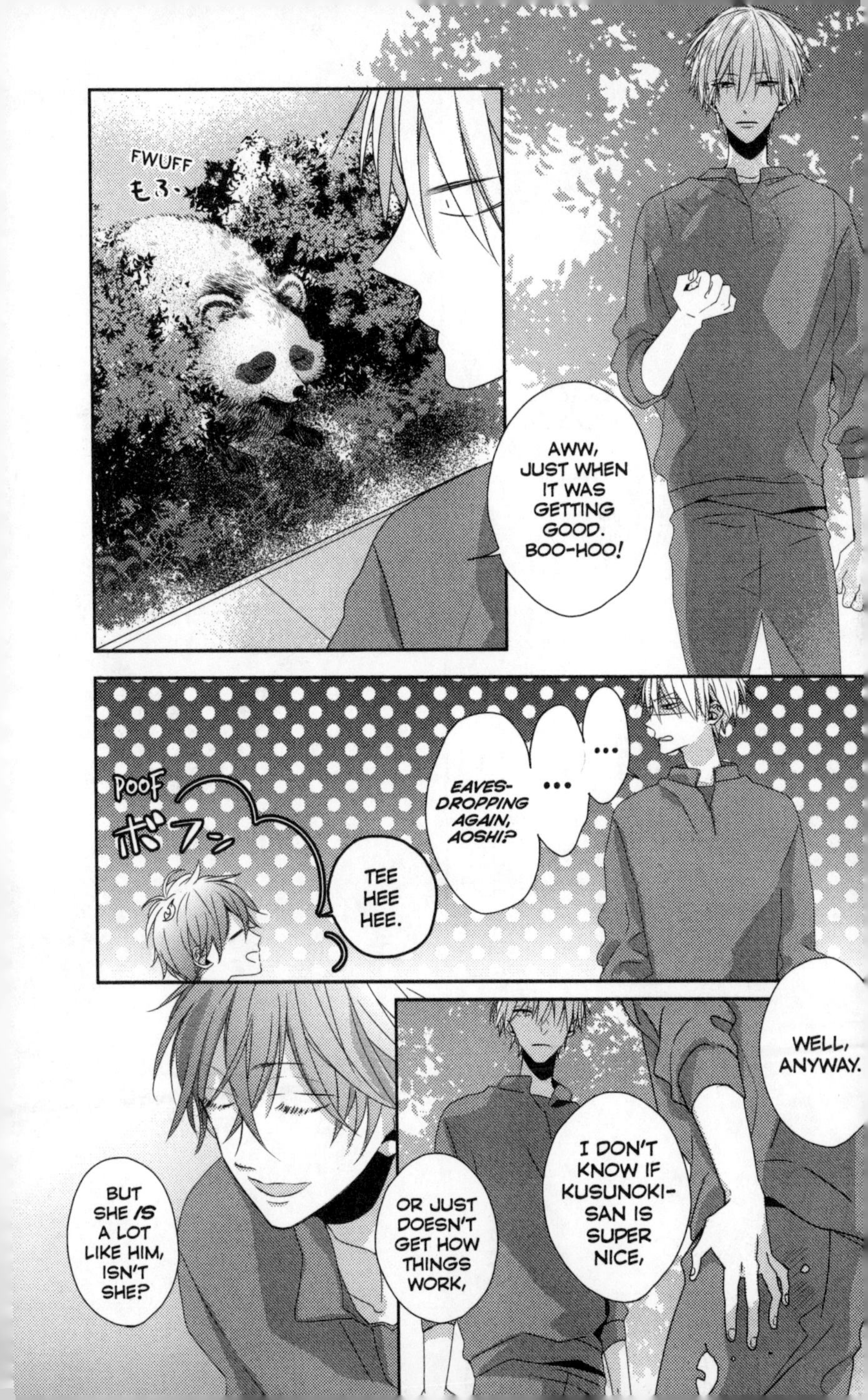
AWW, JUST WHEN IT WAS GETTING GOOD. BOO-HOO!
FWUFF
もふ・
...
...
EAVES-DROPPING AGAIN, AOSHI?
POOF
ボフン
TEE HEE HEE.
WELL, ANYWAY.
I DON'T KNOW IF KUSUNOKI-SAN IS SUPER NICE,
OR JUST DOESN'T GET HOW THINGS WORK,
BUT SHE *IS* A LOT LIKE HIM, ISN'T SHE?

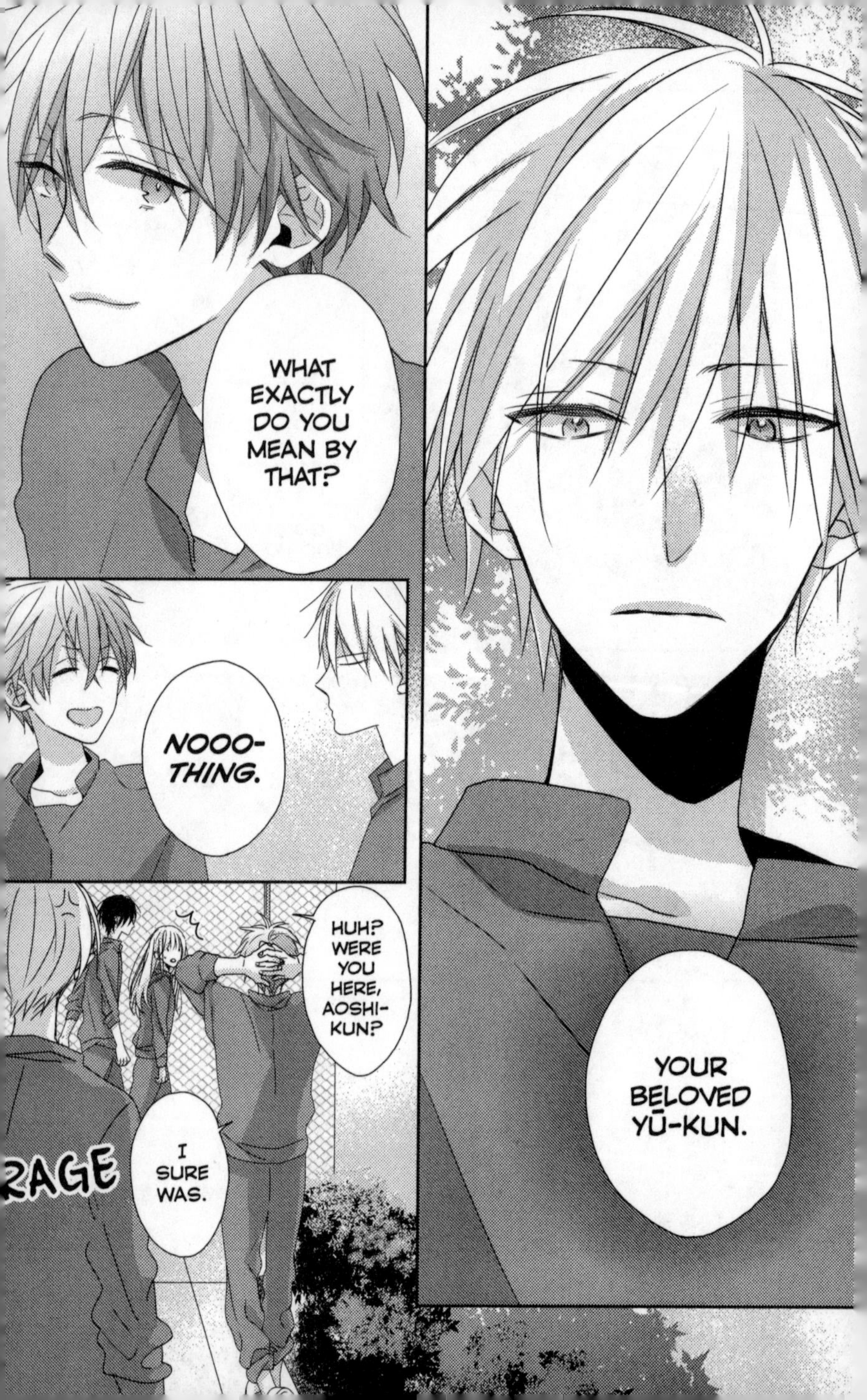
YOUR BELOVED YŪ-KUN.
WHAT EXACTLY DO YOU MEAN BY THAT?
NOOO-THING.
HUH? WERE YOU HERE, AOSHI-KUN?
I SURE WAS.
RAGE

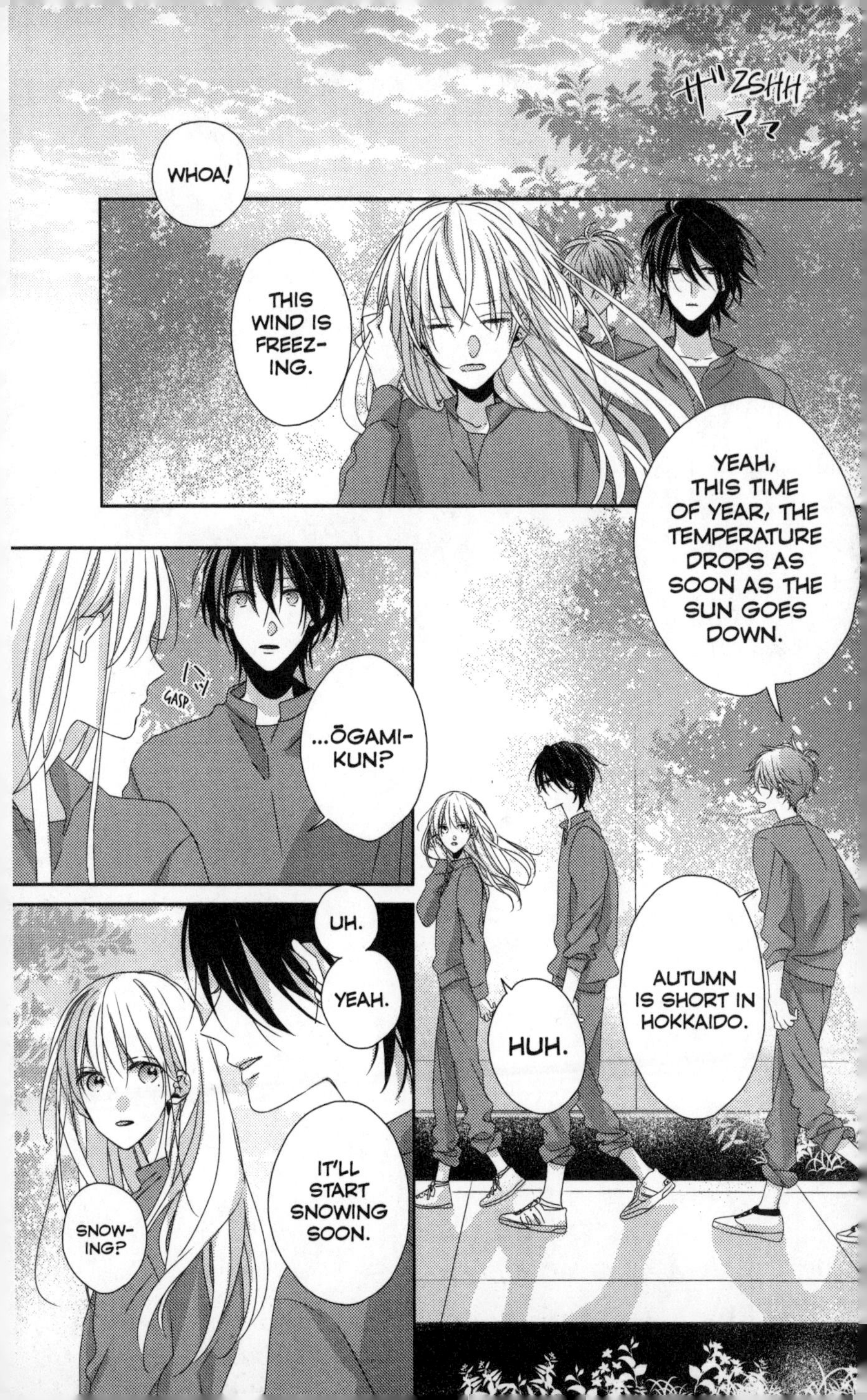
ZSHH
WHOA!
THIS WIND IS FREEZ-ING.
YEAH, THIS TIME OF YEAR, THE TEMPERATURE DROPS AS SOON AS THE SUN GOES DOWN.
AUTUMN IS SHORT IN HOKKAIDO.
HUH.
GASP
...ŌGAMI-KUN?
UH.
YEAH.
IT'LL START SNOWING SOON.
SNOW-ING?

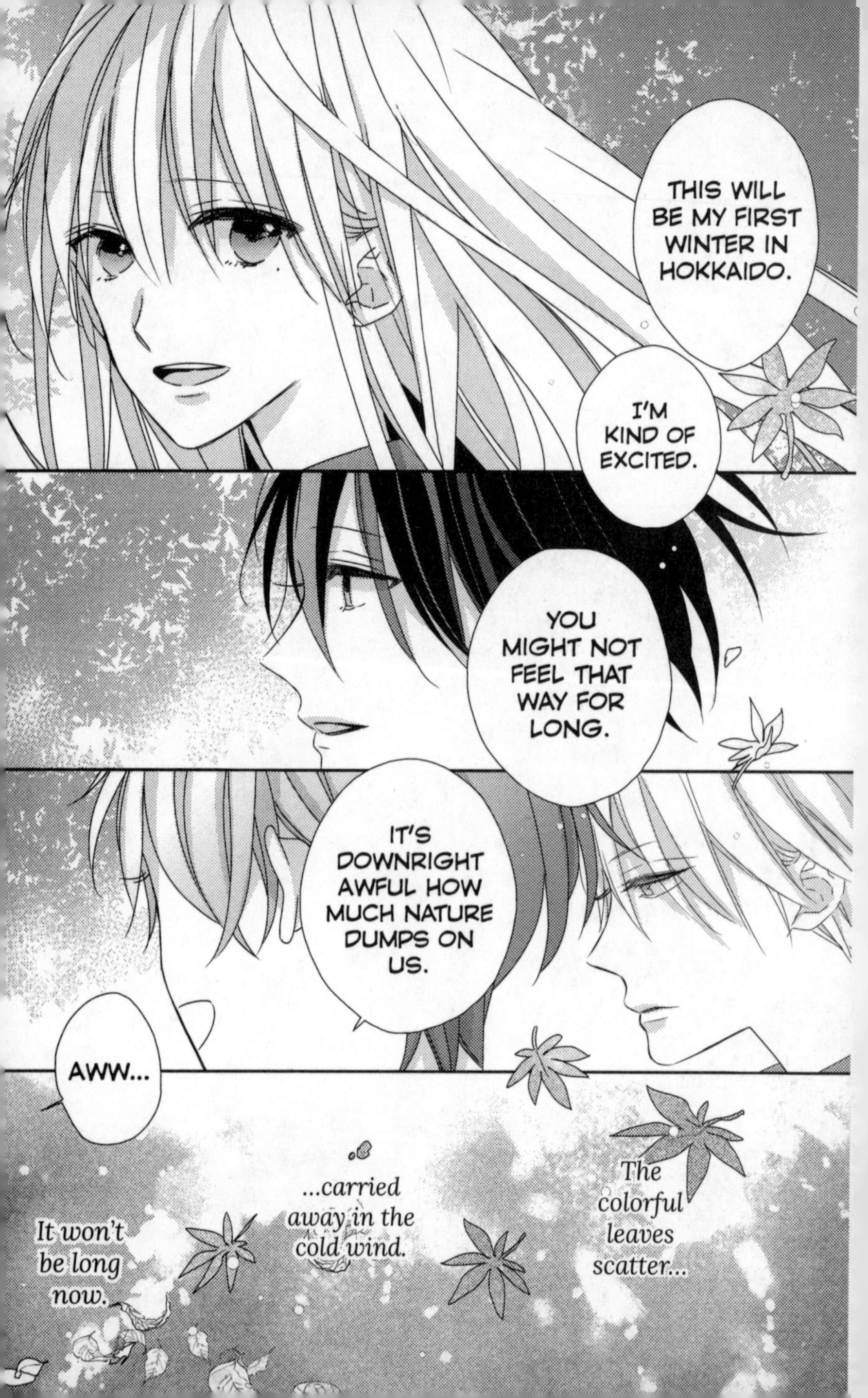
THIS WILL BE MY FIRST WINTER IN HOKKAIDO.
I'M KIND OF EXCITED.
YOU MIGHT NOT FEEL THAT WAY FOR LONG.
IT'S DOWNRIGHT AWFUL HOW MUCH NATURE DUMPS ON US.
AWW...
The colorful leaves scatter...
...carried away in the cold wind.
It won't be long now.

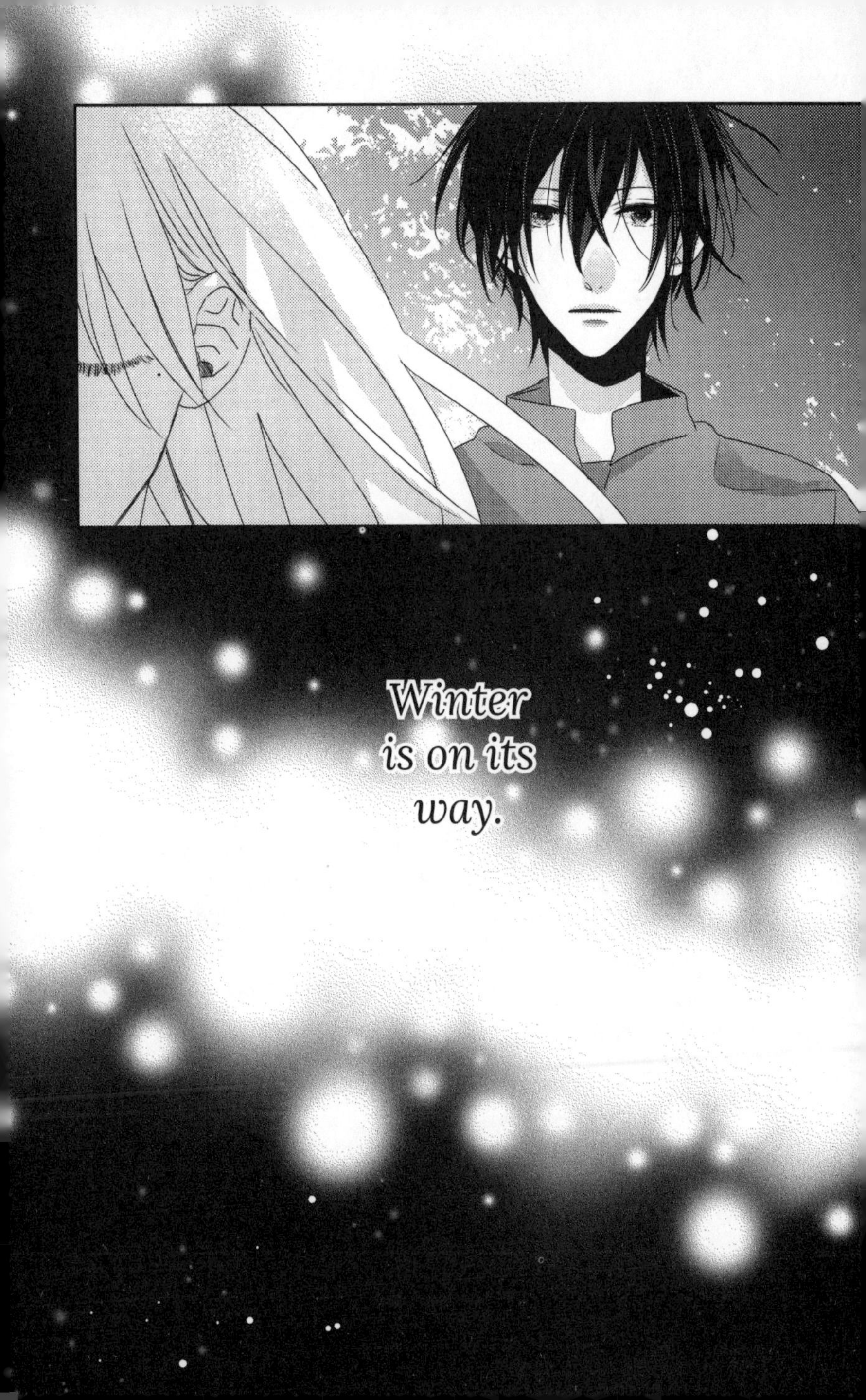
Winter is on its way.

GLANCE
チラ.

That Wolf-Boy is Mine!

Chapter 7

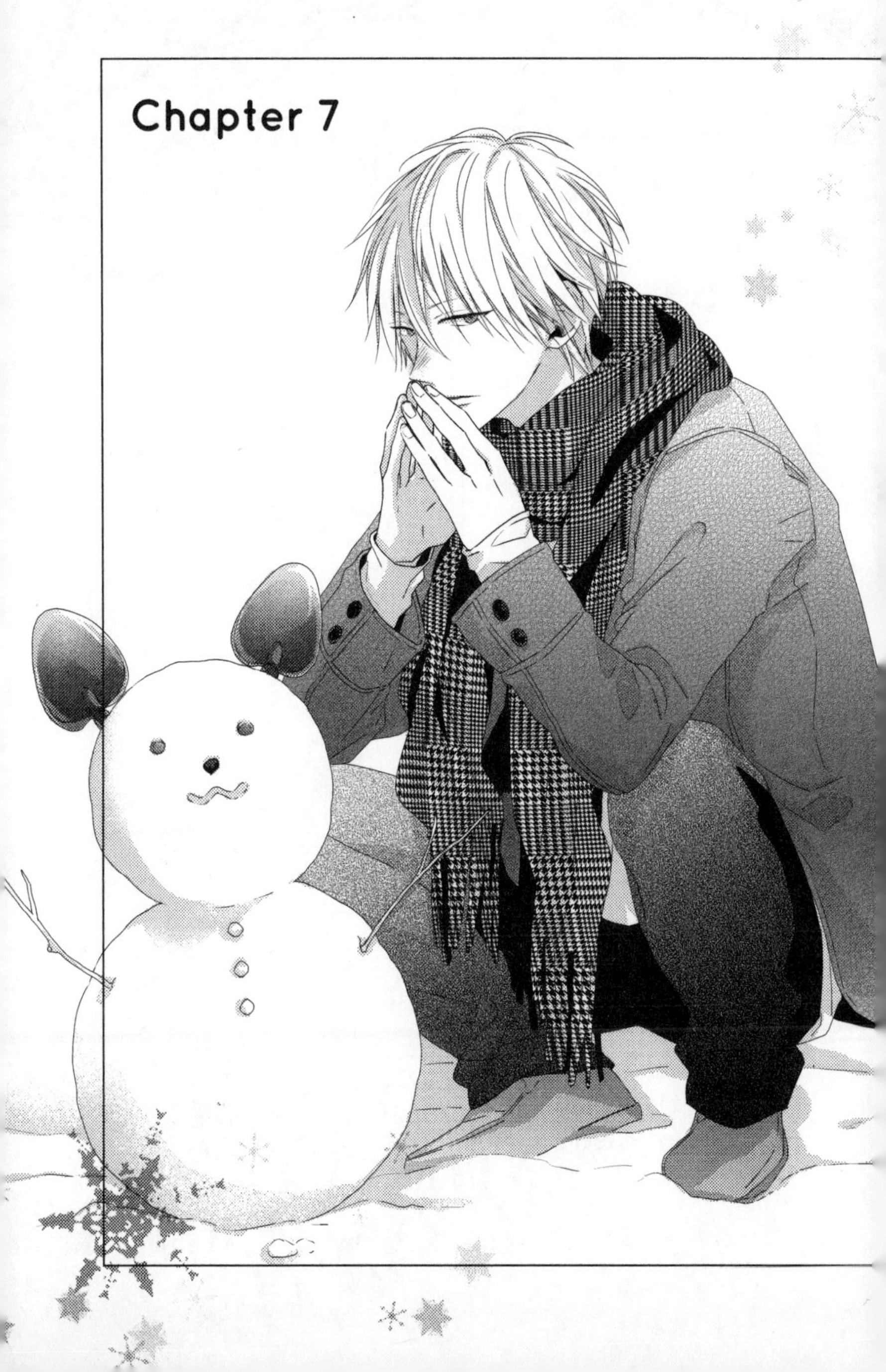

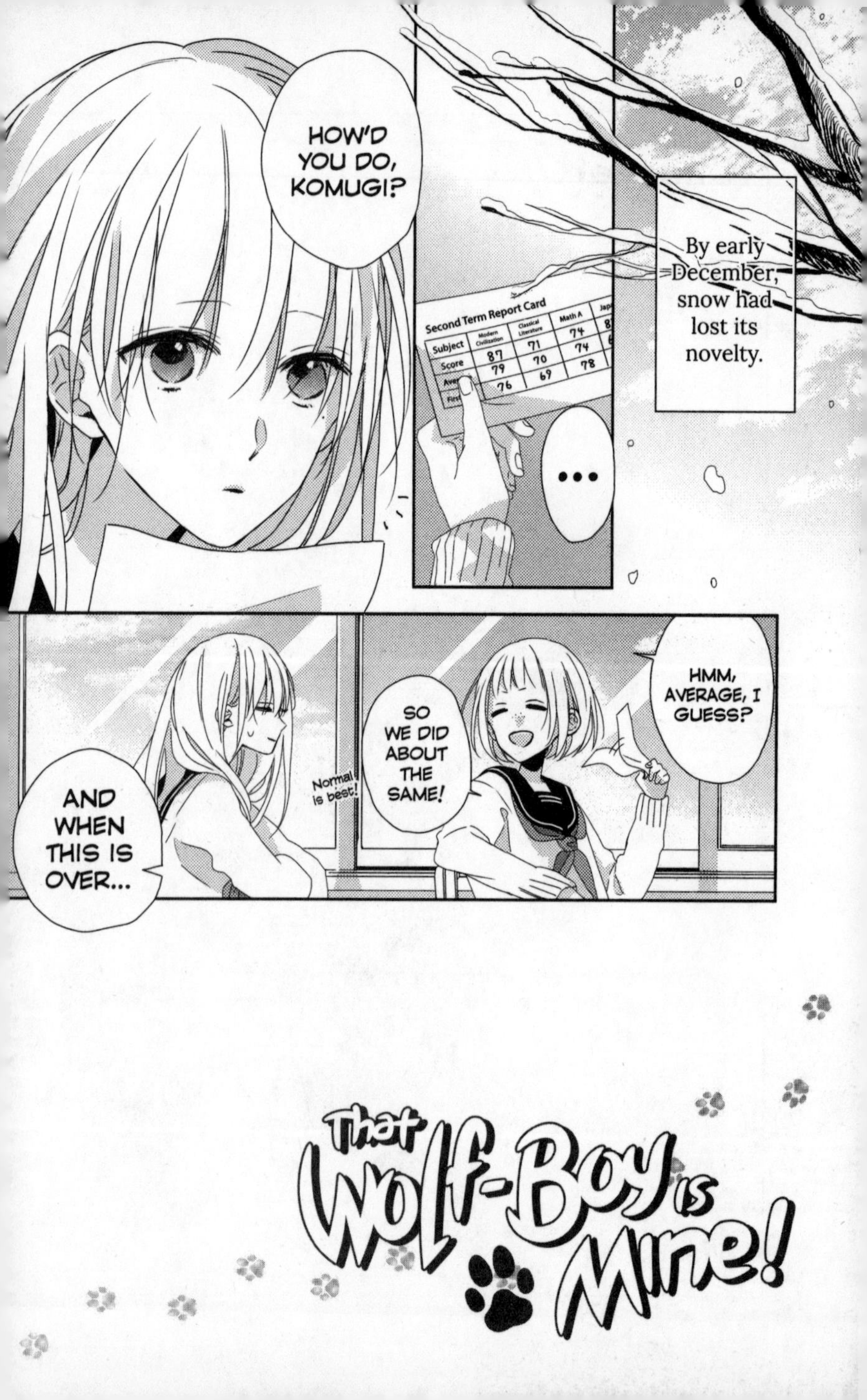
By early December, snow had lost its novelty.
Second Term Report Card
...
HOW'D YOU DO, KOMUGI?
HMM, AVERAGE, I GUESS?
SO WE DID ABOUT THE SAME!
Normal is best!
AND WHEN THIS IS OVER...
That Wolf-Boy is Mine!

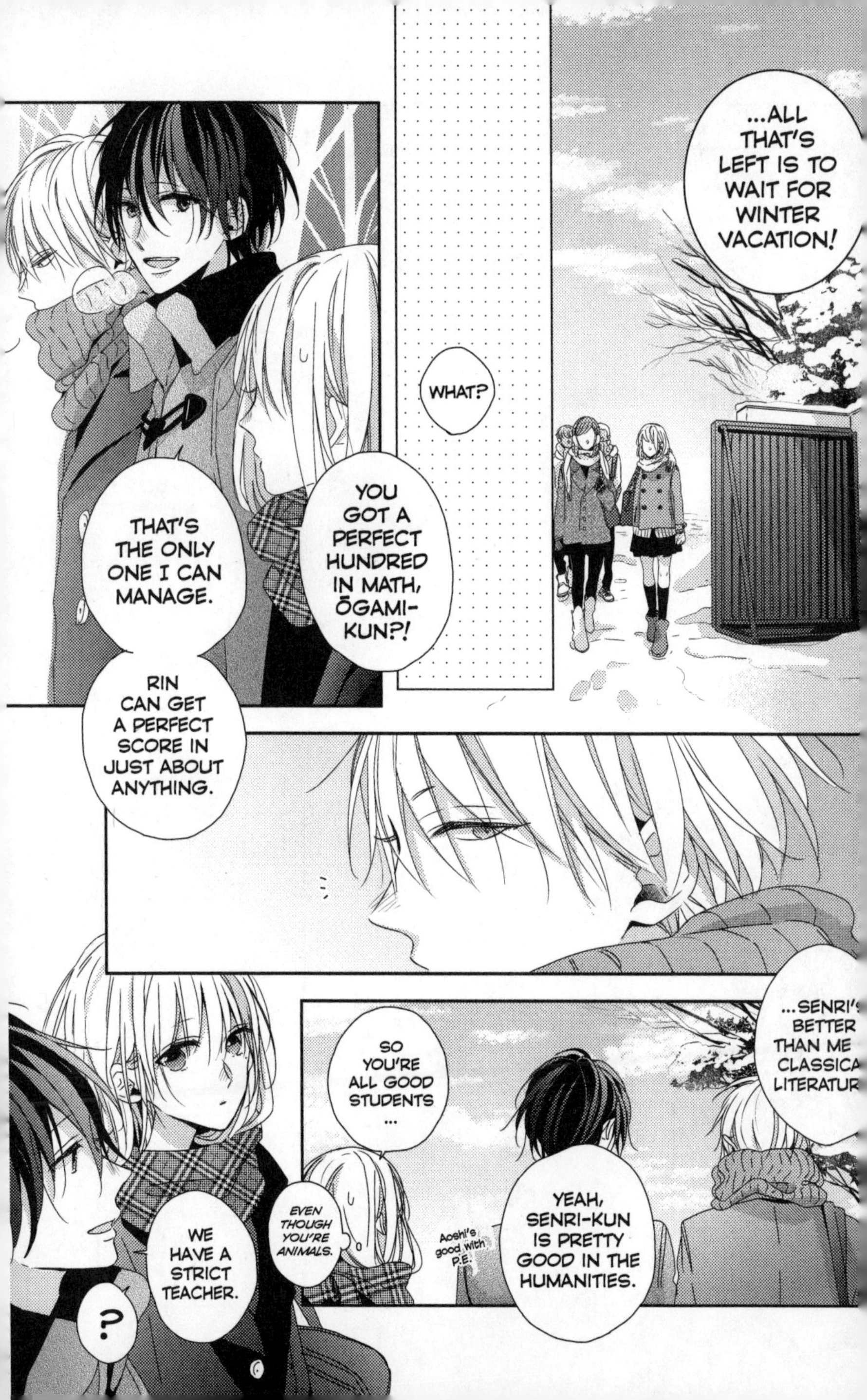
...ALL THAT'S LEFT IS TO WAIT FOR WINTER VACATION!
WHAT?
YOU GOT A PERFECT HUNDRED IN MATH, ŌGAMI-KUN?!
THAT'S THE ONLY ONE I CAN MANAGE.
RIN CAN GET A PERFECT SCORE IN JUST ABOUT ANYTHING.
...SENRI'S BETTER THAN ME CLASSICA LITERATUR
YEAH, SENRI-KUN IS PRETTY GOOD IN THE HUMANITIES.
Aoshi's good with P.E.
SO YOU'RE ALL GOOD STUDENTS ...
EVEN THOUGH YOU'RE ANIMALS.
WE HAVE A STRICT TEACHER.
?

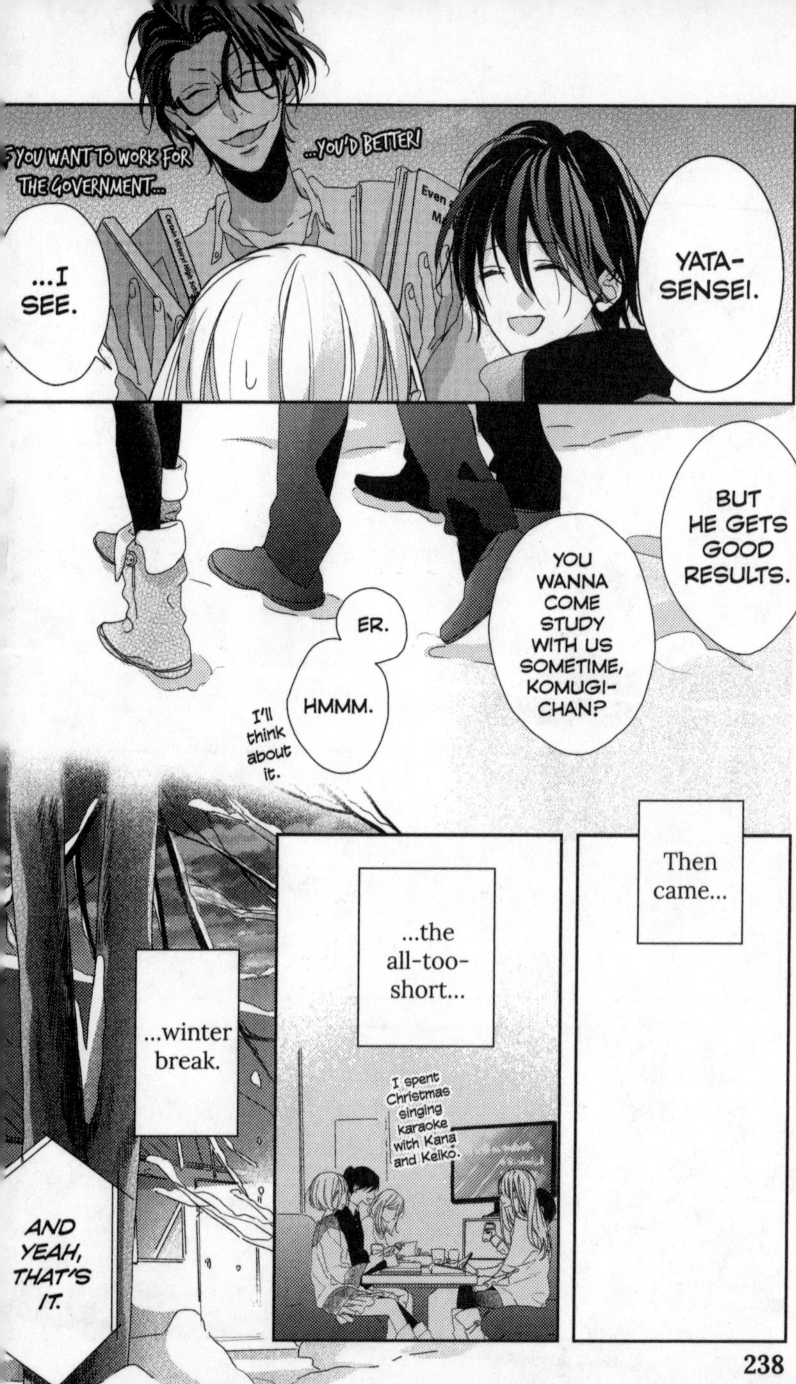
YATA-SENSEI.
...YOU'D BETTER!
F YOU WANT TO WORK FOR THE GOVERNMENT...
...I SEE.
BUT HE GETS GOOD RESULTS.
YOU WANNA COME STUDY WITH US SOMETIME, KOMUGI-CHAN?
ER.
HMMM.
I'll think about it.
Then came...
...the all-too-short...
I spent Christmas singing karaoke with Kana and Keiko.
...winter break.
AND YEAH, THAT'S IT.

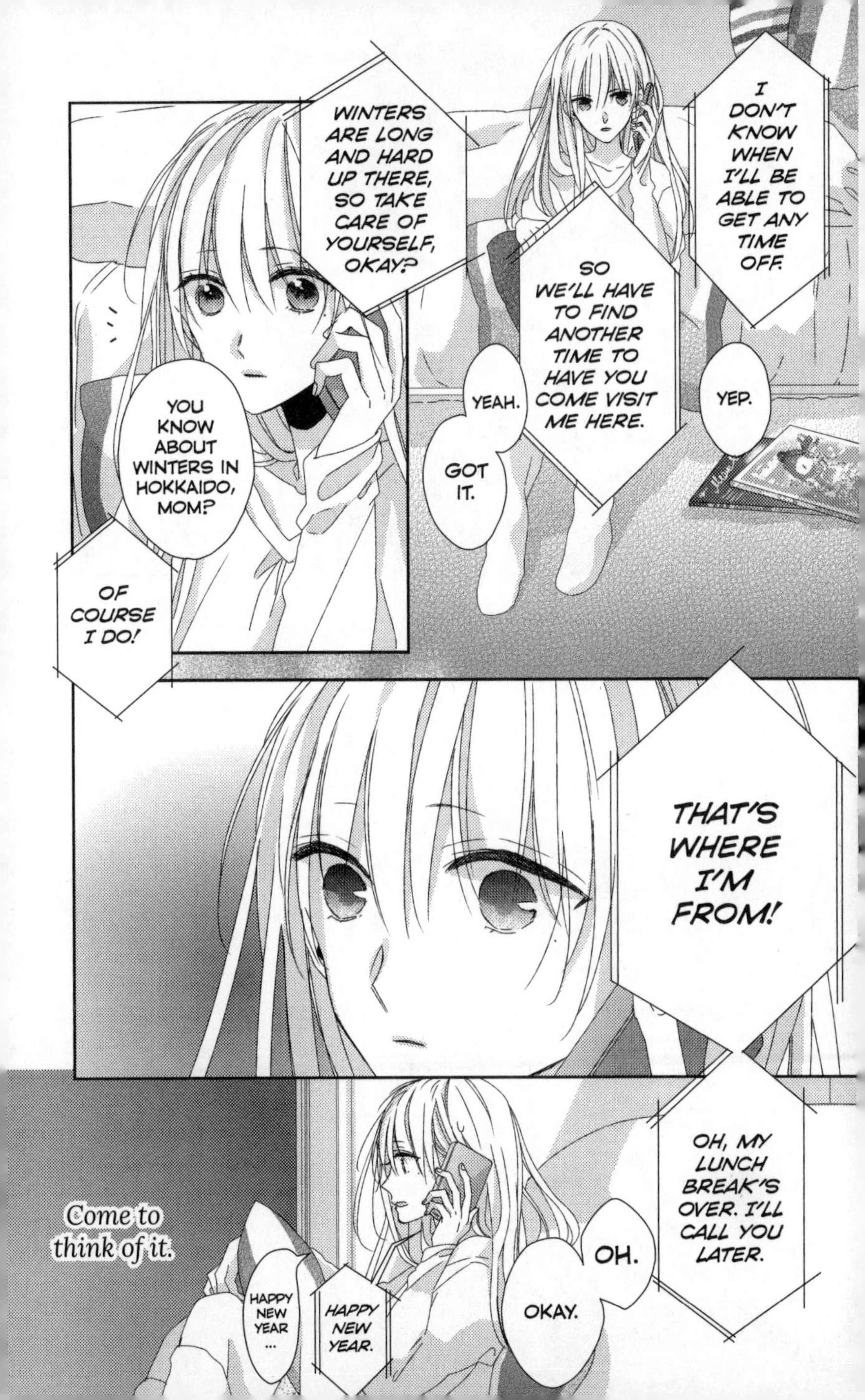
I DON'T KNOW WHEN I'LL BE ABLE TO GET ANY TIME OFF.
YEP.
SO WE'LL HAVE TO FIND ANOTHER TIME TO HAVE YOU COME VISIT ME HERE.
YEAH.
GOT IT.
WINTERS ARE LONG AND HARD UP THERE, SO TAKE CARE OF YOURSELF, OKAY?
YOU KNOW ABOUT WINTERS IN HOKKAIDO, MOM?
OF COURSE I DO!
THAT'S WHERE I'M FROM!
OH, MY LUNCH BREAK'S OVER. I'LL CALL YOU LATER.
OH.
OKAY.
HAPPY NEW YEAR.
HAPPY NEW YEAR...
Come to think of it.

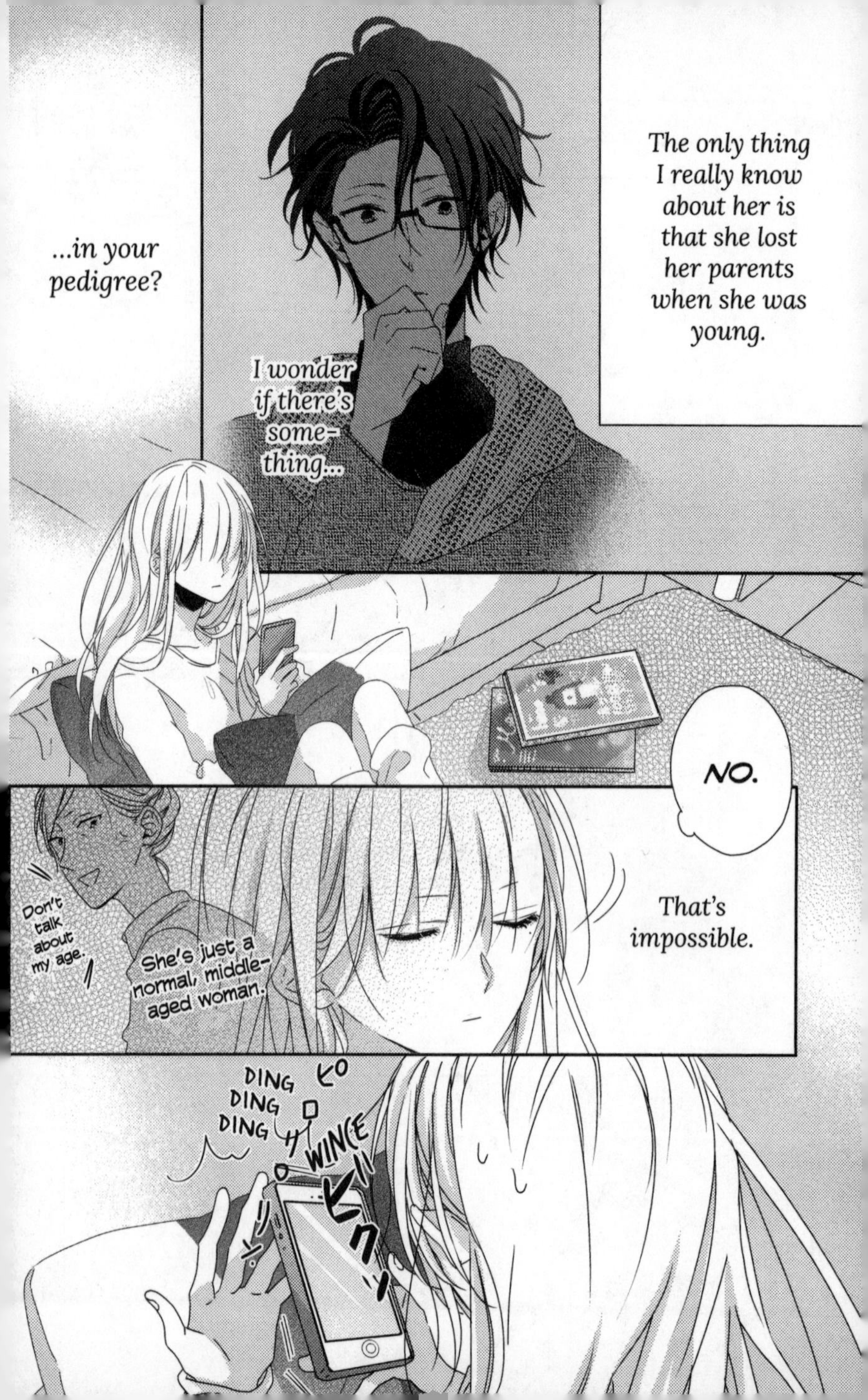
The only thing I really know about her is that she lost her parents when she was young.
I wonder if there's some-thing...
...in your pedigree?
NO.
That's impossible.
She's just a normal, middle-aged woman.
Don't talk about my age.
DING DING DING
WINCE

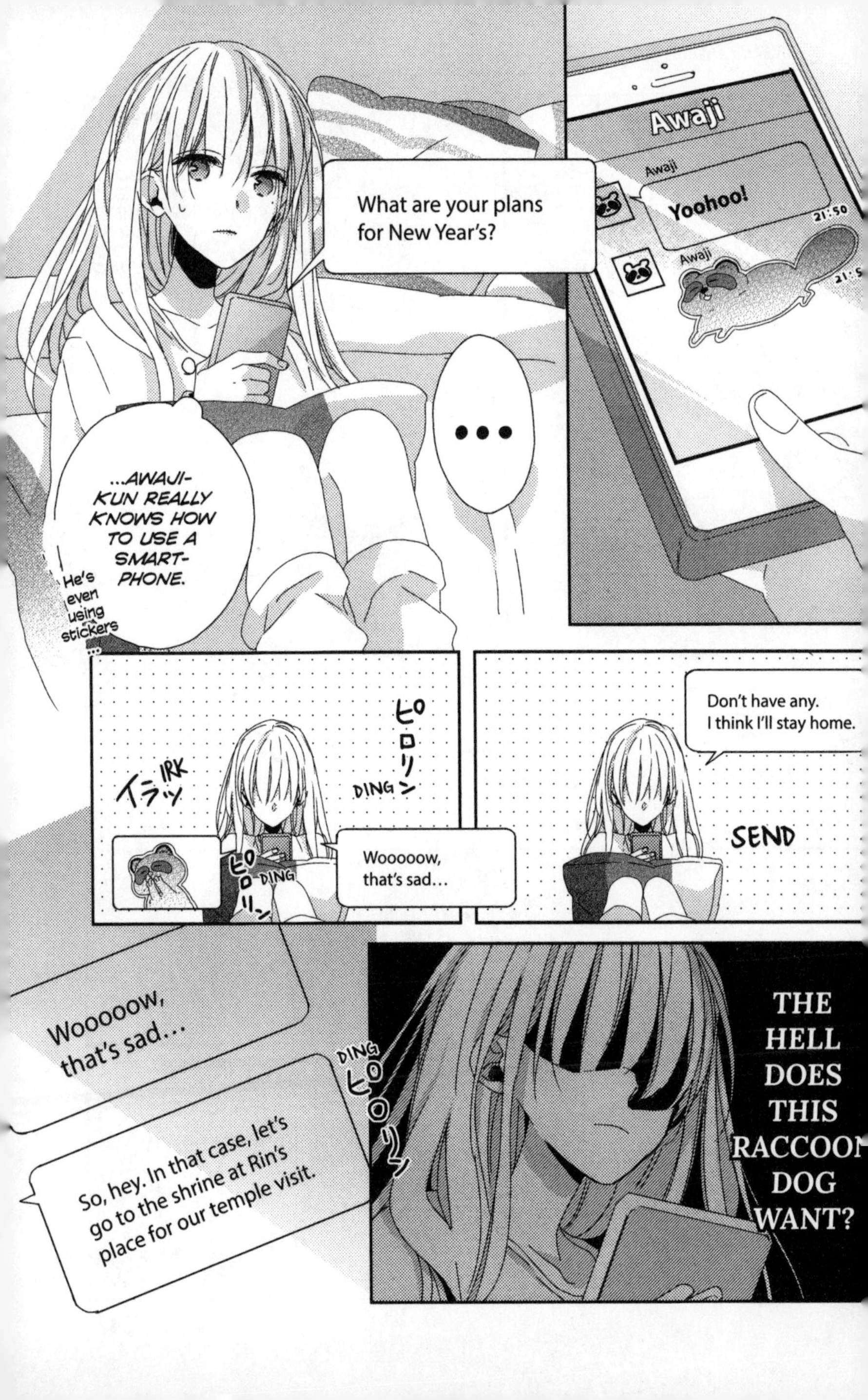
Awaji
Awaji
Yoohoo!
21:50
Awaji
What are your plans for New Year's?
•••
...AWAJI-KUN REALLY KNOWS HOW TO USE A SMART-PHONE.
He's even using stickers...
Don't have any. I think I'll stay home.
SEND
ピロリン DING
Wooooow, that's sad…
ピロリン DING
イラッ IRK
THE HELL DOES THIS RACCOON DOG WANT?
DING ピロリン
Wooooow, that's sad…
So, hey. In that case, let's go to the shrine at Rin's place for our temple visit.

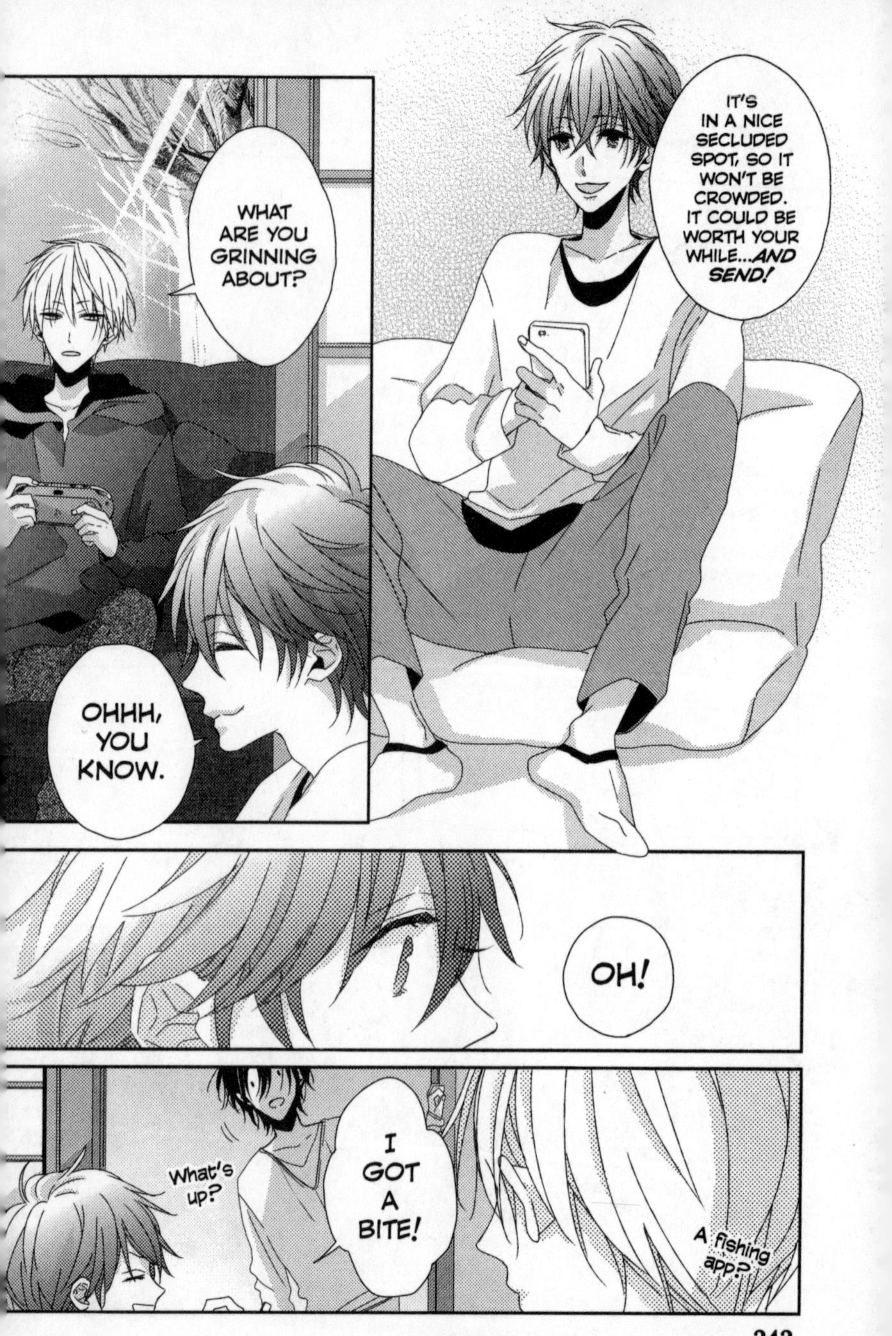
IT'S IN A NICE SECLUDED SPOT, SO IT WON'T BE CROWDED. IT COULD BE WORTH YOUR WHILE...*AND SEND!*
WHAT ARE YOU GRINNING ABOUT?
OHHH, YOU KNOW.
OH!
A fishing app?
I GOT A BITE!
What's up?

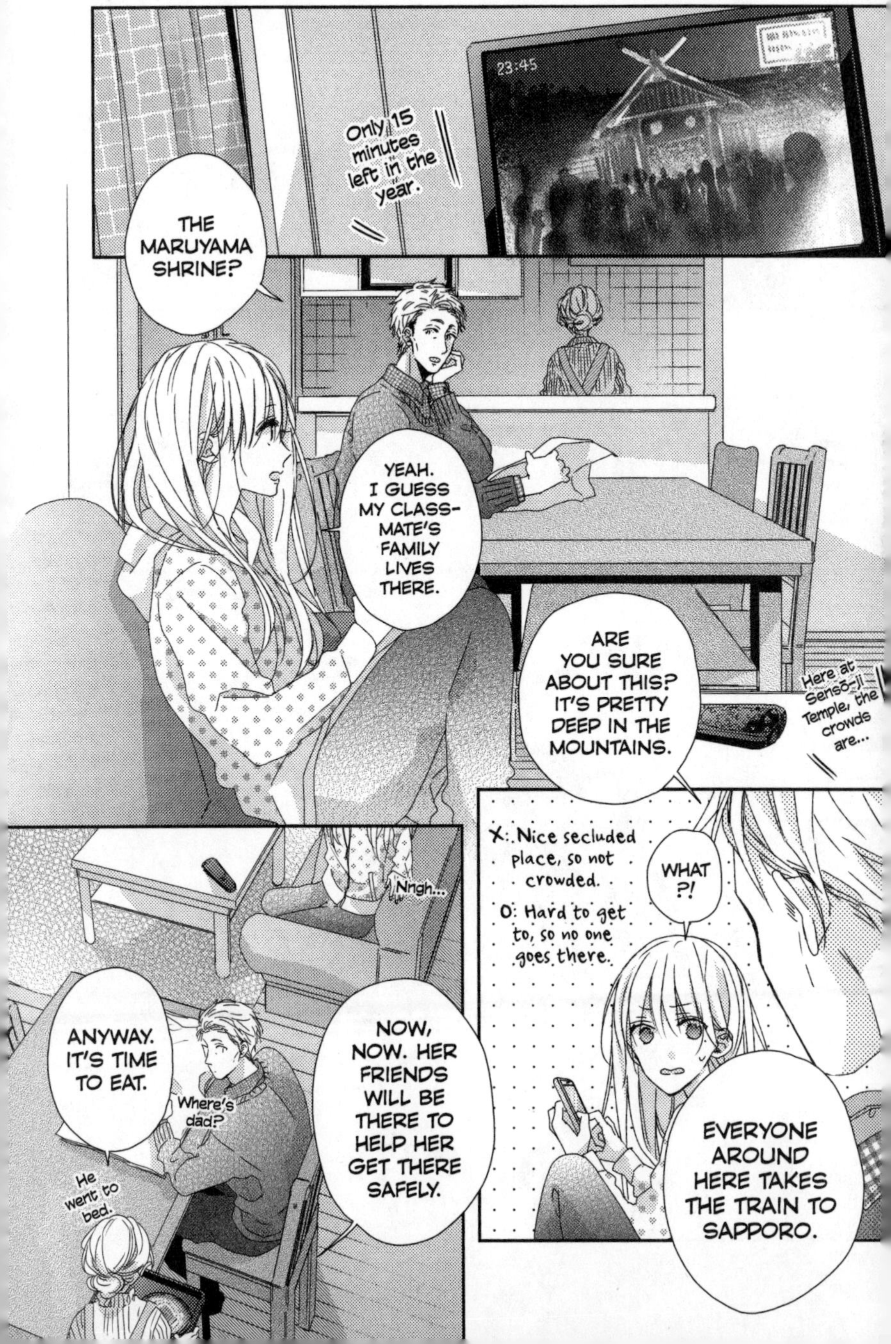
23:45
Only 15 minutes left in the year.
THE MARUYAMA SHRINE?
YEAH. I GUESS MY CLASS-MATE'S FAMILY LIVES THERE.
Here at Sensō-ji Temple, the crowds are...
ARE YOU SURE ABOUT THIS? IT'S PRETTY DEEP IN THE MOUNTAINS.
X: Nice secluded place, so not crowded.
O: Hard to get to, so no one goes there.
WHAT?!
EVERYONE AROUND HERE TAKES THE TRAIN TO SAPPORO.
NOW, NOW. HER FRIENDS WILL BE THERE TO HELP HER GET THERE SAFELY.
Nngh...
ANYWAY. IT'S TIME TO EAT.
Where's dad?
He went to bed.

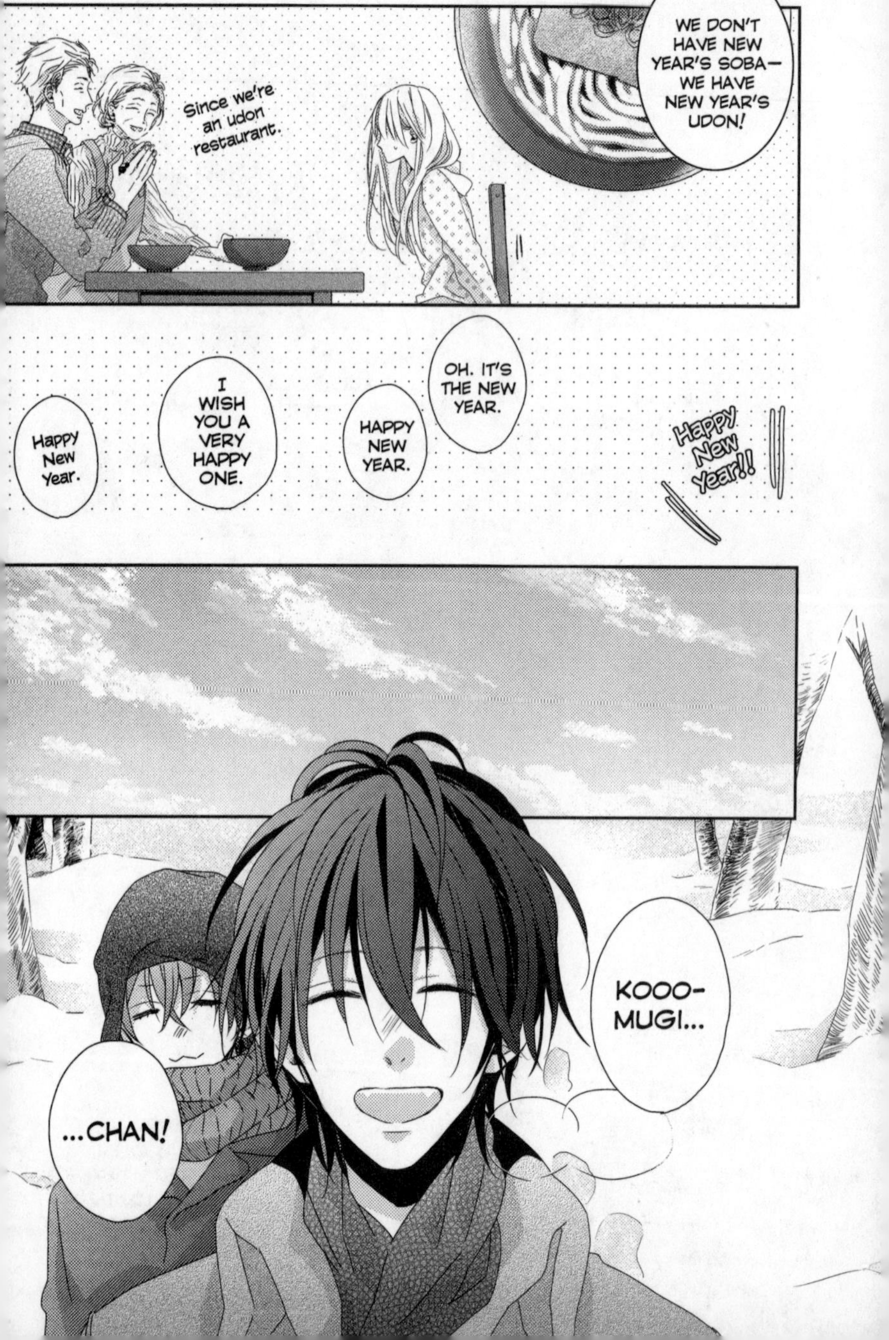
WE DON'T HAVE NEW YEAR'S SOBA— WE HAVE NEW YEAR'S UDON!
Since we're an udon restaurant.
Happy New Year!!
OH. IT'S THE NEW YEAR.
HAPPY NEW YEAR.
I WISH YOU A VERY HAPPY ONE.
Happy New Year.
KOOO-MUGI...
...CHAN!

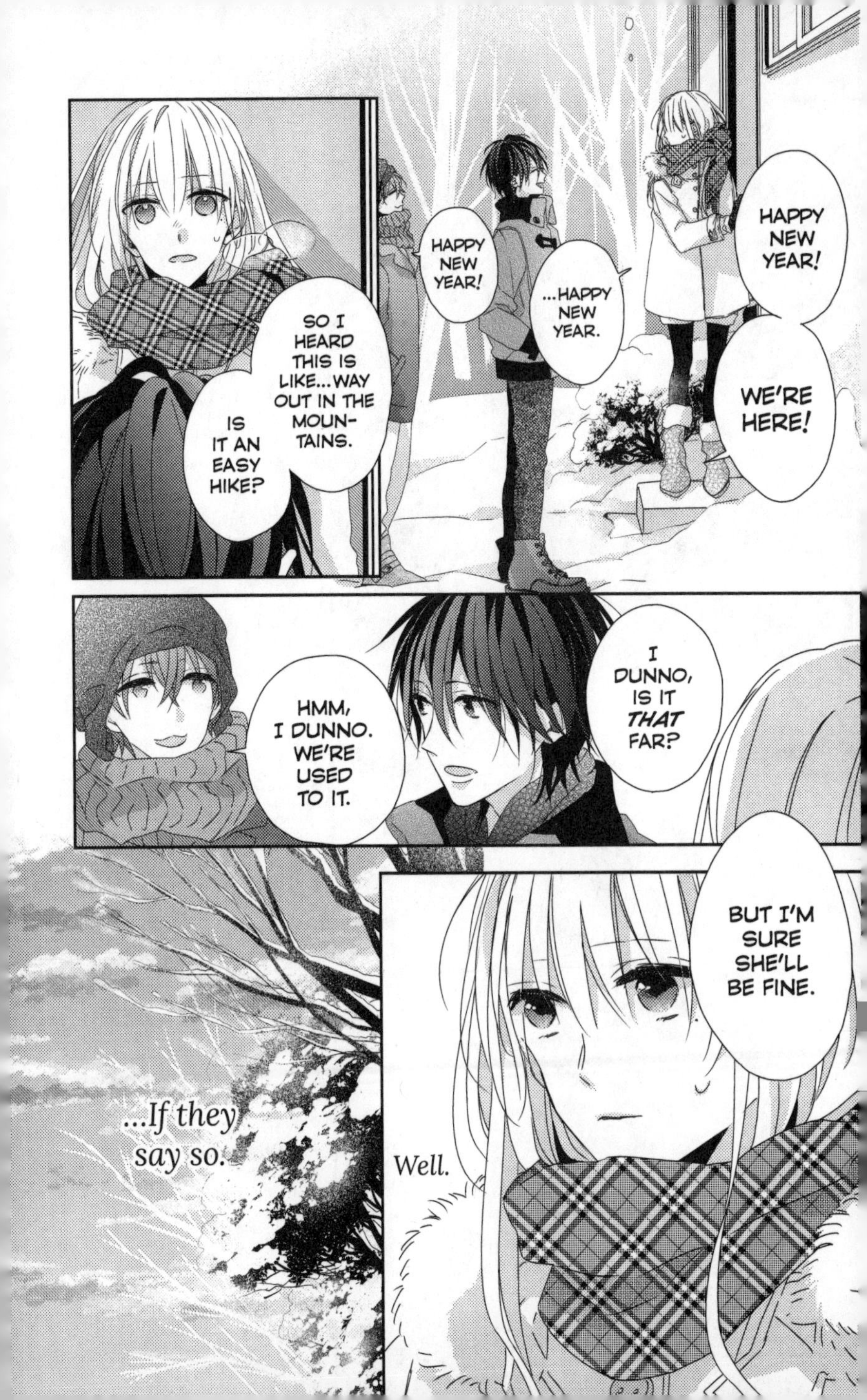
HAPPY NEW YEAR!
WE'RE HERE!
...HAPPY NEW YEAR.
HAPPY NEW YEAR!
SO I HEARD THIS IS LIKE...WAY OUT IN THE MOUN-TAINS.
IS IT AN EASY HIKE?
I DUNNO, IS IT *THAT* FAR?
HMM, I DUNNO. WE'RE USED TO IT.
BUT I'M SURE SHE'LL BE FINE.
Well.
...If they say so.

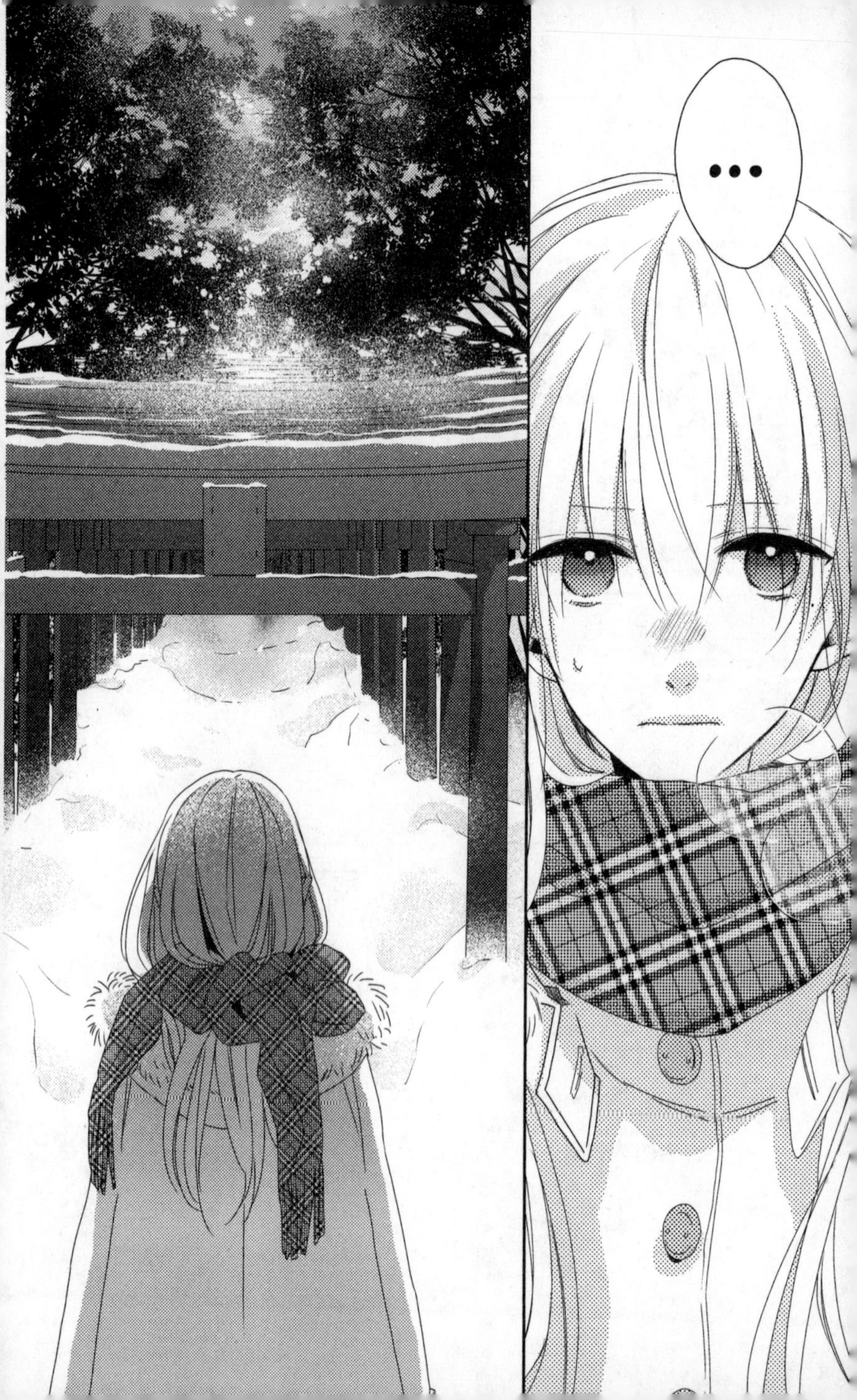
...

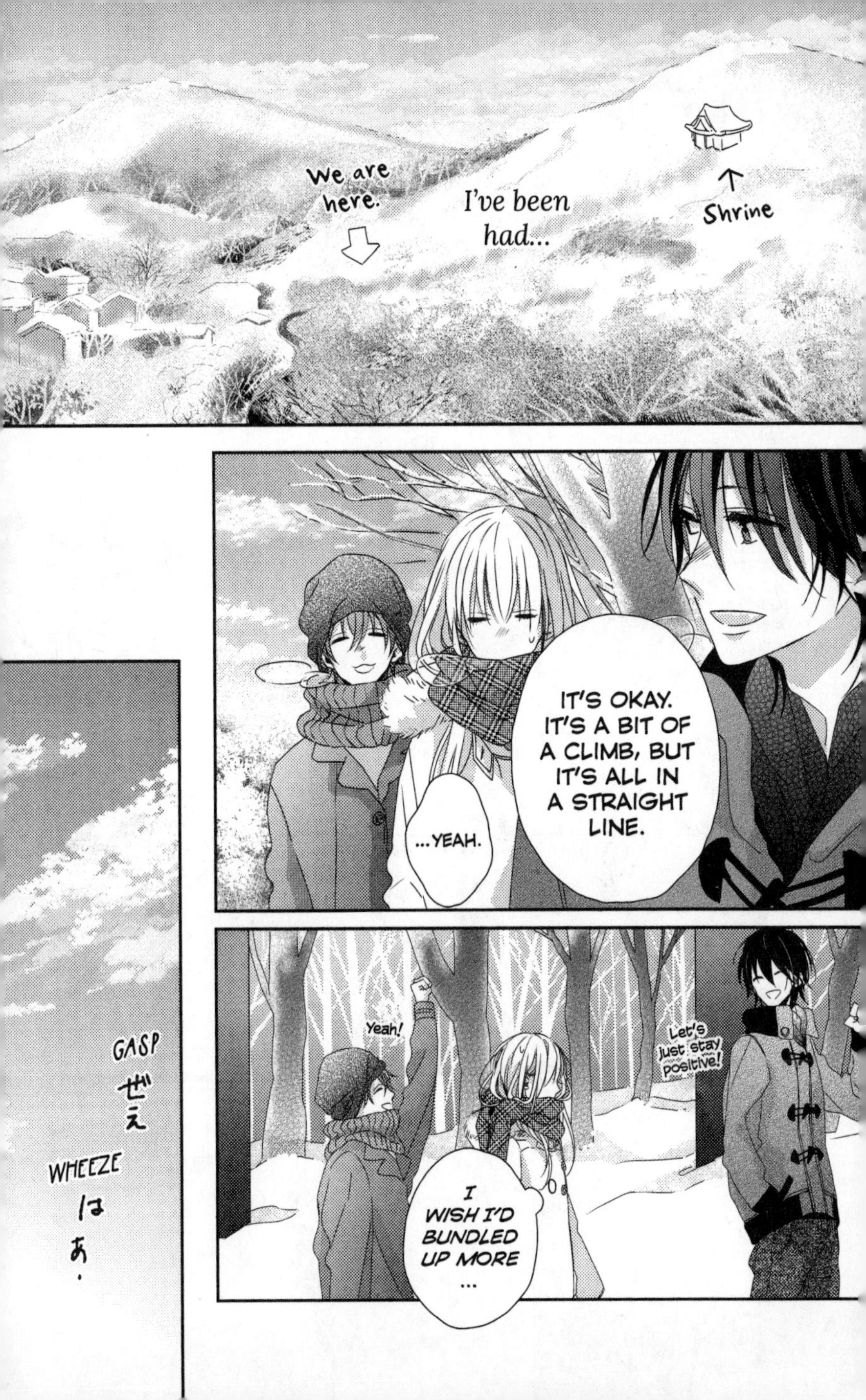
Shrine
I've been had...
We are here.
IT'S OKAY. IT'S A BIT OF A CLIMB, BUT IT'S ALL IN A STRAIGHT LINE.
...YEAH.
Let's just stay positive!
Yeah!
I WISH I'D BUNDLED UP MORE ...
GASP
ぜぇ
WHEEZE
はぁ

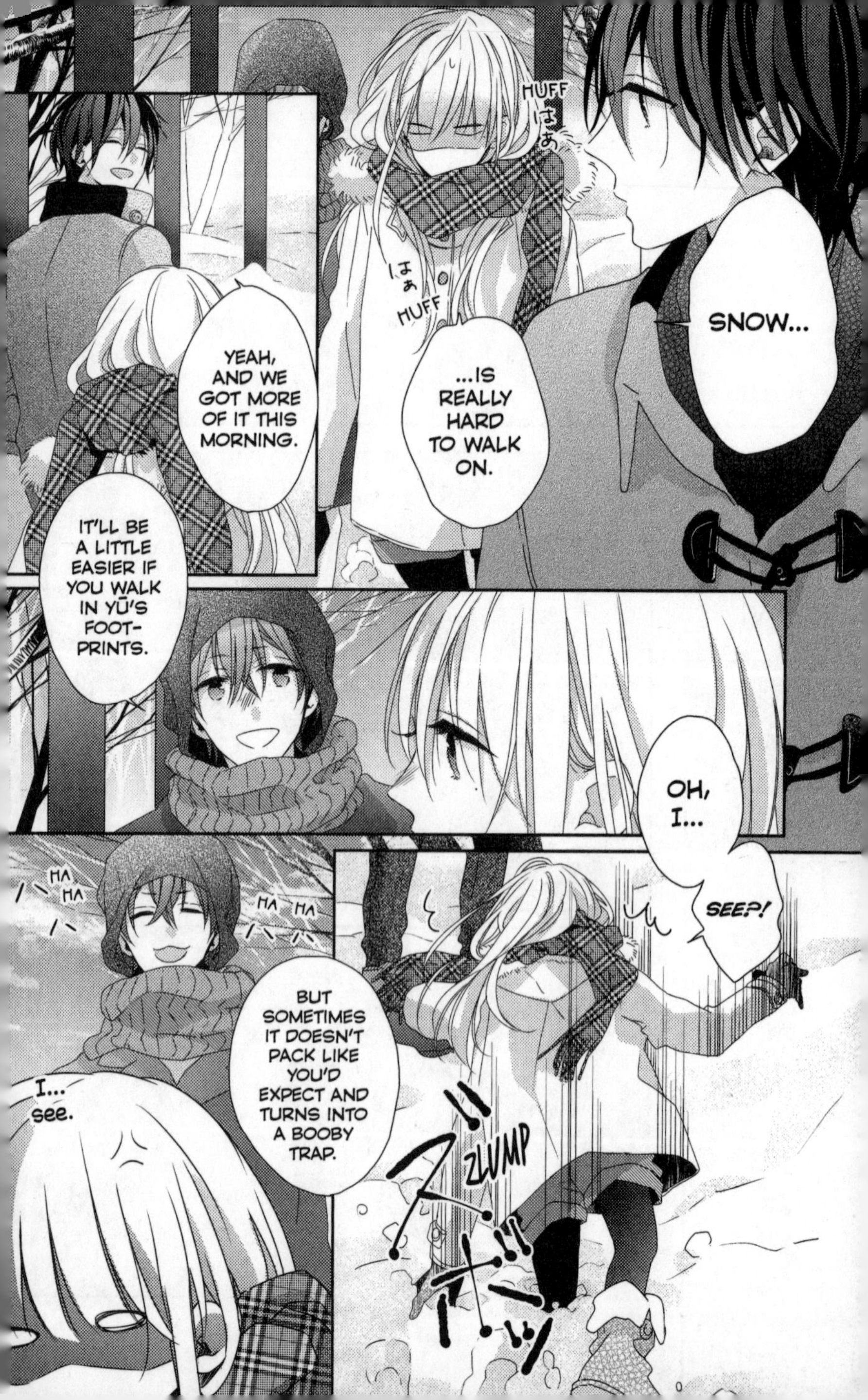
SNOW...
HUFF はぁ
はぁ HUFF
...IS REALLY HARD TO WALK ON.
YEAH, AND WE GOT MORE OF IT THIS MORNING.
IT'LL BE A LITTLE EASIER IF YOU WALK IN YŪ'S FOOT-PRINTS.
OH, I...
SEE?!
ZLUMP
HA HA
HA HA
BUT SOMETIMES IT DOESN'T PACK LIKE YOU'D EXPECT AND TURNS INTO A BOOBY TRAP.
I... see.

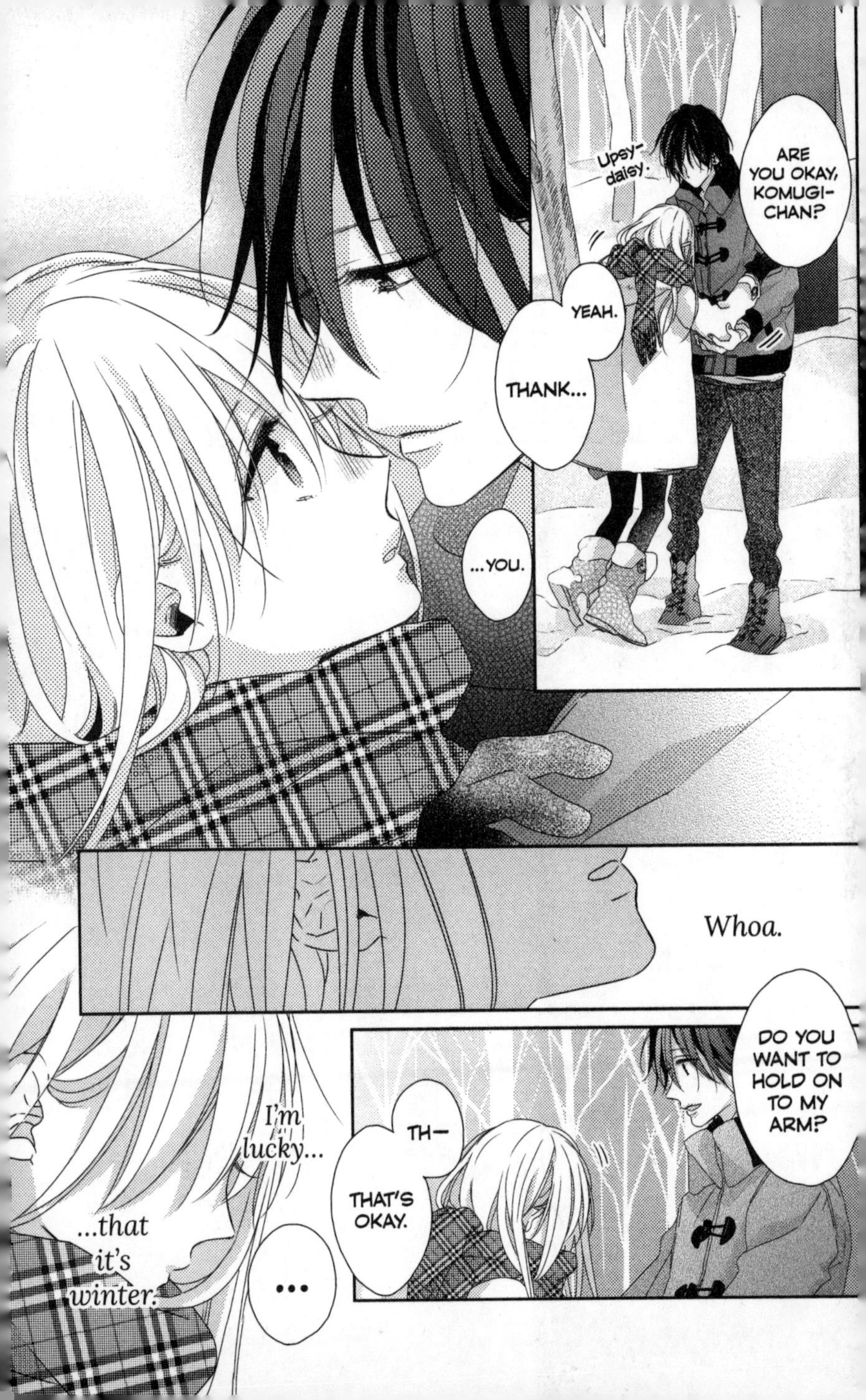
ARE YOU OKAY, KOMUGI-CHAN?
Upsy-daisy.
YEAH.
THANK...
...YOU.
Whoa.
DO YOU WANT TO HOLD ON TO MY ARM?
TH—
THAT'S OKAY.
...
I'm lucky...
...that it's winter.

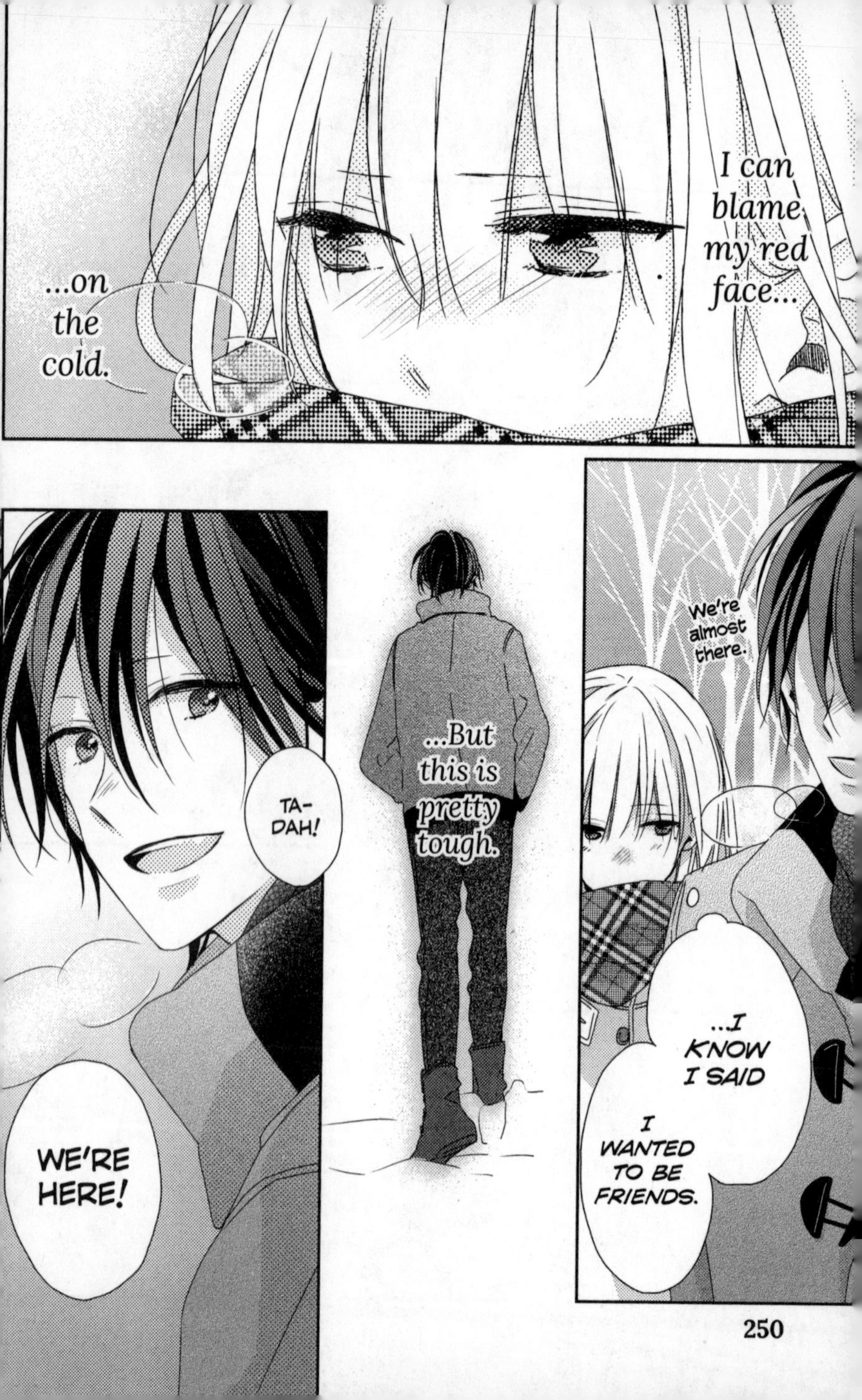
I can blame my red face...
...on the cold.
We're almost there.
...I KNOW I SAID I WANTED TO BE FRIENDS.
...But this is pretty tough.
TA-DAH!
WE'RE HERE!

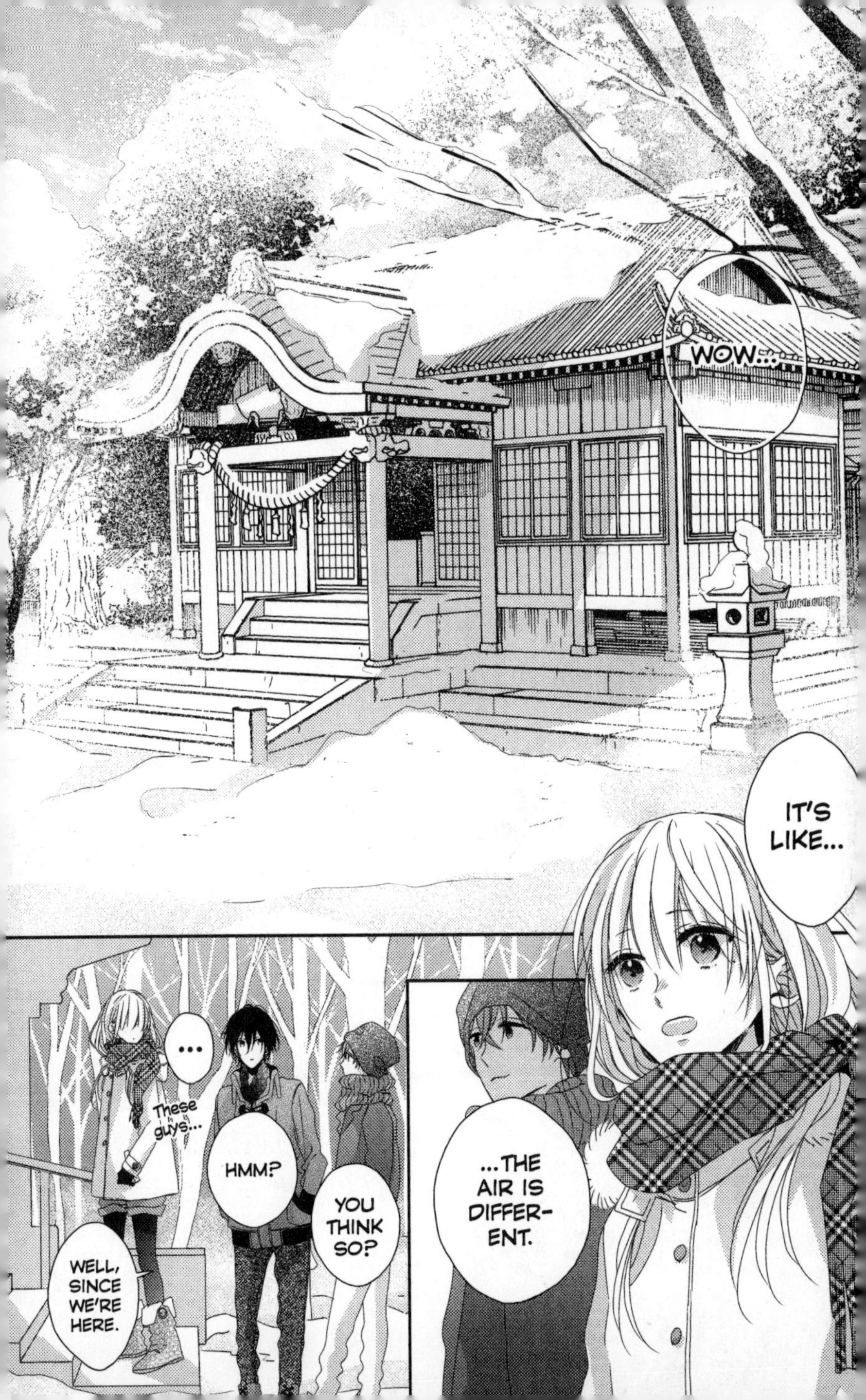
WOW...
IT'S LIKE...
...THE AIR IS DIFFER-ENT.
...
These guys...
HMM?
YOU THINK SO?
WELL, SINCE WE'RE HERE.

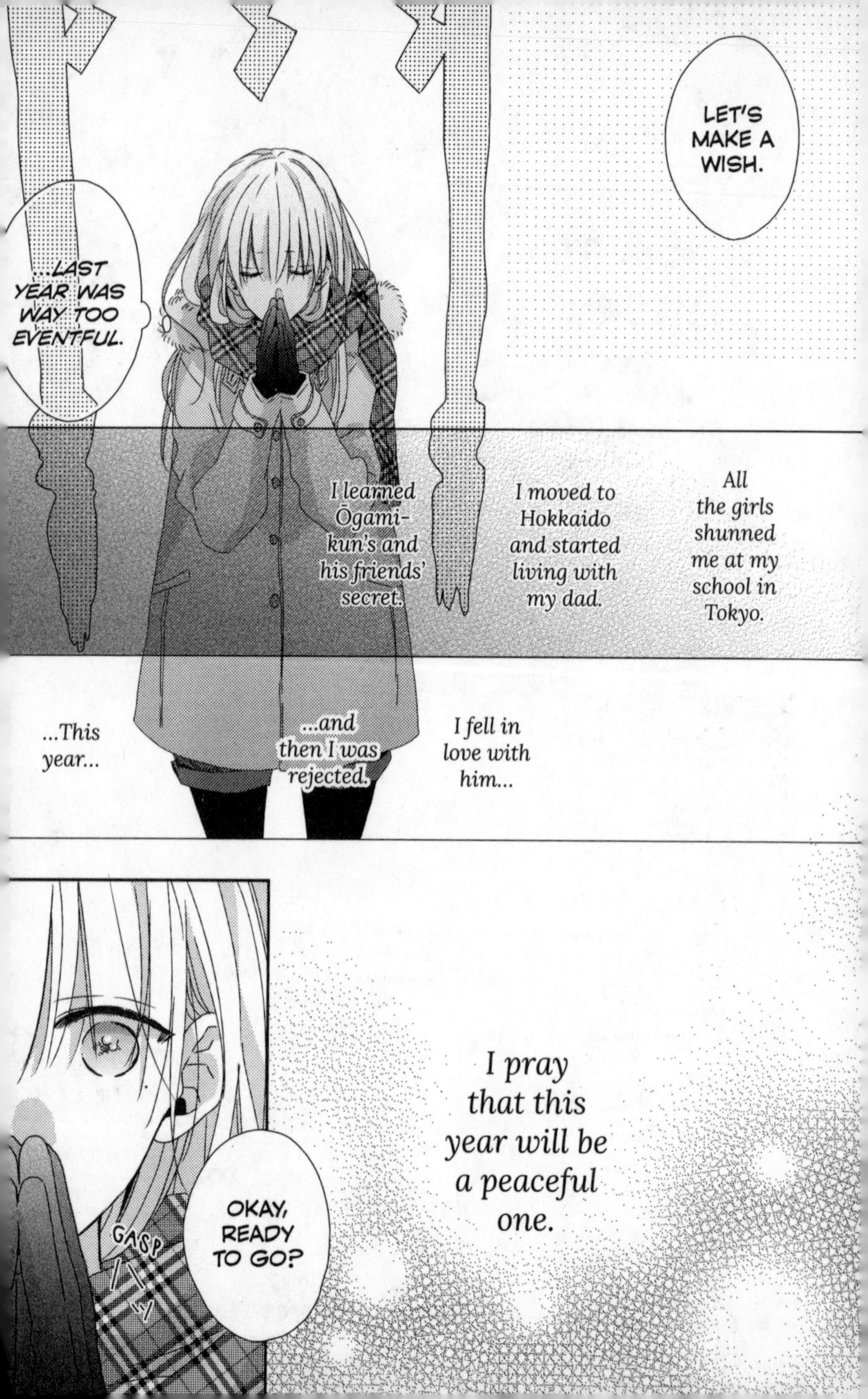
LET'S MAKE A WISH.
...LAST YEAR WAS WAY TOO EVENTFUL.
All the girls shunned me at my school in Tokyo.
I moved to Hokkaido and started living with my dad.
I learned Ōgami-kun's and his friends' secret.
I fell in love with him...
...and then I was rejected.
...This year...
I pray that this year will be a peaceful one.
OKAY, READY TO GO?
GASP

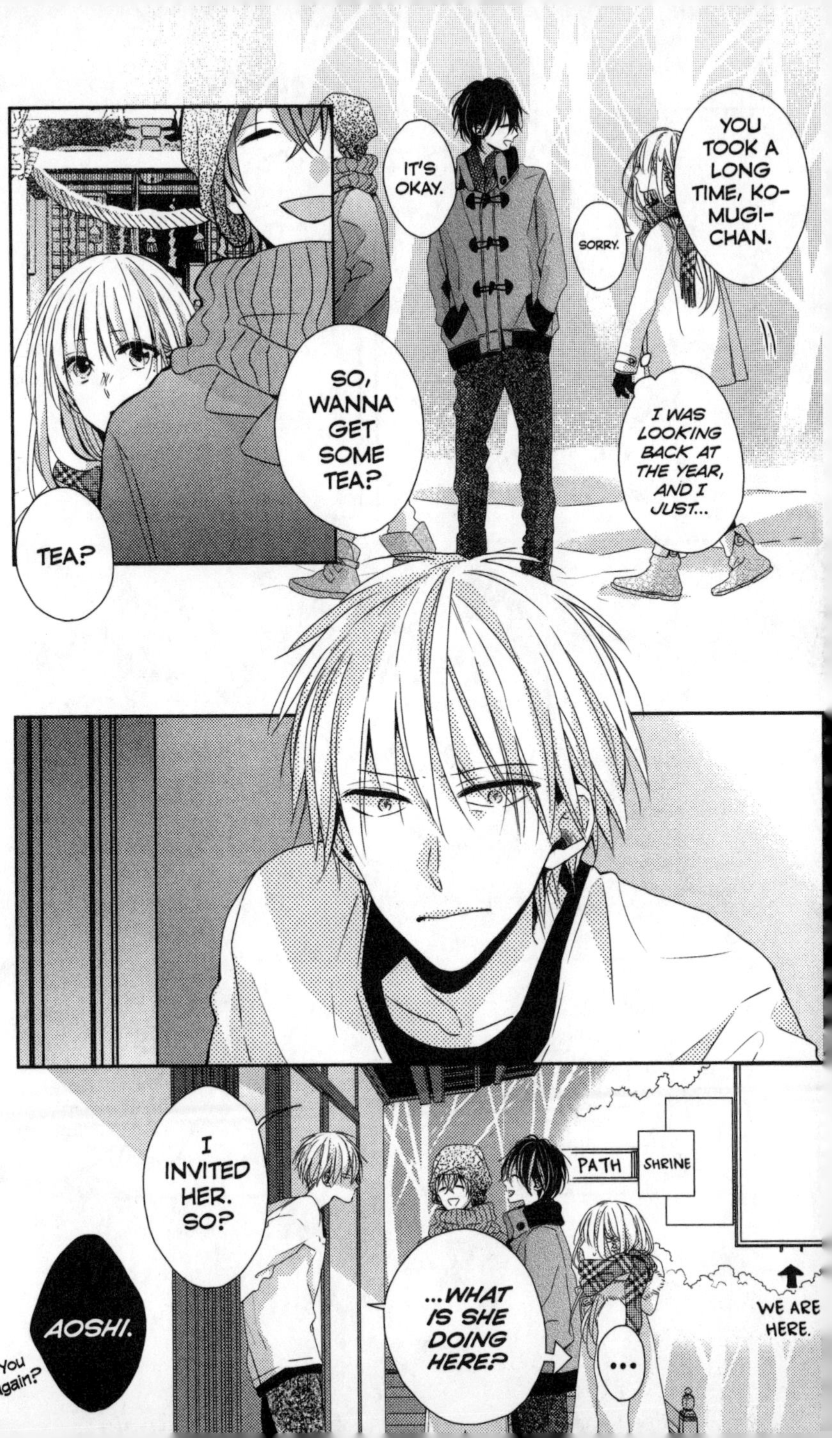
YOU TOOK A LONG TIME, KO-MUGI-CHAN.
SORRY.
IT'S OKAY.
I WAS LOOKING BACK AT THE YEAR, AND I JUST...
SO, WANNA GET SOME TEA?
TEA?
WE ARE HERE.
SHRINE
PATH
...
...WHAT IS SHE DOING HERE?
I INVITED HER. SO?
AOSHI.
You again?

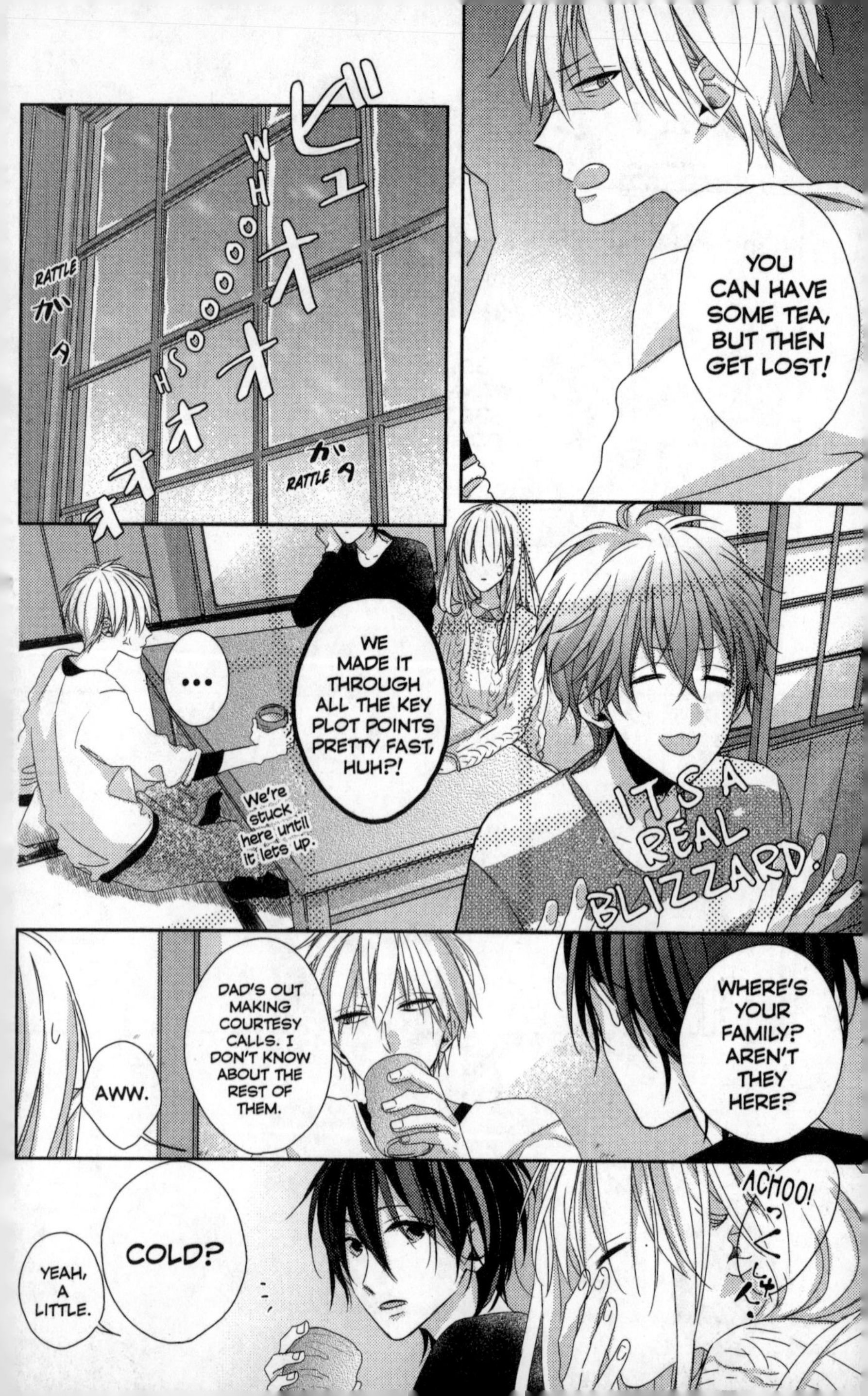
YOU CAN HAVE SOME TEA, BUT THEN GET LOST!
WHOOOOOSH
RATTLE
RATTLE
IT'S A REAL BLIZZARD.
WE MADE IT THROUGH ALL THE KEY PLOT POINTS PRETTY FAST, HUH?!
We're stuck here until it lets up.
...
WHERE'S YOUR FAMILY? AREN'T THEY HERE?
DAD'S OUT MAKING COURTESY CALLS. I DON'T KNOW ABOUT THE REST OF THEM.
AWW.
ACHOO!
COLD?
YEAH, A LITTLE.

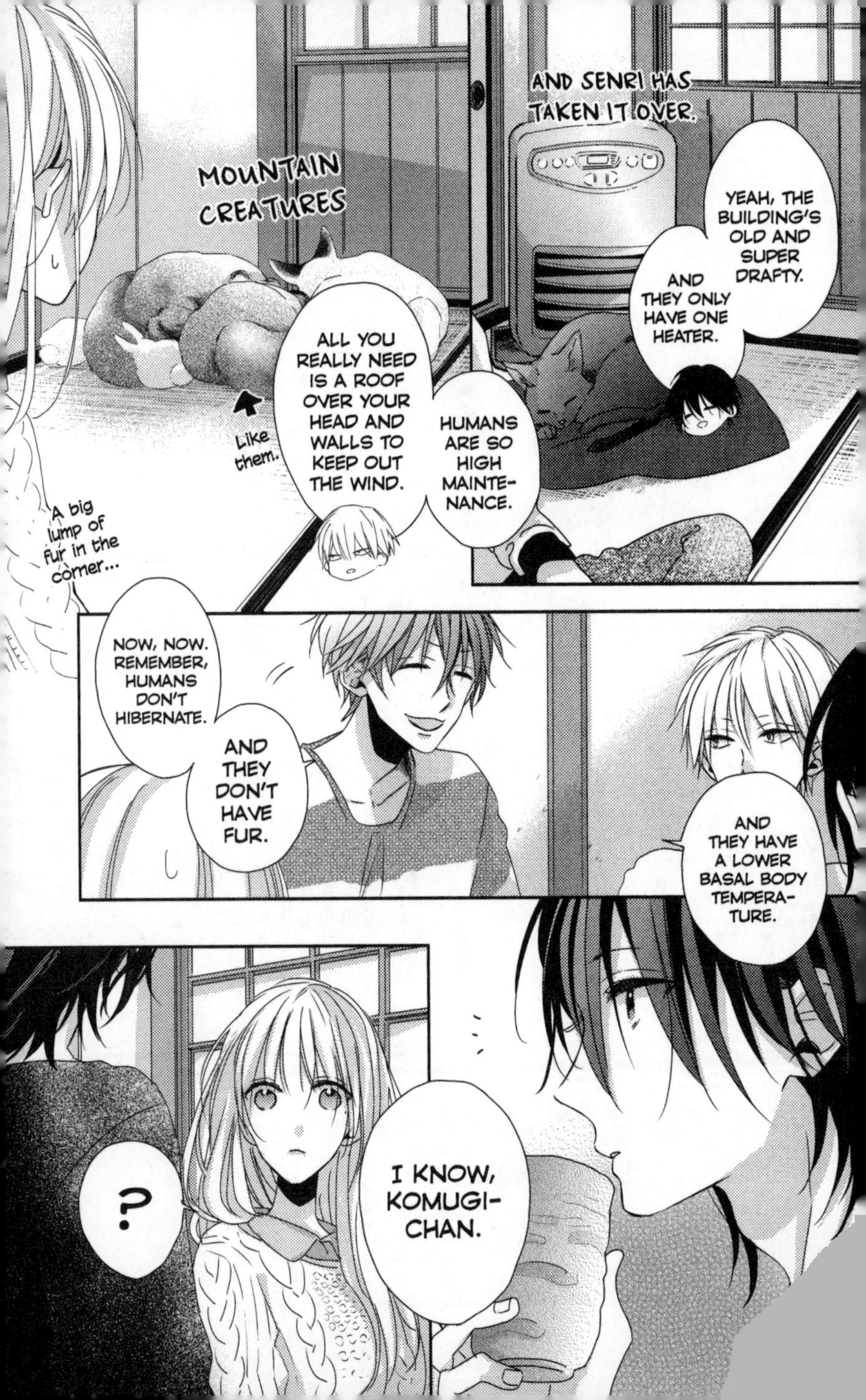
AND SENRI HAS TAKEN IT OVER.
YEAH, THE BUILDING'S OLD AND SUPER DRAFTY.
AND THEY ONLY HAVE ONE HEATER.
HUMANS ARE SO HIGH MAINTE-NANCE.
ALL YOU REALLY NEED IS A ROOF OVER YOUR HEAD AND WALLS TO KEEP OUT THE WIND.
MOUNTAIN CREATURES
Like them.
A big lump of fur in the corner...
AND THEY HAVE A LOWER BASAL BODY TEMPERA-TURE.
NOW, NOW. REMEMBER, HUMANS DON'T HIBERNATE.
AND THEY DON'T HAVE FUR.
I KNOW, KOMUGI-CHAN.
?

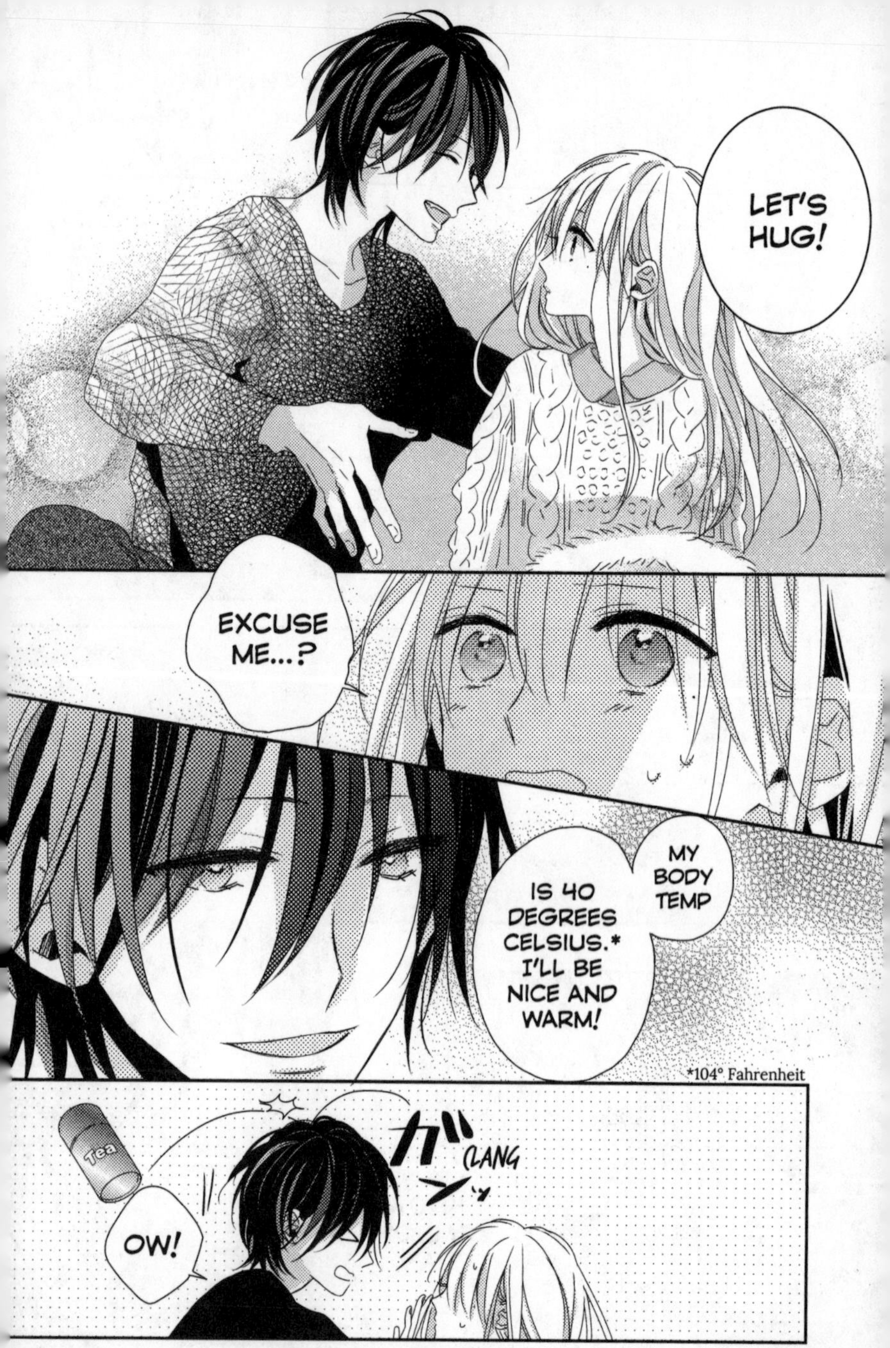
LET'S HUG!
EXCUSE ME...?
MY BODY TEMP
IS 40 DEGREES CELSIUS.* I'LL BE NICE AND WARM!
ガン
CLANG
Tea
OW!
*104° Fahrenheit

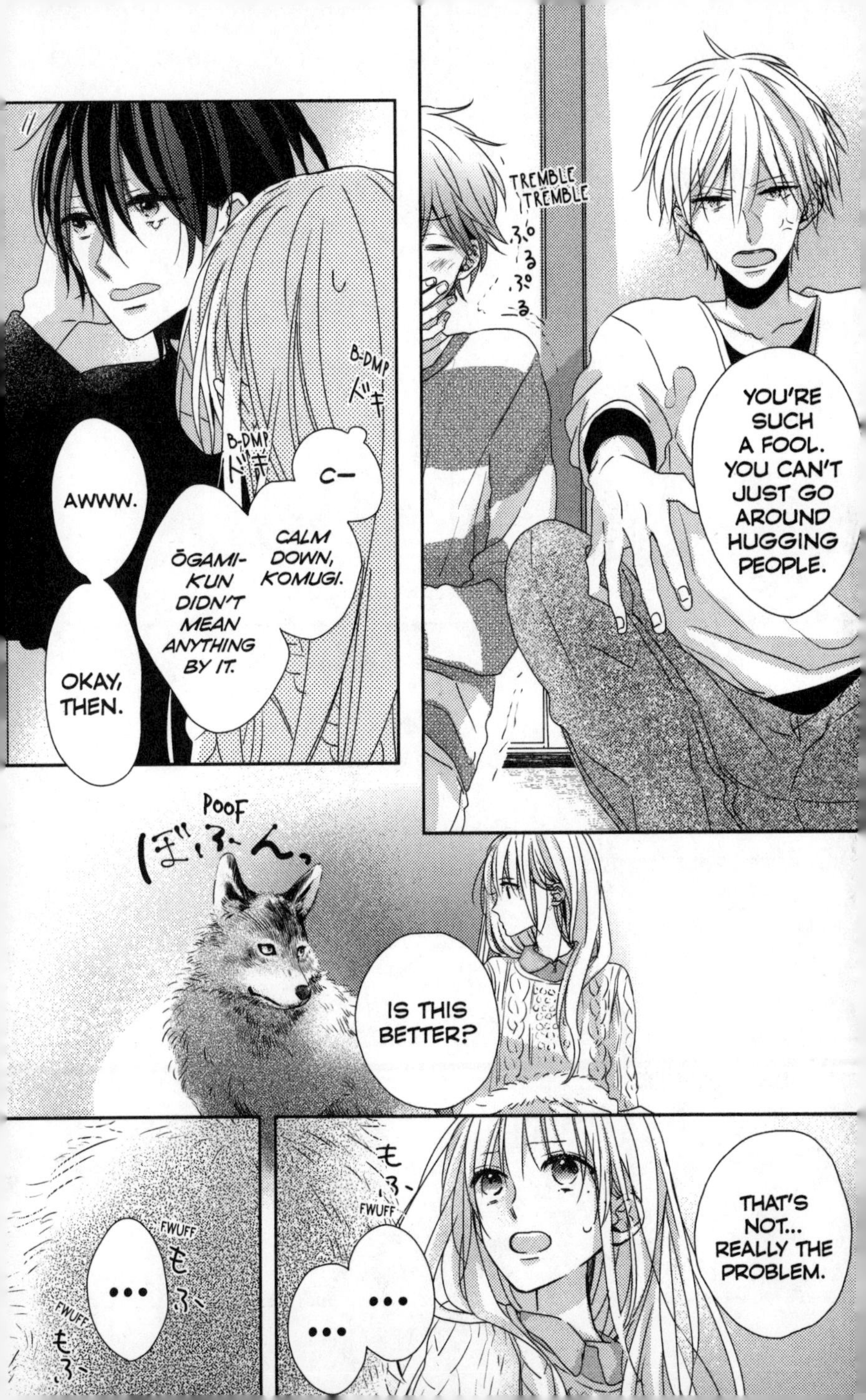
TREMBLE TREMBLE
ぷるぷる
YOU'RE SUCH A FOOL. YOU CAN'T JUST GO AROUND HUGGING PEOPLE.
B-DMP
ドキ
B-DMP
ドキ
C—
CALM DOWN, KOMUGI.
ŌGAMI-KUN DIDN'T MEAN ANYTHING BY IT.
AWWW.
OKAY, THEN.
POOF
ぼふん
IS THIS BETTER?
THAT'S NOT... REALLY THE PROBLEM.
FWUFF
もふ
... ...
FWUFF
もふ
...
FWUFF
もふ

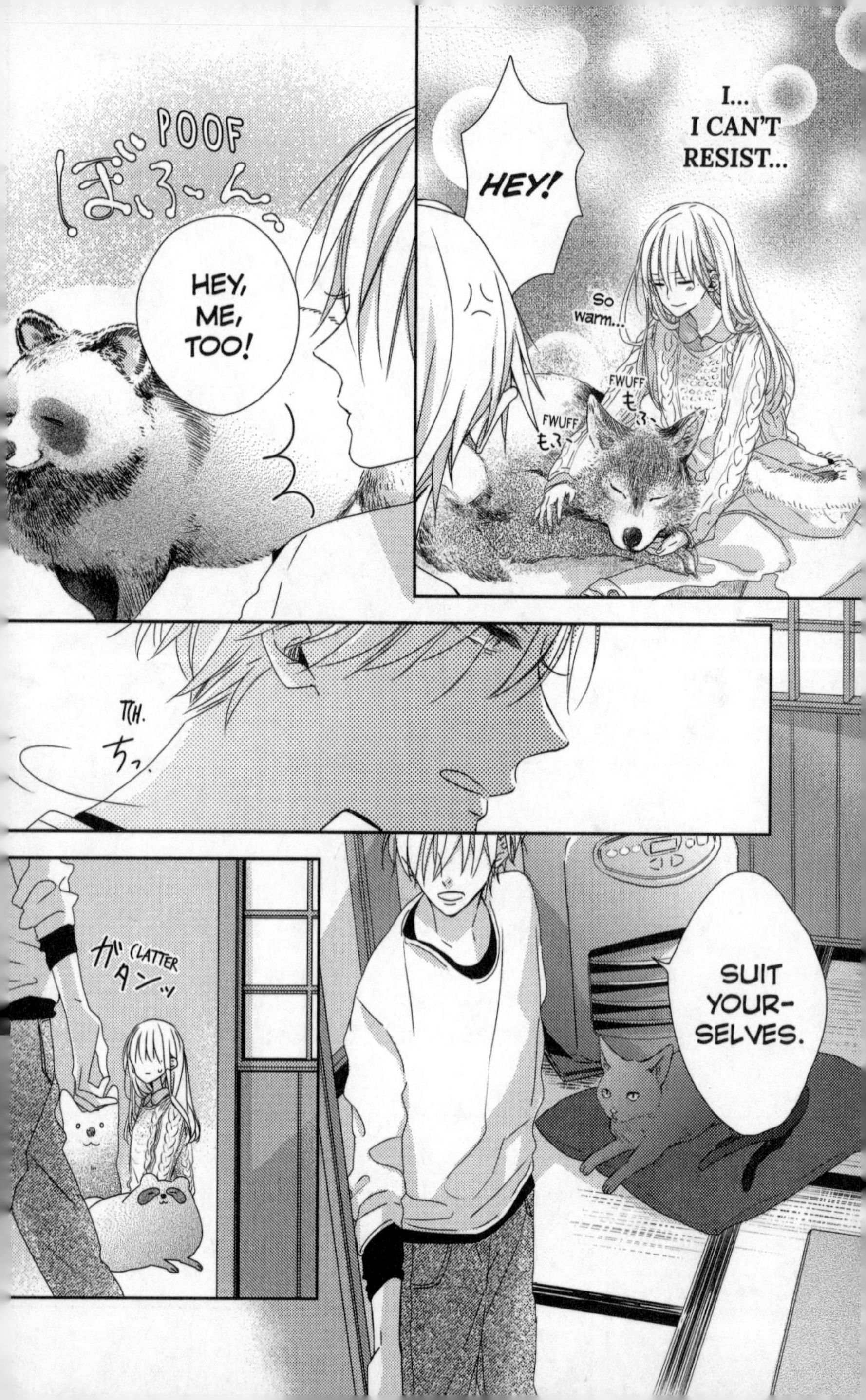
I...
I CAN'T RESIST...
HEY!
So warm...
FWUFF もふ
FWUFF もふ
POOF ぼふ～ん
HEY, ME, TOO!
TCH. ちっ
SUIT YOUR-SELVES.
CLATTER ガタンッ

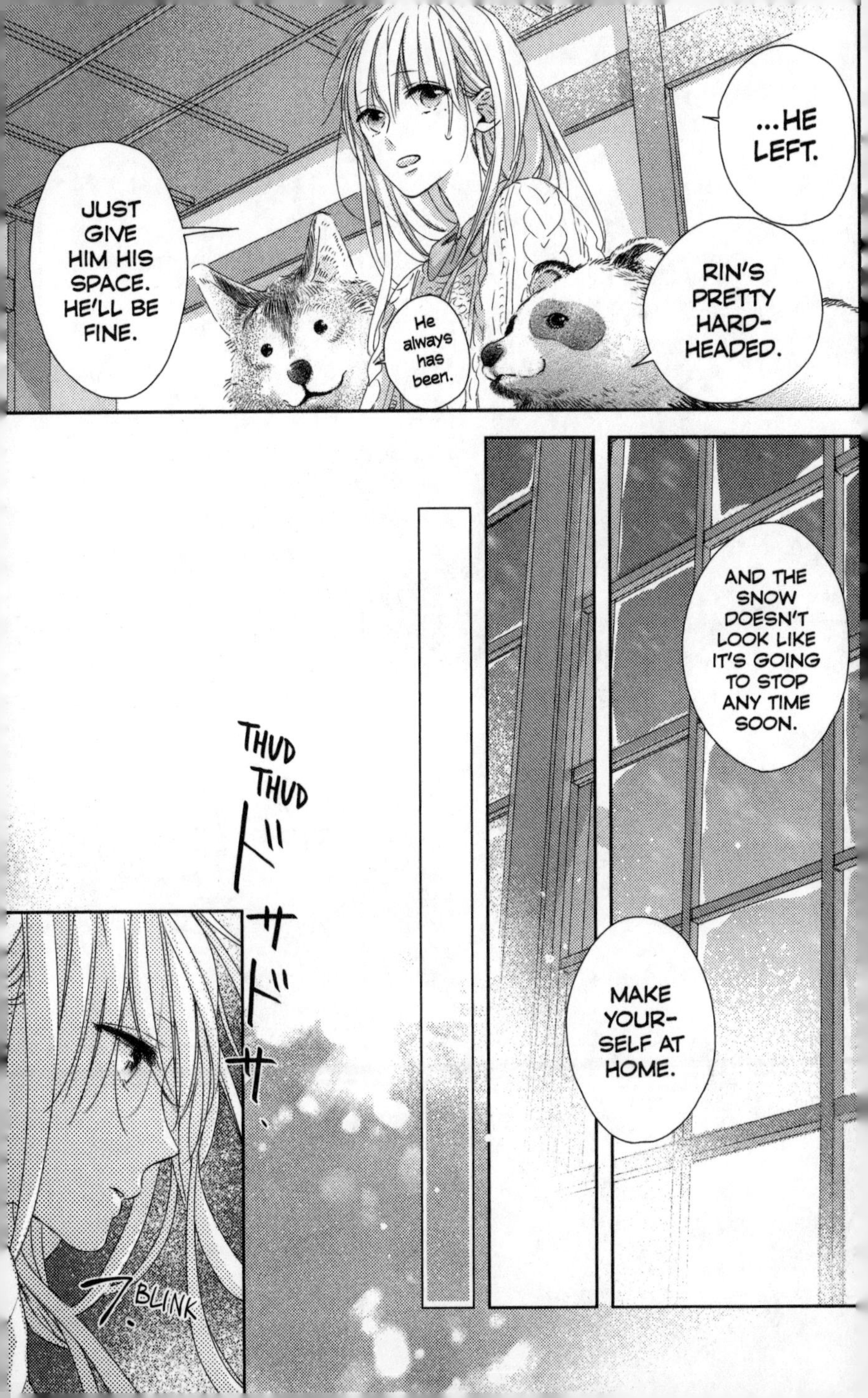
...HE LEFT.
RIN'S PRETTY HARD-HEADED.
He always has been.
JUST GIVE HIM HIS SPACE. HE'LL BE FINE.
AND THE SNOW DOESN'T LOOK LIKE IT'S GOING TO STOP ANY TIME SOON.
MAKE YOURSELF AT HOME.
THUD THUD
ドサドサ
BLINK

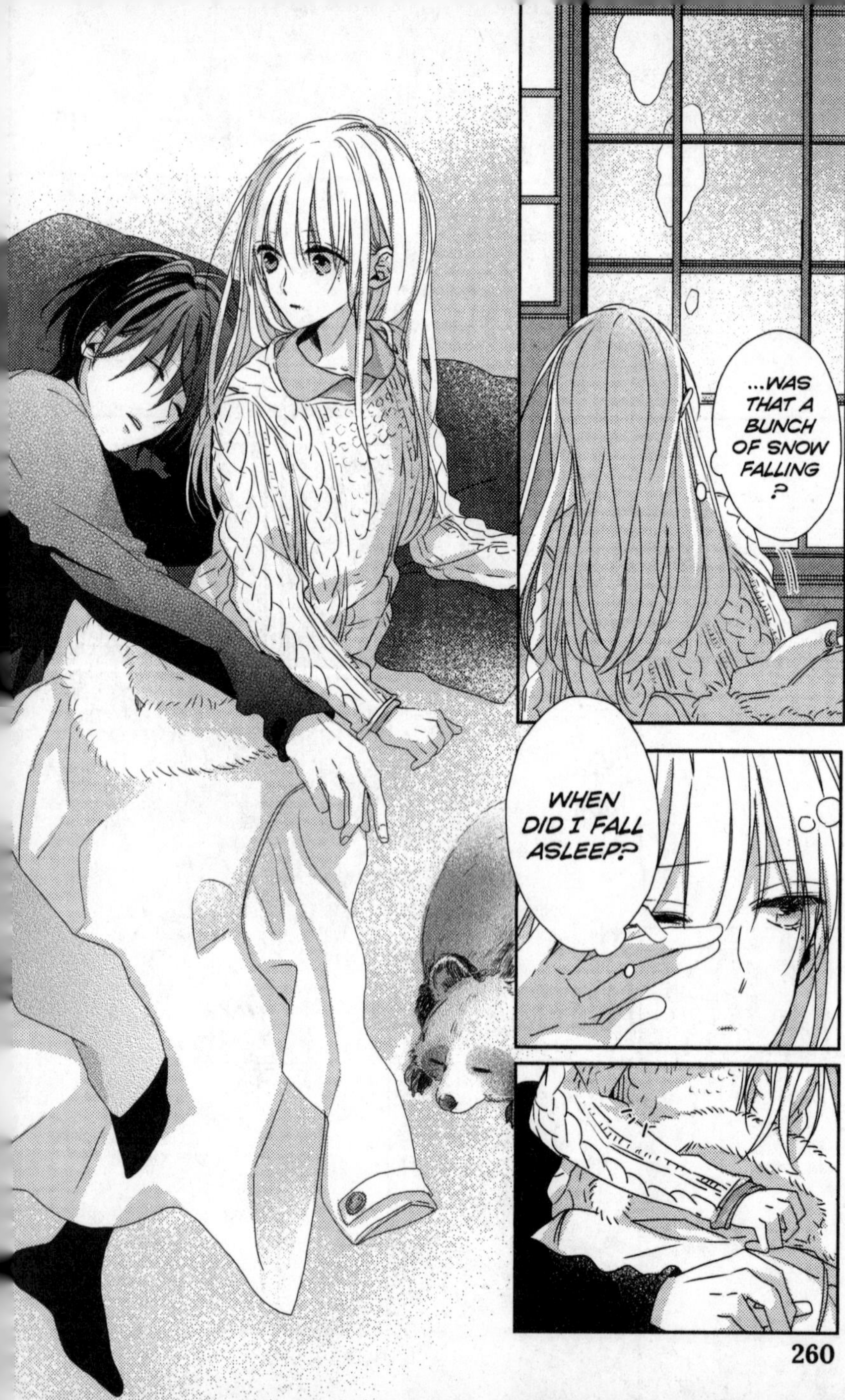
...WAS THAT A BUNCH OF SNOW FALLING ?
WHEN DID I FALL ASLEEP?

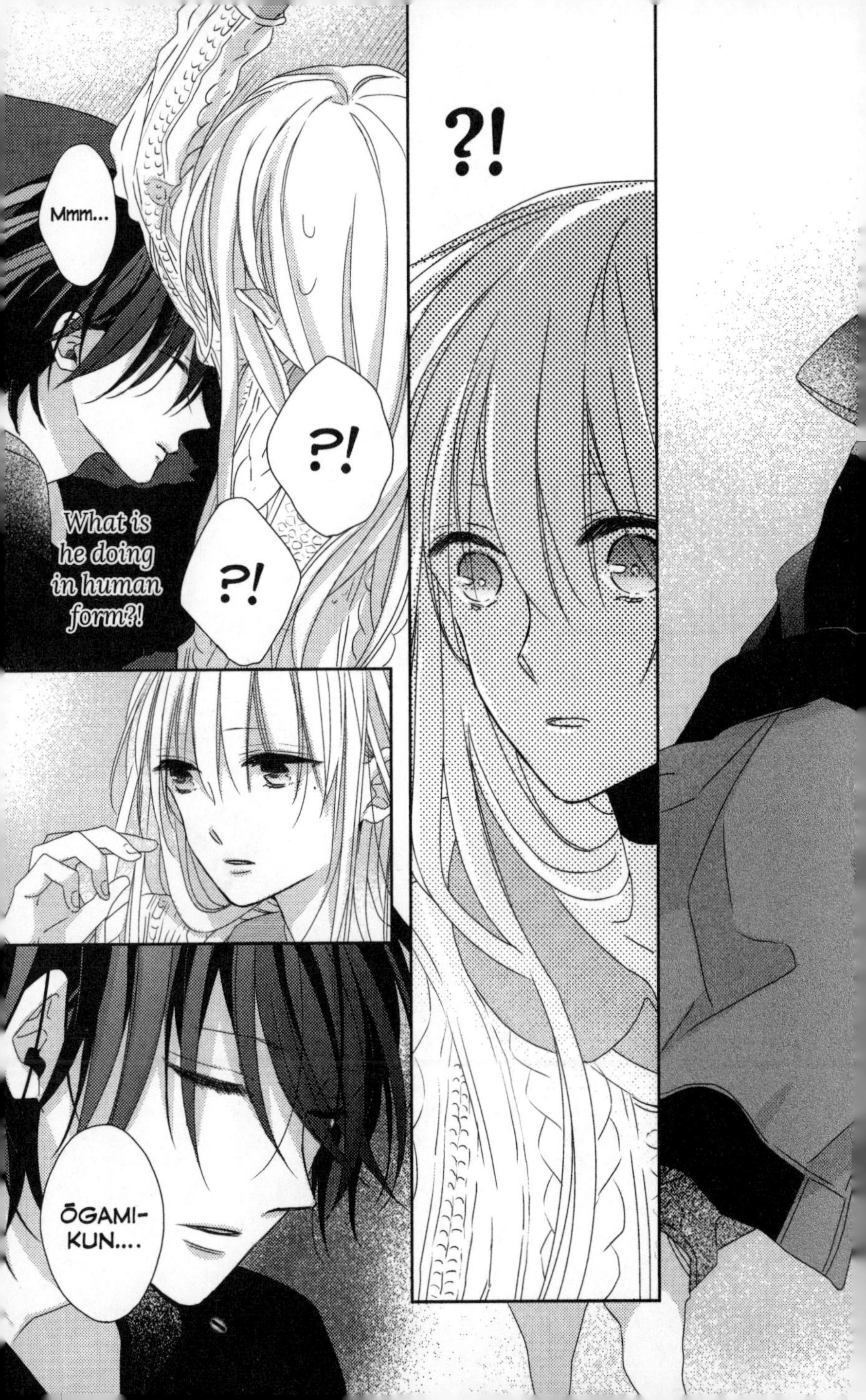
?!
Mmm...
?!
?!
What is he doing in human form?!
ŌGAMI-KUN....

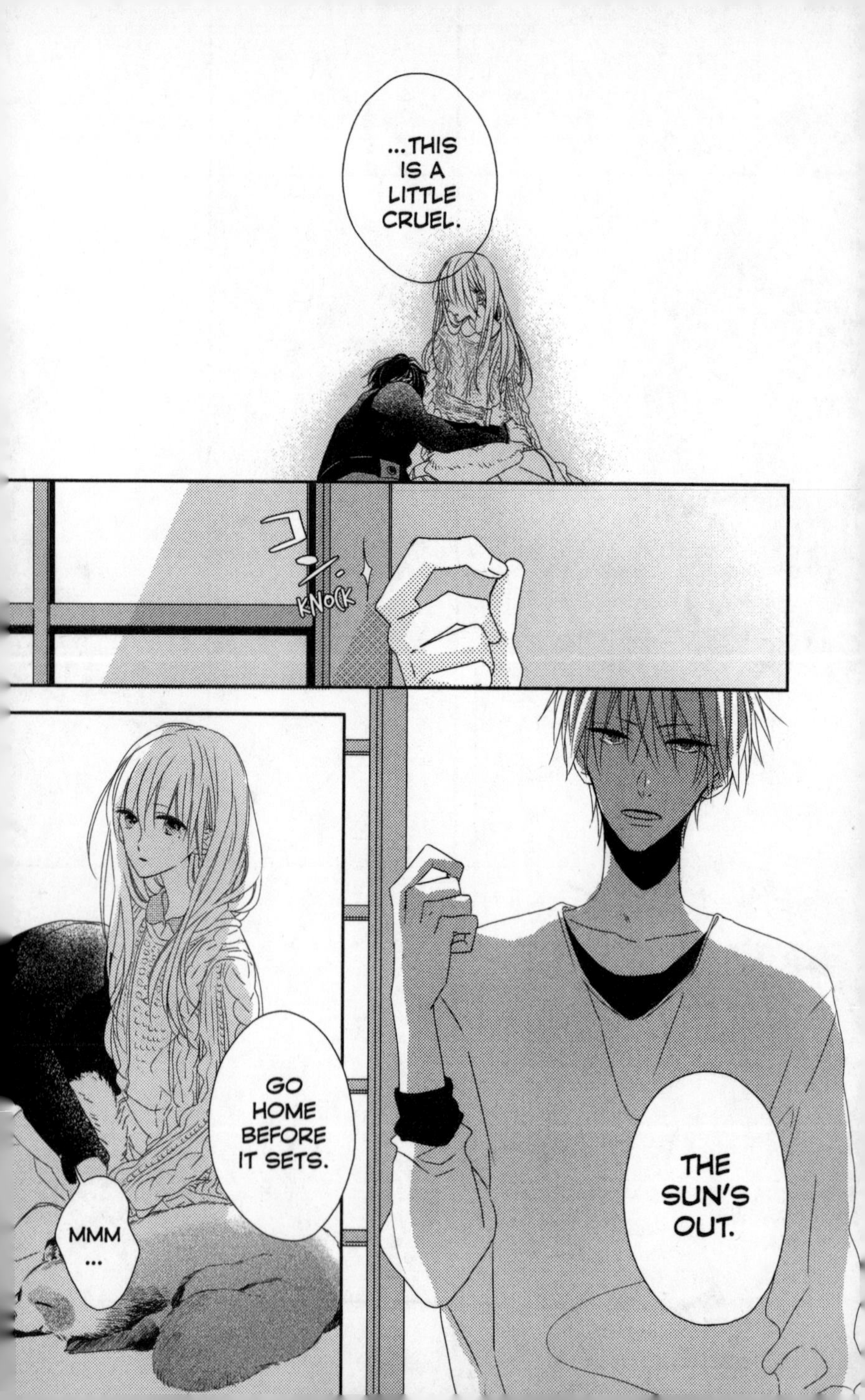
...THIS IS A LITTLE CRUEL.
KNOCK
THE SUN'S OUT.
GO HOME BEFORE IT SETS.
MMM ...

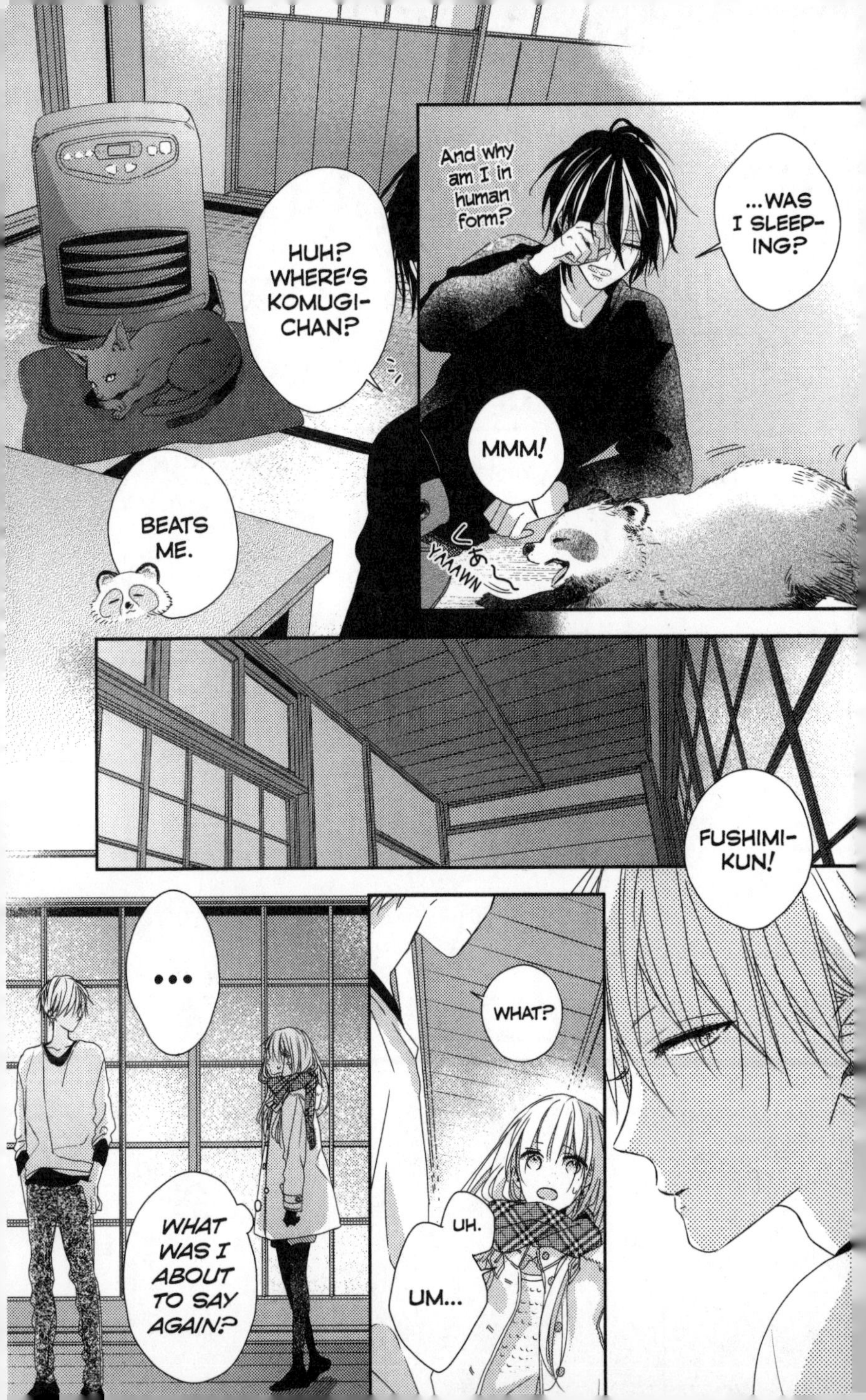
...WAS I SLEEP-ING?
And why am I in human form?
MMM!
くあ
YAAAWN
HUH? WHERE'S KOMUGI-CHAN?
BEATS ME.
FUSHIMI-KUN!
WHAT?
UH.
UM...
...
WHAT WAS I ABOUT TO SAY AGAIN?

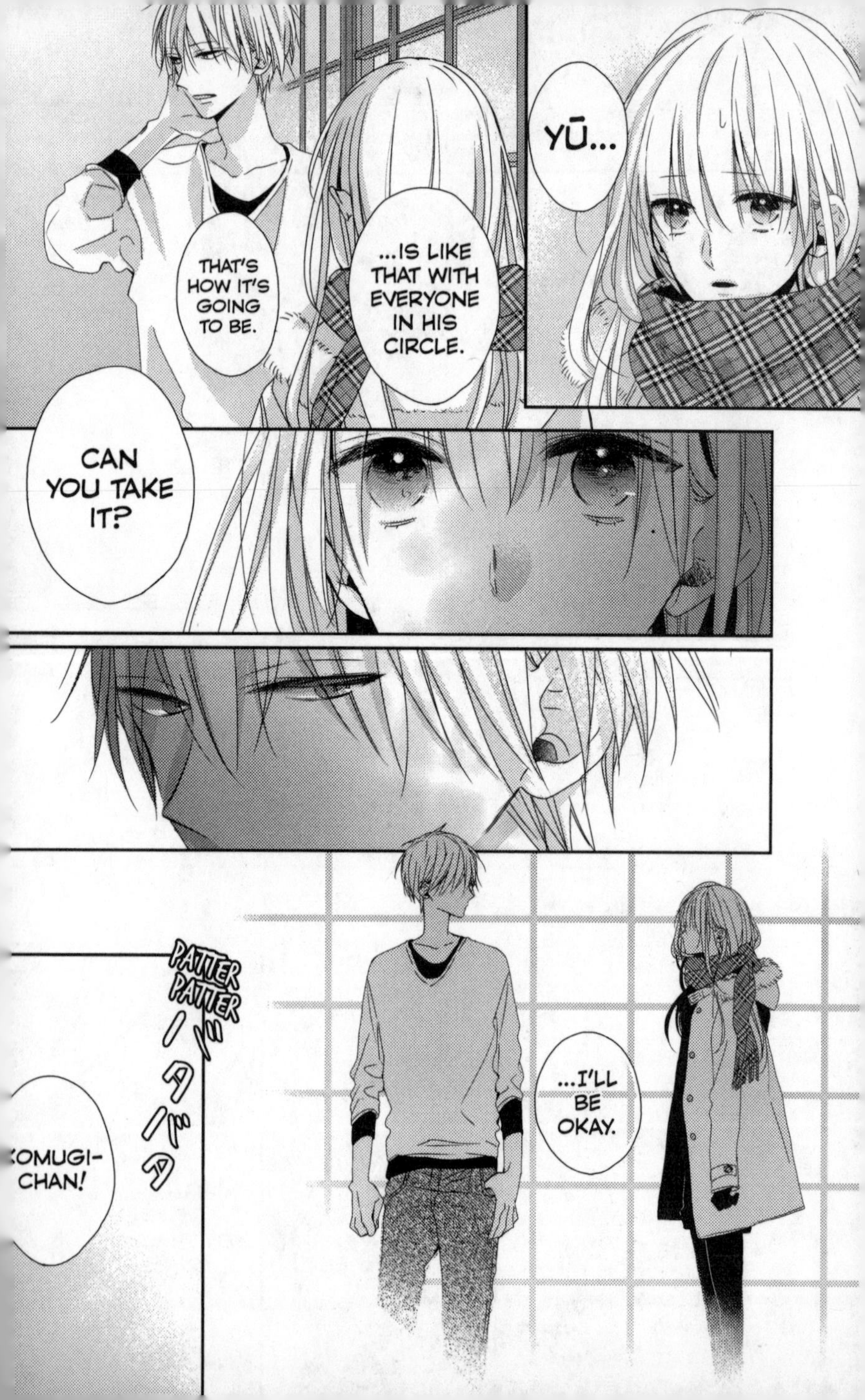

YŪ...
...IS LIKE THAT WITH EVERYONE IN HIS CIRCLE.
THAT'S HOW IT'S GOING TO BE.
CAN YOU TAKE IT?
...I'LL BE OKAY.
PATTER PATTER
KOMUGI-CHAN!

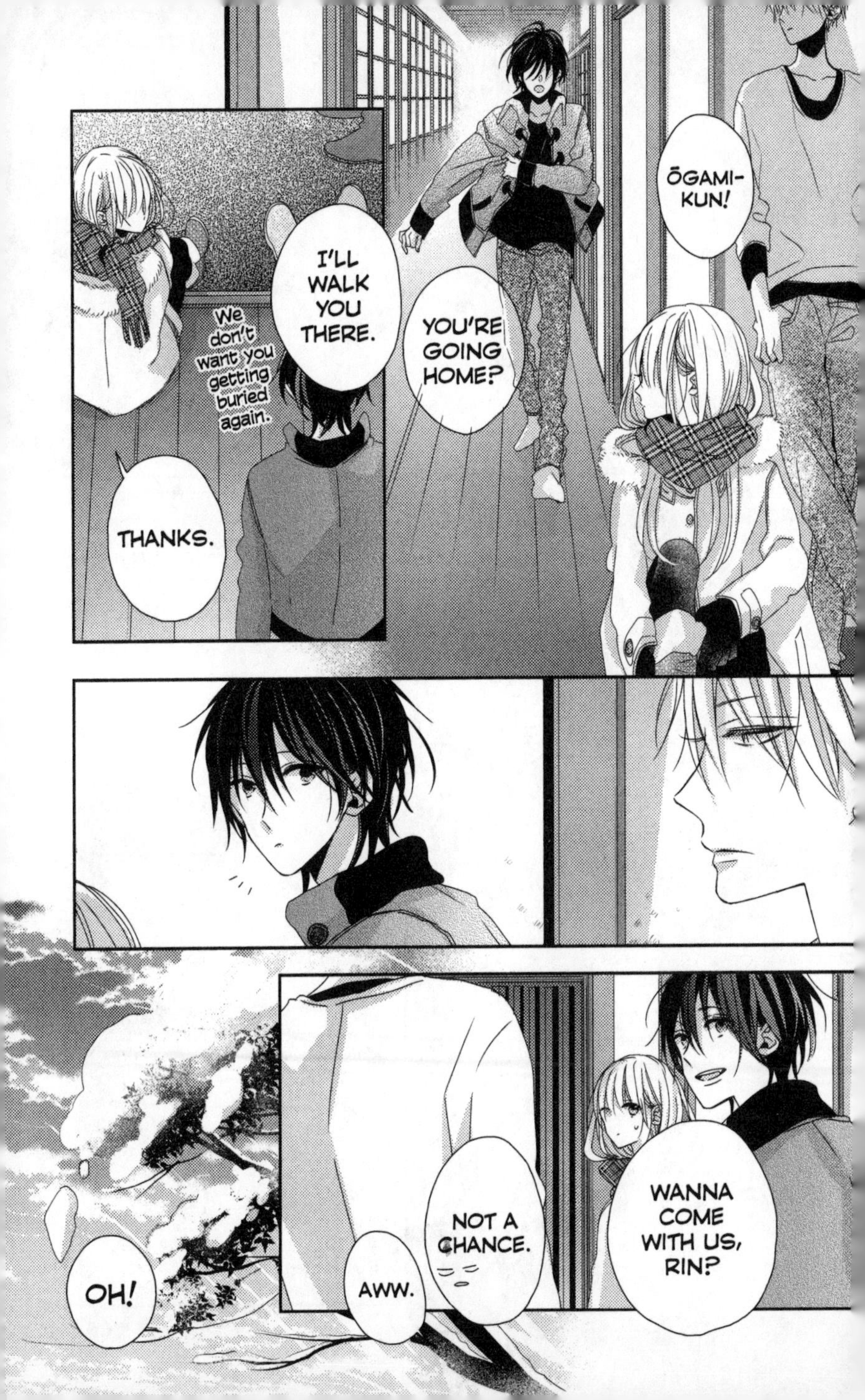
ŌGAMI-KUN!
YOU'RE GOING HOME?
I'LL WALK YOU THERE.
We don't want you getting buried again.
THANKS.
WANNA COME WITH US, RIN?
NOT A CHANCE.
AWW.
OH!

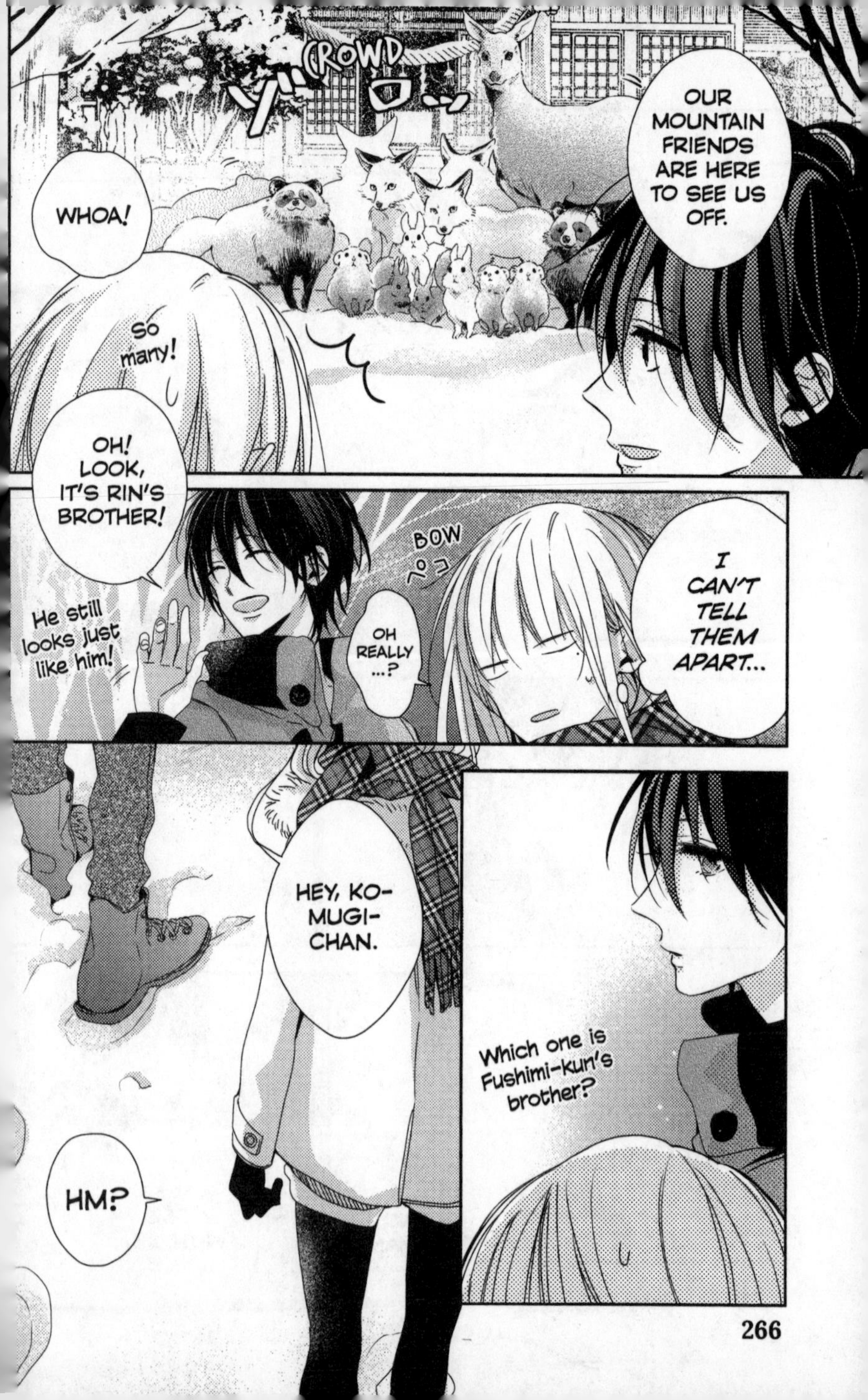
OUR MOUNTAIN FRIENDS ARE HERE TO SEE US OFF.
CROWD
WHOA!
So many!
I CAN'T TELL THEM APART...
BOW
OH REALLY ...?
OH! LOOK, IT'S RIN'S BROTHER!
He still looks just like him!
Which one is Fushimi-kun's brother?
HEY, KO-MUGI-CHAN.
HM?

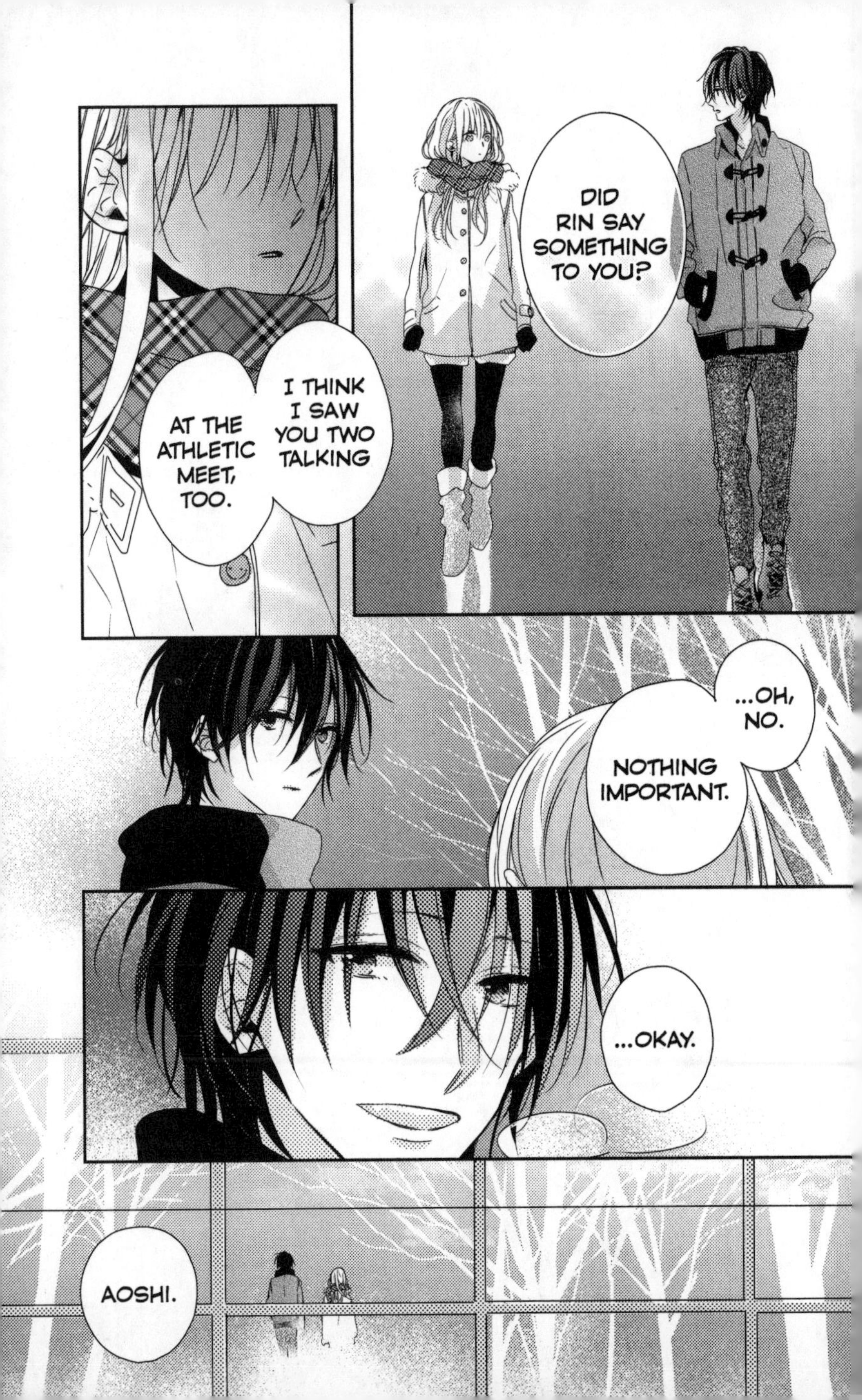
DID RIN SAY SOMETHING TO YOU?
I THINK I SAW YOU TWO TALKING
AT THE ATHLETIC MEET, TOO.
...OH, NO.
NOTHING IMPORTANT.
...OKAY.
AOSHI.

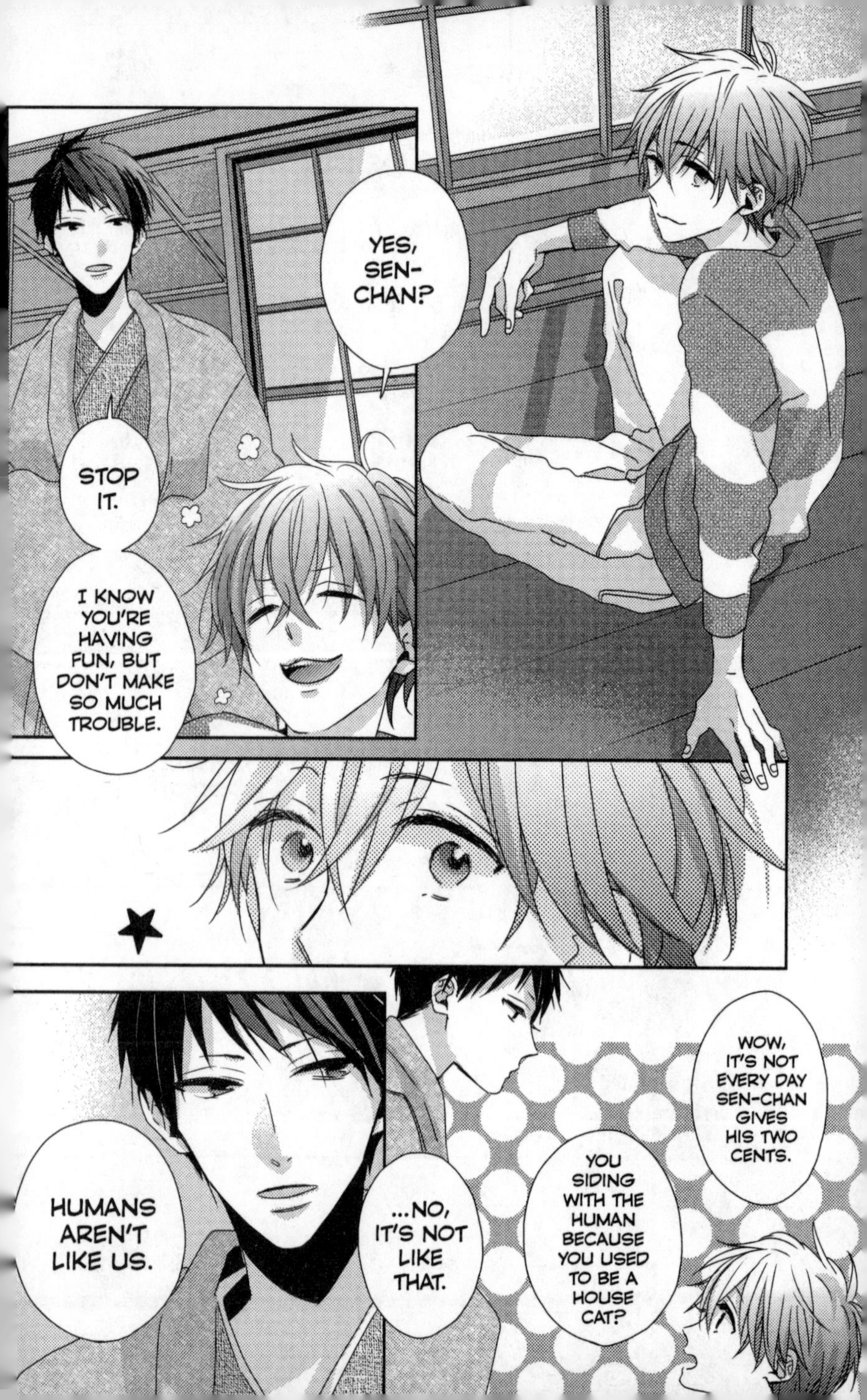
YES, SEN-CHAN?
STOP IT.
I KNOW YOU'RE HAVING FUN, BUT DON'T MAKE SO MUCH TROUBLE.
WOW, IT'S NOT EVERY DAY SEN-CHAN GIVES HIS TWO CENTS.
YOU SIDING WITH THE HUMAN BECAUSE YOU USED TO BE A HOUSE CAT?
...NO, IT'S NOT LIKE THAT.
HUMANS AREN'T LIKE US.

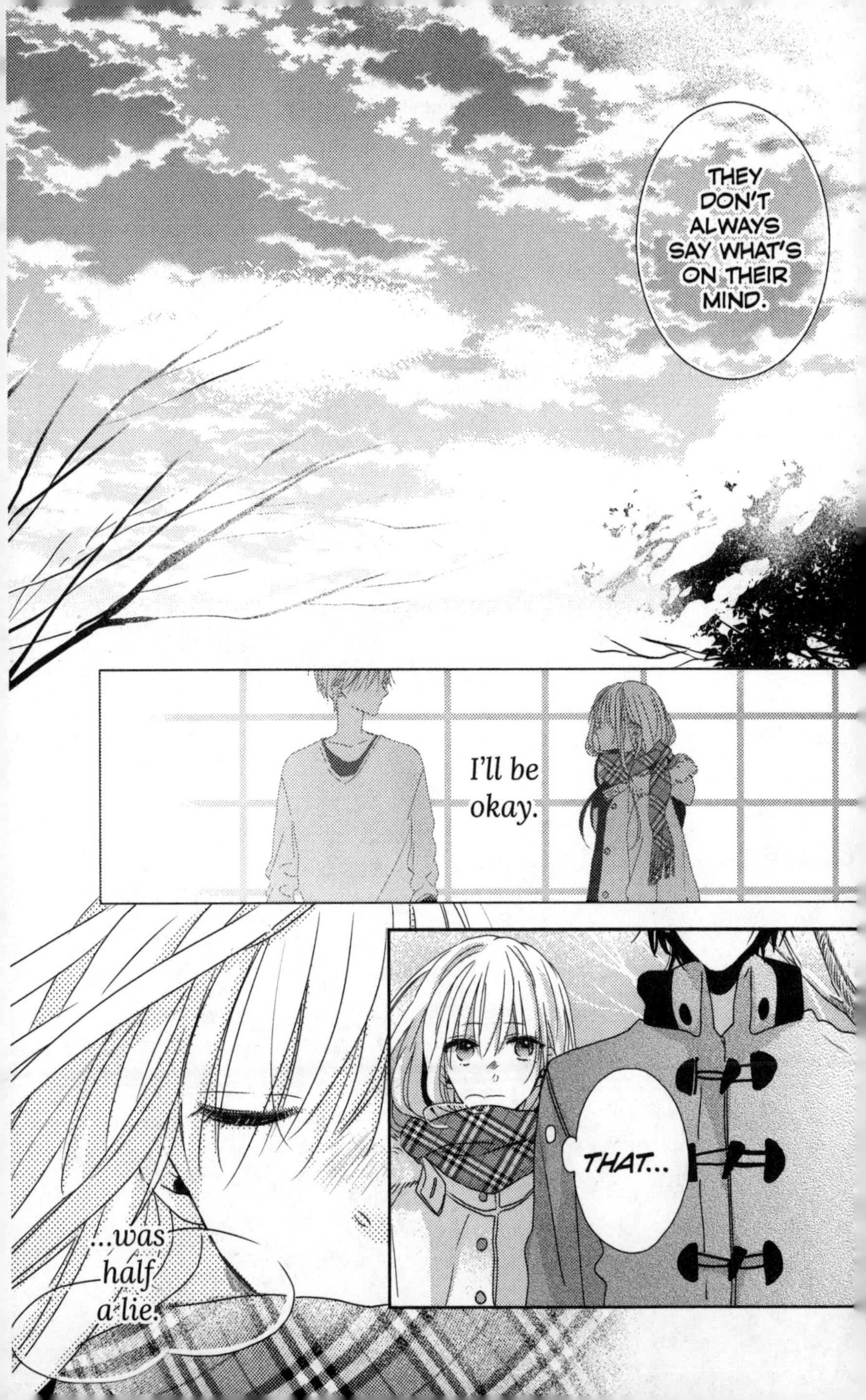
THEY DON'T ALWAYS SAY WHAT'S ON THEIR MIND.
I'll be okay.
THAT...
...was half a lie.

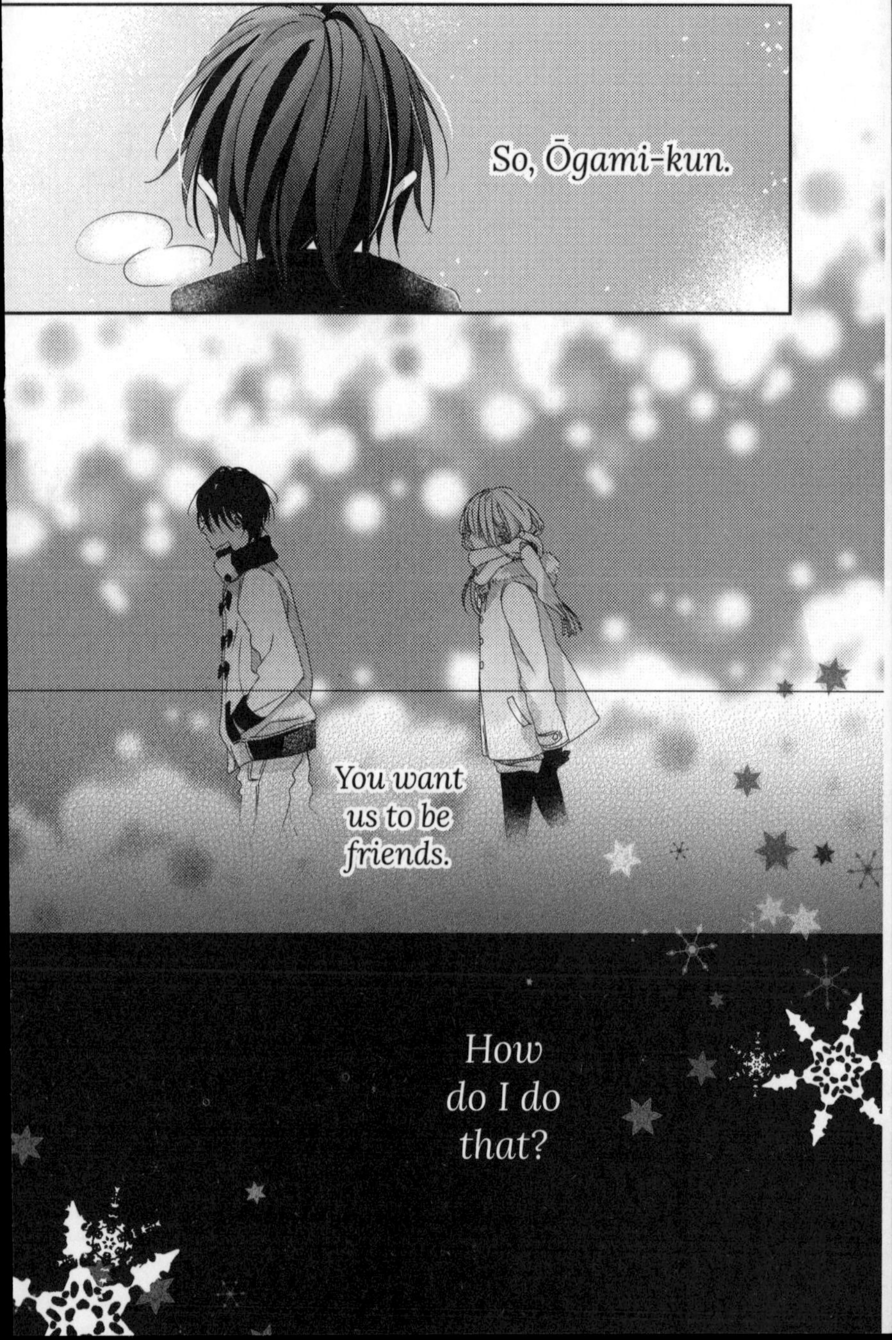
So, Ōgami-kun.
You want us to be friends.
How do I do that?

That WOLF-BOY IS MINE!

That Wolf-Boy is Mine!

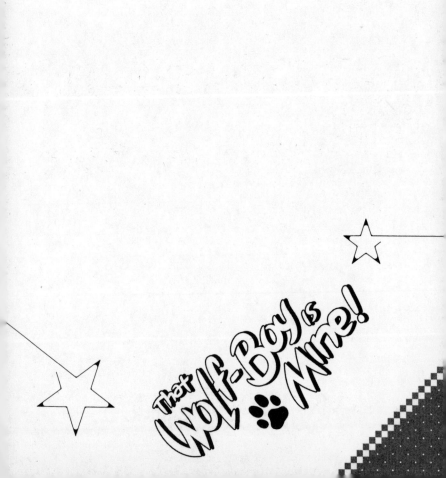

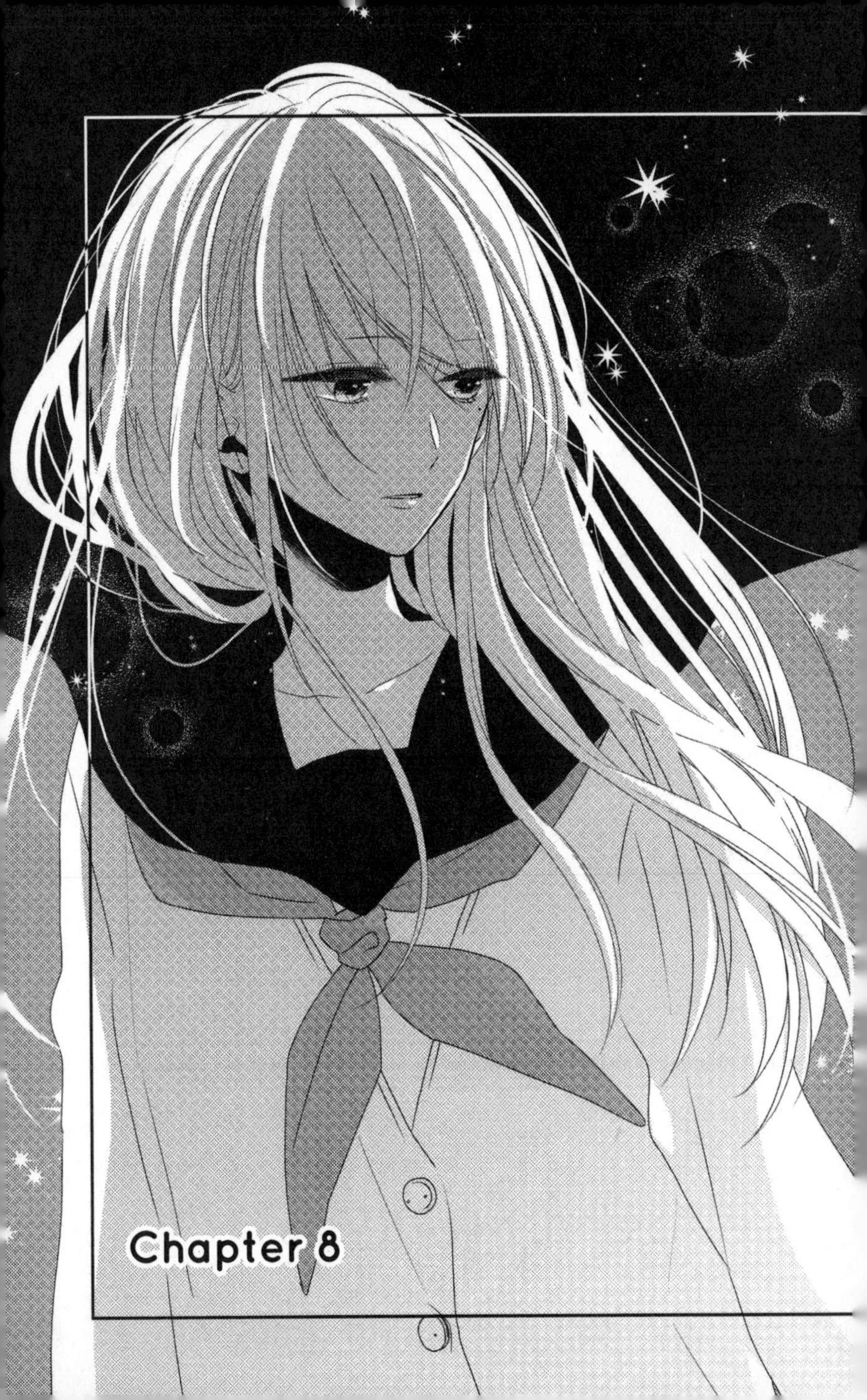
Chapter 8

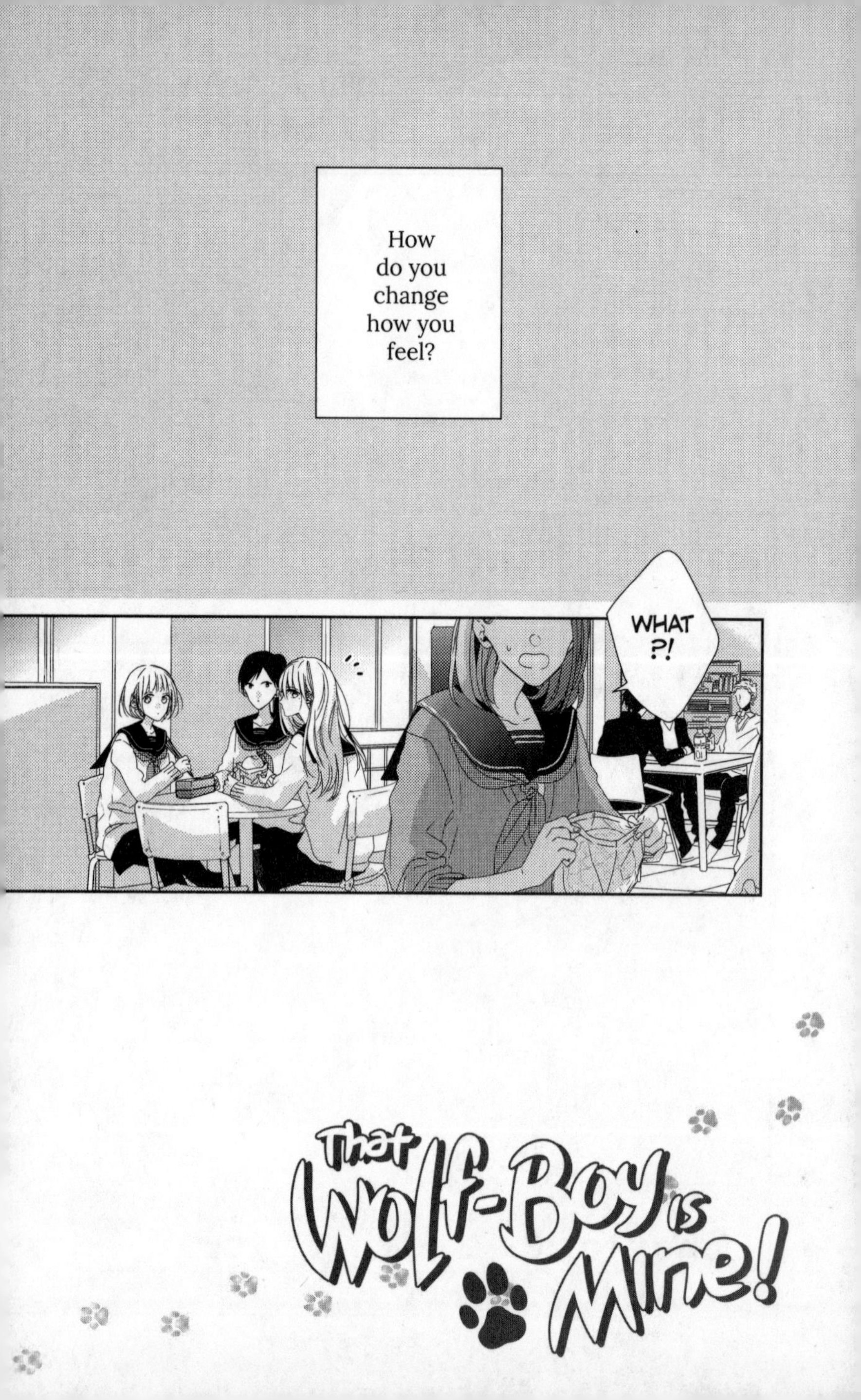
How do you change how you feel?
WHAT ?!
That Wolf-Boy is Mine!

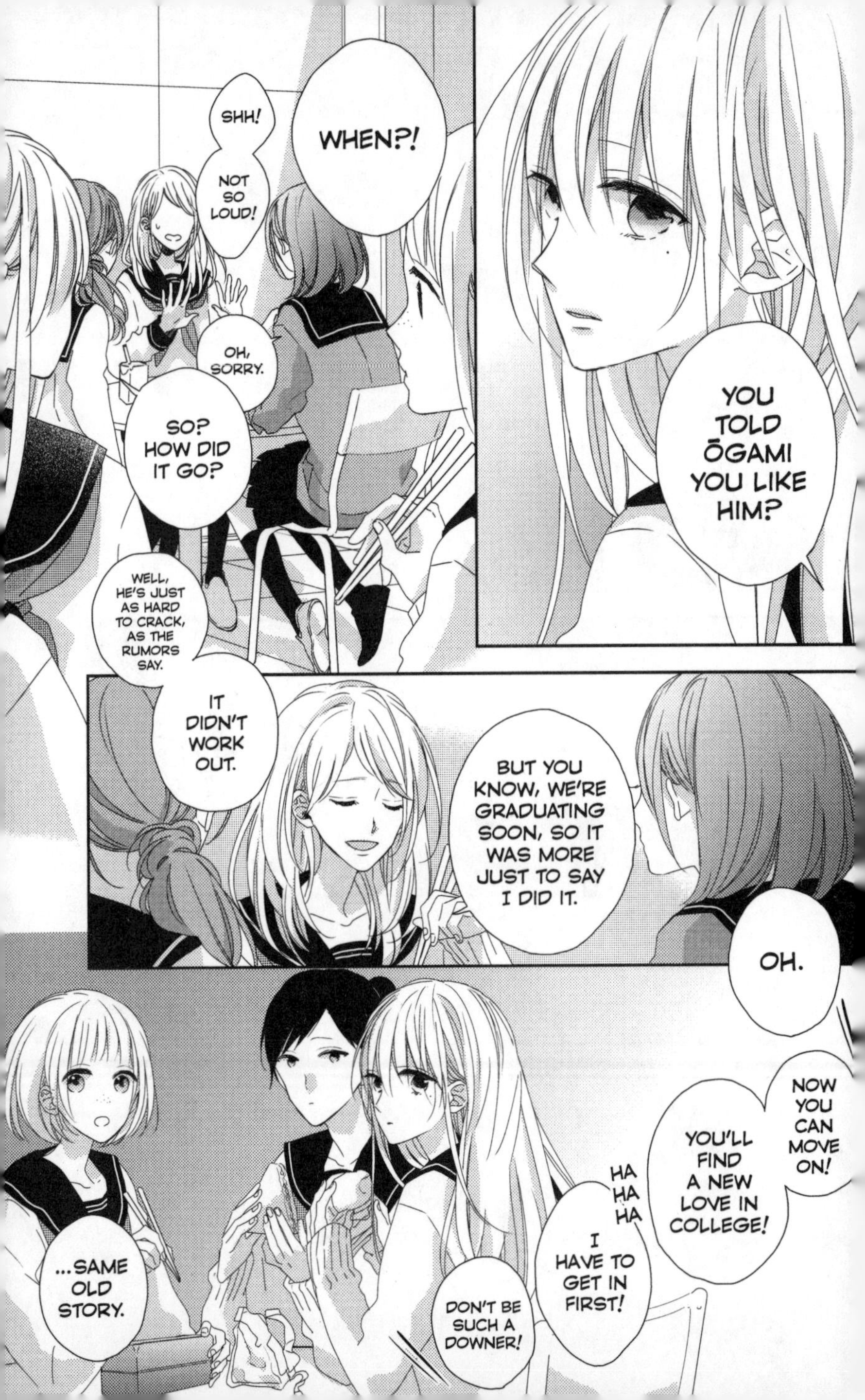
YOU TOLD ŌGAMI YOU LIKE HIM?
WHEN?!
SHH!
NOT SO LOUD!
OH, SORRY.
SO? HOW DID IT GO?
WELL, HE'S JUST AS HARD TO CRACK, AS THE RUMORS SAY.
IT DIDN'T WORK OUT.
BUT YOU KNOW, WE'RE GRADUATING SOON, SO IT WAS MORE JUST TO SAY I DID IT.
OH.
NOW YOU CAN MOVE ON!
YOU'LL FIND A NEW LOVE IN COLLEGE!
HA HA HA
I HAVE TO GET IN FIRST!
DON'T BE SUCH A DOWNER!
...SAME OLD STORY.

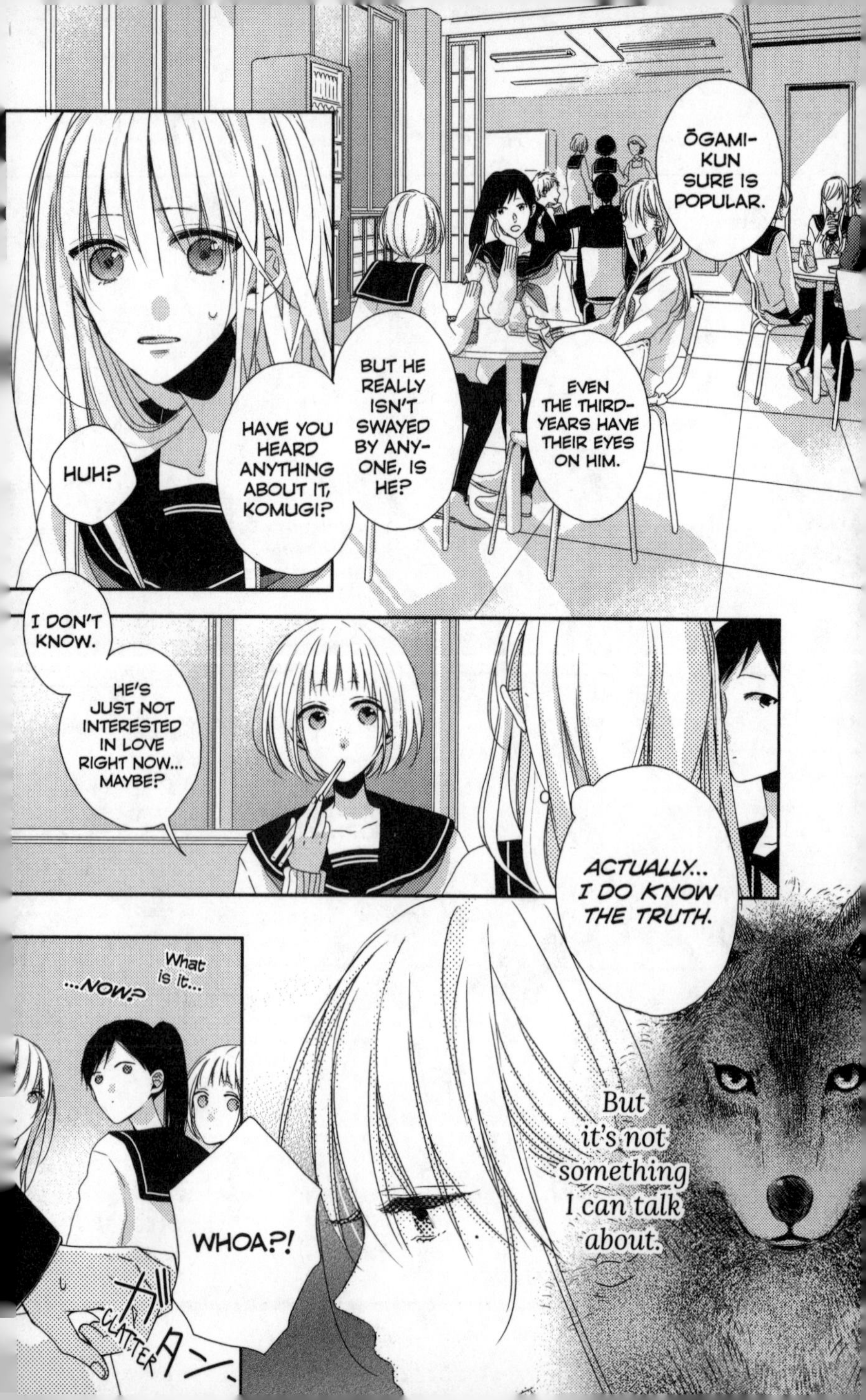
ŌGAMI-KUN SURE IS POPULAR.
EVEN THE THIRD-YEARS HAVE THEIR EYES ON HIM.
BUT HE REALLY ISN'T SWAYED BY ANY-ONE, IS HE?
HAVE YOU HEARD ANYTHING ABOUT IT, KOMUGI?
HUH?
I DON'T KNOW.
HE'S JUST NOT INTERESTED IN LOVE RIGHT NOW... MAYBE?
ACTUALLY... I DO KNOW THE TRUTH.
But it's not something I can talk about.
What is it... ...NOW?
WHOA?!
CLATTER

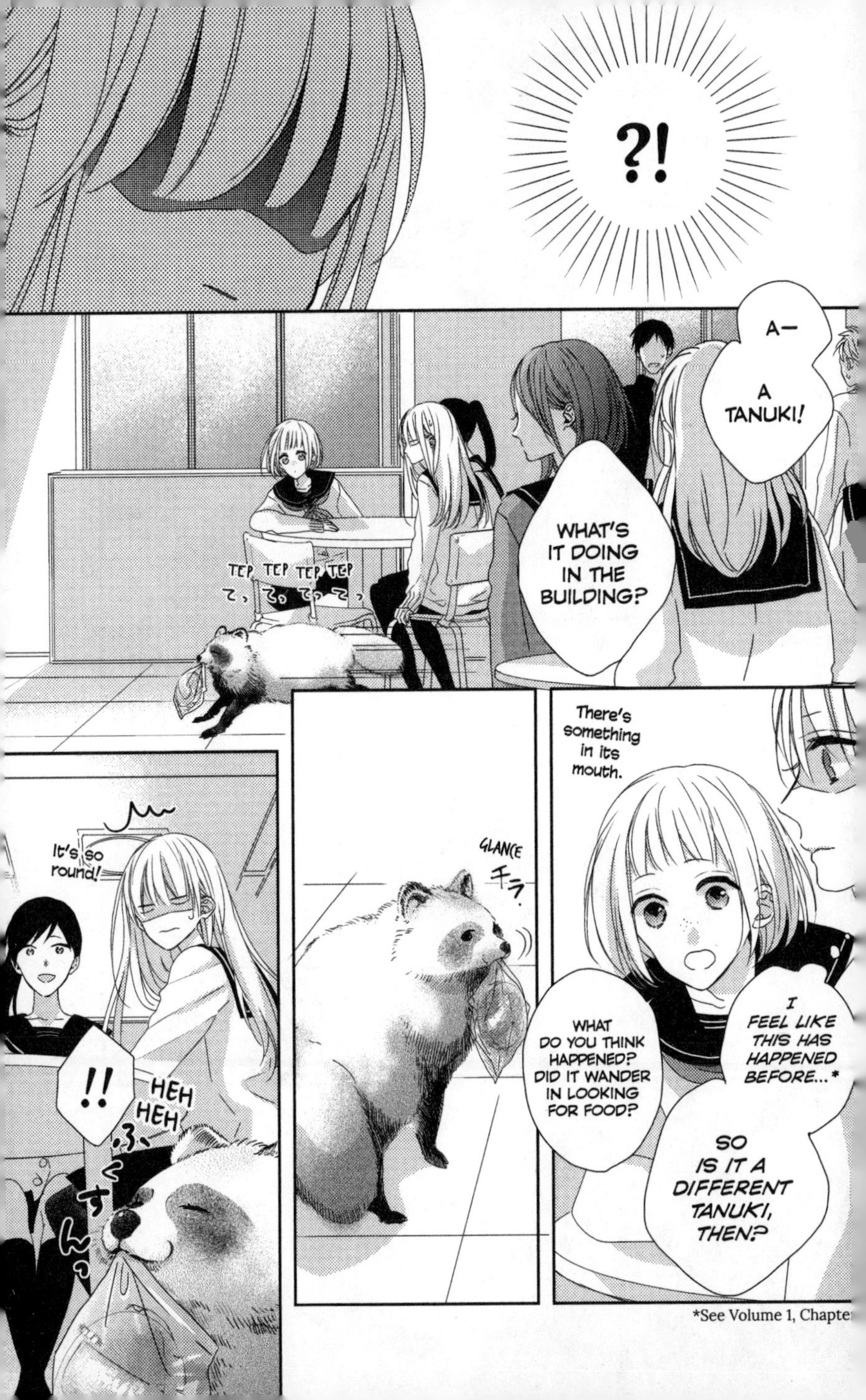
?!
A—
A TANUKI!
WHAT'S IT DOING IN THE BUILDING?
TEP TEP TEP TEP
てってってって
I FEEL LIKE THIS HAS HAPPENED BEFORE...*
There's something in its mouth.
WHAT DO YOU THINK HAPPENED? DID IT WANDER IN LOOKING FOR FOOD?
SO IS IT A DIFFERENT TANUKI, THEN?
GLANCE
チラ
It's so round!
!!
HEH HEH
ふくすんっ

*See Volume 1, Chapte

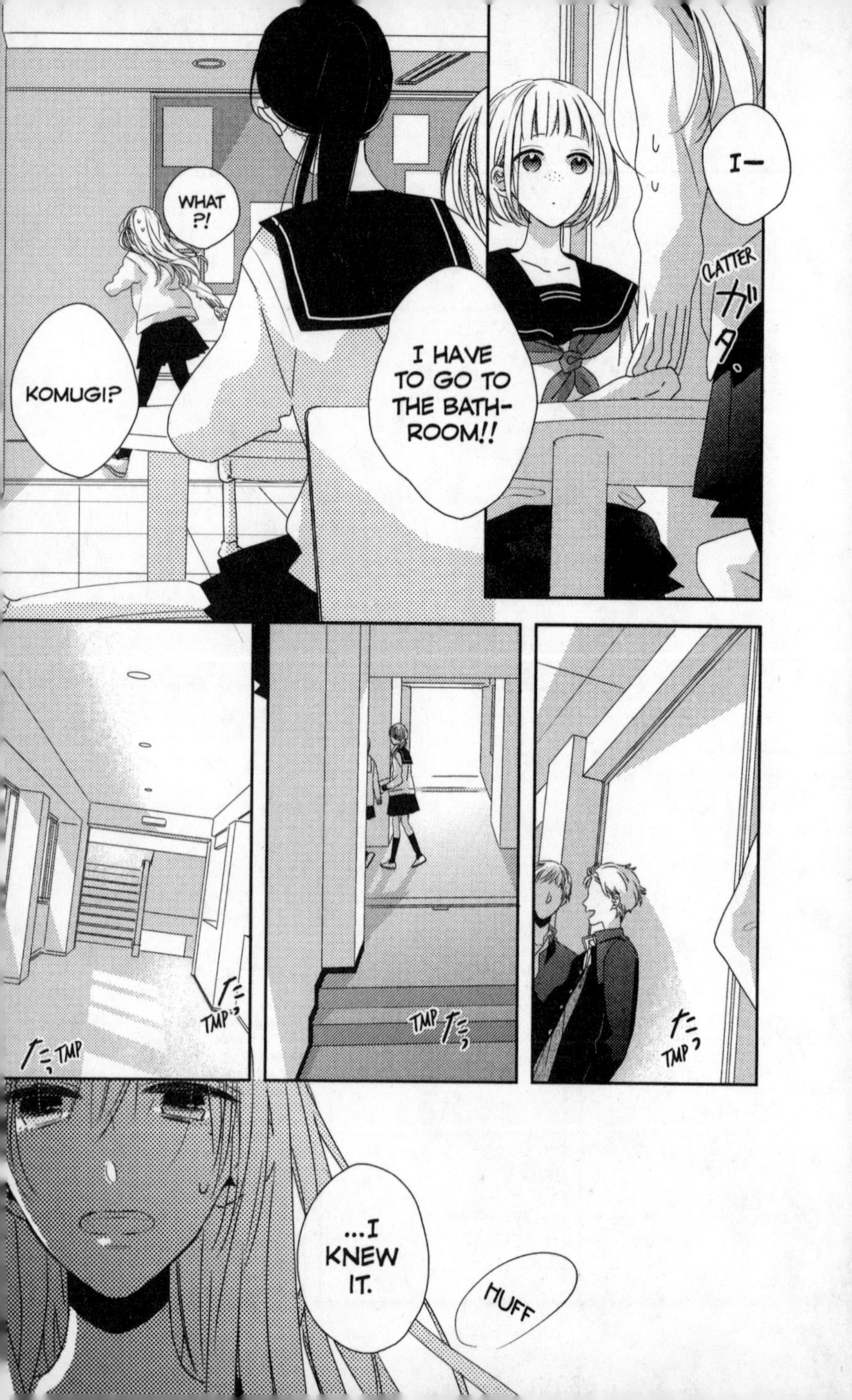
I—
CLATTER
I HAVE TO GO TO THE BATH-ROOM!!
WHAT?!
KOMUGI?
TMP
TMP
TMP
TMP
...I KNEW IT.
HUFF

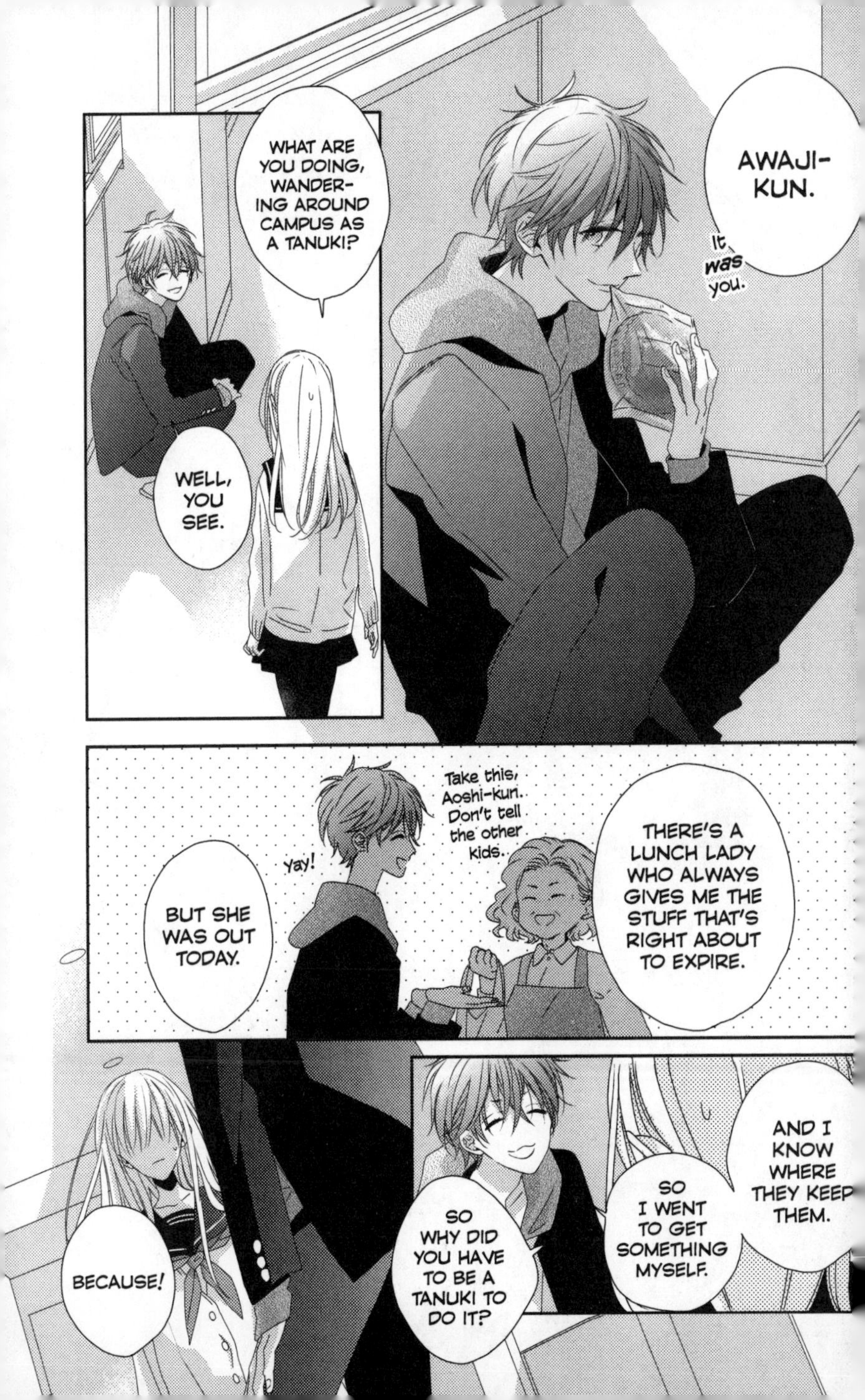
AWAJI-KUN.
It was you.
WHAT ARE YOU DOING, WANDERING AROUND CAMPUS AS A TANUKI?
WELL, YOU SEE.
THERE'S A LUNCH LADY WHO ALWAYS GIVES ME THE STUFF THAT'S RIGHT ABOUT TO EXPIRE.
Take this, Aoshi-kun. Don't tell the other kids.
Yay!
BUT SHE WAS OUT TODAY.
AND I KNOW WHERE THEY KEEP THEM.
SO I WENT TO GET SOMETHING MYSELF.
SO WHY DID YOU HAVE TO BE A TANUKI TO DO IT?
BECAUSE!

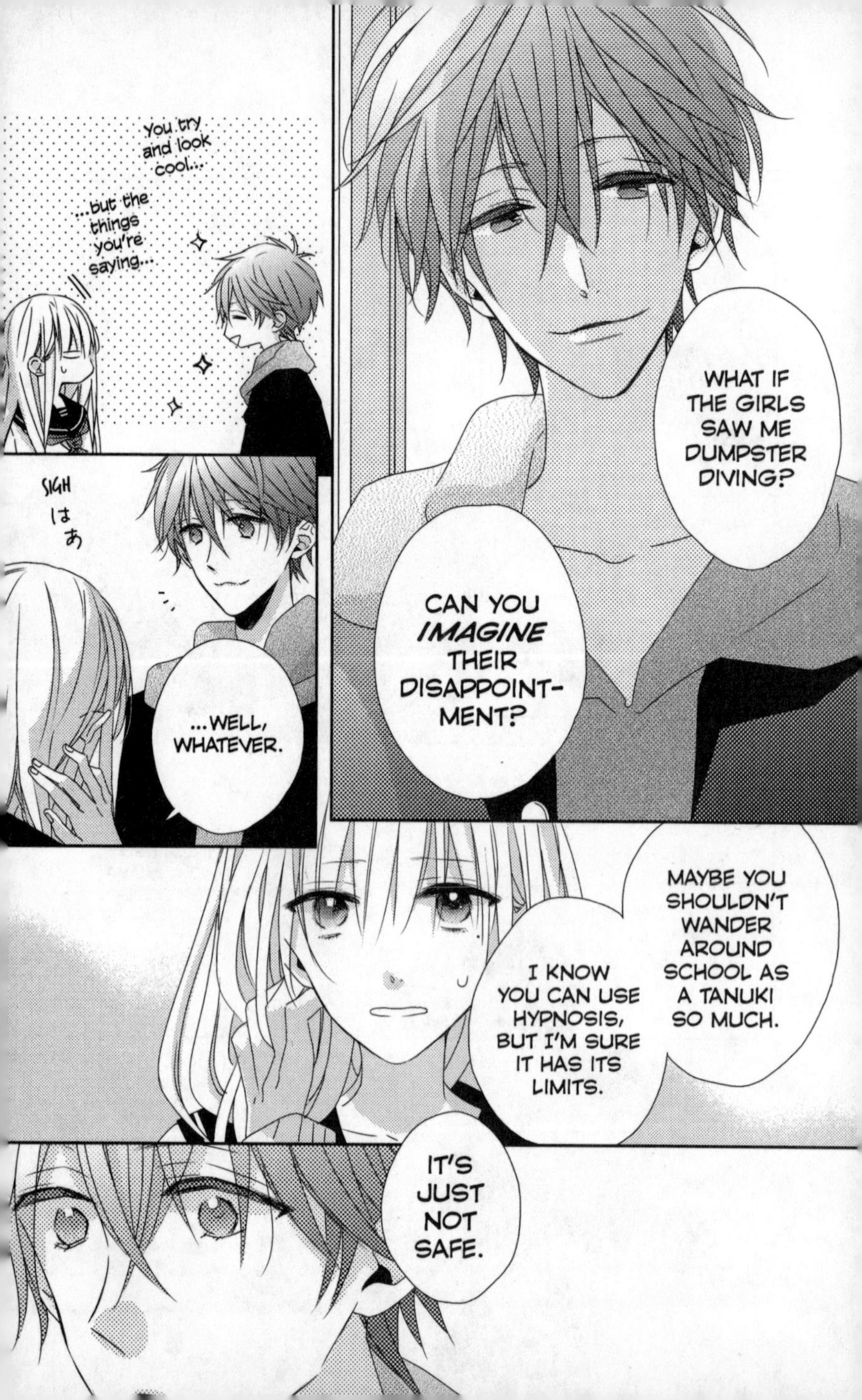
WHAT IF THE GIRLS SAW ME DUMPSTER DIVING?
CAN YOU *IMAGINE* THEIR DISAPPOINTMENT?
You try and look cool...
...but the things you're saying...
SIGH
はあ
...WELL, WHATEVER.
MAYBE YOU SHOULDN'T WANDER AROUND SCHOOL AS A TANUKI SO MUCH.
I KNOW YOU CAN USE HYPNOSIS, BUT I'M SURE IT HAS ITS LIMITS.
IT'S JUST NOT SAFE.

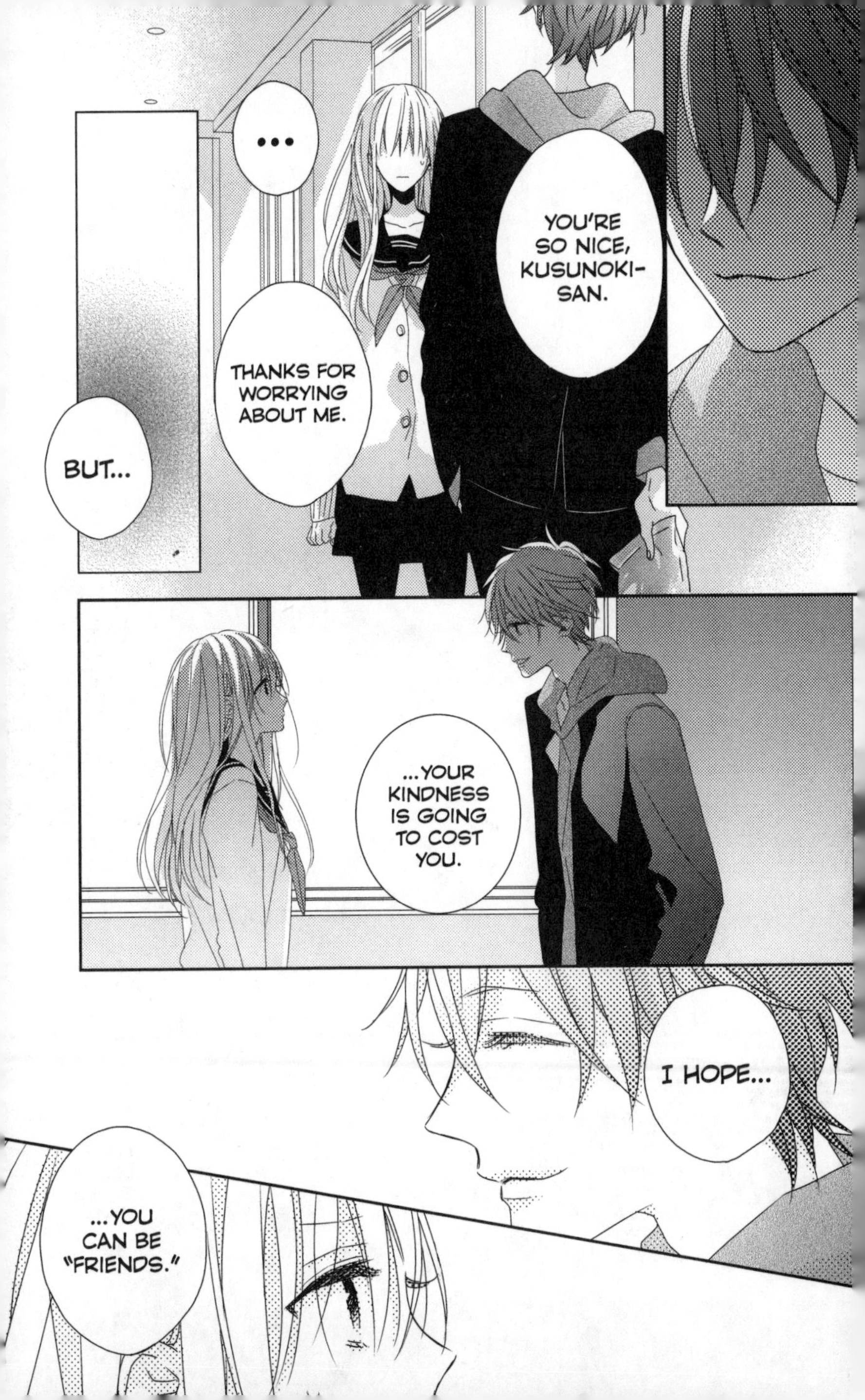
YOU'RE SO NICE, KUSUNOKI-SAN.
...
THANKS FOR WORRYING ABOUT ME.
BUT...
...YOUR KINDNESS IS GOING TO COST YOU.
I HOPE...
...YOU CAN BE "FRIENDS."

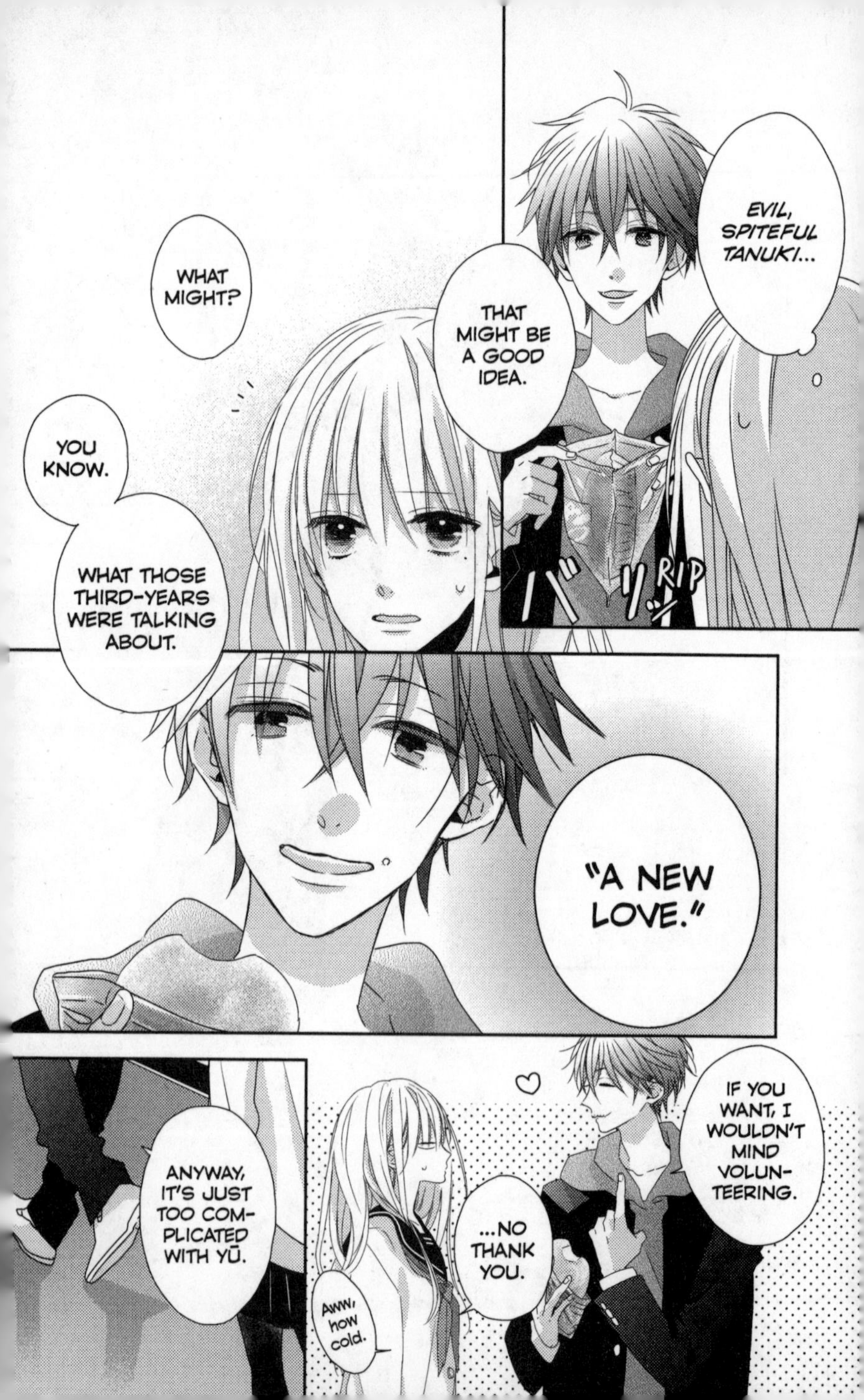
EVIL, SPITEFUL TANUKI...
THAT MIGHT BE A GOOD IDEA.
バリッ RIP
WHAT MIGHT?
YOU KNOW.
WHAT THOSE THIRD-YEARS WERE TALKING ABOUT.
"A NEW LOVE."
IF YOU WANT, I WOULDN'T MIND VOLUN-TEERING.
...NO THANK YOU.
Aww, how cold.
ANYWAY, IT'S JUST TOO COM-PLICATED WITH YŪ.

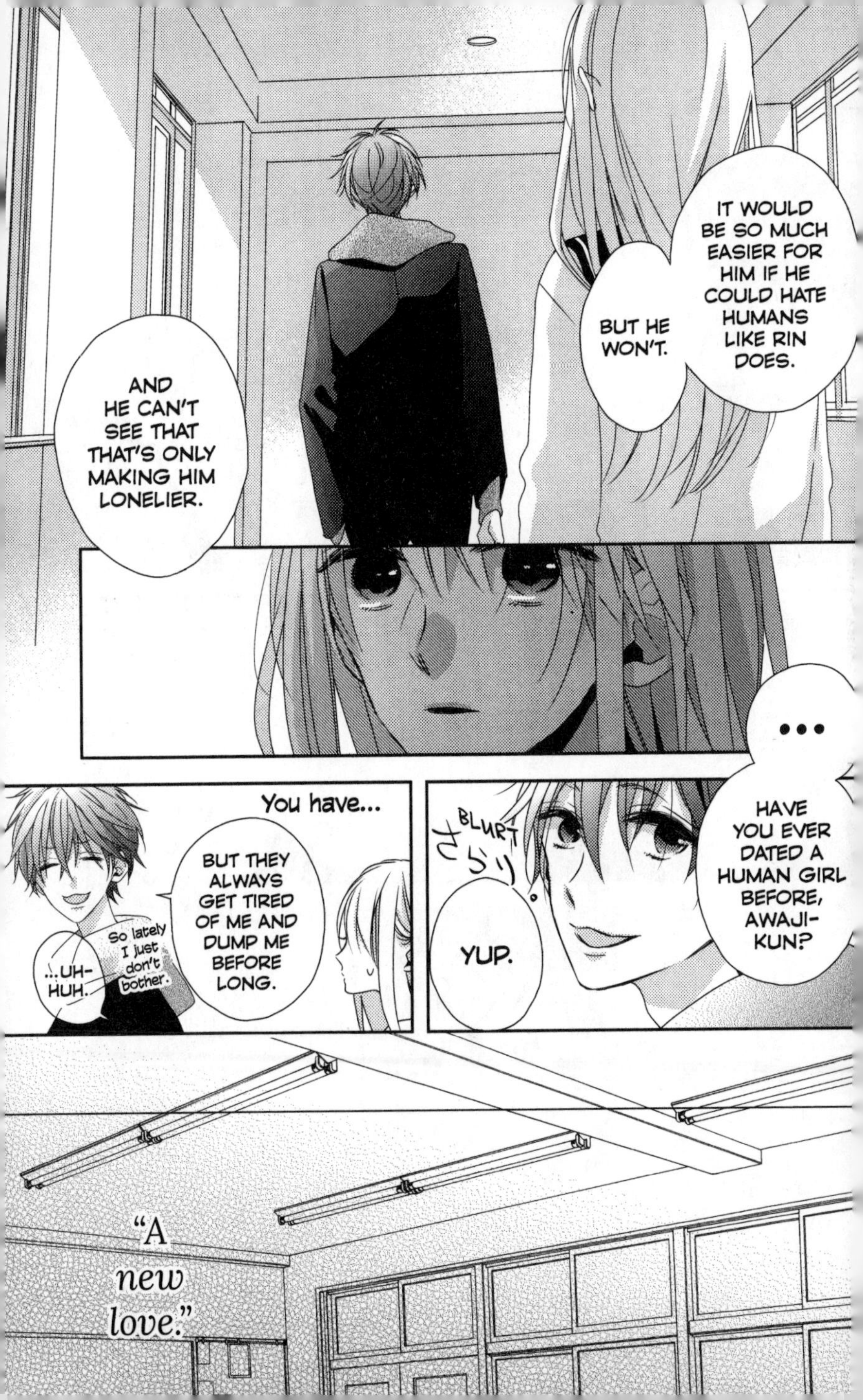
IT WOULD BE SO MUCH EASIER FOR HIM IF HE COULD HATE HUMANS LIKE RIN DOES.
BUT HE WON'T.
AND HE CAN'T SEE THAT THAT'S ONLY MAKING HIM LONELIER.
...
HAVE YOU EVER DATED A HUMAN GIRL BEFORE, AWAJI-KUN?
BLURT
YUP.
You have...
BUT THEY ALWAYS GET TIRED OF ME AND DUMP ME BEFORE LONG.
So lately I just don't bother.
...UH-HUH.
“A new love.”

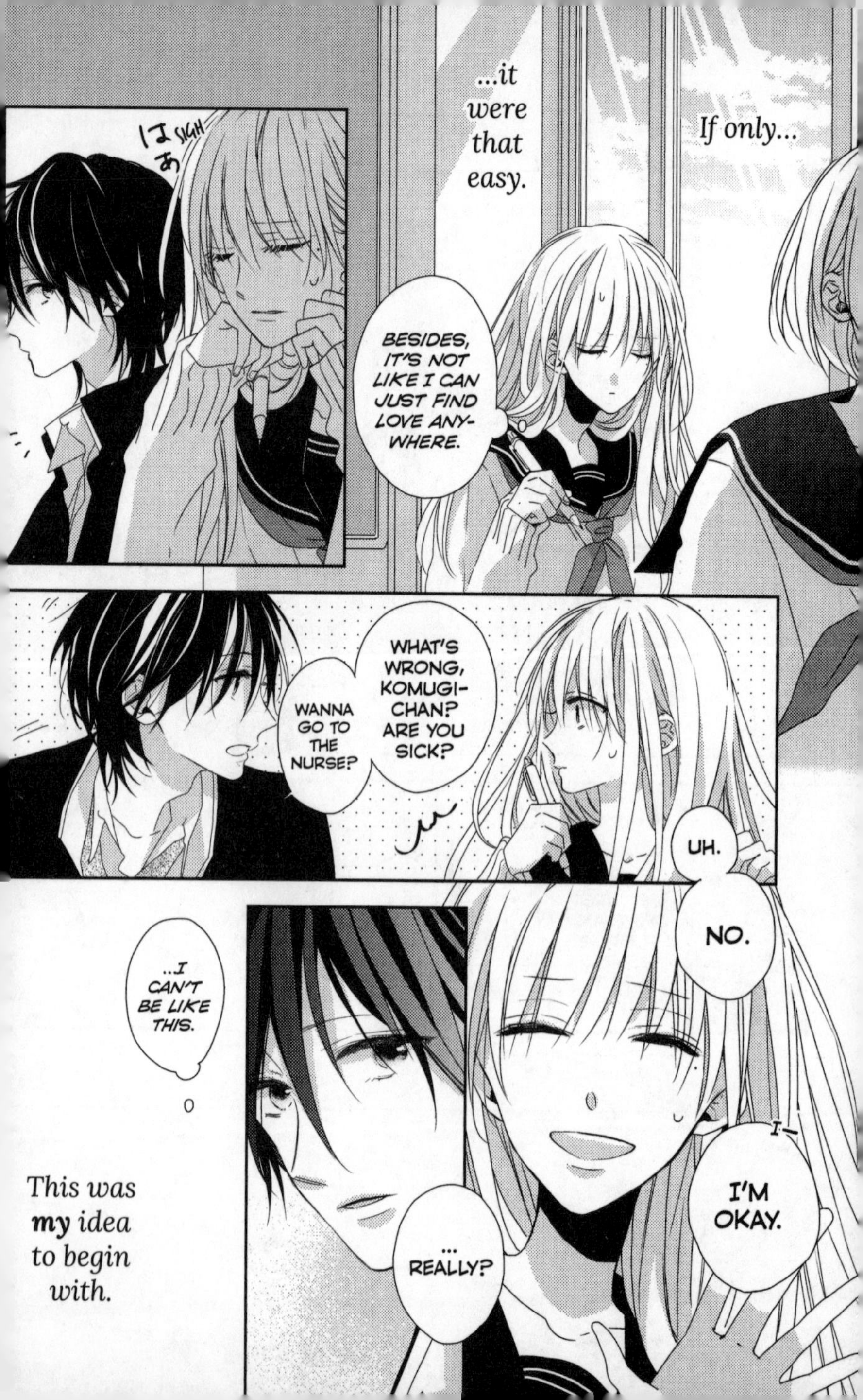

If only...
...it were that easy.
BESIDES, IT'S NOT LIKE I CAN JUST FIND LOVE ANYWHERE.
はあ SIGH
WHAT'S WRONG, KOMUGI-CHAN? ARE YOU SICK?
WANNA GO TO THE NURSE?
UH.
NO.
I—
I'M OKAY.
...REALLY?
...I CAN'T BE LIKE THIS.
This was **my** idea to begin with.

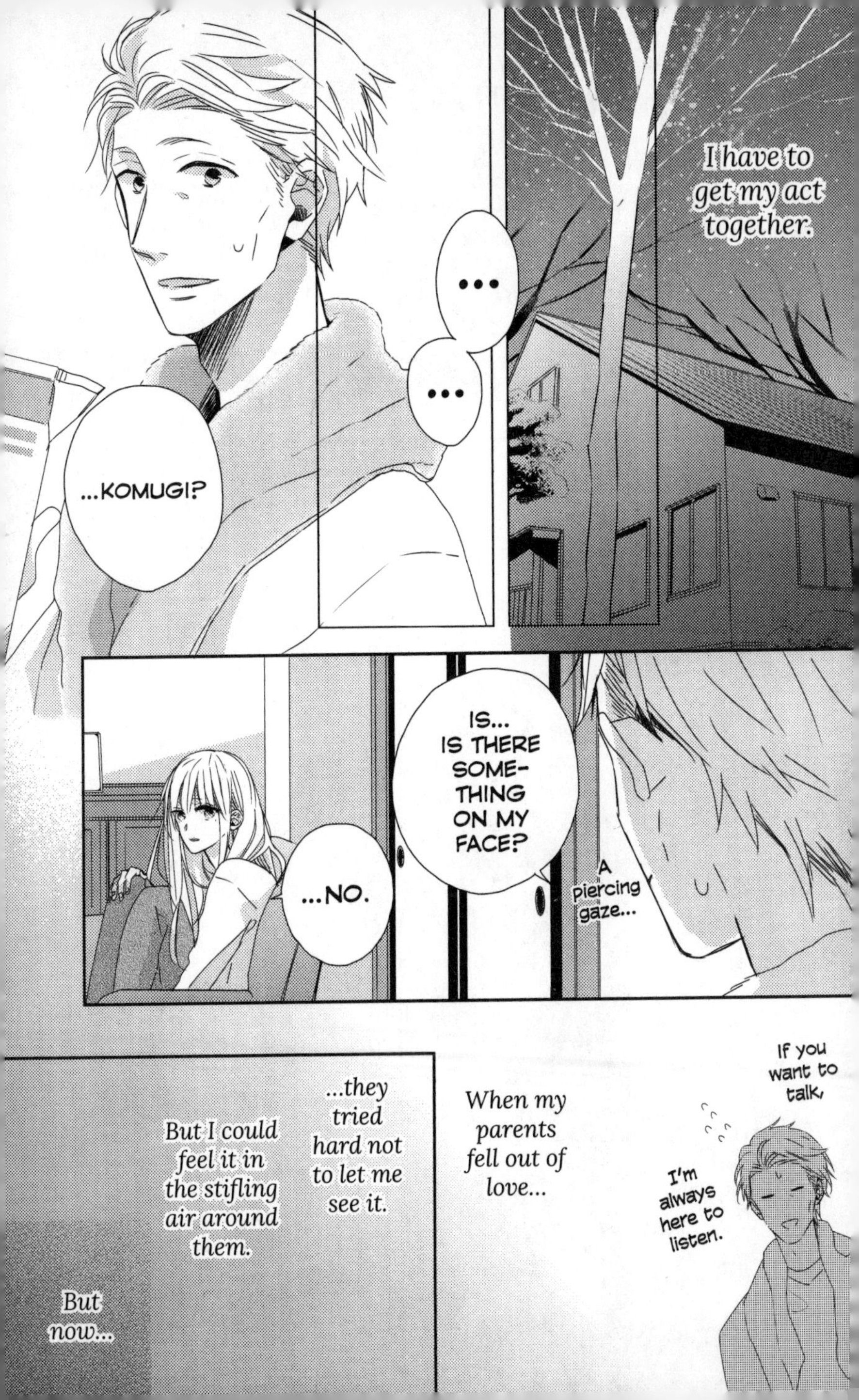
I have to get my act together.
...
...
...KOMUGI?
IS... IS THERE SOMETHING ON MY FACE?
A piercing gaze...
...NO.
If you want to talk,
I'm always here to listen.
When my parents fell out of love...
...they tried hard not to let me see it.
But I could feel it in the stifling air around them.
But now...

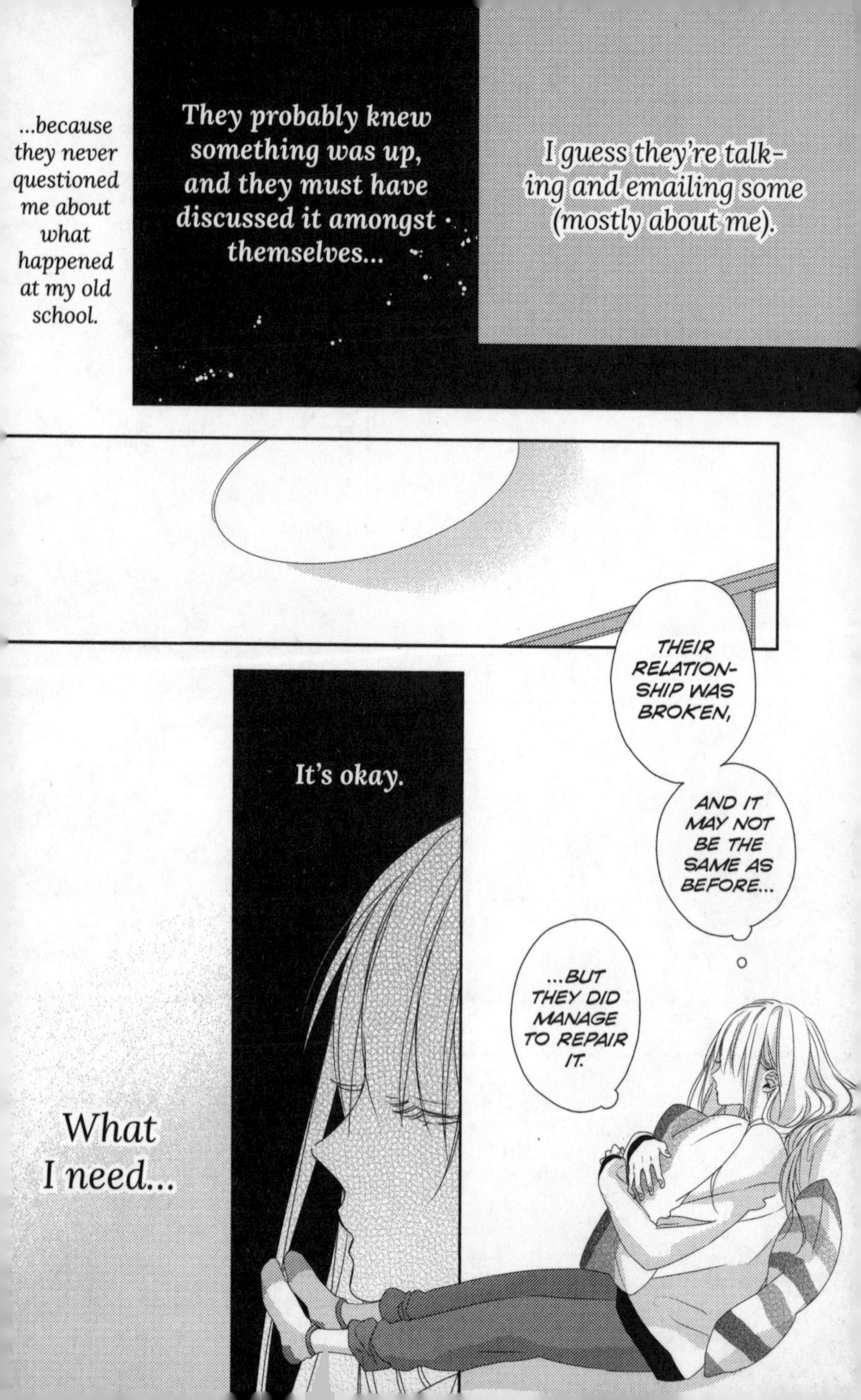
I guess they're talking and emailing some (mostly about me).
They probably knew something was up, and they must have discussed it amongst themselves...
...because they never questioned me about what happened at my old school.
THEIR RELATIONSHIP WAS BROKEN,
AND IT MAY NOT BE THE SAME AS BEFORE...
...BUT THEY DID MANAGE TO REPAIR IT.
It's okay.
What I need...

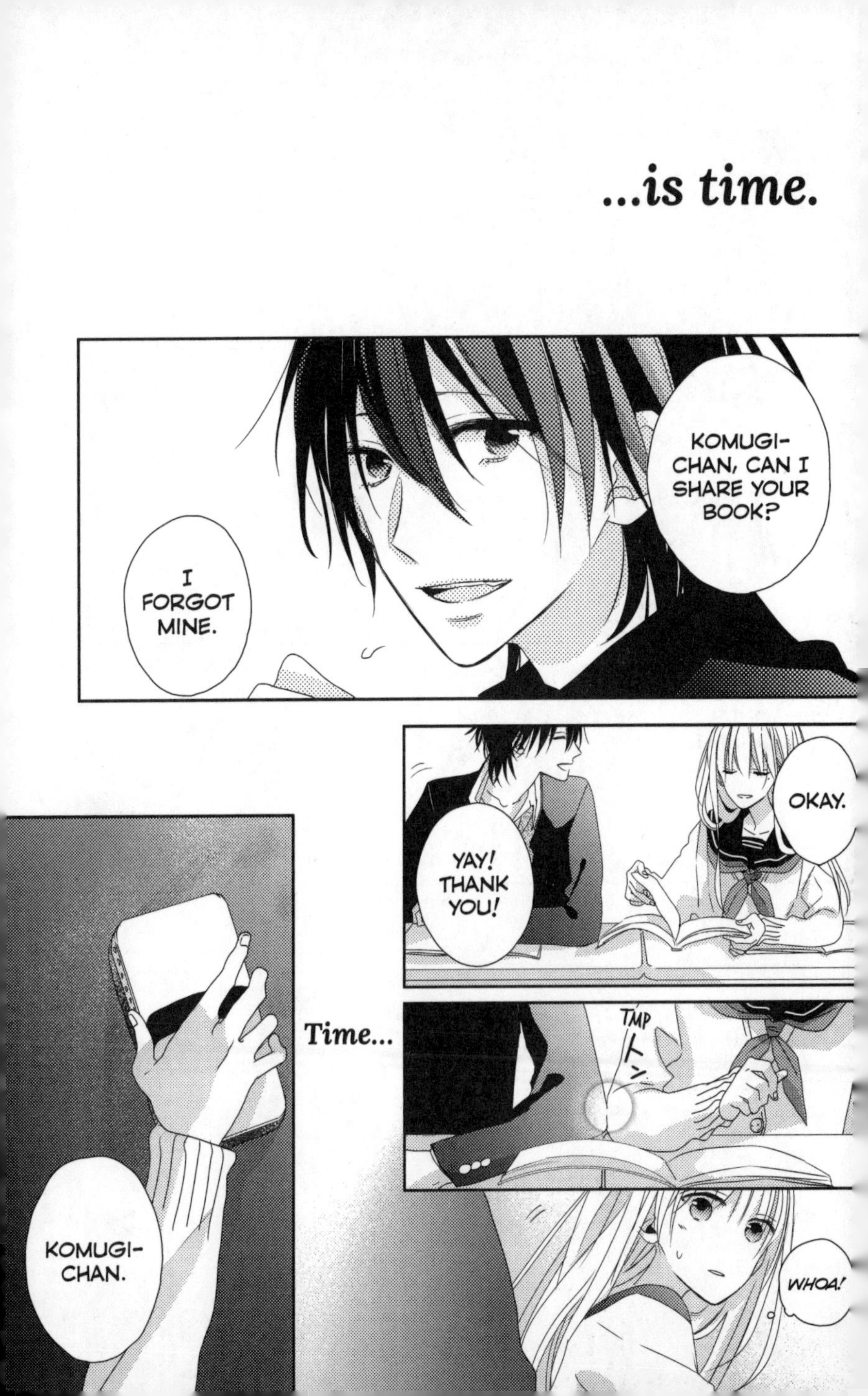
...is time.
KOMUGI-CHAN, CAN I SHARE YOUR BOOK?
I FORGOT MINE.
OKAY.
YAY! THANK YOU!
TMP
Time...
WHOA!
KOMUGI-CHAN.

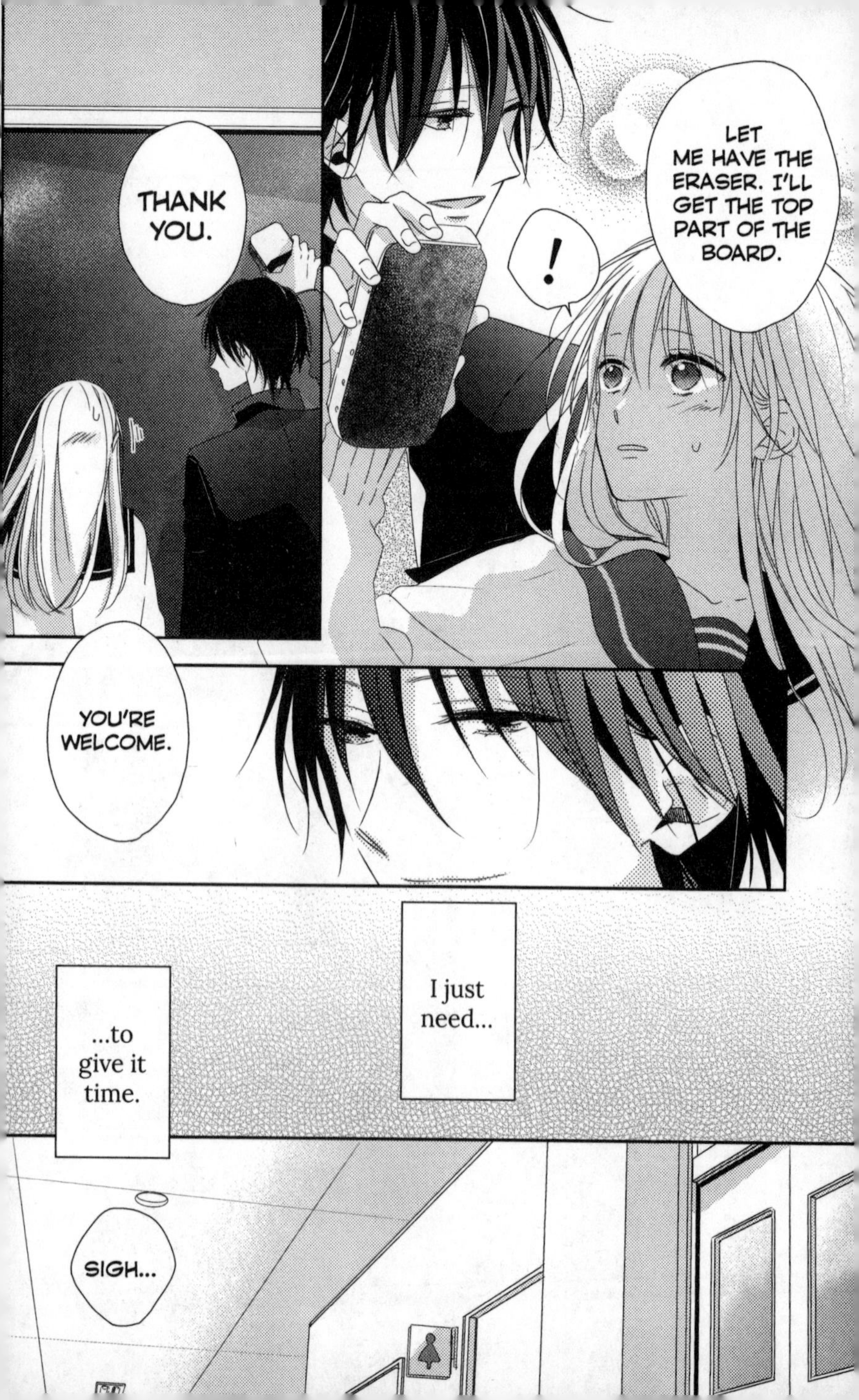
LET ME HAVE THE ERASER. I'LL GET THE TOP PART OF THE BOARD.
!
THANK YOU.
YOU'RE WELCOME.
I just need...
...to give it time.
SIGH...

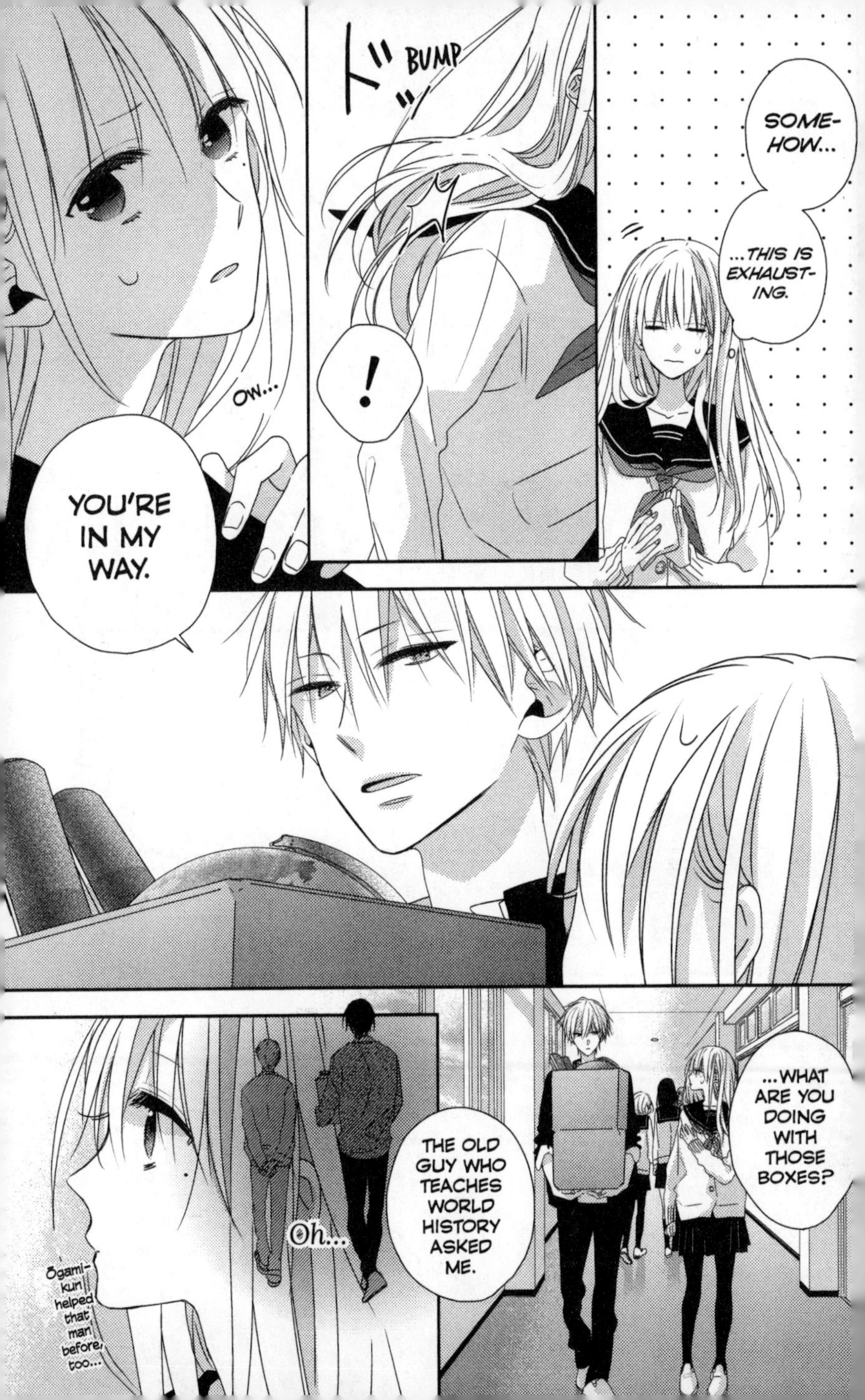
SOME-HOW...
...THIS IS EXHAUST-ING.
ドッ
BUMP
!
OW...
YOU'RE IN MY WAY.
...WHAT ARE YOU DOING WITH THOSE BOXES?
THE OLD GUY WHO TEACHES WORLD HISTORY ASKED ME.
Oh...
Ōgami-kun helped that man before, too...

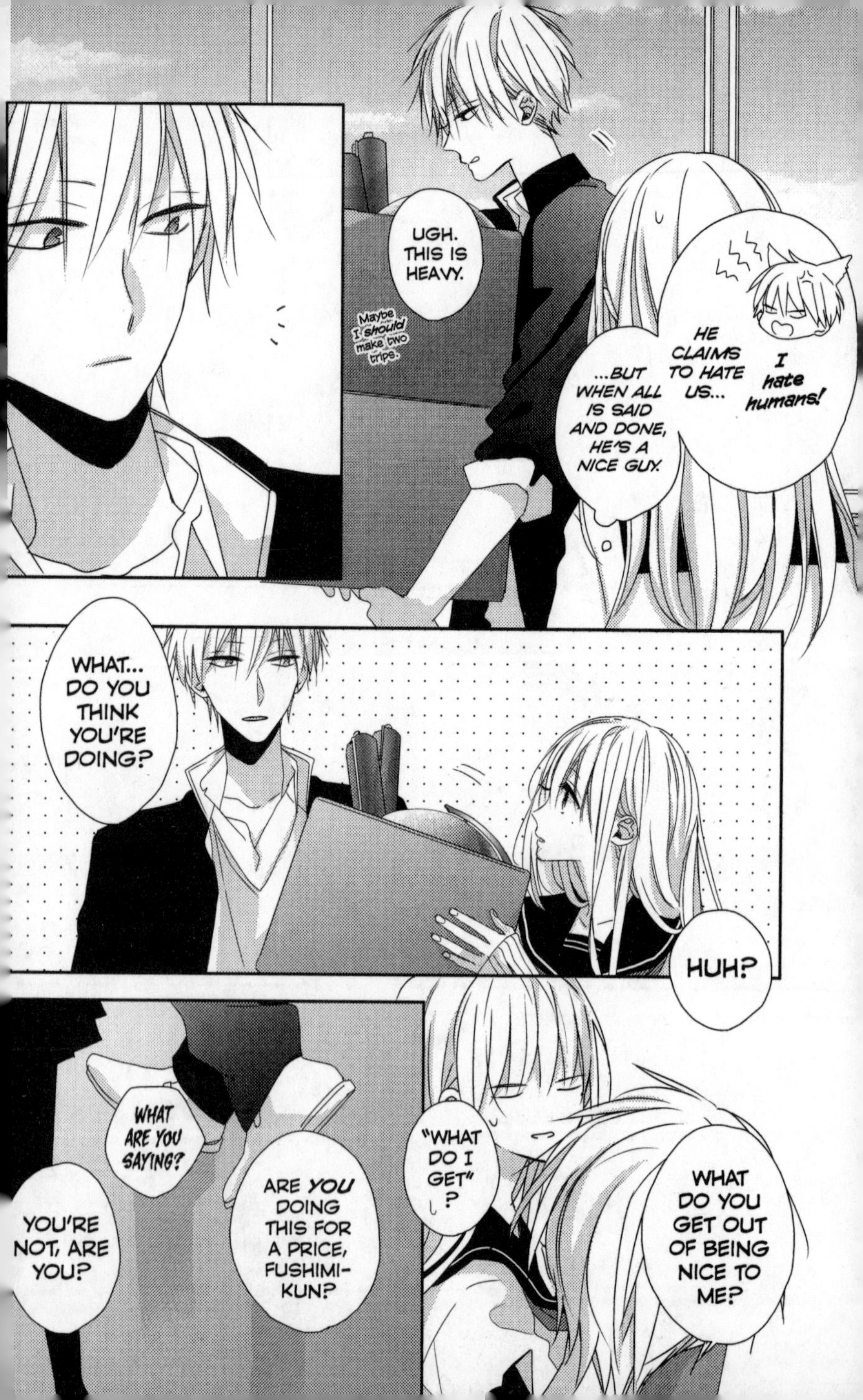
UGH. THIS IS HEAVY.
Maybe I *should* make two trips.
HE CLAIMS TO HATE US...
I hate humans!
...BUT WHEN ALL IS SAID AND DONE, HE'S A NICE GUY.
WHAT... DO YOU THINK YOU'RE DOING?
HUH?
WHAT DO YOU GET OUT OF BEING NICE TO ME?
"WHAT DO I GET"?
WHAT ARE YOU SAYING?
ARE *YOU* DOING THIS FOR A PRICE, FUSHIMI-KUN?
YOU'RE NOT, ARE YOU?

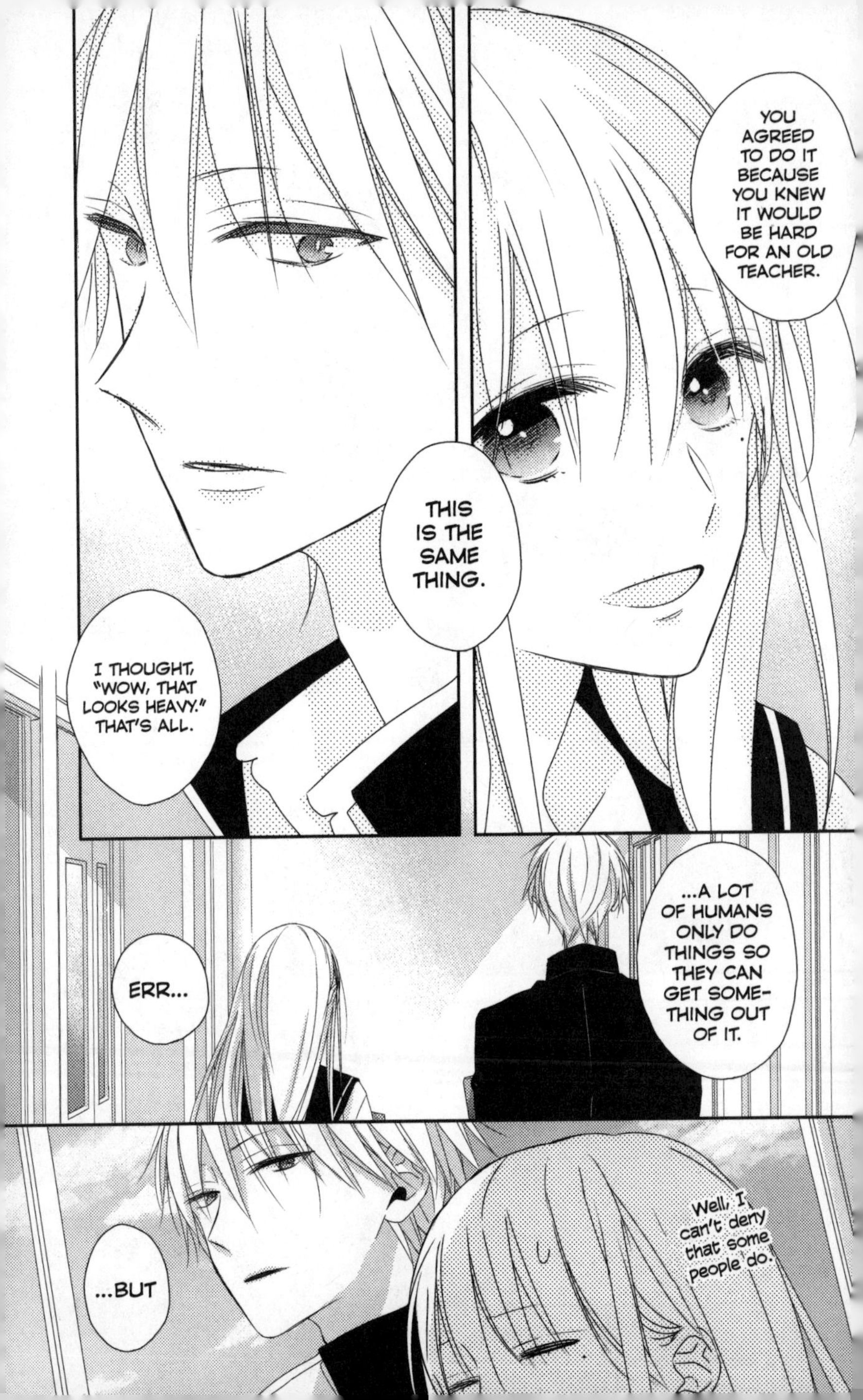
YOU AGREED TO DO IT BECAUSE YOU KNEW IT WOULD BE HARD FOR AN OLD TEACHER.
THIS IS THE SAME THING.
I THOUGHT, "WOW, THAT LOOKS HEAVY." THAT'S ALL.
...A LOT OF HUMANS ONLY DO THINGS SO THEY CAN GET SOME-THING OUT OF IT.
ERR...
Well, I can't deny that some people do.
...BUT

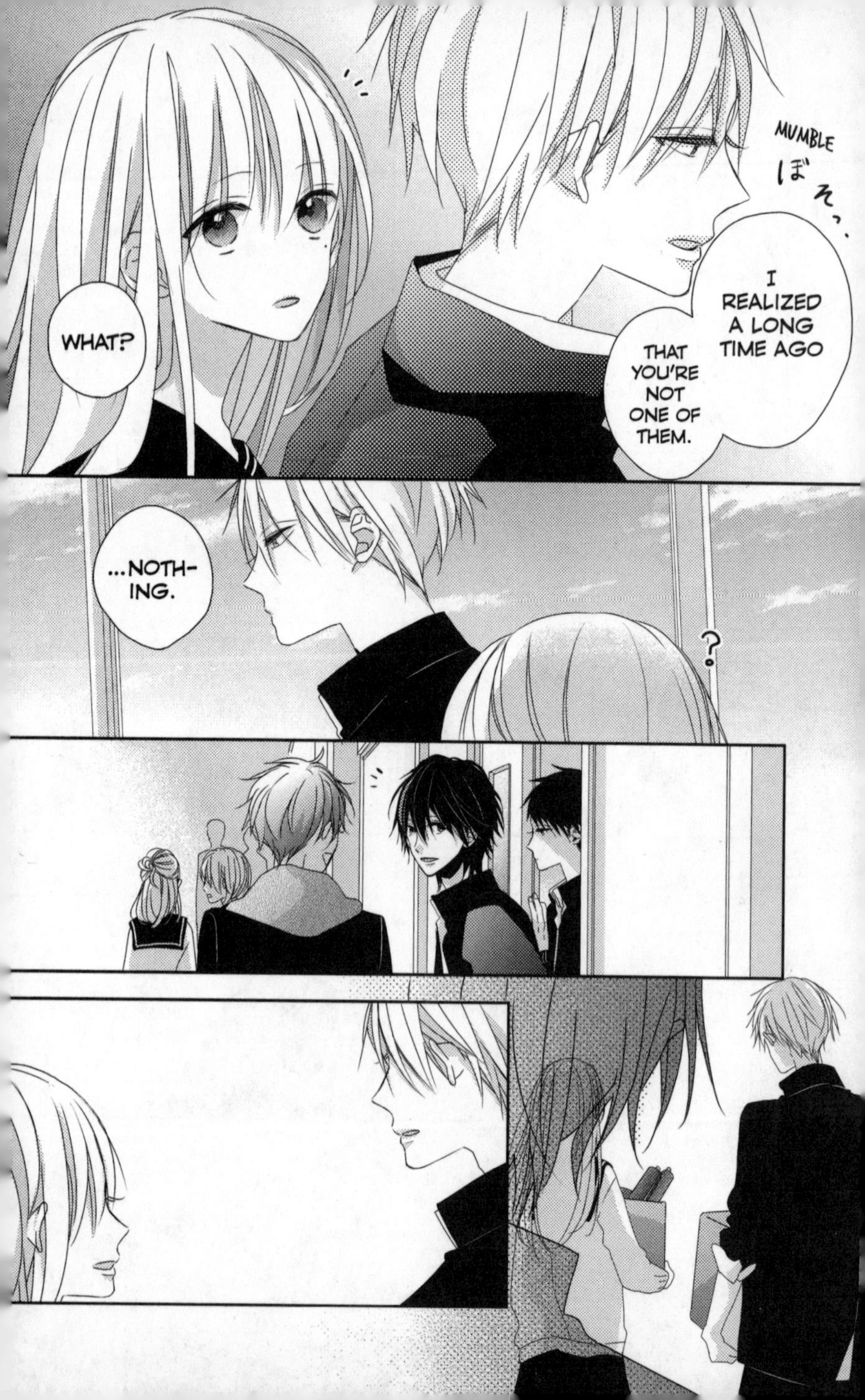
MUMBLE
ぼそっ.
I REALIZED A LONG TIME AGO
THAT YOU'RE NOT ONE OF THEM.
WHAT?
...NOTH-ING.
?

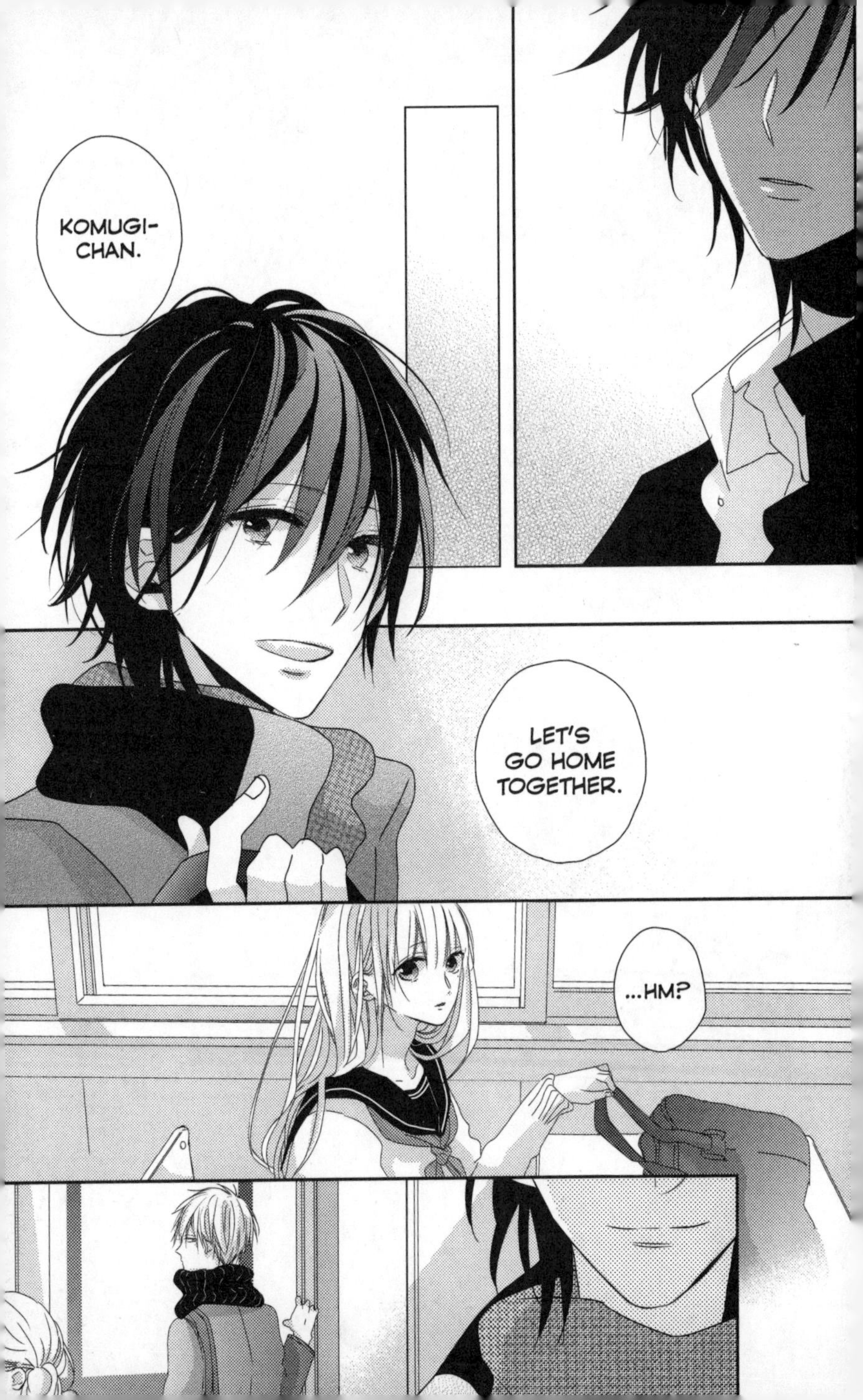
KOMUGI-CHAN.
LET'S GO HOME TOGETHER.
...HM?

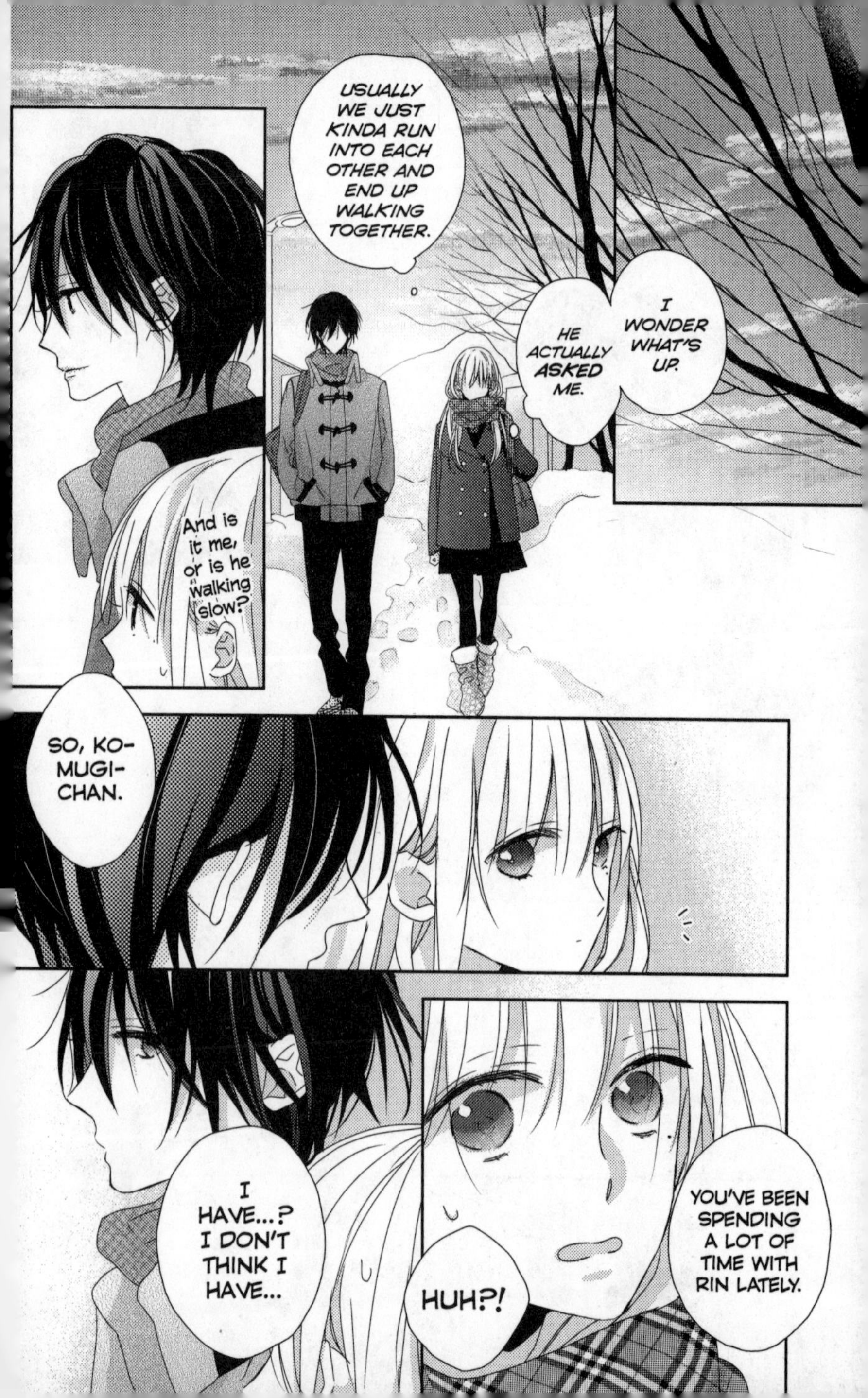
I WONDER WHAT'S UP.
HE ACTUALLY ASKED ME.
USUALLY WE JUST KINDA RUN INTO EACH OTHER AND END UP WALKING TOGETHER.
And is it me, or is he walking slow?
SO, KO-MUGI-CHAN.
YOU'VE BEEN SPENDING A LOT OF TIME WITH RIN LATELY.
HUH?!
I HAVE...? I DON'T THINK I HAVE...

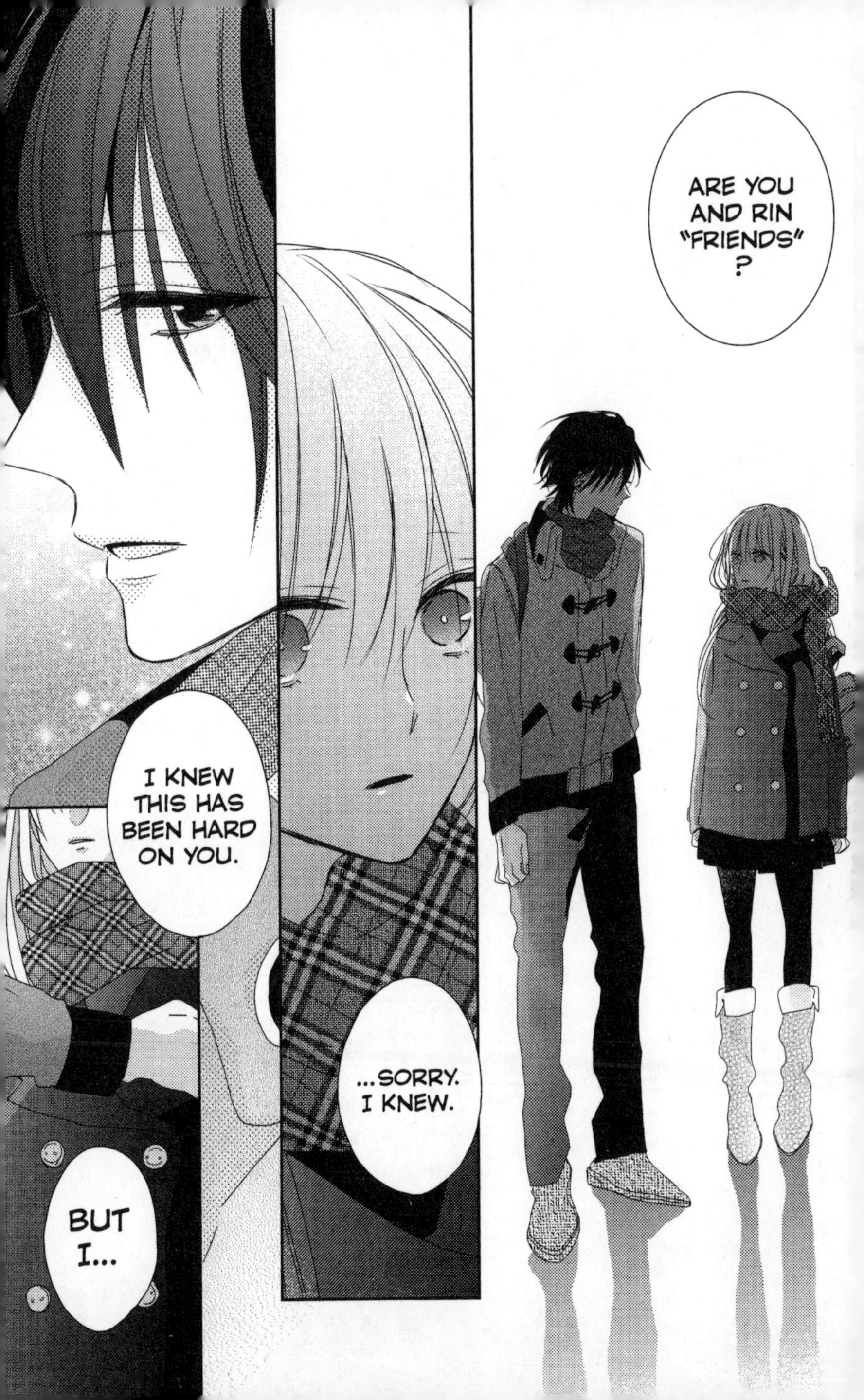
ARE YOU AND RIN "FRIENDS" ?
...SORRY. I KNEW.
I KNEW THIS HAS BEEN HARD ON YOU.
BUT I...

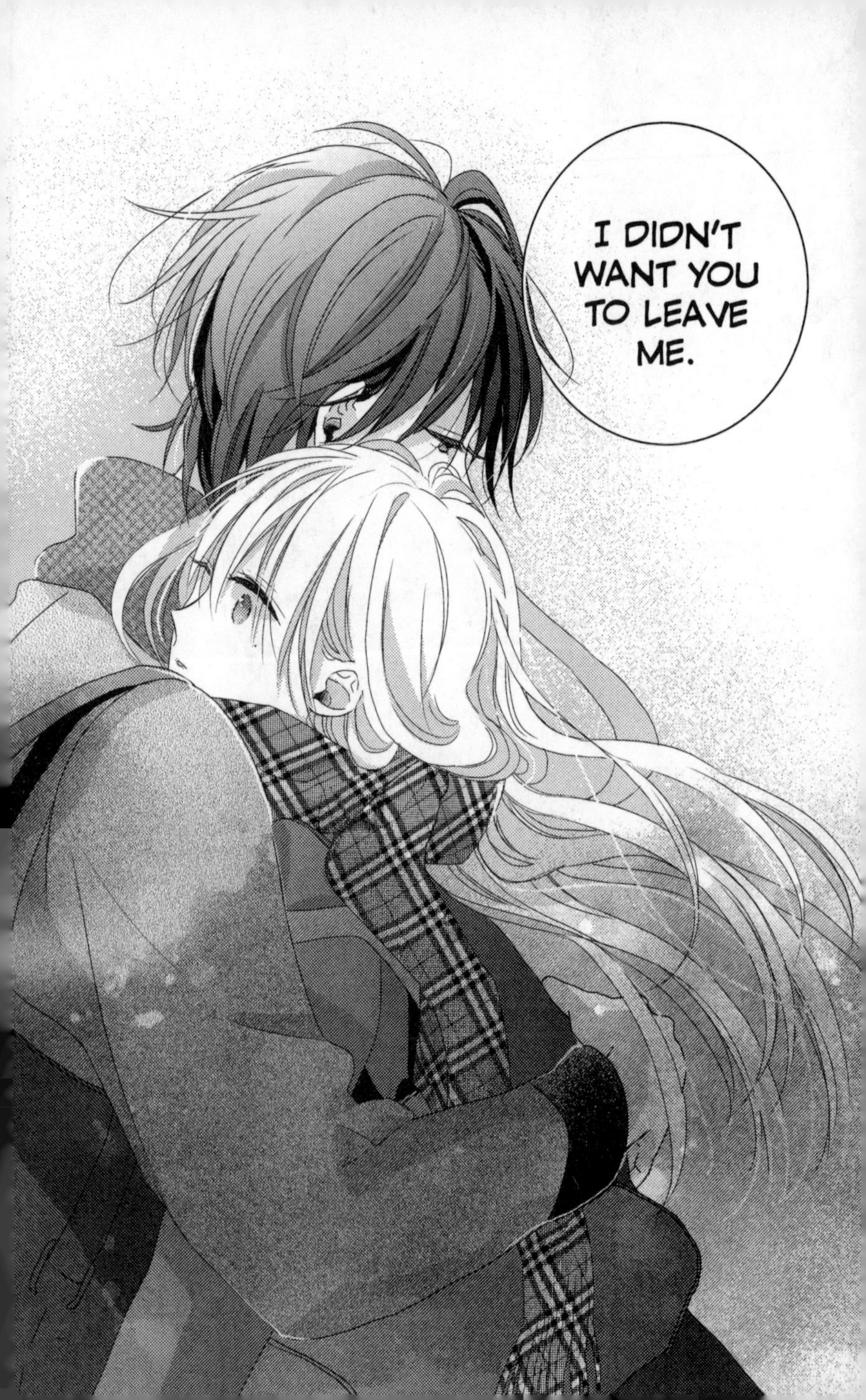
I DIDN'T WANT YOU TO LEAVE ME.

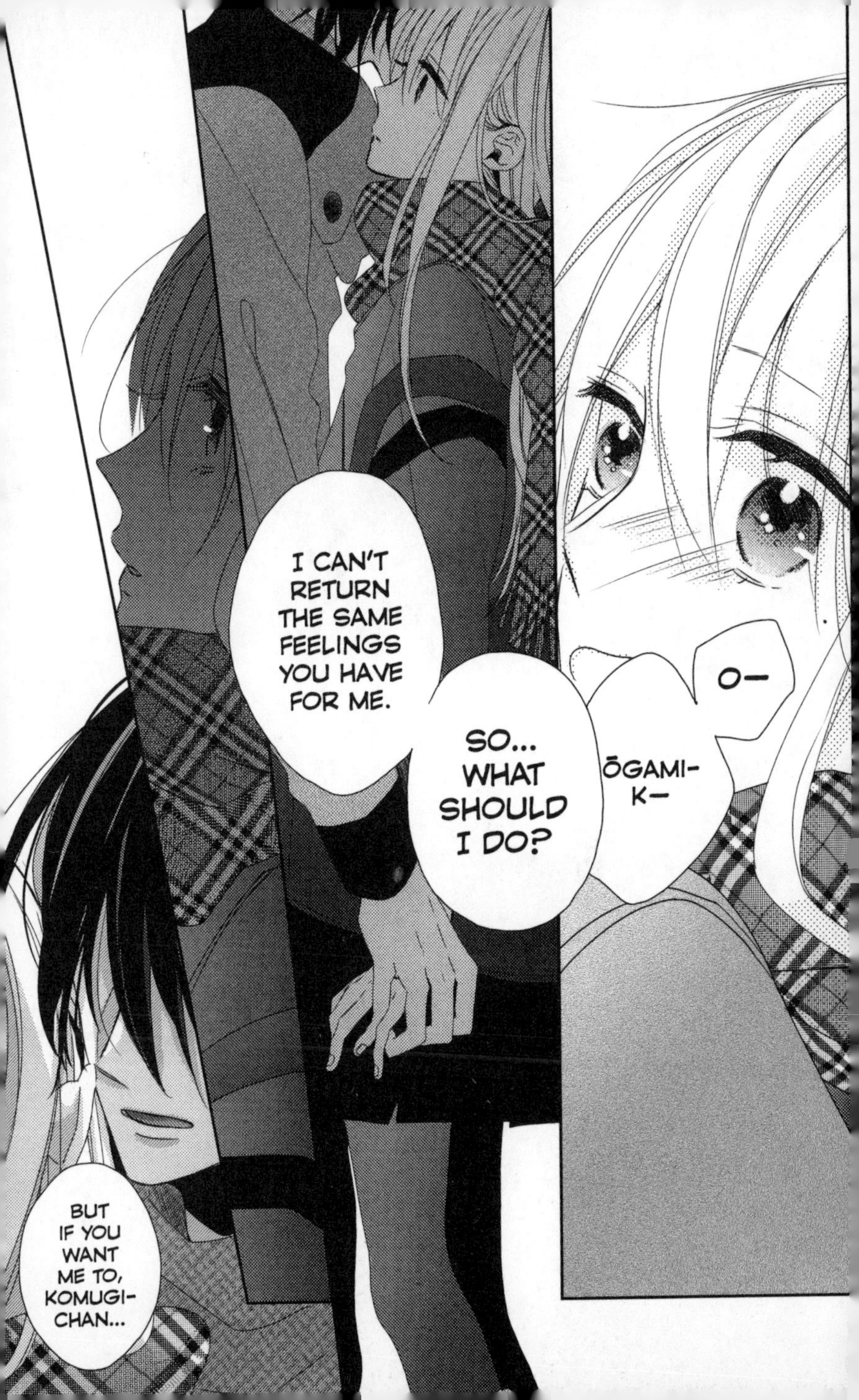
O—
ŌGAMI-K—
I CAN'T RETURN THE SAME FEELINGS YOU HAVE FOR ME.
SO... WHAT SHOULD I DO?
BUT IF YOU WANT ME TO, KOMUGI-CHAN...

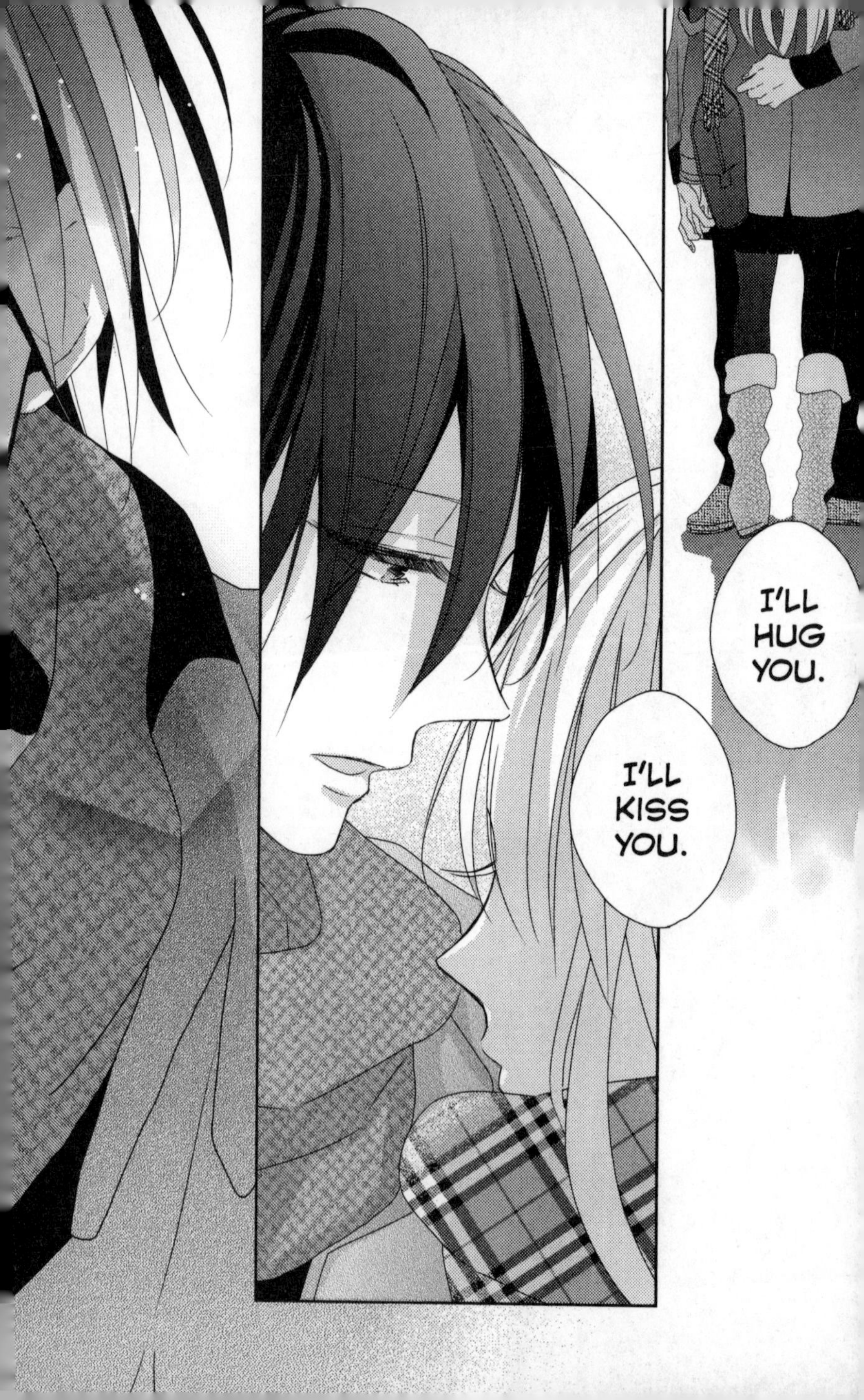
I'LL HUG YOU.
I'LL KISS YOU.

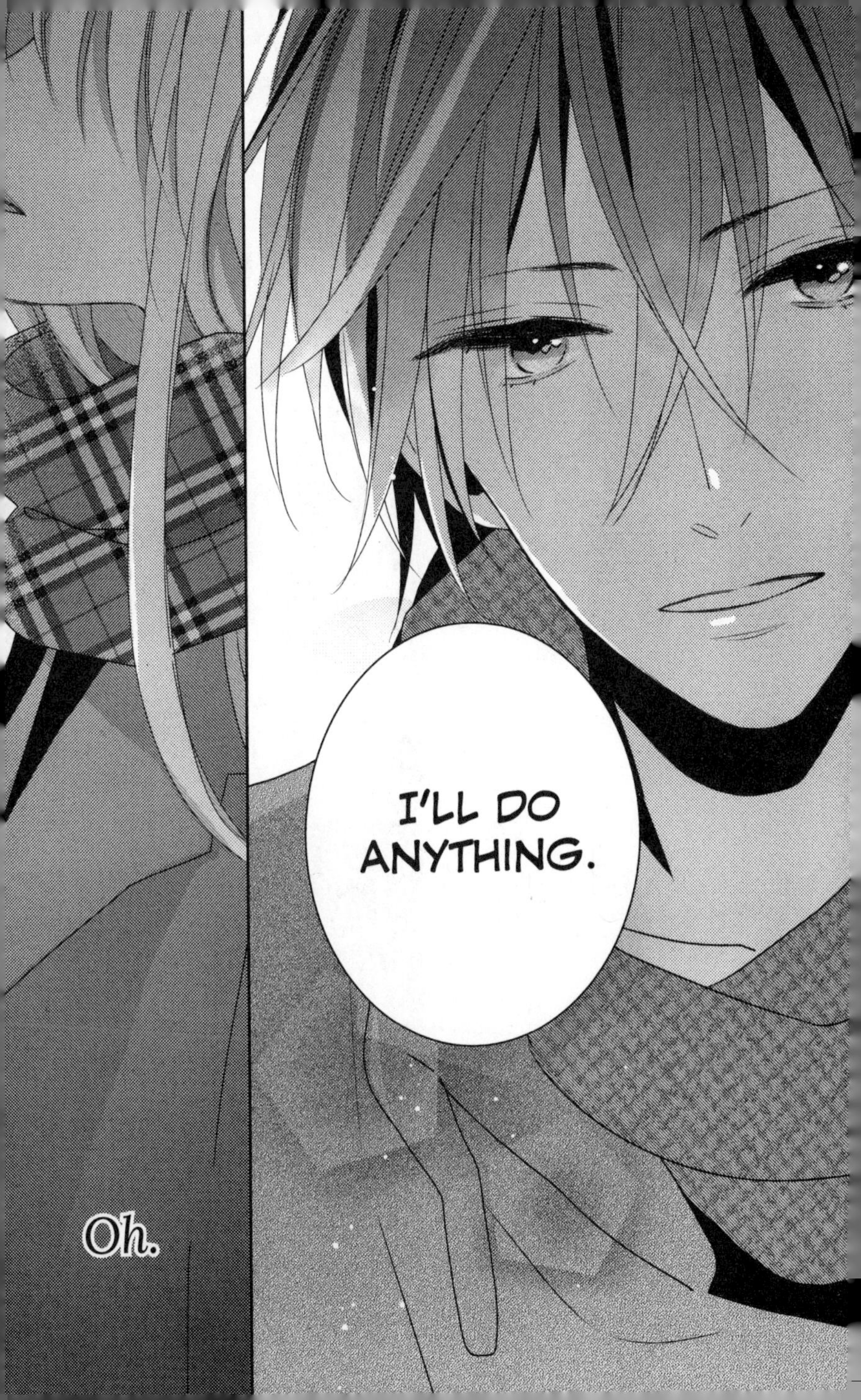
I'LL DO ANYTHING.
Oh.

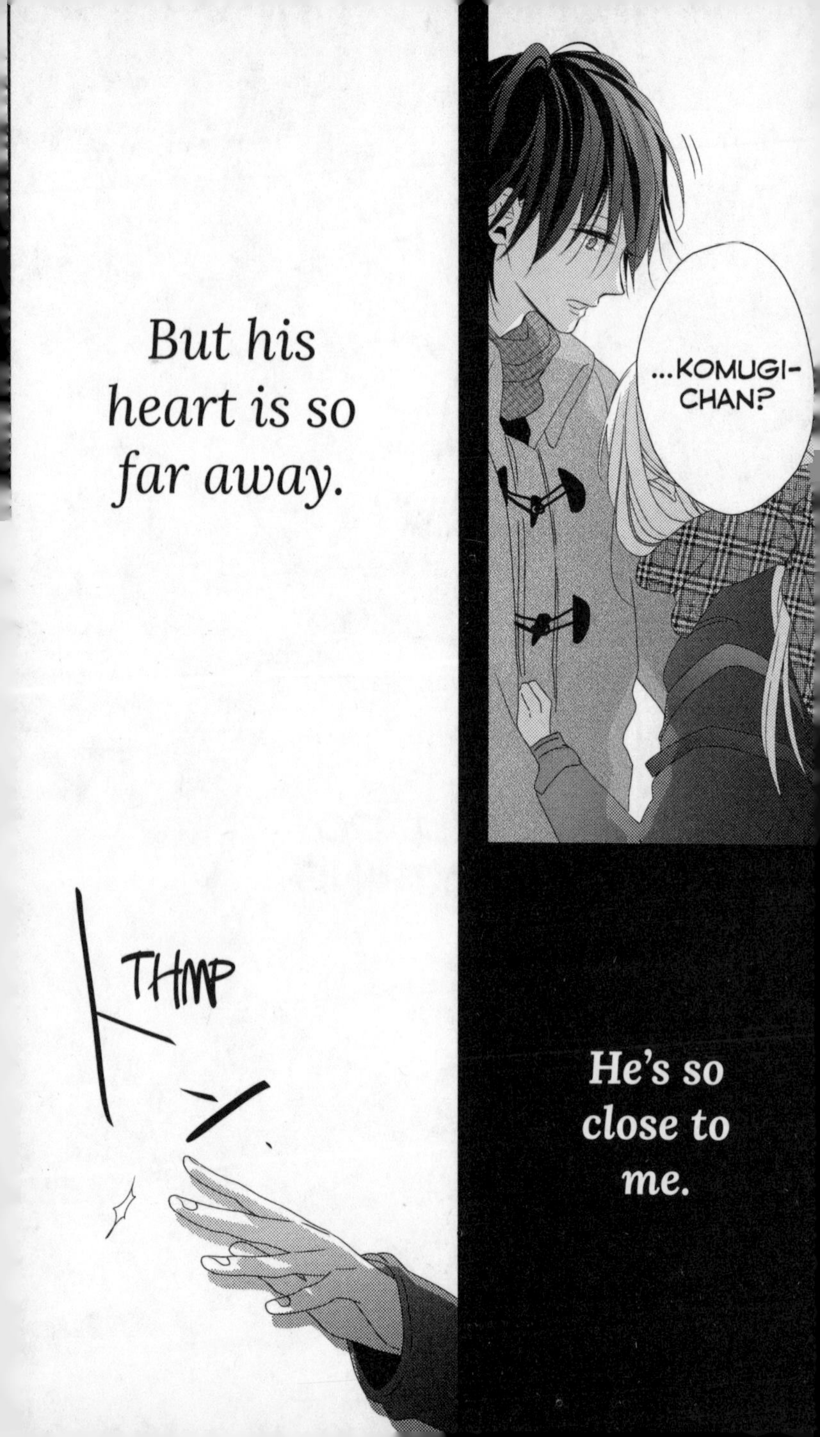
...KOMUGI-CHAN?
He's so close to me.
But his heart is so far away.
THMP

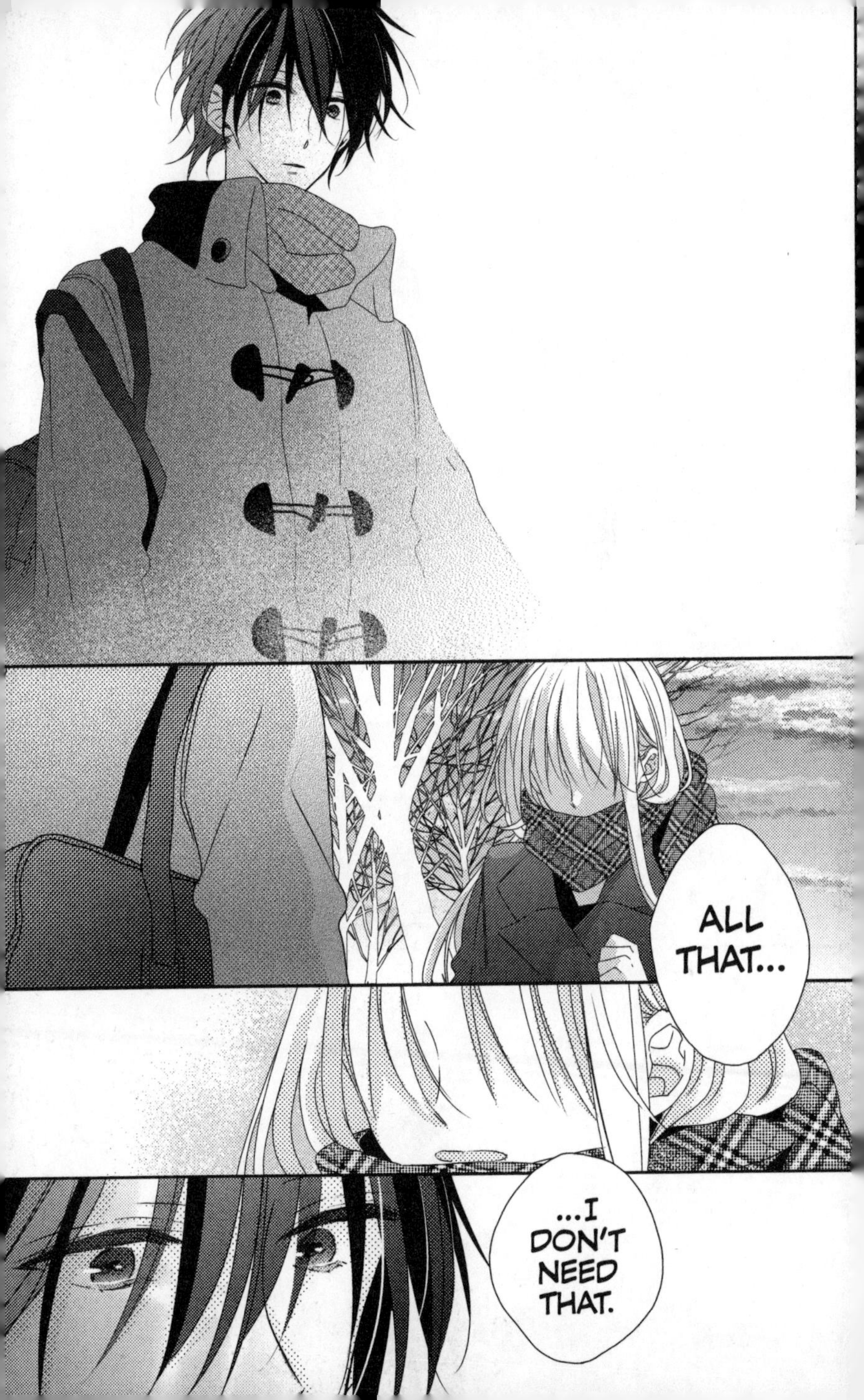
ALL THAT...
...I DON'T NEED THAT.

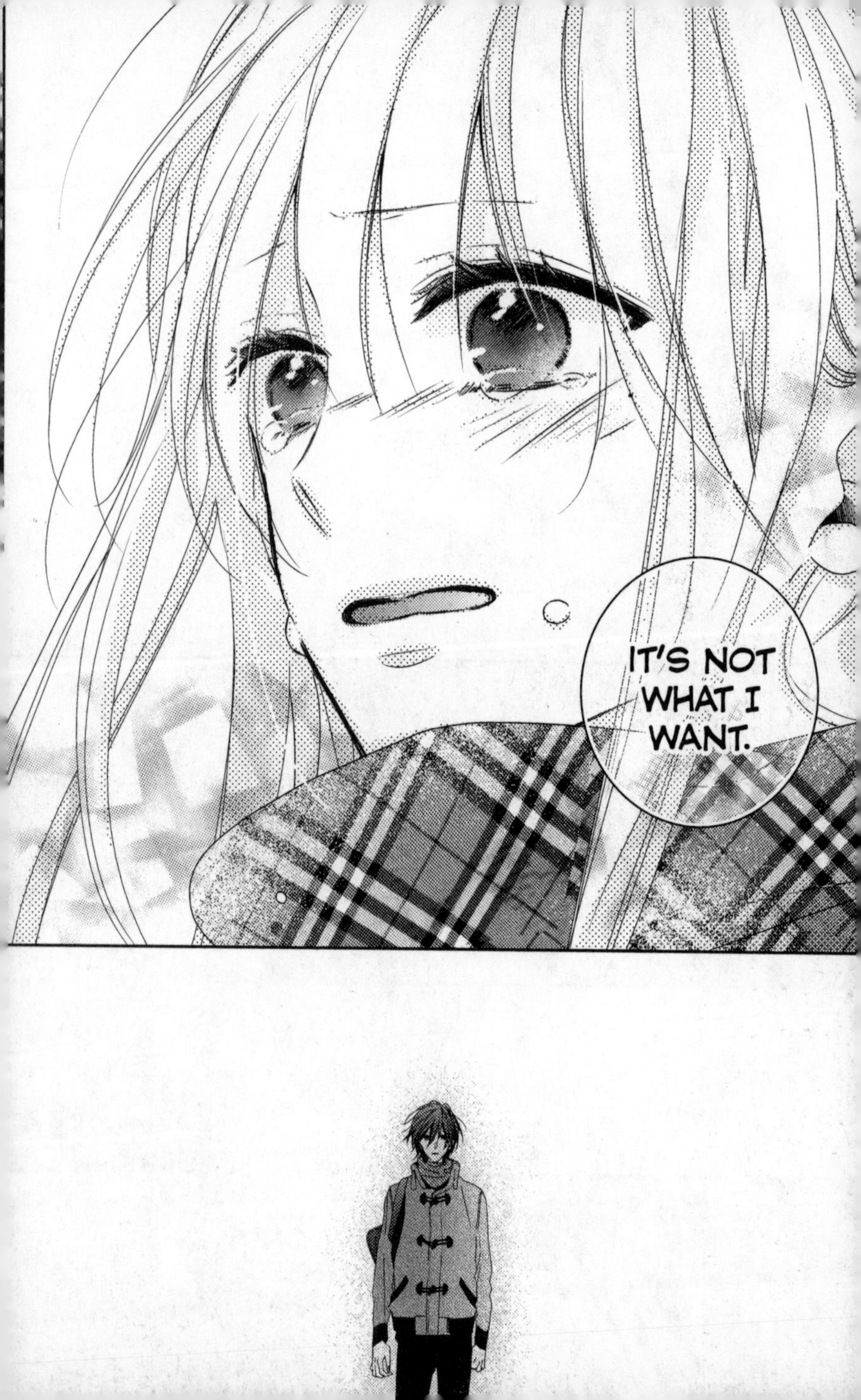
IT'S NOT WHAT I WANT.

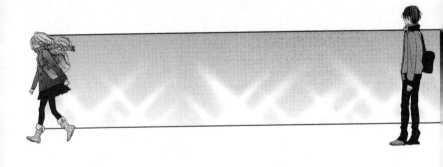

I was so sure
of myself.

But...

...I
was so
wrong.

That
I under-
stood his
solitude.

I
assumed
that I
under-
stood
him.

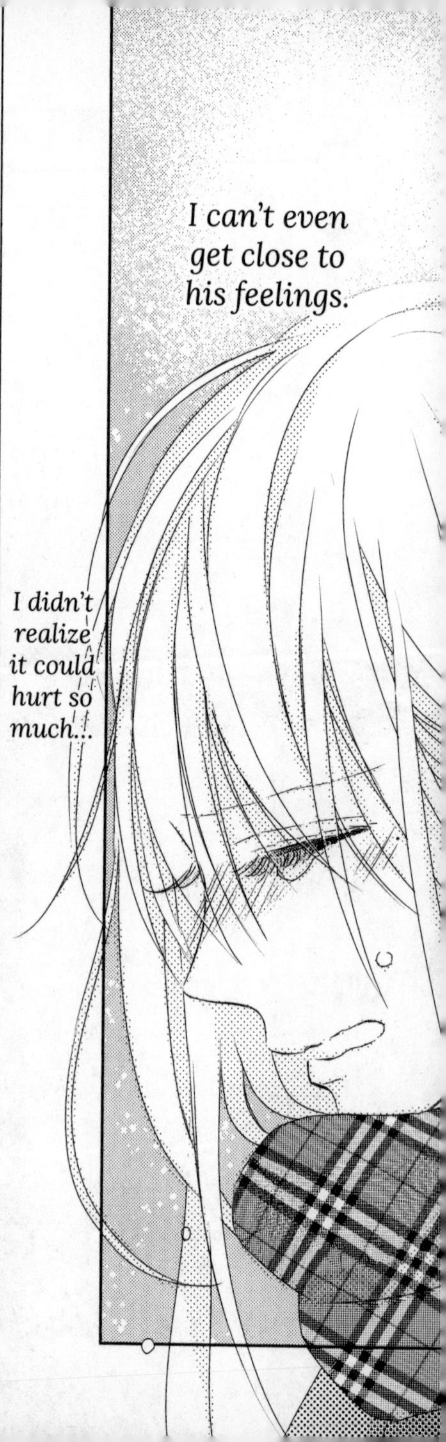
I can't even get close to his feelings.
I didn't realize it could hurt so much...

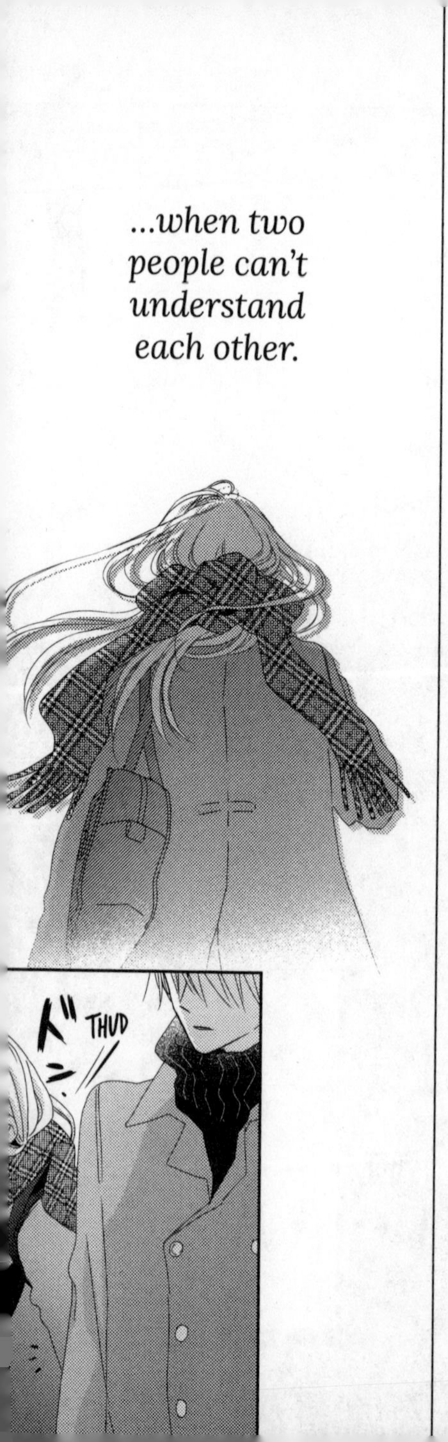
...when two people can't understand each other.
THUD

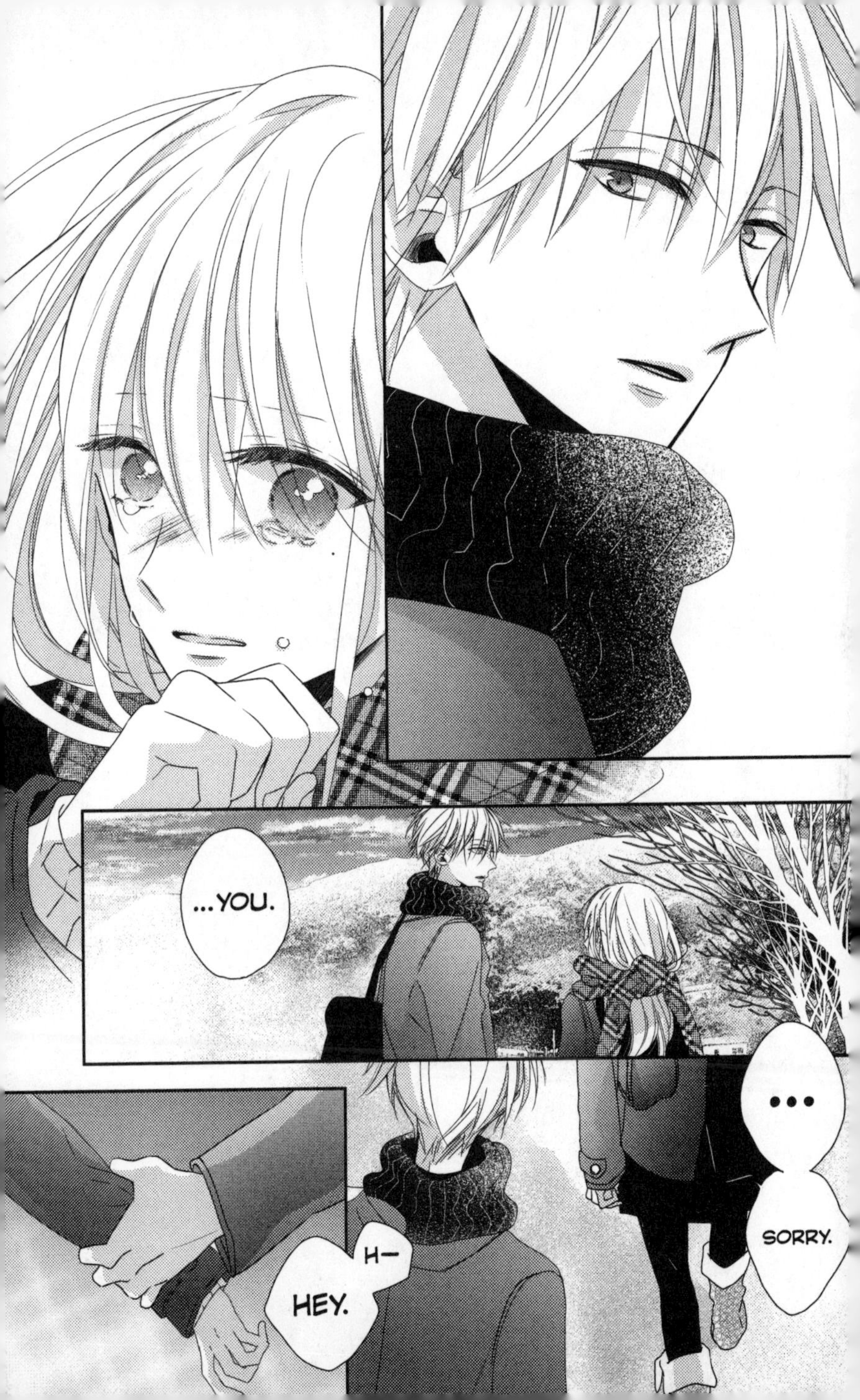
...YOU.
...
SORRY.
H—
HEY.

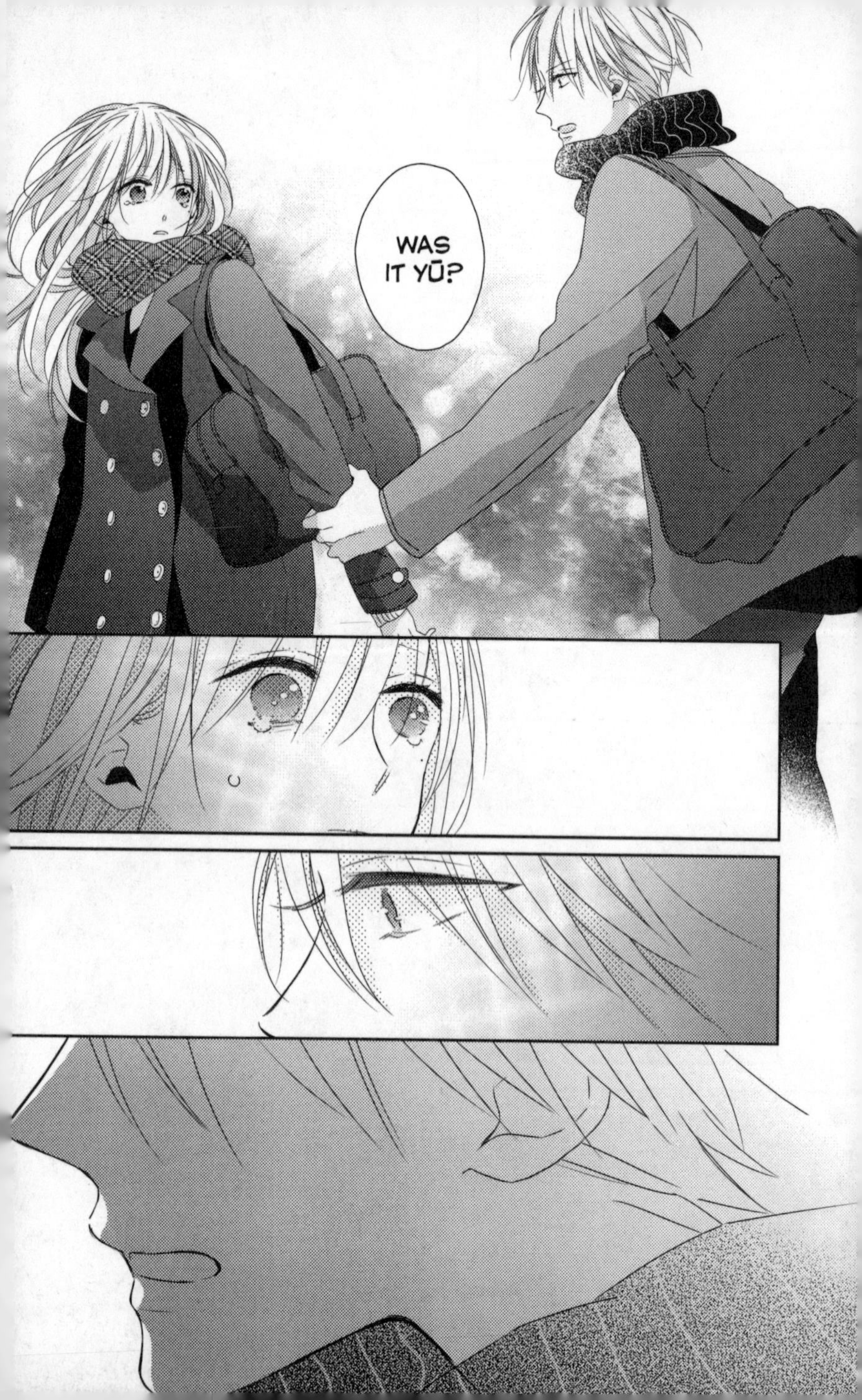
WAS IT YŪ?

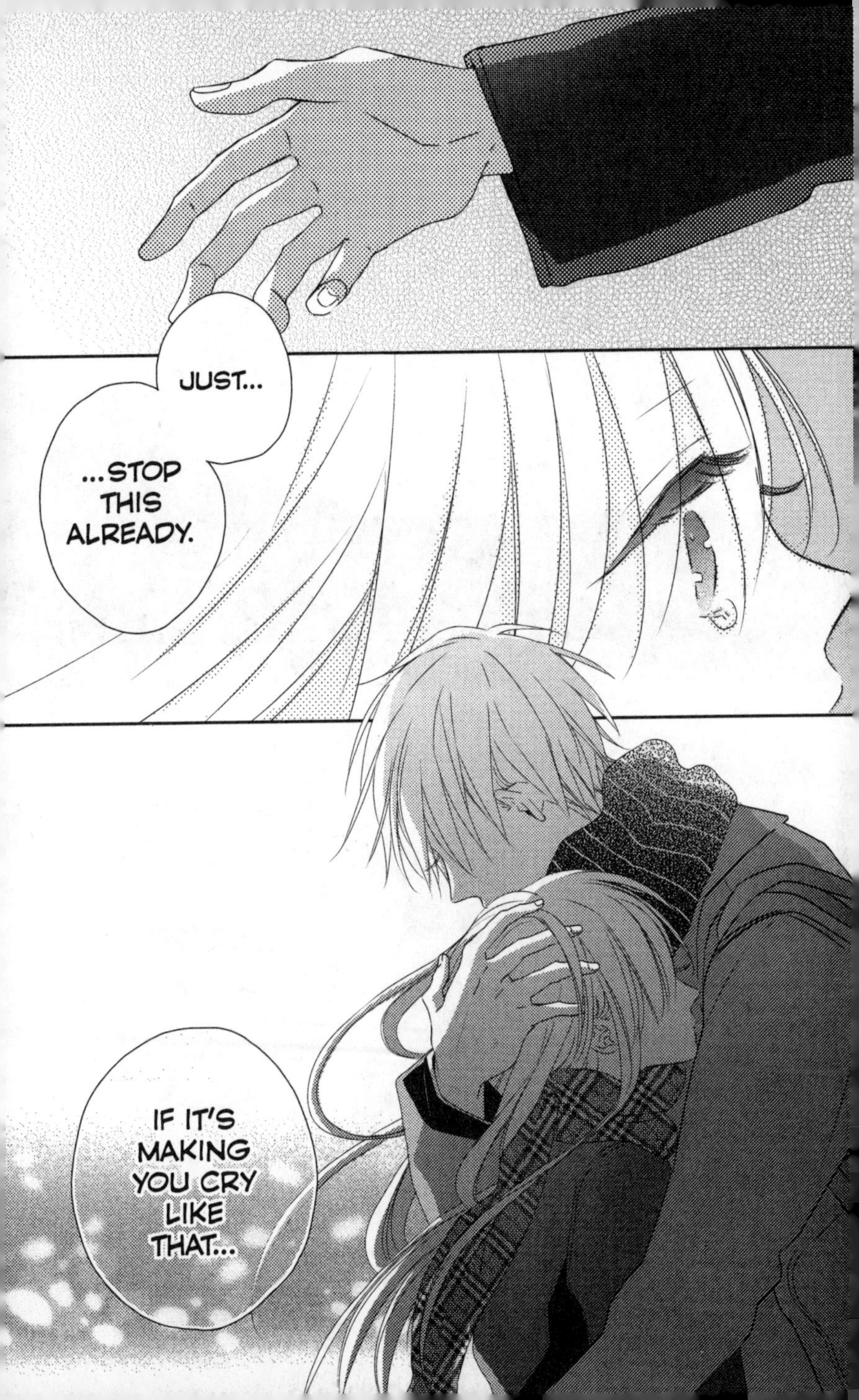
JUST...
...STOP THIS ALREADY.
IF IT'S MAKING YOU CRY LIKE THAT...

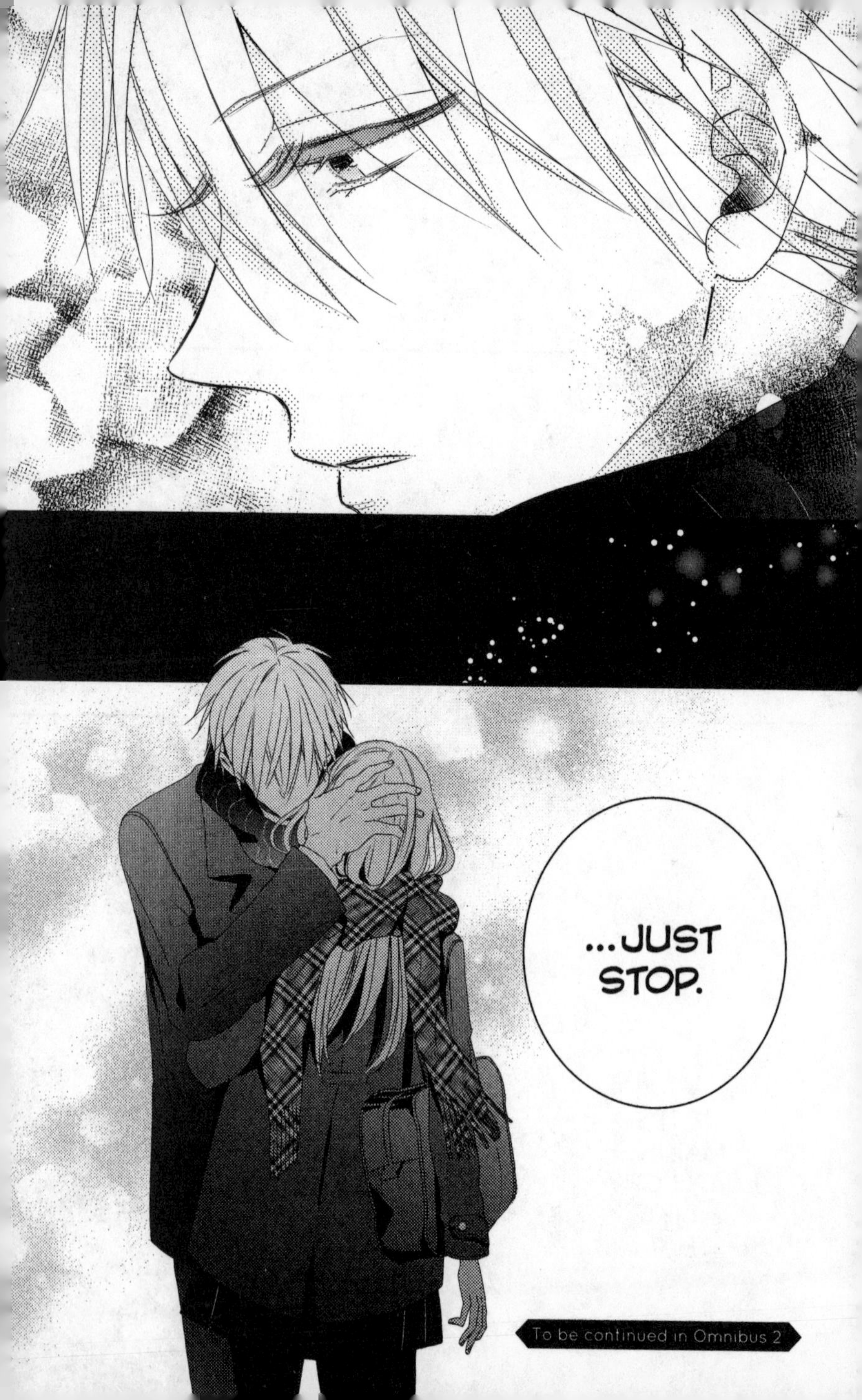
...JUST
STOP.
To be continued in Omnibus 2

That Wolf-Boy is Mine!

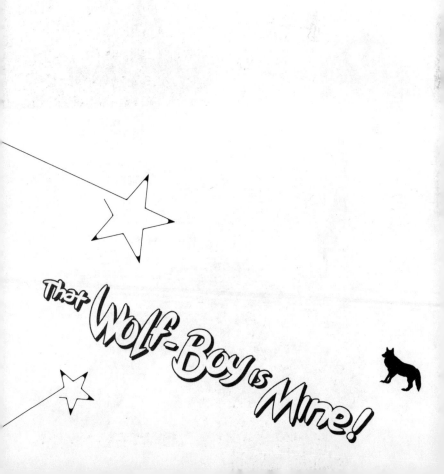

Komugi Kusunoki

Height: 156cm [5'1"]
Birthday: October 16
Blood type: O
Favorite food: Tofu
Least favorite food: Cucumber
Hobby: Reading

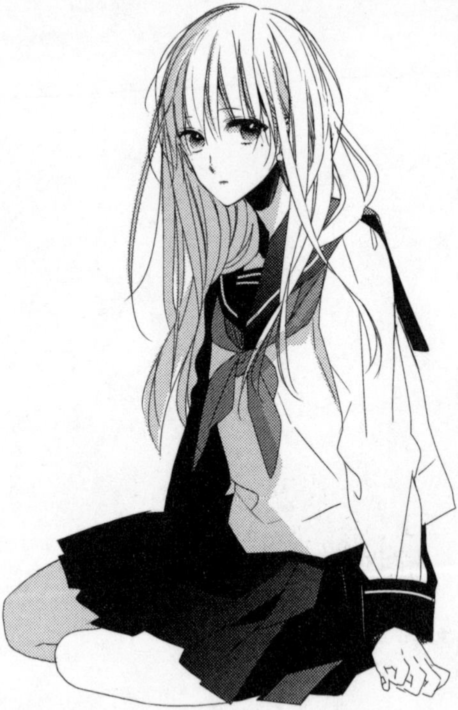

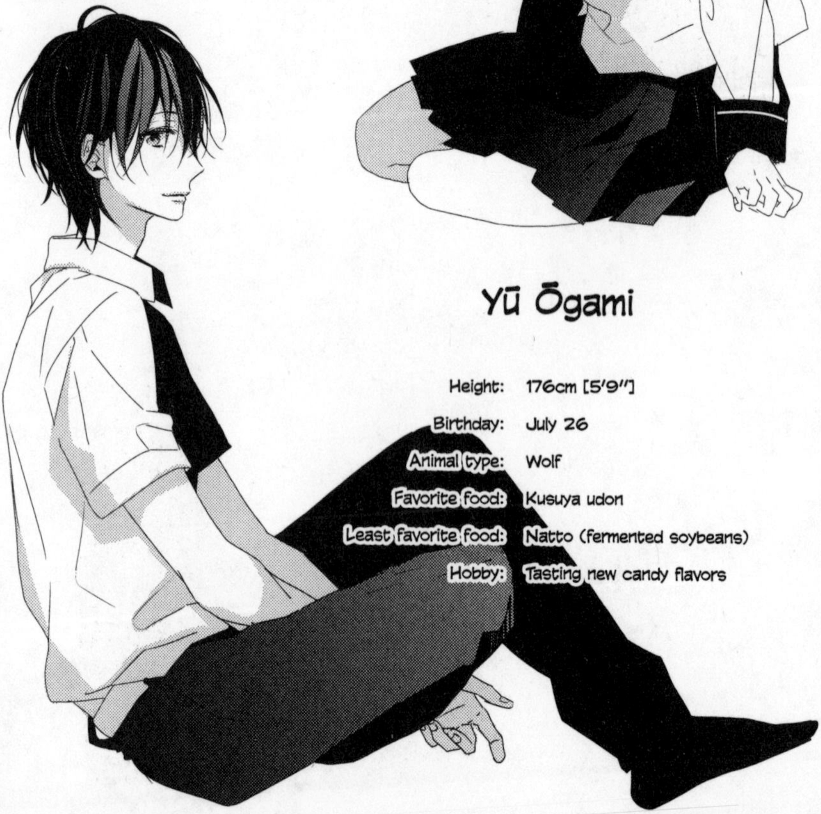

Yū Ōgami

Height: 176cm [5'9"]
Birthday: July 26
Animal type: Wolf
Favorite food: Kusuya udon
Least favorite food: Natto (fermented soybeans)
Hobby: Tasting new candy flavors

Rin Fushimi

Height:	174cm [5'8.5"]
Birthday:	September 23
Animal type:	Fox
Favorite food:	Ramen
Least favorite food:	Ankake (thick saucy topping)
Hobby:	Video games

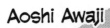

Aoshi Awaji

Height:	173cm [5'8"]
Birthday:	June 15
Animal type:	Tanuki
Favorite food:	Soba noodles
Least favorite food:	Anything sour
Hobby:	Messing with people

Senri Miyama

Height:	171cm [5'7"]
Birthday:	December 23
Animal type:	Two-tailed cat
Favorite food:	Canned tuna
Least favorite food:	Anything spicy
Hobby:	Napping

Kurō Yata

Height:	179cm [5'10"]
Birthday:	Unknown
Animal type:	Three-footed crow
Favorite food:	Saké
Least favorite food:	Nothing in particular
Hobby:	Observing people

Afterword

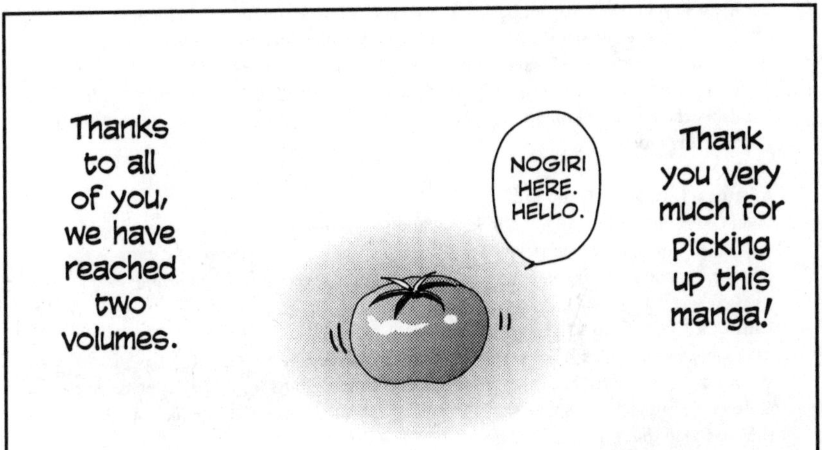
Thank you very much for picking up this manga!
NOGIRI HERE. HELLO.
Thanks to all of you, we have reached two volumes.

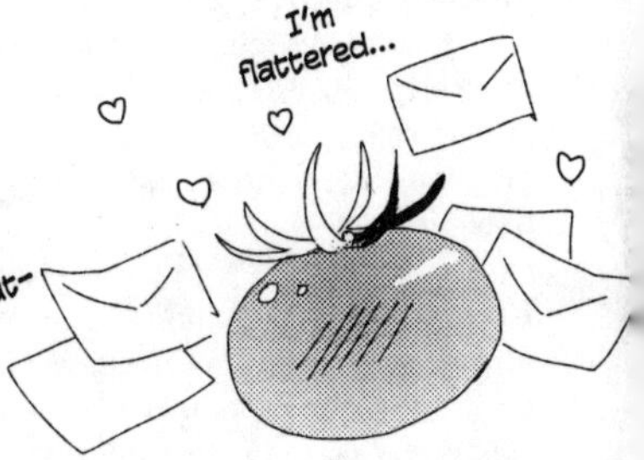
I'm flattered...
I'm so very flattered!

The messages I get on Twitter and in letters really cheer me up.

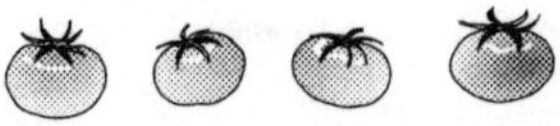

Thank you so much!

- ☆ To my editor-sama
- ☆ Aki Nishihiro-chan
- ☆ A-H-chan
- ☆ All my friends and family
- ☆ Everyone who read this book

I hope you'll read volume three, too!

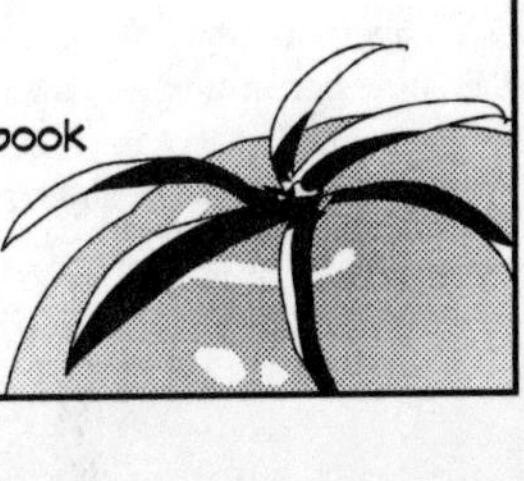

Translation Notes

Ooh, a blazer, page 12

In Japanese schools, there are basically two types of uniforms. At Komugi's new school, the girls wear sailor collars, while the boys wear jackets called *gakuran*. At her old school, the girls wore blazers. Generally speaking, sailor collars and *gakuran* are associated with public schools, while blazers are associated with private schools. In this case, the fact that Komugi wears a blazer adds to the chicness of her having come from the big city.

Komugi, like wheat, page 15

Food names are not uncommon in Japan, and they're especially not uncommon in manga. As Yū kindly explains, *komugi* is the Japanese word for wheat. The name is fitting for the daughter of someone who makes *udon* wheat noodles for a living.

Can I call you Komugi, page 16

In Japan, even in high school, if you don't know someone very well, it can be considered rude to call them by their first name. Normally, Kana would be expected to address Komugi as "Kusunoki-san," but since she wants to be friends, she just asks if they can skip that formality and go straight to a first-name basis.

Tsune-jiichan, page 25

Jiichan translates roughly to "grandpa," and is a friendly title to add to the name of an elderly man, whether or not the speaker is related. Considering that they are still at school, the other students would probably call this gentleman *sensei*, which is the proper title for teachers and other faculty. Thus, we see that Yū considers everyone to be a close friend.

Kitsune udon, page 35

Kitsune udon means "fox udon," and is named after the fox because the main topping for this dish of noodles is *aburaage*, or deep-fried tofu. According to Japanese folklore, *aburaage* is a favorite food of foxes.

Ayakashi Inn, page 68

The name of this particular inn already gave Komugi cause for concern, because *ayashi-sō* (Ayashi Inn) can also mean "seems suspicious" in Japanese. But now, with the addition of the syllable *ka*, the inn becomes a place for the gathering of beings such as Yū and his friends. *Ayakashi* is one of a few blanket terms used to describe supernatural phenomena and creatures. This word and related terms (such as *yōkai*) have been translated many different ways, including ghost, phantom, demon, ghoul, etc., but in this case, it seems to mainly refer to animals that have acquired supernatural powers, including the ability to take a human shape.

Translation Notes

Oinari-san, page 70
Named after a Japanese god of rice and agriculture who is strongly associated with foxes, Oinari-san, or *inarizushi*, is a dish consisting of seasoned rice stuffed inside a pouch of *aburaage* fried tofu.

Animals living among humans, page 71
The stories referenced here are actual parts of Japanese folklore. Though it can't be proven that his mother was the white fox Kuzunoha, Abe no Seimei is a real person who served as an *onmyōji* (practitioner of *onmyōdō* cosmology) for emperors about a thousand years ago. Sōko Tanuki is a tanuki that took human form and worked as a Buddhist priest. His identity was discovered just like Yū's was—while he was napping. But because of his hard work, the priests at the temple made him a page and let him continue to work there.

Two-tailed cat, page 78
According to Japanese folklore, if a cat lives long enough, its tail will split into two and it will become an *ayakashi* known as a *nekomata*.

Otome games, page 98
An otome game is a video game made for *otome*, or "maidens," to simulate fantasies geared for the female gaze. In addition to playing through the main story as the leading lady, the player can also make choices that lead to a romantic ending with one of many male, and sometimes female, characters. Clearly Kana believes that the men in these games are much more worth her while than any real man.

Tsundere, page 133
For readers unfamiliar with Japanese anime and manga tropes, *tsundere* comes from *tsun-tsun* (meaning prickly) and *dere-dere* (meaning lovestruck). A *tsundere* is a character whose first reaction to other people is prickly and mean, but because they care deep down, sometimes those ooey-gooey emotions will show through.

Translation Notes

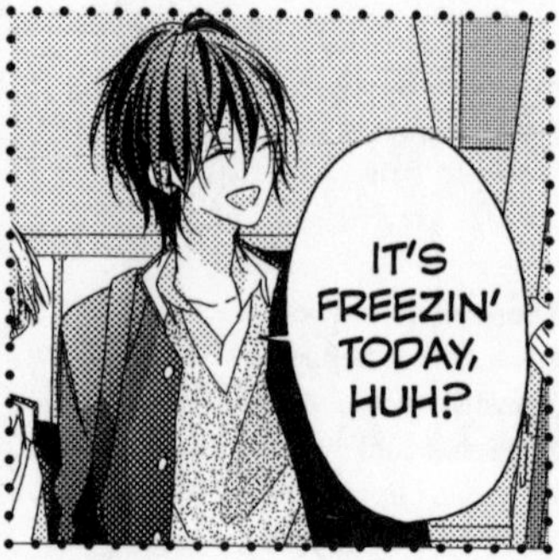
IT'S FREEZIN' TODAY, HUH?

Freezin', page 168
Because this story takes place in Hokkaido, some words that are uncommon in standard Japanese slip into the dialogue. A lot of dialects mixed together in Hokkaido because people from many different regions of Japan once settled there. The term Yū uses here in his regional Hokkaido dialect is *shibareru*, which means "very cold."

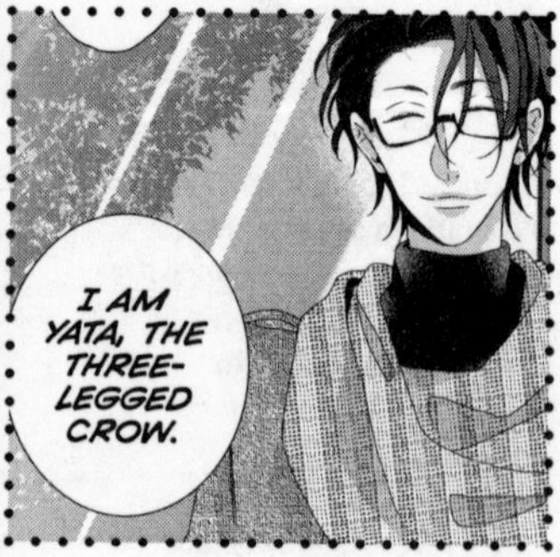
I AM YATA, THE THREE-LEGGED CROW.

Three-legged crow, page 203
The three-legged crow is a part of various Asian mythologies. In Japanese, the *yatagarasu* crow was sent by Amaterasu, the goddess of the sun and universe, to guide one of the nation's first emperors.

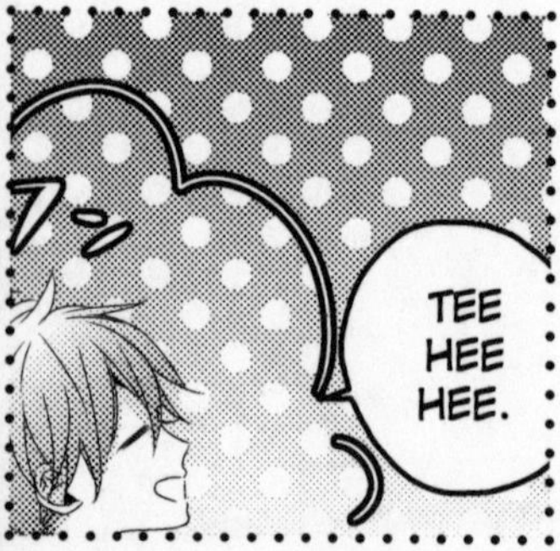
TEE HEE HEE.

Tee hee hee, page 229
To be more precise, Aoshi says "tee hee" followed by a licking sound, as if he were laughing innocently and sticking his tongue out in a cute, childish manner. Incidentally, the leaf on his head is a common accessory for transforming tanuki.

Translation Notes

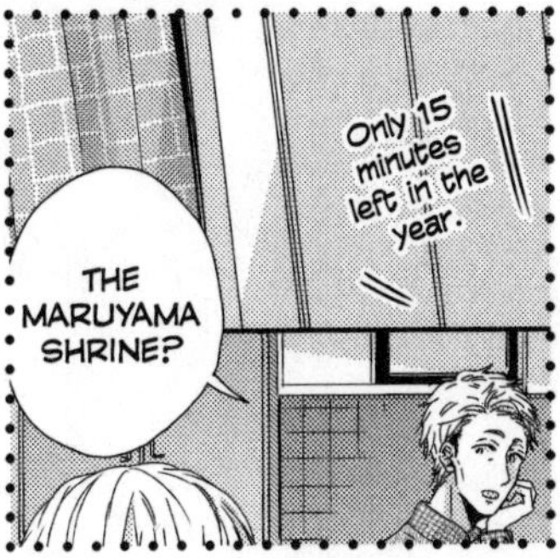
Only 15 minutes left in the year.
THE MARUYAMA SHRINE?

New Year's temple visit, page 243
One of the Japanese New Year traditions is to visit a temple or shrine. Once there, one can make wishes for the new year, make offerings to the temple deities, get amulets and fortunes, etc. People in Hokkaido can go to the Hokkaido Shrine in Sapporo. A popular shrine to visit in Tokyo is Sensō-ji, as mentioned by the New Year's reporters.

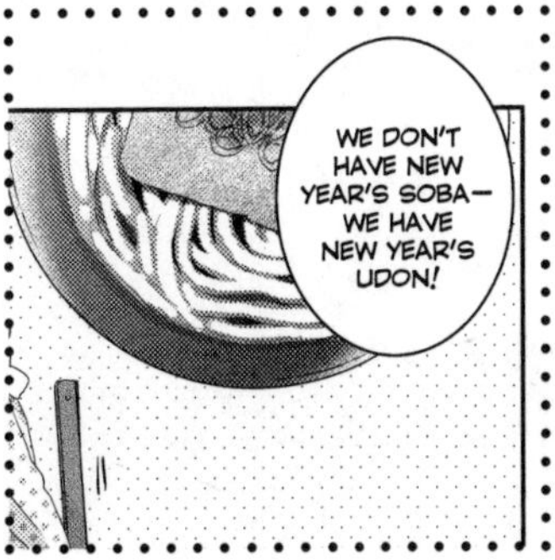
WE DON'T HAVE NEW YEAR'S SOBA—WE HAVE NEW YEAR'S UDON!

New Year's soba, page 244
Another Japanese New Year's tradition is to eat a bowl of soba noodles on New Year's Eve. In Japanese it is called *toshikoshi soba*, or "year-crossing noodles." The noodles are long, representing longevity and long-lasting family fortune, but they're easy to cut, so one can easily cut ties with the hardship and misfortune of the previous year.